Martin Luther on the Bondage of the Will;

MARTIN LUTHER

ON THE

BONDAGE OF THE WILL;

TO THE VENERABLE MISTER

ERASMUS OF ROTTERDAM.

1525.

FAITHFULLY TRANSLATED FROM THE ORIGINAL LATIN

BY

EDWARD THOMAS VAUGHAN, M.A.

VICAR OF ST. MARTIN'S, LEICESTER, RECTOR OF FOSTON, LEICESTERSHIRE, AND SOMETIME FELLOW OF TRINITY COLLEGE, CAMBRIDGE.

WITH A PREFACE AND NOTES.

LONDON:

SOLD FOR THE EDITOR, BY T. HAMILTON, PATERNOSTER-ROW; AND T. COMBE, LEICESTER.

1823.

[Entered at Stationers' Hall.]

BJ1460
.L8
1823a

LL
549239
FEB 8 1941

London: Printed by A. Applegath,
Stamford-street.

TO

HIM

WHO SITTETH UPON THE THRONE

BY THE SIDE OF THE INVISIBLE FATHER,

EVEN JESUS,

MY LORD AND MY GOD!

WHO KNOWETH THAT

NOT BY MY FREEWILL, BUT BY HIS,

THIS WORK,

WHATSOEVER IT BE,

WAS PROMPTED AND UNDERTAKEN,

AND HATH NOW AT LENGTH BEEN EXECUTED,

I DEDICATE IT:

DESIRING THAT HIS WILL, NOT MY OWN,

BE DONE BY IT;

AND FIRM IN THE HOPE, THAT HE WILL USE IT

UNTO THE EDIFYING OF HIS PEOPLE.—

E. T. V.

PREFACE.

I DEEM it expedient to put the reader in possession of the circumstances under which this work was written; for which purpose it is necessary that I premise a rapid sketch of Luther's history, in its connection with Protestantism.

Martin Luther was born in the year 1483, at Isleben, in Saxony. His father, who had wrought in the mines of Mansfield, became afterwards a proprietor in them; which enabled him to educate his son, not only with a pious father's care, but with a rich father's liberality. After furnishing him with the elements in some inferior schools, he sent him at an early age to the University of Erfurth: where he made considerable proficiency in classical learning, eloquence and philosophy, and commenced Master of Arts at the age of twenty. His parents had destined him for the bar; but after devoting himself diligently to the study of the civil law for some time, he forsook it abruptly, and shut himself up in a convent at Erfurth.

Here he became remarkable for his diligence, self-mortification and conscientiousness; occasionally suffering great agitation of mind from an ignorant fear of God. Habitually sad, and at intervals overwhelmed with paroxysms of mental agony, he consulted his vicar-general Staupitius; who comforted him by suggesting, that he did not know how useful and necessary this trial might be to him: 'God does not thus exercise you for nothing, said he; you will one day see that he will employ you as his servant for great purposes.'—'The event, adds the historian, gave ample honour to the sagacity of Staupitius, and it is very evident that a deep and solid conviction of sin, leading the mind to the search of Scripture-truth, and the investigation of the way of peace, was the main spring of Luther's whole after conduct; and indeed this view of our reformer's state of mind furnishes the only key to the discovery of the real motives, by which he was influenced in his public transactions.'

It was not till the second year of his residence in the monastery, that he accidentally met with a Latin Bible in the library, when he, for the first time, discovered that large portions of the Scriptures were withheld from the people. Being sick this same year, he was greatly comforted by an elder brother of the convent, who directed his attention to that precious article of our creed, 'I believe in the remission of sins.' Staupitius, he afterwards remarked, had spoken to him as with the voice of an angel, when he taught him that 'true repentance begins with the love of righteousness and of God;' but the old monk led him up to the source of this love.—There may be, there is, a breathing after righteousness, and a feeling after God, which prepareth the way for this love; but there can be no real righteousness wrought, or real love of it and of God felt, till we have the consciousness of his forgiveness.— His aged adviser represented to him, that this article implied not merely a GENERAL BELIEF—for the devils, he remarked, had a faith of that sort—but that it was the command of God, that each particular person should apply this doctrine of the remission of sins to his own particular case; and referred him for the proof of what he said to Bernard, Augustine and St. Paul.—With incredible ardour he now gave himself up to the study of the Scriptures, and of Augustine's works. Afterwards he read other divines, but he stuck close to Augustine; and held by him, as we find, to his last hour.

In the year 1507, he received holy orders; and in the next year was called to the Professorship of Divinity at Wittemberg, through the recommendation of his friend Staupitius; who thereby gave him an opportunity of verifying his own forebodings concerning him. Here arose his connection with the elector Frederic, of Saxony; which was so serviceable to him in all his after-conflicts. Frederic was tenderly anxious for the credit and success of his infant seminary; and Luther more than fulfilled his expectations, both as a teacher of philosophy and as a public minister. 'Eloquent by nature, and powerful in moving the affections, acquainted also in a very uncommon manner with the elegancies and energy of his native tongue, he soon became the wonder of his age.'

In 1510, he was dispatched to Rome on some important business of his order; which he performed so well as to receive the distinction of a doctor's degree upon his return. Whilst at Rome he had opportunities of noticing the spirit with which religious worship was conducted there— its pomp, hurriedness and politicality; and was thankful to return once more to his convent, where he might pray deliberately and fervently without being ridiculed. He now entered upon a public exposition of the Psalms and Epistle to the Romans; studied Greek and Hebrew with great diligence; improved his taste, and enlarged his erudition, by availing himself of the philological labours of Erasmus (to which he always owned that he had been greatly indebted); rejected the corruptive yoke of Aristotle and the Schoolmen, and rested not, like the satirist who had given him a taste for pulling down, in confusion, but sought and found his peace in erecting a scriptural theology upon the ruins of heathenized Christianity. The true light beamed very gradually upon his mind: from suspecting error he became convinced that it was there; constrained to reject error, he was forced step by step into truth.

Whilst thus employed, with great contention of mind,

in studying, ruminating, teaching and preaching; when now he had been favoured with some peculiar advantages* for ascertaining the real state of religion, both amongst clergy and laity, in his own country, his attention was in a manner compelled to the subject of Indulgences. He had not taken it up as a speculation; he did not know the real nature, grounds, ingredients, or ramifications of the evil. As a confessor, he had to do with acknowledgments of sin; as a priest, he was to dictate penances. The penitents refused to comply, because they had dispensations in their pockets.—What a chef-d'œuvre of Satan's was here! It is not " Sin no more, least a worse thing happen unto thee;" but ' Sin as thou listest, if thou canst pay for it.' Luther would not absolve. The brass-browed Tetzel stormed, and ordered his pile of wood to be lighted that he might strike terror into all who should dare to think of being heretics. At present Luther only said with great mildness from the pulpit, ' that the people might be better employed than in running from place to place to procure INDULGENCES.'†

* In his office of subaltern vicar he had about forty monasteries under his inspection, which he had taken occasion to visit.

† It is not to be inferred that Luther was at this time ignorant of the doctrine of grace, because ignorant of this particular subject. This is the memorable year 1517. In the preceding year, 1516, he thus wrote to a friend. ' I desire to know what your soul is doing; whether wearied at length of its own righteousness, it learns to refresh itself and to rest in the righteousness of Christ. The temptation of presumption in our age is strong in many, and specially in those who labour to be just and good with all their might, and at the same time are ignorant of the righteousness of God, which in Christ is conferred upon all with a rich exuberance of gratuitous liberality. They seek in themselves to work that which is good, in order that they may have a confidence of standing before God, adorned with virtues and merits, which is an impossible attempt You, my friend, used to be of this same opinion, or rather—of this same mistake, so was I, but now I am fighting against the error, but have not yet prevailed.'—' A little before the controversy concerning Indulgences, George, Duke of Saxony, entreated Staupitius to send him some worthy and learned

PREFACE. v

He was sure it was wrong; he would try to check it; would try, with canonical regularity, applying to archbishop and bishop for redress: so ignorant of the principals, sub-ordinates and sub-sub-ordinates in the traffic, that he called upon his own archbishop vender to stop the trade!

See how God worketh. Ambition, vanity and extravagance are made the instrument of developing the abominations of the Popedom, that God may develope himself by his dealings with it. The gorgeous temple, whose foundations had previously been laid, to the wonderment of man, not to the praise and worship of God, must continue to be built; though not one jot may be subtracted from Leo's pomp, sensuality and magnificence, and though his treasury be already exhausted. Profligate necessity leads him to an expedient, which, whilst it reveals his own spirit, and discloses the principles of the government

preacher. The vicar-general, in compliance with his request, dispatched Luther with strong recommendations to Dresden. George gave him an order to preach: the sum of Luther's sermon was this; That no man ought to despair of the possibility of salvation; that those who heard the word of God with attentive minds were true disciples of Christ, and were elected and predestinated to eternal life. He enlarged on the subject, and shewed that the whole doctrine of predestination, if the foundation be laid in Christ, was of singular efficacy to dispel that fear, by which men, trembling under the sense of their own unworthiness, are tempted to fly from God, who ought to be our sovereign refuge.'—Evidence to the same effect may be drawn in abundance from his letter to Spalatinus, written in this same preceding year, containing remarks on Erasmus's interpretations of Scripture, compared with those of Jerome, Augustine, and some of the other Fathers.—' When obedience to the commandment takes place to a certain degree, and yet has not Christ for its foundation, though it may produce such men as your Fabricius's, and your Regulus's, that is, very upright moralists, according to man's judgment, it has nothing of the nature of genuine righteousness For men are not made truly righteous, as Aristotle supposes, by performing certain actions which are externally good— for they may still be counterfeit characters—but men must have righteous principles in the first place, and then they will not fail to perform righteous actions. God first respects Abel, and then his offering'—Milner, iv. Cent xvi. chap. ii.

he administers, could scarcely fail to draw some at least into an inquiry, by what authority they were called to submit to such enormities. This expedient (not new indeed—Julius had adopted it before—but never yet so extensively and so barefacedly practised, as in this instance) was no other than to make gain of godliness, by selling merits for money—by not pardoning only, but even legalizing, contempt and defiance of God, through the distribution of certain superfluous riches of Christ and of his saints, of which the Pope has the key. The price demanded varied with the circumstances of the buyer, so that all ranks of men might be partakers of the benefit. In fact, all orders of men were laid under contribution to ecclesiastical profligacy, whilst the infamous Dominican had some colour for his boast, that he had saved more souls from hell by his Indulgences, than St. Peter had converted to Christianity by his preaching.

Luther inquired, studied, prayed, called on his rulers; and at length, receiving no help but only silence or cautions from authorities, published his ninety-five theses, or doctrinal propositions, upon the subject: which were spread, with wonderful impression and effect, in the course of fifteen days, throughout all Germany.

Tetzel answered them by one hundred and six; which gave occasion to sermons in reply and rejoinder; and so dutiful, so simple-hearted, and so confident in truth, was Luther, that he sent his publications to his superiors in the church, his diocesan and his vicar-general; and requested the latter to transmit them to the Pope.—The cause was now fairly before the public. New antagonists arose. Luther was elaborate and temperate in his answers.—At length the lion was roused. He *had* commended brother Martin for his very fine genius, and resolved the dispute into monastic envy—a rivalry between the Dominicans and the Augustinians: but now, within sixty days, he must appear to answer for himself at Rome;

nay, he is condemned already as an incorrigible heretic, without trial, in the apostolic chamber at Rome, even before the citation reaches him. Through the intercession of his powerful friend the elector, he gets a hearing at Augsburg; if that can be called a hearing, which gives the accused no alternative but admission of his crime and recantation.—Such however was the justice and the judgment which Luther met with at the hands of Cajetan. After going *to* and *beyond* the uttermost of what was right in submission—saving nothing but to write down *the six letters* (REVOCO), which would have settled every thing—though there were other weighty matters in dispute, besides the Indulgences—he left his imperious, contemptuous judge with an appeal which he took care to have solemnly registered in due form of law, " from the Pope ill-informed to the same most holy Leo X. when better informed."—Luther had in his several conferences at Augsburg, written and unwritten, stood distinctly upon his distinguishing ground, ' Scripture against all papal decrees:' it is his glory on this occasion, that he maintained it in the very jaws of the usurper's representative; an abject mendicant monk, as the cardinal haughtily termed him, with all due and unfeigned respect for human superiority, took and acted the language, which two apprehended and arraigned Apostles had used before him, " We ought to obey God rather than men."—Cajetan got no honour at Rome by his negociations at Augsburg; the papal counsellors complained that he had been severe and illiberal, when he ought to have promised riches, a bishopric, and a cardinal's hat. Such were their hot-burning coals to be heaped upon the head of inflexibility!

On his return to Wittemberg, at the close of 1518, Luther meditated to leave Germany and retire into France; but the elector forbad him, and made earnest application to the emperor Maximilian to interpose, and get the controversy settled. Meanwhile, Luther renewed his appeal to the Pope; which was followed, strange to tell, by a new bull in favour of Indulgences, confirming all the ancient abuses, but not even mentioning Luther's name. In his then state of mind, clinging as he still did to the Pope's authority, this document was opportune; as serving to make his retreat impossible. Maximilian's death, which took place early in 1519, increased the elector's power of protecting Luther during the interregnum, and led to more lenient measures at Rome. The courteous Saxon knight was sent to replace the imperious Dominican.—' Martin, said he, I took you for some solitary old theologian; whereas I find you a person in all the vigour of life. Then you are so much favoured with the popular opinion, that I could not expect, with the help of twenty-five thousand soldiers, to force you with me to Rome.'—Luther was firm, though softened: he had no objection to writing submissively to the Pope; as yet he recognised his authority, and it was a principle with him to shew respect to his superiors, and to obey " the powers that be," in lawful things, if constituted lawfully.

In the month of July, 1519, were held the famous disputations at Leipsic; where Luther, who had been refused a safe conduct, if he attempted to appear in the character of a disputant, was at length permitted to take up Carolstadt's half-defended cause, and to answer for himself in opposition to one of the most learned, eloquent and embittered of his papal opponents. Eckius, Luther's quondam friend, had come to earn laurels for himself, and strength for the Papacy; but He who gives the prey assigned it to truth, and made this the occasion of supplying Luther with many able coadjutors. Melancthon's approval of his doctrine and attachment to his person were the offspring of this rencounter. ' At Wittemberg, Melancthon had probably been well acquainted with Luther's lectures on divinity: but it was in the citadel of Leipsic that he heard the Romish tenets defended by all the arguments that ingenuity could devise; there his suspicions were strengthened respecting the evils of the existing hierarchy; and there his righteous spirit was roused to imitate, in the grand object of his future inquiries and exertions, the indefatigable endeavours of his zealous and adventurous friend.'

Here it was, that the question of papal supremacy first came into debate. The act of granting Indulgences assumed the right; but the principle was now brought forwards by Eckius, in malicious wilfulness, for the purpose of throwing scandal upon Luther; who as yet, however, " saw men, but as trees, walking ;" and even maintained the Pope's supremacy, though on inferior grounds. He gave it him by a right founded on human reasons; DIVINE PERMISSION, and THE CONSENT OF THE FAITHFUL. Though Eckius's thirteen propositions, and Luther's adversative ones, had respect chiefly to the papal domination, they comprehended other topics; and much important matter of a more generally interesting nature was elicited and agitated by the discussion. On all the subjects of debate, Luther shewed a mind opening itself to truth, as in the instance just cited; though it may be doubted whether he was yet *fully* enlightened into any. Even on Justification, and on Freewill, though he held the substance of what he taught afterwards, he did not use the same materials, or the same form of defence. Hear his own account, as given in the preface to his works. ' My own case, says he, is a notable example of the difficulty with which a man emerges from erroneous notions of long standing. How true is the proverb, custom is a second nature! How true is that saying of Augustine, habit, if not resisted, becomes necessity! I, who both publicly and privately, had taught divinity with the greatest diligence for seven years, insomuch that I retained in my memory almost every word of my lectures, was in fact at that time only just initiated into the knowledge and faith of Christ; I had only just learnt that a man must be justified and saved not by works but by the faith of Christ; and lastly, in regard to pontifical authority, though I publicly maintained that the Pope was not the head of the church by a DIVINE RIGHT, yet I stumbled at the very next step, namely, that the whole papal system was a Satanic invention. This I did not see, but contended obstinately for the Pope's RIGHT, FOUNDED ON HUMAN REASONS; so thoroughly deluded was I by the example of others, by the title of HOLY CHURCH, and by my own habits. Hence I have learnt to have more candour for bigoted Papists, especially if they are not much acquainted with sacred, or perhaps, even with profane history.'—When the debate was over, Luther calmly reviewed his own thirteen propositions, and published them, with concise explanations and proofs; establishing his conclusions chiefly by an appeal to Scripture and to ecclesiastical history.

These wrestling-matches of ancient times were the seed-bed of the reviving church: the people heard, the people read; and thus, according to Luther's favourite maxim, THE STONE which is to destroy Antichrist WAS CUT OUT WITHOUT HANDS.

In 1520, Miltitz advised a second letter to the Pope. Advancing, as he now was, towards meridian light, he found it difficult to do this with integrity; it may be questioned, whether he succeeded in his attempt. Already he had disclosed to his friend that he had not much doubt but the Pope is the real Antichrist. 'The lives and conversation of the Popes, their actions, their decrees, all, said he, agree most wonderfully to the descriptions of him in Holy Writ.' With what consistency could he still approach him as his authorized head and desired protector, flatter his person, and propose terms of mutual silence? True, the tone of his address is much altered from that of his former letter; he declares many of the abominations of his government; he expressly refuses to recant;

he insists upon his great principle, 'perfect freedom in interpreting the word of God.' He is also peculiarly wise, just, plain and forcible in warning him against the big swelling words, with which his flatterers dignified him: "O my people, they which call thee BLESSED cause thee to err." But we could be glad to see more of frankness and less of compliment; the person not so subtilely separated from the office, the man from his court; wishes and prayers for good suppressed, where he had begun to be persuaded that there could be only curse and destruction. The only plausible defence is, his mind was not yet FULLY made up as to what the Pope is: he had doubts, he thought himself bound to go to the uttermost in endeavours to conciliate, such an appeal would be a touchstone. In estimating the rectitude of this measure, every thing, it is plain, depends upon the degree of light which had then beamed upon his mind: but it is difficult to conceive, that, writing, as he had done, early in this same year to Spalatinus, and writing, as he afterwards did, in the month of June, his treatise on the necessity of reformation, and, in the month of August, his Babylonish captivity, he should, in the intermediate space, have retained a state of mind which, consistently with simplicity, could dictate *his*, or indeed *any* letter of accommodation to Leo.

At length, however, having abundantly proved his David, and convinced him of his foolishness, the Lord took it clean away from him, whilst He sealed up his enemies in theirs. Never was there a more manifest illustration of Jewish blindness and induration—" He hath blinded their eyes, and hardened their heart"—than in the counsels of the Conclave at this period. Leo disdains to be conciliated. After three years' delay, when Lutheranism has now grown to a size and a strength which no fire can burn, the damnatory bull is issued on the 15th of June, 1520, at Rome; and after a further short interval of mysterious silence is published in Germany. It extracted forty-one propositions out of his writings, declaring them all to be heretical, forbad the reading and commanded the burning of his books, excommunicated his person, and required all secular princes to aid in his arrest.

Luther was now quite prepared to receive it; prepared through the judgment which the Lord had now enabled him to form concerning the papal usurpation; and prepared, through the willingness which He had given him to suffer martyrdom for the truth, if called to that issue. The trenches were now fairly opened; the war was begun. His first measure was to publish two Tracts: in one of which he treated the bull ironically, pretending to have some doubts of its authenticity, but still entitling it the execrable bull of Antichrist, and calling upon the emperor and all christian princes to come and defend the church against the Papists; in the other, he gave a serious answer to the forty-one condemned articles, defending the authority of Scripture, and calling every body to study it, without deference to the expositions of men. Having answered, he acted his reply to it. If the bull were valid, it was not to be answered, but obeyed: he would shew, therefore, that he accounted it an illegal instrument. The Pope was the separatist, not he; a bull of Antichrist is a bull to be burnt. He therefore takes the bull, together with the papal decretals, and such parts of the canon law as had respect to the pontifical jurisdiction, and with all due solemnity and publicity commits them to the flames: a measure, which he afterwards proved to have been deliberately adopted— not the effect of heat and rage, but of calm conviction— by selecting thirty articles from the books he had burnt, publishing them with a short comment, and appealing to the public whether he had shewn them less respect than they deserved. The two last of these were, Article 29. 'The Pope has the power to interpret Scripture, and to teach as he pleases; and no person is allowed to interpret in a different way.' Article 30. 'The Pope does not derive from the Scripture, but the Scripture derives from the Pope authority, power and dignity.' He had more, he said, of like kind. Assume his cause to be just, and his bold proceedings were unquestionably right. His was not a case for half-measures. He was either a subject for burning, or a vindicator of the oppressed. What sort of vindicator? Not by the knight-errant's sword, but by such acts as should declare him to be in earnest, and such arguments as should shew that he was not in earnest for nought. His publications at this period, and during the two preceding years, were almost without number. He knew that his life was in his hand; he prized the short interval, as he anticipated, which was allowed him; the cause of Christ, so evidently committed into his hands, was to be maintained, extended, and at length made triumphant, only by the bloodless sword of the Spirit. That sword therefore he would wield with all his might, without cessation, faintness, or weariness. His main expectation was from the word of God simply and intelligibly set forth. He added short practical and experimental treatises—appeals to plain sense and Scripture—but the expounded word was his stay. Hence his great labour in the Epistle to the Galatians; which he first published in the year 1519, and, after fifteen years of additional research, having made it one material subject of his public lectures during all that period, revised, corrected, enlarged, and reedited in 1635.

'I have repeatedly read and meditated on this treatise, says his pious, laborious and philosophical historian, and, after the most mature reflection, am fully convinced, that, as it was one of the most powerful means of reviving the light of Scripture in the sixteenth century, so it will, in all ages, be capable of doing the same, under the blessing of God, whenever a disposition shall appear among men to regard the oracles of divine truth, and whenever souls shall be distressed with a sense of in-dwelling sin. For I perfectly despair of its being relished at all by any but serious, humble and contrite spirits, such being indeed the only persons in the world, to whom the all-important article of justification will appear worthy of all acceptation. The AUTHOR himself had ploughed deep into the human heart, and knew its native depravity; he had long laboured, to no purpose, to gain peace of conscience by legal observances and moral works, and had been relieved from the most pungent anxiety, by a spiritual discovery of the doctrine just mentioned. He was appointed in the counsels of Providence—by no means exclusively of the other reformers, but in a manner more extraordinary and much superior—to teach mankind, after upwards of a thousand years' obscurity, this great evangelical tenet—compared with which how little appear all other objects of controversy! namely, that man is not justified by the works of the law, but by the faith of Christ.'

I cannot deny myself the satisfaction of inserting one extract from this truly spiritual work.—' This doctrine, therefore, of faith must be taught in its purity. Namely, that as a believer, thou art by faith so entirely united to Christ that he and thou are made as it were one person. That thou canst not be separated from Christ; but always adherest so closely to him, as to be able to say with confidence, I am one with Christ; that is, Christ's righteousness, his victory, his life, death, and resurrection, are all mine. On the other hand, Christ may say, I am that sinner; the meaning of which is, in other words, his sins, his death, and punishment, are mine, because he is united and joined to me, and I to him. For by faith we are so joined together as to become one flesh and one bone. We are members of his body, of his flesh, and of his bones; so that, in strictness, there is more of an union between Christ and me, than exists even in the relation of husband and wife, where the two are considered as one flesh. This faith, therefore, is by no means an ineffective quality; but possesses so great excellency, that it utterly confounds and destroys the foolish dreams and imaginations of the Sophisters, who have contrived a number of metaphysical fictions concerning faith and charity, merits and qualifications.—These things are of such moment, that I would gladly explain them more at large, if I could.'*

Luther had many antagonists in his warfare. As his assertive manifestoes were clear, argumentative and decisive; so his answers to those who attacked them were prompt, energetic and full. He neither spurned, nor delayed, nor spared. His admiring historian thinks it necessary to apologize for his vehemence, and for his acrimony. I do not concur with him in the sense of that necessity. God, who made the man, gave him his language. His language was the language for his case, for his hour, for his hearers and readers. Such were the publications wanted; such would be read; they agitated the high, they were understood by the vulgar. His own account of himself, as given at a later period, is worth a thousand apologies. 'I, says he, am born to be a rough controversialist; I clear the ground, pull up weeds, fill up ditches, and smooth the roads. But to build, to plant, to sow, to water, to adorn the country, belongs, by the grace of God, to Melancthon.'—If he had a spirit of rancorous enmity and cold-blooded malice towards his opponents, let him be condemned: but, we all know, severe words may be spoken without a particle of malignity, and a smooth tongue often disguises an

---

* There is a defect in Luther's statement of the believer's union with Christ: he does not mark, he did not discern, its origin and foundation, and its consequent exclusiveness and appropriateness to a peculiar people. He refers it all to his believing, which is the manifestation, realization and effectuation of that relation which has subsisted, not in divine purpose only, but in express stipulation and arrangement, from everlasting, and which has been the source of that very faith, or rather of that energizing of the Holy Ghost, which *he* considers as its parent. But *the thing itself*, the *nature* of this union, is so beautifully described, that, whatever be its defects, I could be glad to give it all currency.

envenomed spirit.—*I am much more disposed to quarrel with his vanity, than with his petulance.*

The obligations which Charles owed to Frederic were such as to secure his protection for Luther, to a certain extent. For his opinions he cared not, though his own prejudices were no doubt on the side of the old system: he cared only for the political bearings of the question; and it was obvious the elector's friend must not be condemned without a hearing. Hence, after much negociation and correspondence, his appearance at Worms is agreed upon. His wise protector gets an express renunciation of the principle, 'Faith not to be kept with heretics,' from Charles, several of the princes countersign his safe conduct; and Luther, as if to face as many devils as there were tiles upon the houses of the selected city, preaches his way up to Worms. His defence there has sometimes disappointed me, and he seems afterwards to have felt that he had been too tame and unexplicit himself. When he speaks, at a still later period, of his boldness; questioning whether he should in that day (but a little before his death) have been so bold—a fact recited triumphantly by many historians—it is with reference to his courage in determining, or rather in proceeding to go up, notwithstanding the strong dissuasives which he met with on his way, that he gives God glory. He who made man's mouth and gives him wisdom, and who hath promised for such very occasions, "I will give you a mouth and wisdom which all your adversaries shall not be able to gainsay or resist," did, no doubt, order his speech in perfect wisdom, at that trying hour. The speech he delivered was the speech for the time and for the case. But the question is, was it the speech we should have looked for from a Luther? We admit there never was such a moment, possibly, since the Apostles' days. All the pomp of Cæsar was before him. But I confess there is more of the, elector Frederic, Spalatinus and Melancthon, than of Paul before Felix, or of Peter and John before the council. Hear his own account. 'I have great misgivings (says he in a letter to Spalatinus some months after), and am greatly troubled in conscience, because, in compliance with your advice, and that of some other friends, I restrained my spirit at Worms, and did not conduct myself, like an Elijah, in attacking those idols. Were I ever to stand before that audience again, they should hear very different language from me.' And again; 'To please certain friends, and that I might not appear unreasonably obstinate, I did not speak out at the diet of Worms; I did not withstand the tyrants with that decided firmness and animation which became a confessor of the Gospel! Moreover I am quite weary of hearing myself commended for the moderation which I shewed on that occasion.'—The dean sets it all down to humility; but I doubt not there was much of well-founded and conscientious self-upbraiding in these acknowledgments.— He maintained his principle, however; 'a free use of the word; the Scripture *for* all, to be freely interpreted *by* all: retract he would, if convinced by Scripture, but not else.' Upon being informed that he was required to say simply and clearly whether he would or would not retract his opinions, ' My answer, said Luther instantly, shall be direct and plain. I cannot think myself bound to believe either the Pope or his councils; for it is very clear, not only that they have often erred, but often contradicted themselves. Therefore, unless I am convinced by Scripture or clear reasons, my belief is so confirmed by the scriptural passages I have produced, and my conscience so determined to abide by the word of God, that I neither can nor will retract any thing; for it is neither safe nor innocent to act against a man's conscience.' There is something particularly affecting in the words which follow: ' Here I stand, I cannot do otherwise. May God help me. Amen.'

Many attempts were made to persuade him in secret; but the upshot was, he would stand by the word: 'rather than give up the word of God, when the case is quite clear, I WOULD LOSE MY LIFE.'*

In the course of three hours after his last interview with the elector Archbishop of Treves (who, though a bigoted Roman Catholic, had shewn strong dispositions to serve him), Luther received an order to quit Worms; only twenty-one days being allowed for his safe conduct, and he not permitted to preach in his way home. A sanguinary edict was then smuggled through the diet: many of the members had left Worms before it was voted; the ceremony of enacting it took place in the emperor's private apartments; the decree was ante-dated, as though it had passed on the 8th instead of the 21st, and Aleander, the Pope's legate, Luther's accuser, who had been much gravelled by the vast consideration and respect shewn to Luther, received it, as a sort of sop and soporific, from the emperor, that he should draw up the sentence.

'The edict, as might be expected, was penned by

* Much was said, in the course of these discussions, about a future council Luther acknowledged the authority of such a council; maintaining only, that it must be legally convened—the civil governor being the alone rightful summoner—and that its decisions must be regulated by the word of God There is more of sound than substance in the recognition of this appeal; upon Luther's principles Waving the difficulty of summoning such a GENERAL COUNCIL, where deputies are to be brought together out of all Christendom, divided as it is into independent states, under various supreme heads; what is the decision at last? The testimony of Scripture is testimony of Scripture to my conscience, only so far as I am led to *understand* Scripture in a sense which is coincident with the general decision. If that decision be contrary to my own deliberate, conscientious and supposedly Spirit-taught views, as a lover of order I bow to the tribunal by submitting to its penalties, whether positive or negative; but I cannot confess myself convinced, or adopt the judgment of the council as my own, without violating Luther's fundamental principle, 'the word my judge.' (See Part II. Sect. XII note ᵏ of the following work.)—Luther's last answer confirms the distinction which I have here been marking; it is to the supposed decision of a council, that his resolution applies.

Aleander with all possible rancour and malice. The first part of it states that it is the duty of the emperor to protect religion and extinguish heresies. The second part relates the pains that had been taken to bring back the heretic to repentance. And the third proceeds to the condemnation of MARTIN LUTHER in the strongest terms. The emperor says, that by the advice of the electors, princes, orders, and states of the empire, he had resolved to execute the sentence of the Pope, who was the proper guardian of the Catholic faith. He declares, that Luther must be looked on as excommunicated, and as a notorious heretic; and he forbids all persons, under the penalty of high treason, to receive, maintain, or protect him. He orders, that after the twenty-one days allowed him he should be proceeded against in whatever place he might be; or at least that he should be seized and kept prisoner till the pleasure of his imperial majesty was known. He directs the same punishment to be inflicted on all his adherents or favourers; and that all their goods should be confiscated, unless they can prove that they have left his party and received absolution. He forbids all persons to print, sell, buy or read any of his books, and he enjoins the princes and magistrates to cause them to be burnt.'

This high-sounding decree was never executed. Charles was too busy, too much entangled with crooked and conflicting politics, too dependent and too needy, to take vengeance for the Pope, at present, in Germany. In 1522, a diet of the empire held at Nuremberg agreed to a conclusion which Luther considered as an abrogation of it. In 1523, a second diet held at the same place, after some considerable difference of sentiment, concurred in a similar recess. The Lutherans were divided between hope and fear, alternately elated and depressed, during some succeeding years. In 1526, when evil had been anticipated, the diet of Spires, after much jangling, terminated favourably. The wrath, however, was but deferred. In 1529, a second diet at Spires went nigh to establish the neglected edict of Worms. The violence, with which it was conducted, led to a Protest of the Lutheran states and princes (whence we have derived our name of Protestants), and was followed by the famous defensive league of Smalcalde. The decree of Augsburg, in 1530, served to confirm the necessity of this league. The most moderate expressions of doctrine, and the most guarded behaviour, had no conciliatory efficacy; force was prepared, and must be repelled by military combination. It is not by strength, however, or by might—human strength and human might—that the Lord wins his battles. That formidable confederacy, which could bring 70,000 men into the field, under the banner of John the Constant, to meet a not more than 8000 of the emperor's, soon melted away like the winter's snow. In 1547, the emperor carries all before him—takes the two great Protestant leaders captive, and makes a spectacle of them to their subjects—establishes his Interim, slays the Protestant witnesses and assumes to be even the MAN OF SIN's master, in his domination over the Lord's heritage. But behold! in three years and a half, the witnesses " whose dead bodies have been lying in the street of the great city, which spiritually is called Sodom and Egypt, where also our Lord was crucified "—even in that Germany which has been called the highway of Europe—are seen standing upon their feet again. The treacherous and intriguing Maurice is made the instrument of bringing deliverance to the Protestants. The emperor becomes, in his turn a fugitive, a panic-struck, and, within a hair's breadth, the captive of his captives; when, at length, the unhoped-for treaty of Passau legalizes Protestantism, and secures to the revived witnesses a seat in the symbolical heavens.

From the disasters, alike as from the triumphs, of these latter scenes Luther was removed by a rapid sickness and premature death, in the year 1546. Fatigue and anxiety had impaired the native soundness and vigour of his bodily frame, and he died an old man, at the age of sixty-three.

The storm which had gathered around his head at Worms was repelled in its onset by a prudent stratagem of the elector's, which he had communicated, it is probable, in secret, to the emperor himself. Having seized his person, by a mock arrest, whilst returning to Wittemberg, he took and hid him in the castle of Wartburg; where he fed and nourished him at his own expense for ten months, and would have continued to do so, if Luther had allowed him, to the end of his days. In this hiding-place which he called his Patmos, comparing himself with St. John as banished to that island by Domitian, he saw many visions of the Almighty, which enlightened his future ministry. He betrayed a good deal of impatience under this seclusion. He complained that his kind detainer fed him too well; that he ate and drank too much, that he grew stupid and sensual. But the truth seems to have been, that stir and bustle and a great to do were his element. He did not like fowling, though he allegorized it, so well as reading lectures to five or six hundred young men, and preaching to half as many thousands. Here, however, the Lord nurtured his Moses, and made him wiser in the art of feeding his sheep; and, if he suffered him to be dull and heavy, he gave him no inclination to be idle. The Yonker,* in his horseman's suit, wrote many tracts; improved himself in the knowledge of Greek and Hebrew, which he studied very diligently with an eye to his projected translation of the Scriptures, and actually accomplished his German version of the New Testament, so as to publish it this same year. These were not the achievements of sloth and sensuality! Of his original works at this period, his answer to Latomus's defence of

* 'During his residence in the castle of Wartburg he suffered his beard and hair to grow, assumed an equestrian sort of dress, and passed for a country gentleman, under the name of Yonker George.'

the Louvain divines was the most elaborate. 'A confutation, says Seckendorff, replete with so much solid learning and sound divinity, that it was impossible to reply to it without being guilty of obvious cavilling or downright impiety,—If the author of it had never published any thing else in his whole life, he would, on account of this single tract, deserve to be compared with the greatest divines which ever existed in the church. At the time of writing it, he was furnished with no other book but the Bible; and yet he interprets the leading passages of the Prophets and the Apostles, and does away the deceitful glosses of sophistical commentators with so much exquisite erudition and ability, that the genuine meaning of the inspired writers cannot but be clear to every pious and attentive reader.'

He dedicates it to Justus Jonas, who had recently been appointed to the presidency of the college of Wittemberg; desiring him to accept it as a sort of congratulatory present, expressing a strong sense of the divine indignation as now poured out upon the visible church, and hinting what he expected from the new president, in the discharge of his office.—'It is my earnest prayer, that you, my brother, who, by your appointment ought to teach the pestilential decretals of Antichrist, may be enlightened by the Spirit of God to do your duty; that is, UNTEACH every thing that belongs to Popery. For though we are compelled to live in Babylon, we ought to shew that our affections are fixed on our own country, Jerusalem. Be strong and of good comfort; and fear not Baalpeor; but believe in the Lord Jesus, who is blessed for evermore. Amen.'

In this treatise, he vindicates himself from the charge of insincerity in having for so long a time submitted to the Pope, and to the received opinions; whilst he declares his grief for having done so, his thankfulness to the Lord Jesus Christ for that insight into the Scriptures, which he deemed a hundred times preferable to the scholastic divinity of the times, and his now full conviction, that the

Pope is that monster of Antichrist, foretold throughout the sacred writings. He expresses himself indifferent to the charge of wanting moderation, and as to sedition, it was no more than the Jews had charged Christ with; the main point in debate, he maintains, is 'THE NATURE OF SIN.' ' If in the passages which I have quoted from St. Paul, says he, it can be proved that the Apostle does not use the word SIN in its true and proper sense, my whole argument falls to the ground; but if this cannot be proved, then Latomus's objections are without foundation. He blames me for maintaining that no human action can endure the severity of God's judgment. I reply, he ought to shudder in undertaking to defend the opposite sentiment. Suppose, for a moment, that any man could say, he has indeed fulfilled the precept of God in some one good work. Then such a man might fairly address the Almighty to this effect: " Behold, O Lord, by the help of thy grace, I have done this good work. There is in it no sin; no defect; it needs not thy pardoning mercy: which, therefore, in this instance I do not ask. I desire thou wouldest judge this action strictly and impartially. I feel assured, that, as thou art just and faithful, thou canst not condemn it; and therefore I glory in it before thee. Our Saviour's prayer teaches me to implore the forgiveness of my trespasses; but in regard to this work, mercy is not necessary for the remission of sin, but rather justice for the reward of merit." To such indecent, unchristian conclusions are we naturally led by the pride of the scholastic system! This doctrine of the sinless perfection of human works* finds no support in Scripture: it rests entirely on a few expressions of the Fathers, who are yet by no means agreed among themselves, and if they were agreed, still their authority is only human. We are directed to prove

* It is the works of the godly that are the subject of inquiry, the charge against which Luther here defends himself is, his having maintained that the very best acts of the best men have the nature of sin.

ALL THINGS and to hold fast that which is good. ALL doctrines then are to be proved by the sacred Scriptures. There is no exception here in favour of Augustine, of Jerome, of Origen, nor even of an antichristian Pope.—Augustine, however, is entirely on my side of the question.... Such are my reasons for choosing to call that SIN to which you apply the softer terms of defect and imperfection. But farther, I may well interrogate all those, who use the language of Latomus, whether they do not resemble the Stoics in their abstract definition of a wise man, or Quintilian in his definition of a perfect orator; that is, whether they do not speak of an imaginary character, such as never was, nor ever will be. I challenge them to produce a man, who will dare to speak of his own work, and say it is without sin.—Your way of speaking leads to most pernicious views of the nature of sin. You attribute to mere human powers that which is to be ascribed to divine grace alone. You make men presumptuous and secure in their vices. You depreciate the knowledge of the mystery of Christ, and, by consequence, the spirit of thankfulness and love to God. There is a prodigious effusion of grace expended in the conversion of sinners: you lose sight of this; you make nature innocent, and so darken or pervert the Scripture, that the sense of it is almost lost in the christian world.'—I make no apology for these instructive extracts. 'The matter of this controversy must always be looked on as of the last importance, if any thing is to be called important, in which the glory of God, the necessity of the grace of Jesus Christ, the exercises of real humility, and the comfort of afflicted consciences are eminently concerned.'

'Luther concludes his book with observing, that he is accused of treating Thomas Aquinas, Alexander, and others, in an injurious and ungrateful manner. He defends himself by saying, those authors had done much harm to his own mind; and he advises young students of divinity to avoid the scholastic theology and philosophy as the ruin of their souls. He expresses great doubts whether Thomas Aquinas was even a good man : he has a better opinion of Bonaventura. Thomas Aquinas, says he, held many heretical opinions, and is the grand cause of the prevalence of the doctrines of Aristotle, that destroyer of sound doctrine. What is it to me, if the Bishop of Rome has canonized him in his bulls ?'

Valuable, however, as this work is, it will admit of no comparison with the truly herculean and apostolic labour, in which he was interrupted by performing it. ' You can scarcely believe, says he, with how much reluctance it is, that I have allowed my attention to be diverted from the quiet study of the Scriptures in this Patmos, by reading the sophistical quibbles of Latomus.' And again; ' I really grudge the time spent in reading and answering this worthless publication—particularly as I was EMPLOYED IN TRANSLATING the Epistles and Gospels into our own language.'

We who sit at ease, and, when we have leisure or inclination to read a chapter in the Bible, have nothing to do but take down our Bible and open it where we please, are apt to forget the labour which it cost to furnish us with that Bible in our native language, and the perils by which we were redeemed into the liberty of reading it with our own eyes, and handling it with our own hands. *We* especially, who have fallen upon times, in which, through the manifest counsel and act of God, out of the supposed three hundred languages and dialects of the earth, versions of the Scriptures are now circulating throughout the whole of the known world in more than one hundred and forty, and to whom it is a rare thing to meet with an individual who has it even in his heart, much less upon his tongue, to put any limits to the circulation of the sacred volume, are ill prepared, by our own feelings and experience, to estimate the boon of a Bible now for the first time edited in the vernacular tongue. But Luther had not only to fight for the right to read, but to labour that they might have whereupon to exercise that right. 'Luther easily foresaw the important consequences which must flow from a fair translation of the Bible in the German language. Nothing would so effectually shake the pillars of ecclesiastical despotism; nothing was so likely to spread the knowledge of pure christian doctrine. Accordingly he rejoiced in the design of expediting the work, whilst his adversaries deprecated the execution of it, more than any heresy of which the greatest enemy of the church could be guilty.' Accordingly, he had begun, and was preparing himself by the more accurate study of the original languages for the completion of his work, when drawn off by Latomus: an enterprise, which required the silence and seclusion of his Patmos for its origination and commencement, but which could not be satisfactorily completed, without larger resources than he possessed there. ' I find, says he, I have undertaken a work which is above my strength. I shall not touch the Old Testament till I can have the assistance of yourself and my other friends at Wittemberg. If it were possible that I could be with you, and remain undiscovered in a snug chamber, I would come; and there, with your help, would translate the whole from the beginning, that at length there might be a version of the Bible fit for Christians to read. This would be a great work, of immense consequence to the public, and worthy of all our labours.'

This arduous task was at length accomplished: the New Testament, as I have already mentioned, being published in 1522; the Old Testament afterwards, in parts, till completed in 1530. ' In this work he was much assisted by the labour and advice of several of his friends, particularly Jonas and Melancthon. The whole performance itself was a monument of that astonishing industry which marked the character of this reformer. The effects of this labour were soon felt in Germany; immense numbers now read in their own language the precious word of God, and saw with their own eyes the just foundations of the Lutheran doctrine.'—What an Ithuriel's spear did the Lord thus enable him to put into the hands of the mass of the people! No wonder that the Papists should cry out and burn.—What, in fact, has upheld the Popedom but ignorance of THE BOOK ? and what is ultimately to destroy it, according to Luther's intelligent and enlightened anticipation of that event, but the knowledge of *the Book?* 'The kingdom of Antichrist, according to the Prophet Daniel's prediction, must be broken WITHOUT HAND ; that is, the Scriptures will be understood by and by, and every one will speak and preach against the papal tyranny from the word of God ; until THIS MAN OF SIN is deserted by all his adherents, and dies of himself. This is the true christian way of destroying him ; and to promote this end, we ought to exert every nerve, encounter every danger, and undergo every loss and inconvenience.'—The wonder is, that, in our days, individuals shall I say ? numbers rather, comprehended in that communion, are zealous for the dissemination of the Scriptures in the spoken language of their country; whilst one of these, towering high above the rest, has been the favoured instrument of distributing more than three hundred thousand copies of a German version of his own, besides many thousands of this very version of Luther's.*

' To decide on the merits of Luther's translation would require not only an exact knowledge of the Hebrew and Greek, but also of the German language ; certainly it was elegant and perspicuous, and beyond comparison preferable to any scriptural publication which had before been known to the populace. It is probable that this work had

* I need scarcely mention the name of Leander Van Ess. But is there no opposition to this work, amongst the Roman Catholics? Are there not divisions and fiercest persecutions amongst them on this very ground? And where, and what, are the Bible Societies of Spain, Portugal, Bavaria and the Italian States?

many defects; but that it was in the main faithful and sound, may be fairly presumed from the solid understanding, biblical learning and multifarious knowledge of the author and his coadjutors. A more acceptable present could scarcely have been conferred on men, who were emerging out of darkness; and the example being followed soon after by reformers in other nations, the real knowledge of Scripture, if we take into account the effects of the art of printing, was facilitated to a surprising degree.'

The papistical plagiarist Emser endeavoured first to traduce, and afterwards to rival and supersede him: but his correct translation was, in fact, little more than a transcript of Luther's (he was himself notoriously ignorant of the German language), some alterations in favour of the Romish tenets excepted; so that Luther was read under Emser's name, and the Lord gave him grace to say with his heart, " Nothwithstanding, whether in pretence or in truth, Christ is preached, and I therein do rejoice, yea, and will rejoice."

It was not without manifesting, from time to time, a considerable degree of impatience, that Luther was detained even for ten months in his solitude: action was his element, and it was painful to him to sit still. 'For the glory of the word of God, and for the mutual confirmation of myself and others, I would much rather burn on the live coals, than live here alone, half alive and useless. If I perish, it is God's will; neither will the Gospel suffer in any degree. I hope you will succeed me, as Elisha did Elijah!'—I could wish he had not written this last sentence to his friend Melancthon.—However, after ten months, the state of his beloved Wittemberg concurred with his own self-centered likes and dislikes, to render it manifestly desirable for the church's welfare, and so, by just inference, the clear will of God, that he should hazard his life and safety by leaving his retreat and returning to his public station in the then capital of infant Protestantism. Melancthon wanted spirits and vigour; the elector wanted boldness and decision; Carolstadt was become tumultuous; the flock was in the state of sheep without a shepherd; the enemy was crying, " There, There." Having already made one short visit by stealth, and finding that an occasional interposition would no longer meet the difficulty, he determined to risk all, and knowing the elector as he did, to act first, and then apologize. Accordingly, he left Wartburg, and wrote his noble letter to him from Borna, on his way, in which he freely opened his motives and expectations, delivering Frederic from all responsibility for his safety, and testifying his entire and alone confidence in the divine protection. Having done so, he pursued his journey with no real or even pretended safeguard, but Him who is invisible.—' I write these things that your highness may know, I consider myself in returning to Wittemberg to be under a far more powerful protection than any which the elector of Saxony can afford me. To be plain, I do not wish to be protected by your highness. It never entered my mind to request your defence of my person. Nay, it is my decided judgment, that, on the contrary, your highness will rather receive support and protection from the prayers of Luther and the good cause in which he is embarked. It is a cause which does not call for the help of the sword. God himself will take care of it without human aid. I positively declare, that if I knew your highness intended to defend me by force, I would not now return to Wittemberg. This is a case where God alone should direct; and men should stand still, and wait the event without anxiety; and that man will be found to defend both himself and others the most bravely, who has the firmest confidence in God. Your highness has but a very feeble reliance on God; and for that reason I cannot think of resting my defence and hopes of deliverance on you.' If I were to put my finger on the most splendid moment of Luther's life, I should fix it at Borna. All the magnanimity, courage and perseverance which he displayed afterwards, were but the acting of that Spirit which he had then evidently received: the fruit and effect of the Lord's most full and most clear manifestation of Himself, as that which he is, to his soul. This enabled him to cast his die in God. He cast it at Wartburg, he declared it at Borna.—His return to Wittemberg was healing, confidence and peace to his scattered, agitated and mistrustful flock.

Luther's valuable life was preserved to the church, for twenty-four years, after his return to Wittemberg. In these, he had first to build, which he found more difficult than to destroy; then, to protect, extend, uphold and perpetuate his infant establishment.* He had to provide against the rapacity of the secular arm, without making ecclesiastics rich; to obtain learned instructors of the people, without feeding hives of drones; to make the untaught teachers; to abolish pomp without violating decency. Often he was at a loss what to advise; and often he was obliged to adopt what was only second best in his own eyes. The press was the great weapon of his warfare, and of his culture; his publications extended to a vast variety of subjects, and it may be truly said, he had thought and knowledge, matter and weight for all. We are to remember, that he was all this while like a vessel living in a storm; not only an excommunicated man (he had excommunicated in return), but an outlaw, under the ban of the empire; whom any body that dared might have seized and delivered up to justice:—is not this the man whom the Lord holdeth with His right hand, keepeth as the apple of His eye, and spreadeth a table for in the midst of his enemies?

Nor were his professed enemies his worst: the slow caution of the elector, the timidity of his coadjutors, the

---

* It was an acknowledged principle with him, as with *our* reformers, to alter as little as possible. He was more of a Cranmer than a Knox.

madness of the people—fleshly heat assuming the name and garb of religious fervour—lust of change—every body must be somebody—envy, debate, clamour, and his own native obstinacy, were more to him than the Eckiuses and the Aleanders, the Conclave and the Emperor!

The character of Luther is sufficiently obvious from this mere hint at his history. Magnanimous, capacious, abstinent, studious, disinterested, intrepid, wise, 'He feared God, he feared none else.' Early in life he had been made to drink deep into the knowledge of his own wickedness, accountableness, lostness and impotency. Melancthon tells of him, that, while he was deeply reflecting on the astonishing instances of the divine vengeance, so great alarm would suddenly affect his whole frame, as almost to frighten him to death. I was once present, when, through intense exertion of mind in the course of an argument respecting some point of doctrine, he was so terrified as to retire to a neighbour's chamber, place himself on the bed, and pray aloud, frequently repeating these words, " He hath concluded all under sin, that he might have mercy upon all." This sensibility of conscience prepared him for a trembling reception of the divine word. We have seen how the Lord threw it in his way. For a considerable time it spake only terrors to him. "THEREIN is the righteousness of God revealed," stirred him up to blasphemy. At length the Lord had pity on him, and opened his eyes, and shewed him that the righteousness of God there spoken of is not His own essential righteousness, which renders Him the hater and punisher of iniquity, but a substance which He has provided to invest sinners withal; and thus, this very expression which had proved a stumbling-block to him became his entrance into Paradise. In process of time, the Lord revealed the mystery of this righteousness somewhat more distinctly to him. He shewed him that the Lord Jesus Christ was in his own person this righteousness; and that to enter into Him, and to put Him on, by faith, was to be righteous, before God; that the merit of Christ was complete for justification; that nothing was to be added, or could be added to it, by a sinner; and that it was received by faith only. Thus far the Lord gave him clearness of sight, though not fulness; and that speedily: after, and beyond this, He left him to blunder; aye, and to the end of his days.—Now therefore, "it having pleased God, who had separated him from his mother's womb, and called him by his grace, to reveal his Son in him, straightway he conferred not with flesh and blood;" "he could not but speak the things which he had heard and seen;" "he was ready not to be bound only, but also to die at Jerusalem for the name of the Lord Jesus."*

God gave three special endowments to this chosen witness; which are the characteristics of his testimony: great knowledge of Scripture, great talent for abstruse and elaborate argumentation, and a singular felicity in addressing the common people.† In illustration of the first of these, his whole works may be appealed to, if his

---

* If his faults be required, he had, *in* him, every fault under heaven. *In him*, that is, in his flesh, dwelt no good thing; that is, dwelt every bad thing. His WITHIN was like ours. "For from within, out of the heart, &c. &c." But if, as should rather be, what came out of him *chiefly*, that is evil, be inquired, his vices, as is the nature of evil, were his virtues run mad. he was obstinate, fierce, contemptuous, vain — He was not unkind, as some would represent him; he had "bowels of mercies." he was not rash; no man more deliberately weighed his words and deeds he was not implacable, witness his attempts to conciliate that greatest of all bears, the Duke George, our *tiger* Henry, Carolstadt, Erasmus, and even the Pope.

† This does not imply that he always interpreted Scripture rightly, or saw all the truth, any more than his skill in arguing implies that he *always* arrived at right conclusions, or proceeded to them by just steps —His excellency in addressing the common people, let it be observed, did not consist in his having one doctrine, or one reason, for them, and another for the learned, he had one Gospel for all, and told it all out to all, but he had powers of language—facility of illustration and simplicity of expression—which made him intelligible and affecting to the most illiterate.

translation of the Bible be not proof enough: for the second, his disputations with Eckius, Latomus and Erasmus—specially the treatise which follows: for the last, all his numerous tracts and sermons, particularly his address to the common people on the breaking out of the rustic war.—His commentary on the Galatians furnishes specimens of the three.

Such was the man, whom the Lord raised up, called forth and employed, as the most prominent, active and efficacious of his *blessed* workfellows, in accomplishing the Reformation! But how strange is it, that man will look but at half of God, and at the surface only of that half, when His whole self stands revealed; and when it is the very aim and contrivance of his operation, to effect that complete display! The Reformation was God's act—an act, inferior only to those of Calvary and of the Red Sea, for manifesting his mighty hand, and his outstretched arm—which he accomplished by doing all in all that Luther did, and all in all that Luther's enemies did; by working in Charles as well as in the Elector; in Leo as well as Luther; in Cajetan, Campeggio, Prierias, Hogostratus, and the whole train of yelping curs and growling mastiffs, which were for baiting and burning the decriers of Babylon, as in Jonas, Pomeranus and Melancthon. Indeed, if we would estimate this transaction aright, as a displayer of God, we must not only inspect the evil workers, visible and invisible, as well as the good, but must mark the steps by which He prepared for his march, and the combinations with which He conducted it; we must see Constantinople captured by the infidel, and the learned of the East shed abroad throughout Christendom; we must see the barbarian imbibing a taste for letters, and the art of printing facilitating the means of acquiring them; we must see activity infused into many and various agents, and that activity excited by various and conflicting interests; we must see rival princes, and vassals hitherto bowed down to the earth, now beginning to ask a reason of their governors; we must see a domineering Charles, a chivalrous Francis, a lustful and rapacious Henry, a cannonading Solyman, a dissipated Leo, a calculating Adrian, a hesitative Clement—German freedom, Italian obsequiousness, Castilian independence, Flemish frivolity, Gallic loyalty, Genoa's fleet and Switzerland's mercenaries, Luther's firmness, Frederic's coldness, Melancthon's dejectedness, and Carolstadt's precipitancy—made, stirred and blended by Him, as a sort of moral chaos, out of which, in the fulness of his own time, He commandeth knowledge, liberty and peace to spring forth upon his captives in Babylon.

Luther describes himself, we have seen, as a rough controversialist: controversy was his element; from his first start into public notice, his life was spent in it.—I hope my reader has learned not to despise, or even to dread controversy. It has been, from the beginning, the Lord's choice weapon for the manifestation of his truth; just as evil has been his own great developer. What are Paul's and John's Epistles but controversial writings? What was the Lord's whole life and ministry but a controversy with the Jews? Luther well knew its uses, and had tasted its *peaceable* fruits : it stirs up inquiry; it stops the mouth of the gainsayers; it roots and grounds the believers. Still, there were three out of his many, from which he would gladly have been spared; they were maintained against *quondam* friends. In the first of these he was all in the right, but not without question; in the second, all in the wrong, without question; in the third, all in the right, without question: without question, I mean, not as respects any public trial which has been held, and judgment given, but before the tribunal of right reason.

'Andreas Bodenstenius Carolstadt, *unheard, unconvicted, banished* by Martin Luther,'—What ! Luther become a persecutor? he who should have been a martyr himself, make martyrs of others ? Not so; but charged with doing so, and appearances against him!—*Honest Carolstadt*—there is some question whether he truly deserves this name—was a turbulent man. He had no hearty relish for Luther's ' broken WITHOUT HANDS ;' though a learned man, and still a professor at Wittemberg, he gave out that he despised learning, and, having placed himself at the head of a few raw and hot-brained recruits, raved at the papal abuses which still remained amongst them, and proceeded to remove them WITH HANDS, by breaking images and throwing down altars. This disorderly spirit gave the first impulse to Luther's return. ' The account of what had passed at Wittemberg, he said, had almost reduced him to a state of despair. Every thing he had as yet suffered was comparatively mere jest and boys' play. He could not enough lament, or express his disapprobation of those tumultuous proceedings; the Gospel was in imminent danger of being disgraced, from this cause.' Carolstadt fled before him; became a factious preacher at Orlamund; was banished by the elector; restored at length through the intercession of Luther; reconciled to him, but without much cordiality; and at length retired into Switzerland, where he exercised his pastoral office in a communion more congenial with his own sentiments, and died in 1531. Such is the *short* of Carolstadt; one of Luther's earliest defenders, who turned to be his rival and his enemy, and with whom he waged a sort of fratricidal war, for some years after his return from Wartburg, in conferences, sermons and treatises: of the last of these, his ' Address to the Celestial Prophets and Carolstadt' is the principal. Of his banishment it is unquestionable that Luther was not the author, though he thoroughly approved it; nay, on his submitting himself, he took great pains to get him restored: he could not succeed with Frederic, he did with John. Still I *have* thought him repulsive, arbitrary, and ungenerously sarcastic in his resistance to this Carolstadt; even as

I *have* thought him unwarrantably contemptuous and exclusive in his comments and conflicts with the Munzerites, and somewhat too confident in shifting off all influence of his doctrine from the rustic war. Hence my expression, 'not without question.' But, on a closer review, I find clear evidence that Carolstadt really was what Luther charged him with being—whimsical, extravagant, false and unsettled in doctrine; a preacher and a practiser of sedition—that he had moreover united himself to Munzer and his associates, and had thereby obtained a niche amongst the Celestial Prophets. I find clear evidence that Stubner, Stork, Cellery, Munzer and the rest were a nest of designing hypocrites; raging and railing, and making pretensions to divine favour, which they neither defined, nor defended.—His test of false prophecy and false profession, too, let it be remarked, is sound, efficacious and practicable; though perhaps founded (I refer to his test of conversion) rather too positively and exclusively upon his own personal experience. Again; I find Luther's doctrine so clear in marking the line of civil subordination that it was impossible for the peasants, or those who made them their stalkinghorse, to urge that Luther had taught them rebellion. Nor was it less than essential to sound doctrine, that he should disclaim, and express his abhorrence of their error.—With the exception of that part of the controversy therefore, which respected his Sacramentarian error, Luther had right on his side: and on that subject, Carolstadt, though right in his conclusion was so defective in his reasoning, so fickle, so versatile, and so disingenuous, that he defeated his own victory.

In the second of these controversies, which, although broached by Carolstadt, soon fell into abler hands, and was at length settled by abler heads than his,* Luther

---

* Zuingle and Œcolampadius, the former at Zurich, and the latter at Basil, were the great defenders of the faith, in this cause; who, notwithstanding the authority, ponderosity, calumniousness, and inflexi-

was lamentably wrong; wrong in his doctrine, and wrong in the spirit with which he defended it:—an affecting monument of what God-enlightened man is; who can literally and strictly see no farther than God gives him eyes to see withal, and for whose good it is not, and therefore for God's glory in whom it is not, that he should see every thing as it really is, but should in some particulars be left to shew, to remember and to feel, " the rock whence he was hewn, and the hole of the pit whence he was digged." Is there any exception to this remark amongst human teachers and writers? Can we mention one, on whose writings this mark has not been impressed, so as to make it legible that we are reading a book of man's, not of God's?

Luther held, that 'the real substance of the Lord's body and blood was in the bread and wine of the Eucharist, *together with* that previous substance which was bread and wine only:' a tenet, involving all the absurdity of popish transubstantiation, together with the additional one, that the same substance is at the same instant of two dissimilar kinds.

bility of Luther, manifested to the uttermost in opposing them, were enabled to " bring forth judgment unto truth." Zuingle's great work is a commentary on true and false religion, published in 1525, to which he added an appendix on the Eucharist Œcolampadius's principal performance is a treatise ' On the genuine meaning of our Lord's words, ' This is my body,' published about the same time: of which Erasmus, in his light and profane way, said, ' it might deceive the very elect,' and, being called, as one of the public censors, to review it, declared to their high mightinesses, the senate of Basil, that it was, in his opinion, a learned, eloquent and elaborate performance—he should be disposed to add ' pious,' if any thing could be pious which opposes the JUDGMENT AND CONSENT OF THE CHURCH Zuingle testified his sense of the importance of the question by remarking in his letter to Pomeranus, ' I do not think Antichrist can be completely subdued, unless this error of consubstantiation be rooted up.' Œcolampadius traces the origin of the doctrine of the REAL PRESENCE to Peter Lombard; and contends that every one of the Fathers had held that the words ' This is my body,' were not to be taken literally.

Now, although the word of God requires us to receive many things as true which are *beyond* the testimony of sense, and *above* the deductions of right reason, it nowhere calls us to receive any thing *contrary* to these. In what page, or chapter, or verse of the Bible are we called to believe a palpable contradiction? This negative applies, by the way, not only to the abstruser articles of the faith, the coexistence of three coequal persons in the one divine essence, the Godman-hood of the Lord Jesus Christ, and the reality of divine and diabolical agency within the human soul, but also to those simpler verities which affirm what are called the moral attributes of God, and have been strangely marred and confounded by neglecting it. Luther, for instance, perplexed to reconcile what is commonly understood by these with his representations of truth, has gone the length of maintaining that we do not know what these are in God: whereas, if justice, faithfulness, purity, grace, mercy, truth &c. &c. be not *essentially* the same sort of principles in God, as in his moral creatures, we can know nothing, we can believe nothing, we can feel nothing rightly concerning him. How these may consist with each other, and with his actings, is a distinct consideration: but it is a bungling, a false, and a pernicious expedient for solving difficulties, to deny first principles; and, if our very ideas of moral qualities, even as respects their essential nature, be impugned and taken from us, we cease to be moral beings.

The tenet of consubstantiation, then, is contradictory both to sense and reason. Four of our senses testify against it, whilst only one can claim to bear witness in its favour. If the disciples heard the Lord affirm it, and if we hear it from their writings, our sight, our touch, our taste, our smell, assure us that it is bread, and nothing but bread, which we are pressing with our teeth.*—The

* It was this *sort* of argument which brought the infidel Gibbon back to the Protestant faith, from which he had been seduced. ... 'That

same body can only be extended in one place at the same instant: the Lord's body therefore, which is at the right hand of God, cannot be in any place where the sacrament is administered; much less in the various places in which it is administered at the same moment; any more than the bread which he held in his hand when he instituted the ordinance could occupy the same place as the hand itself. Luther talked much of *ubiquity*; but what is the ubiquity of the Lord's body? Are we not expressly taught that it is extended, and remains for a season, in one place? "So then, after the Lord had spoken unto them, he was received up into heaven, and sat on the right hand of God;" "Who is gone into heaven, and is on the right hand of God." "Who is even at the right hand of God." "Sit on my right hand, until I make thine enemies thy footstool." "Whom the heavens must receive until the times of restitution of all things."—Besides, what precludes all dispute, He has in reality now no such body and blood to give. "There is a natural body, and there is a spiritual body." "Flesh and blood cannot inherit the kingdom of God." He did indeed turn his spiritual body into a natural one, by miracle, for some moments, at sundry times, after his resurrection, in order that he might give competency to his witnesses—"Even to them which did eat and drink with him after he rose from the dead"—but his abiding, ordinary subsistence, ever since, has been in a body which no teeth could manducate, no lips enclose.

All Luther's stress was upon the words 'This is my body:' he carried that sound and just principle of his, 'Interpret Scripture literally, not tropically, where you can,' to a false and even ridiculous extreme here; in opposition to his own admitted exception, 'unless an evident

---

the text of Scripture which seems to inculcate the real presence is attested only by a single sense, our sight—while the real presence itself is disproved by three of our senses.' See his 'Memoir of my Life and Writings,' vol. i. p. 58.

context, and some absurdity which offendeth against one of the articles of our faith, in the plain meaning, constrain us to such interpretation.' (See Part iv. Sect. iii. p. 239. of the following work.) Is this the only instance of such a form of speech? Circumcision, elsewhere called the token of the Abrahamic covenant, is, in some places, called *the* covenant; the two tables of stone are called *the* covenant; the lamb is called *the* passover; the rock stricken in Horeb is called Christ. Besides, if the bread be consubstantiated into his body, the cup should also be consubstantiated into a testament; " this cup *is* the new testament." And when we have eaten this flesh, and drunken this blood (if such act were possible) by a carnal manducation and deglutition, what has it done for us? As if flesh could nourish spirit; or, as if Christ's flesh (Luther dreamed that it was so) were spirit.'

Luther diminished the impression of his general character as a reasoner, and invalidated the authority of his argumentations, by an elaborate and ingenious obstinacy in this controversy. He gave himself the air of an orator who could descant upon a broomstick, and could defend a bad cause as vehemently as a good one, by exhausting the great powers of his mind in forcible appeals and sophistical illustrations to establish this unfounded tenet. Not that he knew, or thought, he was advocating falsehood—his only palliation is, he was honest; aye, honest to his dying hour; for however he might regret the heat of spirit and of language into which he had gone out against his opponents, he never made any concession with respect to his doctrine, but declared it amidst the concussion and relentings of a severe sickness in 1526, and continued to preach and write upon it to the last. The spirit he had manifested, he *did* regret; and well he might. He had maintained it like a wild bull in a net, calling names, and making devils of his adversaries—who, to say the least, were as pure, as learned and as laborious, if not so commanding in their aspect, so exalted in their sufferings, and so brilliant in their successes, as he—and the rending of the mantle which should have covered Switzerland as well as Germany, and made both one against the foe of both, was more his than theirs.* This

* Take an instance of the toil and sweat of his argumentation; take an instance, or two, of the calumnious fierceness with which he pursued these fraternal adversaries

'But it is absurd to suppose the body of Christ to be in more than a hundred thousand places at once —This is not more absurd than the diffusion of the soul through every part of the body. Touch any part of the body with the point of a needle, and the whole man, the whole soul is sensible of the injury If then the soul be equally in every part of the body, and you can give no reason for it, why may not Christ be every where, and every where equally, in the sacrament? Tell me, if you can, why a grain of wheat produces so many grains of the same species; or why a single eye can fix itself at once on a thousand objects, or a thousand eyes can be fixed at once on a single minute object —Take another example What a feeble, poor, miserable, vanishing thing is the voice of a man! Yet what wonders it can perform—how it penetrates the hearts of multitudes of men! and yet not so as that each person acquires merely a portion of it, but rather as if every individual ear became possessed of the whole. If this were not a matter of experience, there would not be a greater miracle in the whole world. If then the corporeal voice of man can effect such wonders, why may not the glorified body of Christ be much more powerful and efficacious in its operations?—Farther; when the Gospel is preached through the exertion of the human voice, does not every true believer, by the instrumentality of the word, become actually possessed of Christ in his heart? Not that Christ sits in the heart, as a man sits upon a chair, but rather as he sitteth at the right hand of the Father. How this is no man can tell, yet the Christian knows, by experience, that Christ is present in his heart. Again, every individual heart possesses the whole of Christ, and yet a thousand hearts in the aggregate possess no more than one Christ. The sacrament is not a greater miracle than this.'

'The Sacramentarian pestilence makes havoc, and acquires strength in its progress. Pray for me, I beseech you, for I am cold and torpid. A most unaccountable lassitude, if not Satan himself, possesses me, so that I am able to do very little. Our ingratitude, or perhaps some other sin, is the cause of the divine displeasure: certainly our notorious contempt of the word of God will account for the present penal delusion, or even a greater. I was but too true a prophet, when I predicted that something of this kind would happen.—If I had not known

acrimonious controversy, deplorable on many accounts, but not without its direct and collateral benefits, began in from experience, that God in his anger did suffer men to be carried away with delusions, I could not have believed that so many, and so great men, would have been seduced by such trifling and childish reasonings, to support this pestilentious, this sacrilegious heresy.... I am all on fire to profess openly for once my faith in the sacrament, and to expose the tenets of our adversaries to derision in a few words, for they will not attend to an elaborate argument. I would have published my sentiments long ago, if I had had leisure, and Satan had not thrown impediments in my way.... Factious spirits always act in this way. They first form to themselves an opinion which is purely imaginary; and then torture Scripture to support that opinion.... He gave himself seriously to the work, and produced, in the month of February or March, a most elaborate treatise, in the German language, on the words 'Take, eat, this is my body,' AGAINST THE FANATICAL SPIRITS OF THE SACRAMENTARIANS.... They lay no stress on any thing except their Sacramentarian tenet. Devoid of every christian grace, they pretend to the sanctity of martyrs, on account of this single opinion. ... They would persuade one that this was the great, the only concern of the Holy Ghost, when, in reality, it is a delusion of Satan, who, under the pretence of love and concord, is raising dissensions and mischiefs of every kind.'—In the celebrated conference at Marpurg, proposed and accomplished by the landgrave of Hesse in 1529, for the purpose of mutual conciliation and peace—though the Sacramentarians begged hard to be acknowledged as brethren, and even went so far as to own repeatedly, that the body of Christ was verily present in the Lord's Supper, though in a spiritual manner, and Zuingle himself, in pressing for mutual fraternity, declared with tears, that there was no man in the world with whom he more earnestly wished to agree, than with the Wittemberg divines—the spirit of Luther proved perfectly untractable and intolerant. It seems he had come with a mind determined not to budge one inch upon this point. Accordingly, 'nothing more could be gained from him than that each side should shew christian charity to the other as far as they could conscientiously; and that both should diligently pray God to lead them into the truth. To go further, Luther maintained, was impossible, and expressed astonishment that the Swiss divines could look upon him as a christian brother, when they did not believe his doctrine to be true. In such circumstances, however, though there could be no such thing as fraternal union, the parties, he allowed, might preserve a friendly sort of peace and concord; might do good turns to each other, and abstain from harsh and acrimonious language.' The vehemence, in fact, was not confined to one side, though the Swiss had learned more of modern manners than the Lutherans, and could cut deep without appearing to carry a sword;

1524, and continued *to* and *beyond* Luther's death: the churches which pass under his name still retain his dogma.

In the last of these controversies, I pronounce him all in the right; right, I would be understood to mean, as respects his conclusion and his opponent, though he adduces some arguments which might have been spared, and does not always exhibit a full understanding and correct use of his weapons.

Erasmus, who was Luther's predecessor in age by about sixteen years, had done the reformers some service; chiefly by facilitating the knowledge of the ancient languages through his successful researches in literature, but not a little by employing his peculiar talent of ridicule upon some of the grosser abominations of Popery. Not that he had any hearty concern about these; but he was a man born *pour le rire*—he was all for his jest—and monks and friars furnished him with a subject which he did not know how to reject. Like Lucian and Porphyry therefore, he, without seriously meaning it, prepared the way for a better faith, by turning much of the old into derision. He was indignant to be thought a sceptic; and many now-a-days think him hardly used by such an insinuation. But is not every one who trifles with his soul a sceptic? and what is the great multitude of professing Christians but such a company of triflers, who, if they were brought to the test, would act what he said in his irony, ' God has not given every body the spirit of martyrdom?'

Erasmus, however, had committed himself in some degree to the cause of the reformers, by speaking well of

---

whereas the Lutherans growled more than they bit, in this fight.—Still our business is with the wrong of Luther. He provoked first, he spoke worst; their acrimony was no excuse for his. His was the fury of a great man brought to the level of, or even below his equals; whom he would fain count his inferiors, and treat as his vassals.

them, specially of Luther, and acquiescing in many of their dogmas. In 1520, when the bull was preparing, and when the bull was out, he had both written and spoken a very decided language in Luther's favour: 'God had sent him to reform mankind;' 'Luther's sentiments are true, but I wish to see more mildness in his manner;' 'The cause of Luther is invidious, because he at once attacks the bellies of the monks, and the diadem of the Pope.' 'Luther possesses great natural talents; he has a genius particularly adapted to the explanation of difficult points of literature, and for rekindling the sparks of genuine evangelical doctrine, which have been almost extinguished by the trifling subtilties of the schools. Men of the very best character, of the soundest learning, and of the most religious principles, are much pleased with Luther's books; in proportion as any person is remarkable for upright morals and gospel-purity, he has the less objections to Luther's sentiments. Besides, the life of the man is extolled, even by those who cannot bear his doctrines. It grieved him that a man of such FINE PARTS should be rendered desperate by the mad cries and bellowings of the monks.' When pressed by the Pope's legates to write against Luther, he answered, ' Luther is too great a man for me to encounter. I do not even always understand him. However, to speak plainly, he is so extraordinary a man, that I learn more from a single page of his books than from all the writings of Thomas Aquinas.'—Still, as the cause advanced, Erasmus did not advance with it, but receded. Vanity, a love of the praise of men, was his ruling passion; and the particular mode of it, a desire to stand high with great men—with princes, dignified ecclesiastics, and all who were highly thought of—to stand high, specially on the ground of extreme moderation; such as became a man of letters. He would be an Atticus in his day. To join heartily with the reformers was not the way to achieve this object; they were despised by the rulers, and, what was still more provoking, they would not make him a king even among themselves.

> ' Micat inter omnes
> Julium sidus, velut inter ignes
> Luna minores.'—Hor.

But *he* was not that Luna, Luther was that Luna. What was to be done therefore, but to pout, and distinctly separate himself from them; giving the princes clearly to understand, that they were mistaken if they thought him one of them? Thus, by a sort of dexterous manœuvre, he would kill two birds at once; avenge the injury of his ' spreta forma,' and open a way for the sun and stars to shine in upon him. He confessed this in his answer to Luther: ' As yet I have not written a syllable against you; otherwise I might have secured much applause from the great; but I saw I should injure the 'Gospel. I have only endeavoured to do away the idea that there is a perfect understanding between you and me, and that all your doctrines are in my books. Pains have been taken to instil this sentiment into the mind of the princes, and it is hard even now to convince them that it is not so.' Luther would have been glad that the matter should rest here. Erasmus had done all the service he was made for; but let him not become their enemy: he was a successful sharpshooter; some of his shots would hit, annoy and dismay. There were underlings, however, in Luther's camp, as well as in the Pope's: and these had not quite *mind* enough to preserve Luther's line. They would step beyond it; they lampooned the satirist; hinted pretty broadly what he was, and made him little to his great ones. Luther tried to abate the shock of their attack; but it was too late. The enemy had been beforehand with him. Henry of England had implored, Adrian in two epistles had supplicated, duke George had demanded, Tunstall had conjured, Clement had persuaded: and all this, whilst the sting of the wasps was yet sore. Luther makes his last attempt to pacify him: with great forbearance, yet not trenching upon sincerity; with some galling hints as to the real state of the cause, but, as Erasmus himself allowed, with sufficient civility. 'I shall not complain of you, for having behaved yourself as a man estranged from us, to keep fair with the Papists, my enemies; nor that you have censured us with too much acrimony.'....'The whole world must own with gratitude your great talents and services in the cause of literature, through the revival of which we are enabled to read the sacred Scriptures in their originals.—I never wished that, forsaking or neglecting your own proper talents, you should enter into our camp.'....'I could have wished that the COMPLAINT of Hutten had never been published.'....'I am concerned, as well as you that the resentment and hatred of so many eminent persons hath been excited against you. I must suppose that this gives you no small uneasiness; for virtue like yours, mere human virtue, cannot raise a man above being affected by such trials'.....'What can I do now? Things are exasperated on both sides; and I could wish, if I might be allowed to act the part of a mediator, that they would cease to attack you with such animosity, and suffer your old age to rest in peace in the Lord: and thus they would conduct themselves, in my opinion, if they either considered your weakness, or the magnitude of the controverted cause, which hath been long since beyond your capacity. They would shew their moderation towards you so much the more, since our affairs are advanced to such a point, that our cause is in no peril, although even Erasmus should attack it with all his might; so far are we from fearing any of his strokes and strictures.'....'Our prayer is, that the Lord may bestow on you a spirit worthy of your great reputation; but if this be not granted, I entreat you, if you cannot help us, to remain at least a spectator of our severe conflict; and not to join our adversaries; and in particular not to write tracts against us; on which condition I will not publish against you.'

All is in vain: to preserve his gold, to shew his gratitude for what he has already received, and (except he be barbarously treated) to earn more, his pledges must now be redeemed, and out comes the Diatribe.*

He vapours much about the great danger of publishing it: 'no printer at Basil would dare to undertake his or any work which contained a word against Luther.' 'The die is cast, he tells Henry (to whom he had sent a part of the manuscript for his approbation); my little book on Freewill is published: a bold deed, believe me, if the situation of Germany at this time be considered: I expect to be pelted; but I will console myself with the example of your majesty, who has not escaped their outrages.' Conscience speaks out, when he says to Wolsey, 'I have not chosen to dedicate this work to any one, least my calumniators should instantly say that in this business I had been hired to please the great: otherwise I would have inscribed it to you, or to the Pope.' His ruling passion speaks out, when he declares the mighty consequences which he expected from his publication. He writes to Tunstall; 'The little book is out; and, though written with the greatest moderation, will, if I mistake not, excite most prodigious commotions. Already pamphlets fly at my head.'

Such was the birth of the Diatribe; the offspring of a peevish, dissatisfied, vain man; who had tampered with both parties, and pleased neither, but was now sufficiently determined which side he would be of, yet aimed still to preserve his favourite character of moderation. It is the work of a great scholar, but not of a deep thinker; 'of one who had scoured the surface of his question, but by no

---

* He feared losing the pension which he received from England Clement had made him a present of two hundred florins. He had received most magnificent promises from popes, prelates and princes.

means penetrated into its substance;' of one who knew what is in the Bible, but did not understand the Bible: imposing, but not solid; objurgatory and commendative; but neither disproving what he blamed, nor establishing, or even defining, what he approved. Yet is this a performance, such as, not careless persons only, but half the tribe of professedly serious gospellers will defend, and do in substance maintain, in opposition to Luther's; nay, many that call and account themselves Calvinists, or Calvinistic (I am by no means an advocate for names—it is character and principle, not sect or party, that I would uphold), are in heart and understanding, if not avowedly, Freewillers; squaring, as they seek to do, the testimony of Jesus Christ, the Son of God, to the deductions of blinded human reason, and making a God for themselves, by blending shreds and patches of Scripture with shreds and patches of their own imagination, instead of simply studying, lying at the feet of, and inhabiting, that living and true One, whom the Bible has been written and published to make known.—I subscribe *my* testimony to Luther's, that it is tedious, distractive, illusory, false and pernicious.

Luther hesitated about answering it; but at length consented to do so, for reasons which he declares in the introduction of his letter: if he was to answer such a production of such a man upon such a subject, why, it must be done as he has done it—with all his might. He that would see Luther, therefore, may behold him here.

Erasmus replied in two distinct treatises under the name of Hyperaspistes, ' defender as with a shield;' the first, as he tells us, written in ten days, that it might be ready for the ensuing Frankfort fair (the great mart for literature as well as commerce, in that day)—a passionate and hasty effusion, in which he did not give himself time to think; the second, a very long and highly-laboured performance, in which ' he was completely unfettered, and completely in earnest, and, if he had been able, would, without the least mercy, have trampled on Luther, and ground him to powder.' ' *Diis aliter visum.*' ' This second book is very long and very tedious; but the tediousness, of which every reader must complain, is not owing so much to the length of the performance, as to the confusion which pervades it throughout. The *writer* is kept sufficiently alive, amidst great prolixity, by the unceasing irritation of his hostility and resentment; but the reader is fatigued and bewildered, by being led through obscure paths one after another, and never arriving at any distinct and satisfactory conclusion. A close attention of the mind to a long series of confused and jumbled propositions wearies the intellect, as infallibly, as a continued exertion in looking at objects difficult to be distinguished exhausts the powers of the most perfect organs of vision.'

Luther did not rejoin to this twofold reply: he well knew that Erasmus was fighting for victory, not for truth, and he had better things to do than write books merely to repeat unanswered arguments. There was nothing of argument in the Hyperaspistes, which had not been answered in his Bondage of the Will; even as there was nothing in the Diatribe, which had not been in substance advanced and confuted many times before. The Letter, or Treatise, which is now presented to the public must, therefore, be considered as containing Luther's full, final, and, as he deemed it, unrefuted and irrefragable judgment, on the state of the human will.

That state is, according to Erasmus, a state of liberty; according to Luther, a state of bondage. Such is the subject and position brought into debate by Erasmus, and accepted as matter of challenge by Luther.

The accurate Locke, whose name I would ever recite with veneration and gratitude, has shewn that the question is improperly stated. The will, he says in substance, is but a power of the human mind, or, of the man; freedom is also a power of the man; to ask, therefore,

PREFACE.

whether the will be free is to ask whether one power of the man possesses another power of the man: which is like asking, whether his sleep be swift, or his virtue square; liberty being as little applicable to the will, as swiftness of motion is to sleep, or squareness to virtue. The proper question is, not whether *man's will* be free, but whether *man* be free: and this he determines that he is, in so far, and only so far, as he can by the direction or choice of his mind, preferring the existence of any action to the non-existence of that action, and *vice versâ*, make it to exist, or not exist; liberty being a power to act, or not to act, according as we shall choose, or, *will*: If however the improper question be still urged, whether the will be free, it must be changed into this form; *is man free to will?* that is, has he liberty in the exercise of his will? Now this must respect either the act of exercising his will; or the result of that exercise, the thing chosen. As to the former of these, he determines, that, in the greater number of cases, man has not liberty; for when any action in his power is once proposed to his thoughts, as presently to be done, *will he must:* in the latter, he determines, that he cannot but have liberty; he wills what he wills, he is pleased with what he is pleased with. To make a question here, is to suppose that one will determines the acts of another, and that another determines that; and so on *in infinitum.**—In this latter assertion, Luther, it must be remarked, is as explicit as Locke; maintaining expressly, that a compelled will is a contradiction in terms, and should be called *Noluntas*, rather than *Voluntas: non-will*, rather than *will*. (See Part i. Sect. xxiv. p. 69.)

The schoolmen, from whom Luther and Erasmus took this question (Erasmus first on this occasion—but then Luther had taken it up before), made a distinction between the absolute faculty of the will, and that faculty as exercised, or, in action. Their question was not, *an sit libera*

* See Locke's Essay, vol. i. pp. 195—200. b. ii. c. 21.

voluntas, but *an sit liberum arbitrium?* a distinction, in fact, without a difference: because, what is the subject matter about which they were disputing? not a dormant faculty surely, but a faculty such as it is when exercised; for how else can its nature and properties be ascertained? Luther is as perceptive as Locke himself here. Erasmus, in his definition of Freewill, calls it ' that power of the human will by which a man is able to turn himself to those things which appertain to his salvation, or to turn himself away from them:' in reality meaning to interpose a *something* between the will and its actings. Luther, when canvassing this definition, denies that there can be any such *tertium quid;* and uses a language so very like Locke's, that it might well draw from his historian the remark, ' Luther, with as much acuteness as if he had studied Mr. Locke's famous chapter on power, replies &c.' ' But, what is meant by this same power 'applying itself and turning away itself;' except it be this very willing and refusing, this very choosing and despising, this very approving and rejecting; in short, except it be ' the will performing its very office;' I see not. So that we must suppose this power to be ' a something interposed between the will itself and its actings:' a power by which the will itself draws out the operation of willing and refusing, and by which that very act of willing and refusing is elicited. It is not possible to imagine or conceive any thing else here.' See Part iii. Sect. ii. p. 132.

But this false distinction opens a door to the solution of the whole difficulty. Their improper question has been, ' Is the *will* free?' The proper question would be, ' Is the *understanding* free?' that is, has the man's will all the case before it, when he decides upon any given question? A blind understanding will lead to a false determination, though that determination be made without any thing approaching to compulsion. Now this I apprehend to be just the true state of the case: the natural man, having his understanding darkened, being alienated from the life of God, through the ignorance that is in him, because of the blindness of his heart; and being, moreover, possessed by the devil, whose energizing consists in maintaining and increasing his blindness; forms his decisions and determinations upon partial and false evidence. The same observation extends to the spiritual man, in so far as he is not spiritual; in so far as his flesh, through which the devil acts upon him, is allowed in subserviency to the great general principle, ' God's glory in his real good,' to influence the determination of his will. So that it is the judgment, perception, or understanding, not the will, correctly speaking, which is really in bondage; that faculty, which presents objects to the determining faculty, presenting them erroneously, either by suppressing what ought to be made present, or giving a false colour or distorted appearance to that which is, and ought to be, there. This suggestion will explain the paradox, that the will is at the same time free and not free, in popular language: free, inasmuch as from its very nature it cannot be compelled; not free, inasmuch as it acts in the dark: so that it may more fitly be called *blind-will*, than *bond-will;* which is Luther's term. This suggestion will go further; it will explain all mysteries' and all paradoxes: Paul's conflict in Romans vii.—Pharaoh's induration—our own daily experience—nay, the whole system of God's government, in ruling, as he does, a world of moral beings—flee before it. Only such considerations as He makes present can really constitute the materials of any judgment which we form, and consequently of any determination which we can come to, with respect to our own actings: that is, our volitions, whilst free, are subject to His agency, and, through the means of our perceptions, His will becomes ours.—I have adopted throughout, however, the language of the combatants; which is also the language of common life. I speak of the *will* as free, or in bondage; and I use the term Freewill, as expressive of some supposed power in man, separating it into a sort of distinct substance, and almost continually personifying it.

Let it be conceded then, that the question is not correctly worded; that the proper inquiry is, not whether man's will be free, but whether man be free; or rather, as we have just seen, whether his perceptive faculty be clear and entire: still the substance of the debate remains unaltered, and its importance unimpaired. Essentially, we are ascertaining what is the moral state of man; and the considerations, nay, even the expressions, introduced into many parts of the discussion, will shew that it is not an abstract and isolated question about the will which we are entertaining, but an investigation of our Adam soul. What shall be called momentous, if this subject be not so? What can be understood, if this be unknown? Of what sort is the Christ of an ignorant Freewiller? (See Part i. Sect. v. vi. vii. viii.) The truth is, ignorance of the real state of man lies at the root of all religious ignorance, and it is, manifestly, the ordained, arranged and continually operated course of the Lord's dealings with his people to bring them to the knowledge, use and enjoyment of Himself through the means of deep, minute, self-emptying and self-abasing self-knowledge. How can this be, but by opening to us the abyss of impotency as well as crime, of blindness as well as enmity, into which we have freely plunged ourselves?

It is the peculiarity of this treatise to explore the present state of the human soul by the aid of scripture testimonies and scriptural reasonings, exclusively; without one syllable of abstract philosophical investigation beyond what is absolutely necessary to the writing and reading upon it intelligibly.* Luther was not ignorant of metaphysics;

* I was once asked, why, with such an excellent treatise as Jonathan Edwards's, and others, in our own language, I thought it necessary to revive Luther. Here is my answer. Your great metaphysicians decom-

he had been thoroughly trained in Aristotle and the schoolmen: if he forbore to use such weapons, it was because
he disdained them; I should rather say, because, according
to his own testimony as recited already, he had found
them pernicious. Erasmus sometimes compels him to
break a lance of this kind; when he gives full proof that
he could have handled such weapons dexterously, if he
had deemed them to be the weapons of the sanctuary.
One who was no common speculator, and no unskilful
arbitrator, has said of him; 'Even in the metaphysical
niceties, which could not be entirely avoided in this abstruse inquiry, he proved greatly his (Erasmus's) over-
match.' But those who have *really* submitted themselves
to the authority of Scripture, and have drunk deep of it
to know the Father's testimony concerning Jesus, will feel
that, as this subject is the most momentous which can
engage the human soul, so this method of investigating it
can alone be expected to yield a satisfactory conclusion.
They will rejoice therefore, that such a man as Erasmus—
a man well acquainted with the letter of Scripture (so
Luther testifies of him—*qui sic nostra omnia perlustravit*—Part iii. Sect. vi. note ᵉ)—should have delivered his
challenge in the form of an appeal to the canonical
Scriptures only; and that such a man as Luther, who
had penetrated to no inconsiderable depth in the mines

pound man; and, if they could, would decompound God. Your great
theologians do the same. But if we would really know either man or
God, we must first learn to take the Bible for granted—that it is the
word of God—and then study both, as therein drawn and described: not
imagining a God for ourselves, by decking out some we know not what
substratum with a number of what we call attributes; but remember-
ing, that what we hear called His attributes are in reality parts of His
essence, and considering, that it is THAT GOOD ONE who hath devised,
fore-ordained, and in his appointed time manifested the Lord Jesus
Christ as the image of Himself, in his person and in his actings—which
is our God; and that we ourselves are parts of that Adam, by his dealings with, and declarations concerning which, in Christ, He has been,
and is, effecting the manifestation of what He himself is.

of that volume, should have accepted and brought it to issue.

The ORDER of the argumentation is minutely shewn in the Table of Contents which follows, and is afterwards noticed at the head of each Part and Section. I shall only premise therefore, that, after a short Introduction, Luther pursues the order of Erasmus's march (who, desultory as he is, furnishes us with a clue for his labyrinth), first examining his Preface, then his Proem, then his testimonies, then his pretended refutation, and afterwards establishing his own position by direct proof: he concludes the whole with a pathetic address, even as each Part exhibits a specimen of the 'melting mood,' in its close. It is a common idea, that Luther wanted softness; yet the once cloistered, but afterwards conjugal and paternal monk, could weep, be gentle, be compassionate, be a little child.

The FORM of the treatise is epistolary: it is truly nothing else but a LETTER to Erasmus; and therefore I have preferred the division of PARTS to that of CHAPTERS—considering chapters of a letter as anomalous, though we are accustomed to it, I grant, in our distribution of the Scriptures: this division however, it is to be remembered, has no authority, and has led to much misconstruction; Locke advises those who would understand Paul to disregard it. I have only one caution to give with respect to these Parts; which is, that the reader do not suffer himself to take fright at some of the less inviting *gladiations* of the first Part—not that *I* account them uninteresting, but that the work increases in interest, as it proceeds. I trust the reader will find it so, and will remember meanwhile, that we must make a way to the walls, as well as storm them.

I cannot compliment Luther upon his STYLE: the sentences are long, the ideas multifarious; the words often barbarous, their collocation inharmonious. But there is always meaning in what he says, although that meaning be not always obvious, or clear: he is sometimes elaborately eloquent, and often simply so. The language is like the man. He is Hercules with his club, rather than Achilles with his sword; more of a Menelaus than an Ulysses; always forcible, sometimes playful; drawing wires now and then; never leaving a loophole for his adversary to escape through, but dragging him through many of his own.

The EXCELLENCES of this treatise are, a noble stand for truth on its proper ground—God's testimony unmixed with man's testimony (see Part ii. Sect. i—xii.); that ground cleared from objection (Part ii. Sect. xiii. xiv.); an integral part of the truth of God firmly set upon its base (see Part iii. Part iv. Part v.); much of it, besides, collaterally and incidentally asserted or implied—proved, or left to clear and palpable inference: so that a man need not fear to say, ' Give me Luther, and I will give you THE TRUTH.'

But Luther has not given it us, either in this treatise, or elsewhere; the defects of his theological system being manifest in this best of his best,* as well as his other performances: I say ' theological system;' because TRUTH is one vast whole, not a number of disjointed and dissevered propositions—a whole made up of many parts, which, whilst distinct, are yet so closely interwoven and compacted with each other, that it is scarcely possible to discern any one of these as it really is, without discerning each, and all, and that whole. Let those who deny system in the Bible say what they understand by Ἡ ἀλήθεια (*the* truth); let those who deny system in the Bible say why this should be a name for that counsel, or plan, which God is executing in Christ; why it should be a name for Christ; why it should be a name for God.† If God be

---

* ' It may not be impropei to observe, that Luthei himself, many years afterwards, had so good an opinion of it, as to declare, that he could not review any one of his writings with complete satisfaction, unless perhaps his Catechism and his Bondage of the Will.'

† See John i. 17 xiv. 6 Eph. i. 13. iv. 21. Col. i. 5. 1 John v. 20.

himself the only truth, THE TRUE ONE; if Christ be his Image; if the counsel, or system of divine operations, which is *in Him*, be the image of that Image; if the Gospel, or doctrine of the kingdom of God, be the word or declarer of that counsel; we can have no difficulty in understanding why one and the same term should be applied to all these various subjects. They are all, in various regards, THE TRUTH. Nor is it a sound objection to say, 'this revered man did not see it there,' or, 'that revered man did not see it there;' it may be there still: and, if it be not there, God has come short of His object in revelation, which is, not to reveal a proposition, but to reveal HIMSELF. Let every one so study the Bible as to get to know God by it; which he cannot do, except he realize what is there written, IN HIM, and realize it as a whole: let him at the same time take this caution—he is to get his whole, not by murdering or stifling any part, but by giving its fair, well-considered and authenticated meaning to each and every portion of the testimony.

The DEFECTS of this treatise, then, are the defects of Luther's theological system. It was not given to him to discern, that all God's dealings with creatures are referable to one vast counsel, devised, ordained and operated for the accomplishment of one vast end; that this vast end is the manifestation of God; that this counsel is in *all* its parts (not in that only which respects man's redemption, but every jot of every part) laid, conducted and consummated *in* and *by* Christ—the eternally predestinated, and in time very, *risen* GOD-MAN* (see Part ii. Sect. viii. note r. Part iii. Sect. xxxii. note s); much less was it given to him to discern the structure and materials of that counsel by which God is effecting this end—that Adam, meaning not the personal Adam only, but all that was created in him, even the whole human

---

* See, amongst other places, John i 1—14 1 John i. 1, 2. Coloss. i. 15—20. Heb. i. Prov. viii. 22—31. Micah v. 2.

race, is the great and capital subject of His self-manifesting operations. (See Part iii. Sect. xxviii. notes ᵗ ʸ ˣ. Sect. xxxvii. note¹ &c.) Though he had some insight into the mystery of Christ's person (see Part i. Sect. iii.; also Sect. xvi. note ⁿ)—that He was verily God and man, a coequal in the Trinity made man through the Virgin's impregnation by the Holy Ghost, he was not fully led into the mystery that his person is constituted by taking a human person, the spiritualized man Jesus, into union with his divine person, and that he has been acting in this person, as inspired, not by his own godhead, but by the Holy Ghost,* from the beginning—having subsisted as the glorified God-man first predestinately and secretly, up to the period of his ascension; and now, ever since that period, really and declaredly—doing the will of the Father continually, not his own will, by the Holy Ghost's inspiration, not his own; thus exhibiting the Trinity in every act he performs, which is, in deed and in truth, every act of God. His human person, moreover, was marvellously formed, so as to be at the same time both son of Adam and son of God; the Holy Ghost's impregnation gave him a spotless soul; the daughter of Adam gave him a sinful body; thus he became the sinless sinner; thus he that knew no sin was made sin for us, and was in all points tempted like as we are, without sin; that same Holy Ghost which had begotten him sinless, keeping him without sin amidst all the temptations of the world the flesh and the devil, until he had died to sin once, and his mortality had been swallowed up of life.—Into this depth of the mystery of Christ's person,†

---

* See especially Matt. xii. 28. Acts i 1, 2. ii. 22 &c. x. 38

† The essence of Christ's person is God-man-hood: He is God the equal of the Father and of the Holy Ghost: He is man by the conception of the Holy Ghost in the Virgin; He is God-man in one substance, through that union of his God person with his man person, which is effected by the agency of the Holy Ghost, Who, being one in essence with his God person, inhabiteth that manhood of His which he hath generated. What is that manhood so generated? Its essence is a pure,

of which the essential element is ' union yet distinctness'—both as it respects his divine and human person, and as it respects his oneness with us—it was not given to Luther to penetrate. (See as before, Part ii. Sect. viii. note ʳ. Part iii. Sect xxii. note ˢ; also Part v. Sect. xxii. note ᵗ, Sect. xxviii. note º.) Again; although it was given him to see the fact of man's coming into the world guilty (which he ascribes to his being born of Adam (see Part v. Sect. xx.), and that entire vitiation of his nature, as brought into the world with him, which renders him both vile and impotent (a fact which he assumes, and reasons upon, throughout the whole of his treatise, but see especially Part iv. Sect. x.); he was not led to see the mystery of the creation and fall of every individual of the human race, male and female, *in* and *with* Adam.* (See Part iv. Sect. x. note ᶻ. Part v. Sect. xx. note ᴾ.) Again; though it was given him to see the fact that there are elect and reprobate men, God having predestinated some to everlasting life and others to everlasting death; he had no insight into that covenant-standing in Christ, and the appro-

---

spotless, sinless spirit inhabiting (in the days of his flesh, and whilst yet it was flesh and blood) a sinful body Romans i 3, 4 *rightly interpreted*, confirms this satisfying account of the matter. " Who was made of the seed of David according to the flesh, that is, the body; Who was declared to be Son of God with power, according to the spirit of holiness—that is, *according to his spirit which was holy* (the opposition, I maintain, is between *his* flesh and *his* spirit)—*from the period* of his resurrection (ἐξ ἀναστάσεως) The whole teroui of Scripture declaration falls in with this view. His body is his connecting link with manhood, that is, with *Adam-hood*. *Son of man* is not *man* merely, man *any how* begotten, *any how* made, *any how* existent (as the Lord God might have made five hundred species of men), but Son of *Adam*, one who has his being SOME HOW *through* and *of the stock* of Adam.

* The notes referred to are explicit and full, but take an illustration, which may be of use to some, 1. from the case of Rebekah, Genesis xxv. 21—23 (. . . " Two *nations* are in thy womb, and two manner of *people* shall be separated from thy bowels); and 2. from Heb vii, 9, 10. (For he was yet *in the loins of his Father*, when &c)

priateness of His work, consequently, to the elect, which renders God just in acting a difference between them, whilst the original and eternal separation is of a law beyond justice—even of that sovereignty which knows no limit but omnipotency. Thus he was not only left, through his ignorance of God's plan and counsel, without any insight into that blessed and glorious principle which reconciles the spiritual mind to the severity of his appointments—for how, else, shall that paramount end of God-manifestation be accomplished?—but he was even obliged to give up the justice of God (which, both verily and discernibly, is without a flaw in this procedure) and to take refuge in a most pernicious falsehood, ' that we know nothing about God's justice, and must be content to be ignorant what it is, till THE DAY disclose it.' Why, if justice, truth and all other moral excellencies be not in Him essentially what they are in us, and according to our *spiritual* conceptions of HIM, ' chaos is come again:' we know nothing—nothing of God—He has revealed himself in vain. (See Part iii. Sect. xxviii. notes [t] [v] [x]. Sect. xxxvii. note [l]. Part iv. Sect. xv. note [n]. Part v. Sect. xxxiii. note [e].) Again; whilst it was given him to see something of the freeness and completeness of a sinner's justification *in* and *by* Christ, it was impossible, from the very nature of that ignorance which hath already been ascribed to him, that he should see it correctly and perfectly: he neither saw the eternal justification which they received in Christ Jesus, distinctly, personally and individually, before the world began—God engaging to raise them up to Him as his accepted ones, for the sake of the merits of His death; nor did he see with precision what constituted their atonement made in time; nor did he see the state into which they were hereby brought, and have from the beginning been dealt with as though they had been meritoriously brought—a state of gracious acceptance, in which they can bring forth, as He is pleased to enable them, and actually do bring forth, as He is pleased to enable them, fruit unto God: nor did he see that, whilst their crown is a free crown, the Lord has so arranged, and so brings it to pass, that it shall be a righteous thing in God to put a difference between the righteous and the wicked; there being a mind in the one, which is correlative to the manifestation He has made and is making of himself in his new-creation kingdom, whereas in the other there is nothing but enmity to Him, as so displayed. Again; though he had some insight into the nature of Holy-Ghost-influences, the other parts of his ignorance were incompatible with true and correct knowledge here. He did not see that the gift of the Holy Ghost is, in fact, the gift of His personal presence and agency; altogether a super-creation gift, a gift in Christ; had, *when* and *as* God has been pleased to arrange to give it—had therefore, when it be good for his people to have, and withheld, as to manifestation, when it be good that they have it not; in nowise contributing to the justification, properly so called, of a sinner, though enabling the manifestly justified to shew their justification. When I say, ' in nowise contributing,' I mean that none of their acts performed *by* and *in* the Spirit, are what contribute the least particle to their acceptance. They are foreknown freely, predestinated freely, called freely, justified freely (that is, have their absolution from all sin testified to them freely) glorified freely; whilst it is the Holy Ghost who alone enables, nay constrains them to believe, thereby exhibiting in their persons an obedience to the divine commandment,* and putting a badge upon them which declares

* God has given a commandment, " Repent ye, and believe the Gospel;" " And this is his *commandment*, that we believe on the name &c " This command is congruous to that manifestation which he makes of himself in his super-creation kingdom , say rather, is congruous to what He himself is—He being, even as He hath hereby shewn himself to be, the God, who, in perfect harmony and consistency with all other perfections, is love, grace and mercy. The giving of this commandment,

that they are in the number of those for whom Christ according to the will of the Father—thus evinced to be the will of the sacred and coequal Three—in due time died. Luther's ignorance on this subject led him to speak of Adam's having the Spirit, of the Spirit's being our law-fulfiller, and of the Jewish church, as not having been justified by the law, because they had not the Spirit. (See Part iv. Sect. x. note ^{z}. Part v. Sect. x. note ^{z}.) As if the Spirit of grace were a creational, natural, or legal possession! Again; whilst he saw the Law to be a condemning precept, he did not understand its real nature, form and design; that it was an interpolation, typical in all its parts, preparatory, temporary; whose glory was to be done away. (See Part iii. Sect. xxiv. note ^{1}. Part v. Sect. x. xi. xii. xiii.) This ignorance led him to bring it back upon the people of God, instead of banishing it for ever; to heap burdens with his left hand, which he had hardly removed with his right. He was not led to apprehend the distinct nature, as well as end, of Law obedience and Gospel obedience: that obedience to the Law, which he substantially, if not in word, demanded, is not only an obeying *for* life instead of an *acting* of the life given; but is even a denying of God to be what He is and is manifesting himself to be, whilst we profess to be believing in Him, and serving Him.*

and the receiving of his people according to it, falls in with his great design of God manifestation, by drawing out, as it does, what is in man, and shewing HIM as dealing with what *is* so drawn out, according to justice and equity —It no way disparages the freeness of the grace, whilst it manifests to the uttermost the justness of the indignation —Which of the reprobate disobeys the Gospel edict, because he counts himself to be a reprobate? and which of them has any right to deal with himself as such?

* The law is a perfect transcript of creation man's duty, in enigma; *typical emblem* of Christ as the *unblemished* Lamb, and of the law of the Spirit of life which is *laid up* in Him ("Your lamb shall be without blemish," Exod xii 5. . . . "And put the tables in the ark which I had made," Deut. x. 5. . . . "A new covenant . . . I will put my laws into

PREFACE. lxiii

These are some of the principal DEFECTS of Luther's theology:* which he manifests, as might be expected, in their mind, etc." Heb. viii 8—11), and *real teacher* that *Adam* cannot obey his Maker; say rather, that creature, *as* creature, cannot fulfil the law of his sort. But grace has a new MIND to study, and is cast into a mould correspondent to that mind—brought to a mind which is of much higher tone, and of other string, than that which God taught and demanded at Sinai.

* I would be understood as not pretending to make full and accurate references in proof of Luther's *seeings* and *not seeings* (which would, in fact, be to analyze and anatomize the whole of his work), but merely to give a hint at each —And now, I well know how I shall be arraigned of arrogancy, for having dared to controvert his positions, nay more, to judge and to condemn him I can only say, as Luther did at Worms, 'Here I stand. I cannot do otherwise. May God help me Amen'—It is the fashion to speak of Luther and the rest of the reformers as little less than inspired men, and of the æra of the Reformation, as the season of an effusion of the Spirit · the same sort of expression has been applied also to later times, to a *supposed*, and, as I will hope, *real* revival of religion which took place in Whitfield's time. Such expressions are unwarranted : I know but of one effusion, when, " being by the right hand of God exalted, and having received of the Father the promise of the Holy Ghost, Jesus did shed forth that which was seen and heard," on the day of Pentecost. Granting, therefore, what I would by no means dispute, that it has been the Lord's blessed will from the beginning to make peculiar display of his Spirit at certain seasons—as in private and personal experience, so in the community of his people— and not sticking at a word, but calling this, if you please, EFFUSION, what is the extent of the benefit? It is not meant that the atmosphere is impregnated with spiritual influences, so that *all* who live at such a period, and within the circle of it, are made partakers of the boon. Else, whence come the Caiaphases and the Alexanders, the Felixes and the Cæsars? It goes no farther, than that certain persons are peculiarly taught, strengthened and comforted at these seasons, and that the number so instructed and enlivened is greater than in ordinary times. It does not follow, that the blessed Spirit hath, at these seasons, taught and shewn all that ever is to be taught and shewn of God and of his truth. The Bible and other records shew, that there has, on the contrary, been a progression in His teaching, in the manner of revealing, if not in the matter revealed Though all truth be contained in, " And I will put enmity between thee and the woman &c." this truth has been made plainer, in various degrees, since the beginning ; to Abraham, to Moses, to David, to the Prophets, the Evangelists and the Apostles. It would not be adventurous to affirm, that, as the Prophets spake *to* as well as *of* the Apostles' days, so the Apostles have spoken *to* as well

lxiv   PREFACE.

this elaborate treatise. I have dealt fairly, as I believe, both with his excellencies and with his defects. It has been my endeavour to give the most faithful rendering I could to his whole text, and to every word and syllable of it. His excellencies, which, if I have succeeded in my endeavour, cannot be hidden, I have made yet more conspicuous by extricating each point of his argument, and specifying it distinctly, with the numbers 1. 2. 3. &c. prefixed. His errors and defects 1 have endeavoured to obviate and to supply, severally, by telling out THE TRUTH. My statements are ample, but I am not aware that they are prolix. I have desired to consult brevity; and, in some instances, have obtained, as I fear, the reward of

of later times; times yet for to come. Is it sacrilege or blasphemy to say, that what Paul and John wrote and spake shall be better understood, and is even now better understood, *generally in the church*, than it was by their own immediate hearers and leaders, if not by themselves, It would be preposterous surely to affirm, that nothing has been added to the store of evangelical learning, since Luther's time, by the discovery of additional manuscripts, and by the collation of them; by the improved knowledge of the original languages, by the illustrations of travellers, and other sources of intelligence, inquiry and communication. Whilst all other knowledge is progressive, why should biblical knowledge be stationary? Has it, in fact, been so? is it even yet so? And it is plain, this remark does not apply to the elucidation of prophecy exclusively; it extends to the counsel and truth of God Take our fourth Article as a specimen. In Luther's and our reformers' time, I suppose every body expected to rise with a flesh and blood body, as that Article speaks—in spite of Paul's clear words But *now*, we have been taught with what sort of a body the Lord rose, and what sort of an one we may look to be clothed with, ourselves.—(See 1 Cor. xv. 44—54.) See also Bishop Horsley's NINE DISCOURSES ON OUR LORD'S RESURRECTION)—These hints must be my defence against the supposed arrogancy of impugning and correcting Luther. The Reformation did not absorb the spiritual Sun, any more than former or later periods had, or have done so. He still continues to shoot forth his rays, *when* and *as* it pleaseth Him, and those on whom they fall have already received their direction how to deal with them, from his own mouth, where He says, " No man, when he hath lighted a candle, covereth it with a vessel, or putteth it under a bed, but setteth it on a candlestick, that they which enter in may see the light." Luke viii. 16.

laboured brevity, by becoming obscure. But I hope not often so.

The reader must have seen already, that, if I was to publish Luther, it must be with NOTES. I honestly believe, that he would be unintelligible without; as well as defective and fallacious. I have therefore adhered rigidly to two simple principles throughout, 'Luther, all Luther, and nothing but Luther, in the text; my own sentiments, whether agreeing with, or contradicting his, in the notes.'

Now, if it be asked why, in all wonder, have you thought it worth your while to publish Luther at all, when you pronounce his sentiments to be both defective and erroneous; I am not without an answer. With all its defects and errors, *con*fessed and *pro*fessed, I count this a truly estimable, magnificent and illustrious treatise. I publish it therefore, 1. Because I deem the subject all-important. 2. Because I know no other work of value upon this all-important subject, which discusses it by the same sort of argumentation. 3. Because Luther's name is gold with some, and will, I hope, beget readers. 4. Because his *right* is so very right, and so very forcible. 5. Because his very errors and defects throw some rays of light upon their corrector and supplier, claim and obtain a hearing for him, and open a way to the more successful march and entry of truth. The wise Paley remarks, that, if he could but make his pupils sensible of the precise nature of the difficulty, he was half way towards conquering it. Let the reader see what sort of a God, and of a Christ, and of a salvation, Luther, when brought into day, sets before him; and my expectation is, he will cry out for something better.

I have said Luther's name is gold, and Luther, as I trust, will beget readers. Do not let it be supposed that I am therefore leaning upon Luther's arm for the support of truth. That be far from me. I disclaim, as he did, man's authority; what he protested against the *Fathers*, that I protest against *him*, and against every uninspired teacher. The fair and legitimate use of human authority is to awaken attention. What so eminent a man of God has said, is worth listening to, is worth weighing: but, could he now be called before us, he would say, 'Weigh it in the balances of Scripture: I desire to be received no farther than as I speak according to the oracles of God.' High respect is due to the opinions of a godly, God-raised, God-owned man—but he is man, fallible man at last; and this man carried the mark of his fallibility with him to his grave, yea, has left it not in his writings only, but as a frontlet between the eyes of his blindly-devoted followers—who *consubstantiate* with him. "To the law and to the testimony"—Well! but neither will that appeal *ensure* the knowledge of THE TRUTH: all do not know THE TRUTH who search the Scriptures. It is the Scripture as we believe it to be opened to us by the Holy Ghost, which is the guide of our spirit; and, whilst we are bound to yield a certain deference and obedience to the decisions of a lawfully constituted human tribunal—submitting to its inflictions even to the destruction, not of our worldly substance only, but of our flesh—our spirit owns no fetters but those which the Spirit imposes.

I commend this work therefore, both as it respects Luther and as it respects my own part in it, to the candid, patient and anxious consideration of the reader; earnestly requesting him to compare what is here written with the Scriptures, and carrying with him into that comparison a prayer which I here breathe out for him, 'Lord, grant me to understand thy word; preserve me from concluding rashly against any thing that is written in this book, however it may contradict my preconceived opinion; and what is true in it enable THOU me to welcome, digest, hold fast and enjoy!'

I have already hinted that my desire has been to accomplish a *faithful* translation. I believe the Lord has given me my desire. I need scarcely say I have found it a difficult undertaking. Every scholar knows that the work of translation is one of great nicety. There is in every language some *one* word which more precisely than any other corresponds with the given one; but it may often be the rumination of many hours to find that word. This has been much of my toil. Luther's work, above most others, demanded it: he abounds in emphatic and distinctive words. His meaning also, as I have said, is not always unambiguous. He wrote, too, in a dead language: in which, though he doubtless tried his best on this occasion, and was complimented by having it supposed that the elegant pen of Melancthon had assisted him, he was but a clumsy and *middle-aged* composer. He has proverbs, moreover, without end; some German, some classical. ' The Germans, you know (as a very learned friend, whom I consulted in one of my difficulties, obligingly writes to me), are great proverbialists, and many of their allusions are now lost. I have searched a great variety of authors, on a similar inquiry' (he was kind enough to do so now), ' but in vain.'—*I* too, in a much more humble way, have made some search and a great deal of inquiry, but have learned nothing: witness, the Wolf and the Nightingale (p. 79), the beast which eats itself (p. 196), and the palm and the gourd (p. 373). My greatest perplexity has arisen from his in some instances mixing the old with the new, and luring me, like a will o' the wisp, to go after him, because I fancied I had a lantern to guide me, but soon found myself left in darkness.

I fear my notes will incur the censure of two different sorts of reader; each of whom will account many of them superfluous. I can only say none of them have been inserted without thought and design. To the learned I have been anxious to vindicate my accuracy; to the unlearned I have been anxious to give such helps as might enable them to understand me. The learned must bear the burden of my laborious dulness, and the unlearned, of my Latin and Greek.

With respect to my theology, I shall not wonder if I appear more positive and dogmatical to some, than even Luther himself. Let me be understood here. Whilst I make no claim to infallibility, but desire only that my assertions may be brought to the standard of Scripture, I desire to give my reader the full benefit of the firmness and deliberateness with which I have formed, entertained, and advanced my opinion, by omitting all such qualifying and hesitative restrictions, as 'if I mistake not,' 'I believe it will be found,' 'I would venture to affirm &c.' Such subjects require a mind made up in the instructor; and, if he would not invite others to doubt, his language must breathe the indubitative confidence which he feels. Besides, there is an energy, as well as an importance in truth, which inspires, even as it demands, boldness.

I cannot take leave of my reader without desiring him to acknowledge his obligations to the late venerable Dean of Carlisle, Dr. Milner, to whose completion of his brother's valuable history I am indebted, almost exclusively, for my account of Luther: a work of great research; in which, by ransacking a vast body of original documents, and drawing light from sources which former historians had been content to leave unexplored, he has vindicated, illustrated and adorned this dauntless standard-bearer of the Reformation.

POSTSCRIPT.

In the following work, it has been my endeavour to assist the unlearned and those who may not have access to books, by giving some account of the various persons named in it by the author. I believe I have been tolerably consistent in doing so, but am aware that I have left two capital writers without note or comment. I would aim at uniformity therefore, by supplying this deficiency here: Plato is one of these, Augustine is the other. Not only their celebrity, but the frequent reference made to them by Luther (especially to the latter), would render my omission inexcusable.

1. The great PLATO then (for such he truly was), seems to have been no favourite with Luther; who was deeply conscious of the mischievous tendency of his writings as fostering a spirit of proud self-sufficiency, and as having cooperated with other sources of error to contaminate the truth, by exhibiting some semblances of its glory and beauty. In Part iv. Sect. lii. he speaks contemptuously of his 'Chaos'; and in Part ii. Sect. v. of his 'Ideas.' This Plato, however, appears to have been led into some vast conceptions of God (whence he derived them, is another question)—his nature, will, power and operations—into some exalted aspirations after communion with him—and into some elaborate attempts to purify and elevate the morals of his countrymen. Like others who speculated upon God, without God's guidance, he made matter eternal as well as God, though he gave God a supremacy over it, and ascribed to him both the modelling of the world, and

the commanding of it into being. Doubtless, it is a strange jumble which he makes—the world having a soul, nay a compound soul; man with his two souls, and second causes placing a material body round a germ of immortality!—but in his 'chaos,' wild as it is, and that universal soul which was plunged into it and by its agitation brought out order, we see the vestige of corrupted truth; in his 'ideas,' or 'first forms of things,' we see something yet more nearly approaching to reality—even the eternal God devising, ordaining and protruding every thing which exists; and in his ideal world with God reigning in its highest height, as compared with the visible system and its sun, we catch a faint glimpse of the invisible glory, and of that repose which shall be found in the uninterrupted contemplation of the reposing God.—I am not for bringing men back to Platonism, but for letting them see, that even pagan Plato had a conception and a relish beyond many on whom the true light has shone; and for leading them to understand, that revelation and tradition have extended much more widely than they are aware of; so that it ought not to appear strange, if even heathens are dealt with on a ground of knowledge which we may falsely have supposed that they had not the means of possessing. (See Part iii. Sect. xxviii. note ᵛ. Part v. Sect. xxvi. note ᶜ.) 'The notion of a Trinity, more or less removed from the purity of the Christian faith, is found to have been a leading principle in all the ancient schools of philosophy, and in the religions of almost all nations; and traces of an early popular belief of it appear even in the abominable rites of idolatrous worship. If reason was insufficient for this great discovery, what could be the means of information but what the Platonists themselves assign, Θεοπαράδοτος Θεολογια; 'a theology delivered from the Gods,' i. e. a revelation. This is the account which Platonists, who were no Christians, have given of the origin of their master's doctrine. But from what revelation could they derive their information, who lived before the Christian, and had no light from the Mosaic? For whatever some of the early Fathers may have imagined, there is no evidence that Plato or Pythagoras were at all acquainted with the Mosaic writings: not to insist that the worship of a Trinity is traced to an earlier age than that of Plato or of Pythagoras, or even of Moses. 'Their information could only be drawn from traditions founded upon earlier revelations; from the scattered fragments of the ancient patriarchal creed; that creed which was universal before the defection of the first idolaters, which the corruptions of idolatry, gross and enormous as they were, could never totally obliterate.'—' What Socrates said of him, what Plato writ, and the rest of the heathen philosophers of several nations, is all no more than the twilight of revelation, after the sun of it was set in the race of Noah.' (See Horsley's Letters to Priestley, pp. 49, 50.)

I am the rather surprised that Luther should fleer so roughly at Plato, because his beloved Augustine acknowledged obligations to him. ' And first, as thou wouldest shew me how thou resistest the proud, and givest grace to the humble; and how great thy mercy is shewn to be in the way of humility; thou procuredst for me, by means of a person highly inflated with philosophical pride, some of the books of Plato translated into Latin, in which I read passages concerning the divine word similar to those in the first chapter of St John's Gospel; in which his eternal divinity was exhibited, but not his incarnation, his atonement, his humiliation, and glorification of his human nature. For thou hast hid these things from the wise and prudent, and revealed them unto babes; that men might come to thee weary and heavy laden, and that thou mightest refresh them.....Thus did I begin to form better views of the divine nature, even from Plato's writings, as thy people of old spoiled the Egyptians of their gold, because, whatever good there is in any thing, is all thy own; and at the same time I was enabled to escape the evil which was in those books, and not to attend to the idols of Egypt.'—His historian remarks upon this, ' there is something divinely spiritual in the manner of his deliverance. That the Platonic books also should give the first occasion is very remarkable; though I apprehend the Latin translation, which he saw, had improved on Plato, by the mixture of something scriptural, according to the manner of the Ammonian philosophers.'*—Thus Plato, it seems, could hold the candle to an Augustine, whilst he was himself far from the light: but there was truth, we see, and discriminating truth, mixed and blended with his falsehood.

2. AUGUSTINE's errors were those of Luther, increased

* Milner does not appear to have understood what the investigating Horsley has made plain, that neither was Plato an inventor, neither were the Ammonians scriptural improvers of human inventions, but both Plato and those from whom he copied retailers, in fact, of mutilated revelations. ' These notions were by no means peculiar to the Platonic school: the Platonists pretended to be no more than the expositors of a more ancient doctrine; which is traced from Plato to Parmenides; from Parmenides to his masters of the Pythagorean sect; from the Pythagoreans to Orpheus, the earliest of the Grecian mystagogues; from Orpheus to the secret lore of the Egyptian priests; in which the foundations of the Orphic theology were laid. Similar notions of a triple principle prevailed in the Persian and Chaldean theology; and vestiges even of the worship of a Trinity were discernible in the Roman superstition in a very late age; this worship the Romans had received from their Trojan ancestors. For the Trojans brought it with them into Italy from Phrygia. In Phrygia it was introduced by Dardanus as early as in the ninth century after Noah's flood. Dardanus carried it with him from Samothrace, where the personages that were the objects of it were worshipped under the heathen name of the Cabirim. . . . ' The Great or Mighty ones:' for that is the import of the Hebrew name. And of the like import is their Latin appellation, Penates. . . . . Thus the joint worship of Jupiter, Juno and Minerva, the triad of the Roman capital, is traced to that of the THREE MIGHTY ONES in Samothrace; which was established in that island, at what precise time it is impossible to determine, but earlier, if Eusebius may be credited, than the days of Abraham.'—Horsley's Letters to Priestley, pp. 47—49.

by an ignorance of the doctrine of justification: he had
the elements of this doctrine, it is said, but he never put
them together. His case was a very remarkable one.
After a profligate youth, in which he had run to great
excess of riot; after having infected himself with the
poison of the Manichees (see Part iv. Sect. ix. note ⱴ.
Sect. xi. note ʰ); after having sold himself into the service of vain-glory, lasciviousnes, pride and atheism, he
was made to bow down before the true God, and to kiss
his Son. God had hereby signally and specially prepared
him to be the champion of grace in opposition to Pelagianism; which started up in his days a many-varied
monster. By degrees he was led to use his own experience as an interpreter of Scripture; and though, as his
historian tells us, St. Paul's doctrine of predestination was
a doctrine that, with him, followed experimental religion,
as a shadow follows the substance—it was not embraced
for its own sake—yet follow him it did; and he was persuaded of it, and embraced it, and maintained it in much,
though not all of its vigour, against its antagonists. In
fact, how could he defend the doctrine of grace, as his
historian terms it (meaning thereby not grace in its fulness, but only the gift of the Spirit), without it? If his
historian be correct, we have in him a confirmation of the
salutary effect of controversy; it was Pelagianism which
made Augustine understand what he did of predestination:
we have it also exemplified, that, not to know the root and
outline of truth is not to know any branch or feature of
it thoroughly. His historian would commend him for
his moderation, which is here another name for his ignorance; but the reality is, not thoroughly understanding
predestination, which is the root " of the mystery of God,
and of the Father, and of Christ," he did not understand
justification, he did not understand redemption, he did not
understand man's state, he did not understand that grace
of which he was the strenuous and honoured defender.

Grace of the Spirit (properly so called) is but a part of the grace of God the Father, which was given us in Christ Jesus before the world began; and even of that part, of which he spake so sweetly and so feelingly, he did not discern the spring, channel and mouth.—What is to be said of this—how it should have been so arranged to this beloved child, that he should have been left, and kept, and used in his ignorance, is one question; the fact that he was so left is another. The truth is, he and his venerable yoke-fellow Luther are clear confirmers of the position I have maintained in a preceding note (see p. lxiii.) that the light of divine truth is progressive; Augustine knew what Cyprian did not, and Luther knew what Augustine did not—and why is the climax to end with Luther, Calvin and Cranmer? Grace however, though not in all its fulness, yet in all its freeness, was Augustine's theme and Augustine's glory. With such a history going before, how could he teach any thing else? ' The distinguishing glory of the Gospel is to teach humility, and to give God his due honour; and Augustine was singularly prepared for this by a course of internal experience. He had felt human insufficiency completely, and knew that in himself dwelt no good thing. Hence he was admirably qualified to describe the total depravity and apostasy of human nature, and he described what he knew to be true.....Humility is his theme. Augustine taught men what it is to be humble before God. This he does every where with godly simplicity, with inexpressible seriousness. And in doing this, no writer, uninspired, ever exceeded, I am apt to think ever equalled him in any age..... Few writers have been equal to him in describing the internal conflict of flesh and spirit..... He describes this in a manner unknown to any but those who have deeply felt it: and the Pelagian pretensions to perfection oblige him to say more than otherwise would be needful to prove, that the most humble and the most holy have, through life, to combat with in-dwelling sin.... Two more practical subjects he delights to handle, charity and heavenly-mindedness. In both he excels wonderfully... A reference of all things to a future life, and the depth of humble love appear in all his writings; as in truth, from the moment of his conversion, they influenced all his practice.' With all his darkness, therefore, abiding thick upon him (we are not to call darkness light because God commanded the light to shine out of it), He who formeth the light and createth darkness made him light to His church. ' For a thousand years and upwards the light of divine grace, which shone here and there in individuals, during the dreary night of superstition, was nourished by his writings; which, next to the sacred Scriptures, were the guides of men who feared God: nor have we, in all history, an instance of so extensive utility derived to the church from the writings of men.' *Beatus Augustinus* is the title by which he is commonly quoted; and a word from him, for confirmation, was usually made an end of all strife by Luther, Calvin, and all the Oracles of the Reformation, when eleven hundred years had rolled over his ashes.

TABLE OF CONTENTS.

	Page
INTRODUCTION	2—9
PART I.—Erasmus's Preface reviewed	10—77
——— II.—Erasmus's Proem reviewed	78—128
——— III.—Texts for Freewill disproved	129—235
——— IV.—Texts against Freewill maintained	236—380
——— V.—Freewill proved to be a Lie	381—467
CONCLUSION	468—470

PART I.

SECT.
I. Assertions defended.
II. Erasmus a sceptic.
III. Christian truth not hidden.
IV. Scripture falsely accused of obscurity.
V. Freewill a necessary subject.
VI. Erasmus's Christianity.
VII. The same exposed by similes.
VIII. Connection of the subject with true piety.
IX. Erasmus has omitted God's prescience.

SECT.
X. God's prescience flows from Erasmus's concession.
XI. Objection to term 'Necessity.' Necessity of a consequence, &c.
XII. Prevalence of the opinion of ' Necessity.'
XIII. Temerity of Erasmus's moderation.
XIV. All *Scripture* truth may be published safely.
XV. That ' some truths ought not to be published' considered.

CONTENTS.

SECT.
- XVI. Erasmus's three examples considered.
- XVII. Erasmus neither understands nor feels the question.
- XVIII. Peace of the world disturbed.
- XIX. Free confession. The Pope and God at war. The people abuse.
- XX. Respect of persons, time and place pernicious.
- XXI. The Fathers have no authority but from the word.

SECT.
- XXII. 'All things by necessity;' 'God all in all.'
- XXIII. Two reasons why certain paradoxes should be preached.
- XXIV. That 'all human works are necessary,' explained and defended.
- XXV. Erasmus self-convicted: madness of claiming Freewill.
- XXVI. Erasmus reduced to a dilemma.

PART II.

- I. Canonical Scriptures to be the standard.
- II. Excellences of the Fathers not of Freewill.
- III. Luther demands effects of Freewill in three particulars.
- IV. The Saints practically disclaim Freewill.
- V. Luther demands a definition of Freewill.
- VI. Erasmus's advice turned against himself.
- VII. Injustice done to the Fathers.
- VIII. 'That God should have disguised the error of his church,' considered.
- IX. The church hidden.
- X. Judgment of faith distinct from judgment of charity.
- XI. Erasmus's perplexity.
- XII. Two tribunals for the spirits of men.
- XIII. Clearness of Scripture proved.
- XIV. The same.
- XV. Concludes against Freewill.
- XVI. 'All your adversaries shall not be able to resist,' considered.
- XVII. We have this promised victory.
- XVIII. Why great geniuses have been blind about Freewill.
- XIX. That Erasmus has admitted Scripture to be clear.
- XX. Erasmus reduced to a dilemma.
- XXI. Luther claims victory before the battle.

PART III.

SECT.
1. Erasmus's definition of Freewill examined.
II. Definition continued.
III. Definition continued.
IV. Inferences from Erasmus's definition.
V. Erasmus's definition compared with that of the Sophists.
VI. Eccl^{us}. xv. 15—18. considered.
VII. Opinions on Freewill stated.
VIII. Erasmus inconsistent with his definition.
IX. The approvable opinion considered.
X. The approvable opinion further considered.
XI. Freewill not a 'negative intermediate power of the will.'
XII. The approvable opinion compared with the other two.
XIII. Eccl^{us}. xv. 14—18. resumed and expounded.
XIV. Eccl^{us}. at least does not decide for Freewill.
XV. What meant by 'If thou wilt, &c.'
XVI. Use of such forms of address.
XVII. Diatribe insincere in her inference—proves too much—confirms Pelagianism.

SECT.
XVIII. Conclude that Eccl^{us}. proves nothing for Freewill.
XIX. Genesis iv. 7. considered.
XX. Deut. xxx. 19. considered.
XXI. Passages from Deut. xxx. &c. considered.
XXII. His Scriptures prove nothing; his additions too much. Simile of the hand tied. Uses of the law.
XXIII. Isaiah i. 19. xxx. 21. xlv. 20. lii. 1, 2. and some other passages considered.
XXIV. Mal. iii. 7. more particularly considered.
XXV. Ezek. xviii. 23. considered.
XXVI. The true meaning of Ezek. xviii. 23. stated.
XXVII. Ezek. xviii. 23. negatives Freewill, instead of proving it.
XXVIII. How far God may be said to bewail the death he produces.
XXIX. Exhortations, promises, &c. of Scripture useless.
XXX. Deut. xxx. 11—14. considered.
XXXI. Sum of the Old Testament witnesses for Freewill.

CONTENTS.

SECT.
XXXII. New Testament witnesses for Freewill, beginning with Matthew xxiii. 37—39. considered.
XXXIII. The reality of God's secret will maintained.
XXXIV. Matthew xix. 17. and other like passages, considered.
XXXV. Objection, 'that precepts are given, and merit is ascribed to Freewill.'
XXXVI. New Testament precepts are addressed to the converted, not to those in Freewill.
XXXVII. Merit and reward may consist with necessity.

SECT.
XXXVIII. Why there are promises and threatenings in Scripture.
XXXIX. Reason is answered, 'Such is the will of God.'
XL. Apology for not going further. Absurd cavil from Matt. vii. 16.
XLI. Luke xxiii. 34. is *against* not *for* Freewill.
XLII. John i. 12. is all for grace.
XLIII. Objections from Paul summarily despatched.
XLIV. Wickliffe's confession confessed.

PART IV.

I. Erasmus has but two texts to kill.
II. Kills by resolving them into tropes: which he defends by Luther's example.
III. Trope and consequence when only to be admitted.
IV. Luther denies having used trope in his interpretation of—"Stretch out," and "Make you."
V. Diatribe must prove by Scripture or miracle, that the *very* passage in question is tropical.
VI. Erasmus's trope makes nonsense of Moses, and leaves the knot tied.
VII. Necessity still remains, and you do not clear God.
VIII. Diatribe's similes of sun and rain rejected.
IX. Erasmus's two causes for tropicizing considered.
X. That God made all things very good, not a sufficient reason.
XI. How God works evil in us, considered.
XII. How God hardens.

CONTENTS.

SECT.
- XIII. Mistakes prohibited.
- XIV. Pharaoh's case considered.
- XV. Impertinent questions may still be asked.
- XVI. The trope compared with the text.
- XVII. Moses's object is to strengthen Israel.
- XVIII. Paul's reference in Rom. ix. Diatribe obliged to yield.
- XIX. Diatribe's concessions and retractions exposed.
- XX. Where true reverence for Scripture lies.
- XXI. What carnal reason hates.
- XXII. Paul's argument resumed. Diatribe tries to escape but cannot.
- XXIII. 'Necessity of a consequent,' exposed.
- XXIV. The other admitted text defended.
- XXV. Paul defended in his use of Genesis xxv. 21—23.
- XXVI. The same.
- XXVII. Diatribe's evasions of Malachi i. 2, 3. considered.
- XXVIII. The same.
- XXIX. The same.
- XXX. Simile of the potter.
- XXXI. The cavil from 2 Tim. ii. repelled.

SECT.
- XXXII. Reason's cavil from this simile.
- XXXIII. The same.
- XXXIV. That Scripture must be understood with qualifications.
- XXXV. That Luther has always maintained the consistency of Scripture.
- XXXVI. After all Paul stands.
- XXXVII. Gen. vi. 3. maintained.
- XXXVIII. Gen. viii. 21. and vi. 5. maintained.
- XXXIX. Isaiah xl. 2. maintained.
- XL. Episode upon God's help.—Cornelius rescued.
- XLI. Isaiah xl. 6, 7. maintained.
- XLII. The true interpretation of the same
- XLIII. Heathen virtue is God's abhorrence.
- XLIV. Consequences of the assumption that a part of man is not 'flesh.'
- XLV. Luther falsely charged. Authority of the ancients, &c.
- XLVI. Jeremiah x. 23, 24. defended.
- XLVII. Proverbs xvi. 1. defended.
- XLVIII. Much in Proverbs for Freewill.
- XLIX. John xv. 5. maintained.
- L. Inconsistency charged.

f

CONTENTS.

SECT.
- LI. Luther proves his negative.
- LII. 1 Cor. iii. 7. 1 Cor. xiii. 2. John iii. 27.
- LIII. Diatribe's similes naught, and against her. — What she ought to have spoken to.
- LIV. Diatribe's inconsistency and audacity—takes up one subject and pursues another—argues by inversion.
- LV. Solemn conclusion.

PART V.

- I. How Luther proposes to conduct the fight.
- II. Romans i. 18. pronounces sentence upon Freewill.
- III. A published Gospel proves want of knowledge as well as power.
- IV. Freewill neither conceives the truth nor can endure it.
- V. Paul expressly names the chiefest of the Greeks, and afterwards condemns the Jews indiscriminately.
- VI. Paul's epilogue establishes his meaning.
- VII. Paul justified in his quotations.
- VIII. David's condemnation includes power as well as act.
- IX. Paul's big words in Romans iii. 19, 20. insisted upon.
- X. Evasion, that it is ceremonial law of which Paul speaks.
- XI. Paul's meaning is, 'works of the law done in the flesh condemn.'
- XII. All the law does is to shew sin.
- XIII. Confirmed by Gal. iii. 19. and Rom. v. 20.
- XIV. Rom. iii. 21—25. contains five thunderbolts against Freewill.
- XV. The same.
- XVI. The same.
- XVII. Sophists worse than the Pelagians.
- XVIII. Fathers overlooked Paul.
- XIX. Paul's citation of the example of Abraham searched and applied.
- XX. Luther omits much which he might insist upon.

CONTENTS.

SECT.
- XXI. Luther's own view of Paul.
- XXII. Paul's crown.
- XXIII. Grace exemplified in Jews rejected—Gentiles called.
- XXIV. John a devourer.
- XXV. John Baptist's testimony.
- XXVI. Nicodemus's case.
- XXVII. John xiv. 6. forestalled. Way, Truth, &c. are exclusive.
- XXVIII. John iii. 18. 36.

SECT.
- John iii. 27. John iii. 31. John viii. 23.
- XXIX. John vi. 44.
- XXX. John xvi. 9.
- XXXI. Omits ' flesh and spirit.'
- XXXII. Difficulty stated, and exposed.
- XXXIII. The same reproved, and palliated by example.
- XXXIV. Sum of the argument.

ERRATA.

PAGE
22, note P, *for* Chap. ii. *read* Part ii.
60, note l, *for* Chap. i. Sect. iii. note i. *read* Part i. Sect iii. note k.
71, note c, *for* Sect. ix. note d. *read* Sect. ix. note e.
199, side note, *for* Some *read* Sum.
225, note q, *for* y *read* y.

MARTIN LUTHER,

ON THE

BONDAGE OF THE WILL;

TO THE VENERABLE MISTER ERASMUS, OF ROTTERDAM.

1525.

MARTIN LUTHER,
etc.

To the venerable Mr. Erasmus of Rotterdam Martin Luther sends grace and peace in Christ.

INTRODUCTION.

Reasons for the Work.

IN replying so tardily to your Diatribe[a] on Freewill, my venerable Erasmus, I have done violence both to the general expectation and to my own custom. Till this instance, I have seemed willing not only to lay hold on such opportunities of writing when they occurred to me, but even to go in search of them without provocation. Some perhaps will be ready to wonder at this new and unusual patience, as it may be, or fear of Luther's; who has not been roused from his silence even by so many speeches and letters which have been bandied to and fro amongst his adversaries, congratulating Erasmus upon his victory, and chaunting an Io Pæan. 'So then, this Macca-

---

[a] *Diatribe.*] One of the names by which Erasmus chose to distinguish his performance on Freewill. He borrows it from the debates of the ancient philosophers; and would be understood to announce a canvassing of the question rather than a judicial determination upon it. The original Greek term denotes, 1. The place trodden by the feet whilst they were engaged in the debate. 2. The time spent in such debate. 3. The debate itself. Erasmus's Diatribe, therefore, is 'a disquisition, or disputation,' on Freewill. Luther often personifies it.

bæus and most inflexible Assertor has at length found an antagonist worthy of him, whom he does not dare to open his mouth against!'

I am so far from blaming these men, however, that I am quite ready to yield a palm to you myself, such as I never yet did to any man; admitting, that you not only very far excel me in eloquence and genius (a palm which we all deservedly yield to you—how much more such a man as I; a barbarian who have always dwelt amidst barbarism), but that you have checked both my spirit and my inclination to answer you, and have made me languid before the battle. This you have done twice over: first, by your art in pleading this cause with such a wonderful command of temper, from first to last, that you have made it impossible for me to be angry with you; and secondly, by contriving, through fortune, accident, or fate, to say nothing on this great subject which has not been said before. In fact, you say so much less for Freewill, and yet ascribe so much more to it, than the Sophists[b] have done before you (of which I shall speak more at large hereafter), that it seemed quite superfluous to answer those arguments of yours which I have so often confuted myself, and which have been trodden under foot, and crushed to atoms, by Philip Melancthon's invincible 'Common Places.'[c] In

[b] The schoolmen, with Peter Lombard at their head, who arose about the middle of the twelfth century; idolizers of Aristotle; their theology abounding with metaphysical subtilties, and their disputations greatly resembling those of the Greek sophists.

[c] Luther refers to the former editions of Melancthon's 'Common Places,' which contained some passages not found in the later ones; this amongst others. 'The divine predestination takes away liberty* from man: for all things happen according to divine predestination; as well the external actions as the internal thoughts of all creatures.... The judgment of the flesh abhors this sentiment, but the judgment of the

* Not 'choice,' but 'unbiassed choice;' 'freeness and contingency of choice.'—ED.

my judgment, that work of his deserves not only to be immortalized, but even canonized. So mean and worthless did yours appear, when compared with it, that I exceedingly pitied *you*, who were polluting your most elegant and ingenious diction with such filth of argument, and was quite angry with your most unworthy *matter*, for being conveyed in so richly ornamented a style of eloquence. It is just as if the sweepings of the house or of the stable were borne about on men's shoulders in vases of gold and silver! You seem to have been sensible of this yourself; from the difficulty with which you was persuaded to undertake the office of writing, on this occasion; your conscience, no doubt, admonishing you, that with whatever powers of eloquence you might attempt the subject, it would be impossible so to gloss it over that I should not discover the excrementitious nature of your matter through all the tricksy ornaments of phrase with which you might cover it; that *I* should not discover it, I say; who, though rude in speech, am, by the grace of God, not rude in knowledge. For I do not hesitate, with Paul, thus to claim the gift of knowledge for myself,

spirit embraces it. For you will not learn the fear of God, or confidence in Him, from any source more surely than when you shall have imbued your mind with this sentiment concerning predestination.'—It is to passages such as these that Luther doubtless refers in the testimony here given to Melancthon's work; and from the withdrawing of which in subsequent editions, it has been inferred that Melancthon afterwards changed his sentiments upon these subjects. The late Dean of Carlisle has investigated this supposition with his usual accuracy and diligence; and concludes that he probably did alter his earlier sentiments to some extent in later life. Truth, however does not stand *in* man or *by* man. Too much has no doubt been made of supposed changes in the opinions of many learned and pious divines. But after all, what do these prove? We have the same sources of knowledge as they, and must draw our light from the clear spring, not from the polluted and uncertain stream.—See Milner's Eccles. Hist. vol. iv. p. 920—926, first edition.

and with equal confidence to withhold it from you; whilst I claim eloquence and genius for you, and willingly, as I ought to do, withhold them from myself.

So that I have been led to reason thus with myself. If there be those who have neither drunk deeper into our writings, nor yet more firmly maintain them, (fortified as they are by such an accumulation of Scripture proofs) than to be shaken by those trifling or good for nothing arguments of Erasmus, though dressed out, I admit, in the most engaging apparel; such persons are not worth being cured by an answer from me: for nothing could be said or written which would be sufficient for such men, though many thousands of books should be repeated even a thousand times over. You might just as well plough the sea-shore and cast your seed into the sand, or fill a cask, that is full of holes, with water. We have ministered abundantly to those who have drunk of the Spirit as their teacher through the instrumentality of our books, and they perfectly despise your performances; and as for those who read without the Spirit, it is no wonder if they be driven like the seed with every wind. To such persons God would not say enough, if he were to convert all his creatures into tongues. So that I should almost have determined to leave these persons, stumbled as they were by your publication, with the crowd which glories in you and decrees you a triumph.

You see then, that it is neither the multitude of my engagements, nor the difficulty of the undertaking, nor the vastness of your eloquence, nor any fear of you, but mere disgust, indignation, and contempt; or, to say the truth, my deliberate judgment respecting your Diatribe, which has restrained the impulse of my mind to answer you: not to mention what has also its place here, that ever like yourself you with the greatest pertina-

INTRODUCTION.

city, take care to be always evasive and ambiguous.^d More cautious than Ulysses, you flatter yourself that you contrive to sail between Scylla and Charybdis; whilst you would be understood to have asserted nothing, yet again assume the air of an asserter. With men of this sort how is it possible to *confer* and to *compare*;^e unless one should possess the art of catching Proteus? Hereafter I will shew you with Christ's help what I can do in this way, and what you have gained by putting me to it.

Still it is not without reason that I answer you now. The faithful brethren in Christ impel me by suggesting the general expectation which is entertained of a reply from my pen; inasmuch as the authority of Erasmus is not to be despised, and the true christian doctrine is brought into jeopardy in the hearts of many. At length too it has occurred to me that there has been a great want of piety in my silence; and that I have been beguiled by the 'wisdom' or 'wickedness' of my flesh into a forgetfulness of my office, which makes me debtor to the wise and to the unwise, especially when I am called to the discharge of it by the entreaties of so many of the brethren. For, although our business^f be not content with an external

^d *Lubricus et flexiloquus.*] *Lub.* 'one that slips out of your hands, so that you cannot grapple with him.' *Flex.* 'one whose words will bend many ways; as being of doubtful or pliable meaning.'

^e *Conferri aut componi.*] What Erasmus professed to do, and thereupon gave the name of 'Collatio' to his Treatise: 'a sort of "conference" and "comparison" of sentiment; each disputant bringing his opinion and arguments, and placing them front to front with his opponent's.'—Proteus was a sort of Demigod supposed to have the power of changing himself into many forms.

^f *Res nostra.*] 'The ministering of Christ' is the business here spoken of, by a phrase correspondent with 'res bellica,' 'res navalis,' 'res judiciaria,' &c. &c. as being the trade, occupation, and alone concern of Christ's ministers; in whose name he here speaks.

teacher, but besides him who planteth and watereth without, desires the Spirit of God also (that He may give the increase, and being Himself life may teach the doctrine of life within the soul—a thought which imposed upon me); still, whereas this Spirit is free, and breathes, not where we would, but where He himself wills; I ought to have observed that rule of Paul's, "Be instant in season, out of season;" for we know not at what hour the Lord shall come. What if some have not yet experienced the teaching of the Spirit through my writings, and have been dashed to the ground by your Diatribe! It may be their hour was not yet come.

And who knows but God may deign to visit even you, my excellent Erasmus, by so wretched and frail a little vessel of His, as myself? Who knows but I may come to you in happy hour (I wish it from my heart of the Father of Mercies through Christ our Lord) by means of this treatise, and may gain a most dear brother? For, although you both think ill and write ill on the subject of Freewill, I owe you vast obligations, for having greatly confirmed me in my sentiments, by giving me to see the cause of Freewill pleaded by such and so great a genius, with all his might, and yet after all so little effected, that it stands worse than it did before.—An evident proof this, that Freewill is a downright lie; since, like the woman in the Gospel, the more it is healed of the doctors the worse it fares. I shall give unbounded thanks to you, if the event be, that you are made to know the truth through *me*, even as *I* have become more fixed in it through *you*. Howbeit, each of these results is the gift of the Spirit, not the achievement of our own good offices.[g]

[g] *Officii nostri.*] *Off.* 'What a man has to do;' 'his business,' implying relation; as 'munus et officium oculorum,' 'the office or function of the eye.' Hence, 'good office, obligation, kindness conferred.'

We must therefore pray God to open my mouth and your heart and the hearts of all men, and to be himself present as a Teacher in the midst of us, speaking and hearing severally within our souls. Once more; let me beg of you, my Erasmus, to bear with my rudeness of speech, even as I bear with your ignorance on these subjects. God gives not all his gifts to one man; nor have we all power to do all things; or, as Paul says, "There are distributions of gifts, but the same Spirit." It remains, therefore, that the gifts labour mutually for each other, and that one man bear the burden of another's penury by the gift which he has himself received; thus shall we fulfil the law of Christ. (Galat. vi. 2.)

PART I.

ERASMUS'S PREFACE REVIEWED.

SECTION I.

Assertions defended.

I would begin with passing rapidly through some chapters of your Preface, by which you sink our cause and set off your own.[a] And first, having already in other publications found fault with me for being so positive and inflexible in assertion, you in this declare yourself to be so little pleased with assertions that you would be ready to go over and side[b] with the Sceptics on any subject in which the inviolable authority of the divine Scriptures, and the decrees of the Church (to which you on all occasions willingly submit your own judgment, whether you understand what she prescribes, or not) would allow you to do so. This is the temper you like.

I give *you* credit, as I ought, for saying this with a benevolent mind, which loves peace; but if another man were to say so, I should perhaps inveigh against him, as my manner is. I ought not however to suffer even you, though writing with the best intention, to indulge so erroneous

---

[a] *Gravas, ornas.*] The figure is mixed: gr. 'clog, load, weigh down.' Orn. 'beautify with apparel.'

[b] *Pedibus discessurus.*] A Roman phrase taken from their method of voting in the senate, when they dissented from the decree as proposed: they walked over to the opposite side of the house.

an opinion. For it is not the property of a christian mind to be displeased with assertions; nay, a man must absolutely be pleased with assertions, or he never will be a Christian. Now, (that we may not mock each other with vague words^c) I call 'adhering with constancy, affirming, confessing, maintaining, and invincibly persevering,' ASSERTION; nor do I believe that the word 'assertion' means any thing else, either as used by the Latins, or in our age. Again; I confine 'assertion' to those things which have been delivered by God to us in the sacred writings. We do not want Erasmus, or any other Master, to teach us that in doubtful matters, or in matters unprofitable and unnecessary, assertions are not only foolish but even impious; those very strifes and contentions, which Paul more than once condemns. Nor do you speak of these, I suppose, in this place; unless, either adopting the manner of a ridiculous Orator, you have chosen to presume one subject of debate and discuss another, like him who harangued the Rhombus; or, with the madness of an impious Writer, are contending that the article of Freewill is dubious or unnecessary.

SECT. I.

Assertions defended.

^c *Ne verbis ludamur.*] 'That we may not be mocked by words;' 'made the sport of words.'

^d *Velut ille ad Rhombum.*] If you be indeed speaking of such assertions here, you are either a ridiculous orator, or a mad writer: a ridiculous orator, if it be not true genuine Freewill which you are discussing; a mad writer, if it be. Oratory was out of place on such a subject, however sincere and disinterested the speaker might be; but orators were for the most part a venal and frivolous tribe, and some exercised their art unskilfully, whilst others were hired but to amuse and make sport. It is not without meaning, therefore, that Luther puts the orator and the writer into comparison; and if Erasmus is to fill the weightier place of the writer, it is that of one phrensied and blasphemous.—I am indebted to the kindness of a learned friend for the reference, 'velut ille ad Rhombum,' which had perplexed me. I can have no doubt that it is to the fourth Satire of Juvenal, where Domitian is represented as

PART. I. We Christians disclaim all intercourse with the Sceptics and Academics, but admit into our family asserters twofold more obstinate, than even the Stoics themselves. How often does the Apostle having called a council of his senators to deliberate what should be done with an immense 'Rhombus,' or Turbot; with which a fisherman out of fear had presented him. Amongst other counsellors was a blind man, of very infamous character, as an informer, but high in the favour of the Emperor, named Catullus; 'cum mortifero Catullo.'

"Grande et conspicuum nostro quoque tempore monstrum
"Cæcus adulator."

This man extolled the Rhombus exceedingly, pointing to its various beauties with his hand, as if he really saw them. But unfortunately, whilst he pointed to the fish as lying on his left hand, it lay all the while on his right.

"Nemo magis Rhombum stupuit : nam plurima dixit
"In lævum conversus : at illi dextra jacebat
"Bellua :

This was not the only occasion on which he had given scope to his imagination, and praised as though he had eyes:

"...... sic pugnas Cilicis laudabat et ictus,
"Et pegma, et pueros inde ad velaria raptos."—Juv. iv. 113—121.

The force of the comparison, therefore, lies in Erasmus being supposed to discuss the phantom of his own imagination, instead of the real Rhombus. This phantom he might call dubious or unnecessary, without being himself impious; it was the coinage of his own brain : but if he called the real Rhombus, 'the Church's confession of Freewill,' dubious or useless, he wrote gravely, but he wrote sacrilegiously. He has only the alternative, therefore, of being a fool or a madman, if he place Luther's assertion on Freewill amongst the barren and vain.—The word 'præsumere' is used in rather a peculiar, but not unauthorized, sense ; correspondent with our English word, 'presume,' and with its own etymology ; 'preconceive,' 'anticipate,' 'conjecture,' imagine,' —' opinari,' 'credere,' 'conjicere,' 'imaginari.'—I should rather have preferred understanding 'præsumere' in the sense of 'anticipating ;' meaning that he spoke of one subject here in his Preface, and of another in the body of his work. But the illustration does not coincide with this view ; Catullus did not make two speeches : nor do I find any authority for such use of 'præsumere.'—It has a peculiar rhetorical sense of 'pre-occupying ;' that is, 'occupying the adversary's ground before him,' by anticipating and obviating his objections.—But this will not apply here.

Paul demand that Plerophory,[e] or most assured and most tenacious 'assertion' of what our conscience believes! In Rom. x. he calls it 'confession'; saying, "and with the mouth confession is made unto salvation." (Rom. x. 10.) And Christ says, "He who confesses me before men, him will I also confess before my Father." (Matt. x. 32.) Peter commands us to give a reason of the hope that is in us. (1 Pet. iii. 15.) And what need of many words? Nothing is more notorious and more celebrated amongst Christians than Assertion: take away assertions, and you take away Christianity. Nay, the Holy Ghost is given to them from heaven, that He may glorify Christ and confess him even unto death. Unless this be not asserting, to die for confessing and asserting! In short, the Spirit is such an assertor, that He even goes out as a champion to invade the world, and reproves it of sin, as though he would provoke it to the fight; and Paul commands Timothy to "rebuke, and to be instant out of season." (John xvi. 8. 2 Tim. iv. 2.) But what a droll sort of rebuker would he be, who neither assuredly believes, nor with constancy asserts himself, the truth which he rebukes others for rejecting. I would send the fellow to Anticyra.[f] But I am far more foolish myself, in wasting words and time upon a matter clearer than the sun. What Christian would endure that assertions should be despised? This were nothing else but a denial of all religion and piety at once; or an assertion, that neither religion, nor piety, nor any dogma of the faith, is of the least moment.—And why, pray, do you also deal in assertions? 'I am not pleased

SECT. I.

Assertions defended.

[e] Luther has no authority for this interpretation of the term Plerophory; which expresses no more than 'full evidence to a fact, or truth;' or, 'full assurance of that fact or truth.' But in substance he is correct; 'confession' (which amounts to assertion) *is* demanded.

[f] *Antic.*] The famous island of Hellebore; which cured mad people. Hence 'Naviget Anticyram.'—Hor.

PART. I. with assertions, and I like this temper better than its opposite.'

But you would be understood to have meant nothing about confessing Christ and *his* dogmas in this place. I thank you for the hint; and, out of kindness to you, will recede from my right and from my practice, and will forbear to judge of your intention; reserving such judgment for another time, or for other topics. Meanwhile, I advise you to correct your tongue and your pen, and hereafter to abstain from such expressions; for however your mind may be sound and pure, your speech (which is said to be the image of the mind) is not so. For, if you judge the cause of Freewill to be one which it is not necessary to understand, and to be no part of Christianity; you speak correctly, but your judgment is profane. On the contrary, if you judge it to be necessary, you speak profanely and judge correctly. But then there is no room for these mighty complaints and exaggerations about useless assertions and contentions: for what have these to do with the question at issue?

SECT II. But what say you to those words of yours in which you speak not of the cause of Freewill only, but of all religious dogmas in general, ' that, if the inviolable authority of the divine writings and the decrees of the Church allowed it, you would go over and side with the Sceptics; so displeased are you with assertions.'

Erasmus shewn to be a Sceptic.

What a Proteus is there in those words, 'inviolable authority and decrees of the Church!' As if you had a great reverence, forsooth, for the Scriptures and for the Church; but would hint a wish that you were at liberty to become a Sceptic. What Christian would speak so? If you say this of useless dogmas about matters of indifference, what novelty is there in it? Who does not in such cases desire the licence of the Sceptical profession? Nay, what Christian does not, in point of fact, freely use this licence and condemn those who are the sworn captives of any particular sentiment? Unless (as your words almost express) you account Christians, taken in the gross, to be a sort of men whose doctrines are of no value, though they be foolish enough to jangle about them, and to fight the battle of counter-assertion! If, on the contrary, you speak of necessary doctrines, what assertion can be more impious than for a man to say, that he wishes to be at liberty to assert nothing, in such cases? A Christian will rather say, 'So far am I from delighting in the sentiment of the Sceptics, that, wherever the infirmity of my flesh suffers me, I would not only adhere firmly to the word of God, asserting as *it* asserts; but would even wish to be as confident as possible in matters not necessary, and which fall without the limits of Scripture assertion.' For what is more wretched than uncertainty?

Again; what shall we say to the words subjoined, 'to which I in all things willingly submit my judgment, whether I understand what they prescribe, or not'? What is this you say, Erasmus? Is it not enough to have submitted your judgment to Scripture? do you submit it also to the decrees of the Church? What has she power to decree, which the Scripture has not decreed? If so, what becomes of liberty, and of the power of judging those dogmatists: as Paul writes in 1 Cor. xiv. "Let the others judge?" You do not like, it seems, that there should be a judge set over the decrees of the Church; but Paul enjoins it. What is this new devotedness and humility of yours, that you take away from us (as far as your example goes) the power of judging the decrees of men, and submit yourself to men, blindfold? Where does the divine Scripture impose this on us? Then again, what Christian would so commit the injunctions of Scripture and of the Church to the winds, as to say 'whether I apprehend, or do not

SECT. II.

Erasmus shewn to be a Sceptic.

apprehend.' You submit yourself, and yet do not care whether you apprehend what you profess, or not. But a Christian is accursed, if he do not apprehend, with assurance, the things enjoined to him. Indeed, how shall he believe if he do not apprehend? For you call it apprehending here, if a man assuredly receives an affirmation, and does not, like a Sceptic, doubt it. Else, what is there that any man can apprehend in any creature, if 'to apprehend a thing' be 'perfectly to know and discern it'? Besides, there would then be no place for a man's at the same time apprehending some things, and not apprehending some things, in the same substance; but if he have apprehended one thing, he must have apprehended all: as in God, for instance; whom we must apprehend, before we can apprehend any part of his creation.

In short, these expressions of yours come to this: that, in your view, it is no matter what any man believes any where, if but the peace of the world be preserved; and that, when a man's life, fame, property and good favour are in danger, he may be allowed to imitate the fellow who said 'They affirm, I affirm; they deny, I deny;' and to account christian doctrines nothing better than the opinions of philosophers and ordinary men, for which it is most foolish to wrangle, contend and assert, because nothing but contention and a disturbing of the peace of the world results therefrom. 'What is above us, is nothing to us.' You interpose yourself, as a mediator who would put an end to our conflicts by hanging both parties and persuading us that we are fighting for foolish and useless objects. This is what your words come to, I say; and I think you understand what I suppress here, my Erasmus.[g]

---

[g] Luther does not choose to speak out on the subject of Erasmus's scepticism and infidelity, but hints pretty broadly at it. There is but too strong evidence that the insinuation was just; and it constituted the most galling part of his attack. Erasmus's object was to rise upon the ruins of Luther; but

However, let the words pass, as I have said; and, in the mean time, I will excuse your spirit, on the condition that you manifest it no further. O fear the Spirit of God, who searches the reins and the hearts, and is not beguiled by fine words. I have said thus much to deter you from hereafter loading our cause with charges of positiveness and inflexibility; for, upon this plan, you only shew that you are nourishing in your heart a Lucian, or some other hog of the Epicurean sty, who, having no belief at all of a God himself, laughs in his sleeve at all those who believe and confess one. Allow us to be asserters, to be studious of assertions, and to be delighted with them; but thou, meanwhile, bestow thy favour upon thy Sceptics and Academics, till Christ shall have called even thee also. The Holy Ghost is no Sceptic; nor has He written dubious propositions, or mere opinions, upon our hearts, but assertions more assured and more firmly rooted than life itself, and all that we have learned from experience.^h

I come to another head, which is of a piece with this. When you distinguish between christian dogmas, you pretend that some are necessary to be known, and some unnecessary; you say that some are shut up, and some exposed to view.ⁱ Thus, you either mock us with the words of others, which have been imposed upon yourself, or try your hand at a sort of rhetorical sally of your own. You adduce, in support of your sentiment, that saying of Paul's (Rom. xi. 33.) "O the depth of the riches both of the wisdom and knowledge of God;"

Marginal notes: SECT. III. — Christian truth is revealed and ascertained, not hidden.

with what face could the Pope or the Princes prefer an Infidel? See Milner's Eccles. Hist vol iv. 935—945.

^h A beautiful testimony to the confidence inspired into the soul by the Holy Ghost's teachings! We are more sure of the truth of His assertions than that *we live*, and hold them more firmly than we do the results of experience.

ⁱ *Abstrusa, exposita*] *Abst.* 'thrust from us,' as into secret places, 'hidden from view,' like the apocryphal writings. *Expos.* 'set out in broad day,' like goods exposed to sale.

PART I. and that of Isaiah too (Isa. xl. 13.) "Who hath assisted the Spirit of the Lord, or who hath been his counsellor"? It was easy for you to say, these things, either as one who knew that he was not writing to Luther; but for the multitude; or as one who did not consider that he was writing against Luther: to whom you still give credit, as I hope, for some study and discernment in the Scriptures. If not, see whether I do not even extort it from you. If I also may be allowed to play the rhetorician, or logician, for a moment, I would make this distinction: God, and the writing of God, are two things; no less than the Creator, and the creature of God, are two things. Now, that there be many things hidden in God, which we are ignorant of, no one doubts; as he speaks himself of the last day, "Of that day knoweth no man, but the Father." (Matt. xxiv. 36.) And again, in Acts i. "It is not for you to know the times and the seasons." And again; "I know whom I have chosen."[k] (John xiii. 18.) And Paul says, "The Lord knoweth them that are His": (2 Tim. ii. 19.) and the like. But that some dogmas of Scripture are shut up in the dark, and all are not exposed to view, has been rumoured, it is true, by profane Sophists (with whose mouth you also speak here, Erasmus), but they have never produced a single instance, nor can they produce one, by way of making good this mad assertion of theirs. Yet, by such hobgoblins as these, Satan has deterred men from reading the sacred writings; and has rendered holy Scripture contemptible, that he might cause his own pestilent heresies, derived from philosophy, to reign in the Church. I confess indeed

[k] Luther appears to understand this text as most do : 'He knew who those were amongst men, whom he had chosen;' with a supposed reference to eternal election. But the Greek text plainly determines it to mean, 'I know the real character and state of those persons whom I have chosen;' referring to the Twelve exclusively, as those whom he afterwards (xv. 19.) declares himself to have chosen out of the world.

that many passages of Scripture are obscure and shut up; not so much through the vastness of the truths declared in them, as through our ignorance of words and grammar: but I maintain that these do not at all prevent our knowledge of all things contained in the Scriptures. For what, that is of a more august nature, can yet remain concealed in Scripture, now that, after the breaking of the seals, and rolling away of the stone from the door of the sepulchre, that greatest of all mysteries has been spread abroad, that 'Christ, the Son of God, is made man';[1] that 'God is at the same time Three and One;' that 'Christ has suffered for us, and shall reign for ever and ever'? Are not these things known, and even sung in the streets? Take Christ from the Scriptures, and what will you any longer find in them?

SECT III.

Christian truth is revealed and ascertained, not hidden.

The things contained in the Scriptures, then, are all brought forth into view, though some passages still remain obscure, through our not understanding the words. But it is foolish and profane to know that all the truths of Scripture are set out to view in the clearest light, and, because a few words are obscure, to call the truths themselves obscure. If the words be obscure in one place, they are plain in another; and the same truth, declared most openly to the whole world, is both announced in the Scriptures by clear words, and left latent by means of obscure ones. But of what moment is it, if the truth itself be in the light, that some one testimony to it be yet in the dark; when many other testimonies to the same truth, meanwhile, are in the light? Who will say that a public fountain is not in the light, because those

---

[1] " Who was declared to be the Son of God with power, according to the spirit of holiness," (opposed to, " which was made of the seed of David according to the flesh," in the preceding verse) " by the resurrection from the dead." Rom i. 4. *Fractis signaculis.* The stone at the door of the sepulchre was sealed. Matt. xxvii. 65. 66.

PART I.
SECT. IV.

Scripture is falsely accused of obscurity.

who live in a narrow entry do not see it, whilst all who live in the market-place, do see it?"[m]

Your allusion to the Corycian cave,[n] therefore, is nothing to the purpose. The case is not as you represent it, with respect to the Scriptures. The most abstruse mysteries, and those of greatest majesty, are no longer in retreat; but stand at the very door of the cave, in open space, drawn out and exposed to view. For Christ hath opened our understanding, that we should understand the Scriptures. (Luke xxiv. 45.) And the Gospel has been preached to every creature. (Mark xvi. 15. Coloss. i. 23.) Their sound has gone out into all the land. (Ps. xix. 4.) And all things which have been written, have been written for our learning. (Rom. xv. 4.) Also, all Scripture having been written by inspiration of God, is useful for teaching. (2 Tim. iii. 16.) Thou, therefore, and all thy Sophists come and produce a single mystery in the Scriptures, which still remains shut up. The fact, that so many truths are still shut up to many, arises not from any obscurity in the Scriptures, but from their own blindness, or carelessness; which is such, that they take no pains to discern the truth, though it be most evident. As Paul says of the Jews, (2 Cor. iii. 15.) "The veil remains upon their heart." And again, (2 Cor. iv. 3, 4.) "If our Gospel be hid, it is hid to them that are lost; whose hearts the God of this world hath blinded." To blame Scripture, in this matter, is a rashness like that of the man who should complain of the sun and of the darkness, after having veiled his

---

[m] Luther's affirmation and argument is of the greatest importance here. All the truth of God, he maintains, is explicitly and intelligibly declared in Scripture; in some passages more obscurely, through our ignorance of words; in others more manifestly and unequivocally: but there is no truth, no dogma, that is not distinctly taught and confirmed.

[n] A cave of singular virtue in Mount Corycus of Cilicia, supposed to be inhabited by the Gods.

own eyes, or gone from out of the day-light into a dark room to hide himself. Then let these wretches cease from such a blasphemous perverseness as to impute the darkness and dulness of their own minds to the Scriptures of God; which are light itself.

<small>SEC. IV.

Scripture is falsely accused of obscurity.</small>

So, when you adduce Paul exclaiming "how incomprehensible are his judgments" you seem to have referred the pronoun HIS to the Scripture. But Paul does not say how incomprehensible are the judgments of *Scripture,* but of *God.* Thus Isaiah (Isai. xl. 13.) does not say 'who hath known the mind of *Scripture,*' but, "who hath known the mind of the Lord?" Howbeit, Paul asserts that the mind of the Lord is known to Christians : but then it is about "those things which have been freely given to us"; as he speaks in the same place. (1 Cor. ii. 10. 16.) You see, therefore, how carelessly you have inspected these passages of Scripture; which you have cited, about as aptly as you have done nearly all your others in support of Freewill. And thus, your instances, which you subjoin with a good deal of suspicion and venom, are nothing to the purpose ; such as ' the distinction of Persons in the Godhead,' ' the combination of the divine and human nature,' and ' the unpardonable sin :' whose ambiguity, you say, has not even yet been clean removed.° If you allude to questions which the Sophists have agitated on these subjects, 1 am ready to ask what that most innocent volume of Scripture hath done to you, that you should charge her with the abuse, with which wicked men have contaminated her purity? Scripture simply makes confession of the Trinity of Persons in God, of the humanity of Christ, and of the unpardonable sin ; what is there

---

° *Resectum.*] Erasmus's term; taken from 'the *close* cutting of the nails, or hair, or beard ;' or, from ' the excision of the unsound flesh in wounds.' It implies, that all the ambiguity is not yet withdrawn, though some of it may be.

of obscurity, or of ambiguity here? How these things subsist, the Scripture has not told us, as you pretend it has; nor have we any need to know. The Sophists discuss their own dreams on these subjects: accuse and condemn them, if you please, but acquit Scripture. If, on the other hand, you speak of the essential truth, and not of factitious questions, I say again, do not accuse Scripture, but the Arians, and those to whom the Gospel is hid, to such a degree, that they have no eye to see the clearest testimonies in support of the Trinity of Persons in God, and the humanity of Christ; through the working of Satan, who is their God.

To be brief; there is a twofold clearness in Scripture, even as there is also a twofold obscurity: the one external, contained in the ministeriality of the word; the other internal, which consists in that knowledge which is of the heart.^p If you speak of this internal clearness, no one discerns an iota of Scripture, but he who has the Spirit of God. All men have a darkened heart: so that, even though they should repeat and be able to quote every passage of Scripture, they neither understand nor truly know any thing that is contained in these passages; nor do they believe that there is a God, or that they are themselves God's creatures; or any thing else. According to what is written in Psalm xiv.; "The fool hath said in his heart, God is nothing." (Ps. xiv. 1.) For the Spirit is necessary to the understanding of the whole of Scripture, and of any part of it. But if you speak of that external clearness, nothing at all

---

[p] Luther refers back to this passage in the progress of his work. (See below, Chap. ii Sect. xiii) It is not the public ministry of the word, but its instrumentality in general, of which he here speaks. Scripture reveals truth to the ear, and reveals truth to the heart. The former of these he calls an *external* clearness. The word which falls upon the ear is a plain and clear word The other he calls an *internal* clearness. The truth which is contained in Scripture, and conveyed by a clear and plain word, is *understanded* by the heart.'

has been left obscure, or ambiguous; but every thing that is contained in the Scriptures has been drawn out into the most assured light, and declared to the whole world, by the ministeriality of the word.

But it is still more intolerable, that you should class this question of Freewill with those which are useless and unnecessary, and should recount a number of articles to us in its stead, the reception of which you deem sufficient to constitute a pious Christian. Assuredly, any Jew or Heathen, who had no knowledge at all of Christ, would find it easy enough to draw out such a pattern of faith as yours. You do not mention Christ in a single jot of it; as though you thought that christian piety might subsist without Christ, if but God, whose nature is most merciful, be worshipped with all our might. What shall I say here, Erasmus? Your whole air is Lucian, and your breath a vast surfeit of Epicurus?[q] If you account this question an unnecessary one for Christians, take yourself off the stage, pray: we account it necessary.

If it be irreligious, if it be curious, if it be superfluous, as you say it is,' to know whether God foreknows any thing contingently; whether our will be active in those things which pertain to everlasting salvation, or be merely passive, grace meanwhile being the agent; whether we do by mere necessity (which we must rather call suffer) whatever we do of good or evil, what will then be religious I would ask? what, important? what, useful to be known?' This is perfect trifling, Erasmus! This is too much. Nor is it easy to attribute this conduct of yours to ignorance. An old man like you, who has lived amongst Christians and has long revolved the Scriptures, leaves

---

[q] 'Totus Lucianum spiras et inhalas mihi grandem Epicuri crapulam'. *Luc.* One of the most noted satirical blasphemers of Christianity: *Epic.* An atheistic heathen philosopher, who inculcated pleasure and indifference.

us no place for excusing or thinking favourably of him. Yet the Papists pardon these strange things in you, and bear with you, because you are writing against Luther. Men who would tear you with their teeth, if Luther were out of the way and you should write such things! Plato is my friend, Socrates is my friend, but I must honour truth before both. For although you knew but little about the Scriptures and about Christianity, even the enemy of Christians might surely have known what Christians account necessary and useful, and what they do not. But you, a theologian and a master of Christians, when setting about to prescribe a form of Christianity to them, do not, what might at least have been expected of you, hesitate after your usual sceptical manner, as to what is necessary and useful to them; but glide into the directly opposite extreme, and in a manner contrary to your usual temper, by a sort of assertion never heard of before, sit now as judge, and pronounce those things to be unnecessary which, if they be not necessary and be not certainly known, there is neither a God, nor a Christ, nor a Gospel, nor a faith, nor any thing else even of Judaism, much less of Christianity, left behind. Immortal God! what a window shall I say? what a field rather, does Erasmus hereby open for acting and speaking against himself! What could you possibly write on the subject of Free-will, which should have any thing of good or right in it, when you betray such ignorance of Scripture and of piety, in these words of yours? But I will furl my sails, and will talk with you here, not in my own words, (as I perhaps shall do presently) but in yours.

SECT. VI.

Erasmus's Christianity.

The form of Christianity chalked out by you has this article amongst others, that we must strive with all our might; that we must apply ourselves to the remedy of repentance, and solicit the mercy of God by all means; without this mercy, neither the will, nor the endeavour of man, is efficacious. Also, that no man should despair of pardon from God, whose nature it is to be most merciful. These words of yours, in which there is no mention of Christ, no mention of the Spirit; which are colder than ice itself, so that they have not even your wonted grace of eloquence in them; and which, perhaps, the fear of Priests and Kings [r] had hard work to wring from the pitiful fellow, that he might not appear quite an Atheist; do nevertheless contain some assertions: as, that we have strength in ourselves; that there is such a thing as striving with all our strength; that there is such a thing as God's mercy; that there are means of soliciting mercy; that God is by nature just; by nature most merciful, &c. &c. If then any one be ignorant, what those powers are, what they do, what they suffer, what their striving is, what its efficacy, and what its inefficacy; what shall he do? what will you teach him to do? It is irreligious, curious, and superfluous, you say, to wish to know whether our will be *active* in those things which pertain to everlasting salvation, or be only *passive* under the agency of grace. But here you say, on the contrary, that it is christian piety to strive with all our might; and that the will is not efficacious without the mercy of God. In these words, it is plain, you assert that the will does something in matters which appertain to everlasting salvation, since you suppose it to strive; on the other hand, you assert it to be passive, when you say that it is inefficacious without the mercy of God: howbeit, you do not explain how far that activity and that passiveness are to be understood to extend. Thus, you do what you can to make

SECT. VI.

Erasmus's Christianity.

[r] *Pontificum et Tyrannorum*.] These names comprehend the whole tribe of Popes, Cardinals, and Princes, by which the ecclesiastical and civil power of the Roman empire was now administered. *Pont.* 'Priests of high dignity,' generally; not confined to the Pope, but including also his Cardinals. *Tyran.* 'The civil rulers throughout the empire:' in Latin, used more generally in a bad sense, to denote 'usurped authority exercised with fierceness and violence;' but not always.

PART I.
us ignorant what is the efficacy of our own will and what the efficacy of the mercy of God, in that very place in which you teach us what is the conjoint efficacy of both. That prudence of yours, by which you have determined to keep clear of both parties, and to emerge in safety between Scylla and Charybdis, so whirls you round and round in its vortex; that, being overwhelmed with waves and confounded with fears[s] in the midst of the passage, you assert all that you deny, and deny all that you assert.

SEC. VII.

Erasmus's theology exposed by similies.

I will expose your theology to you, by two or three similes. What if a man, setting about to make a good poem or speech, should not consider or inquire, of what sort his genius is; what he is equal to, and what not; what the subject which he has taken in hand requires; but, altogether neglecting that precept of Horace, 'what your shoulders are able to bear, and what is too heavy for them,' should only rush headlong upon his attempt to execute the work; as thinking within himself, that he must try and get it done; and that it would be superfluous and curious to inquire, whether he have the erudition, the powers of language, and the genius, which the task requires? What if a man, anxious to reap abundant fruits from his ground, should not be curious to exercise a superfluous care in exploring the nature of his soil, as Virgil in his Georgics curiously and vainly teaches us; but should hurry on rashly, and having no thought but about finishing his work, should plough the shore, and cast in his seed wherever there is an open space, whether it be sand or mud? What if a man, going to war and desirous of a splendid victory, or having some other service to perform for the state, should not be curious to consider what he is able to effect; whether his treasury be rich enough, whether his soldiers be expert, whether he have any power to exe-

[s] *Confusus*, expresses the state of the mariner's mind: *fluctibus obrutus*, his drowning body.

cute his design; but should altogether despise that precept of the historian, 'before you act, there is need of deliberation,' when you have deliberated, you must be quick to execute;' and should rush on, with his eyes shut and his ears stopped, crying out nothing but "war," "war," and vehemently pursuing his work? What judgment would you pronounce, Erasmus, upon such poets, husbandmen, generals, and statesmen? I will add that simile in the Gospel. If any man, going about to build a tower, sitteth not down first, and counteth the cost, whether he hath wherewithal to finish it; what is Christ's judgment upon that man?

SEC. VII.
Erasmus's theology exposed by similies.

Thus, you command us only to work, and forbid us first of all to explore and measure, or ascertain our strength, what we can do, and what we cannot do; as though this were curious, unnecessary and irreligious. The effect of which is, that, whilst through excessive 'prudence' you deprecate temerity, and make a shew ᵗ of sober-mindedness, you come at last to the extreme of even counselling the greatest temerity. For, although the Sophists act rashness and insanity, by discussing curious ᵘ subjects, yet is their offence milder than yours; who even teach and command men to be mad and rash. To make this insanity still greater, you persuade us that this temerity is most beautiful; that it is christian piety, sobriety, religious gravity, and soundness of mind. Nay, if we do not act it, you, who are such an enemy to assertions, assert that we are irreligious, curious, and vain: ᵛ so beautifully have you escaped your Scylla, whilst you have avoided your Charybdis. It is your con-

ᵗ *Detestaris, prætendis.*] *Detest,* deprecari, amoliri, avertere, deos invocando. *Prætend.,* 'to put forwards as a reason for acting, whether truly or falsely.'
ᵘ *Curiosa.*] Applied in a bad sense to 'things we have no business with,' '*curiosus* dicitur nonnunquam de iis qui nimiâ curâ utuntur in rebus alienis exquirendis.'
ᵛ *Vanos* answers to *supervacaneos* used above, expressing their 'unprofitableness;' 'idle speculators.'

fidence in your own talents which drives you to this point. You think you can impose upon men's minds by your eloquence, to such a degree, that no man shall be able to perceive what a monster you are cherishing in your bosom, and what an object you are labouring to achieve by these slippery writings of yours. But "God is not mocked;" nor is it good for a man to strike upon such a rock as HIM.

Besides, if you had taught us this rashness in making poems, in procuring the fruits of the earth, in conducting wars and civil employments, or in building houses; though it would be intolerable, especially in a man like yourself, you would after all have deserved some indulgence from Christians at least, who despise temporal things. But, when you command even Christians to be these rash workmen, and, in the very matter of their eternal salvation, insist upon their being incurious as to their natural powers, what they can do and what they cannot do; this, surely, is an offence which cannot be pardoned. For, they will not know what they are doing, so long as they are ignorant what, and how much they can do; and if they know not what they are doing, they cannot possibly repent should they be in error; and impenitence is an unpardonable sin. To such an abyss, does that moderate, sceptical theology of yours conduct us!

SEC. VIII.

Absolute necessity of the subject of Freewill in order to true piety.

It is not irreligious, then, nor curious, nor superfluous, but most of all useful and necessary to a Christian, to know whether the will does any thing, or nothing, in the matter of salvation. Nay, to say the truth, this is the very hinge of our disputation; the very question at issue turns upon it.ˣ We are occupied in discussing, what the free will does, what the free will suffers, what is its

ˣ *Status causæ hujus*] 'Status a rhetoribus dicitur quæstio, quæ ex primâ causarum conflictione nascitur; quia in eo tota causa stat et consistit.'

proportion to the grace of God. If we be ignorant of these things, we shall know nothing at all about Christianity, and shall be worse than Heathens. The man who does not understand this subject, let him acknowledge that he is no Christian. The man who censures or despises it, let him know that he is the worst enemy of Christians. For, if I know not, what, how far, and how much, I can, of my own natural powers, do and effect towards God; it will be alike uncertain and unknown to me, what, how far, and how much, God can and does effect in me: whereas God "worketh all in all!" [y]

SEC. VIII.

Absolute necessity of the subject of Freewill in order to true piety.

Again; if I know not the works and power of God, I know not God himself; and if I know not God, I cannot worship, praise, give him thanks, serve him; being ignorant how much I ought to attribute to myself, and how much to God. We ought therefore to distinguish, with the greatest clearness, between God's power and our own power, between God's work and our own work; if we would live piously.

You see then, that this question is the one part [z] of the whole sum of Christianity! Both the knowledge of ourselves, and the knowledge and glory of God, are dependent upon the hazard of its decision. It is insufferable in you, then, my Erasmus, to call the knowledge of this truth irreligious, curious and vain. We owe much to you, but we owe all to piety. Nay, you think yourself, that all good is to be ascribed to God, and you assert this in the description you have given us of your own Christianity. And if you assert this, you unquestionably assert in the same words that

[y] *Omnia in omnibus.*] Not only 'all things in all *men*,' but 'all things in all *things*;' every jot and tittle in every single thing that is done.

[z] *Partem alteram.*] Opposed to 'altera pars' in the next section: considering the sum of Christian doctrine, as divisible into these two integral parts.

PART I. the mercy of God does all, and that our will acts nothing, but rather is acted upon; else, all will not be attributed to God. But, a little while after you declare, that the assertion, and even the knowledge of this truth, is neither religious, pious, nor salutary. However, the mind which is inconsistent with itself, and which is uncertain and unskilled in matters of piety, is obliged to speak so.

SECT. IX.

Erasmus has omitted the question of God's prescience.

The other part of the sum of Christianity, is to know whether God foreknows any thing *contingently*; and whether we do every thing *necessarily*. This part also you represent as irreligious, curious, and vain; as all other profane men do. Nay, the devils and the damned represent it as utterly odious and detestable: and you are very wise in withdrawing yourself from these questions, if you may be allowed to do so. But, in the mean time, you are not much of a rhetorician or a theologian, when you presume to speak and to teach about Freewill, without these parts. I will be your whetstone; and, though no rhetorician myself, will remind an exquisite rhetorician of his duty. If Quintilian proposing to write on oratory should say, 'In my judgment those foolish and useless topics of invention, distribution, elocution, memory, and delivery should be omitted; suffice it to know that oratory is the art of speaking well;' would not you laugh at the artist? This is precisely your method. Professing to write about Freewill, you begin with driving away, and casting off, the whole body, and all the members of this art, which you propose to write about. For, it is impossible that you should understand what Freewill is, until you know what the human will has power to do, and what God does; whether he foreknows, or not? [a]

---

[a] *An præsciat.*] The Newstadt editor inserts the word *necessariò* here. It is not needed. What is foreknowledge, if it be not absolute; i.e. if the event be not inevitable, or necessary?

Do not even your rhetoricians teach you, that, when a man is going to speak upon any matter, he must first speak to the point whether there be such a thing, or no; then, what it is; what are its parts; what its contraries, its affinities, and its similitudes. But you strip poor Freewill, wretched as she is in herself, of all these appendages, and define [b] none of the questions which appertain to her, save the first; whether there be such a thing as Freewill? By what sort of arguments you do this, we shall see presently. A more foolish book on Freewill I never beheld, if eloquence of style be excepted. The Sophists, forsooth, who know nothing of rhetoric, have here at least proved better logicians than you; for in their essays on Freewill they define all its questions; such as, 'whether it be;' 'what it is;' 'what it does;' 'how it is,' &c. &c. Howbeit, neither do even they complete [c] what they attempt. I will therefore goad [d] both you and all the Sophists in this treatise of mine, until ye define the powers and the performances of Freewill [e] to me; yea,

SECT. IX.

Erasmus has omitted the question of God's prescience.

[b] *Definis.*] *Def.* does not express simply what we understand and mean by 'a definition;' but 'a laying out of the subject matter of debate in propositions, and a supporting of those propositions by argument'. Such were Luther's several *Theses*; with ninety-five of which, he first opened his attack upon the Popedom; or rather upon the doctrine of Indulgences: a form of discussion common in those times. Perhaps our English word 'determine' comes nearest to it.

[c] *Efficiunt quod tentant.*] They do not go through with the matter in hand, but leave it short: the 'vires et opera' are still undefined; neither distinctly affirmed, nor satisfactorily proved.

[d] *Urgebo.*] 'Driving, as you would drive cattle,' or an enemy, before you.'

[e] *Liberi arbitrii vires et opera.*] *Voluntas* is 'the faculty of the will at large.' *Arbitrium*, 'the essence, spirit, power of that faculty,' Erasmus maintains this power to be free; Luther, that it is in bondage. Hence 'liberum arbitrium,' 'servum arbitrium.' *Vis*, or *vires* arbitrii, 'the power or powers of this power.' *Vis*, or *vires liberi* arbitrii ; 'the power or powers of this power, as declared by Erasmus to be free;' and so, just corresponds with our idea and term of 'Freewill.' ' You shall define to me, what

PART I.

SECT. X.

God's foreknowledge absolute, flows from Erasmus's confession.

so goad you, with Christ's help, that I hope I shall make you repent of having published your Diatribe.

It is most necessary and most salutary, then, for a Christian to know this also; that God foreknows nothing contingently, but foresees, and purposes, and accomplishes every thing, by an unchangeable, eternal, and infallible will. But, by this thunderbolt, Freewill is struck to the earth and completely ground to powder. Those who would assert Freewill, therefore, must either deny, or disguise, or, by some other means, repel this thunderbolt from them. However, before I establish it by my own argumentation and the authority of Scripture, I will first of all encounter you personally, with your own words. Are not you that Erasmus, who just now asserted, that it is God's nature to be just, that it is God's nature to be most merciful? If this be true, does it not follow, that he is UNCHANGEABLY just and merciful; that, as his nature changes not unto eternity, so neither doth his justice or his mercy change? But what is said of his justice and mercy, must be said also of his knowledge, wisdom, goodness, will, and other divine properties. If these things, then, be asserted religiously, piously, and profitably concerning God, as you write; what has happened to you, that, in disagreement with yourself, you now assert it to be irreligious, curious, and vain, to affirm that God foreknows necessarily? Is it that you think, that, ' he either *foreknows* what he does not *will,* or *wills* what he does not *foreknow?*' If he wills what he foreknows, his will is eternal and immutable, for it is part of his nature: if he foreknows what he wills, his know-

are the powers of this faculty, which is thus supposed and maintained by you to be free.' This is just the crux of modern Freewillers, as it was of Erasmus. They get on pretty well, till they are compelled to define.

ledge is eternal and immutable, for it is part of his nature.[f]

Hence it irresistibly follows, that all which we do, and all which happens, although it seem to happen mutably and contingently, does in reality happen necessarily and unalterably, insofar as respects the will of God. For the will of God is efficacious, and such as cannot be thwarted; since the power of God is itself a part of his nature: it is also wise, so that it cannot be misled. And since his will is not thwarted, the work which he wills cannot be prevented; but must be produced in the very place, time, and measure which he himself both foresees and wills. If the will of God were such as to cease after he has made a work which remains the same, as is the case with man's will when, after having builded a house as he willed, his will concerning it ceases; as it does in death; then it might be truly said, that some events are brought to pass contingently and mutably. But here, on the contrary, so far is it from being the case, that the work itself either comes into existence, or continues in existence *contingently*, by being made and remaining in being when the will to have it so hath ceased; that the work itself ceases, but the will remains. Now, if we would use words so as not to abuse them, a work is said in Latin to be done *contingently*, but is never said to be itself *contingent*.

[f] This abstruse but irresistible deduction from Erasmus's concession may perhaps be stated a little more familiarly, thus: If God does not foreknow all events absolutely, there must be a defect either in his will, or in his knowledge, what happens must either be against his will, or beside his knowledge Either he meant otherwise than the event, or had no meaning at all about the event; or, he foresaw another event, or did not foresee any event at all But the truth is, what he willed in past eternity, he wills now, the thing now executed is what he has intended to execute from everlasting; for his will is eternal. just as the thing which has now happened is what he saw in past eternity; because his knowledge is eternal.

PART I.
The meaning is, that a work has been performed by a contingent and mutable will; such as is not in God. Besides, a work cannot be called a contingent one, except it be done by us contingently and as it were by accident, without any forethought on our part; being so called, because our will or hand seizes hold of it as a thing thrown in our way by accident, and we have neither thought nor willed any thing about it before.

SECT. XI.

Objection to term 'necessity' admitted. absurdity of the distinction between necessity of a consequence and of a consequent.

*I could have wished indeed, that another and a better word had been introduced into our disputation than this usual one, 'Necessity'; which is not rightly applied to the will of either God or man. It has too harsh and incongruous a meaning for this occasion; suggesting the notion of something like compulsion, and what is at least the opposite of willingness, to the mind. Our question, meanwhile, implies no such thing; for both God's will, and man's will does what it does, whether good or bad, without compulsion, by dint of mere good pleasure or desire, as with perfect freedom. The will of God, nevertheless, is immutable and infallible, and governs our mutable will—as Boethius sings, 'and standing fixed, mov'st all the rest'—and our will, wicked in the extreme, can of itself do nothing good. Let the understanding of my reader, then, supply what the word 'necessity' does not express; apprehending by it, what you might choose to call the immutability of God's will, and the impotency of our evil will: what some have called 'a necessity of immutability': not very grammatically or theologically.

The Sophists, who had laboured this point for years, have at length been mastered, and are compelled to admit that 'all events are necessary;' but by the necessity of a *consequence,* as they say, and not by the necessity of a *consequent.* Thus have they *eluded* the violence of this question, but

* N. B. This whole paragraph is omitted in the Nieustadt edition of 1591.

it is by much more *illuding* themselves.[g] I will take the trouble of shewing you, what a mere nothing this distinction of theirs is. By necessity of a consequence (to speak as these thick-headed people do) they mean, that, if God wills a thing, the thing itself must be, but it is not necessary that the very thing which is, should be. For only God exists *necessarily*; all other things may cease to be, if God pleases. Thus they say that the act of God is necessary, if he wills a thing, but that the very thing produced is not necessary. Now what do they get by this play upon words? Why, this, I suppose. The thing produced is not necessary; that is, has not a necessary existence—this is no more than saying, the thing produced is not God himself. Still the truth remains, that every event is necessary; if it be a necessary act of God, or a necessary consequence: however it may not, now that it is effected, exist necessarily; that is, may not be God, or may not have a necessary existence. For, if I am of necessity made, it is of little moment to me that my being or making be mutable. Still I—this contingent and mutable thing, who am not the necessary God—am made. So that their foolery, that all events are necessary, through a necessity of the conse*quence*, but not through a necessity of the conse*quent*, has no more in it than this: all events are necessary, it is true; but though necessary, are not God himself. Now what need was there to tell us this? As if there was any danger of our asserting that the things

[g] *Eluserant, illuserunt*] A play upon the words *eludo, illudo. Elud.* 'to parry off,' 'evade.' A metaphor taken from the gladiator, who, by a dexterous turn of his body, escapes the weapon of his adversary. I do not find any classical authority for understanding 'illudo' with the same reference to the gladiator. It refers to customs of a more general nature; comprehending all sorts of injury inflicted in a way of deception, or derision: 'to sport with,' or 'make sport of;' sometimes 'to *run* in sport.' Thus these Sophists have evaded their adversaries, but they have made fools of themselves.

PART I. made are God, or have a divine and necessary nature. So sure and stedfast is the invincible aphorism, 'All things are brought to pass by the unchangeable will of God:' what they call 'necessity of a consequence.' Nor is there any obscurity or ambiguity here. He says in Isaiah—"My counsel shall stand," and my will shall be brought to pass. (Isa. xlvi. 10.) Is there any schoolboy who does not understand what is meant by these words '*counsel,*' '*will,*' '*brought to pass,*' '*stand?*'

SEC. XII.

Universal prevalence of this persuasion.

But why should these things be shut up from us Christians, so that it is irreligious, and curious, and vain for us to search and to know them; when heathen poets, and the very vulgar, are wearing them threadbare, by the commonest use of them in conversation? How often does the single poet Virgil make mention of fate! 'All things subsist by a fixed law.' 'Every man has his day fixed.' Again, 'If the fates call you.' Again, 'If you can by any means burst the bonds of the cruel fates.' It is this poet's sole object to shew, that in the destruction of Troy and the raising up of the Roman empire from its ruins, fate did more than all human efforts put together. In short, he subjects his immortal Gods to fate; making even Jupiter himself and Juno to yield to it necessarily. Hence they feigned these three fatal sisters, the Parcæ; whom they represent as immutable, implacable, inexorable.

Those wise men discovered (what fact and experience prove) that no man has ever yet received the accomplishment of his own counsels, but all have had to meet events which differed from their expectations. 'If Troy could have been defended by a human right hand, it had been defended even by this,' says Virgil's Hector. Hence that most hackneyed expression in everybody's mouth, 'God's will be done.' Again, 'If it please God, we will do so.' Again, 'So God would have it.'

'So it seemed good to those above.' 'So ye SEC XIII. would have it,' says Virgil. So that, in the minds of the common people, the knowledge of the predestination and foreknowledge of God is not less inherent, we perceive, than the very notion that there is a God: although blessed Augustine, with good reason, condemns fate; speaking of the fate which is maintained by the Stoics. But those who professed to be wise went to such lengths in their disputations, that, at last, their heart being darkened they became foolish, (Rom. i. 22.) and denied or dissembled those things which the poets, and the vulgar, and their own consciences, account most common, most certain, and most true.

I go further, and declare, not only how true these things are (of which I shall hereafter speak more at large from the Scriptures) but also how religious, pious, and necessary it is to know them. For if these things be not known, it is impossible that either faith or any worship of God should be maintained. For this would be a real ignorance of God; with which salvation cannot consist; as is notorious. For if you either doubt this truth, or despise the knowledge of it, that God foreknows and wills all things; not contingently, but necessarily and immutably; how will you be able to believe his promises, and with full assurance to trust and lean upon them? For, when he promises, you ought to be sure that he knows what he promises, and is able and willing to accomplish it: else you will account him neither true nor faithful; which is unbelief, the highest impiety, and a denial of the most high God.

The exceeding temerity and mischievousness of Erasmus's pretended and boasted moderation.

But how will you be confident and secure, if you do not know that he certainly, infallibly, unchangeably, and *necessarily* knows and wills, and will perform what he promises? Nor should we only be certain, that God necessarily and immutably wills and will perform what he has promised;

PART I. but we should even glory in this very thing, as Paul does in Romans iii. saying, "But let God be true and every man a liar." (Rom. iii. 4.) And again, " Not that the word of God hath been of none effect." (Rom. ix. 6.) And in another place, " The foundation of God standeth sure, having this seal, the Lord knoweth them that are his." (2 Tim. ii. 19.) And in Titus i. "which God who cannot lie hath promised before the world began." (Tit. i. 2.) And in Hebrews xi. " He that cometh to God must believe that God is, and that he is a rewarder of them that hope in him." (Heb. xi, 6.)

So then, the christian faith is altogether extinguished, the promises of God and the whole Gospel fall absolutely to the ground, if we be taught and believe, that we have no need to know that the foreknowledge of God is *necessary*, and that all acts and events are *necessary*. For this is the alone and highest possible consolation of Christians, in all adversities, to know that God does not lie, but brings all things to pass without any possibility of change; and that his will can neither be resisted, nor altered, nor hindered. See now, my Erasmus, whither this most abstinent and peace-loving theology of yours leads us! You call us off from endeavouring, nay forbid that we endeavour, to learn the foreknowledge of God and necessity, in their influence upon men and things; you counsel us to abandon such topics, to avoid and to hold them in abhorrence. By this ill-advised labour of yours, you at the same time teach us to cultivate an ignorance of God, (what in fact comes of itself, and even grows to us[h]) to despise faith, to forsake God's promises, and to set at nought all the consolations of the Spirit

[h] *Agnata*] ' What grows to us as a sort of monstrous appendage,' like the *membra agnata et agnascentia* in animals; parts that are more than should be by nature; as a sixth finger, &c.

and the assurances of our own conscience. Injunctions these, which scarcely Epicurus himself would lay upon us!

Not content with this, you go on to call that man irreligious, curious, and vain who takes pains to get the knowledge of these things; you call that man religious, pious, and sober who despises them. What else do you achieve then by these words, but that Christians are curious, vain, and irreligious; and that Christianity is a thing of no moment at all; vain, foolish, and absolutely impious. Thus it happens again, that whilst you would, above all things, deter us from rashness, being hurried, as fools usually are, into the opposite extreme, you teach us nothing but the most excessive temerities and impieties, which must lead us to destruction. Are you aware that your book is, in this part, so impious, so blasphemous, and so sacrilegious, as no where to have its like?

I speak not of your intention, as I have already said, for I do not think you so abandoned as to wish, from your heart, either to teach these things, or to see them practised by others; but I would shew you what strange things a man obliges himself to babble, without knowing what he says, when he undertakes a bad cause. I would shew you also, what it is to strike our foot against divine truth and the divine word, whilst we personate a character in compliance with the wishes of others, and, with many qualms of conscience, bustle through a scene, in which we have no just call to appear.¹ It is not a play or a pastime to teach

---

¹ *Aliorum obsequio*] Erasmus was a *forced* champion, writing to please the Pope and his party, at their special request. *Personam sumimus* He did not really stand in his own person, but was an actor sustaining a part which had been put upon him. *Alienæ scenæ servire* expresses the drudgery of labouring through a character in which he had made himself a volunteer. *Scenæ servire* sometimes signifies ' to temporize ;' but here I prefer retaining the original figure.—This is one of the poi-

theology and piety; in such an employment it is most easy to make that sort of fall which James speaks of,[k] when he says, "He that offendeth in one point becomes guilty of all." (Jam. ii. 10.) For thus it comes to pass, that, whilst we think we mean to trifle but a little, having lost our due reverence for the Scriptures, we soon get entangled in impieties, and are plunged over head and ears in blasphemies. Just what has happened to you in this case, Erasmus! May the Lord pardon and have mercy on you!

As to the fact, that the Sophists have raised such swarms of questions on these subjects, and have mixed a multitude of other unprofitable matters with them, such as you mention; I am aware of this, and acknowledge it as well as you, and have inveighed against it with yet more sharpness, and at greater length, than you. But you are foolish and rash in mixing, confounding, and assimilating the purity of sacred truth with the profane and foolish questions of ungodly men. They have defiled the gold and changed its beautiful colour, as Jeremiah says, (Lam. v. 1.) but gold is not forthwith to be compared to dung and thrown away together with it; as you have done. The gold must be recovered out of their hands, and

soned arrows of Luther's treatise; 'a hireling expectant, with only half his heart in the cause.'

[k] A forced application of James's words; who speaks of a breach of one commandment as subjecting us to the curse of all, because such breach is derogatory to the authority of the Lawgiver. We set ourselves up against the Lawgiver, and impugn his authority by a single wilful breach of a single commandment, with guilt of the same quality, though not of the same extent and aggravation, as if we brake all. Luther applies it to Erasmus's only meaning to have a little sport; but then it is at the expense of Scripture: and such sport, and even the intention of such sport, implies a want of due reverence for Scripture. This first fault leads to all the impiety which follows; and therefore he who is guilty of it, is guilty of all the impieties which follow, though he did not set out with the intention of committing them. 'Guilty of all,' because one *leads* to all; is the *seed* of all.—This is not James's meaning..

the purity of Scripture separated from their dregs and filth: and I have always been aiming to do this; in order that one sort of regard might be paid to the divine word, and another to their trifling conceits. Nor should it move us, that no other advantage has been gained by these questions, than that, with great expense of concord, we have come to love less, whilst we are far too eager to get wisdom. It is not our question, what advantage disputatious Sophists have gained; but how we may ourselves become good Christians: nor ought you to impute to christian doctrine what ungodly men do amiss. For this is nothing to the purpose, and you might have spoken of it in another place, and have spared your paper.

"In your third chapter, you go on to make us these modest and quiet Epicureans by another sort of counsel, not a whit sounder than the two already mentioned: viz. that 'some propositions are of such a nature, that even though they were true and could be ascertained, still it would not be expedient to publish them promiscuously.'¹ Here again, you confound and mix things, as your custom is, that you may degrade what is sacred to the level of the profane, without allowing the least difference between them; and again fall into an injurious contempt of God and his word. I have said before, what is either plainly declared in Scripture, or may be proved from it, is not only open to view, but salutary; and therefore may be with safety published, learned, and known; nay, ought to be so. With what truth, then, can you say, that there are things which ought not to be published promiscuously, if you speak of things contained in Scripture? If you speak of other things, nothing that you have said concerns us; all is out of place, and you have wasted your

All Scripture truth may be published safely.

---

¹ *Prostituere promiscuis auribus.*] *Prostit.* 'publicare,' 'diffamare,' (*pro*, sive *præ*, statuo.) *Promisc.* 'confusus;' hence, 'general,' 'common.'

PART I. paper, and your time in words. Again, you know that I have no agreement, upon any subject, with the Sophists; so that I deserved to have been spared by you, and not to have had their abuses cast in my teeth. It was against me that you were to write in this book. I know how guilty the Sophists are, and don't want you to teach me, having already reprehended them abundantly: and this I say, once for all, as often as you confound me with the Sophists, and load my cause with their mad sayings. You act unfairly, by me in so doing, and you very well know it.

SEC. XV.

The argument 'some truths ought not to be published' is either inconsistent with Erasmus's act, or out of place.

Let us now look into the reasons on which you build your counsel. Though it should be true, that God is essentially present in the beetle's cave, and even in the common sewer, no less than in heaven (which reverence forbids you to assert and you blame the Sophists for babbling so); still, you think it would be irrational to maintain such a proposition before the multitude.

In the first place, babble who may, we are not talking here about the actions of men, but about law and right; not how we live, but how we ought to live! Which of us lives and acts rightly in all cases? Law and precept are not condemned on this account, but rather we by them. The truth is, you fetch these materials of yours, which are foreign to the subject, from a great distance, and scrape many things together from all sides of you, because this one topic of the foreknowledge of God gravels you; and, having no arguments to overcome it with, you try to weary your reader by a profusion of empty words, before you conclude. But we will let this pass, and return to our subject. —Then how do you mean to apply this judgment of yours, that there are some truths which ought not to be proclaimed to the vulgar? Is Freewill one of these? If so, all that I said before, about the necessity of understanding Freewill, returns upon you. Besides, why do you not follow your own counsel, and withhold your Diatribe? If you are right in discussing Freewill, why do you find fault? if it be wrong to so do, why do you discuss it? On the other hand, if Freewill be not one of these subjects, you are again guilty of running away from the point at issue, in the midst of the discussion, and of handling foreign topics with great verbosity, where there is no place for them.

<small>SEC. XVI.</small>

Not that you deal correctly with the example which you adduce, when you condemn it as an useless discussion for the multitude, 'that God is in the cave, or in the sewer.' You think of God too *humanly.* I acknowledge, indeed, that there are some frivolous preachers, who, having neither religion nor piety, and being moved solely by a desire of glory, or an ambition of novelty, or an impatience of silence, gabble and trifle with the most offensive levity. But these men please neither God nor man, though they be engaged in asserting that God is in the heaven of heavens. On the contrary, where the preacher is grave and pious, and teaches in modest, pure, and sound words; such a man will declare such a truth before the multitude, not only without danger, but even with great profit. Ought we not all to teach that the Son of God was in the womb of the Virgin, and born from her bowels? And what difference is there between the bowels of a woman and any other filthy place? Who could not describe them nastily and offensively? Yet we should deservedly condemn such describers, because there is an abundance of pure words to express this substance, of which it has become necessary to speak,[m] with beauty and grace. Christ's own body, again, was human like our own. And what is filthier than this? Shall we therefore forbear to say that God dwelt in him BODILY, as

<small>Erasmus's three examples of truths not to be published, considered.</small>

---

[m] *Eam necessitatem.*

Paul speaks?[n] (Coloss. ii. 9.) What is more disgusting than death? What more horrible than hell? But the Prophet glories that God is with him in death and in hell. (Psa. xxiii.)

The pious mind then does not shudder to hear that God is in death or in hell; each of which is more horrible than the cave or the sewer: nay, since Scripture testifies that God is every where, and fills all things, not only does such a mind affirm that he is in those places, but will, as matter of necessity, learn and know that he is there. Unless, perchance, if I should somehow be seized by a tyrant, and cast into a prison or a common sewer, which has been the lot of many saints, I must not be allowed to invoke my God there; or to believe that he is present with me; until I shall have come into some ornamented temple! If you teach us that we ought to trifle in this way about God, and are so offended with the abiding places of his essence, you will, at length, not allow us to consider him as abiding even in heaven: for not even the heaven of heavens contains him, or is worthy to do so. But the truth is, you sting with so much venom,[o] as your manner is, that you may sink our cause, and make it hateful, because you see it to be insuperable and invincible, by powers such as yours.

The second instance which you adduce, ' that there are three Gods,' is, I confess, a stumbling-block, if it be indeed taught: nor is it true, nor does Scripture teach it. The Sophists, indeed, speak so; and have invented a new sort of logic: But what is that to us?

---

[n] I would crave the reader's particular attention to this description of the human body of the Lord Jesus Christ; that part of his frame which alone connected him and did *really* connect him with the damned substance of his people. It enters into the very entrails of ' the mystery of godliness.'

[o] *Sic odiosè pungis.*] *Pung.* ' cuspide vel aculeo ictum infero.'

SEC. XVI.

With respect to your third and remaining example of confession and satisfaction, it is wonderful with how happy a dexterity you contrive to find fault: every where, as you are wont, just skimming the surface of the subject, and no more, lest you should appear, either, on the one hand, not simply to condemn our writings, or, on the other, not to be disgusted with the tyranny of the pontiffs :[p] a failure in either of which points would be by no means safe for you. So, bidding adieu, for a little while, to conscience and to God, (for what has Erasmus to do with the will of the latter and the obligations of the former, in these matters?) you draw your sword upon a mere outside phantom, and accuse the common people of abusing the preaching of free confession and satisfaction,[q] as their own evil nature may incline them, to the indulgence of the flesh; maintaining, that by necessary confession they are, some how or other, restrained. O, famous and exquisite harangue! Is this teaching theology? To bind with laws and kill, as Ezekiel says, (xxiii. xiii. 19.) the souls which God has not bound. At this rate, you stir up the whole tyranny of the Popish laws against us forsooth, on the ground of their being useful and salutary; because by them also the wickedness of the people is restrained!

But I am unwilling to inveigh against you, as this passage deserves. I will state the matter as it is, concisely. A good theologian teaches thus: the common people are to be restrained by the

[p] *Pontificum' tyrannidem offendere.*] *Offend.* ' aversari,' ' offendi,' ' molestiam capere ,' quasi impingere, incurrere in aliquid, quod displiceat —Another poisoned arrow. Whilst he keeps no terms with Luther, he must still be the friend of liberty. He had gone far in satirizing the reigning abuses. But how galling the exposure!

[q] *Free.*] That is, preaching that these *are* free, that men may observe or neglect them, according to their own individual conscience.

external force of the sword, when they do amiss, as Paul teaches (Rom. xiii. 1—4.); but their consciences are not to be ensnared by false laws, teasing and tormenting them for sins which God does not account sins. For the conscience is bound only by the commands of God; so that this interposed tyranny of the pontiffs, which falsely terrifies and kills souls inwardly, whilst it, to no purpose, harasses the body without, should be entirely taken out of the way. This tyranny does, indeed, compel men to outward acts of confession, and to other burdens; but the mind is not restrained by these things: rather, it is exasperated to an hatred of God and of man. It hangs, draws, and quarters the body outwardly, without effect; making mere hypocrites within; insomuch, that the tyrants who enact and execute laws of this sort are nothing else but rapacious wolves, thieves, and robbers of souls. These wolves and robbers, O most excellent counsellor of souls, thou commendest to us again. In other words, thou proposest the most cruel of soul-slayers to our acceptance; who will fill the world with hypocrites, blaspheming God, and despising him in their hearts; in order that men may be a little restrained in their outward carriage: as if there were not another method of restraining, which makes no hypocrites, and is obtained without destroying any man's conscience; as I have said.

SC. XVII.

Erasmus neither un-

Here you fetch in^s a host of similes; in which you aim to abound, and to be thought very apt and expert. You tell us, forsooth, that there are

---

^{r} *Consul, auctor,* refer to the customs of the Roman Republic, of which the consul was the *guardian* and *adviser;* he was the author, or originator of measures. i.

^{s} *Allegas,* 'afferre aliquid probandi vel excusandi gratiâ.' A forensic expression; these were his witnesses: but what did they prove? only, what a clever fellow this Erasmus is. Illustration is not argument; but here it is manifestly a substitute for it. He amuses, imposes, irritates, and bewilders by his similies, because he has nothing solid wherewith to answer.

some diseases which are borne with less evil than they are removed withal; such as the leprosy and others. You also add the example of Paul, who distinguished between things lawful and things expedient. A man may lawfully speak the truth, you say; to any body, at any time, in any way he pleases; but it is not expedient for him to do so.

SC. XVII. derstands nor feels the vast importance of the question.

What an exuberant orator! but one who does not at all know what he is saying. In a word, you plead this cause as if your affair with me were a contest for a sum of money which is recoverable; or for some other very inconsiderable object: whose loss (as being a thing of far less value than that dear external peace of yours) ought not to move any one to such a degree that he be unwilling to submit, do, and suffer, as the occasion may require; or to render it necessary that the world be thrown into such a tumult. You plainly intimate, therefore, that this peace and tranquillity of the flesh is far more excellent in your eyes than faith, conscience, salvation, the word of God, the glory of Christ, yea, God himself. I declare to you, therefore, and entreat you to lay this up in your inmost soul, that I, for my part, am in pursuit of a serious, necessary, and eternal object in this cause; such and so great an object, that I must assert and defend it, even at the hazard of my life; nay, though the whole world must not only be thrown into a state of conflict and confusion through it, but even rush back again into its original chaos, and be reduced to nothing. If you do not comprehend, or do not feel, these things, mind your own business; and give others leave to comprehend and to feel them, on whom God has bestowed this power.

For I am not such a fool, or such a madman, I thank God, as to have been willing to plead and maintain this cause so long, with such resoluteness, with such constancy, (*you* call it obstinacy) amidst so many hair-breadth escapes with life, amidst so many enmities, amidst so many wiles and snares—in short, amidst the rage and phrenzy of men and devils; for the sake of money, which I neither have nor desire; or for the sake of glory, which, if I would, I could not obtain in a world that is so hostile to me; or for the sake of bodily life, of which I cannot ensure the possession for a single moment. Do you think that *you* are the only person who hath a heart that is moved with these tumults? I, no more than yourself, am made of stone, or born of the Marpesian rocks. But, since it must be so,[t] I choose rather to endure the collisions of a temporal tumult, for asserting the word of God, with an invincible and incorruptible mind, rejoicing all the while in the sense and manifestations of his favour, than to be crushed to pieces by the intolerable torments of an eternal tumult, as one of the victims of God's wrath. The Lord grant that your mind be not such (I hope and wish he may!) but your words sound as though, like Epicurus, you accounted the word of God and a future state to be mere fables; when, by virtue of the doctorial authority with which you are invested, you wish to propose to us, that, in order to please pontiffs and princes, or to preserve this dear peace of yours, we should submit ourselves, and, for a while, relinquish the use of the word of God, sure as that word is,[u] if occasion require; although, by such relinquishment, we relinquish God, faith, salvation, and every christian possession. How much better does Christ advise us, to despise the whole world rather than do this!

SC.XVIII.

Peace of the world

But you say such things, because you do not read, or do not observe, that this is the most con-

---

[t] 'Since I am reduced to this painful alternative of evils.'

[u] *Certissimum.*] Opposed to what Erasmus gave reason to suspect that he accounted it: '*verbum Dei et futuram vitam fabulas* esse putis.'

stant fortune of the word of God, to have the world in a state of tumult because of it. Christ explicitly asserts this, when he says, "I am not come to send peace, but a sword." (Matt. x. 34.) And in Luke, "I am come to send fire on the earth." (Luke xii. 49.) And Paul (2 Cor. vi. 5.) " In seditions," &c. And the Prophet testifies the same thing, with great redundancy of expression, in the second Psalm, when he asserts, that the nations are in a tumult, that the people murmur, that the kings rise up, that the princes take counsel together against the Lord and against his Christ: as though he should say, numbers, grandeur, riches, power, wisdom, justice, and whatsoever is exalted in the world, opposes itself to the word of God. See, in the Acts of the Apostles, what happens in the world through Paul's preaching only, not to mention the other Apostles; how he singly and alone stirs up both Gentiles and Jews: or, as his enemies themselves affirm in that same place, how he troubles[v] the whole world. The kingdom of Israel is troubled under the ministry of Elijah, as king Ahab complains. What a stir there was under the other Prophets! whilst they are all slain with the sword, or stoned; whilst Israel is led captive into Assyria, and Judah, in like manner, to Babylon. Was this peace? The world and its God neither *can* nor *will* endure the word of the true God; the true God neither will nor can be silent. When these two Gods are at war, what can there be but tumult in all the world?

The wish to hush these storms is nothing else but a wish to take the word of God out of the way, and to stay its course. For the word of God comes for the very purpose of changing and renewing the world, as often as it does come; and even Gentile writers bear witness that a

SC XVIII.
———
disturbed, no argument against a dogma, but *for* it.

---

[v] *Conturbat.*] Luther makes it ' troubled waters'; *we*, more correctly, ' the world turned upside down', ἀναστατώσαντες.

change of things cannot take place without commotion and tumult, nay, without blood. It is the part of a Christian, now-a-days, to await and endure these things with presence of mind; as Christ says, "When ye shall hear of wars and rumours of wars, be not afraid, for these things must first be, but the end is not just yet." I, for my part, should say, if I saw not these tumults, the word of God is not in the world: but seeing them, I rejoice in my heart and despise them; most sure, that the kingdom of the Pope and his adherents is about to fall: for the word of God, which is now running in the world, has especially invaded this kingdom. To be sure, I see you, my Erasmus, complaining of these tumults in many of your publications, and mourning over the loss of peace and concord. Moreover, you try many expedients to cure this disorder, with a good intention, as I verily believe; but this is a sort of gout, which mocks your healing hands. For here, to use your own expression, you are, in truth, sailing against the stream; nay, you are extinguishing fire with stubble. Cease to complain, cease to play the physician: this confusion is of God in its origin, and in its progress; nor will it cease, till it has made all the adversaries of the word like the mire of the streets. But it is a lamentable thing, that it should be necessary to admonish you, who are so great a theologian, of these things, as a scholar; when you ought to be filling the place of a master.

This, then, is the proper application of your aphorism (a very excellent one though you misapply it), 'that some diseases are borne with less evil than removed.' Let all those tumults, commotions, troubles, seditions, divisions, discords, wars, and whatsoever other things there are of like kind, with which, for the word of God's sake, the whole world is shaken and clashed together in conflict; be called diseases better borne than cured. These things, I say, being temporal, are borne with less mischief than old habits of evil; by which all souls must perish, except they be changed through the word of God. So that, by taking this word of God away, you take away eternal blessings; God, Christ, the Spirit. But how much better were it to lose the world, than to lose the Creator of the world; who can create innumerable worlds afresh, and who is better than an infinity of worlds! For what comparison is there between temporal and eternal things? Much rather, then, is this leprosy of temporal evils to be borne, than that, at the expense of the slaughter and eternal damnation of all the souls in the world, the world should, by their blood and destruction, be pacified and cured of all these tumults: since one soul cannot be redeemed by paying the whole world for its ransom. You have many beautiful and excellent similies and aphorisms: but when you come to sacred subjects, you apply them childishly, and even perversely;[x] for you crawl on the ground, and have no thought of any thing which is beyond mere human conception. Now, the things which God does are neither childish things, nor civil or human things; but things of God;[y] and such as exceed all human conception. For example; you do not see that these tumults and divisions are marching through the world by divine counsel and operation, and you are afraid the skies should fall: but I, on the other hand, thanks be to God! see good in these storms; because I see other and greater in the world to come, compared with which, these seem but as the whispers of the

SC XVIII.

---

[x] *Perversè.*] 'Distortedly,' in a manner contrary to their real meaning and use. Luther's charge is no less than this: what Erasmus counted evil was really good; and vice versâ.

[y] *Puerilia, civilia, humana, divina.*] *Civ.* 'What relate to man as a citizen'; opposed to 'puerilia', because it was not till a man attained a certain age that he became entitled to them.

PART I.
SC. XIX.

Doubts whether the dogma of free confession be scriptural. The Pope and God cannot be obeyed conjointly. The people must be left to abuse.

gentle breeze, or the murmur of the soft-flowing stream.

But you either deny, or profess not to know, that our dogma of free confession and satisfaction is the word of God.

This is another[z] question: we, however, both know, and are sure, that it is the word of God; and that word by which christian liberty is maintained, in order that we may not allow ourselves to be entrapped into servitude by human traditions and laws. A point this, which I have abundantly proved elsewhere; and, if you should have a mind to try the question, I am ready to plead in support of it, even at your judgment seat;[a] or to debate it with you. Many books of ours are before the public upon these questions.

'Still, however, the laws of the pontiffs ought to be suffered, and to be observed equally with the divine laws, out of love, if both the eternal salvation of men, through the word of God, and the peace of the world, may thus be made to subsist together without tumult.'

I have said before that this cannot be. The prince of this world does not suffer that the laws of his Pope and his cardinals be maintained in consistency with liberty, but has it in his mind to entrap and enchain men's consciences by them. The true God cannot endure this. Thus it is, that the word of God, and the traditions of men, are opposed to each other with an implacable discord,

---

[z] *Hæc alia quæstio est.*] 'Other' than that of the expediency of proclaiming it, as supposed to be acknowledged truth. Free confession is introduced by Erasmus, as his third example of a dogma, which, though true, ought not to be circulated.

[a] *Et tibi dicere.*] Like his 'etiam te judice', in Part ii. Sect. i. means making Erasmus himself the judge.—*Vel conserere manus* might be supposed to allude to an ancient custom, '*ex jure* manu consertum vocare'; when a party expressed his willingness to go with his adversary into the field, if dissatisfied with the award of the tribunal: a species of judicial combat. But I prefer the simpler antithesis of the text.

no other than that with which God himself and Satan oppose each other; and the one undoes the works and subverts the dogmas of the other, like two kings laying waste each other's kingdom. "He that is not with me is against me," says Christ.

Now, with respect to 'the fear that the multitude, who are prone to crimes, will abuse such liberty;' This must be classed amongst those disturbances we have been speaking of, as a part of that temporal leprosy which is to be tolerated; of that evil which is to be endured. Nor are these persons of so great account, that the word of God should be given up in order to restrain their abuse of it. If all cannot be saved, still some are saved; for whose sake the word of God is given: and these will love it the more fervently, and consent to it the more reverently. And what evils, pray, have wicked men not done even before this, when there was no word of God; rather, what good did they? Has not the world for ever overflowed with war, fraud, violence, discord, and all manner of wickedness, so that Micah compares the very best amongst them to a thorn? (Micah vii. 4.) What would he call the rest, think you? Now, indeed, it begins to be imputed to the promulgation of the Gospel, that the world is wicked; because through the good Gospel it more truly appears how wicked the world was, whilst it lived in its own darkness, without the Gospel. So, illiterate men attribute it to literature, that their ignorance has become notorious since letters have flourished. Such are the thanks we render to the word of life and salvation! What a fear, then, must we suppose to have been kindled amongst the Jews, when the Gospel absolved all men from the law of Moses![b] What degree of licence did

---

[b] Luther's expressions are not equivocal here, but irrestrictive and direct. 'absolved *all* men from *the law of Moses*', without excepting any part of that law; and it is essential to

this prodigious liberty not seem to be hereby conceding to wicked men? But the Gospel was not therefore withheld. Wicked men were left to their own ways, and it was charged upon the godly not to use their liberty for an occasion to the flesh. (Gal. v. 13.)

SEC. XX.

Erasmus's counsel about persons, time, and place, pernicious.

"Nor does that part of your counsel or remedy[c] stand good, where you say, 'It is lawful to declare the truth amongst *any* persons, at *any* time, and in *any* manner, but it is not expedient;' and very absurdly adduce Paul's words, "All things are lawful unto me, but all things are not expedient." (1 Cor. vi. 12.)

Paul is not here speaking about doctrine, or about teaching the truth, as you, confounding his words, and drawing them whither you please, would represent him to do. Nay, he would have the truth proclaimed every where, at any time, by any means; insomuch, that he even rejoices that Christ should be preached for an occasion, and out of envy; and expressly testifies, in the very words, that he rejoices if Christ be preached by *any means*.[d] Paul is speaking about the practice and use of doctrine; to wit, of those vaunters of christian liberty, who, "seeking their own,"[e] cared not what stumbling-blocks they made, and what offences they occasioned by them to the weak. The true doctrine is to be preached

his argument that he be understood thus comprehensively.— Else what ground of fear?

[c] Erasmus interposes in the form of an adviser, or physician; reprobating the course pursued by others, and suggesting a better : this was no other than to modify the truth by squaring it to times, places, and persons.

[d] The allusion is evidently to Philip i. 18, which fully justifies his ' quovis modo.' "What then? notwithstanding *every way*, whether in pretence or in truth, Christ is preached; and I therein do rejoice, yea, and will rejoice." The ' every way', or ' by any means', is ' whatsoever *spirit* he be preached with'; ' sincere or insincere.'

[e] "For all seek their own, not the things which are Jesus Christ's." (Philip ii. 21.)

always, openly, steadily, never to be turned aslant, never to be concealed:[f] for there is none occasion of stumbling in it; 'tis the rod of straightness.[g] And who ever empowered you, or gave you the right, to bind the christian doctrine to places, persons, times, cases; when Christ wills it to be published, and to reign in the world with the most perfect freedom? " For the word of God is not bound," says Paul, (2 Tim. ii. 9.) and shall Erasmus bind it? Nor hath God given us a word which is to make selection of places, persons, and times; since Christ says, " Go ye into all the world." He does not say, ' Go to a certain place, and to a certain place go not,' as Erasmus speaks. Again; " Preach the Gospel to every creature." (Mark xvi. 15.) He does not say, ' Preach it to some, to some preach it not.' In short, you prescribe acceptance of persons, acceptance of places, and acceptance of manner; that is to say, TIME-SERVINGS; in ministering the word of God; whereas, this is one great part of the glory of the word, that " there is no acceptance of persons" (as Paul says) and " God respecteth not persons." You see again, how rashly you make war upon[h] the word of God, as though you pre-

[f] *Obliquanda*,] *Obliq.* is sometimes applied to ' the veering and tacking' of ships; but the essential idea is ' bending, or making crooked, what is in itself straight.' It is here opposed to *constanter*, as ' celanda' is to ' palam'. The truth must be preached in its straightness, or perpendicularity, not bent downwards or sideways, that it may be accommodated to the taste, or lusts, or supposed unaptnesses of the hearer.

[g] The allusion is evidently to Psa. xlv. 6. Luther seems to have understood the Gospel or doctrine of Christ by this rod or sceptre; as he does also, though not exclusively, in his exposition of this psalm. (Vide in loco.) I should rather understand it of his own personal conduct, as a prince. But according to Luther's allusion, the truth being a straight or upright rod, he who walks by it will walk straightly, or uprightly, and will not give occasion to others to walk crookedly, or pronely.

[h] The word of God teaches that there is no respect of persons, and that God regardeth not the persons of men. Coloss. iii. 25. Rom. ii. 6. Gal. ii. 6. Ephes. vi. 9. James ii. 1. Luke

ferred your own thoughts and counsels very far before it.

If now we should request you to distinguish times, persons, and modes of speaking the truth for us, when will you determine them? The world will have laid its end to sleep, and time be no more, before you have fixed upon a single sure rule. Meanwhile, what becomes of the teacher's office? where shall we find the souls which are to be taught? Nay, how is it possible that you should lay down any sure rule, when you know no rate by which to estimate persons, times, and modes of speech? But if you assuredly knew such a rate, still you are ignorant of the hearts of men. Unless, indeed, you should choose to adopt this standard for your manner of speaking; for your time and your person; 'teach the truth, so that the Pope shall not be indignant, so that Cæsar shall not be angry, so that the cardinals and princes be not displeased; provide further; that there be no tumults, or commotions in the world, and that the multitude be not stumbled;

xx. 21. Acts x. 34, &c. &c. How contrary is it, then, to the clear testimony of the word, which declares that God mocks all human distinctions; that Jew and Greek, master and servant, or slave, rulers and subjects, pillars of the church, and men disinterested in the church, are alike regarded and disregarded by Him; to have respect to these distinctions, as Erasmus would counsel us, in the ministry of the word! These testimonies are sometimes perverted to mean a denial of God's *electing grace;* which they do not, in the slightest degree, impugn, nor did Luther conceive so. He maintained that grace as firmly as any man. The truth is, 'respect of persons' in Scripture, means ' respect of persons *according to human and earthly distinctions*'; in which regards, God, contrariwise to man, puts no difference between them. *His* distinctions, which he palpably makes, are built upon another foundation. "Where there is neither Greek nor Jew, circumcision nor uncircumcision, barbarian, Scythian, bond nor free; but Christ is all, and in all" (Coloss iii. 11) But then. " Blessed be the God and Father of our Lord Jesus Christ, who hath blessed us with all spiritual blessings (or blessedness) in heavenly places in Christ; *according as He hath chosen us in Him before the foundation of the world,*" &c. Eph. i. 3, 4. &c.

and made worse.' You have already seen, what sort of a counsel this is. But you choose to play the rhetorician after this manner, with idle words, because you must say something.

How much better were it for us wretched men to give to God, who knows all hearts, the glory of prescribing the manner, persons, and times of speaking the truth! He knows the 'what', the 'when', the 'how', and the 'to whom', we ought to speak; and his injunction is, that his Gospel, which is necessary to all, should know no limits of place or time, but should be preached to all men, at all times, and in all places. I have already shewn that the things set forth in the Scripture are such as lie exposed to the view of all men; such as, whether we will or no, must be spread abroad amongst the common people; and such as are salutary. What you also maintained yourself in your Paraclesis, when you gave better counsel than you do now. Let us leave it to those who are unwilling that souls should be redeemed; such as the Pope and his myrmidons; to bind the word of God, and shut men out from eternal life and the kingdom of heaven; neither entering in themselves, nor suffering others to enter in: whose mad rage you, Erasmus, are perniciously serving by this suggestion of yours.

With the same sort of wariness you, in the next place, suggest that we ought not to make public declarations in opposition to any thing which may have been determined wrongly in general councils; lest we should give a handle for despising the authority of the Fathers.

This you say to please the Pope; who hears it with more pleasure than he does the Gospel: ungrateful in the extreme, if he does not, in return, honour you with a cardinal's hat and revenues! Meanwhile, what is to become of those souls which have been fettered and slain by the unrighteous decree? Is this nothing to you? Why, you

SC. XXI.
———

The Fathers not to be set on a level with Christ; their decisions have no authority but from the word.

PART I. always feel, or pretend to feel, that the statutes of men may be observed without any danger; in coincidence with the pure word of God. If they could, I would readily accord with this proposition of yours. So then, if you be still ignorant, I will again inform you, that 'human statutes cannot be observed in conjunction with the word of God.' For the former bind men's consciences, the latter looses them; and they fight one with another like fire and water, except the former be kept freely; that is, as statutes not binding: a thing very contrary to the Pope's will; and which must be so, unless he should wish to destroy and put an end to his own kingdom; which is only kept up by ensnaring and fettering men's consciences, whilst the Gospel declares them to be free. The authority of the Fathers, then, must be set at nought, and all bad decrees (in which number I include all such determinations as are not warranted by the word of God) must be torn in pieces, and thrown to the dogs; for Christ's authority is of another sort than that of the Fathers. In short, if your statement comprehends the word of God, it is a wicked one: if it be confined to other writings, your verbose discussion of the sentiment which you recommend is nothing to me; my assertions have respect to the word of God only.[1]

SC. XXII.

Injuriousness of certain paradoxes, 'all things by neces-

In the last part of your Preface, you seriously dissuade us from this sort of doctrine, and fancy that you have almost succeeded. What is more injurious, you say, than that this paradox should be published to the world, that 'whatsoever is done by us is not done by Freewill, but by mere

[1] Erasmus had said, that bad decisions should be hushed up; and if spoken of, it should rather be said, that they were good at the time, though unseasonable now. Luther replies, if your remark be intended to affect any decision which is founded upon the word of God, the sentiment is impious. With respect to any other sort of decisions, whether you choose to call them pious and holy, or acknowledge them to be faulty, I have nothing to do with them.

necessity'? And that saying of Augustine's that 'God worketh both good and evil in us;' that he rewards his own good works in us, and punishes his own bad works in us'? Here you are rich in giving, or rather, in demanding reasons. 'What a window will this saying open to impiety, if it be commonly published amongst men?. What wicked man will correct his life? Who will think he is loved of God? Who will strive with his flesh?' I am surprised that, in this mighty vehemence and agony of yours, you did not remember your cause, and say, what will then become of Freewill? Let me also become speaker in my turn, Erasmus, and I will ask you, if you account these paradoxes to be the invention of men, why dispute? why boil with rage? Whom are you opposing? Is there a man in all the world, at this day, who has more vehemently inveighed against the dogmas of men, than Luther has done? So that this admonition of yours is nothing to me. But, if you believe these paradoxes to be the word of God, what face have you?[k] what modesty have you? Where is now—I will not say, that wonted sobriety of Erasmus, but—that fearful reverence which is due to the true God; when you assert, that nothing can be affirmed more unprofitably than this word of God? What! I suppose your Creator is to learn from his creature what is useful to be preached, and what not? Yes, this foolish and ill-advised God has not known hitherto what is expedient to be taught; but now at last his master Erasmus will prescribe to him the manner in which he shall be wise, and in which he shall deliver his commands! He, forsooth, would have been ignorant, unless you had taught him, that your inference follows upon his paradox!

SC. XXII.

sity'; 'God all in all'.

[k] *Ubi frons tua.*] The face is the index of sensibility: effrontery is the result of obduracy. Luther's question implies 'you can have no face; you must have a brow of brass, to speak so.'

PART I. If God, then, hath been willing to have such things spoken openly, and spread abroad amongst the common people, without regard to consequences; who are you, that you should forbid him?

Paul the Apostle explicitly declares the same things, in his Epistle to the Romans, open-mouthed, not in a corner, but publicly and before the whole world, in even harsher words; saying, "Whom he will he hardeneth." (Rom. ix. 18.) And again, "God willing to make his wrath known." (Rom. ix. 22.) What is harsher (to the flesh, I mean) than that saying of Christ, "Many are called, but few chosen." (Matt. xxii. 14.) And again, "I know whom I have chosen."[l] (John xiii. 18.) All these sayings, forsooth, if we listen to your suggestions, are amongst the most injurious that can be conceived; inasmuch as they are the instruments, by which ungodly men fall gradually[m] into desperation, hatred of God, and blasphemy.

Here, as I perceive, you reckon that the truth and usefulness of Scripture are to be weighed and decided by the judgment of men, and these no other than the most ungoldly; so that, what they shall be pleased with, and account tolerable, that, verily, is true, is divine, is salutary; and, what shall be otherwise in their eyes, that is straightways useless, false, and pernicious. What do you propose by this counsel, but that God's words should be dependent upon the will and authority of men, so as to stand or fall by them? whereas the Scripture, on the other hand, says, that every thing stands or falls by the will and authority of God; nay, that "all the earth must keep silence before the face of the Lord." (Hab. ii. 20.) To speak as you do, a man must imagine the living God to be nothing else but some light and igno-

[l] See Chap. i. Sect. iii. note '.

[m] *Prolabantur.*] Translate 'sensim devenire,' 'palatim accedere.'

rant sort of Ranter, declaiming in a rostrum; SC. XXII.
whose words you are at liberty, if you choose, to
interpret any how you please; accepting or rejecting them, according to the emotions or affections which you see produced by them in wicked
men. You clearly shew here, my Erasmus, how
sincere you was before, in persuading us to respect the awful majesty of the divine judgments.
When the question was about the dogmas of
Scripture, and there was no need to call for reverence towards them, on the ground of their being
shut up, and hidden from view; inasmuch as
there are none of this sort; you, in words of
great solemnity, threatened us with Corycian
caves, lest we should break in curiously: so as
almost to deter us, by fear, from reading Scripture at all; that very Scripture which Christ and
his Apostles, and even your own pen, elsewhere,
so greatly urge and persuade us to study! But,
here, when we are actually arrived, not at the
dogmas of Scripture and the Corycian cave only,
but truly at the awful secrets of the divine majesty; to wit, why he works in the manner which
hath been mentioned; here, I say, you break
through bolts and bars, and rush forwards, with
all but blasphemies in your mouth; shewing all
possible indignation against God, because you
are not permitted to see the design and arrangement of such a judgment of his!ⁿ Why do not

---

ⁿ *Non licet videre.*] Referring to Augustine's saying, that
'God worketh all things in us; rewarding his own good, and
punishing his own evil.' In a future part of the work, where
this subject is more fully gone into, and to which I defer my
observations on it as here briefly glanced at, I trust it will appear, that the word of God does not really leave us in that
depth of darkness which Luther's language here implies, and
which his fuller statement, hereafter made, affirms. God has
not revealed himself that he might remain hidden; as unknown, or even yet more unknown than he was before; but,
amidst the unsearchableness of his infinity, has, by his counsel
of manifestation, which the Scripture records, unveiled much

you here, also, pretend obscurities and ambiguities? Why do not you both restrain yourself, and deter others, from prying into those things which God hath willed to be kept secret from us, and hath not published in his word? You should have laid your hand upon your mouth here, revering the unrevealed mystery, adoring the secret counsels of the Divine Majesty, and exclaiming with Paul, " Nay, but, O man, who art thou that repliest against God?" (Rom. ix. 20.)

Sc.XXIII. — Answers to Erasmus's objectionary questions, who will take pains, &c.? Two reasons why these things should be preached.

You say, 'who will take pains to correct his life?' I answer, no man; nor will any one be even able to do so; for God pays no regard to your amenders of life, which have not the Spirit, since they are but hypocrites. But the elect and godly will be amended by the Holy Spirit: the rest will perish unamended. For Augustine does not say, that the good works of none will be crowned, nor yet that the good works of all will be crowned; but that the good works of some are crowned. There will be some, therefore, who amend their life. You say, 'Who will believe that he is beloved of God?' I answer, no man will believe so, or be able to believe so; but the elect will believe so: the rest, not believing, will perish; storming and blaspheming, as you do in this place. There will be some, therefore, that believe.

As to what you say, 'that a window is opened to impiety by these doctrines'—What if the disorders resulting from them be referred to that leprosy of tolerable evil, which I have already hinted at? Still, by the same dogmas, a door is at the same time opened to righteousness, and an entrance into heaven, and a way to God, for the

---

of himself to our view, which, before and without it, was, and must for ever have remained, concealed. Luther—prodigy as he was, in his day—had not the clue of God-manifestation to guide him through the labyrinth; and, therefore, counted much that is light, darkness.

elect and godly. Now if, according to your advice, we should abstain from these dogmas, and should hide this word of God from men, so that each one, beguiled by a false persuasion of his safety, should not learn to fear God, and to be humbled, that, through the means of wholesome fear, he may, at length, come to grace and love; then, we shall have nobly closed your window of impiety; but, in its place, we shall open folding doors; nay, pits and gulfs; not only to impiety, but even to the belly of hell; for ourselves and for all men. Thus, we should neither enter heaven ourselves, nor suffer others, who were entering, to go in.

'What is the use or necessity, then, of publishing such things to the world, when so many evils seem to spring from them?'

I answer; it were enough to say, 'God would have these things published: and, as to the principles of the divine will, we have no right to ask them; we ought simply to adore that will, giving glory to God; because He, the only just and wise one, injures no man, and cannot possibly do any thing foolishly or rashly; though it may appear far otherwise to us.' Godly men are content with this answer. But, to be lavish of our abundance,° let it be replied, that 'two things require the preaching of these truths.' The first is, the humbling of our pride, and a thorough knowledge of the grace of God: the second, the very nature of christian faith. For the first, God hath promised his grace, with certainty, to the humbled; that is, to those who bewail themselves in self-despair. But man cannot be thoroughly humbled,

---

° *Super-erogemus.*] 'To lay out and bestow over and above what is due.' *Erogo*, is properly applied to 'public money, exacted and issued upon petition and by order'; thence transferred to 'private expenditure.' *Ut ex abundantiâ super.* implies, that a superabundance of reasons might be alleged, where none is necessary.

PART I.

till he knows that his salvation lies altogether beyond, and out of the reach of his own strength, counsels, desires, will, and works; depending absolutely upon the counsel, will, and work, of another; that is, of God only. For, as long as he is persuaded that he can do the least thing possible for his own salvation, he continues in self-confidence, and does not absolutely despair of himself; therefore, he is not humbled before God, but goes round about anticipating for himself, or hoping, or, at least, wishing to obtain, a place, a time, and some performance of his own, by which he may at length arrive at salvation.[p] On the other hand, he who has not the shadow of a doubt that he is dependent, wholly and solely, upon the will of God—this man is complete in his self-despair; this man chooses nothing,[q] but waits for God to work; this man is next neighbour to that grace of God, which shall make him whole. So that these things are published for the elects' sake; that they may by these means be humbled and brought to know their own nothingness; and so may be saved. The rest resist this sort of humiliation; nay, they condemn the teaching of this self-despair; they would have some very small modicum of power left to themselves. These persons, secretly, remain proud, and adversaries to the grace of God. This, I say, is one reason why these truths should be preached; that the

[p] *Quo tandem perveniat*] The contrast is between that direct-going to God of the truly humbled sinner; and the circuitous, procrastinative, self-centered expectations of the man who does not yet know the whole of his lostness and impotency.

[q] *Nihil eligit*] In direct contrast with the 'sibi præsumit, sperat, optat' of the former sentence; he does not desire or expect any particular combination of time and place, in which he may perform some great work for himself; but lies passive in the hands of God, leaving it to God even to choose for him. The expression reminds us of St. Paul's language, under other circumstances, which was probably in Luther's mind; "yet what I shall *choose* I wot not." (Phil. i. 22.)

godly, being humbled, may come to a real knowledge^r of the promise of grace, may call upon the name of the Lord, and may receive its fulfilment.

SC.XXIII.

The second reason for this preaching is, that, faith being conversant about things which do not appear; to have place for faith, all the things believed must be hidden things. Now, things are never hidden further from us, than when the contrary to them is set before us by sense and experience. Thus God, whilst he makes us alive, does it by killing us; whilst he justifies us, does it by making us guilty; whilst he lifts us up to heaven, does it by plunging us into hell. As saith the Scripture, "The Lord killeth, and maketh alive; he bringeth down to the grave, and bringeth up:" (1 Sam. ii. 6.) of which, this is not the place to discourse at large. Those, who have seen our books, are hackneyed in these topics. Thus He hides his eternal mercy and pity under eternal wrath; his righteousness under iniquity.

This is the highest degree of faith, to believe that He is merciful, who saves so few, and condemns so many; to believe Him just, who, of his own will, makes us necessary objects of damnation;^s thus seeming, according to Erasmus's account, to be delighted with the torments of the wretched, and to deserve hatred, rather than love. If then, I could, by any means, comprehend how this God is pitiful and just, who shews so great wrath and injustice, there would be no need of faith; but now, since this cannot be comprehended, space is given for the exercise of faith, whilst these things are preached and published;

^r *Cognoscant.*] ' Nosco, vel *bene* nosco'; ' to know a person, or thing, not known before,' opposed to ' agnosco.'

^s *Necessariò damnabiles.*] We were so created, have been so generated and brought out into manifest existence, are so constituted and so situated, that we cannot choose but be just objects of God's eternal damnation This necessity is not blind Fate, but arises out of the appointments, arrangements, and operations of God's counselled will.

even as the faith of life is exercised in death,' whilst God is in the very act of killing us. Enough for the present, in a preface.

By this proceeding of theirs, those who assert and defend these paradoxes, do, in fact, better provide against the impiety of the multitude, than you do, by your counsel of silence and abstinence; which, after all, avails nothing. For, if you either believe, or suspect that they are true (being, as they are, paradoxes of no small moment), through that insatiable desire which men have for scrutinizing secret things (then, most of all, when most of all we wish to conceal them), you will cause men to have a much greater desire for learning whether these paradoxes be true, by publishing this caution of yours; you will have set them on fire, no doubt, by your eagerness. Thus it will be found, that none of us has ever yet given such occasion to the promulgation of these things, as you have done by this devout and vehement admonition. You would have acted more prudently, in quite holding your tongue about shunning these paradoxes, if you meant to obtain your wish. All is over now: since you do not absolutely deny that they are true; they can-

---

† *Fides vitæ.*] Luther has some allusion possibly to Job xiii. 15. 'Though he slay me, yet will I trust in him.'—' Faith of eternal life ;' the belief that he shall possess that life, is exercised by the dying man, in the moment when God is killing him. 'What! He give thee life, who is now killing thee?'. Yes; so faith speaks.—Even so, these apparent contradictions to the justice and other perfections of God, *kill faith* ; but it is exercised in the midst of this death. A fine thought! But it will be seen elsewhere, as I trust, that Luther misconceives and overstates this difficulty; through not seeing far enough into the counsel and actings of God. There is manifestly no injustice in the divine procedure; when that procedure is viewed in its real nature and circumstances, *as revealed.* Nor are we without a *manifested* end, which the spiritual mind entirely approves and rejoices in, for that severity, which is so hateful to carnal man. But it requires great depth, as well as distinctness of vision, so to see, as to be verily and indeed satisfied with this mystery of God, by which He is making himself known.

not hereafter be concealed, but will draw every body to the investigation of them, by the suspicion that they are true." Either deny, therefore, that they are true; or keep silence first yourself, if you mean that others should be silent.

SC XXIV.

With respect to the other paradox, that 'whatever we do is done by mere necessity, and not by Freewill;' let us look a little into it here, that we may forbid its being called most pernicious. What I say at present is, when it shall have been shewn that our salvation is placed beyond the reach of our own power and wisdom, depending upon the work of God only (which I hope to prove fully, hereafter, in the body of my discourse), will it not clearly follow, that 'whilst God is not present *as a worker* in us, every thing is evil which we do; and that we do *necessarily* those things which are of no profit to our own salvation?' For, if it is not *we*, but *only* God, that works salvation in us; we do nothing that is profitable to our salvation, whether we will or no, before he works in us. When I say *necessarily*, I do not mean by compulsion; but, as it is said, by a necessity of immutability, not of compulsion: that is, when a man is destitute of the Spirit of God, he does not work evil against his will, through a violence put upon him; as if some one should seize him by the throat, and twist him round; just as a thief or highwayman is carried, against his will, to the gallows; but he works it of his own accord, and with a willing will. But then he cannot, by his own strength, lay aside, restrain, or change this good pleasure, or will to act; but he goes on willing and liking: and, even if he should be compelled from without to do something else by force, still his will remains averse within him, and he is angry with the person who compels or resists him.

The paradox that 'all human works are necessary,' explained and defended.

ᵘ *Suspicione veritatis*] Interdum suspicio est ' opinio,' ' cogitatio,' ' conjectura,' ' levis cognitio.' a sort of ' surmise', that they may be true.

Now, he would not be angry, if his mind were changed, and he were following the force which acts upon him willingly. This is what I at present call 'a necessity of immutability'; that is, the will cannot change itself and turn another way, but is rather provoked the more to will, by being resisted: as is proved by its indignation. This would not be, if the will were free, or possessed Freewill. Appeal to experience. How impracticable those persons are, who cleave to any thing with affection. If these persons cease to cleave, they so cease through violence, or through the greater advantage which they are to derive from something else; they never cease to cleave, but by constraint: whereas, if they have no affection for the thing, they suffer, what may, to go forwards and be done.

So, if, on the other hand, God work in us, the will which has been changed and softly whispered to by the Spirit of God, again wills and acts according to its own sheer lust, proneness, and self-accord, not compelledly; so that it cannot be changed into another sort of will by any opposite excitements, nor overcome or compelled, even by the gates of hell; but goes on willing and liking and loving good, just as it before willed and liked, and loved evil. For, experience again proves, how invincible and constant holy men are, whilst they are goaded on by force to other objects; insomuch, that they are from thence the more provoked to will: just as fire is inflamed by the wind, rather than extinguished! So that, neither in this case is there any freedom in the will to turn itself another way, or will something else, as the free will might choose; so long as the Spirit and God's grace remain in the man.

In short, if we be under the power of the God of this world, being destitute of the work and Spirit of the true God, we are held captive by him

at his will; as Paul says (2 Tim. ii. 26.); so that
we cannot will any thing but what he wills. For
he is himself that strong man armed, who so
keepeth his palace that those are in peace whom
he possesses; lest they should stir up any commotion or thought against him. Otherwise, the
kingdom of Satan, being divided against itself,
could not stand; whereas Christ affirms that it
does stand. And this will of his we do willingly
and cordially, agreeably to the nature of our will;
which, if it were compelled, would not be a Will:
for compulsion is, if I may so speak, more properly *Non-will*.ˣ But, if a stronger than he come
upon him, and, having conquered him, carry us
off as a spoil; then, again, we become servants
and captives through His spirit (which, however,
is royal liberty), to will and do of our own lust,
just what He himself wills. Thus, the human will
is placed, as a sort of packhorse, in the midst of
two contending parties. If God hath mounted,
it wills and goes whither God pleases; as the
Psalmist says, "I am become as a beast of
burden, and I am ever with thee."ʸ (Psa. lxxiii.
22, 23.) If Satan hath mounted, it wills and goes
whither Satan wills. Nor is it in its own choice,
to which of the two riders it shall run, or to seek
its rider; but the riders themselves contend for the
acquisition and possession of it.ᶻ

ˣ *Noluntas*.] 'The negation of will;' a state supposed,
which is inconsistent with the very existence of the faculty:
yet this is what the opponents of 'necessity' would charge its
assertors with maintaining; instead of that constrained but
freely-acted obedience, which is essential to the reality of God's
being God, and man his *moral* creature.
ʸ Our authorized version gives another turn to this passage,
by dividing the verses differently. But the original text is,
"I am foolish, and I did not know that I was behemoth before
thee: and I am always with thee, thou holdest in thy hand my
right hand."
ᶻ Luther does not really mean what his words might seem to
imply, that God and Satan are co-equal rivals for the throne of

PART I.

SC. XXV.

Erasmus convicted by his own concession: folly and madness of man's claiming Freewill.

What: if I shall have proved from your own words, in which you assert Freewill, that there is no such thing as Freewill; so as to convict you of unwarily denying the conclusion which you endeavour, with so much wariness, to establish? Verily, if I do not succeed in this, I swear to revoke all which I have written against you, from the beginning to the end of this book; and to confirm all which your Diatribe either asserts or brings into question against me.[a]

You represent the power of the free will as something very diminutive, and what is altogether inefficacious without the grace of God.

Do not you acknowledge this? I ask and demand, then, if the grace of God be wanting, or be

man's will. Hereafter, it will be found, that he firmly and explicitly maintains the universal and minute sovereignty of God, as the doer of all things. His object here is to shew the governance under which man's will is; that it is under the power and control of the devil, unless and until the Holy Ghost assume the empire of it: when it is still a subject, though the subject of another, and that a freedom-giving master.—The truth, however, is, that God has never given Freewill (if by Freewill is meant an uncontrolled will) to any creature. Man, in his creation state, had the power of choosing, and refusing, as he has now; and the difference between his then state and his now state, consisted in his knowing nothing but good; and, till the moment of trial, having no temptation to choose any thing but good. When that temptation was, for the first time, presented to him, we know how he met it; and the result was a corrupted faculty, which Satan rides as his packhorse. But both his seat and his riding are of the gift, and according to the will, of God; even as his dispossession is, *when, as* and *in whom* God wills; not a moment sooner, or later. Yet all this agency of God in no wise contradicts the reality of a will in man; God's universal and minute government consisting in his setting, or rather procuring to be set, before this faculty, such considerations as shall lead the free-agent possessor of it to choose just what God would have him choose.

[a] *Contra me tum asserit, tum quærit.*] Much of Erasmus's argument consisted of dubitative remark; hinting a fault or objection, rather than boldly stating it; and proposing questions, rather than affirming certainties.

separated from this little something of power; what will it do by itself?[b] It is inefficacious, you say, and does nothing that is good. Then it will not do what God or his grace would have to be done (for we suppose here, that the grace of God is in a state of separation from it), and what the grace of God doeth not, is not good. It follows, therefore, that the free will,[c] without the grace of God, is absolutely not free, but is immutably the captive and slave of evil; since it cannot, of itself, turn to good. Let but this be allowed, and I will give you leave to make the power of the free will not only that small something, but the power of an angel; a power, if you can, that is truly divine. Still, if you shall add this unhappy appendage, that it is inefficacious without the grace of God, you will instantly take away all power from it.—What is an inefficacious power, but no power at all?

To say, then, that the will is free, and has power, but that its power is inefficacious, is what the Sophists call 'an opposite in the adjunct:' as if you should say, the will is free, but it is not free. It is like saying, fire is cold, and earth is hot. Let fire possess even an infernal degree of heat; if it be neither warm nor burn, but be cold and make cold, I will not call it fire, much less hot—unless you choose to consider it as a painting or engraving of a fire. If, however, we should declare Freewill to be that power, which renders

---

[b] *Quid ipsa faciet*] This question is no less than the deathblow to Freewill, how modest soever may be the pretensions made for her. A false candour and a ruinous forbearance say, why attempt to separate what run so closely and so harmoniously together, God's grace and man's exertion? Goodwill to man and zeal for God demand the separation: thus only can man be made to know himself, thus only can God's proper praise be knowingly and unfeignedly rendered to him.

[c] See above, Sect. ix. note [d]. *Lib arb.* 'The power of willing,' thus asserted to be *free. Vis lib. arb.* 'The power of this power, &c. &c.' 'Freewill.'

man a fit substance to be seized by the Spirit and imbued with the grace of God, as a being created to eternal life, or eternal death ; we should speak properly. For we also confess this power (that is, this fitness) in the will; or, as the Sophists speak, this disposable quality and passive adaptedness; which everybody knows to be not implanted in the trees and in the beasts: for God hath not created heaven for geese and ganders; as it is said.[d]

It stands fixed, even by your own testimony, therefore, that we do all things by necessity, and nothing by Freewill; so long as the power of the free will is nothing, and neither does nor can do good, in the absence of grace. Unless you, by a new use of terms, should choose to mean 'completion' by 'efficacy;' intimating, that Freewill can begin and can will a good work, though not complete it; which I do not believe. But more of this hereafter.

It follows, from what has been said, that Freewill is a title which belongs altogether to God; and cannot join with any other being, save the Divine Majesty only. For that Divine Majesty, as the Psalmist sings, can and does effect all that He wills in heaven and in earth. (Psa. cxxxv. 6.) But if this title be ascribed to men, you might just as well ascribe divinity itself to them; a sacrilege which none can exceed. So that, it was the duty of theologians to abstain from this word, when

---

[d] It is necessary to mark with precision the amount of this concession. Man has a *rational* will, (not that his reason is seated in his will, it is a distinct faculty; and we should say more correctly, man has an understanding as well as a will) which brutes have not; and through the means of which he *may* become the subject of spiritual influences There is a spirit in man; and this spirit *may* be renewed and invigorated by the Holy Ghost, so as to discern spiritual objects, and to perform spiritual acts. But how does this affect the reality of the *natural* blindness and impotency of the rational will? It presupposes that reality.

they would speak of human power, and to leave it
for God only; and, having done this, to remove the
same from out of the mouth and discourse of men,
claiming it as a sacred and venerable title for their
God.[e] Nay, if they must by all means ascribe
some power to man, they should teach that it be
called by some other name than 'Freewill;' especially, when as we all see and know, the common
people are miserably seduced and beguiled by
this term; hearing in it, and conceiving from it,
a something very far different from what theologians entertain in their minds, and affirm. For
'Freewill' is too magnificent, extensive, and
copious a term; by which the common people
suppose (as both the force and the nature of the
word require) that a power is meant, which can
turn itself freely to either side, and is of such extent as not to yield or be subjected to any one.
Did they know that the fact is otherwise; and
that scarcely a very small particle of a little spark
is signified by it, and that this very small particle
is quite inefficacious by itself; nay, the captive
and slave of the devil; it would be strange if they
did not stone us, as mockers and deceivers, for
uttering a sound so very far different from our
meaning: and this too, when it is not even a settled
and agreed thing amongst us yet, what we really
do mean! For "he who speaks deceitfully," says
the wise man, "is detestable;"[f] especially, if he
do so in matters of piety, where eternal salvation
is at stake.

Seeing, then, that we have lost the substance

[e] *Nomen.*] He does not mean that God should be called by
this name; but that it is a property, which should be to him
as a name; 'what separates the individual, in the recognition
of others, from all that resemble him.'

[f] *Odibilis.*] I do not find any words like these, either in the
Canonical Scriptures, or in the Apocrypha. Some have supposed Luther to refer to Eccle. xxxvii. 3. "O wicked imagination, whence camest thou in to cover earth with deceit?"

which is expressed by so glorious a name, or rather have never possessed it (the Pelagians, indeed, would have it that we do; beguiled, as you are, by this word); why do we so obstinately retain an empty name, to the mocking and endangering of the common people which believe?

It is just the same sort of wisdom, as that by which kings and princes either retain, lor claim and vaunt themselves to possess, empty titles of kingdoms and countries; when they are almost beggars all the while, and are as far as possible from possessing those kingdoms and countries. This, however, is a folly that may be borne; since they neither deceive nor beguile any one, but feed themselves on vanity, to no profit at all. But in the case before us, the soul-danger and the deception are most injurious.

Who would not laugh at, or rather hate, that unseasonable innovator in the use of words, who, contrary to all common usage, should endeavour to introduce such a mode of speaking as to call a beggar rich; not for having any money of his own, but because some king might perchance give him his? Especially, if he should do this, as though he were in earnest; without any figure of speech, such as antiphrasis or irony. So, if he should call one that is sick unto death a man in perfect health; because some other person, who is in health, might possibly make him whole, like himself. So, if he should call a most illiterate idiot a very learned man; because some other person might possibly give him letters. It is just the same sort of thing which is said here—' man has Free-will': yes, forsooth: if God should give him His. By such an abuse of speech, any man might boast himself of any thing: as for instance, that he is Lord of heaven and earth; that is, if God would but give it him. Such, however, is not the language of theologians, but of stage-players and swaggerers.[g] Our words ought to be plain, pure, sc. xxv. and sober:[h] what Paul calls "sound and irreprehensible." (Tit. ii. 7, 8.)

If, then, we be not willing to give up the term altogether, which would be the safest expedient, and most consistent with piety; still, let us teach men to keep good faith in using it only within certain limits; by which Freewill shall be conceded to man, only with respect to such substances as are inferior to himself, and not to those which are his superiors. In other words, let him know that he has, with regard to his faculties and possessions, a right of using them—of doing, and of forbearing to do—according to his own free will; although this very right be also controlled by God's alone free will, wheresoever he sees fit to interpose. But in his actings towards God, in things pertaining to salvation or damnation, he has no free will, but is the captive, the subject, and the servant, either of the 'will of God, or of the will of Satan.[i]

[g] *Quadruplatorum.*] This name was applied, under the Roman law, to 'public informers,' who gained a fourth part of the accused's goods, or of the fine imposed upon him : or, as others say, because they accused persons, who, upon conviction, used to be condemned to pay *fourfold;* as those guilty of illegal usury, gaming, or the like. But, chiefly mercenary and false accusers, or litigants, were called by this name; and also those judges who, making themselves parties in a cause, decided in their own favour. Seneca calls those who, for small services, sought great returns, ' quadruplatores beneficiorum suorum;' as overrating and exaggerating them.—Luther, however, may possibly have no allusion to these customs, but use the term, according to its essential meaning, for 'a bouncer' or 'exaggerator;' insinuating, that Erasmus's statements were of this kind. But his uniting it with *Histrionum* leads us rather to some notorious class, or community of persons.

[h] *Propria, pura, sobria.*] Prop. ' plain,' as opposed to figurative;' *pur.* ' simple,' as opposed to ' ornamented;' *sobr.* ' temperate,' as opposed to ' extravagant.'

[i] Luther's distinction here is neither profitable, nor just, nor safe.: *unprofitable,* because the amount of the exception is small, and hard to be defined; *unjust,* because God does, in fact, interpose always—" He worketh all things after the coun-

Luther concludes his review of Erasmus's Preface, by reducing him to a dilemma, and making short work of some of his sharp sayings.

I have said thus much on the chapters of your Preface, which even in themselves contain almost the whole of our matter; more of it, I might say, than the body of the book which follows. But the sum of these is what might be dispatched by this short dilemma. Your preface complains either of the words of God, or of the words of man: if, of the words of man, it is all written in vain, and I have no concern with it; if, of the words of God, it is altogether profane. So that, it would have been more profitable to make this our question; are the words, about which we dispute, God's words or man's words? But, perhaps the Proem which follows, and the disputation itself, will discuss this question.

What you repeat in the conclusion of your preface, does not at all disturb me: as 'that you should call my dogmas fables, and useless;' 'that you should say, that we ought rather, after the example of Paul, to preach Christ crucified;' 'that wisdom must be taught amongst them that are perfect;' 'that Scripture has its language variously attempered to the state of the hearers;' which makes you think, that it is left to the prudence and charity of the teacher, to preach what he may deem suitable to his neighbour.

All this is absurdity and ignorance; I also preach nothing but Jesus crucified: but "Christ crucified" brings all these things along with it; and brings, moreover, that very wisdom amongst them that are perfect: since there is no other wisdom to be taught amongst Christians, than that which is hidden in a mystery and belongs to the

---

sel of his own will." "Not a sparrow falleth to the ground without your Father," "He is all (things) in all (things)." *Unsafe;* because, if Freewill be admitted any where, why not every where? who will yield to our authority, when we say, ' it is *here*, but it is not *there*?' The truth is, man is a *free-agent*, though not a *free-willer*, in *spiritual* things, and he is no more in *temporal* things, and in his dealings with the inferior creatures. (See Sect. xxiv. note ᶻ.)

perfect; not to children,[k] of a Jewish and legal people, which glory in works without faith. This is Paul's meaning in 1 Cor. ii. unless you would have 'the preaching of Christ crucified' to mean no more than the sounding out of these letters, 'Christ was crucified.'

As to those expressions, 'God is angry,' 'hath fury,' 'hateth,' 'grieveth,' 'pitieth,' 'repenteth;' when we know that none of these things happeneth to God;

You are looking for a knot in a bulrush.[1] These expressions do not make Scripture obscure, or such as must be modulated according to the varieties of the hearer; except that some people are fond of making obscurities where there are none. These are matters of grammar: the sentiment is expressed in figurative words; but those, such as even schoolboys understand. However, we are talking about doctrines, not about figures of speech, in this cause of ours.

SC.XXVI.

[k] *Pueros.*] *Puer.* opposed to *perfectos;* ἐν τοῖς τελείοις· The men 'of full age', opposed to babes. (1 Cor. ii 6)
[1] *Nodus in scirpo quæritur.*] A proverb for stumbling upon plain ground.

PART II.

LUTHER COMMENTS UPON ERASMUS'S PROEM.

SECTION I.

Canonical Scriptures to be the standard of appeal. Human authority all against Luther—admitted—but depreciated.

Now, therefore, when about to enter upon your disputation, you promise to plead the Canonical Scriptures only, since Luther does not hold himself bound by the authority of any other writer.

I am satisfied, and accept your promise: albeit, you do not make this promise on the ground of judging those other writers unprofitable to the cause, but to spare yourself useless labour; for you do not quite approve this audacity of mine, or whatever else the principle, by which I regulate myself in this instance, must be called.

You are not a little moved, forsooth, by so numerous a series of the most learned men, who have been approved by the common consent of so many ages: amongst whom, are to be found men of the greatest skill in sacred literature, some of the most holy of our Martyrs, and many celebrated for their miracles. Add to these a number of more modern theologians; so many Universities, Councils, Bishops, Pontiffs. In short, on the one side stands erudition, genius, numbers, grandeur, high rank, fortitude, sanctification, miracles, and what not? But on my side, only Wickliff and one other, Laurentius Valla (howbeit Augustine also, whom you pass over, is altogether with me); whose weight is nothing, in comparison with the former.

There remains none but Luther—a private man, a man of yesterday—and his friends: who have neither so much learning, nor so much genius; no numbers, no grandeur, no sanctification, no miracles—they cannot even heal a lame horse. They make a parade of Scripture; which they nevertheless consider to be equivocal,[a] as well as the opposite party. They boast of the Spirit also; but they give no signs of possessing it.—And a great many other particulars; which you could specify, if you pleased.[b]—There is nothing on our side, therefore, but what the wolf acknowledged in the devoured nightingale; 'You are a voice,' said he, 'and nothing else.' 'They talk,' you say; 'and, for this only, expect to be believed.'

I confess, my Erasmus, that you are not without good reason moved by all these things. I was so much affected by them myself for more than ten years, that I think no other person was ever equally harassed by such conflicts: and it was utterly incredible to me, that this Troy of mine, which, for so long a time, and during so many wars, had proved itself to be invincible, could ever be taken. Nay, I call God for a record upon my soul, that I should have continued in my opinion, and should, to this day, be still impressed with the same feelings, if it were not that the goadings of my own conscience, and the evidence of facts, constrain me to judge differently. You can have no difficulty in conceiving, that, although my heart be not a heart of stone, yet if it were one, it might have melted in the struggle and collision with such waves and tides as I brought upon myself, by daring to do an act,

[a] *Quam tamen dubiam habent.*] The pretended ambiguity of Scripture is a point on which Erasmus laid great stress, and which Luther, hereafter, most powerfully and satisfactorily repels.

[b] A vaunting insinuation expressed in the words of Æneas. (Æn. iv. 333, 334); by which Erasmus would lead his reader to understand, that he had a great deal still behind.

which would, as I perceived, cause all the authority of these persons whom you have recounted, to come down, with all the violence of a deluge, upon my own head.[c]

But this is not the place for me to construct a history of my life, or of my works; nor have I taken this book in hand with the design of commending myself, but that I might extol the grace of God. What sort of a man I am, and with what spirit and design I have been hurried into these transactions, I commit[d] to that Being, who knows that all these things have been effected, not by my own Freewill, but by His: howbeit, even the world itself ought to have become sensible of this, long ago. It is evidently a very invidious situation into which you throw me, by this exordium of yours: from which it is not easy for me to extricate myself, without trumpeting my own praises, and censuring so many of the Fathers. But I shall be short. In erudition, genius, numbers, authority, and every thing else, I allow the cause to be tried at your judgment-seat, and acknowledge myself the inferior.[e]

[c] Luther claims respect, here, for three properties of his mind and conduct; conscientiousness, scrupulous investigation of truth, and full consciousness of the evil he was encountering. Not only was his light poured in very gradually, and admitted very cautiously, but, from first to last, he would have been often glad to hold his tongue. When he spoke, or wrote, it was because God's word was in his heart as a burning fire shut up in his bones, and he was weary with forbearing, and could not stay. (Jer. xx. 9)

[d] *Commendo.*] Properly, to 'commit as a deposit into the hands of a trustee.' I leave my character and my conduct, in these particulars, with my God.

[e] Luther considers himself as arrayed, in opposition to the Fathers, before the judgment-seat of Erasmus. His defence must consist of self-praise and abuse of the Fathers. He declines making such a defence, and cuts the matter short by acknowledging his inferiority; and, that in *all* the points of competition which Erasmus had introduced —Dr Milner understands him to reserve three, viz. the Spirit, miracles, sanctification. But this does not appear to be the fair construction and import of the original text. If I collect the

"But if I should turn round upon my judge, and propose these three questions to you, what is the manifestation of the Spirit? what are Miracles? what is Sanctification?' you would be sense aright, he makes two concessions: *etiam te judice;* ' I will allow the cause to be tried even at your judgment-seat;' *omnibus aliis;* ' I reserve not a single point of superiority for myself.' (Did Luther *indeed* mean to contest the palm on any of these three grounds of excellency?)—But then he abates the force of his concessions, by remarking, with respect to those three distinctions which alone are of any value in the number and variety claimed for his adversaries, that, in the first place, Erasmus could not define them; and, in the next, he could not prove concerning any individual of his vaunted host, that he possessed them. (See Miln. Ecclesi. Hist. vol. iv. part ii. p. 863.)

It may be well, just to notice the order, in which Luther hence proceeds, in his animadversions upon Erasmus's Proem. 1. You cannot prove that they possessed these properties. 2. If they had them, they did not come at them by Freewill. 3. Show ye the same. 4. At least *define* the power. 5. How absurd your conduct with respect to the Fathers. 6. Some desultory objections—such as, ' strange that God should have tolerated such errors in his church'; ' Scripture is not clear'— met and repelled. 7. Erasmus reduced to a dilemma.

' By ' manifestation of the Spirit,' Luther (with reference to Erasmus's taunt, ' quem nusquam ostendunt.') means, ' how men are to prove that they have the Spirit dwelling and walking in them.' By ' miracles', how the reality or falsehood of affirmed miracles is to be proved. By ' sanctification', the state of a saint; that is, of one effectually called by the Holy Ghost: this effectual calling, or *separation* of the Spirit, being that act by which the *eternally separated* of the Father (Jude ver. 1.) are drawn into a realized and recognised union with the *separated* one, even the Lord Jesus Christ; *in whom* (Heb. ii. 11.), according to eternal purpose and covenant, they are *separated* to God. So that ' separation *from* and *unto*' constitutes the essence of sanctification; into which the Scripture use of the term is every where resolvable: not a gradual work, the result of repeated actions of the Spirit upon the substance of the natural soul, as human authors fondly teach; but one complete and final operation, by which the natural soul ($\psi v \chi \eta$) is made a spiritual soul ($\pi \nu \epsilon \hat{v} \mu a$); as holy, with respect to its own substance, as it ever will be in eternity. (See 1 Pet. i. 2, 22, 23. 2 Thess. ii. 13. John vi. 37, 44, 63, 64. See also the $\kappa \lambda \eta \tau o \hat{i} s$ $\dot{a} \gamma \acute{i} o i s$, called to be saints,' of the epistolary inscriptions.) Luther very properly distinguishes this ' sanctimonia,' ' sanctum esse vel fuisse', from the ,' habere spiritum;' that is, from the presence of the Holy Ghost *with,* and his consequent actings *in* and *by,* the renewed Spirit.

G

PART II.
found too inexpert and too ignorant (so far as I know you from your letters and from your books) to answer me one syllable. Or, if I should go on, and demand of you, which of all these heroes, of whom you make your boast, you could certainly show to have been, or to be sanctified, or to have had the Spirit, or to have displayed real miracles; my conviction is, that you would have to work very hard, and all in vain.[g] Much that you say is borrowed from common use and public discourse;[h] which loses more than you suppose of its credit and authority, when summoned to the bar of conscience. True is the proverb, 'Many pass for saints on earth, whose souls are in hell.'

SECT. II.

The excellencies of the Fathers were not *of*, or *for* Freewill.

But let us grant you, if you please, that even all of them were sanctified, had the Spirit, and wrought miracles (a concession which you do not ask); tell me, was any one of them sanctified, did any one of them receive the Spirit and work miracles, in the name or by the power of Freewill; or, to confirm the doctrine of Freewill? God forbid; you will say: all these things were done in the name and by the power of Jesus Christ; and in support of the doctrine of Christ. Why, then, do you adduce their sanctification, their having the Spirit, and their miracles, in support of the doctrine of Freewill; for, which they were not given and wrought? Their miracles, therefore, their having the Spirit, and their sanctification, are all ours; who preach Jesus Christ, in opposition to the powers and works of men. Now, what wonder is it, if those men (holy, spiritual, and workers of miracles as they were) being every now and then forestalled by the flesh, have spoken and have acted, according to the flesh? what happened more than once to the Apostles

[g] *Multùm sed frustrà sudatorum.*] Horace's 'sudet multùm frustráque laboret:' implying great and inefficacious toil.

[h] *Ex usu et publicis sermonibus.*] *Us.* 'men's saying what is usually said, what others say.' *Publ. serm.* 'what men talk in public;' contrasted with private meditation and the secret testimony of their own hearts.

themselves, when living under the immediate eye of Christ. For you do not deny, but even assert, that Freewill is not a matter of the Spirit, or of Christ, but a mere human affair; so that the Spirit, which was promised, that he might glorify Christ, cannot possibly preach Freewill. If, therefore, the Fathers have sometimes preached Freewill; assuredly they have spoken by the flesh, as men, and not by the Spirit of God; much less have they wrought miracles, that they might support it. So that your allegation respecting the Fathers, as having been sanctified, had the Spirit, and wrought miracles, is inapplicable: since it is not Freewill, but the dogma of Jesus Christ[i] as opposed to that of Freewill, which is proved thereby.

But come now, ye that are on the side of Freewill, and assert that a dogma of this sort is true; that is, has come from the Spirit of God; still, still, I say, manifest the Spirit, publish your miracles, display your sanctification. Assuredly you, who assert, owe these things to us who deny. The Spirit, sanctification, miracles, ought not to be demanded of us who deny; of you who assert, they ought. Since a negative advances nothing, is nothing, is not bound to prove any thing, nor ought to be proved itself. An affirmative ought to be proved. You affirm the power of Freewill; a human substance. But no miracle has ever yet been seen, or heard of, as performed by God, for any dogma in support of a human thing; but only for one in support of a divine thing. We have it in charge to receive no dogma whatsoever, which has not been first proved by divine attestations. (Deut. xviii. 15—22.) Moreover, the Scripture calls man vanity and a lie;[k] which is in effect saying,

Luther challenges him to shew effects of Freewill, in the three particular excellencies which he has selected out of Erasmus's catalogue.

[i] *Jesu Christi dogma.*] Not ' a dogma taught by Jesus Christ;' but a ' dogma of which He is the subject:' ' the truth as it is in Jesus ;' which is directly opposite to this fancy of Freewill.
[k] Ps. xxxix. 5. lxii. 9.

that all human things are vanities and lies. Come then; come, I say, and prove your dogma in support of a human vanity and lie, to be true! Where is now your manifestation of the Spirit? where, your sanctification? where, your miracles?—I see talents, erudition, and authority—but God hath given these to the Gentiles also.

And yet, it is not great miracles to which we will compel you; such as that of healing a lame horse;[1] lest you should complain of a carnal age:[m] howbeit, God is wont to confirm his doctrines by miracles, without any regard to the carnality of the age. He is not moved by the merits or demerits of a carnal age, but by mere pity and grace; and by a love of establishing souls in solid truth, unto His glory.[n] You are at liberty to work a miracle as small as you please. Nay, by way of provoking your Baal to exertion, I jeer you; and challenge you to create even a single frog, in the name and by the power of Freewill: of which the impious Gentile magicians in Egypt were enabled to create many. For I will not put you to the trouble of creating lice; which they also were not able to bring forth. I will set you a still lighter task: take but a single gnat or louse (since you tempt and mock my God with your fleer about healing a lame horse); and if, with the whole united force, and the whole conspiring efforts, both of your God and of yourselves, you shall be able to kill him—in the name and by the power of Freewill—you shall be proclaimed conquerors; and it

[1] *Equum claudum sanare.*] Erasmus's burlesque illustration of their want of miracles. Luther plays with it : ' we will not call you to practise upon so huge an animal as an horse; we will be content with something less.'

[m] Alluding to the Lord's, "a wicked and adulterous generation seeketh after a sign," Matt. xvi. 4. xii. 39.

[n] Luther confines the design of God in his miracles to the *gracious* object of them : but does not God also design, by these seals set upon his truth, to convict and render inexcusable the reprobate and ungodly ?

shall be admitted that you have maintained your cause, and we will come presently and adore this God of yours—the marvellous slayer of a louse! Not that I deny your having the power even to remove mountains: but because it is one thing to have it asserted, that some act has been performed by the power of Freewill; and another, to have it proved.

What I have said of miracles, I say also of sanctification. If, in so great a series of ages and of men, and of all things which you have named, you shall be able to show a single work (let it be but the lifting up of a straw from the ground); or a single word (let it be but the syllable 'my'); or a single thought (let it be but the feeblest sigh)—proceeding from Freewill—by which they have either applied themselves to grace, or earned the Spirit, or obtained pardon of sin, or have negociated any thing (let it be as diminutive as you please—we will not talk about their sanctification) with God; be ye again the victors, and we the vanquished! But then it must be through the power and in the name of Freewill! For, as to what is done in men through the power of a divine creation, it has Scripture testimonies in abundance. You certainly ought to exhibit some work of this kind, if you would not make yourselves ridiculous teachers, by spreading dogmas throughout the world, with all this superciliousness and authority, about a thing of which you produce no record. For those shall be called dreams, which produce no result whatsoever (the most disgraceful thing imaginable) to persons of so great consequence, living through such a series of ages, men of the greatest erudition and sanctity, who have also the power of working miracles. The issue will be, that we prefer the Stoics before you; who, although they too described a wise man such as they never saw, still endeavoured to exhibit the likeness of some part of him in their own character.

PART II.

SECT. IV.

The saints practically disclaim Freewill,

But you have absolutely nothing to show; not even the shadow of your dogma.

So again, with respect to the Spirit: if, out of all the assertors of Freewill, you can show me one, who hath possessed even so small a degree of strength of mind, or of good feeling, as might enable him to despise a single farthing, to forego a single cast of the die, or to forgive a single word or letter of injury (I will not talk of despising wealth, life, and fame), in the name and through the power of Freewill; take the palm again, and I will be content to be sold as your captive.º You ought at least to show us this, after all your big swelling words ᵖ in boast of Freewill; else, you will again seem to be either wrangling about goats' wool, or, like the noble Argian, seeing plays in an empty theatre.ᵍ

But, in contradiction to your statement, I shall easily shew you that holy men, such as you vaunt yourself to possess, as often as they come to pray or plead with God, approach him in an utter forgetfulness of their own Freewill; despairing of

º *Sub hastam libenter ibimus.*] The custom of selling under the spear was derived from the sales of booty taken in war; in which the spear was set up, and the spoil sold under it, to denote whence the property had been obtained. So constant, however, was the use of the spear in auctions, that ' hasta' is sometimes put absolutely for the auction itself; and ' sub hastâ venire' corresponds to our ' coming under the hammer.' Luther applies it here, in agreement with its original use; ' he will freely come to the spear, that he may be sold as a part of Erasmus's spoil.'

ᵖ *Buccâ verborum.*] ' The puffed or distended cheek' is used to express ' anger,' ' pride,' or ' boastfulness.' Horace has ' iratus buccas inflet;' Persius, ' scloppo tumidas intendis rumpere buccas.'

ᵍ *Land caprind, vacuo theatro.*] The first allusion (Hor. 1. Epist. xviii. 15.) charges him with ' contentious, trifling;' like the man who quarrels with his friend about goats' hair, whether it should be called wool or bristles; ' fighting for straws:' the second—' fuit haud ignobilis Argis'—(Hor. 2. Epist. ii. 128—130, &c.) with indulging ' a *harmless* but *disordered fancy*.'—If you cannot show us any moral effects produced by it, Freewill must be either a thing of no value, or an illusion.

themselves, and imploring nothing but pure grace only; which they acknowledge to be far removed from their own deservings. Such a man does Augustine frequently prove himself to have been; such did Bernard, when, in his dying-hour, he said, 'I have lost my time, for I have lived abominably.'[r] I do not see any power which applies itself for grace alleged in these expressions, but all the power which a man has, accused of absolutely turning away from it.[s] And yet, these self-same holy men sometimes spoke a different language about Freewill, in their disputations. Just what happens, as I perceive, to all mankind: they are one sort of people, whilst intent upon words and reasonings; and another, when feeling and acting. In the former instance, they speak a language which differs from their previous feelings; in the latter, their feelings contradict their previous language. But men are to be measured by their feelings, rather than their discourse; whether they be pious, or impious.

SECT. V.

however they may dispute about it.

But we give you still more: we do not demand miracles, the Spirit, sanctification; we return to the dogma itself: demanding only, that you shall at least shew us, what work, what word, what thought, this power of the free will stirs up, or attempts to perform, in order that it may apply itself to grace. It is not enough to say, 'there is a power,' 'there is a power,' 'there is a certain power, I say, in the free will;' for what is easier than to say this? Nor is this worthy of those most learned and most holy men, who have been approved by so many ages. 'The babe must be named,' as the German proverb has it. You must define what that power is, what it does, what it suffers, what are its accidents. For example; speaking as one most dull of apprehension, I would ask,

Luther demands a definition of Freewill; a specification of its parts, powers, properties, and accidents.

---

[r] *Perditè.*] 'More perditi hominis; flagitiosè,' 'nequiter, corruptè.'

[s] *Non nisi aversa fuerit.*] Opposed to 'ad gratiam sese applicet;' aversation and disgust, instead of desire and seeking.

PART II. is it the office of this power either, to pray, or to fast, or to labour, or to keep under the body, or to give alms, or to do any thing else of this kind, or does it make any attempt at these things? If it be a power, it will be trying to achieve something. But here, you are more dumb than the Seriphian frogs, and fishes.[t]

And how is it possible that you should define it, when, according to your own testimony, you are still uncertain what the power itself is; at variance with each other, and each of you inconsistent with himself? What will become of the definition, when the thing defined means one thing in one place, and another in another?

But, let it be granted, that, since the time of Plato, there has, at length, been some sort of agreement amongst you, about the power itself: let it further be defined, as its office, that it prays, or fasts, or does something of this sort, which still, perhaps, lies concealed in the maze of Plato's 'Ideas.'[u] Who shall assure us, that the dogma is true, that it is, well-pleasing to God, and that we are safe in maintaining it?[x] Especially, when you confess yourselves that it is a human thing, which has not the testimony of the Spirit; for that it

[t] Seriphus was an island in the Ægean sea; one of the Sporades; where, according to Ælian, the frogs never croaked; but, when removed to another place, became more noisy and clamorous than others. The latter part of the story, however, is differently told, and in a manner more consistent with the proverb; that they retained their dumbness, when transferred and mingled with others. Hence the saying, Βάτραχος εκ Σερίφυ, for a silent man, who can neither speak, nor sing.

[u] *Platonis Ideis.*] A term used by Plato to denote the first forms of things; the sort of mental draught, according to which *nature* (in the language of a heathen philosopher—and would it were only professed heathens who speak so!) has framed all her substances 'Plato ideas vocat ex quibus omnia quæcunque videmus fiunt, et ad quas omnia formantur.'

[x] *Nosque tutò rectum agere,* i. e. *in* rectum.] 'More literally, ' safe in going straight forwards.' Quasi ' in rectum agere iter.'

"Iterque
Non agit in rectum."............ ", in rectum exire catervas." ·
LUCAN.

was bandied by the philosophers, and had a SECT. V.
being in the world, before Christ came, and
before the Spirit was sent from heaven. Thus it
is made most certain, that this dogma was not
sent from heaven, but had been born long before,
out of the earth: so that a great deal of testimony
is necessary, to confirm it as certain and true.
Let us, then, be private men and few, whilst
you are even publicans^y and a multitude; let us
be barbarians, and you most learned; let us be
stupid, and you most ingenious; us, men of yesterday, and you older than Deucalion; us, men of
no acceptance; you, men who have received the
approbation of ages; us, in fine, sinners, carnal,
sottish;^z you, men fitted to excite fear in the very
devils, by your sanctity, the Spirit which is in you,
and your miracles. Give us, at least, the right of
Turks and Jews; that of demanding a reason for
your dogma, agreeably to what your great patron
St. Peter^a has commanded you. We ask this,
however, with the greatest modesty; inasmuch

^y *Publicani.*] Not without meaning used here instead of *publici,* as opposed to *privati.* The publicans were govern-
ment-officers, employed in collecting the public revenues;
which they contracted for at a price, and lived upon the produce. They were chiefly of the equestrian order, and held in
honour. ' Erant publicani equites Romani, qui tributa et pub-
lica' vectigalia questûs sui causâ conducebant.' ' Publicani
autem, sunt, qui publico fruuntur.' ' Flos equitum Roma-
norum, ornamentum civitatis, firmamentum reipub. Publica-
norum ordine continetur.'—Luther uses the name, if I understand him aright, equivocally. Whilst he gives them the glory
of publicity, he hints at their support being derived from the
fiscus, and the infamous celebrity which they had acquired by
their exactions. In fact, what were the barefaced traffickers
in Indulgences, such as Tetzel and others, but publicans of
the worst stamp?—I do not find any authority for the word
publicanus, but as referred to this office.

^z *Socordes.*] Quasi *sine corde.* 'Not only sinful, instead of
sanctified; and carnal, instead of having the Spirit; but absolutely without natural intellect and feeling.

^a Referring to 1 Pet. iii. 15. "And be ready always to give
an answer to every man that asketh you a reason of the hope
that is in you, with meekness and fear." *Petrus vester.* 'Your
tutelar saint and pretended founder.'

as we do not demand that it be proved to us, by sanctification, by the Spirit, and by miracles, as we might do according to your own law; which is, to demand these things of others. Nay, we even allow you not to give us any instance of thought, word, or deed in your dogma; but to teach us the simple, naked proposition. Declare the dogma itself, at least; what you wish to be understood by it; what is its form.[b]

If you will not, or cannot give us an example of it, let us at least try to give you one. Imitate the Pope and his cardinals at least, who say, 'Do what we say, but do not according to our works.' Even so, do ye also say what work that power requires to be performed by its subjects, and we will apply ourselves to it; leaving you to yourselves. What! shall we not even gain this from you? The more you exceed us in numbers, the more ancient you are, the greater, the better in all respects than we; by so much the more disgraceful is it to you, that you are not able to prove your dogma—by the miracle of even slaying a louse, or by any very small affection of the Spirit, or by any very small work of holiness—to us, who are a mere nothing in your presence, and are wishing to learn and perform your dogma. Nay, you are not even able to exemplify it in a single deed or word. More than this, you are not even able to declare the very form or meaning of the dogma (such a thing as never was heard of), that *we*, at least, might imitate it. Delightful teachers of Freewill! What are ye now, but a voice, and nothing else? Who are those now, Erasmus, that make boast of the Spirit, and *show*

[b] *Quâ formâ.*] In a dialectic sense. 'A dialecticis sumitur pro specie subjectâ generi.' 'Formæ sunt, in quas genus dividitur.' 'Specificate,' or 'define' it; i. e. enumerate and combine all the several ideas contained in it.—We do not ask miracles, &c.; we do not even ask an example, by way of illustrating it; but we do require a clear and explicit affirmation of what you mean; a full and precise description of the supposed substance.

nothing of it? that only speak, and forthwith
expect to be believed. Are not these admired
ones of yours, the men who do all this; though so
extolled to the skies? who do not even speak,
and yet make such great boasts and demands?[c]

We ask it as a favour, therefore, of yourself
and of your party, my Erasmus, that you would
at least grant to us, that, being terrified with the
danger incurred by our conscience, we may be
allowed to indulge our fears, or at least to defer
our assent to a dogma, which you perceive yourself to be nothing but an empty word, and the
sounding of so many syllables; (to wit, 'There is
such a thing as Freewill;' 'there is such a thing
as Freewill;') if you should even have attained the
summit of your object, and all your positions
should have been proved and allowed. Then,
again, it is still uncertain, even amidst your own
party, whether this mere word has a being or not;
since they are at variance one with another, and
not agreed each with himself. It is a most unfair
thing; nay, the most wretched thing imaginable,
that the consciences of those whom Christ hath
redeemed with his own blood, should be harassed
with the mere phantom of a single petty word,
and that word of doubtful existence. Yet, if we
do not suffer ourselves to be thus harassed, we
are accused of an unheard of pride, for having
despised so many Fathers, of so many ages, who
have asserted the doctrine of Freewill; when the
truth is, that they have laid down no distinct propositions at all concerning Freewill, as you perceive from what has been said; and the dogma of
Freewill is set up under the cover of their name,
whilst its maintainers are unable to exhibit either

[c] *Qui ne dicitis quidem.*] 'You are not even the nightingale.'
(See above, Sect. i.) They had voice enough, when speaking
for themselves; but none with which to answer the questions
and demands of their opponents.

PART II.

SECT. VI.

Erasmus's advice turned against himself: presumption, cruelty, want of discernment, charged upon him.

its species, or its name.^d It is thus; that they have contrived to delude the world with a lying word!^e And here, Erasmus, I summon your own and not another's counsel^f to my aid; who persuadest us above, that we ought to desist from questions of this kind, and rather to teach Christ crucified, and such things as may suffice for christian piety. Such has now, for a long time, been the nature of our questions and discussions. For what else are we aiming at; but that the simplicity and purity of Christ's doctrine may prevail; and that those dogmas, which have been invented and introduced by men, may be abandoned and disregarded. But, whilst you give us this advice, you do not act it; but just the contrary. You write Diatribes; you celebrate the decrees of Popes, you boast in the authority of men, and try all means of hurrying us into those matters which are strangers and aliens from the holy Scriptures, and of agitating unnecessary topics; in order that we may corrupt and confound the simplicity and genuineness of christian piety with the additions of men. Hence we readily perceive, that you have not given us this counsel from your heart; and that you do

^d *Neque speciem neque nomen.*] 'They can neither define it, nor find an appropriate name by which to express it.'

^e *Mendaci vocabulo.*] Though they cannot find a *name* for it, they have got a *word* for it: but that word is a liar; for it proclaims the will to be free, which is really in bondage. Logicians distinguish 'vocabulum' from 'nomen:' the former is arbitrary and general; the latter descriptive and precise. What you cannot *name* (according to this distinction) you may *speak of*. 'Differunt nomina et vocabula; quia nomina finita sunt et significant res proprias; vocabula autem infinita, et res communes designant.'

^f *Appellamus.*] A forensic expression, applied to advocate, witnesses, and judge; but to each, in consistency with its primary meaning of 'addressing a person by name,' προσαγορεύω· Luther would avail himself of Erasmus's own testimony and advice, now that he has shewn the dogma of Freewill to be this unauthorized and unprofitable one. Erasmus had recommended that all such should be suppressed.

not write any thing seriously, but trust to the vain and puerile ornaments of your language,[g] as that which may enable you to lead the world whithersoever you please. Meanwhile you, in point of fact, lead it no whither; for you utter nothing but sheer contradictions throughout the whole, and in every part: so that you would be most fitly characterised by the man who should call you Proteus, or Vertumnus[h] himself; or who should accost you with the words of Christ, and say, "Physician, heal thyself!" It is disgraceful to the teacher, when the fault, which he reproves, reproves himself.[i]

Until you shall have proved your affirmative, therefore, we persist in our negative; and venture to make it our boast at the tribunal of our judge (even though that judge should be the whole band of holy men, which you vaunt yourself as having all on your side; or, rather, should be the whole world); that we do not, and ought not to admit a dogma, which is really nothing, and of which it cannot be shewn, with certainty, what it is. We will, moreover, charge you with an incredible degree of presumption, or insanity, in demanding that this dogma should be admitted by us; without any reason, except that it pleases your High Mightinesses—who are so many, so great, and so ancient—to assert the being of a

[g] *Inanibus bullis verborum*] 'Prettinesses of style' 'Bulla' is properly 'a bubble, made by the boiling of water,' and is thence applied to divers ornaments of dress; particularly to one in the shape of a heart, worn by the Roman youth of which the quality depended upon their rank, or degree of nobility. This they dedicated to the Lares, when they took the manly gown.

[h] Vertumnus had, amongst the Latins, the same property of assuming all shapes, which Proteus had amongst the Greeks.

[i] Luther does not tell us to whom he is indebted for this *metrical* aphorism —Erasmus had played the physician, prescribing silence with respect to some dogmas; his own is shewn to be one of them.

PART II. thing, which you confess yourselves to be a mere
nothing. Is it really a conduct worthy of christian teachers, to delude the poor wretched common people, in the matter of piety, with a mere nothing; as though it were a something of great moment to their salvation! Where is now that sharpness of Grecian wit, which heretofore invented lies, having at least some shew of beauty; but on this subject utters only naked and undisguised falsehoods? Where is now that Latin industry, not inferior to Grecian, which in this instance so beguiles, and is beguiled, with the vainest of words?[k] But thus it happens to unwary, or designing, readers of books: they make those dogmas of the Fathers and of the Saints which are the offspring of their infirmity, to be all of the highest authority; the fault not being that of the authors, but of the readers. Just as if a man, leaning on the sanctity and authority of St. Peter, should contend that all which Peter ever said is true; including even that saying in Matt. xvi. 22. by which, through infirmity of the flesh, he persuaded Christ not to suffer; or that saying, by which he commanded Christ to depart from him out of the ship (Luke v. 8.); and many others, for which he is reproved by Christ himself.

SEC. VII.

Injustice done to the Fathers, by choosing their bad

Men of this sort are like those, who, by way of sneering at the Gospel, go chattering that all is not true which is in the Gospel; and lay hold of that word (John viii. 48.) where the Jews say to Christ, "Say we not well that thou art a Samaritan, and hast a devil?" or that, "He is guilty

[k] Erasmus had bestowed these and some other commendations upon the Greek and Latin Fathers, to the disparagement of the Reformers, as making for *his* side in the argument. Luther asks, whether what they had said on Freewill was a specimen of this richness of invention, and laboriousness of investigation and expression? Here they had not excelled, any more than Erasmus himself: to whom Luther was not backward to ascribe the praise of resembling and even equalling them.

of death;" or that "We have found this fellow subverting our nation, and forbidding to give tribute unto Cæsar." The assertors of Freewill do just the same thing (with a different design, it is true; and not willingly, but through blindness and ignorance), when they lay hold on what the Fathers, having fallen through infirmity of the flesh, say in support of Freewill; and oppose it to what the same Fathers have, in the strength of the Spirit, said elsewhere against it: after which, they go on presently to make the better give place to the worse. Thus it comes to pass, that they give authority to the worse sayings, because they make *for* the judgment of their flesh; and withdraw it from the better, because they make *against* that judgment.

Why do we not rather choose the better? Many such sayings are in the works of the Fathers. To give you an instance: what saying can be more carnal; nay, what saying can be more impious, more sacrilegious, and more blasphemous; than that wonted one of Jerome's? 'Virginity fills heaven, and marriage earth.' As if earth, and not heaven, were the due of those patriarchs, apostles, and private Christians, who have married wives; or heaven were the due of vestal virgins amongst the heathens, without Christ! Yet the Sophists collect these, and like sayings, from the Fathers; maintaining a contest of numbers, rather than of judgment, to get the sanction of authority for them. Just like that stupid fellow, Faber of Constance,[1] who presented his Margaritum (more properly called his stable of Augeas) lately to the

---

[1] John Faber, a native of Suabia; who, from one of his works against the Reformers, probably this very work, was called 'The Mallet of the Heretics.' He was advanced to the see of Vienna in 1531, and died there in 1542. His elevation was supposed to have been the fruit of his zeal against Luther. He entitled it his *Pearl*: but Luther would rather call it his *Dunghill*; with allusion to Hercules's famous labour of removing the long accumulated filth of 3000 oxen.

SEC. VII.

sayings and leaving their good.

PART II.
SEC. VIII.

Objection, 'that God should have disguised the error of his Church,' answered.

public, that the pious and learned might have their nauseating and vomiting draught.

In answer to what you say, 'that it is incredible that God should have disguised[m] the error of his Church for so many ages, and should not have revealed to any of his saints what we maintain to be the very head of evangelical doctrine;' I reply:

First, that we do not say that this error has been tolerated by God in his Church, or in any saint of His. For, the Church is governed by the Spirit of God; the saints are led by the Spirit of God (Rom. viii. 14.); and Christ remains with his Church even unto the end of the world (Matt. xxviii. 20.); and the Church of God is the pillar and ground of the truth.[n] (1 Tim. iii. 15.) These things, I say, we know. For thus speaks even our common creed; 'I believe in the holy Catholic Church:' so that it is impossible for her to err in the least article.[o] And if we should even grant

[m] *Dissimulârit.*] 'Diligenter et astutè celo, occulto, fingo non esse, quod reverà est '

[n] Στῦλος καὶ ἑδραίωμα τῆς ἀληθείας] Luther connects and refers these words, as the older editions of the Scriptures, and our translators, have done; but Griesbach, and others after him, connect them with what follows. A very important sense is thus elicited, "the pillar and ground of the truth (and without controversy great is the mystery of godliness) is God was manifested in the flesh, &c."—But there seems an evident allusion to the ancient tabernacle, with its boards and sockets (the pillars, or uprights, and the silver foundations into which these were grooved; see Exod. xxvi. 15—30.); of which the Church of God is the blessed reality; even as that was the image, or figure.

[o] Luther seems to have inferred the *immaculateness* of the militant and visible Church, from the above, and other like testimonies, 'an *entire* exemption from error in a certain ever-subsistent community of the Lord's people tabernacling in flesh of sin'. The Nineteenth Article of our Church declares, more correctly, 'The visible Church of Christ is a congregation of faithful men, in the which the pure word of God is preached, and the sacraments be duly ministered, *in all those things that of necessity are requisite to the same.* As the Church of Jerusalem, Alexandria, and Antioch have erred, so also the Church of Rome hath erred; not only in their living and manner of ceremonies, but also in matters of faith.'—The same

that some elect persons are held in error all their lifetime, still they must, before death, return into the way; because Christ says (John x. 28.), " No one shall pluck them out of my hand." But this must be your labour and your achievement; even to make it appear, with certainty, that those whom you call the Church, are the Church; or, rather, that those, who all their lifetime were wanderers, have not at length been brought back to the fold, before they died. For it does not directly follow, if God hath suffered all those whom you adduce (scattered through as long a series of ages as you please, and men of the greatest erudition, if you please) to abide in error, that therefore he has suffered his Church to abide in error.

Look at Israel, the people of God: of all their kings, so many in number, and reigning during so long a period, not even one is mentioned, but what erred. And, under Elias the Prophet, to such a degree had all men, and all that was *public*[p] of that people, departed into idolatry; that he thought himself left alone. Yet, in the mean time, whilst God was going to destroy kings, princes, priests, prophets, and whatsoever could be called the people or church of God, he reserved to himself seven thousand men. But who saw or knew these to be the people of God? So then, who will dare to deny, that God hath even now preserved to himself a Church amongst the common people, concealed under those principal men, (for you mention none but men of public office and of name—) and hath left all those to perish, as he did in the kingdom of Israel? since it is God's pecu-

SEC. VIII.

Erasmus must prove what he calls the Church, to be the Church.

---

remark extends to each individual of the faithful Who hath not erred in his *lifetime*? Of whom shall we say, that he *died* without any mixture of error in his creed?—Luther's representation, therefore, requires restriction: of such error as he is disputing about, it holds good.

[p] *Omne quod publicum erat*] 'Men of public station, as opposed to private men.' Luther does not forget Erasmus's *privatus* and *publicus*.

liar, right, and act, to entangle the choice men of Israel, and to slay their fat ones (Psa. lxxviii. 31), but to preserve the dregs and remnant of Israel alive; as Esaias saith.[q]

What happened under Christ himself: when all the Apostles were offended, and he was denied, and condemned by the whole people; scarcely one or two, Nicodemus and Joseph, and afterwards the thief upon the cross, being preserved to him? But were these, at that time, called the people of God? There was, indeed, a people of God remaining, but it was not called so: what was called so, was, not that people. Who knows, whether such may not have been the state of the Church of God always, during the whole course of the world, from its beginning; that some have been called the people and saints of God, who were not really so; whilst others, abiding as a remnant in the midst of them, have been, but have not been called, his people or saints? as is shewn by the history of Cain and Abel, of Ishmael and Isaac, of Esau and Jacob.

Look at the Arian period:[r] when scarcely five

---

[q] Frequent promises are made in this Prophet that ' a remnant shall be left ' " Except the Lord of Hosts had left us a very small *remnant*, we should have been as Sodom," &c. (Is. i. 9) " The *remnant* of Israel and such as are escaped of the house of Jacob .... The *remnant* shall return, even the *remnant* of Jacob, unto the mighty God " " For though my people Israel be as the sand of the sea, yet a *remnant* of them shall return ". (x. 20, 21, 22. Comp. Rom ix. 27.) So Is xi 11—16. But I do not find the expressions ' dregs' and ' remnant' united

[r] *Arrianorum seculum.*] Arianism arose early in the fourth century; about three hundred years before the rise of the Popedom; and, though condemned by Councils, was adopted by several of Constantine's successors, and became a source of grievous persecution to those who were sound in the faith. For an account of its origin and real nature, see Milner's Eccles. Hist. vol. ii pp. 51—54. It was, in substance, a denial of the co-eternity, co-equality, and co-essentiality of the Lord Jesus Christ with the Father. ' Already some secret and ambiguous attempts had been made to lessen the idea of the divinity of the Son of God. While his eternity was admitted by Eusebius the

Catholic bishops were preserved in all the world, and those driven from their sees; the Arians historian, he yet was not willing to own him co-equal with the Father. Arius went greater lengths: he said, 'That the Son proceeded out of a state of non-existence, that he was not before he was made; that he, who is without beginning, has set his Son as the beginning of things that are made; and that God made one, whom he called Word, Son, and Wisdom, by whom he did create us' (Miln. in loc.) Like all the rest of heresy, it is truth corrupted; and the only solid and satisfactory answer will be given to it, not by boldly asserting and proving the real and proper divinity of the Lord Jesus, but by showing forth his whole person in its complexity; made up, as it is, of two persons, a divine person and an human person, held together by an indissoluble union: the secret being, that God does all his works by this complex person's agency, who acts in his human person as plenarily inspired by the Holy Ghost. This person who thus doeth that will of God—of God, even the Trinity—which is referred to the Father personally; does hereby, amongst other subjects of manifestation, especially manifest that which we may well suppose to be the preeminent object of display in the TRI-UNE Jehovah, the threefold personality of his one undivided essence.—I am aware that the term 'union of persons,' as substituted for 'union of natures,' will be deemed objectionable, till it is well considered: but I have the authority of one of the best philosophers I know, for thus entitling the human part of the person of the Lord Jesus Christ. 'That which can contrive, which can design, must be a person. These capacities constitute personality, for they imply consciousness and thought. They require that which can perceive an end or purpose; as well as the power of providing means, and of directing them to their end. They require a centre in which perceptions unite, and from which volitions flow; which is mind. The acts of a mind prove the existence of a mind; and in whatever a mind resides is a person. The seat of intellect is a person.' (Paley's Nat. Theol. pp. 439, 440, 14th Edⁿ.) Now, is it not plain from Scripture, and the admission of all Christians, with a very few heretical exceptions, that the Lord Jesus had this human mind, distinct from his godhead? he had, therefore, according to this description, a person distinct from his divine person—And, what is to hinder that divine person, if the will of God be so, from taking up an human person into union with himself, and acting in that person, from thenceforth, not in his divine person? Is not that union *real*, which subsists between this divine person and this human person; when this human person, having been first generated, is afterwards inhabited, by his co-equal co-essential in the unity of God? Does it not also subsist without for-

PART II. reigning every where, under the public name, and as filling the office,[t] of the Church. Nevertheless, under the dominion of those heretics, Christ preserved his Church; but in such a form, that it was by no means supposed to be, or regarded as, the Church.

Under the reign of the Pope, shew me a single bishop discharging his duty; shew me a single Council, in which matters of piety were treated of;

feiture of distinctness? Is it not also constant and unbroken, when that divine person evermore acts *in* and *by* that human person, putting his godhead as it were into abeyance? Yet, are not his acts and his sufferings the acts and sufferings of the co-equal of the Father, and of the Holy Ghost?' There is no diminution, it is plain, of his essential godhead, in his voluntarily, and to a great end, submitting to act *by* and *in* this creature person; which constitutes him at the same time both creature and Creator: very man doeth the works of God, and very God doeth the works of man.—And, if this complexity of person is thus to be realized in time, what is to hinder that person in God, in whom it is to be realized, from transacting as though he actually were this complex person, *from* and *in* the beginning? Is not Jehovah's will both immutable and irresistible? is it not his propriety, to call things which are not as though they were, and to give realized being to substances which, as yet, exist in predestination? And must he not have acted thus in this particular instance, when he chose a people of mankind to be in this complex person as a head, and gave grace to that people so chosen, before the world began?— Now, therefore, we can meet Arius upon his own ground, and confound him even there Admitting all that he says, and says from the plain text of Scripture, about ' begotten,' ' nonexistence,' ' was not before he was made,' ' God hath made one whom he calls Word, Son, and Wisdom, by whom he did create us ,' this in no wise impugns the co-eternity, co-equality, and co-essentiality of the Lord Jesus Christ with the Father: his human person, *by* and *in* which he has thus been doing all things, *is* the creature which Arius would describe; but he who assumed this person into union with himself is *very God;* which implies, that he is all that God is.

^s *Catholici.*] *Cath* opposed to *heretical;* a Greek term (αἵρεσις αἱρετικὸς) denoting ' selection', or ' partiality,' as opposed to the profession of *the whole faith.*

^t *Publico nomine et officio*] They were publicly called, and recognised as, Christ's Church; and performed its public functions.

and not robes, dignity, revenues, and other profane trifles, which none but a madman can attribute to the Holy Spirit. Yet they are called the Church; when all who live as they did—whatever may be said of others—are in a lost state, and any thing, rather than the Church. Howbeit, under these Christ preserved his Church; yet so, as not to have it called the Church. How many saints, think you, have these sole and special inquisitors[u] of heretical pravity burnt and slain; in the course of some ages, for which they have now reigned? Such as John Huss[v] and the like; in whose time, no doubt many holy men lived, of the same spirit.

Why do you not rather express your admiration at this, Erasmus, that, from the beginning of the world, there have always existed amongst the heathens men of more excellent genius, greater erudition, and more ardent study, than amongst Christians, or the people of God? Just as Christ himself confesses, that the children of this world are wiser than the children of light. (Luke xvi. 8.) What Christian is worthy to be compared with

[u] *Soli isti inquisitores.*] Referring, not to the Inquisition only which was established about the year 1226, the Vaudois and Albigenses being the first objects of it); but to the whole system of espionage, confiscation, excommunication, and violence, with which ' the lamb-like beast' professed to be achieving the extirpation of heresy; whilst he was himself the great heresiarch.

[v] John Huss, and his fellow-martyr Jerom of Prague, were amongst the earlier and most intrepid vociferators against the Papal abuses. They were favoured with much insight into the truth of God, walking in the light, and treading in the steps, of their immediate predecessor, Wickliff; though it has been said, that they struck at the branches rather than the root of Antichrist, not sufficiently exposing the predominant corruptions in doctrine (See Milner, vol iv. p. 275.) They suffered death, under very aggravated circumstances of perfidy, fierceness, and maliciousness, by a decree of the Council of Constance, 1415, 1416; about a hundred years before Luther's time. Huss is supposed to have been Luther's swan; singing of him in his death, as one that should come after.

but Cicero only—not to mention the Greeks—in genius, erudition, and diligence? What shall we then say to have been the hindrance, that none of them hath been able to attain to grace? Certainly they have exercised the free will with all their might: and who will venture to say, that not any one of them hath been most eagerly bent upon arriving at the truth? Yet it must be asserted, that none of them hath reached it. Will you say here also, that it is incredible God should have left so many and so great men to themselves, throughout the whole course of the world, and should have suffered them to strive in vain? Assuredly, if Freewill were any thing, or could do any thing, it must have been something, and have done something, in those men; in some one of them at least. But it has effected nothing; nay, its effect has always been the opposite way. So that Freewill may be fully proved to be nothing, by this single argument; that, from the beginning of the world to the end, no sign can be shewn of it.

SEC. IX.

The Church is not yet manifested, the saints are hidden.

But to return to the point. What wonder, if God suffer all the great ones of the Church to walk in their own ways, when he has so left all nations to walk in their own ways; as Paul says in the Acts? (xiv. 16.) The Church of God is not so vulgar[x] a thing, my Erasmus, as this name, 'The Church of God,' by which it is called; nor do the saints of God meet us up and down every where, so commonly as this name of theirs, 'The Saints of God,' does. They are a pearl and noble gems; which the Spirit does not cast before swine, but, as the Scripture speaks, keeps hidden; that the

---

[x] *Vulgaris*] Properly, 'what is possessed by the common people;' 'ordinary,' 'common,' 'promiscuous;' opposed to 'rare,' 'choice,' 'what is the possession of a few.' The names 'Church of God,' and 'Saints,' are in every body's mouth; but the things signified by these names are select and few.

wicked may not see the glory of God.^y Else, if these were openly recognised by all people, how could it happen that they should be so afflicted and persecuted in the world? as Paul says, "If they had known, they would not have crucified the Lord of glory."^z

I do not say these things, as denying that those whom you mention were saints, or were the Church of God; but because it cannot be proved (should any one be disposed to deny it) that these identical persons were saints, but must be left altogether uncertain: and, consequently, an argument drawn from their saintship is not of sufficient credit^a to confirm any dogma. I call them saints, and account them such; I call, and think them to have been, the Church of God; but by the law of love, not by the law of faith: that is, charity,

Sect. X.

Distinction between judgment of faith and judgment of charity.

^y *Gloriam Dei.*] These substances are not only select, but hidden; 'the Church' is an invisible community, and the saints have no outward badge to distinguish them. If they could be discerned by the eye, that Scripture would be falsified, which saith, 'The wicked shall not see the glory of God.' I do not find this text to which he appears to refer. The Lord's people are expressly called 'his hidden ones.' Ps. lxxxiii. 3. and his act of hiding them is mentioned Ps. xxvii. 5. xxxi. 20. Also the sentiment of 'the wicked not seeing God,' is common in Scripture, though not with this allusion; which is evidently a strained one, though beautiful and just. But I do not find any Scripture which puts the two sentiments together; 'hidden, that the wicked may not see.' 'The Church,' and 'each individual saint,' is a part of that substance, 'the mystical Christ,' which God has ordained and created to his glory.

^z *Dominum gloriæ crucifixissent.*] Here again, we have a strained application of Scripture (1 Cor. ii. 8.); although the sentiment be correct. What the Apostle there says, he says of Christ personally and exclusively; but it is also true, that, in persecuting his people, they act his crucifixion over again. They are animated with the same spirit as the crucifiers; and the Lord himself has said, with application to this very case, "Why persecutest thou *Me?*"

^a *Locum satis fidelem.*] *Loc.* more strictly, 'a fund of arguments;' 'locus' et 'loci,' sunt sedes argumentorum, ex quibus ea tanquam è promptuario petuntur. *Fid.* 'fide dignus,' 'trustworthy;' like πιστός, it expresses either 'one who has faith,' or 'one towards whom faith is exercised.'

which thinketh all good of every man, and is in no wise suspicious, and believes and presumes all good of her neighbours, calls any baptized person you please,[b] 'a saint.' Nor is there any mischief, if she be mistaken: because it is the lot of charity to be deceived; exposed, as she is, to all the uses and abuses of all men; a general helper to the good and to the evil, to the faithful and to the unfaithful, to the true and to the false. But faith calls no man a saint, except he be declared such by a divine judgment. Because it is the property of faith, not to be deceived. So that, whereas, we ought all to be accounted saints mutually, by the law of charity; still, no one ought to be decreed a saint by the law of faith; as though it were an article of faith, that this or that man is a saint. It is in this way, that the Pope, that great adversary of God, who sets himself in the place of God, canonizes his saints: of whom he knows not that they are saints.[c]

How Luther would separate writers, and parts of writings.

This only I affirm, with respect to those saints of yours, or rather of ours; that, since they are at variance amongst themselves, those rather should have been followed who spoke the best things; that is, against Freewill in support of grace; and those should have been left, who, through infirmity of the flesh, have witnessed to the flesh, rather than to the Spirit. Again; those writers, who are inconsistent with themselves, should have been adopted and embraced where they speak after the Spirit, and left where they savour the flesh. This was the part of a christian reader; a clean animal, which parteth the hoof and cheweth the cud.[d] But our course has been, to post-

---

[b] *Quamvis baptisatum.*] Luther states this too broadly: the judgment of charity is moderate and indulgent; but surely there are deflections, both in faith and practice, which place many 'a baptized unbeliever' beyond the bounds of the widest enclosures of charity.

[c] See 2 Thessal. ii. 4.   [d] See Levit. xi. 3. Deut. xiv. 6.

pone the exercise of judgment, and to devour all sorts of meat indiscriminately: or, what is still more unrighteous, by a perverse exercise of judgment, we reject the better and approve the worse, in the self-same authors; and, after having done so, we affix the title and authority of their saintship to those very parts which are the worse: a title which they have deserved for their better parts, and for the Spirit only; not for their Freewill, or flesh.

'What shall we do then? The Church is a hidden community: the saints are not yet manifested. What and whom shall we believe? or, as you most shrewdly argue, who shall assure us? How shall we try their spirit?[e] If you look to erudition, there are Rabbies on both sides. If you look to the life, on both sides are sinners. If you look to Scripture, both parties embrace it with affection. Nor is the dispute so much about Scripture (which is not even yet quite clear) as about the meaning of Scripture.[f] Moreover, there are on both sides men, who, if they do not promote their cause at all by their numbers, their erudition, or their dignity; much less do so, by their fewness, their ignorance, and their meanness. The matter is therefore left in doubt, and the dispute remains still under the hands of the judge: so that it seems as if we should act most prudently in withdrawing, as a body, into the sentiment of the Sceptics; unless we should rather choose to follow your best of all examples, who profess to be just in such a state of doubt, as enables you to testify, that you are still a seeker and a learner of

Erasmus's perplexity and advice stated; in some degree admitted, but amended.

[e] *Unde explorabimus Spiritum*] Referring to 1 John iv. 1. Erasmus talks about *Paul's* recommending to try the spirits, but evidently his allusion is to these words of St John.

[f] *Neque adeo de Scripturâ.*] It is not so much the authority of Scripture, as its right interpretation, which is in dispute. *Quæ necdum* Want of clearness is hinted rather than affirmed; 'necdum' implies, 'notwithstanding all that has been written and decreed about it.'

the truth; inclining to that side which asserts the freedom of the will, only just until truth shall have made herself manifest.'

To this I reply, 'What you say here is the truth, but not the whole truth.'[g] For we shall not try the spirits by arguments drawn from the erudition, life, genius, multitude, dignity, ignorance, rudeness, paucity, or meanness of the disputants. Nor do I approve those, who place their refuge in a boast that they have the Spirit. For I have had a very severe contest this year,[h] and am still maintaining it, with those fanatics who subject the Scriptures to the interpretation of their own spirit. Nay, it is on this ground, that I have hitherto inveighed against the Pope himself; in whose kingdom nothing is more commonly urged, or more commonly received, than this saying, 'That the Scriptures are obscure and ambiguous;' 'that we must seek the interpreting spirit from the Apostolic See of Rome.' There cannot be a more pernicious assertion than this; from which ungodly men have taken occasion to exalt themselves above the Scriptures, and to fabricate just what they pleased: till at length, having quite trodden the Scriptures under foot, we were believing and teaching nothing but the dreams of madmen. In a word, this saying is no human invention, but a mouthful of poison sent into the world by the incredible malice of the very prince of all the devils.

SEC. XII.

There are two tribunals for the

This is *our* assertion; that the spirits are to be tried and proved by two sorts of judgment. One of these is internal; by which, the man who has been enlightened by the Holy Spirit, or special gift of

---

[g] *Neque nihil, neque omnia dicis*] Erasmus says rightly, 'the spirits must be tried,' wrongly, 'that there is no test of them' Also, the tests he proposes are bad

[h] It was in 1525 (the date of his performance), that Luther published his 'Address to the Celestial Prophets and Carolstadt.'

God, for his own sake and for his own individual salvation, doth, with the greatest certainty, judge and discern the dogmas and thoughts of all men. Of this judgment the Apostle speaks, 1 Cor. ii. 15. " He that is spiritual judgeth all things, and is judged of no man." This judgment appertains to faith; and is necessary even to every private Christian. I have called it above 'the internal clearness of Holy Scripture.'¹ Perhaps, this is what was meant by those who have replied to you, 'that every thing must be determined by the judgment of the Spirit.' But this judgment is of no profit to any other person besides ourselves, and is not the subject of inquiry in this cause: nor does any one, I dare say, doubt that this judgment is just what I state it to be.

spirits of men, one private, the other public.

There is, therefore, another judgment, which is external; and by which we, not only for ourselves, but for others, and for the salvation of others, do with the greatest certainty judge the spirits and dogmas of all men. This is the judgment of the public ministry, an outward office, appealing to the word: what belongs chiefly to the leaders of the people, and preachers of the word.ᵏ We use it to confirm the weak, and to

---

¹ See Part i. Sect. iv.

ᵏ *Judicium publici ministerii in verbo*] *Minis* 'The office, or body, of ministers.' *In verbo.* The word is to them, what the law of the land is to a civil judge. *Offic exter.* opposed to an internal function, or operation. Luther refers to the judgment of a synod, or council; a tribunal, to which he always declared himself willing to submit his own obnoxious assertions. He states the matter too broadly, and was guided by an image which he had in his mind of what might be, rather than by any exhibition of this external judgment which he had ever seen, or could appeal to as an example. A synod of real saints might be confidently looked to, as decreeing under the illumination of a light from above. But when has such a synod met since the council of Jerusalem? (Acts xv. 1—31.) If, as it is probable, there be real saints in the council, who is to ensure their being the majority? Whilst great respect, therefore, is due to a judgment of this kind, it cannot be that infallible one, which Luther's commendations might seem to imply.

PART II.— confute the gainsayers. I have called this above
'the external clearness of Holy Scripture.' Our
assertion is, ' Let all the spirits be tried in the
face of the Church at the bar of Scripture.' For
it ought to be a first principle, most firmly maintained amongst Christians, that the Holy Scriptures are a spiritual light, far brighter than the
sun; especially in those things which pertain to
salvation, or are necessary.

SEC XIII. But, since we have now for a long time been
persuaded to a contrary opinion by that pestilent
Clearness saying of the Sophists, ' That the Scriptures are
of Scripture prov- obscure and ambiguous;' I am compelled, in the
ed, by testi- first place, to prove that very first principle of
monies
from the ours, by which all the rest are to be proved:—
Old Testa- what would to philosophers appear absurd and
ment. impossible.

First, then, Moses says (Deut. xvii. 8), that, if
any difficult cause should arise, they must go up
to the place which God hath chosen for his name,

It is not strictly parallel to the ' external clearness' of Scripture; which he refers to, as asserted, Part i. Sect iv. The
testimony may be imperfectly brought out; or the judges may
not have eyes to see it. Would Luther undertake to say, that
he should himself bring all the testimony that is in the Scriptures, to bear upon any given question, or would he, had he
been able to cite it, have convinced the Council of Constance,
or the Council of Trent? After all, the private and internal
judgment which he speaks of; the Spirit shining upon and confirming his testimony by the word, is that which the spiritual
man must, and will, at last resort to, and can alone depend
upon. He is thankful for, and in some sense obedient to, the
judgment of pure synods (pure as such compounds can be expected to be), but to a higher Master he standeth or falleth.
" This I say then, walk in" (or *after*) "the spirit." (Gal. v. 16.)
—Enough for Luther's purpose may, however, be admitted. Let
all dogmas be brought to the standard of Scripture, *publicly;*
let the leaders and counsellors of the people declare upon them,
stating the grounds of their decision. Such judgment will
have its weight, though not paramount; and it will be manifested how slender, or how false, are the foundations of error.
This object is obtained, in a great degree, now, by the free
canvass which religious, as well as other opinions, are made to
submit to, from the press.

and there consult the Priests, who must judge it
according to the law of the Lord. " According
to the law of the Lord," saith he. But how shall
they judge, except the law of the Lord, wherewith
the people must be satisfied, were externally [1] most
plain? Else, it were enough to say, 'They shall
judge according to their own spirit.' Nay, the
truth is, that in every civil government, all the
causes of all the subjects are settled by the laws.
But how could they be settled, except the laws
were most certain, and just like so many shining
lights amongst the people. For, if the laws were
ambiguous and uncertain, not only would it be
impossible that any causes should be decided, but
there could be no certain standard of manners:
since laws are made for this very purpose, that
the manners of the people may be regulated by a
certain model; and the principles by which causes
are to be determined, may be defined.[m] That
which is to be the standard and measure of other
things, ought itself to be by much the surest and
clearest of all things: and such a sort of thing is
the law. Now, if this light and certainty in their
laws be both necessary, and also conceded freely
to the whole world, by a divine gift, in profane
governments (which are conversant about temporal things); how is it possible, that God should
not have granted laws and rules of much greater
light and certainty to his christian people (*his
chosen*, forsooth); whereby to direct their own
hearts and lives individually, and to settle all their
causes? since He would have temporal things to
be despised by his children? For, "if God so

[1] *Externè*] As opposed to a light of the Spirit, *within* the soul

[m] *Causarum quæstiones definiantur.*] The book of the laws lays down and recognises certain broad principles, to which the facts of each case are applied. These principles must be determinately fixed, admitted, and perspicuously affirmed. '*Status causæ*,' is the question of fact, at issue; '*quæstio causæ*,' the law principle to which it is referable.

clothe the grass, which to day is, and to-morrow is cast into the oven, how much more shall he clothe us?"—But let us go on to overwhelm this pestilent saying of the Sophists with Scripture.

The nineteenth Psalm (ver. 8) says, "The commandment of the Lord is lightsome, or pure; enlightening the eyes." I suppose that which enlightens the eyes, is not obscure, or ambiguous.

So the 119th Psalm (ver. 130) says, "The door of thy words enlighteneth; it giveth understanding to thy little ones." Here he attributes to the words of God that they are 'a door,' 'a something set open;' what is exposed to the view of all, and enlightens even the little ones.

Isaiah viii. (ver. 20) sends all questions to the law, and to the testimony; threatening, that the light of the morning shall be denied us, unless we do so.[n]

In Zech. ii.[o] he commands them to seek the law from the mouth of the Priest, as being the messenger of the Lord of Hosts. Pretty messenger or ambassador of the Lord, forsooth, if he speak those things which are both ambiguous in themselves, and obscure to the people; so that *he* is as ignorant of what he speaks, as *they* are of what they hear.

And what is more frequently said to the praise of Scripture, throughout the whole of the Old Testament, and especially throughout that single hundred and nineteenth Psalm, than that it is in itself

---

[n] In our version, it is not a threat, but an explanation of a fact "If they speak not according to this word, it is because there is no light in them."—A testimony equally conclusive as to the clearness of the word; for how are we to compare declarations, and ascertain their conformity with the written word, if that word be not plain?

[o] A false reference. the words are found in Malachi ii. 7. "For the Priest's lips should keep knowledge, and they should seek the law at his mouth; for he is the messenger of the Lord of Hosts."

a most certain and a most evident light? For thus he celebrates its clearness, "Thy word is a lamp unto my feet, and a light unto my paths." (v. 105.) He says not, 'Thy Spirit only is a lamp unto my feet:' albeit, he assigns its office to this also; saying, "Thy good Spirit shall conduct me forth[p] in a right land." Thus, it is called both a 'way' and 'a path;'[q] doubtless, from its exceeding great certainty.

Clearness of Scripture proved, by testimonies from the New Testament

Let us come to the New Testament. Paul says (Rom. i. 2.), that the Gospel was promised by the Prophets in the Holy Scriptures: and in chap. iii. that the righteousness of faith was witnessed by the law and the Prophets. (Ver. 21.) But what sort of a witnessing was this, if obscure? Nay, he not only makes the Gospel 'the word of light,' 'the gospel of clearness,' in all his Epistles; but does this professedly, and with great abundance of words, in 2 Cor. iii. and iv. where he reasons boastfully upon the clearness, as well of Moses as of Christ.[r]

Peter also says (2 Peter i. 19), "We have a very sure word of prophecy; whereunto ye do well that ye take heed, as unto a light that shineth in a dark place." Here Peter makes the word of God a clear lamp, and all other things darkness: and do we make obscurity and darkness of it?

Christ so often calls himself "the light of the world," and John the Baptist "a burning and a shining light;" not because of the sanctity of their lives, doubtless; but because of the word: just

[p] *Deducet.*] Like the προπέμπω of the Greeks, expresses 'the escorting' of a person to his home.

[q] *Via et semita*] *Via*, 'the broad carriage-road,' *semita*, 'the narrow foot-path.'

[r] *Gloriosè disputat*] The Apostle institutes a comparison (in chap iii) between the glory of the Gospel ministry and that of Moses; shewing the superiority of the former. The scope and effect of the comparison is to magnify his own office: but the clearness of both is assumed, as the very basis of the argument; a clearness, indicated in Moses by the glory of his countenance.

as Paul calls the Philippians "bright lights of the world;" "because ye hold fast[s] the word of life," says he. For, without the wo rd,life is uncertain and obscure.

And what are the Apostles about, when they prove their own preachings by the Scriptures? Is it, that they may darken their own darkness to us, by greater darkness? or, is it to prove the more known thing by one more unknown? What is Christ about, in John v. (ver. 39.) when he teaches the Jews to search the Scriptures; as being his witnesses, forsooth? Is it that he may render them doubtful about the faith of him?[t] What are those persons about, in Acts xviii. (ver. 2.) who, on hearing Paul, read the Scriptures day. and night, to see whether those things were so? Do not all these things prove, that the Apostles, as well as Christ himself, appeal to the Scriptures, as the clearest witnesses to the truth of their discourses? With what face, then, do we represent them as obscure?

I beg to know, whether these words of Scripture are obscure or ambiguous, "God created the heavens and the earth;" "and the word was made flesh;" and all those affirmations which the whole world has received as articles of faith: and whence received them, but from the Scriptures? And what are those about, who preach still to this day? Do they interpret and declare[u] the Scrip-

[s] Our translation says " holding forth," Luther says " tenetis:" the original word is ἐπέχοντες· ' exhibeo,' ' præ me fero.' But it must be possessed, before it can be held forth ; and, if on this account they be called " lights," what must the word itself be ?

[t] *De fide sui*] If these witnesses were doubtful, not clear; he would be justifying them in their unbelief, instead of establishing his claim to be received.

[u] *Declarant*] ' Make clear,' or ' cause to be seen ,' it refers to the *matter* of Scripture, as *interpretantur* does to the *meaning of the terms*: an ' avowing,' ' propounding,' or ' distinctly setting forth to the world,' of the testimony, or truth of God, which is contained and shut up in the Scriptures.

tures? If the Scripture, which they declare, be obscure; who is to assure us, that even this declaration of it is certain? Another new declaration? What shall declare that also? At this rate, we shall have an endless progression. In fine, if Scripture be obscure or doubtful, what need was there for it to be declared to us by God from heaven? Are we not sufficiently obscure and ambiguous, without having our obscurity, ambiguity, and darkness increased to us from heaven? What will then become of that saying of the Apostle, "All Scripture, having been given by inspiration of God, is profitable for teaching, for reproving, and for convincing?" (2 Tim. iii. 16.) Nay, it is absolutely useless, Paul! and what thou attributest to Scripture must be sought from the Fathers, who have been received for a long series of ages, and from the Roman see! Thy sentence, therefore, must be revoked, which thou writest to Titus, "That a bishop must be mighty in sound doctrine, that he may be able both to exhort and to refute the gainsayers, and to stop the mouth of vain-talkers and soul-deceivers." How shall he be mighty, when thou leavest him the Scriptures obscure; that is, arms of flax; and, for a sword, light stubble? Then must Christ also recant his own word, who falsely promises us, "I will give you a mouth and wisdom, which all your adversaries shall not be able to resist." How shall they not resist, when we fight against them with obscure and uncertain weapons?—Why dost *thou* also prescribe a form of Christianity to us, if the Scriptures are obscure to thee?

But I think I have long been burdensome, even to men of no sensibility, in making so long delay, and so wasting my forces ᵛ on a proposition which is most evident. But it was necessary to over-

---

ᵛ *Tantas moras traho et copias perdo*] His 'copiæ' are his Scripture testimonies and reasonings.

PART II. whelm that impudent and blasphemous saying, 'The Scriptures are obscure;' that you also might see, my Erasmus, what it is you say, when you deny the Scripture to be quite clear. For you must, at the same time, assent to me, that all your saints, whom you adduce, are much less clear. For who shall assure us of their light, if you make out the Scriptures to be obscure? So that those, who deny the Scriptures to be most clear and most evident,[x] leave us nothing but darkness.

SEC. XV.

The conclusion is, if the dogma of Freewill be obscure, it is not in Scripture.

But here you will say, 'All this is nothing to me; I do not say that the Scriptures are obscure upon all subjects (for who would be mad enough to say so?); but only on this, and the like.' My answer is; neither do I assert these things in opposition to you only, but in opposition to all who think as you do. And again: in opposition to you distinctly; I affirm, with respect to the whole Scripture, that I will not allow any part of it to be called obscure. What I have cited from Peter stands good here; that "the word of God is a lamp shining to us in a dark place."[y] Now, if there be a part of this lamp which shineth not; it will become part of the dark place, rather than of the lamp itself. Christ has not so enlightened us, as wilfully to leave some part of his word dark; when he, at the same time, commands us to give heed to it: for in vain he commands us to give heed, if it doth not shine.

So that, if the dogma of Freewill be obscure or ambiguous; it belongeth not to Christians and to the Scriptures, and should be altogether aban-

[x] *Lucidissimas et evidentissimas.*] *Luc.* 'their testimony unequivocal;' *evid.* 'the terms in which that testimony is conveyed, unambiguous.'—So that they may be compared to some of those beautiful orbs above us; which are not only luminous, but exposed to view.

[y] See above, Sect. xiv. *Stat ibi.* 'qui vigent,' 'in statu suo manent,' 'incolumes sunt,' 'dignitatem suam retinent;' nonnunquam stare dicuntur: opposed to 'concido;' 'loses none of its authority here.'

doned, and ranked amongst those fables, which Paul condemns Christians for wrangling about.[z] For, if it belong to Christians and to the Scriptures, it ought to be clear, open, and evident, and just like all the other articles of the faith: which are most evident. For, all the articles, which Christians receive, ought not only to be most certain to themselves, but also fortified against the assaults of other men, by such manifest and clear Scriptures, that they shut every man's mouth from having power to say any thing against them: as Christ says in his promise, "I will give you a mouth and wisdom, which all your adversaries shall not be able to resist." If, therefore, our mouth be so weak in the behalf of this dogma, that our adversaries can resist it; what he says is false, that no adversary can resist our mouth. So that, we shall either meet with no adversaries, whilst maintaining the dogma of Freewill (which will be the case if it does not belong to us); or, if it do belong to us, we shall have adversaries, it is true; but they shall be such as cannot resist us.

But this inability of the adversaries to resist (since the mention of it has occurred here) consisteth not in their being compelled to abandon their own humour,[a] or being persuaded either to

Meaning and exemplifications of the promise, 'All

---

[z] *Christianis rixantibus.*] Luther does not appear to refer to any single text explicitly, but to the many warnings of this kind, which are dispersed throughout the Epistles to Timothy and Titus. The nearest references seem to be, 1 Tim. i. 4, 6. ("Neither give heed to fables and endless genealogies, which minister questions rather than godly edifying, which is in faith"...."From which some having swerved, have turned aside unto vain jangling") 2 Tim ii 23 ("But foolish and unlearned questions avoid, knowing that they do gender strifes.") And Titus iii 9. ("But avoid foolish questions, and genealogies, and contentions, and strivings about the law, for they are unprofitable and vain")

[a] *Sensu suo cedere*] 'Sensus' is properly, 'the frame of thought, or of feeling,' whatever that be, 'the state of mind.' 'Communis sensus,' which follows just below, is properly, 'the common judgment, or feeling, of mankind;' and is

confess or to be silent. For who shall compel the unwilling to believe, to confess their error, or to be silent? What is more loquacious than vanity, says Augustine?—But their mouth is so far stopped, that they have nothing to say in reply; and, though they say much in reply, yet, in the judgment of common sense, they say nothing. This is best shewn by examples. When Christ had put the Sadducees to silence (Matt. xxii. 23—32.), by citing Scripture, and proving the resurrection of the dead from the words of Moses (Exod. iii. 6.), "I am the God of Abraham, &c.".... "He is not the God of the dead, but of the living—" upon this, they could not resist, or say any thing in reply. But did they, therefore, recede from their opinion?—And, how often did he confute the Pharisees, by the most evident Scriptures and arguments; so that the people clearly saw them convicted, and they themselves perceived it? Still, however, they continued his adversaries. Stephen, in Acts vii.[b] so spake, according to Luke, that "they were not able to resist the wisdom and the Spirit which spake in him." But what was their conduct? Did they yield? So far from it, being ashamed to be overcome, and having no power to resist, they go mad; and, stopping their eyes and ears, suborn false witnesses against him. (Acts vi. 10—14.) See how he stands before the council, and confutes his

---

thence transferred to express a certain imaginary standard of judgment, or court of appeal, the voice of unadulterated and unsophisticated nature, which we call 'common sense.'

[b] This should be Acts vi. (v. 10) There is a good deal of confusion in Luther's reference to this history. He represents the violence with which they rushed upon him at the close of his defence (especially when he had testified ' that he saw the heavens opened, and the Son of man standing on the right hand of God'), as having been expressed before his apprehension and arraignment, and refers the whole transaction to Acts vii.; of which the first incidents are recorded in the preceding chapter.

adversaries! After having enumerated the benefits which God had bestowed upon that people, from their origin, and having proved that God had never ordered a Temple to be built to him (for on this charge he was tried, and this was the point of fact at issue);*c* he at length concedes, that a Temple

c Reus agebatur.] *Re ag.* 'He was arraigned;' *ed quæstione,* ' on this indictment;' this was the law-crime charged *status causæ,* ' the question of fact to be tried.'—Luther intimates, that his address to the council is resolvable into this main subject; ' a defence against the charge of having blasphemed the Temple.' Such being the charge preferred against him, he repelled it, by maintaining that it was nothing criminal to speak against the Temple; for *that* was not God's ordinance. Probably, he had been led by the Holy Ghost, to aim at beating down the idolatrous attachment which the Jews shewed to their Temple, in his reasonings with those who arose and disputed with him. But it is expressly said, "they suborned men which said, We have heard him speak blasphemous words against Moses, and against God." (Acts vi 11.) And afterwards, "And set up false witnesses, which said, This man ceaseth not to speak blasphemous words against this holy place, and the law." (Acts vi 13.)—It should seem, therefore, that more was charged against him, with respect to this blasphemy, than he had really spoken.—Perhaps his defence, or, as I would rather call it, his address; may be correctly said to have had a broader basis than that of merely repelling a charge of having blasphemed the Temple; viz. that of proving, that the great body of their nation had always been " resisters " of the Holy Ghost; and by inference, therefore, that they were such now, in what they had done to Jesus From the Patriarchs downwards, their plans and efforts had always been in direct opposition to the counsel and purpose of God, as declared to them by those in whom the Holy Ghost spake (See Heb. i 1, 2. Gr.) Whatever was the accusation, and however he might design to repel it, the clue to his discourse seems to be found in vv. 51—53 " Ye stiffnecked and uncircumcised in heart and ears, ye do always resist the Holy Ghost"—(not as striving *in their own souls,* but as testifying in those whom God sent to be his instruments for drawing out the enmity of their carnal mind)—"as your fathers did, so do ye "—On this broader basis, however, he contrives to build an answer to his own peculiar charge respecting the Temple; by shewing, that this very Temple furnished one proof of their resistance to the Holy Ghost—their idolized Temple had not originated from God, but was man's device. It was, in fact, David's own suggestion, which he was forbidden to execute, and was rather acquiesced in, than appointed of God (just as in the former case of appointing

had indeed been built to him, under Solomon. But then he abates the force of his concession,[d] by subjoining after this manner; "Howbeit the Most High dwelleth not in temples made with hands :" and, in proof of this, he alleges the last chapter of the Prophet Isaiah, " What house is this that ye build unto me?" (Isa. lxvi. 1.) Tell me, what could they say now, against so plain a Scripture ? But they, nothing moved by it, remained fixed in their own sentiment. Which leads him to inveigh against *them* also:[e] " Ye uncircumcised in heart and ears, ye do always resist the Holy Ghost." ' They resist,' he says; whereas, in point of fact, they were not able to resist.

Let us come to the men of our day.[f] When John Huss disputes after this manner against the Pope, from Matt. xvi. 18, &c. " The gates of hell prevail not against my Church." (Is there any

[a king, 1 Sam viii—xii) ; when the honour of building it was appropriated to Solomon. (2 Sam. vii. 1 Chron. xvii.) God's Temple (not only the spiritual one, but the material fabric also) was deferred till the latter times (Ezek. xl.—xlviii) ; and Solomon's was but an abortive birth, arising from the precocity of man: the Lord giving way, as it were, to man's device, that he might shew him its instability and vanity. God instituted a tabernacle ("Our fathers had the tabernacle of witness in the wilderness, as he had appointed, speaking unto Moses, that he should make it according to the fashion that he had seen " Acts vii. 44. &c. &c)—a fabric more suited to the then state of his Church and nation—but the well-meaning vanity of his aspiring worshippers, would have a stately temple : as if walls and roofs could contain him! " Howbeit the Most High &c."

[d] *Subsumit.*] I do not find any authority for this word; but, taking the general principle of the preposition *sub*, when used in composition (*secretly, diminutively*) , the amplification in the text seems most nearly to express the author's meaning. ' Tandem concedit ..... At ibi subsumit :' *subs* implies ' a secret, or partial, retraction of his concession.'

[e] *Unde et in eos*] In contradistinction to their fathers.

[f] The Council of Constance, A. D. 1415 was Luther's day; and even *our* day, as compared with that of Christ and his first Martyr.

obscurity or ambiguity in these words?) But against the Pope, and his abettors, the gates of hell *do* prevail; since they are notorious for their manifest impiety and wickednesses all the world over. (Is this also obscure?) Therefore the Pope and his partisans are not that Church of which Christ speaks.—What could they hereupon say against him; or how could they resist the mouth, which Christ had given him? Yet they *did* resist, and persevered in their resistance, till they burnt him: so far were they from altering their mind. Nor does Christ suppress this, when he says, 'the adversaries shall not be able to resist.' They are adversaries, says he; therefore they will resist. If they did not resist, they would not be adversaries, but friends; and yet they shall not be able to resist. What is this, but to say, that, resisting, they shall not be able to resist?

SC. XVII.
————

Now, if we also shall be able so to confute Free-will, as that our adversaries cannot resist; even though they retain their own humour, and, in spite of conscience, hold fast their resistance; we shall have done enough. For I have had abundant experience, that no man chooses to be conquered; and, as Quintilian says, 'there is no one who would not rather seem to know, than to be a learner:' although it be a sort of proverb in every body's mouth amongst us (from use, I should rather say abuse, more than affection), 'I wish to learn; I am ready to be taught; and, when taught better things, to follow them. I am a man; I may err.' The truth is, men use such expressions as these, because, under this fair mask, as under a shew of humility, they are allowed confidently to say, 'I am not satisfied; I do not understand him; he does violence to the Scriptures; he is an obstinate assertor:' because they are sure, forsooth, that no one can suspect such

We must be content with this sort of victory. Our adversary will not confess himself beaten.

PART II. humble souls, as theirs, of being pertinacious in their resistance to truth; and of making a stout attack upon her, when now they have even recognised her presence.[g] So then, it ought not to be ascribed to their own perverseness, that they keep their old mind; but to the obscurity and ambiguity of the arguments, with which they are assailed.

This was just the conduct of the Greek philosophers also: that none of them might seem to yield to another, even though manifestly overcome, they began to deny first-principles; as Aristotle recites. Meanwhile, we kindly persuade ourselves and others, that there are many good men in the world, who would be willing to embrace the truth, if they had but a teacher who could make things plain to them; and that it is not to be presumed, that so many learned men, through such a series of ages, have been in error, or that they have not thoroughly understood the truth. As if we did not know, that the world is the kingdom of Satan: in which, besides the blindness adherent as a sort of natural excrescence to our flesh, spirits even of the most mischievous nature having dominion over us, we are hardened in that very blindness; and now no longer held in chains of mere human darkness, but of a darkness imposed upon us by devils.

SC. XVIII. 'If the Scriptures then be quite clear, why have men of excellent understanding, you say, been for so many ages blind upon this subject?' I answer, 'they have been thus blind, unto the praise and glory of Freewill: that this magnificently boasted power, by which man is able to apply himself to those things which concern his everlasting salva-

Why great geniuses have been blind about Freewill: viz. that they might

[g] *Pertinaciter resistere, fortiter impugnare.*] The unsuspected case was the real case notwithstanding all his ostentatious professions of humility, Erasmus was not only rejecting clearest evidences of truth—which is bad enough—but even fighting against *what he knew to be truth*—which is far worse.

tion; this power, I say, which neither sees what it sees, nor hears what it hears—much less understands or seeks after these things; might be shewn to be what it is. For to this belongs, what, Christ and his Evangelists so often assert from Isaiah, "Hearing, ye shall hear and shall not understand; and seeing, ye shall see and shall not perceive." What does this mean, but that the free will, or human heart, is so trodden under foot of Satan, that, except it be miraculously[h] raised up by the Spirit of God, it cannot of itself either see or hear those things which strike upon the very eyes and ears, so manifestly as to be palpable to the hand: such is the misery and blindness of the human race. For it is thus, that even the Evangelists themselves, after expressing their wonder how it should happen that the Jews were not taken with the works and words of Christ—which were absolutely irresistible and undeniable—reply to their own expressions of wonder, by citing this passage of Scripture:[i] by suggesting, forsooth, that man, left to himself, seeing sees not, and hearing hears not. What can be more marvellous? "The light," saith he, "shineth in darkness, and the darkness apprehendeth it not."

SC.XVIII.
——
expose Freewill.
But no wonder, that the natural man is blind to the things of God.

[h] *Mirabiliter suscitetur*] Mir. would express either the *nature* or the *degree* of influence exerted; but here it must be the *nature* — the very least degree of the Holy Ghost's regenerating energy, applied to the natural soul, produces this result, an energy which admits not of degrees. One soul is not more *regenerated* than another: and every such act of regeneration is a miracle; an exercise of super-creation grace and of supernatural power, effecting a supernatural constitution and state, in those that are the subjects of it. "Except a man be *begotten from above*, he cannot see the kingdom of God." "Except a man be begotten of water and of the Spirit, he cannot enter into the kingdom of God." "Of his own will *begat* he us by the word of truth." "Every one that doeth righteousness hath been *begotten* of him."

[i] See especially John xii. 37—41. It is remarkable that this passage of Isaiah is quoted more often than any other in the New Testament; being found in each of the Evangelists, in Acts xxviii, and in Rom. xi.

(John i. 5.[k]) Who would believe this? who ever heard the like? that the light shineth in darkness; and yet the darkness remains darkness, and is not made light?

Besides, it is nothing wonderful, that men of excellent understanding have for so many ages been blind in divine things. In human things, it would be wonderful. In divine things, the wonder rather is, if one or two be not blind; whilst it is no wonder at all, if all, without exception, be blind. For what is the whole human race, without the Spirit, but the kingdom of the devil, as I have said; a confused chaos of darkness? Whence Paul calls the devils, "the rulers of this darkness;" and says (1 Cor. ii. 8.), "None of the princes of this world knew the wisdom of God!" What do you suppose that he thought of the rest, when he asserts that the princes of the world were slaves of darkness? For, by princes, he means the first and highest persons in the world: whom you call men of excellent understanding. Why were all the Arians blind? Were there not, amongst them, men of excellent understanding? Why is Christ "foolishness" to the Gentiles?[1] Are there not amongst the Gentiles men of excellent understanding? Why is he to the Jews "a stumbling-block?" Have there not been amongst the Jews men of excellent understanding? "God knoweth the thoughts of the wise," says Paul;

[k] *Apprehendunt*] More proper than our version 'comprehend;' which implies 'compassing about,' and so (translatively) 'taking in the whole of a substance:' οὐ κατέλαβεν αὐτό· 'did not lay hold of it, so as to possess it;' 'did not receive,' or 'admit' the 'light;' but (as Luther explains it) remained darkness still. See Sleusner in v. καταλαμβάνω· 'excipio,' 'admitto'

[1] 1 Cor. i. 23. Our authorized version, and most copies, read "Greeks." by which St. Paul frequently denominates that part of the world which is not Jewish; as Rom. i. 16. It would seem to give more point to Luther's antithesis here: but "Gentiles" is the more authentic reading. See Griesbach's text and note in loc.

"for they are vain." He would not say, " of men," as the text itself has it;[m] but singles out 'the first and chiefest amongst men:' that from these we may estimate the rest of them.

But I shall perhaps speak more at large of these things, hereafter. Suffice it, for an exordium, to have premised 'that the Scriptures are most clear;' and 'that, by these our dogmas may be so defended, as that our adversaries shall not be able to resist.' Those dogmas, which cannot be so defended, are other people's; and do not belong to Christians. Now, if there be those who do not see this clearness, and are blind, or stumble, in this sunshine; these, on the supposition that they are ungodly men, shew how great is the majesty and power of Satan in the sons of men: even such, that they neither hear nor apprehend the clearest words of God. Just as if a man, beguiled by some sleight of hand trick, should suppose the sun to be a piece of unlighted coal, or should imagine[n] a stone to be gold! On the supposition that they are godly persons, let them be reckoned amongst those of the elect, who are led into error some little, that the power of God may be shewn in us: without which, we can neither see, nor do any thing at all. For, it is not weakness of intellect (as you complain), which hinders the words of God from being apprehended: on the contrary, nothing is more adapted to the apprehension of the words of God, than weakness of intellect. For, it is because of the weak, and unto the weak, that Christ both came, and also sends his word. But it is the mischievousness of Satan, who sits and reigns in our weakness, resisting the

[m] Psalm xciv. 11.
[n] *Putet, sentiat.*] *Put.* is rather matter of reasoning and argument; *sent.* rather matter of sense. Both are intermixed here, though each has its distinct appropriation: he thinks about the sun, he handles the stone.—A double error is pointed out by the illustration. These ungodly men *assert* what is not, and *deny* what is.

PART II.

SC. XIX.

Erasmus shewn to have admitted that Scripture is clear.

word of God. If it were not for this acting of Satan, the whole world of men would be converted by one single word of God, once heard; nor would there be any need of more.°
And why do I plead long? why do we not finish the cause together with this exordium, and give sentence against you, on the testimony of your own words? according to that saying of Christ, "By thy words thou shalt be justified, and by thy words thou shalt be condemned."ᴾ (Matt. xii. 37.) You assert, ' that the Scripture is not clear upon this point:' and then, as though the sentence of the judge were suspended, you dispute on both sides of the question, advancing all that can be said both *for* and *against* Freewill. This is all that you seek to gain by your whole performance; which, for the same reason, you have chosen to call a Diatribe rather than an Apophasis,ᑫ or any thing else: because you write with the intention of bringing all the materials of the cause together, without affirming any thing. If the Scripture, then, be not plain, how comes it that those of whom you make your boast; that is, so numerous a series of the most learned men, whom the consent of so many ages hath approved even to this very day; are not only blind upon this

° Luther does not distinguish here, as he ought to do, between what Satan *has made of us*, and what Satan *personally does in us*. The soul of man, in its natural state, is so blinded and hardened and satanized, that, even if there were no immediate agency of his upon any individual soul, the effect of ' one', or even ' many' words of God (unaccompanied by his quickening Spirit) would not be such as Luther describes; but it would still reject the truth!

ᴾ A forced application of the words. The Lord is there speaking of the words being a sure index of the mind. Luther seems to have got some confusion into his mind, from Luke xix. 22 " Out of thine own mouth will I judge thee, &c."

ᑫ A Greek term, which may express either 'affirmation' or ' negation;' but here clearly denotes the former: with allusion either to the ' explicit avowal of private opinion;' or, to ' the judge delivering his sentence in court.'

subject, but even rash and foolish enough to define and assert Freewill from the Scripture, as though that Scripture were positive and plain. The greater number of these men come recommended to us, you say, not only by a wonderful knowledge of the sacred writings, but by piety of life. Some of them, after having defended the doctrine of Christ by their writings, gave testimony to it with their blood. If you say this sincerely, it is a settled thing with you, that Freewill has assertors endowed with wonderful skill in the Scriptures; who have borne witness to it as a part of Christ's doctrine with their blood. If this be true, they must have considered the Scripture as clear: else, how should they be said to possess a wonderful skill in the sacred writings? Besides, what levity and temerity of mind would it have been in them, to shed their blood for a thing that is uncertain and obscure? This is not the act of Christ's martyrs, but of devils.

'' ʳ Now, therefore, do you also ' set before your eyes and weigh with yourself, whether you judge, that more ought to be attributed to the prior judgments ˢ of so many learned men, so many orthodox men, so many holy men, so many martyrs, so many ancient and modern theologians, so many universities, so many councils, so many bishops, and so many popes—who have thought the Scriptures clear, and have confirmed their opinion by their blood, as well as by their writings—or to your

ʳ *Jam et tu pone*] Luther here retorts Erasmus's own words upon him. "Et tamen illud interim lectorem admonitum velim, si etc ...ut tum denique sibi ponat ob oculos tam numerosam seriem eruditissimorum virorum etc....tum illud secum expendat, utrum plus tribuendum esse judicet tot eruditorum, tot orthodoxorum etc..... præjudiciis, an unius aut alterius privato judicio.'

ˢ *Præjudicus*] A forensic term, expressing either, 1 ' precedents which apply to an undecided cause,' or, 2. ' matters relating to the cause in hand, which have already been decided;' or, 3. ' a previous judgment of the cause itself;' as here. These men had sat in judgment upon this question before, and had decided it.

PART II. own single judgment—which is that of a private individual—denying the Scriptures to be clear:' when, it may be, you have never sent forth one tear, or one sigh, for the doctrine of Christ. If you believe these men to have thought correctly, why not follow their example? If otherwise, why boast yourself with such a puffed cheek and such a full mouth; as if you would overwhelm me with a sort of tempest and flood of words: which falls, however, with still greater force upon your own head, whilst *my* ark rides aloft in security. For you, in the same instant, attribute the greatest folly and temerity to these so many and so great ones; when you write, that they were most skilful in the Scriptures, yet have asserted by their pen, by their life, and by their death, a sentiment which you nevertheless maintain to be obscure and ambiguous. What is this but to make them most ignorant in knowledge, and most foolish in assertion? I, their private despiser, should never have paid them such honour, as you, their public commender, do.[t]

SEC. XX.

Erasmus reduced to a dilemma.

I hold you fast then, here, by a horned syllogism, as they call it:[u] for one or other of these two things must be false; either what you say, ' that these men were worthy to be admired for their knowledge of the sacred writings, life and martyrdom;' or what you say, 'that the Scripture is not plain.' But, since you would rather choose

[t] *Privatus* &c.] The substance is, ' Insignificant Luther, whom Erasmus taunted with his obscurity, and with his contempt of these great men (though, in fact, he had only shaken off the yoke of their undue authority, without expressing any sentiment of contempt), would never have so vilified them in his privacy, as Erasmus—the man of name and fame—was doing by his public extolment of them.'

[u] *Cornuto syllogismo*] *Corn. syll* Dilemma; so called, because the horns of the argument are, in this kind of syllogism, so disposed, that to escape the one you must run upon the other. The term ' horns' is applied to argumentation, from a certain disposition of forces, as well naval as military, in which they resemble the horns of the crescent moon.

to be driven upon this horn of the two, 'that the Scripture is not plain' (what you are driving at throughout your whole book); it remains, that you must have pronounced them to be most expert in Scripture, and martyrs for Christ, either in fun or in flattery—certainly not seriously—merely to throw dust in the eyes of the common people, and to give Luther trouble, by loading his cause with hatred and contempt, through vain words. However, I pronounce neither true; but both false. I affirm, first, that the Scriptures are most clear; secondly, that those persons, so far as they assert Freewill, are most ignorant of the Scriptures; thirdly, that they made this assertion neither with their life, nor by their death, but only with their pen—and that, under absence of mind.

I do therefore conclude this little disputation,[v] thus. 'By Scripture—seeing that it is obscure—nothing certain has yet been determined, or can be determined, on the subject of Freewill; according to your own testimony.' That, 'by the lives of all men, from the beginning of the world, nothing has been shewn in support of Freewill,' is what I have argued above. Now, to teach any thing which is neither enjoined by a single word *in* Scripture, nor demonstrated by a single fact *out* of Scripture; is no part of christian doctrine, but belongs to the true stories of Lucian :[x] except that Lucian—sporting as he does, on ludicrous subjects, in mere jest and wittingly—deceives nobody and hurts nobody. But

---

[v] *Disputatiunculam*] *Disp.* The diminutive implies 'a discussion subordinate to the main point in debate'

[x] See Part i. Sect v. note q. Lucian, the Epicurean philosopher of Samosata, in Syria, ridiculed all religions; and served Christianity, without meaning it, pretty much as Erasmus was doing—by depreciating the fashionable and reigning idolatry. He died wretchedly, A. D. 180.—Much of his writings is in dialogue—Erasmus's favourite composition—with which he interweaves many 'true stories,' of very doubtful credit.

PART II. these antagonists of ours play the madman on a serious subject—even one pertaining to eternal salvation—to the destruction of innumerable souls.

SEC. XXI.

Luther claims victory already, but will proceed.

Thus, too, I might have put an end to this whole question about Freewill; since even the testimony of my adversaries is on my side, and at war with theirs: whilst there is no stronger proof against an accused person, than his own proper testimony against himself. But, since Paul commands us to stop the mouths of vain babblers, let us take the very pith and matter of the cause in hand; treating it in the order in which Diatribe pursues her march. Thus, I will first confute the arguments adduced in behalf of Freewill; secondly, defend our own confuted ones; and, at last, make my stand for the grace of God, in direct conflict with Freewill.

PART III.

LUTHER CONFUTES ERASMUS'S TESTIMONIES IN SUPPORT OF FREEWILL.

SECTION I.

Erasmus's Definition of Freewill examined.

And first, as in duty bound, I shall begin with your very definition of Freewill; which is as follows:

'Moreover, by Freewill here, I mean that power of the human will, whereby a man is able to apply himself to those things which lead to eternal salvation, or to turn himself away from them.'

With great prudence, doubtless, you lay down a naked[a] definition here; without opening any part of it, as is customary with others: afraid of more shipwrecks than one! I am, therefore, compelled to beat out the several parts of it, for myself. The thing defined, if it be strictly examined, is certainly of wider range than the definition: it is, therefore, what the Sophists would call a defective definition; such being their term for those which do not fill up the thing defined.[b] For I have shewn above, that Freewill belongs to none but God only. You might, perhaps with propriety, attribute *will* to man; but to attribute *free* will to him, in *divine* things,[c] is too much: since the term Freewill, in the judgment of all ears, is

---

[a] 'Bald and bare;' without any appendage of amplification, resolution of parts, or illustration.
[b] The idea is that of a mould not filled up: the definition is not commensurate with the thing defined.
[c] See Part i. Sect xxv. note l.

PART III.
properly applied to 'that which *can* do, and which *does*,' towards God, whatsoever it pleases; without being confined by any law, or by any command. You would not call a slave free, who acts under the command of his master. With how much less propriety do we call a man, or an angel, free: when they live under the most absolute subjection to *God* (to say nothing of sin and death), so as not to subsist for a moment by their own strength.

Instantly, therefore, even at the very doors of our argument, we have a quarrel between the definition of the name, and the definition of the thing; the word signifying one thing, and the thing itself being understood to be another. It would be more properly called *vertible* will, or *mutable* will. For thus Augustine, and after him the Sophists, extenuates the glory and virtue of that word *Free;* adding this disparagement to it, 'that they speak of the vertibility of the free will.' And so it would become us to speak, that we might avoid deceiving the hearts of men by inflated, vain, and pompous words: as Augustine also thinks, that we ought to speak in sober and plain words, observing a fixed rule. For, in teaching, a dialectic simplicity and strictness of speech is required; not big swelling words, and figures of rhetorical persuasion.[d]

SECT II.
Definition continued.
But, lest I should seem to take pleasure in fighting for a word, I will acquiesce, for the moment, in this abuse of terms; great and dangerous as it is; so far as to allow a 'free' will to be the same as a 'vertible' will. I will also indulge Erasmus with making Freewill 'a power of the *human* will;' as though Angels had it not: since, in this performance, he professes to treat only

[d] 'A fixed rule,' opposed to whim, taste or chance; 'sober,' opposed to 'extravagant;' 'plain,' or 'proper,' opposed to 'figurative;' 'strictness of speech,' (i.e. words used in their own genuine and natural sense) opposed to 'metaphor;' 'logic' opposed to 'rhetoric.'

of human Freewill: else, in this particular also, the definition had been narrower than the thing defined.

I hasten to those parts of the definition on which the subject hinges. Some of these are sufficiently manifest; others flee the light, as though a guilty conscience made them afraid of every thing: yet a definition ought to be the plainest and most certain thing in the world; for to define obscurely, is just like not defining at all. These parts are plain: 'a power of the human will;' also, ' by which a man is able;' also, ' unto eternal salvation:' but those words, ' to apply himself;' and again, 'those things which lead;' and again, ' to turn away himself;' are words of the hoodwinked fencer.[e] What shall we then divine that saying, ' to apply himself,' to mean? Again, ' to turn away himself?' What are those words, ' which lead to eternal salvation?' What corner are they slinking into? I have to do, as I perceive, with a very Scotus or Heraclitus;[f] who wears me out with two sorts of labour. First, I have to go in search of my adversary, and to grope for him in the dark, amidst pitfalls, with a palpitating heart (a daring and dangerous en-

[e] *Andabatæ*] 'A man fighting in the dark, with his eyes blinded:' a name given (quasi ἀναβαται sive ἀνταναβαται) to certain fencers, or gladiators, who fought on horseback with their eyes covered; or, more properly, ' to the man *who went up into the chariot to fight with the charioteer.*' It was one of the games of the Circus, of which the peculiarity consisted in the conflict being maintained in the dark. Jerome has the expression, ' More andabatarum, gladium in tenebris ventilans;' with allusion to the former of these customs.

[f] *Scotus*] The celebrated Duns Scotus, a Franciscan, the great opponent of Thomas Aquinas, the Dominican. He acquired the name of the ' subtile' doctor; as his opponent did that of the ' angelic.' *Heraclitus*, the weeping philosopher, was characterised as ' tenebrosus,' or ' obscure;' from the enigmatical style in which he communicated his reveries. Socrates is said to have expressed an admiration of some of his pieces, so far as he could understand them; but to have intimated the danger there was of being drowned in his incomprehensible depths.

terprise); and, if I do not find him, to fight with hobgoblins, and beat the air in the dark, to no purpose. Secondly, if I shall have dragged him into the light; then at length, when I am worn out with the pursuit, I have to close with him in equal fight.

By 'a power of the human will,' then, is meant, as I suppose, an ability, or faculty, or disposedness, or suitedness, to will, to refuse, to choose, to despise, to approve, to reject, and to perform whatever other actions there are of the human will. But, what is meant by this same power ' applying itself and turning away itself;' except it be this very willing and refusing, this very choosing and despising, this very approving and rejecting; in short, except it be 'the will performing its very office;' I see not. So that we must suppose this power to be 'a something interposed between the will itself and its actings:' a power, by which the will itself draws out the operation of willing and refusing, and by which that very act of willing and refusing is elicited. It is not possible to imagine or conceive any thing else here. If I be mistaken, let the fault be charged upon the author who defines, not upon me who am searching out his meaning. For, it is rightly said by the jurists, that the words of him who speaks obscurely, when he might speak more plainly, are to be interpreted against himself. And here, by the way, I could be glad to know nothing of these Moderns,[g] with whom I have to do, and their subtleties: for we must be content to speak grossly,[h] that we may teach and understand. 'The things which lead to eternal salvation,' are the words and works of

[g] *Moderni.*] Quasi *hodierni.* The subtle doctor and his contemporaries, together with those who had preceded them, from Peter Lombard downwards, were but men of 'to-day;' as compared with the ancient logicians, and with the Fathers. Also, the Schoolmen were divided into three classes, like the Academics; old, middle, and new. Scotus was of the last.

[h] *Crassè.*] 'Dull, heavy, fat-headed;' as contrasted with their wire-drawn refinements.

God, I suppose: which are set before the human will, that it may either apply itself to them, or turn away from them. By the words of God, I mean as well the Law as the Gospel: works are demanded by the Law; faith by the Gospel.' For there are no other things that lead either to the grace of God, or to eternal salvation, save the word and work of God: since grace, or the Spirit, is the life itself; to which we are led by the word and work of God.[k]

But this life, or eternal salvation, is a thing incomprehensible to human conception; as Paul cites from Isaiah (1 Cor. ii. 9.): "What eye hath not seen, nor ear heard, neither hath entered into the heart of man, are the things which God hath prepared for them that love him." For this also is placed amongst the chief articles of our faith; in confessing which we say, 'and the life everlasting.' And what the power of Freewill as to receiving this article is, Paul declares in 1 Cor. i. 10. "God," saith he, "hath revealed them to us by his Spirit." As if he should say, 'except the Spirit shall have revealed them, no man's heart will know or think any thing about them; so far is it from being able to apply itself thereunto, or to covet them.'

Consult experience. What have the most excellent wits amongst the heathens thought of a

---

[i] Luther speaks here, as theological writers commonly do. But the truth is; the Law required faith, and the Gospel requires works · though the *form* of the two several dispensations was such as Luther represents them   The Law was designed to shut the Church up unto faith; the Gospel, to open it, by that faith which is itself a work (for " this is the work of God that ye believe on Him whom He hath sent " John vi. 29) to those works which alone are acceptable to God, viz the actings and manifestations of a self-emptied, contrite, and believing soul.

[k] He speaks not of any particular word or work of God, but of his whole word, and of his whole work, excepting only what he does, by his special grace, in and upon the hearts of his people.

PART III.

future life, and of the resurrection? Has it not been, that, the more they excelled in genius, the more ridiculous did the resurrection, and eternal life, appear to them. Except you will say, that those philosophers and other Greeks, who called Paul a babbler,[1] and an assertor of new Gods, when he taught these things at Athens, were not men of genius. Porcius Festus calls Paul a madman, in Acts xxvi.[m] (ver. 24.) for preaching eternal life. What does Pliny bark about these things, in his seventh book? What says Lucian, so great a wit? Were these men stupid? Nay, it is true of most men, even at this day, that the greater their genius and erudition, the more they laugh at this article, and account it a fable; and that openly. For, as to the secret soul, no man positively, except he be sprinkled with the Holy Ghost, either knows, or believes in; or wishes for eternal salvation, even though he may make frequent boast of it with his voice and with his pen. Would to God that you and I, my Erasmus, were free from this same leaven! so rare is a believing mind, as applied to this article.—Have I hit the sense of your definition?

SECT. IV.

Inferences from Erasmus's definition.

So then, Freewill, according to Erasmus, is a power of the will, which is able, of itself, to will and not to will the word and work of God; by which word and work, it is led to those things which exceed both its sense and thought.—But

---

[1] *Babbler*] Σπερμολόγος is a term of contempt, applied properly to persons who went about the forum picking up the seeds and crumbs, or whatever else might fall between buyer and seller, and making a living out of them Hence applied to a loose, ignorant, unordered, and unmeasured speaker; one who retails the sort of refuse, common-place scraps, which he has picked up in the streets. *New Gods,* not in the invidious, or disparaging sense of demons, or of δαίμονες, but some additional deities · objects of worship, having the same sort of claim to reverence which the rest of their multiplied divinities had.

[m] He says, Acts xxiv.; but the allusion is manifestly to Acts xxvi.

if it be able to will and to refuse, it is able also to love and to hate. If it be able to love and to hate, it is able also, in some small degree, to do the deeds of the Law, and to believe the Gospel: because if you will, or refuse a certain thing, it is impossible but that you must be able to work something towards it, by means of that will, even though you be not able, through another's hindering, to finish it. Now, since death, the cross, and all the evils of the world are numbered amongst those works of God which lead to salvation; the human will must be able to choose even death and the man's own destruction. Nay, it is able to will all things; whilst it is able to will the word and work of God. For, what can there be any where, that is below, above, within, or without, the word and work of God; save God himself?" And what is now left to grace, and the Holy Spirit? This is manifestly to attribute divinity to Freewill: since to will the Law and the Gospel, to reject sin, and to choose death, is the property of divine virtue exclusively; as Paul teaches in more places than one.

Hence it appears, that no man, since the Pelagians' days, has written more correctly on Freewill, than Erasmus has. For I have said before, that Freewill is a term peculiar to God, and expresses a divine perfection. However, no man has attributed this divine power to it hitherto, except the Pelagians: for the Sophists, whatever they may think, certainly speak very differently about it. Nay, Erasmus far exceeds the Pelagians: for they attribute this divinity to the whole of the free will, Erasmus to half of it. They make Freewill to consist of two parts; a power of dis-

---

n *Intrà extrà*] ' On *this* side of it, or *beyond* it ·' which, when joined with the preceding words ' infrà, suprà,' express ' the universal comprehension of the word and work of God ;' as containing ' all that is above, beneath, and on all sides of us'— with only one exception.

cerning, and a power of choosing: of which they feign the one to belong to the understanding, and the other to the will; as the Sophists also do. But Erasmus, making no mention of the power of discerning, confines his praises to the power of choosing, singly; and so deifies a sort of crippled and half-begotten Freewill. What would he have done, think you, if he had been set to describe the whole of this faculty?

Yet, not content with this, he even exceeds the heathen philosophers. For they have not yet determined 'whether any substance can put itself into motion;' and on this point, the Platonics and Peripatetics differ from each other, throughout the whole body of their philosophy. But, according to Erasmus, Freewill not only moves itself, but applies even to those things which are eternal; that is, incomprehensible to itself; by its own power. A perfectly new and unheard-of definer of Freewill; who leaves heathen philosophers, Pelagians, Sophists, and all others, far behind him! Nor is this enough: he does not even spare himself, but even disagrees and fights with himself, more than with all the rest. He had before said, 'the human will is altogether inefficacious without grace;' (did he say this in jest?) but now, when he defines it seriously, he tells us that the human will possesses that power, whereby it is efficacious to apply itself to those things which are belonging to eternal salvation; that is, to those things which are incomparably above its power. Thus Erasmus is, in this place, superior even to himself also.°

SECT. V.

Erasmus's definition

Do you perceive, my Erasmus, how, by this definition, you (without meaning it, as I suppose) betray yourself to be one who understands nothing

---

° Erasmus has made Freewill greater than itself. Luther puns upon this, and intimates that he has even out-heroded Herod here; not only exceeding philosophers, &c. but even his own extravagant self.

SECT. V.

compared with that of the Sophists.

at all about these things, or who writes on them in sheer thoughtlessness and contempt, without proving what he says, or what he affirms. As I have remarked before, you say *less*, and claim *more*, for Freewill, than all the rest of its advocates have done: inasmuch as you do not even describe the whole of Freewill, and yet assign every thing to it. The Sophists (or at least their father, Peter Lombard) deliver what is far more tolerable to us, when they affirm, that 'Freewill is the faculty of first discerning good from evil, and then choosing good or evil according as grace be present, or be wanting.'[p] He agrees entirely with Augustine, that 'Freewill, by its own strength, cannot but fall; and has no power, save to commit sin.' On which account, Augustine says, it should be called *Bondwill*, rather than Freewill; in his second book against Julian.

But you represent the power of Freewill to be equal on both sides, inasmuch as it can, by its own strength, without grace, both apply itself *to*, and turn away itself *from* good. You are not aware how much you attribute to it by this pronoun 'itself,' or 'its own self;' whilst you say, 'it can apply itself!' In fact, you exclude the Holy Spirit with all his power, as altogether superfluous and unnecessary. Your definition is therefore damnable, even in the judgment of the Sophists; who, if they were not so maddened against me by the blindings of envy, would rave at your book rather than mine. But, since you attack Luther, you say nothing but what is holy and catholic,[q] even though you contradict both yourself and them. So great is the patience of the saints.[r]

[p] They ascribed the power of discerning, *out of hand;* but the power of choosing good, *conditionally.*

[q] *Catholicum.*] Cath 'Ad omnes pertinens,' 'quod ubique et apud omnes disseminatum est, et ab omnibus recipi debet.' 'What all are bound to receive as true.'

[r] A sarcastic allusion to Rev. xiii. 10. xiv. 12.

PART III. I do not say this as approving the sentence of the Sophists on Freewill, but as thinking it more tolerable than that of Erasmus; because they approach nearer to the truth: but neither do they affirm, as I do, that Freewill is a mere nothing. Still, inasmuch as they affirm (the Master of the Sentences[s] in particular) that it has no power of itself without grace, they are at war with Erasmus; nay, they seem to be at war also with themselves, and to be torturing one another with disputes about a mere word: being fonder of contention than of truth, as becometh Sophists. For, suppose a Sophist of no bad sort to come in my way, with whom I were holding familiar conversation and conference upon these matters in a corner; and whose candid and free judgment I should ask, in some such way as this: 'If any one should pronounce *that* free to you, which, by its own power, can but incline to one side (that is, to the bad side); having power, it is true, on the other side (that is, on the good side)—but that, by a virtue not its own; nay, simply by the help of another: could you refrain from laughing, my friend?' For, upon this principle, I shall easily make it out that a stone, or the trunk of a tree, has Freewill; as being that which can incline both upwards and downwards; by its own power, indeed, only downwards; yet, by another's help, and by that only, upwards also. And thus, as I have before said, by an inverted[t] use of all languages and words, we shall at length come to say, 'No man is all men;' 'nothing is every thing:' as referring the one term to the thing itself, and the

---

[s] Master &c. A title with which Peter Lombard was dignified, from his work entitled 'The Sentences;' by which he was supposed to have rendered the same service to Divinity, which Gratian, his contemporary, had done to Law. He was the father of scholastic theology, which succeeded to that of the Fathers; his work being considered as the great source of that science, in the Latin church. He died A. D. 1164.

[t] 'Turning words topsy-turvy.'

other to some other thing, which is no part of it, but may possibly be present to it and befal it.ᵘ

It is in this way, that, after endless disputings, they make the free will to be free by an accident: viz. as being that which may be made free by another. But the question is about the freedom of the will, as it is in itself, and in its own substance: and if this be the question resolved, there remains nothing but an empty name for Freewill, whether they will or no. The Sophists fail in this also; that they assign a power of discerning good from evil, to Freewill. They also lower regeneration, and the renewal of the Holy Ghost; and claim that extrinsic aid, as a sort of outward appendage to Freewill:ᵛ of which I shall say more hereafter. But enough of your definition: let us now see the arguments which are to swell out this empty little word.ˣ

The first is that taken from Ecclᵘˢ. xv. (vv. 15—18.) "The Lord made man from the beginning, and left him in the hand of his own counsel. He added his commands, and his precepts. If thou shalt be willing to keep his commandments, and to perform acceptable faithfulness for ever, they shall preserve thee. He hath set fire and water before thee; stretch forth thy hand unto whether

Ecclᵘˢ xv. 15—18. considered.

ᵘ For example; 'Nothing is all things.' Why, God made all things of nothing. You might call that 'nothing,' 'all things;' but it would be, by referring the term 'nothing' to the thing itself, and 'all things' to 'the existent one,' who being present communicates being (which he has in himself) to this 'nothing.'

ᵛ *Velut externè affingunt*] The gift of the Spirit, though of course not inherent, they represented as inseparably attached to the free will; and so, communicated as matter of course.

ˣ *Inflatura.*] A figure taken from blowing a bladder, or from raising a bubble, or from making a musical instrument to sound aloud: 'to give size, or substance, or sound, to this empty, speechless thing.'

thou wilt. Before man is life and death, good and evil, whether him liketh shall be given him."[y]

Although I might justly reject this book, for the moment I admit it; that I may not lose my time by involving myself in a dispute about the books received into the Hebrew canon: which you ridicule and revile not a little; comparing the Proverbs of Solomon and the Love-song (as you by an ambiguous sort of jeer entitle it) with the two books of Esdras, Judith, the history of Susannah and of the Dragon, and Esther.[z] This last, however, they have received into their canon; although, in my judgment, deserving, more than all the rest, to be excluded. But I would answer briefly, in your own words: ' the Scripture is obscure and ambiguous in this passage;' it therefore proves nothing with certainty: and, maintaining as we do the negative, I demand of you to produce a place which proves what Freewill is, and what Freewill can effect, by clear words. Perhaps you will do this on the Greek calends.[a] Howbeit, to avoid this necessity, you waste many good words in marching over the ears of corn,[b]

---

[y] The Greek text, from which our authorized version is a faithful translation, omits the words ' conservabunt te,' and ' adjecit mandata et præcepta sua.' Also in verse 17; ' bonum et malum.' The Syriac, or vulgar Hebrew, in which this book was originally written, is lost; although Jerom professes to have seen it. What Jesus the Son of Sirach produced in the Syriac, his grandson translated into Greek, for the benefit of his countrymen in Egypt; who, by long disuse, had forgotten the Hebrew tongue.

[z] ' The rest of the chapters of the Book of Esther, which are found neither in the Hebrew, nor the Chaldee.'

[a] *Græcas calendas.*] ' A day that will never come;' a Latin proverb taken from the Greeks having no calends to their months, as the Latins had.

[b] *Super aristas incedis.*] Applied proverbially, to ' one who affirms nothing absolutely;' he skims the ears of corn, fearing to set his foot on them.

and reciting so many opinions on Freewill, that you almost make Pelagius evangelical.[c] Again; you invent four kinds of grace, that you may be able to assign some sort of faith and charity, even to the heathen philosophers. Again; you invent that threefold law of nature, works, and faith: a new figment, by which you enable yourself to maintain, that the precepts of the heathen philosophers have a mighty coincidence with the precepts of the Gospel. Then again; you apply that affirmation in Psalm iv. "The light of thy countenance has been marked upon us, Lord;"[d] which speaks of the knowledge of the very countenance of God (that is, of an operation of faith) to blinded reason. Now, let any Christian put all these things together, and he will be obliged to suspect that you are sporting and jesting with the dogmas and worship of Christians. For I find it most difficult indeed to attribute all this to ignorance, in a man who has so thoroughly ransacked[e] all our documents, and so diligently treasured them up and remembered them. But I will abstain for the present, content with this short hint; till a fitter opportunity shall offer itself. But let me beg of you, my Erasmus, not to tease *us* any more in this way, with your 'Who sees me?' nor is it safe, in so weighty a matter, to be continually

---

[c] *Pelagius.*] The great heresiarch of Freewill, in the fifth century, a native of Wales, and as is supposed, a monk of Bangor; who exchanged his original name of Morgan, for the more imposing one of Pelagius.

[d] *We* read Psalm iv 6. "Lord lift thou up," &c. as a prayer, but it may with equal propriety be read as an affirmation.

[e] *Nostra omnia sic perlustravit*] I refer the ' nostra omnia' to the sacred records, ' the authorized documents of Christianity;' not the writings of Luther and his friends. *Perlustr.* does not express ' real insight into the things contained in those documents,' but ' complete outside inspection.' This is just the sort of knowledge which Luther would choose to ascribe to him, and which is amply sufficient to exempt him from the plea of ignorance.

142 BONDAGE OF THE WILL.

PART III.

SEC. VII.
Opinions on Freewill stated.

playing at making Vertumnuses of words, with every body.[f]

You make three opinions on Freewill, out of one; accounting that a harsh one,[g] which denies that a man can will good without special grace; which denies that he can begin any thing good, denies that he can go on with any thing good, denies that he can complete any thing good. But though harsh, you account it highly approvable. It approves itself to you, as leaving man in possession of desire and endeavour, but not leaving him any thing to ascribe to his own powers. The opinion of those who maintain that Freewill can do nothing but sin; that only grace works good in us; seems still more harsh to you: but most of all, that opinion which affirms Freewill to be an empty name, God working both good and evil in us. It is against these two last opinions, that you profess to write.

SEC. VIII

Erasmus inconsistent with his definition.

Do you even know what you are saying, my Erasmus? You make three opinions here, as if they were the opinions of three different sects; not perceiving, that it is the same thing declared in different words, with a twofold variety, by us, the same persons, and professors of one sect. But let me warn you of your carelessness, or dullness of intellect; and expose it.

I ask then, how does the definition of Freewill, which you have given above, correspond with this first opinion of yours; which you declare to

---

[f] ' *Us*,' opposed to ' *every body*.' He represents him as *playing at peep* with the learned, and as deceiving *the people* by his tricks upon words, by which he gave the same word as many faces as Vertumnus. He plagued the wise; he deceived the vulgar. Vertumnus had many faces: hence, ' Vertumnis verborum ludere,' ' to *play at* making words like Vertumnus;' that is, different in appearance, whilst really the same. Erasmus could say and unsay every thing, by his copiousness, versatility, and ambiguity of words.

[g] Erasmus does not introduce the word ' harsh' in describing this first opinion; Luther ascribes it to him, as implied in his description of the other two.

be highly approvable? For you have said, that Freewill is a power of the human will, by which a man can apply himself to good: But here you say, and approve its being said, that a man cannot will good, without grace. Your definition affirms what its illustration denies; and there is found 'a yea and nay' in your Freewill: so that you at the same time both approve and condemn us; nay, condemn and approve yourself, in one and the same dogma and article.[h] Do you not think it good, that it applies itself to those things which pertain to everlasting salvation? This is what your definition attributes to Freewill; and yet there is no need of grace, if there be so much of good in Freewill that it can apply itself to good. So then, the Freewill which you define, is a different thing from the Freewill which you defend; and Erasmus has two Freewills more than others have, and those quite at variance with each other.

But, dismissing that Freewill which your definition has invented, let us look at this contrary one, which the opinion itself sets before us. You grant, that a man cannot will good without special grace; and we are not now discussing what the grace of God can do, but what man can do without grace. You grant therefore, that Freewill cannot will good. This is nothing else, than that it cannot apply itself to those things which appertain to eternal salvation, as you sung out in your definition. Nay, you say a little before, that the human will is so depraved, that, having lost its liberty, it is compelled to serve sin, and cannot restore itself to any better sort of produce. If I do not mistake, you represent the Pelagians to have been of this opinion.—Now, I think there is no escape here for my Proteus. He is caught and

The approvable opinion considered.

---

[h] The definition says, 'can apply itself to those things, &c.' The approvable opinion says, 'cannot will good.'

PART III. held by open words; to wit, the will, having lost its liberty, is driven into, and held fast in, the service of sin. O exquisite Freewill which, having lost its freedom, is declared by Erasmus himself to be the servant of sin! When Luther said this, 'nothing had ever been heard that is more absurd;' 'nothing could be published that is more mischievous than this paradox;' Diatribes must be written against him!

But perhaps nobody will take my word for it, that Erasmus has really said these things: let this passage of Diatribe be read, and it will excite wonder. Not that I am greatly surprised. The man who does not account this a serious subject, and is never affected with the cause he is pleading, but is altogether alienated from it in heart, and is tired of it, and chills under it, or nauseates it—how can such an one do otherwise than here and there say absurd things, incongruous things, discordant things? pleading the cause as he does, like a drunken or sleeping man, who belches out 'yes,' 'no,' as the sounds fall variously upon his ears. It is on this account, that rhetoricians require feeling in an advocate; and much more does theology require such a degree of emotion in her champion, as shall render him vigilant, sharpsighted, intent, thoughtful, and strenuous.

SECT. X.

The approvable opinion further considered.

If then Freewill, without grace, having lost her freedom, is obliged to serve sin, and cannot will good; I should like to know what that desire, what that endeavour is, which this first and approvable opinion leaves to a man?¹ It cannot be good desire, it cannot be good endeavour: because he cannot will good; as the opinion says, and as you have conceded. Evil desire, therefore, and evil endeavour are alone left; which, now that liberty is lost, are compelled to serve sin.—And what is meant, pray, by that saying 'This opinion leaves

¹ ' It leaves man in possession of desire and endeavour,' &c.'

TEXTS FOR FREEWILL DISPROVED. 145

desire and endeavour, but leaves not that which SEC. XI.
may be ascribed to the man's own powers?' Who
can conceive this? If desire and endeavour be
left to Freewill, why should they not be ascribed
to it? If they are not to be ascribed, how can
they be left? Are this desire and endeavour,
which subsist before grace, left even to that very
grace which is to come, and not to Freewill; so
as to be at the same time left, and not left, to this
same Freewill? If these be not paradoxes, or
rather monsters, I know not what monsters are.

But perhaps Diatribe is dreaming, that there is Freewill
a something between this being able to will good, not 'a ne-
and not being able to will good, which is the mere gative, in-
power of willing; distinct from any regard to good power of
or evil. Thus, we are to evade the rocks by a the will.'
sort of logical subtilty; affirming, that there is, in
the will of man, a certain power of willing, which
cannot indeed incline to good without grace, and
yet even without grace does not forthwith will
only evil: a pure and simple power of willing;
which may be turned by grace upwards to good,
and by sin downwards to evil. But what then
becomes of that saying, ' having lost its liberty,
it is compelled to serve sin?' Where then is
that ' desire and endeavour' which is left?
Where is that power of applying itself to those
things which belong to eternal salvation? For that
power of applying itself to salvation cannot be a
mere abstract power of willing, unless salvation
itself be called nothing.—Then, again, desire and
endeavour cannot be a mere power of willing;
since desire must lean and endeavour some
whither, and cannot be carried towards nothing,
or remain quiescent. In short, whithersoever
Diatribe shall be pleased to turn herself, she cannot escape contradictions, and conflicting expressions: so that even Freewill herself is not so much
a captive, as Diatribe who defends her. She so en-
tangles herself, in her attempts to give liberty to

L

the will, that she gets bound with indissoluble chains, in company with her freedmaid.

Then, again, it is a mere fiction of logic, that there is this middle faculty of mere willing in man; nor can those prove, who assert it. Ignorance of things, and servile regard to words, has given birth to this fancy; as if the will must straightway be such in substance, as we set it out in words. The Sophists have numberless figments of this sort. The truth rather is, what Christ says, "He that is not with me is against me." He does not say, 'He that is not with me, nor against me, but in the middle.' For, if God be in us, Satan is absent, and only to will good is present with us. If God be absent, Satan is present, and there is no will in us but towards evil. Neither God, nor Satan, allows a mere abstract power to will in us; but, as you have rightly said, having lost our liberty, we are compelled to serve sin; that is, we *will* sin and wickedness; we *speak* sin and wickedness; we *act* sin and wickedness. See into what a corner Diatribe has been driven, without knowing it, by invincible and most mighty truth; who has made her wisdom folly, and compelled her, when meaning to speak *against* us, to speak *for* us, and against herself: just as Freewill does, when she attempts any thing good; for then, by *opposing* evil, she most of all does evil, and opposes good. Thus Diatribe is much such a speaker, as Freewill is an actor. Indeed, the whole Diatribe itself is nothing else but an excellent performance of Freewill, condemning by defending, and defending by condemning;[k] that is, twice a fool, whilst she would be thought wise.

The first opinion, then, as compared with itself, is such as to deny that man can will any thing good, and yet to maintain that desire is left to him;

---

[k] 'Not only ruining her own cause, but establishing her adversary's.'

TEXTS FOR FREEWILL DISPROVED.

and yet that this desire also is not his. Let us now compare it with the other two.—'The second is harsher, which judges that Freewill has no power but to commit sin.' This, however, is Augustine's opinion; expressed in many other places, and specially in his treatise on the Letter and Spirit (the fourth or fifth chapter, if I am not mistaken), where he uses these very words.

SEC. XII.
opinion compared with the other two.

'That third opinion is the harshest of all, which maintains that Freewill is an empty name, and that all we do is necessarily under the bondage of sin.' Diatribe wages war with these two. Here, I admit that probably I may not be German enough, or Latinist enough, to enunciate the subject matter perspicuously; but I call God to witness, that I meant to say nothing else, and nothing else to be understood, by the expressions used in these two last opinions, than what is asserted in the first opinion. Nor did Augustine, I think, mean any thing else; nor do I understand by his words any thing else, than what the first opinion asserts. So that the three opinions recited by Diatribe are, in my view, but that one sentiment, which I have promulgated. For, when it has been conceded and settled, that Freewill, having lost her freedom, is compelled into the service of sin, and has no power to will any thing good; I can conceive nothing else from these expressions, but that Freewill is a bare word; the substance expressed by that word having been lost. Lost liberty my art of grammar calls no liberty at all; and to attribute the name of liberty to that which has no liberty, is to attribute a bare name to it. If I wander from truth here, let who can recal me from my wanderings; if my words be obscure and ambiguous, let who can make them plain, and confirm them. I cannot call lost health, health; and if I should ascribe such a property to a sick man, what have I given him but a bare name?

But away with such monstrous expressions!

PART III. For, who can bear that abuse of language, by which we affirm that man has Freewill; yet, with the same breath, assert that he has lost his liberty, and is compelled into the service of sin, and can will nothing good. Such expressions are at variance with common sense, and absolutely destroy the use of speech. Diatribe is to be accused, rather than we; she blurts out her own words as if she were asleep, and gives no heed to what is spoken by others. She does not consider, I say, what it is, and of what force it is, to declare that man has lost his liberty, is compelled to serve sin, and has no power to do any thing good. For, if she were awake and observant, she would clearly see that the meaning of the three opinions, which she makes diverse and opposite, is one and the same. For the man who has lost his liberty, who is compelled to serve sin, and who cannot will good—what shall be inferred more correctly concerning this man, than that he does nothing but sin, or will evil? Even the Sophists would establish this conclusion by their learned syllogisms. So that Madam Diatribe is very unfortunate in entering the lists with these two last opinions, whilst she approves the first, which is the same with them; again, as her manner is, condemning *herself*, and expressing approbation of my sentiments, in one and the same article.

SC. XIII. 'Let us now return to the passage in Ecclesiasticus; comparing that first opinion, which you declare to be approvable, with *it* also, as we have now done with the other two. The opinion says, 'Freewill cannot will good.' The passage from Ecclesiasticus is cited to prove, that ' Freewill is nothing, and can do nothing.' The opinion which is to be confirmed by Ecclesiasticus, then, declares one thing, and the passage from Ecclesiasticus is alleged to confirm another. As if a man, going to prove that Christ is Messias, should adduce a passage which proves that Pontius

Ecclesiasticus xv. 14—18. resumed, and expounded.

Pilate was Governor of Syria; or something else, which is as wide from it as the extreme notes of the double octave.¹ Just such is your proof of Freewill here: not to mention, what I have dispatched already, that nothing is here clearly and certainly affirmed, or proved, as to what Freewill is, and can do. But it is worth while to examine this whole passage.

In the first place, he says, 'God made man in the beginning.' Here he speaks of the creation of man, and says nothing, hitherto, either about Freewill, or about precepts.

It follows; 'and left him in the hand of his own counsel.' What have we here? Is Freewill erected here? Not even here is any mention made of precepts, for which Freewill is required; nor do we read a syllable on this subject, in the history of the creation of man. If any thing be meant, therefore, by the words 'in the hand of his counsel,' it must rather be, what we read in the first and second chapters of Genesis: 'Man was appointed lord of the things which were made, so as to have a free dominion over them;' as Moses says, "Let us make man, and let him have dominion over the fishes of the sea, &c." Nor can any thing else be proved from these words. For in that state, man had power to deal with the creatures according to his own will, they being made his subjects; and he calls this man's counsel, in opposition to God's counsel. But after this, when now he has declared man to have been thus constituted the ruler, and to have been left in the hand of his own counsel; he goes on,

"He added his own commands and precepts." To what did he add them? Why, to the counsel and will of man; and over and above that establishment of the dominion of man over the rest of

---

¹ *Quod disdiapason conveniat.*] A Greek proverb, denoting the greatest possible dissimilitude.

the creatures. By these precepts, he took away from man the dominion over one part of his creatures (the tree of the knowledge of good and evil, for instance), and rather willed that it should not be free. Having mentioned the adding of precepts, he next comes to man's will towards God, and the things of God.

" If thou shalt be willing to keep the commandments, they shall preserve thee, &c." From this place, then, ' if thou shalt be willing,' the question about Freewill begins. So that we may learn from the Preacher, that man is divided between two kingdoms; in the one of which, he is borne along by his own will and counsel, without any precepts or commandments from God; to wit, in the exercise of his relations to the inferior creatures. Here he reigns, and is lord, as having been left in the hand of his own counsel. Not that God so leaves him, even here, as not to cooperate with him in all things; but that he leaves him a free use of the creatures, according to his own will, not restricting him by laws or injunctions. Just as if you should say, by way of comparison, ' The Gospel has left us in the hand of our own counsel, to rule over the creatures, and use them as we please; but Moses and the Pope have not left us in this counsel, but have restrained us by laws, and have rather subjected us to *their* wills.'—But in the other kingdom, man is not left in the hand of his own counsel, but is borne along, and led by the will and counsel of God. So that, as in his own kingdom, he is borne along by his own will, without the precepts of another; so, in the kingdom of God, he is borne along by the precepts of another, without his own will. And this is what the Preacher affirms, " He added precepts and commands; If thou wilt, &c. &c."[m]

[m] I object to this distinction, as I have already done to the same in substance (Part ii. Sect. xxi.), nor can I believe it to

TEXTS FOR FREEWILL DISPROVED.

If these things then be quite clear, we have proved that this passage from Ecclesiasticus makes against Freewill, not for it; as subjecting man to the precepts and will of God, and withdrawing him from his own will. But if they be not quite clear, I have at least made out, that this passage cannot be brought to support Freewill, as being capable of quite a different interpretation from theirs: such, for instance, as I have just mentioned; which is so far from being absurd, that it is most sound, and is consonant to the whole tenour of Scripture: whereas theirs is repugnant to that testimony, and is fetched from this single passage, in contradiction to the whole volume besides. We stand firm, and without fear, therefore, in our good sense of the words, which

SEC XIV. Ecclesiasticus at least does not decide for Freewill.

have been in the mind of the Apocryphal writer. Man had not *Freewill* given to him, in the exercise of one set of his relations (those to the creatures, for instance), more than in another. Dominion and superiority did not confer Freewill. He was, in reality, made accountable for his use of the creatures, they were not given to him to do what he pleased with. But, if it had been so, this would not have prevented his liability to have his will moved by a power *without* him. Insubjection and unaccountableness are of a perfectly different nature from Freewill. A despot may be ruled *within*, as well as a slave But, taking the writer to mean that he was left to do his own will—this does not necessarily imply more than that he was left a free agent. and this he *was* left, with respect to all his relations, higher as well as inferior and so are we. The difference between Adam's state before his fall, and ours who have been begotten out of him since—after having fallen *in* and *with* him—consisteth not in his having been any way independent of God—which *we* are not—or having had a will that was inaccessible to divine control—which *we* have not—but only in his ignorance of, and freedom from evil He knew only good, and the devil had as yet no part in him But, even in that state, he did only, and only could do, what God willed that he should do, and, though *without excuse* in choosing evil (as having faculties and capacities, and being placed in circumstances, by and in which he ought at once to have rejected the temptation), did so choose, through the operation (not compulsory indeed, but efficacious) and according to the will, of Him who doeth all things. whose glory as well as prerogative it is, to govern a world of *free agents*.

negatives Freewill, until they shall have confirmed their affirmative, harsh, and forced one.

When the Preacher therefore says, "If thou shalt be willing to keep the commandments, and to maintain acceptable faith, they shall preserve thee;" I do not see how Freewill is proved by these words. The verb is in the conjunctive mood ('If thou wilt'); which asserts nothing indicatively. Take an example or two. 'If the devil be God, he is worthy to be worshipped.' 'If an ass fly, he has wings.' 'If the will be free, grace is nothing.' The Preacher should have spoken thus, if he had meant to assert the freedom of the will: 'Man can keep the commandments of God;' or, 'Man has power to keep the commandments.'

SEC XV.
What meant by 'If thou wilt, &c'

But here Diatribe will cavil, that 'the Preacher, in saying "If thou wilt keep," intimates that there is a will in man to keep, and not to keep; for what meaning is there, in saying to a man who has no will, 'If thou wilt.' Would it not be ridiculous to say to a man that is blind, 'If thou wilt see, thou shalt find a treasure?' or to a deaf man, 'If thou wilt hear, I will tell thee a pretty story?' This would be only laughing at their misery.

I answer; these are the arguments of human reason, who is wont to pour out a flood of such wise sayings: so that I have not now to dispute with the Preacher, but with human reason, about an inference.[n] That lady interprets the Scriptures of God by her own consequences and syllogisms; drawing them whither she will. I shall undertake my office very willingly, and with full confidence of success, because I know that she chatters nothing but what is foolish and absurd; the most of

---

[n] *De sequela*] 'What follows, or is supposed to follow, from an assertion proved or admitted, but is not the immediate point in debate.' 'Consequence,' 'deduction,' 'inference.'

TEXTS FOR FREEWILL DISPROVED. 153

all; when she sets about shewing her wisdom on SEC. XV.
sacred subjects.

Now if, in the first place, I should ask how it is proved to be intimated, or to follow, that man has in him a will that is free, as often as it is said 'If thou wilt,' 'if thou shalt do,' 'if thou shalt hear;' she will say, ' because the nature of words, and the custom of speech amongst men, seem to require so.' She measures the things and words of God, then, by the things and usage of men. What can be more perverse than this; when the one sort of things is earthly, and the other heavenly? Thus she betrays her foolish self; how she thinks nothing, but what is human, of God.

But what if I should prove, that the nature of words and custom of speech, even amongst men, is not always such as to make those persons objects of ridicule, who have no power to comply with the demand, as often as it is said to them, ' If thou wilt,' ' if thou wilt do,' ' if thou wilt hear?' How often do parents mock their children, by bidding them come to them, or do this or that, for the mere purpose of making it appear how utterly incapable they are of doing so, and of forcing them to call upon the parent for his helping hand! How often does the faithful physician command his proud patient to do or leave undone things which are either impossible, or noxious, that he may drive him to that knowledge of his disease, or of his weakness, through making trial of himself, to which he could not lead him by any other means! What is more frequent, or more common, than words of insult and provocation, if we would shew, either to friends or to enemies, what they can do, and what they cannot do? I mention these things, only by way of manifesting to human reason, how foolish she is in attaching her inferences to the Scriptures; and how blind she is, not to see that these inferences are not always realized, even in human words

PART III. and actions: yet, if she but see them fulfilled now and then, presently she rushes forwards with precipitation, and pronounces that they take place generally, in all human and divine forms of speech. Thus she contrives to make an universal of a particular, as the manner of her wisdom is.

SEC. XVI.
Use of such forms of address.

Now, if God deal with us as a father with his childen, to shew us our impotency, of which we are ignorant; or as a faithful physician, to make our disease known to us; or if he insult us, as his enemies, who proudly resist his counsel, and by proposing laws to us (which is the most convincing way of doing it), say, 'Do, hear, keep;' or, ' if thou shalt hear, if thou shalt be willing, if thou shalt do;' will it be a just inference from hence, 'So then we can will freely, else God is mocking us?' Is not this rather the inference, ' So then God is making trial of us, whether we be friends or foes; that, if we be his friends, he may lead us to the knowledge of our impotency, by the law; or, if we be proud enemies, then indeed he may truly and deservedly insult and deride us.'[o] This is the reason why God gives laws; as Paul teaches.[p] For human nature is so blind as not to know its own strength, or rather its own disease; and is, besides, so proud as to think that it knows and can do all things. Now, God has not any more effectual remedy for this

---

[o] It is not Luther's business to state whence this difference of reception arises; which is only through the free favour of God, making some to be his friends, by his Spirit working in due season, whilst he leaves others in their native enmity. Luther would not hesitate to assign this cause, but he has here only to do with the fact, that the Lord tries and evinces these different characters of men, by such calls to obedience

[p] " Therefore by the deeds of the law there shall no flesh be justified in his sight; for by the law is the knowledge of sin." (Rom. iii 20) "Moreover, the law entered that the offence might abound." (Rom. v. 20) " Wherefore then serveth the law? It was added because of transgressions." (Gal. iii. 19) " Wherefore the law was our schoolmaster to bring us unto Christ." (Ibid. 24.)

pride and ignorance, than the propounding of his law; of which I shall say more in its proper place. Let it suffice to have taken but a sip of the cup here, that I might confute this inference of foolish, carnal wisdom, 'If thou wilt—therefore the will is free.' Diatribe dreams that man is sound and whole; just such as he is in the sight of his fellow men, in mere human affairs. Hence it is, that she cavils and says, ' Man is mocked by such words as ' if thou wilt,' ' if thou wilt do,' ' if thou wilt hear,' except his will be free.' ' But Scripture declares man to be corrupt and captive; and not only so, but a proud despiser of God, and one ignorant of his corruption and captivity. So she plucks him by the sleeve, and endeavours to awaken him by such words as these, that he may own, even by sure experience, how incapable he is of any of these things.

But I will become the assailant myself in this conflict; and will ask, ' If thou dost indeed think, Madam Reason, that these inferences stand good (if thou wilt—therefore thou canst will freely), why dost thou not follow them ? Thou sayest, in that approvable opinion of thine, that Freewill cannot will any thing good. By what sort of inference, then, will it at the same time flow, as you say it does, from this passage, ' If thou shalt be willing to keep,' that man can will freely, and cannot will freely ? Do sweet water and bitter flow from the same fountain ? Are you not, even yourself, the greater mocker of man here; when you say that he is able to keep what he cannot even will, or wish ? It follows therefore, that neither do you on your part think it a good inference, ' If thou wilt—therefore thou canst will freely;' though you maintain it so vehemently: or else, you do not, from your heart, affirm that opinion to be approvable, which maintains that man cannot will good.'—Reason is so entrapped in the inferences and words of her own wisdom, as not to know what she says, or what

Diatribe insincere in her inference.

she is talking about. Unless it be (as is indeed most worthy of her), that Freewill can only be defended by such arguments as mutually devour and make an end of each other : just as the Midianites destroyed themselves, by a mutual slaughter, whilst making war against Gideon and the people of God.

Proves too much. But let me expostulate, still more at large, with this wise Diatribe. The Preacher does not say, 'If thou shalt have a desire or endeavour to keep, which is, nevertheless, not to be ascribed to thine own powers;' as you collect from his words; but 'If thou wilt keep the commandments, they shall preserve thee.' Now, if we would draw inferences, such as you in your wisdom are wont to do, we shall infer, 'therefore man can keep the commandments:' and thus, we shall leave not only a little bit of a desire, or a sort of endeavouring, in man; but shall ascribe to him the whole fulness and abundance of power to keep the commandments. Else, the Preacher would be mocking the misery of man, by commanding him to keep, when he knew him to be unable to keep. Nor would it be enough, that he should have desire and endeavour: not even thus would the Preacher escape the suspicion of using mockery; he must intimate that he has in him a power of keeping.

Confirms Pelagianism. But let us suppose this desire and endeavour of Freewill to be something. What shall we say to those (the Pelagians, I mean) who, from this passage, were used to deny grace altogether, and to ascribe every thing to Freewill? Without doubt, the Pelagians have gained the victory, if Diatribe's consequence be allowed. For the words of the Preacher import keeping, and not merely desiring or endeavouring. Now, if you shall deny to the Pelagians the inference of 'keeping;' they will, in their turn, much more properly deny to you the inference of 'endeavouring:' and, if you take away complete Freewill from them, they will take from you that little particle of it which you say remains; not allowing you to claim for a particle, what you have denied to the whole substance. So that, whatever you urge against the Pelagians, who ascribe a whole to Freewill from this passage, will come much more forcibly from us, in contradiction to that little bit of a desire which constitutes *your* Freewill.^q The Pelagians too will so far agree with us as to admit, that, if their opinion cannot be proved from this passage, much less can any other be proved from it: since, if the cause is to be pleaded by inferences, the Preacher makes the most strongly of all for the Pelagians; forasmuch as he speaks expressly of entire keeping. 'If thou wilt keep the commandments.' Nay, he speaks of faith also: 'If thou wilt keep acceptable faith.' So that, by the same inference, we ought to have it in our power to keep faith also: howbeit, this faith is the alone and rare gift of God; as Paul says.^r

In short, since so many opinions are enumerated in support of Freewill, and there is not one of them but what seizes upon this passage of Ecclesiasticus for itself; yet those opinions are different and contrary; it must follow, that they deem the Preacher contradictory and opposite, each to the other severally, in the self-same words. They

---

^q *Totum libero arbitrio tribuentibus*] The Pelagians spake more wisely than many who oppose them. They maintained 'the integrity of Freewill,' an absolute power of willing good. Freewill is Freewill; and, if there be any thing of it in man, there is the whole of it.

^r Luther refers, no doubt, to Ephes. ii 8 "For by grace are ye saved through faith; and that not of yourselves it is the gift of God." His interpretation, if I understand the text aright, is incorrect . it is not 'faith' that is spoken of as the gift of God, but 'his whole salvation.' The truth of his affirmation, however, though not fairly deducible from this text, is unquestionable , and may be shewn, as well from particular testimonies, as from the general tenour of Scripture Matt. xvi. 17. John vi. 44, 65. Ephes 1. 19. Coloss. ii. 12. (to which many others might be added) are decisive.

158 BONDAGE OF THE WILL.

PART III. can, therefore, prove nothing from him. Still, if that inference be admitted, he makes for the Pelagians only, against all the rest: and so makes against Diatribe; who cuts her own throat here.[s]

SC.XVIII. But I renew my first assertion; viz. that this passage from Ecclesiasticus patronises none absolutely of those who maintain Freewill; but opposes them all. For that inference, 'if thou wilt—therefore thou canst,' is inadmissible; and the true understanding of such passages as these is, that, by this word and the like, man is warned of his impotency; which, as being ignorant and proud, if it were not for these divine warnings, he would neither own nor feel.

Conclude that Ecclesiasticus proves nothing for Freewill, whether what is said be understood of Adam, or of men generally.

And here I speak, not of the first man only, but of any man, and every man; though it be of little consequence, whether you understand it of the first man, or of any other whatsoever. For, although the first man was not impotent through the presence of grace; still God shews him abundantly by this precept, how impotent he would be in the absence of grace. Now if that man, having the Spirit,[t] was not able to will good; that is,

[s] *Suo ipsius gladio jugulatur*] By quoting a passage for herself, which directly contradicts her.

[t] *Cum adesset Spiritus.*] Luther assumes that Adam, in his creation state, had the Spirit, of which there is no proof, and the contrary seems evidently to have been the fact. Made perfect after his kind, it was no part of his creation dues or gifts to have the Spirit. He was formed to glorify God, as his creature: which implies a substance distinct from, and existing in a state of severance from his Creator; like a piece of mechanism put out of the hand of its artificer. He was left to himself, therefore, having his own high moral powers and acquirements, but no extrinsic aid; to make trial and to shew, what man in his entireness is, and what he would become through temptation, if not inhabited by his Creator. This trial and manifestation would furnish an inference with respect to other creatures; even as the same inference had already been furnished by the angelic nature. But this trial could not have been made, and this exhibition therefore could not have been effected, if he had possessed the Spirit; or, in other words, if he had been united to God. So united, he could not have been overcome. That union, therefore (as Luther, and others with

obedience; while as his will was yet new, and good was newly proposed to him,ᵘ because the Spirit did not add it; what could we, who have not the Spirit, do towards good, which we have lost? It was shewn therefore, in that first man, by a terrible example, for the bruising under of our pride, what our Freewill can do when left to itself; yea, when urged and increased continually, yet more and more, by the Spirit of God. The first man could not attain to a more enlarged measure of the Spirit, of which he possessed the firstfruits, but fell from the possession of those firstfruits. How should we, in our fallen state, have power to recover those firstfruits, which have been taken from us? Especially, since Satan now reigns in us with full power; who laid the first man prostrate by a mere temptation, when he had not yet got to reign in him.—It were impossible to maintain a stronger debate against Freewill, than by discussing this text of Ecclesiasticus, in connection with the fall of Adam: but I have not room for such a descant here, and perhaps the matter will present itself elsewhere. Meanwhile, let it suffice to have shewn, that the Preacher says just nothing in support of Freewill here (which its advocates, however, account their principal testimony); and that this and similar passages, 'If

him, would say), was dissolved; the Spirit which he had possessed was withdrawn during his temptation Then, was he any longer the same substance, or person, which had received the command? On this representation, the command was given him, *having the Spirit*; and he was tried, *not* having the Spirit—So demonstrable is it, that Adam had not the Holy Ghost; whose *in-dwelling* 'doth not appertain to the *perfection* of man's nature.'—But the argument from Adam's state to ours is quite strong enough, without this unwarranted assumption of Luther's. He that was just come out of the hands of his Creator, made in his image, and pronounced by him to be 'very good,' could not stand against a single and solitary temptation: what should *we* do therefore?

ᵘ As opposed to that 'stale and rejected' thing which good is to us.

PART III. thou wilt,' 'if thou wilt hear,' 'if thou wilt do,' declare not what man can do, but what he ought to do.'

SEC. XIX. Another passage is cited by our Diatribe from the fourth chapter of Genesis, where the Lord says to Cain, "The desire of sin shall be subject to thee, and thou shalt rule over it." 'It is shewn here, says Diatribe, that the motions of the mind towards evil may be overcome, and do not induce a necessity of sinning.'

Gen. iv. 7. considered.

This saying, 'that the motions of the mind towards evil may be overcome,' is ambiguous; but the general sentiment, the consequence, and the facts compel us to this understanding of it,^{x} that, 'it is the property of Freewill to overcome its own motions towards evil, and that those motions do not induce a necessity of sinning.' Why is it again omitted here, 'which is not ascribed to Freewill?'^{y} What need is there of the Spirit, what need of Christ, what need of God, if Freewill can overcome the motions of the mind towards evil? What has again become of that approvable opinion, which says that Freewill cannot even *will* good? Here, however, victory over evil is ascribed to

---

^{v} I cannot help regretting that Luther, after the example of his opponent, has given so much space to this Apocryphal testimony from Ecclesiasticus. I could have been glad, if he had not only stood upon his right, which he hints at in the opening of his discussion, declining to answer; but had used the occasion to protest against the honour put upon this book, and the rest of its brothers and sisters, by binding them up in our Bibles and reading them in our churches.—The collateral matter of the argumentation, however, is highly valuable; and Luther could afford to make his adversary a present of an argument. Here, indeed, he may almost be said to have taken a culverin to kill flies withal. For, is it not *Adam*, clearly, of whom the Preacher speaks; whose will is not the matter in debate? and what, as we have seen, is said even of that will, which might not be said of ours? It was left free to choose; and *if* it should choose good, good would result from that good.

^{x} *Vi sententiæ, consequentiæ et rerum huc cogitur.*

^{y} Referring to the 'satis probabilis opinio;' 'sed non relinquat, quod suis viribus ascribat.' See above, Sect. vii.

this substance, which neither wills nor wishes good. Our Diatribe's carelessness is beyond all measure here.—Hear the truth of the matter in few words. I have said before, man has it shewn to him, by such expressions as these, not what he can do, but what he ought to do. Cain is told, therefore, that he ought to rule over sin, and to keep its lustings in subjection to himself. But this he neither did, nor could do, seeing, he was now pressed to the earth by the foreign[z] yoke of Satan. It is notorious, that the Hebrews frequently use the future indicative for the imperative: as in the twentieth chapter of Exodus; 'Thou shalt not have any other Gods,' 'Thou shalt not kill,' 'Thou shalt not commit adultery;' and numberless such like instances. On the contrary, if the words be taken indicatively, according to their literal meaning,[a] they would be so many promises of God, who cannot lie; and so, nobody would commit sin, and there would be no need therefore of these precepts. In fact, our translator would have rendered the words better in this place, if he had said, ' Let its desire be subject to thee, and do thou rule over it.' Just as it ought also to have been said to the woman, ' Be subject to thy husband, and let him rule over thee.'— That it was not said indicatively to Cain, appears from this: it would in that case have been a divine promise; but it was not a divine promise, for the very reverse happened, and the very reverse was done by Cain.[b]

[z] *Alieno imperio.*] ' A dominion *out* of himself,' so that he was no longer his own master.

[a] *Ut sonant*] The sound, as opposed to the sense, or real import.

[b] I admit Luther's principle, but demur to the application of it, both here and in the parallel to which he refers, Gen. iii. 16. The original passage is one of great difficulty I incline to the interpretation which our authorized version gives to it; and refer the words which are immediately under remark, as that appears to do, not to *sin*, but to *Abel.* " If thou doest well, shalt

PART III.
SEC. XX
Deut. xxx. 19. considered.

Your third passage is from Moses, "I have set before thy face the way of life and of death; choose that which is good," &c. &c. 'What could be said more plainly,' says Diatribe? 'He leaves freedom of choice to man.'

I answer, what can be plainer than that you are blind here? Prithee, where does he leave freedom of choice? In saying, 'choose?' So then, as soon as Moses says 'choose,' it comes to pass that they do choose! Again, therefore, the Spirit is not necessary: and since you so often repeat and hammer in[c] the same things, let me also be

---

thou not be accepted? and if thou doest not well, sin lieth at the door. And unto thee shall be his desire, and thou shalt rule over him." Well, and not well, have relation to the then known will of God. Was Cain ignorant, with what sort of offering God was to be approached?—Whatever might be said of later times, Cain must have heard all about Eden, the serpent and the woman, the serpent's seed and the woman's seed, and must have *seen* the coats of skins. Cain despised "the way;" he would none of Christ.—Then, God's words are adapted to quiet, and to instruct him. We know that a man can no more come by Christ, except it be given him from above, than he can come by the law. But this was not the thing to be shewn him, he was to be reminded of the alone way of access, that he might make the fullest developement of himself, if he should continue to neglect and despise it: and, since jealous and angry fears were now arising in his mind with respect to his brother; chiefly, lest he should lose the earthly superiority attached to his primogeniture; he is pacified with an assurance (connected, doubtless, with the fore-mentioned condition), that this dominion should remain in his hands; an assurance conveyed in words very nearly resembling those by which Eve was warned of her subjection to Adam. The Septuagint gives another turn to the former part of the verse, but clearly refers the latter as I do; and so in Gen. iii. 16 — According to this view, the words of this text have nothing to do with Freewill, though it seems the Hebrew Rabbins, as well as Luther and Erasmus, thought they had. (See Pole's Synops in loc.)—If they must be referred to sin, not Abel; Luther's interpretation is correct, and his answer unanswerable —If the words be taken *indicatively*, they are a promise of God, which was broken as soon as made.

[c] *Inculces*] A figurative expression from 'treading in with the feet;' hence applied to those efforts by which, like the pavier ramming down his stones, we aim to drive or beat our

allowed to say the same thing many times over. If there be freeness of choice[d] in the soul, why has your approvable opinion said that the free will cannot will good? Can it choose without willing, or against its will?—But let us hear your simile.

It would be ridiculous to say to a man standing in a street where two ways meet, 'you see two ways, enter which you please;' when only one is open.

This is just what I said before, about the arguments of carnal reason: she thinks that man is mocked by an impossible precept; whereas we say, he is admonished and excited by it to see his own impotency. Truly then, we are in this sort of street; but only one way is open to us: or rather, no way is open.[e] But it is shewn us by the law, how impossible it is for us to choose the one—that leading to good, I mean—except God give his Holy Spirit: how broad and easy the other is, if God allow us to walk in it. Without mockery then, and with all necessary gravity, it would be said to a man standing in the street, 'enter which of the two you please;' if, either he should have a mind to appear strong in his own eyes, being infirm; or should maintain that neither of these ways is shut against him.

The words of the law then, are spoken not to affirm the power of the will, but to enlighten blind reason; that she may see what a nothing her light

meaning into a person's head. Erasmus not only repeats, but pursues long desultory arguments, heaping one upon another, to prove his point.

[d] *Libertas eligendi*] Choice there must be, or there is no will; but that choice may be made under a wrong bias. This is properly the question of Freewill, viz. whether the will be under such a bias, or not.

[e] *Imo nulla patet*] Referring to what he has said before, 'about God's doing every thing;' and our doing all we do, by necessity. So, even the way of evil is only broad and easy, 'si Deus permittat.'

PART III. is, and what a nothing the power of the will is. "By the law is the knowledge of sin," says Paul; he does not say the 'abolition,' or the 'avoidance,' of it. The 'principle[f] and power of the law has for its essence the affording of knowledge, and that only of sin; not the displaying of any power, or the conferring of any.

For this[g] knowledge, neither *is* power, nor *confers* power, but instructs; and shews that there is no power in that quarter, and how great is the infirmity in that quarter. For what else can the knowledge of sin be, but the knowledge of our infirmity and of our wickedness. Nor does he say, ' by the law comes the knowledge of virtue, or good:' but all that the law does, according to Paul, is to cause sin to be known.

This is that passage from which I drew my answer, ' that by the words of the law man is admonished and instructed what he ought to do, not what he can do;' that is, to know his sin, not to believe that he has some power. ' So that, as often as you cast the words of the law in my teeth, I will answer you, my Erasmus, with this saying of Paul; "By the law is the knowledge of sin," not power in the will. Take now some of your larger Concordances, and heap together all the imperative verbs into one chaos (so they be not words of promise, but words of exaction and law), and I shall presently shew you, that by these is always intimated not what men do, or can do, but what they ought to do. Your grammar-masters, and boys in the streets, know this; that by verbs

---

[f] *Tota ratio et virtus legis.*] *Rat.* a word of very extensive and various signification, expresses ' the nature, order, object, structure, and relations of any substance.' ' Principle' seems best to express it here. as comprehending both design and constitution. *Rat. et virt.* The law is both framed for this purpose, and effects it.

[g] I insert ' this;' because the two *this*, which follow, make it plain, that it is not knowledge in general, but this knowledge in particular, of which he speaks.

of the imperative mood nothing else is expressed, but what *ought* to be done: what *is* done, or *may be* done, must be declared by indicative verbs.

How comes it then, that you theologians, as if you had fallen into a state of second childhood, no sooner get hold of a single imperative verb, than you are foolish enough to infer an indicative; as if an act were no sooner commanded, than it becomes straightway, even of necessity, a thing done, or at least practicable. For how many things happen between the cup and the lip,[h] to prevent what you have ordered, and what was moreover quite practicable, from taking place: such a distance is there between imperative and indicative verbs, in common and most easy transactions. But you'—when the things enjoined, instead of being near to us as the lip is to the cup, are more distant than heaven from earth—and, moreover, impracticable—so suddenly make indicatives for us out of imperatives, that you will have the things to have been kept, done, chosen, and fulfilled, or about to be so, by our own power; as soon as ever the word of command has been given, ' do, keep, choose.'[k]

In the fourth place, you adduce many like verbs of choosing, refusing, keeping; as, 'if thou shalt keep,' 'if thou shalt turn aside,' 'if thou shalt choose,' &c. &c. from the third[l] and from the thirtieth chapter of Deuteronomy. 'All these

Passages from Deut. xxx. &c. considered.

---

[h] *Inter os et offam*] 'The mouth and the cake;' but I have preferred the more common proverb.

[i] *Et vos*] It would be read with more spirit in the form of a question —' And do you so suddenly make, &c.'

[k] Luther is abundant in reply to this passage from Deuteronomy. 1. It proves too much. 2 Not ridiculous, if the way be supposed shut. 3 The law gives knowledge of sin. 4. Imperative verbs are not indicatives

[l] The reference to Deut. iii. appears to be incorrect: these expressions are all found in the xxxth; and the like to them in xxvii. xxviii. xxix. But chap. iii. is a mere narrative.

BONDAGE OF THE WILL.

PART III. expressions, you say, would be unseasonable, if man's will were not free to good.'

I answer, you also are very unseasonable, my Diatribe, in collecting Freewill from these verbs! For you professed to prove only desire and endeavour in your Freewill, and adduce no passage which proves such endeavour, but a string of passages, which, if your consequence were valid, would assign 'a whole' to Freewill.[m] Let us, then, distinguish here again between the words adduced from Scripture, and the consequence which Diatribe has appended to them. The words adduced are imperative, and only express what ought to be done. For Moses does not say, you have strength or power to choose, but 'choose, keep, do.' He delivers commands to do, but does not describe man's power of doing. But the consequence added by this sciolous Diatribe infers, ' therefore man can do these things; else they would be enjoined in vain.' To which the answer is, '.Madam Diatribe, you make a bad inference, and you do not prove your consequence: it is because you are blind and lazy, that you think this consequence follows, and has been proved.' These injunctions; however, are not delivered unseasonably, or in vain; but are so many lessons by which vain and proud man may learn his own diseased state of impotency, if he try to do what is commanded. So again, your simile is to no purpose, where you say;

'Else it would be just as if you should say to a man, who is so tied and bound, that he can only stretch out his arm to the left, See! you have a cup of most excellent wine at your right hand, and a cup of poison at your left:'

---

[m] *Totum*, opposed to *particula ejus reliqua*; ' that small remaining particle of Freewill which Erasmus professed to support and prove:' his texts would make it an integer, not a fraction. See above, Sect. iv.

stretch out your hand to whichsoever side you please.'

I have a notion that you are mightily tickled with these similes. But you do not perceive all the while, that, if your similes stand good, they prove much more than you have undertaken to prove; nay, that they prove what you deny, and would have to be disapproved; namely, that Freewill can do every thing. For, throughout your whole treatise, forgetting that you have said 'Freewill can do nothing without grace,' you prove that 'Freewill can do every thing without grace.' Yes, this is what you make out, at last, by your consequences and similes, that, either Freewill, left to herself, can do the things which are said and enjoined, or they are idly, ridiculously, and unseasonably enjoined. Howbeit, these are but the old songs of the Pelagians; which even the Sophists have exploded, and you have yourself condemned. Meanwhile, you show by this forgetfulness and bad memory of yours, how entirely you are both ignorant of the cause, and indifferent to it. For what is more disgraceful to a rhetorician, than to be continually discussing and proving things foreign to the point at issue; nay, to be continually haranguing against both his cause and himself?[n]

I do therefore affirm again, that the words of Scripture adduced by you are imperative words, and neither prove any thing, nor determine any thing, on the subject of human power, but prescribe certain things to be done, and to be left undone: whilst your consequences or additions, *His Scriptures prove nothing; his additions to Scripture, too much.*

---

[n] *Contra causam et seipsum*] Not only in opposition to the cause he was advocating, but even to his own admissions and assertions.—But what a string of charges is here!—*Sciolist!* a mere smatterer in learning and knowledge.—*Pelagian!* which every ' would-be' orthodox disclaims—*negligent, desultory, undiscerning, heartless!* quam nihil vel intelligas vel afficiaris causæ!

and your similes, prove this, if they prove any thing, that Freewill can do every thing without grace. This proposition, however, is not one which you have undertaken to prove, but have even denied: so that proofs of this kind are nothing else but the strongest disproofs. For let me try now, whether it be possible to rouse Diatribe from her lethargy. Suppose I should argue thus: when Moses says, 'choose life, and keep the commandment;' except a man can choose life and keep the commandment, it is ridiculous in Moses to enjoin this upon man: should I by this argument have proved, that Freewill can do nothing good; or that it has endeavour, but not of its own power?° No, I should have proved, by a pretty bold sort of comparison,ᵖ that, either man can choose life and keep the commandment, as he is ordered to do; or Moses is a ridiculous teacher. But who would dare to call Moses a ridiculous teacher? It follows therefore, that man can do the things commanded him. This is the way, in which Diatribe is continually arguing against her own thesis; by which she engaged not to maintain any such position as this, but to show a certain power of endeavouring in Freewill: of which, however, she makes little mention in the whole series of her arguments, so far is she from proving it. Nay, she rather proves the contrary: so as to be herself rather, the ridiculous speaker and arguer every where.ᑫ

° *Sine suis viribus*] He plays upon ' the approvable opinion ;' which leaves endeavour, but does not leave it to be ascribed to Freewill's own power

ᵖ *Satis forti contentione.*] *Cont* is sometimes used in a rhetorical sense to express one of the parts of an oration; ' disputatio sive disceptatio,' opposed to ' quæstio.' or ' controversia ;' what might properly be called ' the argumentation :' but is here used in another rhetorical sense, to express ' contrast, comparison, or antithesis;' ' Moses's folly,' set in array against ' man's power.'

ᑫ She imputed this to Luther : she would make either him or Moses absurd , the real absurdity lay in adducing arguments, which either proved nothing; or proved the opposite.

- With respect to its being ridiculous, according to the simile you have introduced, that a man tied by the right arm should be bidden to stretch out his hand to the right, when he can only stretch it out to the left; would it be ridiculous, I ask—if a man, who was tied even by both hands, should proudly maintain, or ignorantly presume, that he could do what he pleased on both sides of him—to bid such a man stretch out his hand to whichsoever side he likes; not with the design of laughing at his captive state, but that the false presumption of his own liberty and power may be evinced, or that his ignorance of his captivity and misery may be made notorious to himself. Diatribe is always dressing up for us a man of her own invention, who either can do as he is bidden, or at least knows that he cannot. But such a man is no where to be found: and if there were such a man, then it would indeed be true, that, either impossibilities are enjoined ridiculously, or the Spirit of Christ is given in vain.[r]

SC. XXII.
Simile of the hand tied.

But the Scripture sets before us a man, who is not only bound, wretched, captive, sick, dead, but who adds this plague of blindness (through the agency of Satan his prince) to his other plagues, and so thinks himself at liberty; happy, unshackled, able, in health, alive. For Satan knows, that, if man were acquainted with his own misery, he should not be able to retain a single individual of the race in his kingdom: because God could not choose but at once pity and help him, when now he had come to recognise his misery, and cry out for relief: seeing, he is a God so greatly extolled throughout the whole Scripture, as being near to the contrite in heart, that, in the sixty-first chapter of Isaiah (vv. 1—3.), Christ declares himself to have been even sent

Uses of the law, though impracticable.

[r] If he can do what is bidden, there is no need of the Spirit; if he knows he cannot, there is no longer any use for prescribing it.

into the world by Him, for the purpose of preaching the Gospel to the poor, and healing the broken-hearted. So that, it is Satan's business to keep men *from* the recognition of their own misery; and to keep them *in* the presumption of their own ability to do all that is commanded. But the legislator Moses's business is the very opposite of this: HE is to lay open man's misery to him by the law, that, having hereby broken his heart, and confounded him with the knowledge of himself, he may prepare him for grace,ˢ and send him to Christ, and so he may be saved for ever. What the law does, therefore, is not ridiculous, but exceedingly serious and necessary.ᵗ

Those who are now brought to understand these matters, understand at the same time, without any difficulty, that Diatribe proves absolutely nothing, by her whole series of arguments; whilst she does nothing but get together a parcel of imperative verbs from the Scriptures, of which she knows not either the meaning or the use. Having done so, she next adds her own consequences and carnal similes, and thus mixes up such a potent cake,ᵘ that she asserts and proves more than she had advanced, and argues against her very self. It would not be necessary, therefore, to pursue my rapid courseᵛ through her

---

ˢ *Ad gratiam*] Not, what is often understood by grace, 'the gift of the Spirit,' but, what grace truly is in its essence, 'the free favour of God.'

ᵗ *Ridicula* . *seria* . *necessaria*.]. Ridiculous may have respect either to the *laugher*, or the *laughed at*; what we do in sport, or suffer as objects of sport The law neither mocks, nor makes a fool of herself, though her ordinances be impossible to man; neither mocks, by calling merely to expose; nor subjects herself to derision, by speaking where she has nothing to gain.

ᵘ *Offam* seems to be some allusion to Cerberus. Æn. vi. 420.

ᵛ *Percurrere.*] Luther applies the same term to his review of Erasmus's preface, implying short and lively animadversion rather than grave and elaborate research. So, just afterwards, 'recensere;' 'enumeration,' or 'recital,' rather than 'investigation.'

several proofs any further; since they are all dismissed by dismissing one, as all resting upon one principle. Still, I shall go on to recount some of them, that I may drown her in the very flood in which she was meaning to drown me.[x]

In Isaiah i. (ver. 19.) we read, "If ye shall have been willing, and shall have heard, ye shall eat the good of the land:" where it would have been more consistent, as Diatribe thinks, to have said, 'If *I* be willing;' 'If *I* be unwilling;' on the supposition of the will not being free.

The answer to this suggestion is sufficiently manifest, from what has been said above. But what congruity would there be, in its being said here, 'If *I will*, ye shall eat of the good of the land?' Does Diatribe, of her excessive wisdom, imagine that the good of the land could be eaten *against* the will of God; or that it is a rare and new thing for us to receive good, only if HE will?

So in Isaiah xxx.[y] "If ye seek, seek; turn ye, and come." 'To what purpose is it that we exhort those who have no power at all over themselves? Is it not just as if we should say to a man bound with fetters, move yourself that way;' says Diatribe?

Say rather, to what purpose is it that you quote passages, which, of themselves, prove nothing; but by adding a consequence; that is, by corrupting their meaning; ascribe every thing to Freewill: whereas only a sort of endeavour, and that not ascribable to Freewill, was to be proved?

Marginal: SC.XXIII. Isaiah i 19. xxx 21. xlv. 20. lii 1. 2. and some other passages considered; they prove too much; no distinction between Law and Gospel, &c.

[x] *Obruatur copiâ*, seems to be some allusion to the dragon, Rev. xii 15. " And the serpent cast out of his mouth water, as a flood, after the woman, that he might cause her to be carried away of the flood "

[y] The reference seems to be to verse 21, where our translation has it, " And thine ears shall hear a word behind thee, saying, This is the way, walk ye in it, when ye turn to the right hand, and when ye turn to the left.".

PART III. — 'I would say the same of that testimony in Isaiah xlv. " Assemble yourselves, and come; turn to me, and ye shall be saved:" and of that in Isaiah lii. " Arise, arise, shake thyself from the dust, loose the chains from off thy neck." Of that also in Jeremiah xv. " If thou wilt turn, I will turn thee; and if thou wilt separate the precious from the vile, thou shalt be as my mouth." But Zechariah makes still more evident mention of the endeavour of Freewill, and of the grace which is prepared for the endeavourer. He says, " Turn ye to me, saith the Lord of Hosts, and I will turn to you, saith the Lord."[z]

In these passages, our Diatribe discovers no difference at all between law words and gospel words. So blind and ignorant is she forsooth, that she does not see what is Law and what is Gospel. Out of the whole of Isaiah, she brings not a single law word, except that first one, ' If ye shall have been willing.' All the other passages are made up of gospel words; by which the contrite and afflicted are called to take comfort from offers of grace.[a] But Diatribe makes law

[z] Isa xlv. 20 lii. 1, 2. Jerem. xv. 19. The reference made to Zechariah seems properly to belong to Malachi iii. 7. See above, Part ii. Sect xiii note.º.

[a] *Verbo gratiæ oblatæ*] The expression, ' offers of grace,' is exceptionable, as implying freeness of choice; in direct contrariety to Luther's position and arguments. The truth is, that, whilst he abhorred free choice, he liked free offers. I could have been glad if he had expressed his meaning more definitely; which is little else than ' the promises of God received in such wise as they be *generally set forth* to us in holy Scripture,' that is, received ' as promises of free favour made to persons of a certain character; and not to individuals, *as such.*' What but these are the very and legitimate stay of God's eternally foreknown, elect, predestinated; and now quickened child; in the day of his tearing and smiting? . Is he to hear a voice, or see a vision, or receive some providential token, personal to himself, before he presumes to call upon the name of the Lord? Are not these, " Ho, every one that thirsteth;" " To this man will I look," " Come unto me, all ye that travail and are heavy-laden,"; " The same Lord over all is rich

words of them. And pray what good will *he* do in theology, or in the Scriptures, who has not yet got so far as to know what the Law is, and what the Gospel is; or, if he does know, disdains to observe the difference? Such an one must confound every thing; heaven and hell, life and death; and will take no pains to know any thing at all about Christ. I shall admonish my Diatribe more copiously upon this subject hereafter.

Look now at those words of Jeremiah and Zechariah: 'If thou wilt turn, I will turn thee;' and, 'Turn ye to me, and I will turn to you.' Does it follow, 'Turn ye,' therefore ye can turn? Does it follow, 'Love the Lord thy God with all thine heart,' therefore thou shalt be able to love him with all thine heart? What is the conclusion, then, from arguments of this kind, but that Freewill needs not the grace of God, for she can do every thing by her own power? How much more properly are the words taken, just as they stand!^b 'If thou shalt have been turned, I also will turn thee;' that is, if thou shalt leave off sinning, I also will leave off punishing; and if, when thou art converted, thou shalt lead a good life, I also will do thee good, and will turn thy captivity and thy evils.^c But it does not follow

unto all that call upon Him"—his warrant for drawing near, and his first words of consolation '—But these, at last, are not 'offers' of grace, by which God throws himself, as it were, at the knees and feet of his creatures—subjecting himself to a refusal, nay, with full assurance that he must receive one, except he superadd a special and distinct impulse of his own to secure acceptance—but testimonies of his own mouth, and hand, and ordinances, borne to those souls which he, in his own good time, has made ready to welcome them, that he will bind up, and heal, and own, these poor destitutes, amidst the gathered remnant of his heritage

^b *Verba, ut posita sunt*] 'Without additions,' such as Erasmus's

^c I do not know that any reasonable objection can be made to Luther's paraphrase of Jeremiah xv 19, and Malachi (he calls him Zechariah) iii. 7. But the quotation from Jeremiah

PART III. from these words, that a man can turn to God by his own power; nor do the words affirm this: they simply say, 'If thou art converted;' admonishing man what he ought to be. Now, when he shall have known and seen this, he would seek the power, which he hath not, from the source whence he might have it,[d] if Diatribe's Leviathan (her appendage and consequence, I mean) did not come in the way, saying, ' It would in vain be said, " Turn ye," except a man could turn by his own power.'—What sort of a saying this is, and what it proves, has been declared abundantly.

It is the effect of stupor or lethargy to suppose that Freewill is established by those words, 'Turn ye,' ' If thou shalt turn,' and the like; and not to perceive, that, upon the same principle, it would also be established by this saying, " Thou shalt love the Lord thy God with all thy heart;" since the *demand* in the one case, is equivalent to the *command*[e] in the other. Nor is the love of God, and of all his commandments, less required than our own conversion; since the love of God is our true conversion. And yet no man argues Freewill from that commandment of love, whilst all argue

seems perfectly out of place : it is a personal matter between the Lord and his Prophet, a converted man : what has this to do, then, with the question of Freewill ?

[d] *Quærat unde possit.*] I have been inclined to connect these words with the preceding sentence; 'by which he is admonished what he ought to be ; and having understood and discovered this, *is admonished* to seek the power which he hath not whence he might get it ; if Diatribe should not intervene,' &c.—The punctuation, however, forbids this connection, and it does not appear to be Luther's meaning. He imputes it to Diatribe's false suggestion, if man, warned that he ought to turn to God, does not find out his own impotency, and seek his conversion from God. But there is much more that goes to this seeking, than Luther seems to include in it: under the clearest light, men will still resist conviction ; and the heart to seek, is as much a gift, as conversion itself.

[e] More literally, ' since the meaning of the *commander* and the *demander* is equal on both sides.'

TEXTS FOR FREEWILL DISPROVED.

it from those words, 'If thou shalt be willing,' 'If thou shalt hear,' 'Turn,' and the like. If then it followeth not from that saying, 'Love the Lord thy God with all thy heart,' that Freewill is any thing, or has any power, assuredly neither doth it from those, 'If thou wilt,' 'If thou hearest,' 'Turn ye,' and the like: which either demand less, or demand less vehemently, than that 'Love God,' 'Love the Lord.'[f]

Whatever reply, therefore, is made to that saying, 'Love God,' forbidding to conclude Freewill from it; the same shall be made to all other expressions of command or demand, in forbiddance of the same conclusion: namely, that by the command to love is shewn 'the matter of the law,'[g] what we ought to do; but not the power of the human will, what we can do; or rather, what we cannot do. The same is shewn by all other expressions of demand. It is evident, that even the schoolmen, with the exception of the Scotists and the Moderns,[h] assert, that man cannot love God with his whole heart. From whence it follows, that neither can he fulfil any of the other commandments; since they all hang on this, as Christ testifies. Thus, it remains as a just conclusion, even from the testimony of the scholastic doctors, that the words of the law do not prove a power in the free will, but show what we ought to do, and what we cannot do.

But our Diatribe, with still greater absurdity, not only infers an indicative sense from that say-

sc xxiv.

Mal iii 7. more particularly considered.

---

[f] *Dilige Deum. Ama Dominum.*] *Dil* and *am.* are here used as of like import : sometimes they are put in contrast, and that variously ; *diligo* being sometimes the stronger, and sometimes the weaker term. In distinguishing them, 'amo' may be understood to denote the love of appetite, and 'diligo' the love of reason.

[g] *Forma legis*] More literally, ' the shape, mould, or image of the law ;' ' what is comprehended in it.'

[h] *Scotistis et Modernis.*] See above, Part iii. Sect. ii. notes f g.

ing of Zechariah, 'Turn ye unto me;' but maintains, that it even proves a power of endeavouring in Freewill, and grace prepared for the endeavourer.

And here, at last, she remembers her 'endeavour;' and, by a new art of grammar, 'to turn,' with her, signifies the same as 'to endeavour:' so that the sense is, 'Turn unto me;' that is, 'endeavour to turn,' and 'I will turn to you;' that is, 'endeavour to turn' to you. At last, then, she attributes endeavour even to God; intending perhaps to prepare grace for *His* endeavourings also. For, if 'to turn' signifies 'to endeavour' in one place; why not in all?

Again, in that passage of Jeremiah, 'If thou shalt separate the precious from the vile;' she maintains that not only 'endeavour,' but even 'freedom of choice,' is proved: what she had before taught us to have been lost, and to have been turned into a necessity of serving sin. You see then, that Diatribe truly possesses a free will in her handlings of Scripture; by which she compels words, of one and the same form, to prove endeavour in one place, and free choice in another; just as she pleases.

But bidding adieu to these vanities, the word 'turn' has two uses in Scripture; a legal, and an evangelical one. In its legal use, it is an exacter and commander; requiring not endeavour only, but change of the whole life; as Jeremiah frequently uses it, saying, 'Turn ye every one from his evil way;' 'Turn to the Lord:' where it evidently involves an exacting of all the commandments. When used evangelically, it is a word of divine promise and consolation; by which nothing is demanded *from* us, but the grace of God is offered *to* us. Such is that of Psalm cxxvi. 'When the Lord shall turn again the captivity of Zion;' and that of Psalm cxvi. 'Turn again then unto thy rest, O my soul!' And so Zecharias contrives to dispatch both sorts of preaching (law as well as grace) in a very short compendium. It is all law, and the sum of the law, when he says, 'Return unto me:' it is grace, when he says, 'I will return unto you.' As far, therefore, as Freewill is proved by that saying, 'Love the Lord,' or by any other saying of any particular law; just so far, and no farther, is it proved by this summary law word 'Turn.' It is the part of a wise reader of Scripture then, to observe what are law words, and what are grace words; that he may not jumble them all together, like the filthy Sophists, and like this yawning Diatribe.[1]

[1] Luther's distinction between law words and gospel words, as applied by him in these two sections, severally, and comparedly, is arbitrary, indefinite, and unavailing. *Arbitrary*; inasmuch as he pretends not to have any recognised authority for it, and applies it inconsistently; sometimes calling words of exhortation or command 'gospel words;' and sometimes confining that term to words of promise, as opposed to them. 'Turn ye unto me', is a law word; 'I will turn to you' is a gospel word. *Indefinite*; because he gives no fixed rule by which to determine what is one, and what is the other; but, according to his own account, leaves it to the discerning reader. *Unavailing*; because a gospel precept is not less impracticable than a law one to the free will.—In my view, he confounds matters; for 'return,' or 'repent,' is surely not a law precept, but a gospel one: the law knows nothing of repentance.—The truth is, he has given his answer to all these testimonies already. They are requirements; call them law requirements, if you will, or gospel requirements; 'they are something for man to do;' and, as he very properly argues, they are meant to shew him what he ought [to do,] but imply not any power either towards Law, or towards Gospel. The law is, properly, 'the law of the Ten Commandments;' under which, speaking less precisely, may be comprehended all those precepts which fall in with the nature and design of that 'transcript of the creation law of man;' but nothing which regards his relations as a fallen, or as a restored creature.— Luther speaks confusedly, as other writers do, on this subject; not discerning the origin, design, and nature of that institution.—The law *spake* not till Moses; spake only to the Jews; or then visible church of God; was a preparation for, and a fore-preached Gospel. A law word therefore, *rightly understood*, is also a gospel word: a word which prepareth, by compelling a sense of need; and which—whilst it "shuts up unto

N

178   (BONDAGE OF THE WILL.

PART III.
SC. XXV.
Ezek. xviii. 23. considered.

For see now, how she treats that famous passage in Ezekiel xviii. " As I live, saith the Lord, I would not the death of a sinner, but rather that he be converted and live." First, "It is so often repeated, says she, in the course of this chapter," " shall turn away," " hath done," " hath wrought;" in respect both of good and evil. Where then are those who deny that man does any thing? What an excellent consequence is here! She was going to prove desire and endeavour in Freewill; but she proves the whole act, every thing done to the uttermost, by Freewill! Where now are they who maintain the necessity of grace and of the Holy Spirit? For this is her ingenious way of arguing: ' Ezekiel says, "If the wicked man shall turn away from his wickedness and do justice and judgment, he shall live.—Why then the wicked man presently does so, and can do so.' Ezekiel intimates what ought to be done; Diatribe considers this as what is done, and has been done; again introducing a new sort of grammar, by which she may teach us that it is the same thing to owe, as to have—the same thing to be enacted, as to be performed—the same thing to demand, as to pay.

After this, she lays hold on that sweetest of gospel words, ' I would not the death of a sinner,' and gives this turn to it;—' Does the holy Lord deplore that death of his people, which he works in them himself?' If he would not the death of a sinner, verily, it is to be imputed to our own will if we perish. But what can you impute to a being,

the faith which should afterwards be revealed," and which now has been revealed—*impliedly* promises and *exhibits* Him, who was to be, and who now has been and is, its fulfiller and perfecter.
— ^k *Sic versat.*] *Vers.* implies a forced application of it; as if you should turn a body, that is already in motion, out of its natural course; or give motion to one that is at rest.

who has no power to do any thing, either good or evil?'

SC. XXVI.

Pelagius also sang just the same sort of song; when he ascribed not desire and endeavour only, but complete power of fulfilling and doing every thing to Freewill. For these consequences prove this power, as I have before said, if they prove any thing; and therefore fight as stoutly, and even more so, against Diatribe herself (who denies this power in Freewill, and sets up endeavour only); as against us who deny Freewill altogether. But without dwelling upon her ignorance, I will state the matter as it really is.

It is a gospel word, and a word of sweetest consolation to poor miserable sinners, when Ezekiel says, "I would not the death of a sinner, but rather that he should be converted and live, by all means." As is that of the thirtieth Psalm also, "For his wrath is but for a moment, and his will towards us life rather than death." And that of the thirty-sixth Psalm, "How sweet is thy mercy, Lord!" Also, "Because I am merciful." And that saying of Christ, in Matthew xi, "Come unto me, all ye that labour, and I will refresh you." Also, that of Exodus, "I do mercy to them that love me, unto many thousands." Nay, what is almost more than half of the Scripture but mere promises of grace, by which mercy, life, peace, and salvation are offered to men?¹ And what other import have words of promise than this, "I would not the death of a sinner?" Is it not the same thing to say, 'I am merciful,' as to say, 'I am not angry,' 'I do not wish to punish,' 'I do not wish you to die,' 'I wish to pardon you,' 'I wish to spare you?' Now, if these divine promises did not stand in the word, to raise up those whose consciences have been wounded with the sense of sin, and terrified with

The true meaning of Ezek. xviii 23. stated.

¹ See above, Sect xxiii. note.

the fear of death and judgment, what place would there be for pardon, or for hope? What sinner would not despair? But, as Freewill - is not proved by other words of pity, or promise, or consolation, so neither is it proved by this, "I would not the death of a sinner."

But our Diatribe, again confounding the distinction between law words and words of promise, makes this place of Ezekiel a law word, and expounds it thus: 'I would not the death of a sinner;' that is, 'I would not that he should sin mortally, or become a sinner guilty of death; but rather that he should turn away from his sin, if he hath committed any, and so should live.' For, if she did not expound it so, it would not serve her purpose at all: but such an exposition entirely subverts and withdraws this most persuasive word of Ezekiel, 'I would not the death of a sinner.' If we are determined so to read and understand the Scriptures, by the exercise of our own blindness, what wonder if they be obscure and ambiguous? For he does not say, "I would not the sin of a man," but 'I would not the death of a sinner;' clearly intimating, that he speaks of the punishment of sin, which the sinner is experiencing for his sin; that is, the fear of death.' Yes; He raises up and consoles the sinner, when now laid on this bed of affliction and despair, that he may not quench the smoking flax, or break the bruised reed, but may excite hope of pardon and salvation: that so he may rather be converted (converted, I mean, to salvation from the punishment of death) and live; that is, be happy, and rejoice in a quiet conscience.[m]

For this also must be observed, that, as the

---

[m] His state as a sinner is a state of eternal death, the just punishment of his sin; and of this state he has the beginning in his 'now' realizing apprehensions of it. When *converted*, he is delivered from this state of punishment; and when he *lives*, he is brought into the joy of this changed state.

TEXTS FOR FREEWILL DISPROVED. 181

voice of the law is sounded forth only over those who neither feel nor acknowledge their sin (as Paul speaks in Rom. iii. "By the law is the knowledge of sin"); so the word of grace comes but to those who, feeling their sin, are afflicted and tempted to despair. Thus it is, that, in all law words, you see sin charged by shewing us what we ought to do: just as, in all words of promise, on the other hand, you see the misery, which sinners (that is, those who are to be raised up from their dejection by them) labour under, intimated: as here, the word 'I would not the death of a sinner', expressly names death and the sinner; the very evil which is felt, as well as the very man who feels it. But in this word 'Love God with all thy heart' there is pointed out the good we owe, not the evil we feel; that we may be brought to acknowledge how incapable we are of doing that good.

So then, nothing could have been more unaptly adduced in support of Freewill, than this passage from Ezekiel; which even fights against it most lustily. For herein is implied, how Freewill is affected, and what it is able to do, when sin has been discovered, and when now the matter is to turn itself to God: it is herein implied, I say, that it could do nothing but fall into a still worse state, adding desperation and impenitence to its other sins, unless God should presently come to its succour, and should recall and raise it up,[n] by his word of promise. For God's eagerness in promising grace to restore and raise up the sinner, is a very mighty and trustworthy argument, that Freewill of herself cannot but fall from bad to worse; and, as the Scripture says, "to

Margin: SC.XXVII

Margin: Ezek xviii. 23 negatives Freewill, instead of proving it.

---

[n] *Revocaret et erigeret.*] *Revoc.* implies 'departure;' the soul has gone further and further off from God, through despair of mercy. *erig.* implies 'fallen,' 'thrown down,' 'prostrated;' like Saul before the witch of Endor.

PART III. the nethermost hell."º Do you think that God is so light-minded as to pour out words of promise thus fluently, when they are not necessary to our salvation, for the mere pleasure of talking? You see then from this fact, that not only do all law words stand opposed to Freewill, but even all words of promise do utterly confute it. In other words, the whole Scripture is at war with it. So that this saying 'I would not the death of a sinner' has no other object, as you perceive, than that of preaching and offering divine mercy through the world;P which none but those who have been afflicted and harassed to death receive with joy and gratitude. These do so, because the law has in them already fulfilled its office, by teaching the knowledge of sin: whilst those who have not yet experienced this office of the law, and who neither acknowledge their sin, nor feel their death, despise the mercy promised in that word.q

º The Psalms abound with expressions of this sort: see especially the 38th and 88th; from the latter of which these words appear to be a quotation. "For my life draweth nigh unto the grave (v. 3); or, according to the older version, "to hell." (v. 2.)

P See above, note ª. The account I have there given of Luther's meaning is abundantly confirmed here. Mercy is to be preached, and what *he* calls 'offered,' generally to all men; but only those in whom the law has done its office (and whom did Luther understand by these, but God's elect?) will receive it. *His* offer, therefore, is a nugatory offer to all but the elect; and these *must* receive; not ' physically ' must, but ' morally.'

q Luther's answer to Erasmus's argument from Ezek. xviii. 23, is threefold. 1. It proves too much. 2. It proves no more than other gospel words; that is, words of promise and mercy. 3. Such words prove against Freewill, by implying, that without them man could only despair.

See above, note i, where I have objected to this distinction between law words and gospel words, and to the statements generally made respecting the Law, as though it were opposed to the Gospel. Luther is chargeable here with arguing 'per sequelam,' for which he so much blames Erasmus; 'God's

TEXTS FOR FREEWILL DISPROVED.

But, as to why some are touched by the law and others not, so that the former take in, and the latter despise, the grace offered; this is another word of promise proves that man could only despair without it.'—The true answer to Erasmus's argument from this text (which, according to Luther's distinction, is a gospel word—but then there is quite, as much supernatural help necessary to make a gospel word availing, as to fulfil a law one—) is, that it proves nothing on either side. Inferences may be drawn both ways; against as well as for, and for as well as against: but the affirmation respects only *the mind of God*. He declares that he wills not death. What does this assert concerning the natural powers of man?—For a more full view of the doctrine set forth in this and like texts, and of their place in the great scheme of God-manifestation, see the next Section and its notes.

^r Luther has given what he considers the true answer to Erasmus's objection drawn from this text; 'it is a gospel word, for the consolation of the law-stricken;' and declares that we have no right to ask any more questions. I do not approve the exact point to which he brings the debate, nor can I agree with him that it ought to end just here. Luther speaks, and many others like him, as if only the law (meaning thereby the law of the Ten Commandments) could do the office of abasing and prostrating man; which, in effect, assumes that the law was given to man from the beginning, and that Moses's giving of it was but a republication: else how were those saints emptied of self and prostrated, who lived before Moses; such as Abel, Enoch, Noah, and the rest? But what proof is there of the law having been given from the beginning? Express proof is afforded in Rom v. that the law was not till Moses. "For until the law sin was in the world: but sin is not imputed when there is no law. Nevertheless death reigned from Adam to Moses, &c." (vv. 13, 14) The truth is, it is not the law, but the Holy Ghost (using the law, it is true, as his instrument more generally, where it has been given, but by no means universally so using it)—who needeth not the law, but has proofs enough to supply of man's sin, of his " earthly, sensual, devilish " mind; without having recourse to that summary of creation duty—that humbles, empties, and makes ready for the manifold Scripture declarations of God's entire readiness to receive the penitent *freely* These are indeed made such of God, and can only be made such by him; though it is not his plan usually to tell us how we have come, and alone can come, to this mind, when he testifies his love and good-will towards it. So that the question arising from this admitted state of things, ' some receive, others do not receive, this and like gospel words,' is not properly why some are law-stricken;' or, more correctly, why some are prostrated, and self-emptied; and self-despairing; but why some have the

S.XXVIII.

How far God may

PART III.

he said to bewail the death he produces.

question, and one not treated by Ezekiel in this place. He speaks of God's preached and offered mercy, not of that secret and awful will of his, by the counsel of which he ordains whom and what sort of persons he wills to be made capable of receiving, and to become actual participants of his preached and offered mercy. This will of God is not the object of our researches, but of our reverent adoration; as being by far the most venerable secret of the divine majesty, which he keeps locked up in his own bosom, and which is much more religiously[s] prohibited to us, than the Corycian caves to the countless multitude.

When now Diatribe cavillingly asks, 'whether the holy Lord bewails that death of his people which he produces in them himself?' a suggestion too absurd to be entertained:

I answer, as I have already done, we must argue in one wise concerning God, or the will of

Holy Ghost, and others have not; which is, in other words, why is there 'an election of grace?'—I cannot agree with Luther, that we have no right to ask this question; or, in other words, that the Scripture does not afford an answer to it; for *here* is the secret of God.

If it be asked why such a man is elect, and such a man is not elect, it is most true, we have no answer; this *is* God's secret; we have nothing to do with it. But if the question be, why are there elect and non-elect, we have to do with it, and can give an answer: it is *to the manifestation of God; which* is the end of all his counsels, and of all his operations.—For some observations on Luther's accepted aphorism. ' Quæ supra nos, nihil ad nos,' and upon ' his *apparent* setting out of two Gods,' with one of which we have nothing to do; and for the correct answer to Erasmus's insidious question, ' Does God deplore &c.' see notes [t], [v], [x], which follow.

[s] *Religiosius.*] ' By religious considerations.'—The multitude might look into the entrance; priests might enter into the penetralia; but the multitude might not go in to explore: if they did, they were filled with terrors; appalling sights confounded them : just so, and with still more fearful apprehensions of a religious nature, we are prohibited, says Luther, from attempting to penetrate the secret of God. But the question is, where this secret begins ? Luther says, ' in the fact, that some are touched by the law, and others not.'

God, insofar as that will is proclaimed to us, revealed, offered to our acceptance, made the ground of worship; and in another wise, concerning God, insofar as he is unproclaimed, unrevealed, unoffered, and unworshipped. So far as God hides himself, and chooses to be unknown by us, we have nothing to do with him. Here is the true application of that saying, 'What is above us, is nothing to us.' And lest any one should suppose this to be my distinction, let him know that I follow Paul, who writes to the Thessalonians concerning Antichrist (2 Thess. ii. 4.) "That he would exalt himself above all that is proclaimed of God, and that is worshipped;"†

S.XXVIII.
————

† *Super omnem Deum prædicatum et cultum*]. Literally, 'above all the proclaimed and worshipped God.' I question the soundness of Luther's interpretation of this text, and of the argument consequently, which he draws from it, although the distinction which he labours to establish is, with some modification and amplification, the root of the answer to the objection. "Who opposeth and exalteth himself above all that is called God, or *that is an object of worship*," is the more correct rendering of the original text. The meaning seems to be, that this Antichrist would both oppose himself to, and exalt himself above, every object of worship, both true and false, 'every being that is *called* God, and every substance which is worshipped.' It has therefore nothing to do with distinct views and considerations respecting the true God; but only marks the extravagant claims which this Antichrist would make, and which would be allowed by his votaries, as compared with the several objects of worship received in the world.—The word of God, however, doth clearly recognise a distinction between God, regarded as the legislator, governor, and judge of his moral creation—or in any other relations which he may have been pleased to assume towards the whole, or certain parts, of that creation—and God regarded as he is in himself, and as separated from such relations · as also, between that will of His which he hath revealed for our obedience (what may therefore be called his legislative will), and that free, infinite, and eternal will of His, from which this legislative will has emanated, and by which, in perfect consistency with all his assumed relations, and with that of legislator amongst the rest, he regulates his own conduct (what may therefore be called, by way of distinction, his personal will): in other words, between his commands and his mind.—God, who made the worlds, the alone Being, subsisted in his trinity of co-

plainly intimating, that a man might be exalted above God, so far as he is proclaimed, and wor-
equal persons, infinite, and all-blessed, before he made them. Is it presumptuous to say why he made them? Has he not unequivocally told us? His end is, as it must be, seated in himself.* He will shew himself—WHAT HE IS—so far as infinite can be shewn to finite, to certain moral and intelligent creatures, whom he will make capable of apprehending, adoring, and enjoying him, in their measure. Hence the whole counsel, process, series, and results of creation; in which I include all that belongs to Creator and creature-ship. Hence the true distinction between the hidden and revealed God: which is properly no other than God the revealer and God the revealed; creation in this wide extent being only God's revealer; and having in reality revealed much of him, whilst there is much at last in God which is not, cannot be revealed. Thus, we see that this hidden God, or rather this absolute God (so called because not circumscribed by relations; which relations, however, can only be such as he has seen fit to assume; and which he has seen fit to assume, for the one great end of self-manifestation), is the same God with the revealed and circumscribed God; and that, so far from being an unknown God in this regard, he has revealed himself in his relative and circumscribed capacity, for the very purpose of making himself known (so far as the incomprehensible can be made known) in this absolute and uncircumscribed capacity.

So, again, with respect to his secret and his revealed will; or, as I have more correctly distinguished them, his personal and his legislative will; whilst these are distinct, they are neither opposed to each other, nor unconnected with each other—his legislative will subserves his personal will, and is his ordained and specially-devised instrument for accomplishing it: by which accomplishment, his great purpose, in submitting himself to his various creator relationships (to wit, self-manifestation) is achieved.†

Luther does not seem to have apprehended the union and concordance of these two distinct views, in which both God and his will are set forth to us, whilst he so strongly marks their distinctness; and thus, his answer (not being *the whole truth;* that is, not being THE TRUTH; which consists in an harmonious combination of many parts) has an air of evasion and sophistry (to which he seems not to have been insensible himself), and is, in reality, unsatisfying and repulsive. Is it true, that the proverb, 'What is above us, is nothing to us,' has its rightful application here? Is it true, that we have nothing to

---

* See Vaughan's Calvinistic Clergy defended, p. 64—73. 2d Ed.
† In the observations which follow, I do not confine myself to the words immediately under review, but comprehend the whole of Luther's expressions and reasonings in this and the three succeeding paragraphs.

shipped; that is, above that word and worship by which God is made known to us, and main- do with this God of majesty, as Luther calls him; the absolute God? What is the knowledge of God—that last, highest, best gift of promise—but the knowledge of *this* God? the communication of which is, as we have seen, the very end of creation and of revelation.—Again ; is it true, that the revealed God, or relative God, wills only life? or, according to Luther's own way of stating it, that God has revealed himself in his word only, as that God who offers himself to all men, and would draw all men unto himself?—Why then does he tell us, in that selfsame word, that in very deed for this cause he had raised Pharaoh up, for to shew in him His power; and that His name might be declared throughout all the earth?—That it was of the Lord to harden the hearts of the Canaanites, that they should come against Israel in battle, that he might destroy them utterly, and that they might have no favour, but that he might destroy them, as the Lord commanded Moses?—That Hophni and Phinehas hearkened not unto the voice of their father, because the Lord would slay them?—That he smells a sweet savour of Christ in them that perish?—That whom he will he hardeneth?—That there are those ordained of old to condemnation?—Those appointed to stumble at the stone?—Those whom he has commanded to fill up the measure of their iniquities?—That he is, in short, a potter having power over the clay, and using that power?—Has he proclaimed all this concerning himself in his word; does he, moreover, make that word his great instrument of bringing these things to pass; and is it true nevertheless, that his word stands in contrast, nay direct opposition, to himself, so that we are wisely counselled to attend to his word in contrast, and even in opposition, to God who gave it?—Had Luther discerned the simple end of creation and revelation, ' God manifesting himself as what he really is in his essence' (in which essence, hatred of that which is contrary to himself is as much a part as love of that which is like himself); and seen that by means of creation and revelation, God is actually effecting this end—he would not have talked of salvation being the revealed God's alone work; nor have said that we have to do with his word, but not with himself; nor have warned us that we have nothing to do with His inscrutable will (including therein all that Luther includes therein)—when that inscrutable will is made matter of instruction in his word, and is declared to be what he is continually fulfilling in us; what the Lord Jesus thanks his Father for; and what his people find to be their great source of light, and strength, and joy.—How remarkable it is, that Luther should here silence his gainsayer with " Nay, but O man, who art thou that repliest against God?" when, with the interval of only a single verse, the Holy Ghost had furnished him with a clue to the whole

S. XXVIII.

tains intercourse with us. But, if God be regarded, not as he is an object of worship, and as he is proclaimed, but as he is in his own nature and majesty, nothing can be exalted above him, but every thing is under his powerful hand.

God must be left to himself then, so far as he is regarded in the majesty of his own nature; for in this regard we have nothing to do with him; nor is it in this regard that he hath willed to be dealt with by us: but, so far as he is clothed with his word, and displayed to us thereby; that word, by which he has offered himself to our acceptance; that word, which is his glory and beauty, and with which the Psalmist celebrates him as clothed; so far, and so far only, we transact with him. In this regard, we affirm that the holy God does not bewail that death of his people, of which he is himself the worker in them; but bewails that death which he finds in his people, and is taking pains to remove it. For this is what the proclaimed God is about, even taking away sin and death, that we may be saved. For "he hath sent his word and healed them."[u] But the God which is hidden in the majesty of his own counsel of God, and with an answer to those very questions which he says it is not lawful to ask, or possible to get resolved. "What if God, willing to shew his wrath, and to make his power known, endured with much long suffering the vessels of wrath fitted to destruction: And that he might make known the riches of his glory on the vessels of mercy, which he had afore prepared unto glory, even us, whom he hath called, not of the Jews only, but also of the Gentiles?"—Luther both speaks and means incorrectly here; but he says rather more than he means. It is not against the sober, hallowed use of the knowledge of this inscrutable will (for though there be that which is inscrutable in it, there is also that in it which may be known, for he has told it to us), but against those who denied, or confounded, or impugned, or reviled these distinctions, and would hear nothing of his sovereign majesty, and of his secret counsel, that he is aiming his dart here.

[u] Psalm cvii. 20. Luther applies this healing 'to all men;' but the Psalmist declares it only of 'those who cry unto the Lord in their trouble and in particular dispensations of his hand.'—This is not all men.

nature, neither bewails nor takes away death; but
works life and death, and all things in all things."

" Yes—and works life and death, and all things in all things,
through the agency of that proclaimed, or relative God; and
in perfect consistency with—*yea, by means of*—that legislative* will, which regulates man's duty as his moral creature.
It is as the proclaimed or relative God, not as the hidden or
absolute God, that he both saves and destroys; and this, by
means of his legislative enactments, not in contradiction to
them. The power which he gives to his elect and saved, and
which he withholds from the reprobate and damned, is distinct
from these legislative enactments; and, whilst it proceeds
from the relative God, proceeds not from him in his legisla-
torial relation, but in another, which is distinct from and not
commensurate with it; although its subjects be also subject to
that relation, and to its requirements. It is no part of the
legislator's office to give power, or to withhold it. He may
do either. He may work any thing, every thing, upon,
around, above, beneath him, so he but leave the subject of
his enactments a free agent: and this God does, and ever has
done.

 Thus it was in creation strictly so called; God, having assumed
the relation of Creator to man, gave him a law (Gen. ii. 17.)
"But of the tree of the knowledge of good and evil, thou
shalt not eat of it; for in the day that thou eatest thereof
thou shalt surely die." It was no part of his relation, as Creator,
either to withhold temptation from his creature, whom he had
" made upright," " in his own image," " good," " very
good" (but, as we have before noticed,† not having the Holy
Ghost, and therefore not held as by a chain to God, but sub-
sisting in a state of severance from him); nor yet to sustain
him by new powers (additional to those which he had received
at his creation), in a crisis of temptation. The result was that
he fell; and that the whole human race (which had been
created in him, and of which the several individuals had a distinct personal subsistence in him, and were parts of his substance, when, having first apostatized in heart, he did afterwards put forth his hand, and did take, and did eat) shared in
his ruin.—It is by the instrumentality of this law then, that
God both saves whom he personally wills to save, and destroys
whom he personally wills to destroy: saving those to whom,
by a super-creation relation which was given them in Christ
Jesus before the world began, he vouchsafes his special grace;
and, destroying those from whom, in perfect consistency with all
creation dues and obligations, he withholds the same.

* By ' legislative,' I shall be understood to mean all which can be
called ' enactment,' as given by God, of whatever kind; whether to one
nation, or to the whole world; whether Law or Gospel. See note ‡ above.
† Sect. xviii. note ‡.

PART. III. For, when acting in this character, he does not bound himself by his word, but has reserved to himself the most perfect freedom in the exercise of his dominion over all things. But Diatribe beguiles herself through her ignorance, making no distinction between the proclaimed God, and the hidden God; that is, between the word of God, and God himself. God does many things which he has not shewn us in

Thus it was in God's dealings with the nation of Israel, and with his visible church, as for a season co-extensive with that nation. When now he had formed the seed of Abraham into a nation, and had assumed the relation of king to that people, he gave them a law; by which, instrumentally, he kept them for his own, so long as it was his personal will to keep them, and scattered them when it was the counsel of his personal will to scatter them.* By the same law instrumentally, He, in their ecclesiastical relation, saved whom he would save, through the bestowal of a grace which was not of their covenant; whilst he at the same time destroyed whom he would destroy, through the withholding of that grace, in perfect consistency with the provisions of the same.

Thus it is also in the Gospel Church, and in the commanded preaching of the Gospel to all nations, and tongues, and people. God, in the relation of the offended sovereign of the human race, commandeth all men every where to repent; giving them what may be called the law of repentance and faith, and demanding of them a state of mind which is suited to their condition as fallen and guilty creatures. 'Repent ye, and believe the Gospel.'† By this legislative will of his, instrumentally, he fulfils the counsels of his personal will; saving whom he has predestinated to save, and destroying whom he has predestinated to destroy.

* Israel, like Adam in Paradise, broke the law: nearly as soon as it was given him; but, by so doing, he prepared the way for all God's future dealings with him.

† Implicitly, but not explicitly, this is the demand, and the alone demand, which God has made upon man, even the whole human race, since the Fall; and shall continue to be so, till his mystery be finished by the Lord's second coming. The form of this demand has been varied, the knowledge of it has been varied; the law, eminently so called, has been interposed to the church, God has "winked at times of ignorance;" but a Manasseh's humbledness of mind, with a peradventure of mercy—the only demand which, in consistency with the recognition of those primary transactions in the Garden, and with the realities of the case, could be made—is in truth the only demand which has been made upon the sons and daughters of fallen Adam, from the period of the ejection out of Paradise until now: a demand which has served to mark the only difference that can ever be found to subsist between the several apostate members of an apostate head; viz. continued apostasy in some, and restoration in others.

TEXTS FOR FREEWILL DISPROVED. 191

his word. He also wills many things which he s.xxviii.
has not shewn us that he wills, in his word. For
instance; he wills not the death of a sinner—
according to his word, forsooth—but he wills it
according to that inscrutable will of his. Now
our business is to look at his word, and to leave
that inscrutable will of his to itself: for we must
be directed in our path by that word, and not by
that inscrutable will. Nay, who could direct
himself by that inscrutable and inaccessible will?
It is enough for us barely to know, that there is a
certain inscrutable will in God.—What that will
wills, why it so wills, and how far it so wills, are
matters which it is altogether unlawful for us to inquire into, to wish for knowledge about, to trouble
ourselves with, or to approach even with our touch.
In these matters, we have only to adore and to fear.
So then, it is rightly said, 'If God wills
not death, we must impute it to our own will
that we perish.' Rightly, I say, if you speak
of the proclaimed God. For he would have all
men to be saved, coming, as he does, with his
word of salvation to all men; and the fault is in
our own will, which does not admit him; as he
says, in Matt. xxiii. " How often would I have
gathered thy children, and thou wouldest not ?"—
But why this majesty of His does not remove this
fault of our will, or change it in all men (seeing
that it is not in the power of man to do so); or
why he imputes this fault of his will to man, when
man cannot be without it; these are questions
which it is not lawful for us to ask; and which,
if you should ask them, you would never get
answered. The best answer is that which Paul
gives in Romans ix. " Who art thou that repliest
against God?" Let these remarks suffice for this
passage of Ezekiel, and let us go on to the rest.[x]

[x] Luther has in substance given the right answer to this
cavil from Ezekiel, but has given it, as we have seen, in an
exceptionable form; exceptionable, as it respects the distinc-

PART III.
———
SC. XXIX.
———
Exhortations, pro-

After this, Diatribe objects that the exhortations with which the Scripture so much abounds, together with all those manifold promises, threatening which he institutes, 'hidden God and revealed God;' and exceptionable, in that he does not show the sameness of this God, which is thus distinguishingly regarded. "It is to be remembered, that the words bear only by inference and consequence upon the question of Freewill (which is the question in debate), whatever be the correct interpretation of them; neither does Erasmus represent them fairly. Erasmus speaks of *wailing* and working: but where does Ezekiel say that God ",wails?" He says only, 'I would not.' Erasmus argues, 'God deplores; therefore, it is not his doing that they die; therefore, it is their own doing; therefore, there is Freewill.' It is inference two deep; each of which requires proof. 'What if their death be self-wrought? Why may they not have previously forfeited their Freewill, and therefore die under bondwill? We might hold ourselves excused, therefore, from entering at all into this cavil; it is truly *nihil ad nos*.
But there are reasons why we should rather meet it in the face; and the answer has, by-implication, been given to it already,—Some would say, why not at once knock it down with " Secret things belong unto the Lord ?" (Deut. xxix. 29.), a convenient text for a perplexed disputant! My answer is, that text does not apply here. The Prophet is not speaking of the *principles* of divine conduct, but of those providential events and arrangements by which God realizes and fulfils them. It was in the counsels of God to bring the nation of Israel to obedience at the last, through a long course of tergiversation and punishment: but they had at that time the word given to them (" the word is nigh thee, even in thy mouth, and in thy heart; that is, the word of faith, which we preach." Compare Rom. x. 5—10. with Deut. xxx. 11—14.), which they would at length obey. Now, they had nothing to do with these intermediate events which God would bring about; it was theirs to use that commandment (or rather that Gospel which the commandment fore-preached)—looking through the type to the reality—which he commanded them that day.— Besides, if we were at liberty to use this text here, we must learn from it, that we have nothing to do with election and reprobation at all; as some are fond enough of admonishing us. For it is not a question, who is individually of the one class, and who of the other, that is here to be answered; but whether there really be such distinctions, and why there are such. (See above, note ʳ.) —Then ˏmeeting- the question fairly, though not fairly attached to the question of Freewill, how does this assertion in Ezekiel comport with the God-willed death of a sinner?
 Not to insist upon the peculiarities of the case to which this

TEXTS FOR FREEWILL DISPROVED.

ings, expostulations, upbraidings, beseechings, blessings and cursings, and all those numerous solemn declaration of God is annexed (the house of Israel was brought into peculiar relations to God, and the case of an Israelite was therefore considerably different from that of uncovenanted transgressors); not to notice the ambiguity of Erasmus's expression 'his people' (God works no death in his people properly so called, though he works death in many who have a name to be his people, and are not), without insisting that the original words אֶחְפֹּץ יֶחְפָּץ as well as the θέλω, not βούλομαι, of the Septuagint, express inclination rather than determination—and so the sentiment conveyed may be no more than what our translators have assigned to them, 'have I any pleasure at all,' 'for I have no pleasure;' implying only such a reluctance as is not inconsistent with a contrary decision—though Luther, as well as Erasmus, makes it 'nolo;' waving all such objections, which do not shield the vitals of the truth, though they may serve to parry off a blow from its extremities (for clearly here is God at least declaring his dislike of that death which he nevertheless inflicts, and which we affirm that he wills); the true account of the matter, and that which comprehends all possible cases, has been furnished in the two preceding notes; asserted in note t, and illustrated by examples in note u.

The relative God, in his character of Israel's legislator and sovereign, declares in this chapter that he will deal henceforth both nationally and spiritually with that people, each man according to his own ways, and, in effect, preaches the Gospel to each individual of them, saying, 'Repent, and live.' At the twenty-third verse,* he signifies that he has no pleasure in the death of him that dieth. in the three last verses, he exhorts and remonstrates, and repeats his gracious assurances —But it does not belong to these and such like relations, to give grace and power, and, without such grace and power, exhortations promises and threatenings are all, and alike, vain But is God therefore to withhold them? Man, without this superadded grace, ought to obey them, ought, though he cannot; cannot, through a self-wrought impotency And are there no reasons, no satisfying reasons, why God should give them? Are not these amongst his choicest instruments, whereby he effects the manifestation of himself; manifestation of himself, through the manifestation of what is in man, " that thou mightest be justified when thou speakest, and clear when thou judgest "—·His elect obey, his non-elect harden themselves yet the more, under his outward calls.—Thus, whether the case set forth in Ezekiel be considered as the peculiar case of the national Israel, or

SECT. XXIX.

mises, &c. of Scripture useless.

---

* Erasmus quotes the text unfairly, by joining the oath of v. 3 with v. 23; but it is no part of it.

194　　　　BONDAGE OF THE WILL.

PART III. swarms of precepts, are without meaning necessarily,[y] if no one has it in his power to keep what is commanded.

Diatribe is always forgetting the question at issue, and proving something different from what she undertook to prove: nor does she perceive, how much more strongly every thing she says makes against herself than against us. For she proves from all these passages a liberty and power of keeping all the commandments, by force of the inference which she suggests from the words quoted; when all the while she meant only to prove 'such a Freewill as can will nothing good without grace, together with a sort of endeavour, which is not to be ascribed however, to its own powers.' I see no proof of such endeavour in any of the passages quoted; I see only a demand of such actions as ought to be performed: what I' have indeed said too often already, if it were not that such frequent repetition is necessary, because Diatribe so often blunders upon the same string,[z] putting off her reader with an useless profusion of words.

SC. XXX. Nearly the last passage which she adduces from the Old Testament, is that of Moses in Deut. xxx.
Deut. xxx. 11—14. considered. "This commandment, which I command thee this

the general case of the visible church having the Gospel preached to it (that Gospel which is in one view a statute, enactment, or commandment; whilst, in another view, it is the Jubilee trumpet, by which the Holy Ghost proclaims liberty to the Lord's captives); we see in it, at last, but a farther exemplification of what has been shewn already, the relative God revealing the absolute, and his legislative fulfilling his personal will —Luther meant nothing *contrary* to this statement, though his language might seem to imply it.

[y] *Frigere necessariò.*] *Frig.* A metaphor taken from vegetable or animal substances, which are nipped with cold. These exhortations, &c. have no warmth, no life, no power, no meaning in them, without Freewill.

[z] 　　　　　　　　　'Ut citharœdus
Ridetur, chordâ qui semper oberrat eâdem.'
　　　　　　　　　　　　　　, Hor. Art. Poet. 355.

day, is not above thee, nor far off from thee, nor placed in heaven, that you mightest say, who of us is able to ascend up into heaven, to bring it down to us, that we may hear and fulfil it? But the word is very near to thee, in thy mouth and in thy heart, that thou mayest do it." Diatribe maintains it to be declared in this place, that we not only have power to do what is enjoined, but that it is even downhill work to do so; that is, easy, or at least not difficult.

Thanks to you for your immense learning! If then Moses so clearly pronounces that there is not only a *faculty* in us, but even a *facility* of keeping all the commandments; why submit to all this toil? Why have we not at once produced this passage, and asserted Freewill in a field that is without opponent.[a] What need have we any longer of Christ? what need of the Spirit? We have at length found a place which stops every mouth, and distinctly pronounces not only that the will is free, but that the observance of all the commandments is easy! How foolish was Christ to purchase that unnecessary Spirit for us at the price of his own out-poured blood, that it might be made easy to us to keep the commandments; a facility, which it now seems that we possess by nature! Nay, let Diatribe herself recant her own words, in which she said that Freewill can will nothing good without grace: and let her now say, that Freewill is of so great virtue as not only to will good, but even with great ease to keep the chiefest and all the commandments. O see what is the result of having a mind which feels no interest in the cause pleaded! see how impossible it is, that this mind should not betray itself! Is there any longer need to confute Diatribe? Who can confute her more thoroughly than she confutes her own self? This, forsooth, is the animal which devours

---

[a] *Libero campo*] I understand it ' liber ab hoste, seu antagonistâ :' but I do not find any parallel.

PART III. its own stomach.[b] How true is the proverb, 'a liar ought to have a good memory!'

I have spoken on this passage in my commentary upon Deuteronomy.[c] I shall therefore treat it concisely here, shutting out Paul from our discussion, who handles this passage with great power, in Rom. x. You perceive that nothing at all is affirmed here, nor one single syllable uttered, about facility or difficulty, about the power or the impotency, of Freewill or of man, to keep or not to keep the commandment: except that those who entangle the Scriptures in the net of their own consequences and fancies, do thereby render them obscure and ambiguous to themselves,

[b] *Se ipsam comedit*] What this animal is, and whether real or fabulous; I must leave in some doubt. The lobster comes nearest to the description: of which it is said; 'At the same time that they cast their shell, they change also their stomach and intestines. The animal, while it is moulting, is said to feed upon its former stomach, which wastes by degrees, and is at length replaced with a new one.'—Bingley's Animal Biography, vol. iii. p. 511. But the pelican seems the more probable allusion here; whose method of taking its sustenance from its pouch, might well account for the figment of its eating itself, or preying on its own stomach The scolopendra discharges its own bowels, in order to disgorge the hook, and the scorpion, inclosed with burning coals, stings itself to death: but neither of these seems applicable here The name *bestia* is said to be ascribed properly to wild and noxious animals, but not confined to these; whilst *bellua* expresses size rather than fierceness.

[c] See Luther's commentary on Deuteronomy, in loco: where he notices and chides this unjustifiable use, which the Sophists make of it. He gives another turn to the "secret things" of the preceding chapter; considering them as secrets revealed to Israel, that he may obey. Also, he understands St. Paul's application of this text as an accommodation of the original words, not a quotation according to their true sense, as spoken by Moses. But his comment will be found strongly to confirm the view which I have given of this text, in note [x]. Moses's word can only be fulfilled, he says, under the Gospel: yet Moses says, "See, I have set before thee *this day* life and death, &c." Then what more natural, than to understand him as calling upon them to see the Gospel in their Law, and to yield a gospel obedience to that Law? which every spiritual Israelite no doubt did.

for the purpose of making what they please of them. But now, if you have no eyes, turn your ears at least to what is here spoken, or strike your hand over the letters.[d] Moses says, 'it is not above thee, nor placed afar off, nor seated in heaven, nor beyond the sea.' What is the meaning of 'above thee?' 'afar off?' 'seated in heaven?' 'across the sea?' Will they even make our grammar and the commonest words obscure to us, till they make it impossible for us to say any thing that is certain; just to carry their point, that the Scriptures are obscure?

According to my grammar, it is not quality or quantity of human strength, but distance of place, which is meant by these words. It is not a certain power of the will, but a place which is above us, that is expressed by 'above thee.' So the words 'afar off,' 'across the sea,' 'in heaven,' do not denote any power in man, but a place removed from us upwards, to the right hand, to the left hand, backwards or forwards. There may be those perhaps, who will laugh at my thick-headed way of speaking, when with out-stretched hands I present a sort of chewed morsel[e] to these full-grown gentlemen, as though they had not yet learned their A B C, and teach them that syllables must be combined into words. But what can I do, when I see men hunting for darkness in the midst of such clear light, and studiously wishing to be blind, after reckoning up such a series of ages to us, so many geniuses, so many saints, so many martyrs, so many doctors; and after vaunting this passage of Moses with such vast authority, although they deign not to inspect the

[d] *Manibus palpa*] 'If you cannot see, or hear, submit to have your finger put upon each letter, that you may trace it out;' as a child is taught to read.

[e] *Præmansum porrigentem*] Præm. A word of doubtful authority, but well fitted to express the first process in the art of teaching, by which the scholar eats as it were out of the master's mouth.

syllables of which it consists, or to put so much of constraint upon their own thoughts as to consider for once the passage of which they make their boast. Go tell us now, Diatribe, how it comes to pass, that one obscure individual sees what so many public characters and the nobles of so many ages have not seen. Assuredly, this passage proves them to have been not seldom blind, were it but a little child that should sit in judgment upon them.

Then what doth Moses mean by these most obvious and most clear words, but that he has discharged his office as a faithful lawgiver to perfection? Having brought it to pass that there should be no cause, why they did not know, and have in array before them, all the commands of God; and that no place should be left to them for urging by way of excuse, that they did not know or had not commandments, or must seek them from some other quarter. The effect of which would be, that, if they should not keep them, the fault would be neither in the law, nor in the lawgiver, but in themselves; since they have the law, and the lawgiver has taught them, so that there is no plea of ignorance remaining for them, but only a charge of negligence and of disobedience. 'It is not necessary,' says he, 'to fetch laws from heaven' or from the parts beyond the seas, or from afar off; nor canst thou pretend either that thou hast not heard them, or that thou dost not possess them: thou hast them near to thee, they are what thou hast heard by the command of God from my lips; thou hast understood them with thine heart, and hast received them to be read and expounded by the mouth of the Levites,[f] which are in the midst of thee, con-

---

[f] *Tractandas accepisti.*] In Deut. xxxi. 9—13. the ordinance is, "And Moses wrote this law and delivered it to the priests, the sons of Levi, which bare the ark, the covenant of the Lord, and unto all the elders of Israel. And Moses commanded them, saying, At the end of every seven years, in the solemnity

tinually: this very word and book of mine is witness. It remains only that thou mayest do them.'—What is here ascribed, pray, to Freewill? Save that she is required to fulfil the laws which she has, and the excuse of ignorance and want of laws, is taken away.ᵍ

These are nearly all the texts which Diatribe adduces from the Old Testament in support of Freewill; by releasing which,ʰ we leave none remaining, which are not released as well as they —whether she bring more, or be intending to bring more—since she can bring nothing but a parcel of imperative, or conjunctive, or optative verbs, by which is signified not what we can do, or are doing (as I have so often replied to Dia-

SC.XXXI.

Some of the Old Testament witnesses for Freewill.

---

of the year of release, in the feast of tabernacles, when all Israel is come to appear before the Lord thy God, in the place which he shall choose, thou shalt read this law before all Israel, in their hearing. Gather the people together," &c. &c. See also vv. 24—26. Also Josh. viii. 31—35. Also Nehem. viii. 1—8. Also 2 Chron. xvii. 7—9. xxx. 22.—I render the expression 'ore assiduo' *continually :* but, if I could have found authority for the use of the word 'assiduus,' I should rather have given it a reference to what is said in Nehemiah, "And the Levites caused the people to understand the law, &c. So they read in the book in the law of God *distinctly*, and gave the sense, and caused them to understand the reading." —Luther is correct then in suggesting, that the Levites (including the priests under this name) were to *handle* or discourse on the law to the people, not simply to read it: and, although he anticipates the injunction as given on this occasion, it had in substance been given before (see Deut. x. 8, 9.), at the second delivering of the Tables.

ᵍ I do not quite fall in with Luther's interpretation of this text, as I have hinted in note ˣ of Sect. xxviii. and note ᶜ of Sect. xxx.—(Why are we to shut out Paul in our interpretation of it? Is not the Holy Ghost the best commentator upon the Holy Ghost's words?)—But I do not the less resist its application in support of Freewill. 'The thing required is nigh thee; what ought to be in thy mouth and in thy heart.' Is it therefore immediately and necessarily there? and that, of our own giving and getting?'

ʰ *Quibus solutis.*] *Sol.* ' Quod ligatum est, a vinculis libero;' 'the bands of these captive texts having been loosed:' they had been tied and bound in the service of Freewill.

tribe so often repeating the same thing); but what we ought to do, and what is required of us, to the end that our own impotency may become notorious to us, and the knowledge of sin be vouchsafed. These texts indeed, if they prove any thing, through the addition of consequences and similes which are the invention of human reason, prove that Freewill possesses not only endeavour, or some small particle of desire; but an entire power and, the freest ability to do all things,[1] without the grace of God, and without the aid of his Holy Spirit.

So that nothing is further from the thing proved by this whole discourse, trodden into us, as it has been, by continual repetitions, than the proposition which she had undertaken to prove; namely, 'that approvable opinion, by which Freewill is determined to be so impotent that it can will nothing good without grace, and is compelled to serve sin, and possesses endeavour which is not to be ascribed to its own energies:' a monster forsooth, which can at the same time do nothing by its own energies, yet possesses a power of endeavouring, in its own energies; and so consists by a most manifest contradiction.[k]

SECT. XXXII.

New Test. Scriptures for Freewill, beginning with Mat. xxiii. 37—39. considered.

We come now to the New Testament, where a large force of imperative verbs is again mustered in the wretched service of Freewill, and the auxiliaries of carnal reason, such as consequences and similes, are fetched in: like a picture, or a dream, in which you should see the king of the flies, with his lances of straw and shields of hay, set in battle array against a real and well-appointed army[1] of human warriors.—Such is the kind of

---

[1] *Totam vim,* opposed to a fraction; *liberrimam potestatem,* 'the absolute and unrestrained use of this integral power.'

[k] *Quæ constat contradictione manif.*] 'Its constituting elements are power and no power; which cannot subsist together: what becomes of the compound then?

[1] *Veram et justam aciem.*

TEXTS FOR FREEWILL DISPROVED.

warfare which the human dreams of Diatribe carry on against troops of divine testimonies.

First marches forth, like the Achilles of the flies, that text in Matt. xxiii. "O Jerusalem, Jerusalem, how often would I have gathered thy children together, and thou wouldest not?" 'If all things are done by necessity, says she, might not Jerusalem have justly answered the Lord, Why consume thyself with vain tears? If thou wast unwilling that we should listen to the Prophets, why didst thou send them? why impute to us what has been done by thine own will, our necessity?' So much for Diatribe.—My reply is, granting for the moment, that this inference and proof of Diatribe's is good and true; what is proved, pray? that approvable opinion, which says that Freewill cannot will good? Why, here is proved a will that is free, every whit whole, and able to do every thing which the Prophets have spoken! Diatribe did not take upon herself to prove this sort of will in man. Nay, let Diatribe herself be the respondent here, and let her tell us why, if Freewill cannot will good, it is, imputed to her that she did not hear the Prophets; whom, as being teachers of good, it was not possible for her to hear, through her own strength? Why does Christ weep vain tears,[m] as though they could have willed, what he assuredly knew that they could not will? Let Diatribe deliver Christ from a charge of madness, I say, in support of that approvable opinion of hers, and straightway our opinion will have been liberated from this Achilles of the flies. So that this text

---

[m] Luther seems to have confounded this passage in Matt. xxiii. with Luke xix. 41—44. " And when he was come near, he beheld the city, and wept over it." &c &c. It is remarkable that the words which are so closely parallel in Luke xiii. were not spoken at the same time with those recorded in Matt xxiii. The latter were spoken in the Temple at the close of the Lord's public ministry: the former, whilst he was yet in Galilee.

of Matthew either proves a complete Freewill, or fights against Diatribe herself, as stoutly as against us, and lays her prostrate with her own weapons."

I assert, as I have done before, that the secret will of God, as regarded in the majesty of his own nature, is not matter of debate ;° and that the rashness of man, which, through a continual perverseness, is always leaving necessary topics to attack and encounter it, should be called away and withdrawn from occupying herself in scrutinizing those secrets of His majesty, which it is impossible to penetrate,P seeing He dwelleth in light which no man can approach unto; as Paul testifies. (1 Tim. vi. 16.) Let her rather occupy herself with the incarnate God, or (as Paul speaks) with Jesus the crucified: in whom are all the treasures of wisdom and knowledge, but hiddenly.q He will teach her abundantly what she ought to know, and what not. It is the incarnate God then, which speaks here. '*I* would, and thou wouldest not.' The incarnate God, I say, was sent into the world for this purpose, that he might be willing, that he might speak, that he might do, that he might suffer, that he might offer^r all

---

n *Suo illam jaculo.*] Nothing less than a complete Freewill can repel the objection here brought by Diatribe : therefore, either there is a complete Freewill—which she denies—or all such objections have no weight at all.

° Luther expresses this more briefly, but obscurely: 'de secretâ illâ voluntate majestatis non esse disputandum.'

P *Scrutandis. attingere*] Scrut comes nearest to our 'rummage:' 'videtur esse a scrutis, quasi sit ita in loco aliquo prætentare, et versare omnia, ut etiam *scruta* misceantur.' Hence applied to a dog hunting by the scent. It expresses the search for a thing, rather than the improper handling of the thing found. So Luther applies it here ; as is plain from 'attingere :' ' the attaining to, or reaching the thing which was gone after.'

q See 1 Cor. i. 23. ii. 2. Coloss. ii. 3. In this latter text, Luther gives the sense strictly according to the original, which our version does not; ἐν ᾧ εἰσι. . . . ἀπόκρυφοι.

r See above, Sect. xxiii. note ˢ.

things which are necessary for salvation, unto all men: although he stumbles upon many, who, being either left or hardened by that secret will of His majesty, receive him not; willing as he is, speaking, working, offering as he does: which is just what John says, 'The light shineth in darkness, and the darkness comprehendeth it not:' and again, 'He came unto his own, and his own received him not.'

Thus, it is the act of this incarnate God to weep, wail, and groan over the destruction of the wicked, whilst the will of Majesty leaves and reprobates some, on purpose that they may perish: nor ought we to inquire why he does so, but to reverence God, who is both able and willing to do such things.—No one, I suppose, will here cavil, that the will of which it is said, 'how often would I,' was exhibited to the Jews even before God's incarnation; inasmuch as they are charged with having slain the Prophets which lived before Christ, and, by so doing, with having resisted his will. Christians know, that every thing which was done by the Prophets was done by them in the name of that Christ which was to come; of whom it had been promised that he should become the incarnate God. So that whatsoever has been offered to man by the ministers of the word from the beginning of the world, may be rightly called the will of Christ.*

* Luther gives two answers to this cavil from Matt. xxiii.—1. It is equally inconsistent with Diatribe's statement., 2. It is the incarnate God, not the God of Majesty, who here speaks. I must strongly object to this latter solution. It implies a difference, nay a contrariety, between the mind of God and the mind of Christ; and thus destroys the very end for which Christ came—even the manifestation of God as His express image—by not only negativing the fulfilment of that design, but absolutely intimating that he has given us false views of God, by shewing a mind which is the reverse of His: as though *He* willed salvation, where *God* wills destruction. Yet he tells us, " I came not to do mine own will but the will of Him that sent me." " My meat is to do the will of Him that sent me, and to finish his work." " I do nothing of my-

PART III.
———
SECT.
XXXIII.
———
The reality of God's secret will maintained

'But reason, who is quick-scented and saucy, will say here, 'An admirable refuge this, which self; but as my Father hath taught me, I speak these things." "I have manifested thy name unto the men that thou gavest me out of the world." And truly, though we shall know far more of God hereafter than we can know here—so that "Whether there be knowledge, it shall vanish away"—our knowledge of God shall still be derived to us through Christ ("the lamb which is in the midst of the throne shall feed them, and shall lead them unto living fountains of waters"), and we shall never know any thing of God contrary to that which Jesus has exhibited of Him.

The true answer to this cavil, however, has in substance been given already. (See Sect. xxviii. notes ᵗ ᵛ ˣ.) God standing in peculiar relations to Israel, as his typical nation and his visible church, had from the beginning been calling that people to repentance. Their history, their institutions, their lively oracles, their ordinary and extraordinary ministers, had caused them to be peculiarly, and above the rest of mankind, without excuse, even before Christ came. These were so many ' *I woulds, and ye would nots* :' not Christ saying and willing one thing, and the Father another; but Christ by the Father's commandment calling to them, and they refusing But now he had come personally and visibly amongst them, and could say, "If I had not come and spoken unto them, they had not had sin, but now they have no cloak for their sin. He that hateth me, hateth my Father also. If I had not done amongst them the works which none other man did, they had not had sin; but now have they both seen and hated both me and my Father." (John xv. 22—24) And what is all this, but God in certain assumed relations uttering his voice to those connected with him by these relations (in other words, declaring his legislative will), which those, to whom it is uttered, ought without doubt to obey; and which if they did obey, they would according to his promise live. But ' ought to obey' is not ' therefore have power to obey,' and ' have not power to obey,' is not ' therefore the command is given in vain.' Here is, man manifested ; and God, by his dealings with him. If Israel ' would,' he would have been gathered ; if Jerusalem ' would,' she would have remained unto this day. But it was only by a grace not belonging to those relations by which God had at that period connected himself with Israel, that Israel could then have been made willing : he had all given to him which belonged to those relations; to withhold trial, or to administer super-creation and super-covenant grace that he might stand, was no part of the dues which God had made himself debtor to him to perform ; and therefore Israel—justly, and no more than justly, tried—having manifested what was in him with such aggravations of guilt, incurred a sentence which is declared to have been the requital of all the righteous blood

you have discovered: so then, as often as you are pressed by the force of your adversary's argu-

that had been shed upon the earth from Abel to Zecharias. (vv. 35, 36.)—The guilt of that generation was indeed extreme; but who shall say that it was not the concentrated guilt of the intermediate ages and generations of that people, together with their own, which was so shortly to be visited upon them? Carnal reason will not hear of the children being visited for their fathers' sin; but both Scripture and experience testify this reality to the spiritual mind.—The incarnate God, then, has no will contrary to the God of Majesty; or more intelligibly, Christ's will and the Father's are one; Christ's tears (see above, note [m]) imply not any repugnance to the divine counsel, the legislative is here, as in the former instances, the executor of the personal will— With respect to the tears which he shed over that woe which he was shortly to inflict, and of which he well knew the length and breadth, the depth and height, it may be remarked, that the Lord Jesus had a human soul, as part of his complete human person, distinct from his divine person (See Part ii. Sect. viii. note [r]), and that such expressions might, without impropriety, be referred to that part of his complex frame. "We have not an high priest which cannot be touched with the feeling of our infirmities, but was in all points tempted like as we are, yet without sin." He had all the *sinless* feelings of a man, and might therefore not incongruously weep at such a woe. But where is the contradiction to Scripture and right reason in understanding God himself to be moved with compassion at the very grief and pain which He in just judgment inflicts? "Therefore my bowels are troubled for him." "Have I any pleasure at all in the death of him that dieth?" "For he doth not afflict willingly, nor grieve the children of men."

It is pleasing to notice, how nearly Luther approximates to the truth—viz. 'That Christ was eternally fore-ordained *as Christ*, and did by a covenant subsistence assume his person and personal relations, as the risen God-man, before the foundation of the world'—in the defence which he makes against the cavil, 'Christ was not yet come.' He declares that every thing was done by the Prophets in His name, and that all expressions of mercy from the beginning may be rightly called the will of Christ which will, according to his representation of it, is perfectly distinct from that of the Father (his language implies, *contrary to it*), so that there must have been a distinct *agency* of Christ from the beginning. Verily, this is so; though not exactly as he understood and would have represented it and I have often been surprised that, whilst most of those who know any thing of Christ are ready enough to acknowledge, that regard was had to his *sacrifice* from the begin-

PART III. ments, you have but to run back to this terrible will of sovereignty, and you compel your antagonist to silence, when he has become troublesome; just as the astrologers evade all questions about the motions of the whole heavens, by their invention of Epicycles.'[t]

I answer, 'It is not my invention but a direction confirmed by the divine Scriptures. Thus speaks ning (for how else could any soul of man, as Abel, Enoch, Abraham, David, &c. &c. have been pardoned and accepted);' so few distinctly recognise his personal subsistence and agency, *as Christ*, from the same period; although it be in this regard that he is called " the Word," " the Word of life," " the life," " that eternal life," &c. and although a distinct personal agent, to use the blessed materials of his future coming and dying in the flesh—*as a Priest-king*—was not less necessary to the salvation and glorification of every individual of the saved who lived and died before those events had been realized; than was the article of his death.—In what Luther says about abstaining from what he calls ' the secret will of majesty,' he speaks indistinctly, injuriously, and contradictorily: *indistinctly*, because there is an use as well as an abuse of such inquiries, which he ought to have discriminated; *injuriously*, because his observations would go the length of deterring men from even the recognition of such a will, and so would mar the joy and fear and gratitude and love of the Lord's people; *contradictorily*, because he afterwards recognises and makes assertions about it. Christ forsooth *impinges* upon some of God's reprobates!—Still, a hint or two may be borrowed with advantage from Luther's statement. God, in addressing himself to the world as he does by the 'every where to be preached' Gospel, does clearly set himself forth to as many as have a heart in any degree softened and turned towards him, in the form and character of the Father of mercies not willing that any should perish. Such ought not to be deterred and affrighted by the knowledge that he has his reprobates. The melting heart is not the heart of a reprobate. But is he to shut his eyes to the fact that God has his reprobates? Nay, that fact combined with the consciousness of his own personal impotency, turns unto him for a testimony. Neither can he regard God as he ought now, or in any future stage of his experience, without it; for without it, the God whom he serves is not the true God.

[t] *Epicycles.*] 'A little circle, whose centre is in the circumference of a greater: or a small orb, which, being fixed in the deferent of a planet, carries it round its own axis, whilst it is itself carried round the axis of the planet.—An invention of some bungling philosophers to account for the anomalies of planetary motion.'

TEXTS FOR FREEWILL DISPROVED.

Paul in Rom. ix. "Why doth God complain then? Who shall resist his will? O man, who art thou that contendest with God?" "Hath not the potter power?" and the rest. And before him, Isaiah, in his 58th chapter, had said, "For they seek me daily, and desire to know my ways, as a nation which hath done righteousness: they ask of me the ordinances of justice, and desire to draw near to God." In these words, I imagine, it is abundantly shewn to us, that it is not lawful for man to scrutinize the will of sovereignty.ᵘ Besides, this question is of a kind which most of all leads perverse men to attack that awful will; so that it is especially seasonable to exhort them to silence and reverence, when we prosecute it. In other questions, where the matters treated of are such as admit of explanation, and such as we are commanded to explain, I do not proceed so.

Now if a man will not yield to my admonition, but persists in scrutinizing the counselsᵛ of that will,

---

ᵘ This text does not seem to bear upon the point in hand; viz. that we ought not to scrutinize the personal will of God; or, as he terms it, 'the will of majesty,' or sovereignty. Luther understands ' their seeking of God daily, and desiring to know his ways, and asking of him the ordinances of justice;' as if they not only complained of God's appointments towards them being unjust, but were prying curiously into the secret springs of them. But does God, speaking by his Prophet, really mean any more than that they were hypocrites and formalists, yet expected the acceptance of true and devout worshippers? Accordingly they were answered by shewing them that their fasts were not such as he had chosen, and that the worship which he accepts is the reverse of theirs. 'Ask of me the ordinances of justice,' are the only words which bear at all upon the subject, and these do not necessarily imply, or with any probability here imply, 'a spirit of curiousness.'

ᵛ *Rationem scrutari*] *Rat.* More literally, *the method* of that will. 'Ratio' expresses most nearly the 'all about it.' *Scrut.* (see last Section, note ᵖ) does not necessarily denote a bad state of mind; though clearly so here. a mind which doubts the fact that God has such a will, questions his right to have it, and cavils at its decisions. To inquire what the word of God has recorded concerning this will with deep reverence;

208 . BONDAGE OF THE WILL.

PART III. I let him go on and fight with God, as the giants did of old; waiting to see what sort of triumphs he carries off, and very sure in the mean time, that he will withdraw nothing from our cause, and confer nothing upon his own. For it will remain fixed, that either he must prove Freewill to be capable of doing every thing, or the Scriptures which he quotes must contradict his own position. Whichsoever of these be the issue, he lies prostrate as the conquered man, and I am found standing upon my feet, as the conqueror.[x]

SECT. XXXIV.

Matt. xix. 17. and other like passages considered.

Your second text is Matthew xix. 17. " If thou wilt enter into life, keep the commandments." 'With what face could it be said, "If thou wilt," to a man whose will is not free.' So says Diatribe.

To whom I reply; does this saying of Christ's

and meekly, rejoicingly, to submit to that record; would not be making war as the giants of old did against Jupiter.

[x] See here a confirmation of my remark in Sect. xxviii. note [t], that it is against the impugners and deniers of that will which is distinct from God's legislative will, not against its sober investigators and maintainers, that Luther is protesting! His answer to the cavil from Matt xxiii. and like passages is, ' Aye, but there is another will behind this, which is contrary to this, and which we must be content to leave, with asserting it. God as revealed, or, as he afterwards describes him, Christ, the incarnate God, wills only life; but there is another will of God, a will not expressed by this incarnate God, which wills death; and therefore these things which appear to prove Freewill (by inference) may still be said, and yet man be in bondage: because, whilst he deplores, he doth also not deplore. This latter will is not to be searched into, or acted upon; it is only to be asserted and believed deny it, if you dare, you will only be running your head against the wall, making war against God —For objections to this statement, and for a more consistent answer to the cavil, &c. &c. see note [s] of the last Section.—Luther says worse than he means, but he means ignorantly. It had not been given him to know the mystery of God and the Father, and of Christ: He did not understand how that God is not hiding himself behind Christ, but making himself seen in Christ; so that it shall be truly said, " He that hath seen me hath seen the Father: if ye had known me, ye should have known my Father also; and from henceforth ye know him, and have seen him." (John xiv. 9. 7.)

then establish that the will is free? Why, you meant to prove that Freewill can will nothing good, and will necessarily serve sin, if grace be out of the way. With what face then do you now make it all free?

The same shall be said to the words, 'If thou wilt be perfect,' 'if any man will come after me,' 'whosoever will save his soul,' 'if ye love me,' 'if ye abide in me.' (Nay, let all the conjunctions 'if,' and all the imperative verbs, as I have said,[y] be collected together—by way of assisting Diatribe in the number, at least, of her quotations.) 'All these precepts are unmeaning,[z] she says, if nothing be attributed to the human will. How ill does that conjunction, 'if' agree with mere necessity!'

I answer; if they be unmeaning, it is your own fault that they are so, or rather are nothing at all: you make this nonentity of them by asserting that nothing is ascribed to the human will, so long as you represent that Freewill cannot will good, and here on the other hand representing, that it can will all good; unless it be, that the same words are both hot and cold in the same instant, as you use them, at once asserting every thing and denying every thing.[a] Truly I am at a loss to think, why an author should have been pleased to say the same thing so many times over, forgetting his thesis perpetually, unless perchance, through mistrust of his cause, he had a mind to gain the victory by the size of his book, or to wear out his adversary by making it tedious and burthensome to peruse.—By what sort of consequence, I would ask, does it follow that will and power must

---

[y] See above, Sect. xx.
[z] *Frigent*] See above, Sect. xxix. note [y].
[a] It is you who take away all warmth and life from such passages as these, by making the will a contradiction; it can do nothing, it can do all things: these assertions destroy each other, and leave a nought as the result, unless they mean opposite things, such as 'yes,' and 'no,' at the same instant.

P

forthwith be present to the soul, as often as it is said, 'If thou wilt,' 'if a man will,' 'if thou shalt be willing.' Do not we most frequently denote impotency and impossibility, rather than the contrary, by such expressions? As in these examples: 'If thou wilt equal Virgil in singing, my Mævius, thou must sing other songs;' 'If thou wilt surpass Cicero, my Scotus, thou must exchange thy subtilties for the most consummate eloquence;' 'If thou wilt be compared with David, thou must utter Psalms like his.' By these conditionals, it is plain that things impossible of attainment to our own powers are denoted; whilst by a divine power all things are possible to us. 'Thus it is with the Scriptures also: what may be done in us by the power of God, and what we cannot do of ourselves, is declared by such like words. Besides, if such things were said about actions absolutely impossible, (as those which even God also would never at any time do by us, then would they be rightly called either cold or ridiculous, as being said to no purpose. But the truth is, these expressions are used not only to show the impotency of Freewill, which causes that none of these things be done by us; but at the same time to intimate that all such things are, at some time or other, about to be and to be done—howbeit by another's power, even God's: if we quite admit that there is in such like words some intimation of things which are to be done, and which are possible. As if a man should interpret them thus: 'If thou shalt be willing to keep the commandments;' that is, 'If thou shalt at some time possess a will (thou wilt possess it however, not of thyself, but of God—who will give it to whom it shall be his will to give it) to keep the commandments, they also shall preserve thee.' Or, to speak more freely, these verbs, particularly the conjunctive verbs, seem to be inserted thus on account of God's predestination also—as being that which we do not know—and to involve it: as if they should mean to say, 'If thou wilt,' 'If thou shalt be willing'—that is, 'If thou shalt be such in the sight of God as that he shall count thee worthy of this will to keep the commandments—thou shalt be saved.' Each of these two things is couched under this trope:[b] namely, that; on the one hand we can do nothing of ourselves, and on the other, whatever we do, God worketh it in us. I should speak thus to those who would not be content to have it said, that our impotency only is expressed by these words, but would maintain, that a certain power and ability of doing those things which are enjoined, is proved by them. Thus it would at once be true, that we could do none of the things commanded, and could at the same time do all of them; if we should apply the former assertion to our own powers, the latter to the grace of God.[c]

Thirdly, Diatribe is affected by this consideration: 'Where there is such frequent mention of good and bad works, says she; where there is mention of reward; I do not see how there can

SECT. XXXV.

Erasmus's objection that precepts are given, and

---

[b] *Tropo*] Any figurative mode of speech, as opposed to one that is plain, simple, and straight forward; whatever be the particular nature of the obliquity: whether grammatical, as here; or rhetorical.

[c] Luther gives three answers to these texts. 1. Erasmus inconsistent with himself. 2. They teach human impotency. 3. They insinuate the possibility of divine help, and glance at his predestinative favour—In some instances, doubtless, as in Matthew xix. and its parallels (Mark x. Luke xviii.), a peculiar design may also be traced—the teaching of the natural man's impotency, and the hint at what God, according to his eternal purpose, will do in his people—but all these, multifarious as they are, may be resolved into, 'the Lawgiver speaks:' whose voice implies not either power in man, or promise in God. The end is not always conviction of sin in mercy; sometimes it is "whom he will he hardeneth," but always, it is man made to shew what he is, unto the more perfect manifestation of God by him. See Sect. xxviii. notes [t] [v] [x].

PART III.

merit is ascribed to Freewill, considered.—Erasmus inconsistent with himself.

be place for mere necessity. 'Neither nature, nor necessity, says she, hath merit.'ᵈ Nor, do I forsooth, understand how there can be this place; save, that the 'approvable opinion' asserts mere necessity in saying that Freewill can will nothing good, but here attributes even merit to it. 'Freewill has made such advances during the growth of this book and disputation, of Diatribe's, that now she not only has desire, and endeavour, for her own (howbeit, by a strength not her own); nay, she not only wills and does good, but even merits eternal life; because Christ says, in the fifth, of St. Matthew, (ver. 12), "Rejoice, and be exceeding glad, for your reward is abundant in the heavens." *Your* reward; that is, Freewill's reward: for so Diatribe understands this text, making Christ and the Spirit, to be nothing; for what need is there of these, if we have good works and merits through Freewill?—I mention this, that we may see how common it is for men of excellent abilities to be wont to show a blindness in matters which are manifest to even a dull and uncultivated mind; and how weak an argument drawn from human authority is, in divine things: where divine authority alone has weight.ᵉ

SECT. XXXVI.

New Testament precepts are addressed to the con-

Two distinct topics must here be spoken to: first, the precepts of the New Testament; and secondly, merit. I shall dispatch each of these in few words, having spoken of them rather prolixly on other occasions. The New Testament properly consists of promises and exhortations, just as the Old properly consists of laws and

ᵈ *Natura, necessitas.*] By ' nature,' in this connection, I suppose he means ' an inherent, settled, constitution of things;' which produces actions involuntarily : by ' necessity,' ' a compulsory influence' exercised upon such a constitution, from without.

ᵉ The inconsistency is Erasmus's . his Freewill is necessity, but, according to *him,* is the subject of reward.

threatenings. For, in the New Testament, the Gospel is preached; which is nothing else but a discourse offering the Spirit, together with grace, unto that remission of sins which hath been obtained for us by the crucifixion of Christ: and all this gratuitously, because the mercy only of God the Father befriends us, unworthy as we are, and deserving damnation, as we do, rather than any thing else. Then follow exhortations, to stir up those who are already justified, and have obtained mercy, unto a strenuousness in bringing forth the fruits of that freely-bestowed righteousness and of the Spirit, and unto the acting of love in the performance of good works, and unto the bearing of the cross and of all the other tribulations of the world with a good courage. This is the sum of all the New Testament.—How entirely ignorant Diatribe is of this matter, she abundantly shows in not knowing how to make the least difference between the Old Testament and the New; for she sees almost nothing in either, save laws and precepts, by which men are to be formed to good manners. What new birth is;— what renewal, regeneration, and the whole work of the Spirit; she sees not at all: to my utter wonder and astonishment, that a man who has laboured so long and so studiously in the Scriptures should be so perfectly ignorant of them.

So then, this saying, "Rejoice and be exceeding glad, for much is your reward in the heavens," squares just about as well with Freewill as light agrees with darkness. For Christ therein exhorts not Freewill, but his Apostles (who not only were in a state above Freewill, as being already partakers of grace and just persons; but were even established in the ministry of the word; that is, in the highest station of grace), to bear the tribulations of the world. But we are engaged in discussing Freewill, specially as she subsists without grace; who is instructed by laws and threatenings (that is, by the Old Testament) into

PART III. the knowledge of herself, that she may run to the promises set forth in the New.'

'Such is Luther's representation of the New Testament as contrasted with the Old, and of the Gospel. The New is 'promises and exhortations;' the Old is 'law and threatenings.' The Gospel is 'the Spirit, and grace unto salvation, offered to all men; through Christ, who died for all.'*—For some objections to this statement, as it respects 'offers of grace,' see above, Sect. xxiii, note ª; as it respects the opposition between the Law and the Gospel, see above, Sect. xxiv. note ¹.—The Gospel is certainly to be preached to all; to the reprobate as well as to the elect; but with what propriety this can be called 'an *offer* of grace' to all, or to any, may be fairly questioned: much more, with what consistency such language can be used by one who so stoutly maintained, as Luther did, both the impotency of the natural man, and the God-made difference between the elect and the reprobate. With such views as Luther had of the atonement, as though Christ had shed his blood for those from whom it was the Father's good pleasure to hide the mysteries of his kingdom; and with such a want of insight into the first principle of divine counsel, operation, and revelation—even God's design of manifesting himself; in short, with such a want of insight into God; it was impossible that he should not speak inconsistently. Indeed it would be little, if inconsistency were all. Such language is illusive, perplexing, and subversive to man; and, whilst it aims to beautify God, defames him! He is correct, however, to some considerable extent: he nobly asserts, that salvation is altogether gratuitous, the produce of the Father's mercy, conferred upon the hell-deserving through the alone merit of Christ's death. He nobly asserts, that the preceptive parts of the New Testament are for the called and justified only.—But why is the Old Testament to be thus set in array against the New? Where is 'the law and threatenings' in the book of Genesis? What more truly Evangelical words are to be found in the New Testament, than in Isaiah and the other Prophets; in the Psalms, and in Luther's favourite book of Deuteronomy? 'The Old Testament, as our 7th Article wisely speaks, is not contrary to the New: for both in the Old and New Testament everlasting life is offered to mankind by Christ, who is the only mediator between God and man, being both God and man.'—The truth is, even the Law itself, as I have already remarked, is 'Gospel in enigma;' and the scribe that is instructed in the New Testament finds the Old its best commentator and confirmer; what has instructed the same family in its tenderer years, and now makes the "young men" perfect.—I should speak rather differently

* Note, he *distinguishes* between the Spirit and grace, though not very correctly; it is the Spirit as given to the justified, of which he speaks; but this is part of the grace of God; that is, "of the things which are freely given to us of God."

But as to merit, or a reward being proposed, what is this but a sort of promise? This proves not that we have any power; for nothing else is expressed by it, but that, if a man shall have done this or that thing, then he shall have a reward. But our question is, not *how*[g] a reward, or *what sort* of a reward, shall be rendered to a man; but whether we can do those things to which a reward is rendered. This was the thing to be proved. Is it not a ridiculous consequence: The reward of the judge is proposed to all that are in the course; therefore all can run and obtain? If Cæsar shall have conquered the Turk, he shall enjoy the kingdom of Syria: therefore Cæsar can conquer, and does conquer the Turk. If Freewill rules over sin, it shall be holy to the Lord; therefore Freewill is holy to the Lord.— But I will say no more about these superlatively stupid and palpably absurd reasonings; save, that it is most worthy of Freewill to be defended by such exquisite arguments. Let me rather speak to this point; that 'necessity has neither merit,

<small>SECT. XXXVII.

Merit and reward may consist with necessity.</small>

of the Apostles. They *were to be* what he describes, with the exception of one of them; but they *were not* this yet. If they could be truly said to know Christ at all, till the day of Pentecost was fully come, they knew him " after the flesh." (2 Cor v. 16) But it is not to the Twelve exclusively, that the Lord addresses these words (Matt. v 12), nor of them exclusively that he speaks. His precepts were for the regulation of *their* conduct, and of the conduct of all his converted people (whilst walking through the wilderness of this world *in his kingdom*), as they should hereafter be called, one by one, into vital union with him : that union, of which his elect have the sacrament in their baptism, but the reality, when either before or after the receiving of that sacrament, the Spirit has been given, to convert and to dwell in them.—Luther's argument, however, is not shaken by this distinction. The Lord speaks *as* to real members of his kingdom, to persons therefore, who are above and beyond that state of Freewill which is the matter of dispute.—Already Luther has shewn Erasmus inconsistent with himself in arguing from this text (see Sect. xxxv.): his second answer is, ' this text (to which all other New Testament precepts might be added) does not apply,'

[g] *Quo modo.*] *How,* in point of action; what he must do that he may be entitled.

PART III. nor reward." If we speak of a necessity of compulsion, it is true: if we speak of a necessity of immutability, it is false.[h] Who would give a reward, or impute merit, to an unwilling workman? But to those who wilfully do good or evil, even though they cannot change this will by their own power, there follows, naturally, and necessarily, reward or punishment; as it is written, "Thou wilt render unto every man according to his works." It follows naturally, 'if you plunge into water, you will be suffocated; if you swim out, you will save your life.'

To be brief; in the matter of merit, or reward, the inquiry is either about the worthiness, or about the consequence, of actions. If you look at worthiness, there is no such thing as merit; there is no such thing as reward. For, if Freewill can will nothing good of itself, and wills good only through grace (we are speaking, you know, of Freewill as separate from grace, and are inquiring what power is proper to each), who does not see that this good will, together with its merit and its reward, is of grace only? And here again, Diatribe is at variance with herself in arguing the freedom of the will from merit, and is in the same condemnation with me whom she opposes: since it fights equally against herself as against me, that there is merit, that there is reward, that there is liberty; after she has asserted, as she does above, that Freewill can will nothing good, and has undertaken to prove such a sort of Freewill.

If you look at the consequences of actions, there is nothing either good or bad, which has not its reward. And we get into mistakes from this cause, that, in speaking of merits and rewards, we agitate useless considerations and questions about the worth of actions—which is none—when

[h] For this distinction, see above, Part i. Sect. xi. Sect. xxv.

we ought to be debating only about the consequences of them. For hell and the judgment of
God await the wicked by a necessary consequence, even though they themselves neither desire, nor think of such a reward for their sins;
nay, though they exceedingly detest and, as Peter
says, execrate it.¹ In like manner, the kingdom
awaits the godly, though they neither seek it, nor
think of it themselves; being a possession prepared for them of their Father, not only before
they were themselves in existence, but even before the foundation of the world.

Nay, if these latter were doing good that they
might obtain the kingdom, they never would
obtain it; and would belong rather to the community of the wicked, who, with an evil and
mercenary eye, "seek their own,"ᵏ even in
God. But the sons of God do good through a
gratuitous good pleasure;' not seeking any reward, but simply seeking the glory, and aiming
to do the will, of God: they are prepared to do
good, even though according to an impossible
supposition, there were no such thing as either
kingdom or hell-fire. I think these things are
quite sure from that single saying of Christ in
Matt. xxv. "Come ye blessed of my Father,
receive the kingdom, which hath been prepared

¹ *Detestentur, execrentur.*] For proper meaning of 'detes-
tor,' see above, Part i. Sect. vii. note ᵗ. It is opposed to
'obtestor;', as calling God to witness, unto evil and not unto
good. '*Malum alicui imprecari, Deos testes ciendo ;*' '*execrari.*'
Here, however, I understand it literally, according to its
derived meaning; and so, 'exsecror;' which properly denotes
'removing out of sacred relations,' or subjecting to a curse —
The allusion is to 2 Pet. ii. 10—15. "But these.... speak evil
of the things they understand not, and shall utterly perish in
their own corruption; and shall receive the reward of unrighteousness." Βλασφημοῦντες. The original text makes the
reference plainer than our version.

ᵏ "All seek their own, not the things which are Jesus
Christ's." (Phil. ii. 21.) Not content with seeking their own
glory, &c. &c. in their dealings with man, they seek it even
from the hands of God: *He* is to do them good, not himself.

PART III. for you from the foundation of the world." How do they earn that, which is even now theirs, and which was prepared for them before they were born? So that we should speak more correctly, if we should say, the kingdom of God doth rather earn us for its possessors, than we it; placing merit where they place reward, and reward where they place merit. For the kingdom is not *to be* prepared, but *hath been prepared*; but the children of the kingdom are *to be prepared*, not themselves *to prepare* the kingdom: that is, the kingdom earns her children, not the children the kingdom. Hell, in like manner, doth rather earn her children, and prepare them, than they it; since Christ says, "Depart ye cursed into everlasting fire, which hath been prepared for the devil and his angels."[1]

Erasmus objects, that 'so much mention of good works and reward, in Scripture, is inconsistent with mere necessity; which can have no merit.'

Luther answers, though not exactly in this order: 1. Merit and reward are as inconsistent with *your* Freewill (which can will nothing good) as with mine. 2. Reward is a matter of promise; which implies nothing of power, the alone thing in question. 3. Merit and reward are not inconsistent with a necessity of immutability, though they be inconsistent with a necessity of compulsion. (See above, note h.) Merit is not necessarily merit of worth; reward may be a consequence of actions, in which there is no merit of worth. 4. The kingdoms of heaven and hell earn their children, severally, not they them.

The two first of these answers are valid; and, if it were merely so many rounds of the boxer, or so many grapplements of the wrestler, of which we are watching the result, we must give the palm to Luther: he has supplanted, he has knocked down his antagonist. But we want to hear something against merit and reward; and here, Luther is evasive and subtle in his reasoning, though correct in his conclusion. Necessity of immutability does not necessarily imply absence of merit; because that which the will cannot do for itself, it may be changed by another to do. Luther has supplied the basis of a solid and satisfactory answer, in his fourth reply; whilst he has neither opened it, nor appears to be sensible of its force and marrow. "The kingdoms earn their children severally, not they them."

Then what mean those declarations which promise the kingdom and threaten hell? What

SECT. XXXVIII.

Why there are promises and threatenings in Scripture.

Upon Luther's principles, it is impossible to give a solid answer to the objection of 'merit.' For, if Christ has died alike for all; if he has done and suffered the same both for the elect and for the reprobate; so that there is no difference between them, as far as respects HIS merit (which is the essence of the doctrine of Universal Redemption); then, either there must be merit in the individuals of the elect, or there is with God repect of persons: HE makes a different award to some from what he does to others, alike meritorious or unmeritorious, through partiality. Nor will it suffice to say (as Luther does), this reward is mere matter of consequence, like the man swimming out of water, &c. God sees *somewhere* that which makes it the demand of His justice that he should put a difference: and, since this is not in Christ, it must be in the individuals themselves. The true answer is, that God has assumed distinct, super-creation relations to his elect, in Christ; which render it imperative upon him to give them grace and glory, each in its season. This is the true meaning of the kingdom of heaven earning her sons: there are relations of and belonging to that kingdom, which communicate the power that is necessary to the inheriting of that kingdom, in consistency with all that God is, and to the manifestation of him as that God which he is. So again, with respect to the kingdom of hell: that kingdom has relations which have procured its inhabitants and inheritors. The devil has had a power given to him, by which he has drawn legions into his service, and is bringing those legions to be his companion in torments; legions, not of devils only, but of reprobate and accursed men: from which number, as equally ruined by the devil and self-destroyed with the rest, the elect people of God, through their super-creation relations to him in Christ, or, as it has just now been expressed, through the relations of the kingdom of God (of which God, of his distinguishing favour, has given to them to be members), are rescued. Merit and reward are made nearly as much a stumbling-block to the maintainers of free grace, as the sin and impotency of the natural man are to the merit-mongers: with this difference, that the stumbling-blocks which may be thrown upon the path of truth are superable and removable, whilst falsehood may pass by, and cover over, but she cannot expose and expel her stumbling-blocks. Too often, however, the sincere and strenuous advocates of truth defend her cause weakly, and even dangerously.—Who will be satisfied, for instance, with that answer to an objection brought against the truth, which assumes that there is no such thing as "recompense of reward" in the Bible; no soldier's crown; no servant's wages; no agonistic palm; no "for" to the call of the blessed of my Father; or that all these things and meaneth that word "reward," so often repeated as it is, throughout the Scriptures? "Thy work-

sayings are resolvable into what Christ personally hath done; and might, if, according to that will of his and of the Father's which is represented as no other than perfectly arbitrary, he saw fit to do so, be bestowed upon his enemies and blasphemers, just as righteously as upon his servant-friends? (See John xv. 15.)

The true objection to merit and reward is, that, as generally understood and represented, they suppose something of good in the natural man; in that self-ruined, self-damned, and self-made-impotent thing which has merited Hell before he was born into the world, and can merit nothing but Hell.—But, what now if it please God to give to this self-ruined, self-made-impotent thing new powers, under a new relation, and by a new title? Is there any thing to prevent God from accepting an equivalent, if such can be found, for that punishment which is the just reward of this his moral creature's sin; and, of his own free, sovereign and distinguishing favour (as it respects the subject of his infinite, everlasting, and inestimable bounty), placing him in new relations, and endowing him with new capacities as the fruit of those relations? And why may not this new-made creature, so related, so capacitated, and so connected, act in a manner worthy of those relations, and so entitle himself to those results which the God of all grace has seen fit to attach to the maintenance and fulfilment of those relations?—This is just the state and case of the eternally foreknown, elect, predestinated, given and received people of God, in Christ Jesus, their grace and glory Head. Contemplated as now already self-destroyed and fallen in Adam; under express sentence of death, with all that awful hereafter which was implied though not expressed in that sentence; the Lord Jesus, by making himself sin for them, and dying with them, renders it consistent in God to raise them up from the dead, and to bring them out into a new state of being, with new relations, capacities, enjoyments and privileges, in him. In a figure, they are said to have risen with Christ; in reality, the indubitability of their future rising was *publicly* sealed, and manifested to the whole world, by his rising :—I say publicly, because it had been secretly sealed, in the eternal covenant transactions of the Three in Jehovah, before the worlds. "This is that grace which was given us in Christ Jesus before the world began." (2 Tim. i. 9.) Regeneration, in its most correct view, is a partial-fulfilment of the personal resurrection of the Lord's elect: it is the resurrection of the soul or spirit. "The hour is coming, *and now is,* when the dead shall hear the voice of the Son of God, and they that hear shall live." (John v. 25.) By it they are brought into a resurrection state; are shewn to be of those who shall hereafter rise with a body like *His*; and

hath a reward," saith he. "I am thy exceeding great reward." Again; "Who rendereth unto are now called to serve him in an intermediate state, as " God's workmanship, created in Christ Jesus unto good works, which God hath before ordained that we should walk in them."* (Ephes. ii. 10.) Thus they are, essentially, grace receivers of grace powers, called and enabled to act in a manner worthy of a grace reward. Here is reward then, not of mere consequence, but of merit: of merit, which has worth or dignity in it, yet is all the while grace; free, distinguishing, sovereign grace. Thus grace reigneth; but it is THROUGH RIGHTEOUSNESS: which means, if the connection of those words be duly observed, not merely through Christ's being personally righteous; but through, and in a way of righteousness, as it respects the persons of his people. (Rom. v. 20, 21. compare with the whole of Rom. vi. which follows, specially from ver. 14 to ver. 23.)—Many, doubtless, will cavil at this statement; but it is for lack of distinguishing things which essentially differ; it is for lack of understanding the true nature, origin, design, constituent subjects, and provisions of the kingdom of God; it is for lack of understanding that the members of that kingdom are persons already saved (" Who hath saved us, and called us with an holy calling;" " for by grace ye are saved;" " unto us which are saved, it is the power of God"); not men striving for life to get life, but already-living men; not natural men, but men joined unto the Lord, and who are one spirit with him; which constitute the reward-earning community: concerning whom, it is God's glory that they, being brought out, as they are, in the face and heart of the world— a world made up of hypocrites, or false professors of his name, on the one hand; and of declared enemies and persecutors on the other—" should walk worthy of the vocation wherewith they are called;" " should walk worthy of God, who hath called them to his kingdom and glory;" " should be counted worthy of his kingdom," and should manifest him to be the righteous God in recompensing rest (their consummation and bliss) to them, when he recompenseth tribulation to them that have troubled them."—If this statement be duly apprehended,

* When we speak of good works, people are apt to run immediately into the idea of law works, as if the Ten Commandments were to be brought back again: not considering, that good is a relative term; and that good works, therefore, must be those which are consistent with the relations under which we stand, when performing them. If it were possible for renewed man, in the days of his flesh, to keep the whole law, he would not thereby do good works. The law is for creation man; the Gospel is for super-creation man. It is the obedience of a redeemed sinner, to which he is called in Christ Jesus; an obedience analogous to that fuller and more distinct manifestation of God, which he has made of himself in his new, after-creation kingdom. To this obedience, as many as have been created, or builded, in Christ Jesus from the very first, as Abel, &c. have been called and brought, according to their measure of faith.

PART III.
─────
every man according to his works." And Paul
in Romans ii. (saith," "{To those who by the
patience of good works, seek for eternal life;"
and many like sayings. The answer is, that all these sayings prove
nothing but a consequence of reward, and by no
means a worthiness of merit;ᵐ that those, for-

it will give their legitimate force and meaning to numberless
passages of Scripture, which some bring forward to contradict
the truth of God, and others pare down and mutilate to maintain it.—The essence of the distinction too, that the grace
which earneth reward is truly super-creation grace, furnishes a
sure test by which to try and convict hypocrites. How common is the language, ' O, I know I have nothing that I have
not received.' Yes, but how hast thou received it? Grace is
that principle in the divine mind which makes distinctions:
grace is not only favour, but free favour; not only free favour,
but separating favour; in the case we are considering, is separating favour, shewn in a way of mercy; that is, shewn to those
who have deserved a contrary sort of treatment. Hast thou
received then by a new and super-creation title; which puts
a difference between Adam's alike self-destroyed and wholly-destroyed sons? Or, is it that thou hast cultivated thy natural
powers; or, if it pleaseth thee rather, hast improved that gospel-grace which is bestowed on all, and has put all into a
capacity of working out their own salvation? The answer
will unmask the man: grace knows itself, and knows its
origin.

In asserting that the kingdom of hell has earned, and is earning, its subjects through a power which God has given to the
devil, I would be understood to intimate that the devil could
neither be, nor continue to be, without the will of God; and
that hell is filled through his agency: by which, in perfect
consistency with all creation relations and obligations, ruin
was originally brought upon man; and by which he secures
and retains to himself that spoil, which it is the Father's good
pleasure that he should carry off, to HIS glory.

ᵐ *Sequelam mercedis, meriti dignitatem.*] The expression seems
inverted; 'worthiness of merit,' for merit which has worth in
it; the meaning clearly is, ' reward follows as a consequence,
but there is nothing of meritorious worthiness in the subject.'
Luther, in what follows, overstates the matter of disinterestedness; and afterwards virtually contradicts himself. We are
not called to be insensible to the end, but urged to keep it in
view; and why, but as a source of encouragement? which he
presently affirms. What, indeed, is that *following because,*
but an admission of the same thing?—The cure for servility
is, "to the praise of the glory of his grace"—" *saved*

sooth, who do good, do it not through a servile and mercenary disposition to gain eternal life, but still seek eternal life; that is, are in the way by which they shall arrive at and obtain eternal life. So that, to seek eternal life, is painfully to strive, and with urgent labour to endeavour, because it is wont to follow after a good life. Now, the Scriptures declare that these things will take place, and will follow after a good or evil life; in order that men may be instructed, admonished, excited, terrified: for, as by the law is the knowledge of sin and admonishment of our impotency, yet is it not inferred from this law that we have any power; even so, we are admonished and taught, by those promises and threatenings, what follows after that sin and impotency of ours, which the law has pointed out to us; but nothing of worthiness is ascribed by them to our merit.

Wherefore, as law words stand in the place of instruction and illumination, to teach us what we ought to do; and, as the next step, what we cannot do; so words of reward, whilst they intimate what is to happen, stand in the place of exhortation and threatening, to stir up, comfort, and revive the godly,[n] that they may go on, persevere, and conquer, in doing good, and enduring evil, least they should be weary or broken-hearted. Just as Paul exhorts his Corinthian converts, saying, "Quit yourselves like men;" "knowing that your labour is not in vain in the Lord."[o]

already—'the triumph sure'—'Christ magnified by my body'—'God does all our works in us'—'we will do what he enables'—'we will suffer what he appoints to us'—'happy by the way.'—'how much more happy when in my Father's house'.—There is nothing mercenary here; but the end is neither hidden, nor undesired.—See above, note l.

[n *Excitantur, consolantur, eriguntur.*] *Exc.* is a more general term, applicable to any that want excitement; but *erig.* applies especially to those who have fallen or been cast down, and so want raising up. How beautifully this process is described in Ezek. xxxiv.!

[o] Luther quotes these words as if they were parts of the

PART III.

SECT. XXXIX.

Reason objects to this account, but is answered 'such is the will of God.'

Thus, God revives Abraham by saying, 'I am thy exceeding great reward.' Just as if you should cheer a person, by telling him that his works assuredly please God: a sort of consolation which the Scripture frequently uses. Nor is it a small degree of consolation for a man to know, that he pleases God; though nothing else should follow from it; which is, however, impossible. All that is said about hope and expectation must be referred to this consideration, that the things hoped for will certainly take place; although godly men do not hope, because of the things themselves, or seek such benefits for their own sake. So, again, ungodly men are terrified and cast down by words of threatening, which announce a judgment to come, that they may cease and abstain from evil; that they may not be puffed up; that they may not grow secure and insolent in their sins.—Now, if reason should turn up her nose here, and say, 'Why would God have these impressions to be made by his words, when no effect is produced by such words, and when the will cannot turn itself either way? why doth he not perform what he doth, without taking notice of it in the word (seeing he can do all things without the word; and seeing the will neither has more power, nor performs more, of itself, through the hearing of the word, if the Spirit be lacking to move the soul within; nor would have less power, or perform less, though the word were silent, if the Spirit were vouchsafed; since all depends upon the power and work of the Holy Ghost); my reply is,—God has determined to give the Spirit *by* the word, and not *without* it, having us for his cooperators, to sound *without* what he alone and by himself breathes *within,* just where he pleases; producing effects, which he could no doubt accomplish

same sentence : but the one is part of 1 Cor. xv. 58. the other of 1 Cor. xvi. 13.

without the word, but which it is not his pleasure so to do. And who are we, that we should demand the reason why God wills so? It is enough for us to know that God wills so; and it becomes us to reverence, to love, and to adore this will, putting a restraint upon rash Reason. Even Christ, in Matt. xi. assigns no other cause for the Gospel being hidden from the wise and revealed to babes, than that so it seemed good to the Father.[p] So he might nourish us without bread, and he has, in point of fact, given us a power of being nourished without bread, as he says in Matt. iv. " Man is not nourished by bread alone, but by the word of God."[q] Still, it hath pleased him to nourish us inwardly by his word, through the means of bread; and that bread fetched into us from without.[r]

It stands good, therefore, that merit is not proved by reward; in the Scriptures, at least: and again, that Freewill is not proved by merit; much less such a Freewill as Diatribe has undertaken to prove; one which cannot will any thing good, of itself. For, if you should even concede that there is such a thing as merit, and should

---

[p] Here we are reminded again of the defect of Luther's views. It is not arbitrary will, but counselled will of God accomplishing the best end by just and necessary means, which gives occasion to this arrangement. The declaration of his truth, by the word, to the self-made-impotent is necessary to the manifestation of himself, through his dealings with them ' The " Even so, Father," would be enough; but he has been so kind as to show us more, and there are places and seasons where this ' more' should be brought into sight. See Sect. xxviii notes [t] [v] [x].

[q] The original text in Deuteronomy viii. says, פָּל־מוֹצָא,

" Every that proceedeth," meaning no doubt, as the Lord quotes it, ' every word of command which he gives.'

[r] Thus it is God's word which imparts its power of nourishing to the natural bread; but still he is pleased to use that bread so, the spiritual bread of the word only nourishes when he gives the word for it to do so; but still he uses that spiritual bread, when he wills to nourish.

PART III. add those wonted similes and consequences of Reason; as, that commandments are given in vain; that reward is promised in vain; that threatenings are held forth in vain; except there be Freewill: if any thing be proved by these arguments, I say, it is that Freewill can of herself do every thing. For, if she cannot do every thing for herself, that consequence of reason retains its place; 'therefore it is vain to command, it is vain to promise, it is vain to hold out threatenings.' Thus is Diatribe continually disputing against herself, whilst opposing me. The truth meanwhile is, that God alone worketh both merit and reward in us, by his Spirit; but he announces and declares each of these to the whole world, by his outward word; in order that his own power and glory, and our impotency and ignominy, may be proclaimed even amongst the ungodly, the unbelieving, and the ignorant; although none but the godly understand that word with the heart, and keep it faithfully; the rest despising it.

SEC XL.
Apology for not consideiing all his pretended texts separately — Absuid cavil from Matt. vii. 16.

And now, it would be too tiresome to repeat the several imperative verbs which Diatribe enumerates out of the New Testament; always appending her own consequences, pretending that all these expressions are vain, superfluous, unmeaning, absurd, ridiculous, nothing at all, except the Will be free. I have already declared, to a high degree of nauseating repetition, what an absolute nothing is made out by such expressions as these; which, if they prove any thing, prove an entire Freewill. Now, this is nothing else but a complete overturning of Diatribe; who undertook to prove such a Freewill as can do nothing good, and serves sin; but does really prove one which can do every thing: so ignorant and so forgetful of her own self is she continually. They are mere cavils then, when she argues, 'ye shall know them by their fruits,' saith the Lord: by fruits, he

TEXTS FOR FREEWILL DISPROVED.

means works. He calls these works ours: but they are not ours, if all things be performed by necessity.

SEC. XLI.

What! are not those possessions most rightly called ours, which we have not made ourselves, it is true, but have received from others? Why should not those works then be called ours, which God hath given to us by the Spirit? Shall we not call Christ ours, because we have not made him, but only received him? On the other hand, if we make all those things which are called ours, why then we have made our own eyes for ourselves, we have made our own hands for ourselves, we have made our own feet for ourselves; unless we are forbidden to call our eyes, hands, and feet ours! Nay, what have we, which we have not received; as Paul says? Shall we then say, that these possessions are either not ours, or they have been made by our ownselves? But let be now, let be that these fruits are called ours, because we have produced them; what then becomes of grace and the Spirit? For he does not say, ' by their fruits, which are in some very small degree and portion theirs, ye shall know them.'[s]—These, rather, are the ridiculous, the superfluous, the vain, the unmeaning sayings— nay, a parcel of foolish and odious cavils, by which the sacred words of God are polluted and profaned.

Thus too, that saying of Christ upon the cross is sported with;[t] "Father, forgive them; for they know not what they do." (Here, when you would expect a sentence attaching[u] Freewill to the

Luke xxii. 34 is *against* not *for* Freewill.

[s] Erasmus argues, it is necessary to their being called 'ours,' that they be done by our own natural powers. Then they are *wholly* done by our natural powers; for he calls them *ours*, without addition or subtraction —Then there is no Spirit and grace in our good works —Another of the ' nimis probats.'

[t] *Luditur*] ' Ludo se, delectationis causâ, exercere.' I do not know any classical authority for this passive form of the verb 'ludo '—*Verbum*, &c. luditur.

[u] *Astrueret*.] ' Juxtà struo,' ' propè extruo:' not *superstructure*,' but 'additional or contiguous structure.'—It is the

PART III. testimony adduced, she betakes herself again to her consequences.) 'How much more justly, says she, would he have excused them by saying that they were those who had not a free will, and could not, if they would, do otherwise!' And yet; that sort of Freewill which can will nothing good, though it be the one in question, is not proved by this consequence; but that sort of Freewill which can do every thing; which no one contends for, and which all deny, except the Pelagians.—But now, when Christ expressly says that they know not what they do, does he not at the same time testify, that they cannot will good? For, how can you will what you do not know? There can be no desire, surely, for an unknown thing. What can be more stoutly affirmed against Freewill, than that it is in itself such a perfect nullity, as not only to be incapable of willing good, but even of knowing how much evil it is doing, and what good is. Is there any obscurity in any word here? "They know not what they do." 'What is there remaining in Scripture, which may not, by the suggestion of Diatribe, prove Freewill, when this most clear and most adversative saying of Christ is to her an affirmation of it? ' A man might just as easily say, that Freewill is proved by that saying, "The earth was empty' and void;" or by that, "God rested on the seventh day:" and the like. Then will the Scriptures be ambiguous and obscure indeed! nay, they will mean all things, and mean nothing, in the same moment. But such audacious handling of the word of God argues a mind signally contemptuous both towards God and towards man; which deserves no patience at all.[x]

flying off from the proof alleged, in pursuit of something more remote; to which Luther here objects.
[v] *Inanis.*] *We* say, 'without form;' but Luther has it 'without substance;' having nothing in it, or upon it.
[x] Luther answers, 1. It is inference. 2. The text is against you. 3. Such use of Scripture is criminal.

So, again, that saying in John i. "To them gave he power to become the sons of God," she takes in this wise: 'How can power be given to them, that they should become the sons of God, if there be no liberty in our will?'

This passage, also, is a cudgel[y] for Freewill— such as nearly all the Gospel of John is—but adduced in support of it. See, I pray you, John is not speaking of any work of man's, whether great or small; but of the actual renewal and transmutation of the old man, who is a son of the devil, into the new man; who is a son of God. This man is simply passive (as they speak), and does nothing, but is altogether a thing made. For John speaks of his being made: "to be made the sons of God," he says; by a power freely given to us of God, not by a power of Freewill which is natural to us.[z]

But our Diatribe infers from hence, that Freewill is of such power, as to make sons of God; prepared else to determine, that this saying of John is ridiculous and unmeaning. But who has ever extolled Freewill to such a height, as to give it the power of making sons of God; especially such a Freewill, as can will nothing good; the one, which Diatribe has taken up to prove.[a] But let this pass with the rest of those consequences, so often repeated; by which, if any thing is proved, it is nothing else, but what Diatribe denies; namely, that Freewill can do every thing. What John means is this: that, by Christ's coming into the world, a power is given to all men, through the Gospel (that Gospel by which grace is offered, and not work demanded), which

[y] *Malleus*] More properly, 'a mallet;' ' fabrile instrumentum ad tundendum.'

[z] *Vi insita*] *Ins* properly, 'what is inserted as a graft;' but transferred to signify 'what is natural, innate, inherent.' ' Nativus, innatus, ingenitus.'

[a] *Assumsit*] Scil. ad probandum. What he elsewhere expresses by ' probandum suscepit.'

PART III. is magnificent in the extreme; even that of becoming the sons of God, if they be willing to believe! But this being willing, this believing in his name, as it is a thing which Freewill never knew, never thought of before; so is it a thing, which she is yet much further from being able to attain to, by her own powers. For how should reason imagine that faith in Jesus, the son of God and of man, is necessary; when she does not even at this day comprehend, nor can believe, even though the whole creation should as with an audible voice proclaim it, that there exists a person, which is at the same time both God and man. On the contrary, she is the more offended by such preaching; as Paul testifies in 1 Cor. i. so far is she, from being either willing or able to believe.[b]

John, therefore, proclaims those riches of the kingdom of God which are offered to the world by the Gospel, not the virtues of Freewill: intimating at the same time, how few there are that receive them; because Freewill, forsooth, resists the proposal, her power being nothing else, through the dominion which Satan has over her, but even to spurn the offer of grace, and of

[b] We have here, Luther's usual, exceptionable expression about 'offers.' (See Sect. xxiii. note [a]); and his mention of the person of Christ suggests over again the importance of the distinction which I remarked in Part ii. Sect. viii. note [r]. If we do not keep the divine and the human *person* of Christ distinct, but regard him simply as a person who has put another *nature*, the human *nature*, upon his former and eternal, divine nature; his whole history and the things said of him are a Babel: not so, if we be brought to apprehend him as the co-equal of the Father and of the Holy Ghost acting *in* and *by* a human person which he has taken up into union with himself.—The text evidently proves nothing for Freewill: it only says "as many as received him;" without saying by what power; whether natural or supernatural. I do not agree with Luther, in its being the making of the old man into the new man: it is the state of privilege and glory, into which the son of Adam and child of the devil has been brought, by that preceding process of transmutation.

that Spirit, which would fulfil the law. So exquisite is the force of her desire and endeavour to fulfil the law!—But, hereafter, I shall shew more at large, what a thunderbolt this text of John's is against Freewill. Meanwhile, I am not a little indignant, that passages so clear in their meaning and so powerful in their opposition to Freewill, should be cited by Diatribe in her favour : whose dulness is such, that she discovers no difference between law words and words of promise; for, having first of all established Freewill, most ridiculously, by law testimonies, she afterwards reaches the highest height of absurdity,[d] by confirming it with words of promise. This absurdity, however, is easily explained, by considering with what an averse and contemptuous mind Diatribe engages in the discussion. To her it is no matter, whether grace stand or fall; whether Freewill be laid prostrate or maintain her seat; if she may but prove herself the humble servant of a conclave of tyrants, by uttering a number of vain words to excite disgust against our cause.

After this we come to Paul also, the most determined enemy to Freewill, who is nevertheless, compelled to establish Freewill by what he says in Rom. ii. " Or despisest thou the riches of his goodness and patience and longsuffering? or knowest thou not that his goodness leadeth thee to repentance?" How can it be, that contempt of the commandment is imputed, where the will is not free? How can it be, that God invites to repentance, when he is the author of impenitence? How can it be, that damnation

SC.XLIII.

Objections from Paul summarily dispatched.

[c] See note * upon note f, Sect. xxxvi.
[d] *Ineptissimè longè absurdissimè.*] *Inept.* The weaker term ; denoting properly, 'unaptness,' impertinence,' 'silliness;' *absurd*, 'the extreme of incongruity and extravagance.' '*Ineptus* est tantùm non aptus ; *absurdus*, repugnans, abhorrens : itaque absurdus majus quiddam significat;' velut qui *surdis auribus* audiri dignus est.

is just, when the judge constrains to the crime?[e] I answer, let Diatribe look to these questions. What are they to me? She has told us, in her approvable, opinion, that Freewill cannot will good, and compels us necessarily into the service of sin. How is it then, that contempt of the commandment is imputed to her; if she cannot will good, and if she have no liberty, but be under a necessary bondage to sin? How is it, that God invites to repentance, when he is the author of man's not repenting; in that he deserts, or does not confer grace upon him, when, being left alone, he cannot will good? How is it, that the damnation is just, where the judge, by withdrawing his help, makes it unavoidable that the ungodly man be left to do wickedly; since, by his own power, he can do nothing else?—All these sayings recoil upon the head of Diatribe : or, if they prove any thing, prove (what I have said) that Freewill can do every thing; in contradiction to what she has said herself, and every body else. These consequences of reason annoy Diatribe, throughout all her Scripture quotations. It is ridiculous and unmeaning, forsooth, to attack and exact,[f] in such vehement language, when there is not one present who can fulfil the demand? The Apostle, all the while, has it for his object to lead ungodly and proud men to the knowledge of themselves and of their own impotency, by the means of these threatenings; that, having humbled them by the knowledge of sin, he may prepare them for grace.[g]

[e] Referring, no doubt, to Rom. iii. 5—8.
[f] *Invadere et exigere*] *Inv.* expresses the assault upon the person : ' in aliquem locum vado;' ingredior (et ferè cum aliquâ vi, aut impetu), aggredior, irrumpo, irruo. *Exig.* ' extrà ago;' educo Sæpè est reposcere, flagitare, in re pecuniariâ: itemque, exigendo obtinere.—The figure is that of a bailiff seizing a man's person and demanding payment of a debt.
[g] It is not necessary to suppose this ulterior design, neither will it extend to all the cases which the Apostle had in view; though such effect is frequently produced by the instrumen-

TEXTS FOR FREEWILL DISPROVED.

SC. XLIV.

Wickliff's confession confessed.

And why need I recount, one by one, all the texts, which are adduced from Paul's writings; when she does but collect a number of imperative or conjunctive verbs, or such expressions as Paul uses in exhorting Christians to the fruits of faith?[h] Diatribe however, by adding her own consequences, imagines[i] to herself a Freewill of such and so great virtue, that, without grace, it can do every thing which Paul the exhorter prescribes? Christians, however, are not led by Freewill, but by the Spirit of God. (Rom. viii. 14.) Now, to be led is not to lead ourselves, but to be driven along, just as the saw or the hatchet[k] is driven along by the carpenter. And here, least any one should doubt Luther's having said such absurd things, Diatribe recites his words: which I deliberately own; avowing, as I do,[l] that Wickliff's

tality of these Scriptures. Such appeals are amongst the strong manifesters of what is *in* man; *in* him as what he has made himself, not as what God made him; *in* him, therefore, without excuse. By such manifesters, God, as his pleasure is, both hardeneth and converteth. In chap. ii. it is an exposure of the heart of the Jew as boasting himself against the heathen; in chap iii. it is the infidel disporting himself against the truth: whose damnation is shewn to be just by the language which he uses; the language of a heart, which has *made itself* vile.

[h] See Sect. xxxvi. note [f] Gospel precepts, whether from the Lord's mouth, or Paul's pen, are words to the Lord's called *only*; shewing how the saved should walk: that we, *having been delivered out of the hands of our enemies, might serve him without fear, in holiness and righteousness before him, all the days of our life.* (Luke i. 74, 75.)

[i] *Concipit.*] ' Translatè ponitur pro efformare, comprehendere, intelligere;' ' forms an idea.'

[k] I cannot think Luther very happy in this illustration: the hatchet and the saw have no *choice* in the hand of the carpenter; but *we* are *led freely*, *delightingly*.

[l] *Quæ sanè agnosco. Fateor. enim.*] Qu. sa. ag. expresses the perfect self-possession and consciousness with which he acknowledges the words as his. *Sanè.* ' Sanâ mente aut sensu, ubi nihil fuci aut fraudis est.' But it is not honesty and simplicity, so much as calmness, sobriety and stedfastness of judgment, that he claims for himself, in the recognition and restatement of what he had advanced. *Fateor, enim* 'implies avowal made under circumstances which might tempt to the

PART III. article ('all things are done by necessity;' that is, by the unchangeable will of God; 'and our will, though not compelled, indeed to do evil, is incapable of doing any good by its own power'")

suppression of it. His adversaries were the persons to make *confession* of the evil at Constance; not he; on his part, it was proclamation of accordant, not antagonistic, sentiment; but still, it was testimony borne in adversity—borne, as with a halter round his neck.

"Mors sola *fatetur*
" Quantula sint hominum corpuscula."—Juv. x. 171, 2.

Death testifies; but it is, as an unwilling and compelled witness: she would rather boast of her prey, than proclaim its littleness.
ᵐ This splendid paradox of Wickliff's has been brought into discussion already (see Part ii Sect. xxii.), and is the very essence of divine truth, though so offensive to the enemies of truth, and of many who account themselves its advocates. Wickliff, with all his blemishes, was a truly great man; enlightened to see and teach much of the mystery of God; more, I am ready to say, than many that came after him and carried off his palm. Most of these acknowledged his worth indeed: for, more than a century, those who had light did not disdain to acknowledge that they walked in *his* light; such as the Lollards, Huss, Jerome, and others. Erasmus *gives* him to Luther; and Luther is not ashamed to receive and confess him. Certainly, my friend the Dean has not done him justice; yet he tried, I admit, and meant to do it him. But this necessity, was what the Dean did not thoroughly relish, though he tolerated it: and so he apologized, where Wickliff himself would have gloried; and when he professes to give a brief sketch of 'his doctrines as extracted from his writings and other authentic documents,' whilst he admits that 'his distinguishing tenet was, undoubtedly, the election of grace,' he does not tell us what he held about it, nor even mention this paradox, which seems to have been considered as the centre and heart's core of his creed.—The Dean appears to have attached too much importance to Melancthon's judgment, who was so warped by the Sacramentarian Controversy, in which Wickliff's name was drawn out against the Lutherans, that he went to a great extreme in denying Wickliff's light; declaring 'that he had found in him, also, many other errors' (beside this on the sacrament), 'and that he neither understood nor believed the righteousness of faith.'— I admit that he had much darkness mingled with his light; confusion with his clearness; pusillanimity with his boldness; sophistry with his plainness; rashness with his honest zeal for reform. But I am rather inclined to measure a man by what he has of good, than by what he has also of evil; and when I see Wickliff acknowledged as the first open champion and

was falsely condemned by the Council of Constance;ⁿ or rather by conspiracy and sedition. Nay, even Diatribe herself defends him, in conjunction with me; asserting, as she does, that Freewill can will nothing good by its own powers, and serves sin *necessarily;* though, in the course of her proof, she establishes the direct contrary.

sc. XLIV.

declarer against the abominations of Antichrist; when I read such profound and luminous testimonies to the "hidden wisdom" in his writings; when I hear martyrs calling him their apostle, and a Cobham 'solemnly professing before God and man that he never abstained from sin till he knew Wickliff—but that after he became acquainted with that virtuous man and his despised doctrines it had been otherwise with him;' when I recollect, that he was the first who gave the Bible to our nation in English; and vindicated the right of the common people to read it; when I find the more determined of the reformers of the sixteenth century owning him as their forerunner, and their revilers casting him in their teeth: I am ashamed to ask what doctrine he held about tithes; to doubt his sincerity, because his circumstances drew him into an undesirable degree of mixture with carnal statesmen; to weigh the words which he dropped, in the hour of the power of darkness, in a pair of scales; and to 'rejoice in finding evidence,' as the result of much pious search, ᵗ that this celebrated champion *did belong* to the church of Christ.' Huss in the flames, and the Swift receiving his unintombed ashes, shall be my witnesses that he spake by the Holy Ghost.

ⁿ We have heard of the Council of Constance already (see Part ii. Sect. viii. note ᵛ); it was numerous, turbulent, and long: it put down three Popes, and erected one; raved about reform, and confirmed sword-preaching;* condemned a dead saint, and burnt two living ones; denied necessity, made a Sigismund blush, and did one good thing amidst all these bad ones, by setting Councils above Popes.

* Outrages of the Teutonic knights in Poland and Prussia; where they obtained a professed subjection to the Gospel by fire and sword!

PART IV.

LUTHER DEFENDS CERTAIN TESTIMONIES AGAINST FREEWILL.

SECTION I.

Erasmus has but two Texts to kill.

LET what has been said suffice in answer to Diatribe's first part, in which she endeavours to establish the reality of Freewill; and let us now consider her second part, in which she seeks to confute the testimonies on our side of the question: those, I mean, by which its existence is negatived. You will see here what a man-raised smoke is, when opposed to God's thunders and lightnings!

First then, after having recited innumerable texts of Scripture in support of Freewill, as a sort of army too dreadful to encounter (that she may give courage to the confessors and martyrs, and all the holy men and women who stand up for Freewill; and may inspire fear and trembling into all who are guilty of the sin of denying it); she pretends that the host which comes to oppose Freewill is contemptible in point of numbers, and goes on to represent that there are but two passages which stand conspicuous above the rest on this side of the argument: having nothing in her mind, as it should seem, but slaughter, and making sure of accomplishing it without much trouble. One of these is from Exod. ix. " The Lord hardened Pharaoh's heart:" the other is from Malachi i. " Jacob have I loved, but Esau have I hated." Strange, what an odious and unprofitable SECT. II. discussion Paul did take up, in the judgment of Diatribe, when he expounded both these at large to the Romans! In short, if the Holy Ghost were not a little knowing in rhetoric, there would be danger lest his heart should melt within him, through this great reach of art in pretending such vast contempt; and, lest absolutely despairing of his cause, he should yield the palm to Freewill, before the trumpet has called the champions into the lists. Presently, however, I shall come up as the reserve[a] to these two Scriptures, and shew my forces also : and yet, where such is the fortune of the battle, that one man puts ten thousand to flight, what need is there of forces? If one text of Scripture shall have conquered Freewill, her innumerable forces will be of no use to her.

Here therefore Diatribe has discovered a new method of eluding the plainest texts, by choosing to understand a trope in the simplest and clearest forms of speech. As, in the former instance, when pleading for Freewill, she eluded[b] the force of all the imperative and conjunctive law words by adding inferences, and superadding similes of her own invention;[c] so now, on her setting out to plead

Kills by resolving them into tropes: which he defends by Luther's example.

---

[a] *Succenturiatus.*] 'Succenturiati dicuntur, qui explendæ centuriæ gratiâ subjiciunt se ad supplementum ordinum.'—Luther would consider himself as 'the leader of an army of reserve;' though such army would be unnecessary, since the two invalidated texts would keep their ground.—*Pugnæ fortuna.* Luther speaks here, 'more Ethnicorum;' who, it is well known, ascribed every thing to Fortune, erecting temples and altars to her, and accounting 'Fortunatus' ('favoured of fortune') the most illustrious title they could ascribe to their generals. But Luther well knew the God of battles; nor meant to ascribe their *issue* to any other than Him; " even the Lord strong and mighty, the Lord mighty in battle!"

[b] *Elusit.*] It was *evading* the natural and legitimate interpretation of those words, when she practised with them so as to pass them off for assertives.

[c] *Adjectas. affictas.*] *Adj.* 'addere,' 'adjungere :' *affict.* ' sæpius est *fingendo addere.*'

against us, she turns and twists all words of divine promise and affirmation just which way she pleases, by discovering a trope in them: that Proteus may be alike inapprehensible, on both sides.[d] Nay, she demands this for herself with great superciliousness at *our* hands; because *we*, as she pretends, are wont also ourselves to make our escape from the pursuer, when hard pressed,[e] by discovering tropes. In that passage, for instance, 'Stretch out thine hand to whichsoever thou wilt;' that is, 'grace shall stretch out thy hand to whichsoever she wills.' 'Make you a new heart;' that is, 'grace shall make you a new heart:' and the like.[f] It seems a great shame then, if Luther may have leave to introduce so violent and forced an interpretation; but we may not so much as be allowed to follow the interpretations of the most approved doctors. You see then, that our dispute here is not about the text, as it is in itself;[g] nor, as in former instances, about inferences and similies; but about tropes

[d] *Utrobique.*] In both parts of the discussion; the former, where Freewill is maintained; the latter, where its opponents are repelled. *Incomprehensibilis.* 'Uncatchable;' if there were such a word!

[e] *Ubi urgemur, elabi.*] *Elab.* The primary idea is that of the snake slipping out of the hand, or water gliding secretly from its source; which is tranferred to 'silent escape from a pursuing enemy.' *Urgr.* is the *state* of one driven along by the goad or spear, when he can advance no further. (See Part i. Sect. ix. note [d].) 'In this state, says Erasmus, they cry out " trope," " trope ;" as a sort of new discovery which they have made.'

[f] *Extende manum. Facite vobis.*] See above, Part iii. Sect. vi,— Ezek. xviii. 31.

[g] *Non de textu ipso.*] Since it is not interpretation, must refer to genuineness. It is not, as the question was about Eccle[us]. xv. where the authority of the book quoted is doubtful; or other texts which might be named, where the soundness of some particular verse or word might be disputed, though the book were authorized; but whether the acknowledged text is to be understood tropically, and whether certain proposed interpretations be admissible.

TEXTS AGAINST FREEWILL MAINTAINED.

and interpretations. 'O when shall it be, as some will say, that we get a plain and pure text,[h] without inferences and tropes, for and against Freewill? Has Scripture no such texts? And shall the cause of Freewill be for ever an undecided one? one, not settled by any sure text, but driven like a reed by the winds; because nothing is brought forwards in debating it, save a number of tropes and inferences, the production of men quarrelling mutually with each other?'

Let us rather judge, that neither inference, nor trope, ought to be admitted into any passage of Scripture, unless an evident context,[i] and some absurdity, which offendeth against one of the articles of our faith, in the plain meaning,[k] constrain us to such interpretation and inference: on the contrary, that we ought every where to stick close to that simple, pure and natural sense of words, which both the art of grammar, and the common use of speech as God created it in man, direct us to.[l] For, if any man may, at his pleasure, invent inferences and tropes for Scripture; what will all Scripture be, but a reed shaken by the winds, or a sort of Vertumnus? Then it will indeed be true, that nothing certain can be affirmed or proved, as touching any article of faith; since you may quibble it away by some pretended trope.[m] Rather, let every trope be avoided,

SEC. III.

Trope and consequence, when only to be admitted.

[h] *Simplicem, purumque.*] *Simp.* 'Free from figure.' *Pur.* 'Free from human additions.'
[i] *Circumstantia verborum evidens.*
[k] *Absurditas rei manifestæ.*
[l] *Quam grammatica.... habet.*] Luther had no doubt whence the use of speech was derived to man (μέροπες ἄνθρωποι); however some heathen, and demi-heathen, philosophers may have made it matter of speculation: even from him, who prompted its exercise when he brought the animals unto Adam to see what he would call them (Gen. ii. 19, 20); and who afterwards came down to confound that *one* language which he had given. (Gen. xi. 5—9.)
[m] *Quod non queas aliquo tropo cavillari.*] You have but to insinuate, that the texts brought to prove it are figurative, and do not mean what they seem.

as the most destructive poison, which Scripture herself does not compel us to receive. See what has befallen that great trope-master Origen,[n] in expounding the Scriptures! What just occasion does he afford to the calumniating Porphyry![o] insomuch, that even Jerome[p] thinks it of

[n] Origen of Alexandria, the great father of mystical and allegorical interpretation, suffered martyrdom in the 69th year of his age, A. D. 254.—There was much, no doubt, to condemn in him, but something also to commend. Whilst strangely defective in his perceptions of divine truth, he was learned, upright, disinterested, and laborious : a man of conscience and of magnanimity. Philosophy and literature were his bane. He did much mischief to the church by his style of interpreting Scripture, not only in rendering human fancies for a season fashionable, to the exclusion of plain truth; but, as a remote consequence, by bringing even the sober use of types and figures—that pregnant source of lively and particularizing instruction—into the contempt with which it has now for some ages been loaded.—Two sentences of his are worthy to be preserved. On the words, " We conclude that a man is justified by faith " (Rom. iii.) he says, ' The justification of faith only; is sufficient; so that, if any person only believe, he may be justified, though no good work hath been fulfilled by him.' On the case of the penitent thief, he writes, ' He was justified by faith, without the works of the law ; because, concerning these, the Lord did not inquire what he had done, before; neither did he stay to ask what work he was purposing to perform after he had believed;—but, the man being justified by his confession only, Jesus who was going to Paradise, took him, as a companion and carried him there.'—His Hexapla furnished the first specimen of a Polyglot.

[o] Porphyry, a Platonic philosopher, who lived in the same century with Origen, made great use of his fanciful interpretations, in reviling Christianity. From the serious pains taken by the ancient Christians to confute him, it may be presumed that his works (which are now chiefly lost) were subtle and ingenious ; but his testimony, like that of most other infidels, has been made to redound to the establishment, instead of, the subversion, of the Gospel. (See Chap. xxi. Cent. iii. of Milner's Ecc. Hist. where a remarkable assemblage of testimonies to this conclusion is skilfully adduced : and see, especially, vol. ii. of Fry's Second Advent, where Gibbon is made the same sort of unintentional witness.)—Porphyry censures Origen for ' leaving Gentilism, and embracing the barbarian temerity :' whereas Origen was, in fact, brought up under christian parents, and a man of christian habits from his youth. He compliments Origen upon his skill in philosophy, but ridicules

TEXTS AGAINST FREEWILL MAINTAINED.

little avail to defend Origen. What has come to
the Arians, through that trope of theirs, by which
they make Christ a mere nuncupative God?ᑫ
What has come to these new prophets in our day,
who, in expounding Christ's words, 'This is my
body,' find a trope, one of them in the pronoun
'this;' another in the verb 'is;' a third in the
noun 'body?'ʳ It is the result of my observa-

his introduction of it into the Scriptures; which, as this enemy
justly teaches, abhor such an associate.

ᵖ Jerome, the renowned monk of Stridon, in Pannonia,
had a good deal of the spirit of Origen. Luther says,
even Jerome: a man of prodigious learning, lively eloquence,
and vigorous mind, but of small discernment in the truth;
one taught of man, more than of God. He was born under
Constantine, A. D. 331, the contemporary of Augustine, and his
opponent; ever, and all his days, a controversialist· peevish
and vain; self-righteous and superstitious; but sincere and
devout.—To him the Romish church owes her Vulgate. ' In
his very voluminous expositions, he speaks at random is allegorical beyond all bounds, and almost always without accuracy
and precision; lowers the doctrine of illumination in 1 Cor. ii.
to things moral and practical, hints at something like a first
and second justification before God; asserts predestination, and
as it were retracts it; owns a good will as from God in one
place, in another supposes a power to choose to be the whole of
divine grace, never opposes fundamental truths deliberately,
but though he owns them every where, always does so defec-
tively, and often inconsistently. It must be confessed, the
reputation of this Father's knowledge and abilities has been
much overrated. There is a splendour in a profusion of ill-
digested learning, coloured by a lively imagination, which is
often mistaken for sublimity of genius. This was Jerome's
case; but this was not the greatest part of the evil. His
learned ignorance availed, more than any other cause, to give a
celebrity to superstition in the christian world, and to darken
the light of the Gospel. Yet, when he was unruffled by contradiction, and engaged in meditations unconnected with superstition, he could speak with christian affection concerning the
characters and offices of the Son of God.' (See Miln. Eccl.
Hist. vol ii. p. 481.

ᑫ *Deum nuncupativam.*] A sort of titular God; one called
so, but not really so —See above, Part ii. Sect viii. note ʳ.

ʳ Luther, as we all know, is not very sound here. His *consubstantiation* of the sacramental elements avoids a trope; but
the trope here falls in with his admitted exception, 'Scripture
herself compels us to receive it.' The same portion of matter
cannot be extended in two places at the same moment. The

BONDAGE OF THE WILL.

PART IV.

SECT. IV.

Luther denies having used trope in his interpretation of "Stretch out" and "Make you."

tion, that, of all the heresies and errors which have arisen from false expositions of Scripture, none have proceeded from understanding words in that simple sense in which they are bandied amongst men almost all the world over; but from neglecting their simple use, and affecting tropes or inferences which are the laboured offspring of their own brain.

For example; I do not remember, that I have ever applied such a violent sort of interpretation to the words ' Stretch out thine hand to whichsoever, thou wilt,' as to say, ' Grace shall stretch out thine hand to whichsoever she wills.'— ' Make you a new heart ;' that is, ' Grace shall make you a new heart;' and the like: although Diatribe traduces me, in a published treatise, as having spoken thus. In fact, she is so distracted and beguiled' by her tropes and inferences, that she does not know what she says about any body. What I have really said is, ' when the words " stretch forth thy hand, &c. &c." are taken simply according to their real import, exclusive of

bread therefore, which the Lord held in his hand whilst instituting the ordinance, could not at the same instant be bread and hand, or bread and body. The same is true of the cup: it must have been a distinct substance from the hand which held it; and therefore could not be really the Lord's blood; which could indeed only be drunk *as poured out*, and at the instant when He spake, was yet in his veins.—Add to this, the simple but decisive illustration which was suggested to Zuingle's mind in a dream, and which was so greatly blessed in the use he was afterwards led to make of it. 'You stupid man, why do not you answer him from the twelfth of Exodus, as it is there written, " It is the Lord's passover."'—Luther calls the Sacramentists promiscuously ' the new prophets :' not very ingenuously, for even Carolstadt disclaimed all connection with the Celestial Prophets, as they were called—whilst Zuingle and Œcolampadius, in whom the sinews of the contest were, afforded no pretence for such imputation —Miln. Eccles. Hist. vol. iv. chaps. vi. ix. pp. 772—810, 990, &c. 1127. 8.

' *Distenta et illusa.*] *Dist.* ' Distractus, duplici curâ occupatus ; cui duo simul res, diversis partibus, curam injiciunt.' Rectiùs à ' distineo,' quàm ' distendo,' ducitur.

tropes and inferences, they express no more than a demand that we stretch out our hand: by which demand, is intimated to us what we ought to do; according to the nature of the imperative verb, as explained by grammarians, and applied in common speech.'

Diatribe, however, neglecting this simple use of the verb and dragging in her tropes and inferences by force, interprets thus: " Stretch out thine hand;" that is, 'thou canst stretch out thine hand by thine own power:' " Make you a new heart;" that is, ' ye can make you a new heart.' " Believe in Christ;" that is, ' ye can believe.' Thus, it is in her account the same thing whether words be spoken imperatively, or indicatively; if not, she is prepared to represent Scripture as ridiculous and vain. Yet these interpretations, which no scholar[t] can bear, may not be called violent and far-fetched,[u] when used by theologians; but are to be welcomed, as those of the most approved doctors who have been received for ages !"

But it is very easy for Diatribe to allow of tropes and to adopt them in this text: it is no matter to her, whether what is said be certain or uncertain. Nay, her very object is to make every thing uncertain; counselling as she does, that all

[t] *Nulli grammatico ferendas.*] *Gram.* ' ad grammaticam pertinens :' but this term, it seems, was especially applied to those who interpreted classical writers; such as Donatus, Festus, Nonnius, Asconius and others; not to teachers of grammar: differing from *grammatista,* which is sometimes used invidiously.

[u] *Affectatas*] So, in the last section, ' affectatis proprio cerebro tropis ' ' nimio, aut pravo, *affectu* et studio cupitus, quæsitus.' ' De re majore studio et curâ conquisitâ et elaboratâ.' Our English term ' affected,' opposed to ' natural,' implies the same thing. what is factitious, and the result of effort. It is not ' the design, wherewith,' that is marked in these two passages, but ' the labour and search employed.'

[v] *Has ... probatissimorum sunt doctorum*] The sentence is not grammatical.

dogmas on Freewill should be left to themselves, rather than investigated. It would have been enough for her, therefore, to get rid of sayings by which she feels herself to be hard pressed, in any way she can.* But I—who am in earnest and not in sport, and who am in search of most indubitable truth, for the establishing of the consciences of men—must act very differently. For me, I say, it is not enough that you tell me, there *may be* a trope here. The question is, whether there *ought* to be; and *must* be a trope here. If you have not shewn me, that there must necessarily be a trope here; you have done nothing. Here stands the word of God, "I will harden Pharaoh's heart." If you tell me, it *must* be understood, or *may be* understood, 'I will permit it to be hardened;' I hear what you say, that it may be so understood. I hear that this trope is commonly used in popular discourse; just as, 'I have ruined you; because I did not instantly correct you, when you were going astray.' But this is not the place for such sort of proof. It is not the question, whether such a trope be in use. It is not the question, whether a person might use it in this passage of Paul's writings. The question is, whether it would be safe for him to use it, and certain that he used it rightly, in this place; and whether Paul meant to use it. We are not inquiring about another man's—the reader's use of it—but about Paul's, the author's own use of it.

What would you do with a conscience which should question you in this way? 'Lo, God the author of the book says, "I will harden Pharaoh's heart." The meaning of the word 'harden', is obvious and notorious. But a human reader tells me, ' to harden, in this place, is to *give occasion of hardening*, inasmuch as the sinner is not

---

* Utcunque amoliri dicta.] *Amol.* dicr. prop. de iis qui magno conatu et molimine dimoventur.

TEXTS AGAINST FREEWILL MAINTAINED. 245

instantly corrected.' With what authority, with SECT. V.
what design, with what necessity, is that natural
meaning of the word so tortured for me? What
if my interpreting reader be mistaken? Where
is it proved, that this torturing of the word ought
to take place here? It is dangerous, it is even
impious, to torture the word of God, without
necessity, and without authority. Will you next
tutor this labouring little soul,[y] 'Origen thought
so?' Or thus; 'cease to pry into such matters,
seeing they are curious and vain.' She will reply,
'Moses and Paul ought to have had this admonition given to them, before they wrote; or rather,
God himself. To what end do they distract us
with curious and vain sayings?'

This wretched evasion of tropes, then, is of no *Diatribe*
service to Diatribe; but we must keep strong *must*
hold of our Proteus here, till he make us perfectly *prove, by*
sure that there is a trope in this identical passage, *or miracle,*
either by the clearest Scripture proofs, or by *that the*
evident miracles. We do not give the least be- *sage in*
lief to her mere thinking so, though it be backed *question is*
by the toil and sweat of all ages.[z] But I go fur- *tropical.*
ther, and insist that there can be no trope here,
but that this saying of God must be understood
in its simplicity, according to the literal meaning
of the words. For it is not left to our own will
to make, and re-make, words for God as we please:
else what would be left in all Scripture, which

[y] *Animulæ.*] We are reminded of the Emperor Adrian's
'Animula vagula blandula.' *Anim.* vel contemptûs, vel blanditiæ
causâ. Here, it implies 'tenderness:' a weakling soul, tenderly felt for, by the Lord and by his messengers.

[z] *Industriâ consentiente.*] *Indust.* ' Vis ingenii quâ quippium
excogitamus, et adipiscimur. Itaque supra naturam et ingenium
addit studium, et artem, et laborem.' He refers to the 'affectatis tropis' and 'affectatas interpretationes,' which he reprehended in the last section. There was much of scholastic art
and cloistered industry in them; but he must have light from
heaven—the Holy Ghost's testimony either in the word, or in
some palpable, new-wrought miracle—before he would be satisfied that there is a trope in these words.

does not just come back to Anaxagoras's philosophy,[a] 'Make what you please of any thing.' Suppose I should say, "God created the heavens and the earth;" that is, 'he set them in order; but he did not make them out of nothing.' Or, 'He created the heavens and the earth;' that is, the angels and the devils, or the righteous and the wicked. Upon this principle, a man has but to open the book of God, and by and by he is a theologian.[b] Let it be a settled and fixed principle then, that, when Diatribe cannot prove that there is a trope in these passages of ours which she is refuting,[c] she be obliged to concede to us, that the words must be understood according to their literal import; even though she should prove that the same trope is of most frequent use elsewhere, both in all parts of Scripture and in common discourse. If this principle be admitted, all our testimonies which Diatribe meant to confute, have been defended at once; and her confutation is found to have effected absolutely nothing, to have no power, to be a mere nothing.

When she interprets that saying of Moses, therefore, "I will harden Pharaoh's heart," to mean 'My lenity in bearing with a sinner, leads others, it is true, to repentance, but it shall render Pharaoh more obstinate in his wickedness;' this is a pretty saying, but there is no proof that she

---

[a] Anaxagoras, a philosopher of Clazomenæ, the preceptor of Socrates, amongst many other paradoxes, is said to have insisted that 'snow was black, because made of water.'

[b] *Quis non.... Theologus*] If a man's own whimsies, without search or proof, are to be protruded as doctrines and interpretations of Scripture; we have but to open the book and consult our fancy, and straightway we may dub ourselves divines.

[c] *Quos diluit.*] *Dil.* properly 'lavando aufero,' as the water washes the sides of the canal, or the heavy rain washes away the labours of the husbandman: hence transferred to the removal of filth from any substance, and particularly, in a forensic sense, to the purging of a charge. '*Diluere crimen* est purgare, refellere, criminibus respondendo et accusationes refutando.' 'Si nollem ita diluere crimen, ut dilui.'—Cic. pro Milon.

TEXTS AGAINST FREEWILL MAINTAINED. 247

ought to speak so; and we, not content with a mere 'ipse dixit,' demand proof.

So she interprets that saying of Paul's plausibly; "He hath mercy on whom he will have mercy, and whom he will he hardeneth;" that is, 'God hardeneth, when he doth not instantly chastise the sinner; he hath mercy, when he presently inviteth to repentance, by afflictions.' But what proof is there of this interpretation?

So that of Isaiah, "Thou hast made us to err from thy ways, thou hast hardened our heart from thy fear."[d] What if Jerome, following Origen, interpret thus; 'The man is said to seduce who does not straightway call back from error.' Who shall assure us that Jerome and Origen interpret this passage rightly? And what if they do? It is our compact, that we will contest the matter not on the ground of any human teacher's authority, but on that of Scripture only. Who are these Origens and Jeromes then, which Diatribe, forgetting her solemn covenant, throws in my teeth? when as, of the ecclesiastical writers, there be none almost, who have handled the Scriptures more foolishly and more absurdly, than Origen and Jerome.

In a word, such a licentiousness of interpretation comes to this; by a new and unheard of sort of grammar all distinctions are confounded: so that, when God says, "I will harden Pharaoh's heart," you change persons and understand him to say, 'Pharaoh hardens himself through my lenity.' 'God hardens our heart;' that is, we harden our own hearts, through God's deferring to punish us. "Thou, O Lord, hast made us to err;" that is, we have made ourselves to err, through thy not chastising us. So, 'God's having mercy,' no longer signifies 'his giving grace,' or 'exer-

---

[d] Isaiah lxiii. 17. Our authorized version reads it as a question, "O Lord, why hast thou made us to err, &c."

cising compassion,' 'forgiving sin,' 'justifying,' or 'delivering from evil;' but, on the contrary, 'his inflicting evil and punishing.' You will at last make it out by these tropes, that God had pity on the children of Israel, when he carried them away into Assyria and to Babylon: for there it was that he chastised his offenders, there it was that he invited them to repentance by afflictions. On the other hand, when he brought them back and gave them deliverance, he did not pity, but harden them; that is, by his lenity and pity, he gave occasion to their being hardened. Thus, the sending of Christ the Saviour into the world, shall not be called an act of mercy in God, but an act of hardening; since by this mercy he hath given men occasion to harden themselves. On the other hand, in having laid Jerusalem waste, and destroyed the Jews unto this very day, he shows mercy towards them; inasmuch as he chastises them for their sin, and invites them to repentance. In carrying his saints to heaven at the day of judgment, he will not perform an act of mercy but of induration: inasmuch as, he will give them an opportunity of abusing his goodness. In thrusting the wicked into hell; herein, he will shew mercy, because it will be chastising the sinner. Who ever heard, pray, of such compassions and such wraths of God as these?

What, if good men are made better by the for-

---

e *Perdidit.*] '*Ἀπολλύω, ἀποβάλλω*, destruo, everto, deperdo: Si vocem spectes, est a *per et do*; si notionem, a *περθω*, vasto, esse videtur.' There is a miraculous peculiarity in Israel's case, as a nation: perishing, he does not perish; destroyed, he still is preserved. I had therefore hesitated to render *perd.* according to its natural and proper meaning, and was disposed to adopt 'give up,' 'abandon,' 'cast off,' or 'scatter;' which would not, it seems, have been incongruous with its essential meaning.' But why should Luther have used this term in preference to the others; and has not their dispersion been in fact their *destruction*, as a state, city, and nation?

bearance, as well as by the severity of God; still, when we speak of good and bad men promiscuously, these tropes will make the mercy of God wrath, and his wrath mercy, by a most perverse use of speech: since they call it wrath, when God is conferring benefits; and pity, when he is inflicting judgments. Now, if God shall be said to harden, when he is conferring benefits and bearing with evil;[f] and shall be said to have mercy, when he is afflicting and chastising; why is he said to have hardened Pharaoh rather than the children of Israel, or even the whole world? Did he not confer benefits upon the children of Israel? does he not confer benefits upon the whole world? does he not bear with the wicked? does he not send his rain upon the evil and upon the good?—Why is he said to have had compassion on the children of Israel, rather than upon Pharaoh? Did he not afflict the children of Israel, in Egypt and in the desert?[g] I grant that some abuse, and others rightly use, God's wrath and goodness. But you define hardening to be 'God's indulging the wicked with forbearance and kindness;' 'God's having compassion to be' that he does not indulge, but visits and cuts short. So far as God is concerned therefore, he does but harden by perpetual kindness; he does but shew mercy by perpetual severity.[h]

[f] *Benefacit tolerat.*] *Benef.* "heapeth his benefits;" *tol.* "endureth with much long-suffering."

[g] If God hardens by conferring benefits, why is he said to have hardened Pharaoh rather than the children of Israel? If God shews mercy by afflicting, why is he said to have had mercy on Israel in afflicting him, and not on Pharaoh?

[h] Luther admits that there is a different effect produced in different characters, 'the good profit by both good and evil,' 'some use, and others abuse, both kindness and wrath.' But the question here is, what character shall we assign to God's dispensations of judgment and of mercy as falling *generally* upon men; upon good and evil intermixed: *cum simul de bonis et malis loquimur?* The result will be, God's mercy is anger; and his anger, mercy —The truth is, God does harden by

PART IV.
────
SECT. VI.

Erasmus' trope makes nonsense of Moses, and leaves the knot tied.

But this is the best of all, that, 'God is said to harden, when he indulges sinners with forbearance; and to pity, when he visits and afflicts; inviting to repentance by severity.' What did God omit, pray, in the way of afflicting, chastising, calling Pharaoh to repentance? Do we not number ten plagues, as inflicted in that land? If your definition stands good; that, 'to have mercy is straightway to chastise and call the sinner;' assuredly, God had mercy upon Pharaoh. Why then does not God say, I will have mercy upon Pharaoh, instead of saying I will harden Pharaoh's heart? For, when he is in the very act of pitying him; that is, as you will have it, of afflicting and chastising him; he says, 'I will harden him;' that is, as you will have it, 'I will do him good, and will bear with him:' what can be more monstrous to hear, than this? What has now become of your tropes, your Origen, your Jerome, and your most approved doctors; whom the solitary individual, Luther, is rash enough to contradict? But it is the foolishness of the flesh which compels you to speak thus; sporting as she does with the words of God, which she cannot believe to have been spoken in earnest.

The text itself therefore, as written by Moses, proves incontrovertibly, that these tropes are mere inventions, and of no worth in this place; and that something very different and far greater—over and above the bestowal of benefits, together with affliction and correction—is meant by the words, "I will harden Pharaoh's heart:" since we cannot deny that both these expedients were tried in Pharaoh's case, with the greatest care

mercies as well as judgments; and does soften by judgments, as well as mercies: but both the hardening and the softening are distinct from the dispensations which are made the instrument of producing them. It is a variety in the spirit which meets with them, and upon which they act, which causes variety in the result.

TEXTS AGAINST FREEWILL MAINTAINED.

and pains. For what wrath and correction could be more urgent, than that which he was called to endure, whilst stricken with so many signs and plagues, that even Moses himself testifies the like were never seen! Nay, even Pharaoh himself was moved by them more than once, as though he repented: albeit, not moved to purpose,' nor abidingly. At the same time, what forbearance and kindness could be more abundant, than that which so readily took away his plagues, so often forgave his sin,^k so often restored his blessings, so often removed his calamities? Each sort of dispensation, however, is unavailing; the Lord still says, 'I will harden Pharaoh's heart.' You see then, that even though your hardening and your mercy (that is, your glosses and tropes) should be admitted in their highest degree, use, and exemplification—such as they are exhibited to us in Pharaoh—there still remains an act of hardening; and the hardening of which Moses speaks must be of one sort, and what you are dreaming of, another.

But since I am fighting with men of fiction and with ghosts, let me also be allowed to conjure up my ghost and imagine, what is impossible, that the trope which Diatribe sees in her dream is really used in this passage; that I may see how she evades the being compelled to affirm, that we do every thing by God's alone will, and by a necessity that is laid upon us; as also, how she will excuse God from being himself the author[1] and blameworthy cause of our induration. If it be true, that God is said to

Necessity still remains, and you do not clear God.

---

^j *Permovetur.*]—' Valdè movetur .' what goes *through* the substance, and disturbs it throughout; not merely stirs the surface and margin.

^k *Remittit peccatum*] So far as withdrawing present judgment may be taken as a sign of forgiveness . but was his sin blotted out? any one of the sins which had instrumentally provoked the visitation?

^l *Autor et culpa.*

PART IV. harden us, when he bears with us through an exercise of his lenity, and does not forthwith punish us; each of the two following principles still remains. First, man, does nevertheless necessarily serve sin. For, when it has been granted that Freewill can not will any thing good (and such a sort of Freewill is what Diatribe has undertaken to prove), it is made no better by the forbearance of a long-suffering God, but is necessarily made worse; unless through the mercy of God, the Spirit be added to it. So that all things still happen by necessity; as it respects us.

Secondly, God seems to be as cruel in bearing with men out of lenity, as he is thought to be through our representation; who say, that he hardens in the exercise of that inscrutable will of his.[m] For, since he sees that Freewill can will nothing good, and is made worse by his lenity in bearing with us, this very lenity exhibits him in the most cruel form, as one that is delighted with our calamities: seeing he could heal them, if he would; and could avoid bearing with us if he would; or rather, could not bear with us, except it were his will to do so: for who could compel him to do so, against his will? If that will therefore remains, without which nothing happens in the world; and it be granted, that Freewill can will nothing good; all that is said to excuse God, and to accuse Freewill, is said to no purpose. For Freewill is always saying; 'I cannot, and God will not: what can I do?' Let him shew me mercy, forsooth, by afflicting me; I am never the forwarder for it, but must be made worse; except he give me the Spirit. This he does not give; which he would give, if it were his will to do so: it is certain therefore, that he wills not to give it.'[n]

[m] *Volendo voluntate illâ imperscrutabili.*] See above, Part iii. Sect. xxviii. notes t v x.

[n] Luther's drift is, 'There must be a will of God distinct

TEXTS AGAINST FREEWILL MAINTAINED.

SEC. VIII.
———
Diatribe's similes of sun and rain rejected.

"Nor are the similes, which she adduces, at all to the purpose, when she says, 'As mud is hardened by the self-same sun which melts wax; and, as the cultivated ground produces fruit by means of the self-same shower from which the untilled sends forth thorns; even so, by the self-same forbearance of God, some are hardened and others converted.'

"We do not divide Freewill into two different sorts, making one to be mud and the other wax; or one to be cultivated ground, and the other neglected ground: but we speak of one sort of Freewill, which is equally impotent in all men; which is nothing else but the mud, nothing else but the untilled ground, in these comparisons—seeing it is what cannot will good. Nor does Paul say that God, in his character of the potter, makes one vessel to honour and another to dishonour, out of a different lump of clay; but " of the SAME lump, saith he, the potter maketh, &c." So that, as the mud always becomes harder, and the uncultivated ground more thorny, by the sun and rain, severally; even so, Freewill is always made worse, as well by the indurating mildness of the sun as by the liquefying violence of the rain.° If the definition of Freewill then be one, and its impotency the same in all men; no reason can be assigned, why one man's Freewill attains to grace, and another man's does not; if no other cause be declared than the forbearance of an enduring God and the correction of a pitying one: for it is assumed, by a definition which makes no distinctions, that Freewill in every man is a power which can will nothing good. Then it will

from that which he has revealed for the regulation of man's conduct: what he calls 'the inscrutable will,' or 'will of the hidden God.'—My quarrel against him is, that he does not shew the connection and coincidence between these two wills; and does not shew a reason for this apparently harsh conduct. See, as before.

° *Tempestate pluviæ liquefaciente.*

follow, that neither does God elect any man, neither is there any place left for election; but man's Freewill alone elects, by accepting or rejecting forbearance and wrath. But deprive God of his wisdom and power in election, and what do you make him but a sort of phantom of fortune; whose nod is the rash ordainer of all things?[p] Thus, we shall at length come to this, that men are saved and damned, without God's knowing it: seeing, he has not separated the saved and the damned by a determined election; but— bestowing on all, without distinction, first a kindness which bears with them and hardens them; then a pity which corrects and punishes them— has left it to men, to determine whether they will be saved or damned; and himself, meanwhile, has just stepped out perhaps to a banquet of the Ethiopians, as Homer describes him.[q]

Aristotle also paints just such a God for us;[r]

[p] *Cujus numine omnia temerè fiunt.* Chance is the God.

[q] Ζεὺς γὰρ ἐπ' Ὠκεανὸν μετ' ἀμύμονας Αἰθιοπῆας
Χθιζὸς ἔβη μετὰ δαῖτα· Θεοὶ δ' ἅμα πάντες ἕποντο·
Δωδεκάτῃ δέ τοι αὖθις ἐλεύσεται Οὔλυμπόνδε·
ILIAD, A. 423—425.

[r] Aristotle, the disciple and opponent of Plato, the tutor of Alexander, the great master of rhetoric, belles lettres, logic, physics, metaphysics, and heathen ethics, was in theology little better than an Epicurean; one of those 'who have learned that the Gods spend a life without care.' (Hor. 1. Sat. v. 101.) It is said in excuse for the less explicit parts of his system, that ' he attached himself to the principles of natural philosophy, rather than those of theology.' He maintained the existence of a God as the great mover of all things, which have been put into motion *from* eternity, and will continue in motion *to* eternity. Thus he maintained the eternity of matter as well as of God. He *painted* this God finely: 'the necessary being;' ' the first, and the most excellent of beings;' 'immutable, intelligent, indivisible, without extension:' ' He resides above the enclosure of the world,' ' He there finds his happiness in the contemplation of himself.'—How apt is the expression, by which Luther describes him as *painting* God! *(pinxit)* a rhetorical term applied to that sort of discourse ' which is embellished with tropes and figures, such as display much genius, but charm by their sweetness, rather than edify by their intelligence.'

one who sleeps, for example, and suffers any that will, to use and to abuse his goodness and his severity.' And how can reason judge otherwise of God, than Diatribe here does? For, as she herself snores away, and despises divine things;

Aristotle's God, then, is one who keeps order in the heavens, but interferes in a very limited degree with earth. ' All the movements of nature are *in some sort* subordinated to him; He *appears* to be the cause and principle of every thing; He *appears* to take some care of human affairs But, in all the universe, He can look upon nothing but Himself; the sight of crime and of disorder would defile his eyes : He could not know how to be the author either of the prosperity of the wicked, or of the misery of the good. His superintendence is like that of the master of a family, who has established a certain order of things in his household, and takes care that the end which he has in view be accomplished, but shuts his eyes to their divisions and their vices, and only takes care to obviate the consequences of them He stamped the impress of his will upon the universe, when first he projected it like a ball from his hand ; and it is by a general, 'not minute, superintendence, that he sustains it. The perpetuation of the several species of beings is his grand object: which he secured by his one first impulse.'*—Has Luther calumniated this philosopher? Yet was this heathen teacher made the great model for instruction to the christian church, both as to form and substance, for many ages. During the second period of the reign of the schoolmen, which began early in the thirteenth century, his reputation was at its height the most renowned doctors wrote elaborate commentaries upon his works. The predominance of his philosophy—' a philosophy, which knew nothing of original sin and native depravity; which allowed nothing to be criminal, but certain external flagitious actions; and which was unacquainted with any righteousness of grace, imputed to a sinner'—was itself a corruption, and the fruitful source of other corruptions, which cried aloud for reformation, and which THE REFORMERS of the sixteenth century exposed and suppressed. (See Miln. Eccles. Hist. vol. iv. p. 283.)

*. *Correptione.*] The word has occurred several times before, and I have rendered it by ' correction,' ' chastening,' ' severity.' It properly denotes ' the snatching of a substance hastily up,' and is applied sometimes to the seizure of the body by disease. Hence, it is transferred to a figurative ' cutting short.' "At that time the Lord began to cut Israel short" (2 Kings x. 23.), and so, to ' reprehension, chiding and chastisement ' in general.

* I am indebted to the Abbé Barthelemi's Anacharsis for this concise but eloquent view of Aristotle's Theology, vol. v. chap. lxiv.

PART IV. so, she judges even of God, that he in some sort snores away; and, having nothing to do with the exercise of wisdom, will and present power[1] in electing, separating and inspiring, has committed to men this busy and troublesome work of accepting and rejecting his forbearance and his wrath. This is what we come to, whilst coveting to mete out, and excuse God, by the counsel of human reason; whilst, instead of reverencing the secrets of His Majesty, we break in to scrutinize them—overwhelmed with his glory, instead of uttering one single plea in excuse for him, we vomit forth a thousand blasphemies! We forget our ownselves also the mean while, and chatter, like mad people, both against God and against ourselves, in the same breath; though our design is to speak with great wisdom, both for God and for ourselves. You see here, in the first place, what this trope and gloss of Diatribe's makes of God: but do you not also see, how vastly consistent she is with herself in it? She had before made Freewill equal and alike in all, by including all in one definition; but now, in the course of her disputation, she forgets her own definition, and makes a cultivated Freewill one, and an uncultivated Freewill another; setting out a diversity of Freewills, according to the diversity of works, habits, and characters; one that can do good, another that cannot do good: and this, by its own powers, before grace received; by which powers of its own, she had laid it down in her definition, that Freewill could not of itself will any thing good. Thus it comes to pass, that, if we will not leave to the sole will of God both the will and the power to harden, and to shew mercy, and to do every thing; we must ascribe to Freewill herself the power of doing every thing, without grace: although we have denied that it can do any thing good without grace.

[1] *Sap. vol. præsentiâ elig. discern. inspir. omissâ.*

TEXTS AGAINST FREEWILL MAINTAINED.

The simile of the sun and rain, then, is of no force as to this point. A Christian will use that simile with far greater propriety, considering the Gospel to be that sun and rain (as Ps. xix. and Heb. vi. do); the cultivated ground, the elect; the uncultivated, the reprobate. The former of these are edified and made better by the word; the latter are offended and made worse: whereas Freewill, when left to herself, is in all men the uncultivated ground; yea, the kingdom of Satan. SEC IX.

Let us also look into her reasons for imagining this trope in this place. It seems absurd, says Diatribe, that God, who is not only just but also good, should be said to have hardened a man's heart in order to manifest his own power by the man's wickedness. So she runs back to Origen; who confesses, that God gave occasion to the induration, but flings back the blame upon Pharaoh: Origen has, besides, remarked that the Lord said, " For this cause have I *raised thee up:*" He does not say, ' for this cause have I *made thee.*' No: for Pharaoh would not have been wicked, if he had been such as God made him; God having beheld all his works, and they were very good. So much for Diatribe. Erasmus's two causes for tropicizing considered.

Absurdity, then, is one of the principal reasons for not understanding Moses's and Paul's words in their simple and literal sense. But what article of faith is violated by this absurdity, and who is offended by it? Human reason is offended: and she forsooth, who is blind, deaf, foolish, impious and sacrilegious in her dealings with all the words and works of God, is brought in here to be the judge of God's works and words. Upon the same principle, you will deny all the articles of the christian faith; inasmuch as it is the most absurd thing possible, and, as Paul says, "to the Jews a stumbling block, and to the Gentiles foolishness," that God should Absurdity not a sufficient reason.

s

PART IV. become man, the son of a virgin; that he should have been crucified; that he should be sitting at the right hand of the Father. It is absurd, I say, to believe such things. Let us therefore invent some tropes like those of the Arians, to prevent Christ from being God *absolutely*.ᵘ Let us invent some tropes like those of the Manicheans,ᵛ to prevent

---

ᵘ *Simpliciter*, opposed to *figuratively*. See Sect. iii. note.ᑫ

ᵛ The Manichees, so called from Manes their founder, arose in the reign of the Emperor Probus, A. D. 277. ' Like most of the ancient heretics, they abounded in senseless whims, not worthy of any solicitous explanation. This they had in common with the Pagan philosophers, that they supposed the Supreme Being to be material, and to penetrate all nature. Their grand peculiarity was to admit of two independent principles, a good and an evil one, in order to solve the arduous question concerning the origin of evil. Like all heretics, they made a great parade of seeking truth with liberal impartiality, and were thus qualified to deceive unwary spirits, who, far from suspecting their own imbecility of judgment, and regardless of the word of God and hearty prayer, have no idea of attaining religious knowledge by any other method than by natural reason.' ' Like all other heretics they could not stand before the Scriptures. They professedly rejected the Old Testament, as belonging to the malignant principle; and, when they were pressed with the authority of the New, as corroborating the Old, they pretended the New was adulterated.— Is there any new thing under the sun ? Did not Lord Bolingbroke set up the authority of St. John against St. Paul ? Have we not heard of some parts of the Gospel as not genuine, because they suit not Socinian views ? Genuine christian principles alone will bear the test, nor fear the scrutiny of the WHOLE word of God.'—Augustine, who lived about a century after they had first arisen, describes them to the life; after having himself smarted under the poison of their arrows, for about twelve years seduced partly by their subtile and captious questions concerning the origin of evil, partly by their blasphemies against the Old Testament saints.— With respect to the person of Christ, their heresy was like that of the Gnostics, or Docetæ. worthy children of Simon Magus ! They held that the Lord Jesus Christ had no proper humanity, the mere phantasm of a man having glided, as Luther here describes it, through the virgin's womb, and afterwards expired upon the cross.—' Yet though my ideas were material, says Augustine, I could not bear to think of God being flesh. That was too gross and low in my apprehensions. Thy only begotten son appeared to me as the most lucid part of thee, afforded for our salvation. I concluded that such a

TEXTS AGAINST FREEWILL MAINTAINED.

his being a real man; and let us make him out to be a sort of phantom, which glided through the virgin (like a ray of the sun through a piece of glass), and was crucified. A nice way of handling Scripture!

And yet these tropes get us no forwarder, and do not serve to evade the absurdity: for it still remains absurd in the eye of reason that this just and good God should demand impossibilities of Freewill; and when Freewill cannot will good, but by necessity serves sin, should nevertheless impute it to her; and so long as he withholds the Spirit, should not be a whit more kind, or more merciful, than if he were to harden or permit men to be hardened. Reason will be again and again repeating, that these are not the acts of a kind and merciful God. These things so far exceed her apprehension, and she so wants power to take even her own self captive, that she cannot believe God to be good if he should act and judge so; but setting faith aside, demands that she should be able to touch and see and comprehend how it is that He is just and not cruel. Now she would have this sort of comprehension if it were said of God, 'he hardens nobody, he damns nobody; on the contrary, he pities every body, he saves every body;' so as that hell should be destroyed, and the fear of death removed, and no future punishment dreaded. Hence it is, that she becomes so boisterous and so vehement[x] in ex-

SECT. IX.

Does not remove the difficulty.

---

hature could not be born of the Virgin Mary, without partaking of human flesh, which I thought must pollute it. Hence arose my fantastic ideas of Jesus, so destructive of all piety. Thy spiritual children may smile at me with charitable sympathy, if they read these my confessions, such however were my views.'—Milner in Augustine's Confessions, Eccles. Hist. vol. ii. pp 314—327.

[x] *Æstuat et contendit.*] *Æst.* denoting violent heat in general, is especially applied to the boiling and swelling of the sea, when it ebbs and flows, or rises in surges and waves. *Contend,* expresses the full stretch of every nerve and muscle in close conflict.

cusing and defending the just and beneficent God. Faith and the Spirit, however, judge differently; they believe God to be good, although he should destroy all men. And of what use is it, that we are wearied to death with these elaborate speculations that we may be enabled to remove the blame of induration from God to Freewill. Let Freewill do what she can, with all her means[y] and all her might in exercise, she will never furnish an example of avoiding to be hardened where God has not given his Spirit, or of earning mercy where she has been left to her own powers. For, what is the difference whether she be hardened or deserve to be hardened; since hardening is necessarily in her, so long as that impotency, by which, according to Diatribe herself, she cannot will good, is in her. Since the absurdity then is not removed by these tropes, or, if removed, is removed but to make way for greater absurdities, and to ascribe all power to Freewill; away with these useless and misleading tropes, and let us stick to the pure and simple word of God.

SECT. X.

That God made all things very good not a sufficient reason.

'The other principal reason why this trope should be received is, that the things which God hath made are very good: and God does not say, I have made thee for this very thing, but for this very thing I have raised thee up.'

First I answer, that this was said before the fall of man, when the things which God had made were very good. But it follows presently, in the third chapter, how man was made evil, deserted of God and left to himself. From this man, so corrupted, all men are born, and born

---

[y] *Totq mundo totisque viribus*] *Mundus* is properly 'the stuff of the world'—the materials of which it is constituted—and is transferred thence to all kinds of furniture and provision—specially to 'women's dress and ornaments:'. 'instrumentum ornatûs muliebris.' I would not be sure that Luther has not some allusion to 'Madam Diatribe's' adornments here.

wicked; Pharoah amongst the rest. As Paul says, "We were all by nature the children of wrath, even as others." God therefore did make Pharaoh wicked; that is, out of a wicked and corrupted seed. As he says in the Proverbs of Solomon, " The Lord hath made all things for himself, yea, even the wicked man for the day of evil" (not indeed by creating wickedness in him, but by forming him out of an evil seed and ruling him.) It is not a just conclusion therefore, ' God formed the wicked man, therefore he is not wicked.' For how can it be that he is not wicked, springing as he does from a wicked seed? As he says in Psalm li. " Behold I was conceived in sins." And Job says, " Who can make clean that which has been conceived of unclean seed ?" For although God does not make sin, still he ceases not to form and to multiply a nature which has been corrupted by sin, through the withdrawal of the Spirit: just as if a carpenter should make statues of rotten wood. Thus men are made just such as their nature is, through God's creating and forming them of that nature.[z]

[z] Luther has not exactly hit the nail upon the head here. He declares that God makes ' wicked man,' and that he so makes him, through the faultiness of the materials which he has to work with, being fitly compared to ' a carpenter who should make statues of rotten wood' Moreover, this faultiness of the materials arose from the sin of the first man; who was created having the Spirit, what he elsewhere calls ' the firstfruits of the Spirit,' (Part iii. Sect xviii) which he lost by his sin and fall ; being thenceforth deserted of God, and left to himself—I deem both these propositions objectionable and false. Neither doth God *make* sinners ; neither did he withdraw the Spirit from Adam by reason of his sin, and so, through him, from the race which has sprung from him , for he never had it—When God created man in his own image, he created every man The substance of every individual man and woman which exists, hath existed, and shall exist till the trumpet shall sound and the dead shall be raised, was enclosed in the first man, Adam. No new matter of human kind has been brought into existence since that moment, no human being has been *created* there-

PART IV. Secondly, I answer, if you will have those words, "were very good," to be understood of fore, posterior to it. (See Locke's Essay, book ii. chap. xxvi. sect. 2.) Nor was this creation the mere production of a mass of human substance, like so much clay in the hands of a potter which was afterwards to be moulded into distinct vessels. Distinctness and individuality of subsistence was given to the several individuals of the human race in that instant. This appears, as well from other considerations which might be stated, as from these eminently; 1. Man is spoken *of*, and spoken *to*, as plural. (" Let *them* have dominion." " Male and female created he *them*." " God blessed *them*, and God said unto *them*, Be *ye* fruitful and multiply." " And called *their* name Adam, in the day when they were created.") 2. God is declared to have *created* them male and female : a fact which the Lord Jesus refers to (Matt. xix. 4, 5. Mark x. 6.), as indicative of his Father's will concerning marriage. (It is clearly not the formation of Eve to which he refers, but that act of creation which distinctly preceded the making of the help-meet.) 3. God is said to have *chosen* his people to be in Christ before the foundation of the world ; which implies that the whole race was contemplated as personally and individually subsistent, in a state prior to the exercise of that choice.—Having thus given a distinct personal subsistence to every individual of the human race in Adam, when the Lord God added the procreative power, and gave command to exercise it; *essentially* he did make every individual : the substance about to come forth, in the Lord's time, into manifest existence and distinct personal agency, was already formed ; the power and the authority which would be necessary to its production, were superadded. Then, if this was God's ' condidit' (Luther's term—' made,' ' formed,' ' builded '), hath *He* made ' wicked man ?' Is not that saying of the Preacher hereby, and hereby only, shewn to be true, " God hath made man upright ?" (Eccles. vii. 29.)— The only consideration, which can have any shew of involving God in the propagation of the wicked, is, that he did not at once destroy the offender, and those who had offended *in him*. But, without here suggesting counsel and design (we are dealing with facts), the living substances were formed ; the power and the authority for production had been given ; a curse was upon them, which they must be brought out into manifest existence that they might be seen and known to bear.—I cannot but remark, that these, or some such reasons, which arise out of the reality of their previous distinct subsistence, seem absolutely necessary to the vindication of God from the charge of propagating sin.—If it be asked then, but how could those who had no eye to see, no ear to hear, no hand to put forth, commit an act of disobedience ? The answer is, Adam was the sole personal agent (" By *one man* sin entered into the world ;"

the works of God after the fall, you will observe they are spoken not of us, but of God. He does

" by *one man's* offence death reigned by one ," " by the offence of *one* judgment came upon all men to condemnation") , but every individual of the race was enclosed in, and was part of his substance, so that he could not do any thing in which *any* one of them was not one with him —My head offendeth ; but where is my hand and my foot, in the transgression and in its punishment ?—That this is the Scripture view of the fall—' one personal agent ; but every human being partaker with him in the offence'—is decisively shewn from Romans v. 12. Whether εφ' ᾧ be rendered *in whom*, ("through him *in whom* all sinned"—which I greatly prefer), or *for that*. the words which follow make it plain, that ' all men' are dealt with—or rather, all men, from Adam to Moses, *were* dealt with—on the ground of the first transgression —I have no other clue to my own character ; I have no other clue to my own state Nor can I otherwise explain what is thus made clear in the spirit and behaviour of other men.—And does not the church of England recognise this account of the matter in her baptismal service, when she prays that the *infant* ' may receive remission of his *sins* by spiritual regeneration;' and afterwards instructs the priest to speak to the god-fathers and god-mothers in this wise ; ' Ye have prayed that our Lord Jesus Christ would vouchsafe to release him of *his sins*.' *What* sins ?—This is the reality of ' original sin ,' whence flowed ' original guilt ;' whence flowed ' depravation of nature,' so commonly mistaken for it. This alone constitutes every son and daughter of fallen Adam a fallen creature , not merely child of the fallen, but themselves, individually and personally, fallen from their own original uprightness, *in him* —I have hinted that this is not the place to speak of counsel and design , with which all this was done : but it is obvious that hereby a way was made for that further and more complete developement of God (by the assumption of new relations), which could not be made by simple creation, but to which creation was the stepping-stone. (See Part iii. Sect. xxviii. notes ᵗ and ᵛ)

Luther is again in mistake (see Part iii Sect. xviii note ᵘ) about the creation state of man , speaking as though the possession of the Spirit were a part of his endowments —' Desertus a Deo ac sibi relictus' .. ' naturam peccato, subtracto spiritu, vitiatam '—The Lord God having formed his animal structure out of the dust of the ground—a compound mass— breathed into his nostrils breath of " lifes," and man became a living soul. This continuity of soul and body—simple soul, and compounded body—soul, which was an image of Him that is a Spirit ; and body, in which he resembled and was partaker with the brutes—constituted his essential nature ; the solution of which continuity constitutes death. So constituted,

not say, man saw the things which God had made; and they were very good: Many things he had capacities with which to learn, and sources of instruction from which to derive much knowledge of God. The Lord God conversed with him face to face, and he dwelt amongst the teaching creatures of His hand, even as he was himself the most teaching of all creatures. But where is the Spirit? meaning the Holy Ghost. Had he possessed this—had the Spirit dwelt and walked in Him—that is, been continually present with Him, acting *in* Him and *by* Him—he had possessed union with God : a privilege which was not essential to his condition and relation as the moral creature of God, but which might, or might not, be added to it. That it was not added is plain, as from other considerations, so from this ; that if it was added, then it was either conquered in the temptation, or withdrawn previous to it. I know not what a conquered Holy Ghost can mean, and if withdrawn prior to the temptation, its withdrawal would constitute him a different creature from that to which the temptation law had been given.*—But now, being simply a creature, and therefore mutable, he was liable to fall by temptation. Accountability implies account to be rendered, account implies trial, trial implies the presence of that in the tried substance which may be turned to evil. Was not this precisely Adam's state and constitution ? 'Good,' 'very good,' as he came out of the hands of his Creator, his good might be made evil. Those appetites and passions, the appendages of his will, which, in his creation, and until evil was suggested from without, were pure, fixed on fit objects, and acted in purity ; were liable to be turned to other objects, and thus to become evil. Desire of knowledge, desire of pleasant food, taking pleasure in what is beautiful to the eye— all of which were sound and pure in creation—might thus, *by suggestions thrown in*, become evil. as infectious fever, or the serpent's bite, poisons healthful blood If no evil were suggested, there would continue only good, the suggestion, by being entertained, mars them.—Then, was God debtor to Adam, to withhold temptation from him ; or to minister super-

---

* Luther's misapprehension has much to do with a mistake about the Spirit's actings He seems to have thought, as many now do, that there might be a sort of 'fast and loose' *playings* of the Spirit. The Spirit, when given, acts in earnest and efficaciously —Would Luther say, ' does he always act efficaciously in the Lord's called people, *now ?*' I answer, the cases are not parallel. *We* have the Spirit not as our own, and in our Adam selves, but in Christ. When *we* fall, it is not ' the Spirit conquered,' but the Spirit not energizing : what could not have happened to Adam —Luther's expressions are ambiguous as to the period when the Spirit was withdrawn; whether before, or after the temptation In a former note (Part iii. Sect. xviii. note t) I have dealt with him as representing it to have been withdrawn before the temptation A careful comparison of the several passages in which he refers to it leads me to conclude, that he supposed it not withdrawn till after the sin had been committed.

seem very good to God, and are so; which to us appear very bad, and are so. Thus afflictions, calamities, errors, hell, nay all the best works of God, are, in the sight of the world, very bad and damnable. What is better than Christ and the Gospel? but what more hateful to the world? How those things then shall be good in the sight of God, which are evil in our eyes, is a mystery known to God only, and to those who see with God's eyes; that is, who have the Spirit. But there is no need of so subtile a strain of argumentation just yet.[a] The former answer is sufficient for the present.

It is asked perhaps, how God can be said to work evil in us; as for example, to harden, to give men up to their lusts, to tempt, and the like? We ought, forsooth, to be contented with the words of God, and simply[b] to believe what they affirm; since the works of God quite surpass all description. But, by way of humouring reason, which is another name for human folly, I am content to be silly and foolish, and to try if I can at all move her by turning babbler.[c]

In the first place, even reason and Diatribe concede that God worketh all things in all things; and that nothing is effected, or is efficacious without him. He is omnipotent; and this appertaineth to his omnipotency, as Paul says to the

How God works evil in us considered.

creation aid, fortified as he was by creation endowments, to keep him from falling; or to heal his wounds, and restore soundness and peace to him, when as he had *freely* fallen?

[a] *Tam acutâ disputatione.*] A sharp, keen, refined distinction: something like what is ascribed to the " word of God" (Heb. iv. 12.) " piercing even to the dividing asunder of the soul and spirit, and of the joints and marrow." *Disp.* ' the act of disputing,' or ' the debate held.'

[b] *Simpliciter credere*] ' Simply,' as opposed to arguments and investigations. Faith receives *implicitly* what God *explicitly* declares.

[c] *Balbatiendo.*] Properly, to ' lisp, stammer, or stutter.' There seems to be some allusion to 2 Cor xi. " Would to God ye could bear with me a little in my folly · and indeed bear with me." " I speak as a fool." " I speak foolishly,"

PART IV. Ephesians.[d] Satan then and man having fallen from God, and being deserted by him, cannot will good; that is, cannot will those things which please God, or which God wills. They are turned perpetually towards their own desires, so that they cannot but seek what is their own, and not his.[e] This will and nature of theirs therefore, which is thus averse from God, still remains a something. Satan and the wicked man are not a nothing, having no nature or will, though they have a nature which is corrupt and averse from God. This remainder of nature, therefore, in the wicked man and in Satan, of which we speak, seeing it is the creature and work of God, is not less subject to omnipotency and to divine actings, than all the other creatures and works of God.

Since then God moves and actuates all things in all things, it cannot be but that he also moves and acts in Satan and in the wicked. But he acts in them according to what they are, and what he finds them; that is, since they are averse from him and wicked, and are hurried along by this impulse of the divine omnipotency, they do only such things as are averse from him and wicked: Just as a horseman, driving a horse which is lame in one or two of his feet, drives him according to his make and power; and so the horse goes ill. But what can the horseman do? he drives the horse such as he is in a drove of sound horses; he makes him go ill, the others well;[f] it cannot be otherwise, unless the horse be cured. By this illustration you see how it is, that, when God works in bad men and by bad men, evil is the result; but it cannot be that God doeth wickedly, although he works evil by the agency of evil

[d] Ephes. i. 2.
[e] Self is their idol, to the dethronement of God. Their own interests and gratification, not God's, are sought Philip. ii. 21.
[f] *Illo male, istis bene.*] More literally, 'he does well with, and he does ill with.' *Agit cum* must be understood.

men, because he, being good himself, cannot do wickedly;[g] but still he uses evil instruments which cannot escape the seizure and impulse of his power. The fault therefore is in the instruments; which God does not suffer to remain idle, that evil is done; God, meanwhile, himself being the impeller of them. Just as if a carpenter should cut ill by cutting with an axe that is 'toothed and sawed.' Hence it arises, that the wicked man cannot but go astray and commit sin continually; inasmuch as being seized and urged by the power of God, he is not allowed to remain idle; but wills, desires, acts, just according to what he is.[h]

[g] This is very much like saying '*doeth* good because he *is* good, and *is* good because he *is* good'—It is too much like the 'ipse dixit' of the Pythagoreans.

[h] The amount of Luther's explanation of the mystery of God's agency in the wicked, as given in his *folly*, is, 1. That they are still real existences. 2. Still God's creatures. 3. That he works all things in them, even as he does in all his creatures. 4. That he works in them according to their nature: that hence he does all their evil in them, but does no evil himself. All this is true, but it is baldly told, and wants opening, confirmation, and some additions. He ought to shew us how man came to be what he is, in consistency with God's voluntarily contracted obligations to him; he ought to shew us the nature and manner of his agency in the wicked, he ought to shew us how God, in consistency with himself, ordained and wrought the fall, and continues wicked man in being, yea, works wickedness by him, instead of destroying him and putting an end to the reign of evil —I say, he ought to have shewn these things; because, though he talks of 'silliness' and 'foolishness,' and 'babbling,'* it is plain that he means a serious and sober solution of the difficulty —Then, with respect to the first of these shewings, man, as we have seen in a former note,† had a constitution imparted, and a state assigned to him, in which trial was implied, and in which he ought to have overcome temptation. There was no dereliction of the Creator's engagements, no withdrawal of any possession or privilege, no gainsaying discession or addition, with respect to God's previous announcements, either in the operation of the fall, or in the inflictions which followed it. The mutability of the creature, as simple creature—the accountability of moral creature—and the distinct source (not creation, but super-

* *Libet ineptire, stultescere, et balbutiendo tentare.*
† See above, Sect. x. note z.

PART IV.
SEC. XII.
How God hardens.

These are sure and settled verities, if we, in the first place, believe that God is omnipotent; creation) of the Spirit's *within* energizings—unveil a just God; that is, one who leaves nothing undone which he had *freely* bound himself to do, and does nothing which he ought not to do.—Then, with respect to the second of these shewings, Luther compares God's agency in the wicked to a drover driving on a lame horse (he means it not irreverently); which excites the idea of physical rather than moral influence · but the truth is, God acts in the wicked as in the righteous, by setting, or causing to be set, such considerations before the will, as constrain it to choose his will. This is moral necessity; such a will so addressed cannot choose differently.—Then, with respect to the third of these shewings, God's most gracious and everlasting design of making himself known *to*, and enjoyed *by*, certain creatures of his hands, according to what He really is, affords the ample and adequate reason for all. that complex, yet simple, system of operation, by which he has been dealing with man from the creation to this hour, and shall continue *to* and *throughout* eternity to deal with him:—with man, his great manifester, not only in the blessed human person of the Lord Jesus Christ (see Part ii. Sect. viii. note '), but also in every individual substance of the whole human race; which is made to manifest *itself*, that he may manifest *himself* by his doings with it —A sight like this justifies wisdom to her children and, although these considerations may seem to apply themselves exclusively to God's dealings with the wicked; or at farthest, with men; they will require but little extension, to comprehend all creatures. Evil has been introduced into the creation of God, and is not destroyed, but continues therein, and shall so continue, unto God's glory . because he could not be manifested as what he is—the union and concentration of all moral excellency—THE TRUTH, THE LOVE, THE POWER, THE WISDOM—the good one—without it.—And what is this ' evil,' which has thus come into, and thus abides in God's world? a person—as we are apt to account it, having scriptural authority for so speaking of it; but thinking so of it, too often to our hurt?—Hear what a venerable confessor of the Church has to say about it.* ' I now began to understand, that every creature of thine hand is in its nature good, and that universal nature is justly called on to praise the Lord for his goodness.' (Psalm cxlviii) The evil which I sought after has no positive existence, were it a substance, it would be good, because every thing individually, as well as all things collectively, is good. Evil appeared to be a want of agreement in some parts to others. My opinion of the two independent principles, in order to account for the origin of evil, was without foundation.† Evil

* Augustine's Confessions, in Miln. Eccl. Hist. vol. ii. p. 342.
† See above, Sect. ix. note ʳ,

and, in the second, that the wicked man is the creature of God, but being averse from him, and left to himself, without the Spirit of God, cannot will or do good. God's omnipotence causes that the wicked man cannot escape the moving and driving of God; but, being necessarily subjected to God, he obeys him. Still his corruption, or aversation from God, causes that he cannot be

is not a thing to be created ; let good things only forsake their just place, office and order, and then, though all be good in their nature, evil, which is only a privative, abounds and produces positive misery. I asked what was iniquity, and I found it to be no substance, but a perversity of the will, which declines from thee, the supreme substance, to lower things, and casts away its internal excellencies, and swells with pride externally.'—If it be true then, that the creature, *as creature*, is essentially mutable (what Augustine, and the schoolmen after him, applies to the now corrupted state of the human will* being equally applicable to the will of man—to the will of every moral *creature*—in its essence; viz. that it is vertible), if there subsist what may fitly be compared to a chord in every moral creature, which may be so touched as to yield a jarring note, and by its vibration to produce discord throughout the whole instrument ; if this chord, which is not in itself evil, may be so touched by that which is not evil neither, but good (is not self-love such a chord, and is not the sense of God's incomparable excellency, or the intimation of superiority in some other like creature of God's, or the suggestion of some flaw, blemish, or deficiency in the creature itself—each of which ought only to excite humility, submission, and gratitude—such a touch?); can we have any difficulty in conceiving how Satan was withdrawn from his uprightness, when as he was yet only good, and nothing but good was to be heard and seen around him ?— I am not ignorant that some would divert us altogether from contemplations of this kind but why are we told so much about the devil, if we are to have no thoughts about his history and origin ? We are taught that ' pride was his condemnation' (1 Tim. iii. 6), " that he was a murderer from the beginning, and abode not in the truth" (John viii. 44.) ; " that he kept not his first estate, but left his own habitation" (Jude 6.) , " that there was war in heaven." (Rev. xii. 7.†) Who shall be ashamed to meditate and explore what God hath revealed unto his own justification (Rom. iii. 4.) and to our furtherance and joy of faith ? (Phil. i. 25.)

* See Part iii Sect i
† I am aware, that these words are in their connection to be understood prophetically, but there was a foundation for the allusion.

PART IV. moved and dragged along, according to good. God cannot relinquish the exercise of his omnipotency because of the wicked man's aversation; neither can the wicked man change his aversation into good will. Thus it comes to pass, that he of necessity errs and sins perpetually, until he be rectified by the Spirit of God. Howbeit, in all these Satan as yet reigns in peace and keeps his palace in quietness, in subordination to this impulse of the divine omnipotency. After this follows the business of hardening; which is in this wise. The wicked man, as I have said (and the same is true of Satan his prince also), is occupied altogether with himself and his own matters; he does not inquire after God, nor care for those things which are God's; but seeks his own wealth, his own glory, his own works, his own wisdom, his own power; a kingdom, in short, of his own; and what he wants is to enjoy these things in peace. Now, if any one resist him, or have a mind to diminish ought from these possessions, his aversion, indignation, and rage with which he is stirred up against his adversary, are not less vehement than his desire with which he pursues after these possessions: and he is just as incapable of restraining his rage as he is of restraining his desire and pursuit; and just as incapable of restraining his desire as of putting an end to his existence: of which he *is* incapable, inasmuch as he is the creature of God, though a vitiated one.

This is the history of that rage of the world against God's Gospel. That stronger than he, which is to conquer the quiet possessor of the palace, comes by the Gospel; condemning those desires of glory and riches, and of his own wisdom and righteousness; in short, every thing in which he confides. This same provoking of the wicked, which is effected by God's saying or doing something contrary to their wishes, is the hardening and burdening of them. For, whereas they

are averse of themselves through the very corrup- SEC.XIII.
tion of their nature, they are also turned yet more
out of the way, and made worse, by being resisted
and robbed, under their averseness. Thus, when
God was proceeding to snatch his usurped dominion out of the hands of the wicked Pharaoh, he
provoked him, and did yet more harden and
weigh down his heart by assailing him with the
words of Moses, who threatened to take away
his kingdom, and to withdraw the people from his
dominion: meanwhile, he gave him not the Spirit
within, but allowed his own wicked and corrupt
nature, in which Satan was reigning, to grow red
hot, to boil over, to rage and get to its height,
accompanied with a sort of vain confidence and
contemptuousness.

Let not any one think therefore, that God, Mistakes
when he is said to harden, or to work evil in us prohibited.
(for to harden is to make evil), does so by creating
evil as it were anew in us: just as you might
fancy a malignant vintner, full of mischief himself,
whilst none is in his vessel, to pour or mix poison into or with the same; the vessel all the
while doing nothing itself, save that it receives
or endures the malignancy of the mixer. For
when they hear it said, that God works both good
and evil in us, and that we are subjected to
the operations of God by a mere passive necessity; many seem to fancy, that man, a good sort
of creature, or at least not a bad one, is, in some
such way as this, made the subject of a bad work
of God's. These persons do not sufficiently
consider what a restless sort of actor God is, in
all his creatures, and how he suffers none of them
to have a holyday. But let him who would have
any understanding about such sayings settle it
thus with himself; that God works evil in us
(that is, by us), not through any fault of his, but
through our own faultiness: we being by nature
evil, and God good, he hurries us along by means

PART IV. of his own agency (such is the nature of his omnipotency), and, good as he is in himself, cannot do otherwise than work evil by an evil instrument; which he makes a good use of however (such is his wisdom), by turning it to his own glory and our salvation.[i]

In like manner, he finds the will of Satan evil without creating it so; what has become such, through God's deserting of him, and Satan's sinning; and finding it so, he lays hold, of it in the course of his operations, and moves it whithersoever he will: yet this will does not cease to be evil, because God thus moves it. Just so, David says of Shimei (2 Sam. xvi. 10.), "Let him curse, for God hath commanded him to curse David."— How does God command him to curse? such a malignant and wicked act! There was no external commandment of this kind to be found any where. David then has regard to this consideration, that the omnipotent God speaks, and it is done; that is, he doeth all things by his eternal word. So then, the divine agency and omnipotency seizes hold of the will of Shimei, together with all his members—that will which was already evil, and which had aforetime been inflamed against David; who met him just at the right moment, as having deserved such a cursing,—and even the good God commands (that is, he speaks the word and it is done) this curse, which is poured out by a wicked and blasphemous organ, inasmuch as he seizes hold of that organ, and carries it along with him in the course of his own agency.

SEC. XIV.
Pharaoh's case considered.

Thus he hardens Pharaoh, when he presents his words and works to his wicked and evil will; which that will hates, through innate faultiness,

[i] The wheels of God's omnipotent providence (see Ezek. i. 15—21.) carry the evil as well as the good along with them in their goings. and this unto God's glory; but is it unto salvation also?—This is Luther's defective view.

no doubt, and natural corruption. Now, when God does not change this will inwardly by his Spirit, but persists in presenting and obtruding his words and works; and when Pharaoh, on the other hand, considering his strength, wealth and power, confides in them, through the same natural pravity; it comes to pass, that, being puffed up and exalted by his own fancied greatness, on the one hand, and being rendered a proud despiser by the meanness as well of Moses as of the word of God which comes to him in an abject form, on the other; he is first hardened, and then more and more provoked and aggravated, the more Moses urges and threatens him. This evil will of his, however, would not of itself be stirred up to action, or hardened; but since the omnipotent actor drives it along as he does the rest of his creatures, by an inevitable impulse, will it must. Add to this, that He at the same time presents from, without that which naturally irritates and offends it; so that Pharaoh cannot avoid being hardened any more than he can avoid the agency of the divine omnipotence, and the aversation or malignancy of his own will. So that Pharaoh's hardening by God is completed thus; he sets before his maliciousness that which he of his own nature hates from without; after this he ceases not to stimulate that evil will, just such as he finds it, by his own omnipotent impulse within. The man meanwhile, such being the wickedness of his will, cannot but hate what is contrary to himself, and confide in his own strength. Thus he is made obstinate to such a degree, that he neither hears nor has any understanding, but is hurried away under the possession of the devil, like one mad and raving.^k

^k Luther's account of 'hardening' is, 1 God actuates the wicked as well as the rest of his creatures, according to their nature. 2. Satan is in them unresisted and undisturbed. 3. They can only will evil. 4. God thwarts them by word, or

PART IV. If this view of the case be satisfactory, I have gained my cause; we agree to explode tropes and or deed, or both. All this is correct; but it is not the whole of the matter; neither does he put the several parts of the machinery together, cleverly; neither does he shew an end. (See above, Sect. xi. note ʰ. All these things are *of* God, *through* God, and *to* God. (Rom. xi. 36.) The natural man has been brought into the state in which he is, *of, through,* and *to* him. And what is that state? earthly, sensual, devilish soul (James iii. 16.), possessed by the devil; to whom it was given up, as a prey, in the day of apostasy. Luther distinguishes the ' moving and driving,' or ' seizing and moving,' of God, from his ' word and work.' It is a fine image, which he draws of God giving motion to ' all creature.' But if this idea be examined, it will be found to amount to no more than that God keeps all his creatures in a state of being which is accordant to their nature; and that the wicked therefore are, by the necessity of their nature, kept by him in a state of activity, and not allowed to be torpid, or, as Luther facetiously expresses it, ' to have a holy-day.' Particular actings of God, then, upon this substance of the human soul, such and so related, are what he expresses by God's ' thwarting word and work :' but this thwarting word and work extends only to the outside of the man ; *foris offert— foris objicit.* All this while, Satan's is an agency with which, as it respects others, God does not interfere : he is no agent, no minister of His. You might almost judge from his language in some places (contradicted it is true by others), that he accounted Satan a sort of independent chief.—Now here, if I mistake not, the root of the matter lies. Satan *is* an agent and minister of God. (See Job i. 11. 1 Kings xxii. 19—23. 1 Chron. xxi. 1. Compare 2 Sam. xxiv. 1. Zech. iii. 1—3.) Nor can I understand the expressions so repeatedly applied to the case of Pharaoh, " I will harden Pharaoh's heart;" nor " Whom he will he hardeneth;" nor " God hath given them the spirit of slumber;" nor " Thou hast hid these things from the wise and prudent;" and the like—without recurring to this agency : which obviously meets their full and express import, whilst nothing else, or less, does.—And what is the effect of this agency but such as hath been already ascribed to the operation of God? (see note ʰ, as before) hereby ' He sets, or causes to be set, such considerations (it might be added, and causes such to be withheld—for Satan throws dust into men's eyes; hinders them from seeing, as well as causes them to see wrongly) before the mind of His free-agent, as *morally* constrain him to choose what He hath willed.—O what is there that can give peace under the realizing consciousness of his being and agency, but the assurance that he is in truth only this agent of God for good, and nothing but good, to his chosen?—God's hardening, therefore, I define *generally* to be ʳ that special opera-

the glosses of men, and to understand the words of God literally, that it may not be necessary to make excuses for God, or accuse him of injustice. When he says, I will harden Pharaoh's heart, he speaks in plain language, as if he should say, I will cause that the heart of Pharaoh shall be hardened; or, that it shall be hardened through my doings and workings. How this is effected, we have heard: it shall be by my exciting his own evil will inwardly by that general sort of impulse by which I move all things, so that he shall go on under his own bias, and in his own course of willing; nor will I cease to stimulate him, nor can I do otherwise. I will at the same time present him with a word and a work, which that evil bias of his will fall foul of; since he can do nothing else but choose ill, whilst I stimulate the very substance of the evil which is in him, by virtue of my omnipotency.

Thus was God most sure, and thus did he with the greatest certainty pronounce, that Pharaoh should be hardened, as being most sure, that Pharaoh's will could neither resist the excitement of his omnipotency, nor lay aside its own maliciousness, nor receive Moses as a friend when presenting himself to him as an adversary; but that his will would remain evil, and he would necessarily become worse, harder and prouder, whilst,

---

tion of God upon the reprobate soul, by which, through the agency of Satan (whose Lord and rider he is), combined with his own outward dispensations of word and work, he shuts and seals it up in its own native blindness, aversation and enmity towards himself' There have been however, and doubtless are, certain *special* and splendid exemplifications of this operation, each having its minuter peculiarities, whilst the same essential nature pervades all.—Pharaoh is one of these —Indeed the whole history of the Exodus is one of the most luminous displays, which the Lord God hath ever made, of the design he is pursuing and accomplishing in having and dealing with creatures; second only to the marvellous and complicated history of the Lord's death · whereunto also it was appointed; whereunto also it hath been recorded.

PART IV. in pursuing his own natural bias and course, he encountered an opposition which he did not like, and which he despised through a confidence in his own powers. Thus, you see it here confirmed even by this very assertion, that Freewill can do nothing but evil; seeing that God, who neither is mistaken through ignorance, nor lies through wickedness, so confidently promises the hardening of Pharaoh's heart; being sure forsooth, that an evil will can will only evil, and, if a good which contravenes its own lust be proposed to it, can only be made worse thereby.[1]

SEC. XV.

Impertinent questions may still be asked.

It remains therefore, that a man may ask, 'Why doth not God cease from that very stimulation of his omnipotency by which the wicked man's will is stirred up to continue in its wickedness, and to wax worse?' I answer, 'This is to desire that God should cease to be God, for the sake of the wicked, if you wish his power and agency to cease; in fact, it is to desire that God should cease to be good, least they should be made worse.'—But why doth he not at the same time change those evil wills which he excites? This appertaineth to the secrets of his Majesty; in which his judgments are incomprehensible. We have no business to ask this question; our business is to adore these mysteries: and if flesh and blood be offended here and murmur, let it murmur, pray: it will get no forwarder however; God will not be changed for these murmurs. And what if ungodly men go away scandalized in great numbers? The elect will remain notwithstanding.—The same answer shall be given to those who ask, 'Why he allowed Adam to fall,

[1] "Let my people go that they may serve me," is a good demand, but is directly contrary to Pharaoh's will, its course and propensity. (See the preceding note)—Luther makes this act of God negative; save, as respects God's general and particular operations in his providence. He does not change the will, he keeps his moral creature in being; he thwarts his inclinations.—What is Satan, meanwhile; and what does he ?

and why he goes on to make all of us, who are infected through the same sin; when he might have kept him from sinning, and might either have created us from another stock, or have purged the corrupted seed first?' He is God: whose will has no cause or reason [m] which can be prescribed to it for rule and measure; seeing it hath no equal or superior, but is itself the rule of all things. If it had any rule or measure, or cause or reason, it could not any longer be the will of God. For what he wills is not right, because he ought to will so, or ought to have willed so: on the contrary, because he wills so, therefore what is done must be right. Cause and reason are prescribed to the creature's will, but not to the Creator's; unless you would set another Creator over his head.[n]

By these considerations the trope-making Dia-

[m] *Nulla est causa, nec ratio.*] *Cau.* is the correlative of effect; 'what gives origin to this will' *rat.* 'the principle, rate, method, and design of its operations,' which supposes some extrinsic standard. There is no such source, or standard, for God's will no cause which produces it, no rightness which it exemplifies.

[n] The defects of Luther's theology are strongly manifested in this paragraph. He has no answer to give, where a satisfactory one is at hand God continues to move the wicked, because it is for his glory that they should go on to act, just such as they are —For the same cause he ordained and brought about, or, as Luther speaks, *permitted* Adam's fall.—God does not *create* * wicked men (See above, Sect. x. note [z].)—God's will is cause and reason to itself · but he *has* a reason for all he does; and this reason, so far as respects his actings with which we have to do, is resolvable into self-manifestation. (See former notes.)—As to these and such like questions, which Luther judges it improper to ask, the whole matter is, doth the word of God furnish an answer to them, or not' If it does, we are bound to entertain them and supply the true

* Strange that he should use the word 'creare,' as applied to our *generation* from Adam —' When a thing is made up of particles which did all of them before exist, but that very thing, so constituted of preexisting particles, had not any existence before; this, when referred to a substance produced in the ordinary course of nature by an internal principle, but set on work by and received from some external agent or cause, and working by insensible ways which we perceive not, we call generation.'—Locke's Essay, vol. 1. chap. xxvi sect. 2.

PART IV.
———
compared
with the
text.

tribe is sufficiently confuted, I think; but let' us come to the text itself, that we may see what sort of agreement there is between herself and her trope. It is customary with all those who elude arguments by tropes, to despise the text itself stoutly, and make it their only labour to pick out some one word, and torture it with tropes, and crucify it by the sense they impose upon it, without having the least regard to the surrounding context, or to the words which follow and precede, or to the author's scope or cause. Thus it is with Diatribe here: nothing heeding what Moses is about, or what is the aim of his discourse, she snatches this little word 'I will harden' (which offends her) out of the text, and fashions it after her own pleasure; not at all considering in the meanwhile, how it is to be brought back and inserted again into the text, and to be fitted in so as to square with the body of the text. This is just the reason, why Scripture is accounted not quite clear, by those most learned doctors who have had the greatest possible acceptance amongst men for so many ages. What wonder? The sun himself could not shine if such tricks were played with him.°

But to omit what I have already shewn, that Pharaoh is not properly said to be hardened because he is endured by God with lenity, and not forthwith punished; since he was chastened with so many plagues: if to endure through the divine lenity, and not straightway to punish, be called hardening, what need was there for God

answer. How much better than to leave the caviller strong in his unanswered cavils! And what is the result? a *known* God instead of an *unknown*; a God whom we revere, admire, and delight in, when we should otherwise only tremble and shudder before him!

° *Artibus petitus*] Pet. ' made the subject of attack; whether by violence, stratagem, or supplication:' probably has allusion here to some magical incantations by which sorcerers pretended to darken the sun!—See Hor. Epod. v. xvii.

so often to promise that he would (as a future act) SE. XVII.
harden Pharaoh's heart, when now the miracles
were in performance—Pharaoh all the while being
a man who, before these miracles, and before this
hardening, having been endured through the
divine lenity, and not punished, had inflicted so
many evils upon the children of Israel, in his full-
blown pride, the offspring of his prosperity and
wealth? So then, this trope is nothing at all to
the purpose here; since it might be applied promiscuously to all who sin under the endurance of
divine indulgence. At this rate, we might say
that all men are hardened: since there is no man
who does not commit sin; and no man could
commit sin, if he were not endured with divine
indulgence. This hardening of Pharaoh therefore is something different from, and beyond, that
general endurance of the divine lenity.ᴾ

Rather, Moses's object is not so much to an- Moses's
nounce Pharaoh's wickedness, as God's truth and great ob-
mercy: that the children of Israel may not for- such re-
sooth mistrust the promises of God, by which he peated tes-
had engaged to liberate them. This deliverance to God's
being a vast thing, he forewarns them of its dif- design and
ficulty, that their faith may not falter; knowing hardening
as they thus would, that all these things had been is to
predicted, and were receiving such an accom- strengthen
plishment, through the arrangement of that very Israel.
person who had given them the promises. Just
as if he should say, I am delivering you, it is most
true; but you will hardly believe it, Pharaoh will
make such a resistance, and will so put off the
event. But trust in my promises not a whit
the less: all this very putting-off of his will be
effected by my workings, that I may perform the

ᴾ The word *lenitas*, which occurs so frequently in this passage, properly denotes 'softness,' 'gentleness,' 'kindness,' as
opposed to 'roughness,' 'harshness,' 'severity;' and seems
most aptly to express that 'forbearance,' or 'indulgence,'
with which the Lord God suffereth long, and is kind.

more and the greater miracles, to confirm you in your faith, and to shew my power; that you may hereafter place the greater confidence in me with respect to all other things.—This is just what Christ also does, when he promises the kingdom to his disciples at the last supper: he foretels very many difficulties—his own death, and their manifold tribulations—that when the event should have taken place, they might hereafter believe in him much more.[q]

Indeed, Moses sets this meaning very clearly before us, when he says, " But Pharaoh shall[r] not let you go, that many signs may be wrought in Egypt." And again : " To this end have I stirred thee up, that I might shew in thee my power, and that my name might be declared in all the earth." You see here, that Pharaoh is hardened for this very purpose, that he may resist God, and may put off the redemption of Israel; in order that occasion may be made for shewing many signs, and for declaring the power of God; to the end, that he may be spoken of and believed in, throughout all the earth. What is this else, but that all these things are spoken and done to confirm faith, and to comfort the weak, that they may freely trust in God hereafter, as the true, the faithful, the powerful and the merciful One? As if he would say to his little ones in softest words, ' Be not terrified by Pharaoh's hardness of heart; I am the worker of that very hardness also, and I hold it in my own hands; I who am your deliverer will use it with no other effect, than that it shall cause me to work many signs, and to declare

---

[q] " Now I tell you before it come (*Judas's treachery*), that, when it is come to pass, ye may believe that I am He." " And now I have told you before it come to pass (*his going to the Father*), that, when it is come to pass, ye might believe." " But these things have I told you (*their own persecutions*), that, when the time shall come, ye may remember that I told you of them."—(John xiii. 19. xiv. 29. xvi. 4.)

[r] Exod. vii. 4. xi. 9.

my greatness, to the end that ye may believe in me."*

Hence that saying, which Moses repeats after nearly every plague, " And the heart of Pharaoh was hardened, that he did not let the people go, as the Lord had spoken." What is this saying, " As the Lord had spoken," but that God might be seen to be true, who had declared beforehand that he should be hardened? If there had been any vertibility here, any freeness of will in Pharaoh, such as had power to incline towards either side; God could not with such certainty have foretold his induration—but since the Promiser here is one who can neither be mistaken, nor tell a lie, it was necessarily and most assuredly to come to pass, that he should be hardened; and this could not be, unless the induration were altogether without the limits of man's power, and stood only in the power of God: just as I have described it above; to wit, God was certain that he should not omit the general exercise of his omnipotency in the person of Pharaoh, or because of Pharaoh; seeing, it is what he even cannot omit.

Furthermore, he was equally sure that the will of Pharaoh, naturally wicked and averse from Him, could not consent to the word and work of God which was contrary to it; so that, whereas

* Luther circumscribes the design. Doubtless, God would comfort and encourage his people by these acts and predictions: but self-manifestation was His one ultimate object; and in order to this, the confounding, and the rendering yet more inexcusable, of his enemies, as well as the emboldening of his beloved ones—Was there not also a manifestation of what human nature is, hereby made in his own people? Did they *all* believe, after all these signs? Whence those hankerings after Egypt? Whence those, " It had been better for us to have served the Egyptians?"—The whole is resolvable into that great first principle, ' God shewing what he is, by his dealings with the human nature as exhibited both in the elect and in the reprobate—in his friends and in his enemies' But what a maze, or rather what a mass of inconsistency, is this history, and not this history only but all the Bible, without that principle?

PART IV. the impulse to will was preserved inwardly in Pharaoh by God's omnipotency, and a contradictory word and work of God was thrown to meet it from without,' nothing else could be the result, but a stumbling and a hardening of the heart, in Pharaoh. For, if God had omitted the acting of his omnipotency in Pharaoh at the moment when he threw the contradictory message of Moses into his path, and if Pharaoh's will be supposed to have acted itself alone, by its own power; then possibly there might have been ground for questioning to which of the two sides it would have inclined itself. But now, seeing that he is driven and hurried along to an act of willing—no violence, it is true, being done to his will, because he is not forced against his will; but a natural operation of God hurrying him away to a natural acting of his will, such an one as it is, and that is a bad one—it follows that he cannot but run foul" of the word, and by so doing be hardened.—Thus, we see that this text fights manfully against Freewill: inasmuch as God who promises cannot lie; and if he does not lie, Pharaoh's heart cannot but be hardened.

t *Occursu objecto.*] It is contrived that this word and work of God should come into contact with the edge of the will excited into action by omnipotency, through an act like that of throwing a bone to a dog, or casting a stumbling-block in the path of a traveller.

u *Impingere.*] *Imp* (*se* scilicet subaudito) est ' ire impactum;' ' præcipitem ferri in aliquid.'—Here, as before, we have God's actuation, the man's will, and the *trying, provoking* dispensation. But there seems a little confusion in the admission concerning the man's (Pharaoh's) own will, as separated from the divine impulse. He seems now to make the *crisis* of the evil lie there. I can understand that there might be *inertness* in the case which he supposes : but if there be an act of will, in an *essentially* bad will, I cannot understand how it should be other than evil. (See above, note k.)—The case is merely hypothetical, put for the sake of illustration (but, like many other intended illustrations, confusing rather than distinguishing the object on which it would shine), and impossible : for God acts always, and therefore actuates the wicked always; that is, keeps them in their place and state as moral *agents*— which is a state of activity.

But let us look at Paul also, who adopts this passage from Moses in Rom. ix. How sadly is Diatribe tormented here; she twists herself into all manner of shapes, to avoid losing Freewill. One while she says it is the necessity of a conse-*quence*, but not the necessity of a conse*quent*. One while it is an ordered will, or will signified,[v] which may be resisted; whereas a will of good pleasure is that which cannot be resisted! One while the passages adduced from Paul do not oppose Freewill, because they do not speak of the salvation of man. One while the foreknowledge of God presupposes[x] necessity; another while it does not. One while grace prevents the will— causing it to will—accompanies it on its way, and gives the happy issue. One while the first cause effects every thing; another while it acts by second causes, itself doing nothing. By these and such like mocking words, she only aims to get time, and to snatch the cause meanwhile out of our sight, and drag it some whither else. She gives us credit for being as stupid and heartless, or as little interested in the cause, as she herself is. Or as little children, when frightened or at play, cover their eyes with their hands, and think nobody sees them, because they see nobody; even so Diatribe, not being able to bear the rays, or rather the lightnings, of the clearest possible words, uses all sorts of pretences to make it appear that she does not see the real truth; that she may persuade us, if possible, to cover our eyes, so as not even to see it ourselves. But all these are the marks of a convinced mind, which

Sidenote: SE.XVIII. Paul's reference to this passage in Rom. ix. Diatribe hard put to it—obliged to yield.

[v] *Ordinatam seu voluntatem signi.*] The distinction amounts to that of 'regulated' and 'absolute:' will limited and restrained by ordinance, or by some outward sign which has revealed it; and will of pure, uncontrolled good pleasure. The former of these, it is intimated, may be resisted; the latter cannot.

[x] I understand *ponit* in a logical sense, ' takes for granted;' assumes as a *datum*.

struggles rashly against invincible truth. That figment of the necessity of a consequence as differing from the necessity of a consequent, has been confuted already. (Part i. Sect. xi.) Let Diatribe invent and re-invent, cavil and re-cavil, as much as she pleases, if God foreknew that Judas would be a traitor, Judas necessarily became a traitor; nor was it in the power of Judas, or of any creature, to do otherwise, or to change his will, though he did what he did by an act of willing, and not by compulsion. But to will that act was the operation of a substance which God put into motion by his own omnipotency, as he also does every thing else. For it stands as an invincible and self-evident proposition, that 'God neither lies, nor is mistaken.' The words under our consideration are not obscure or doubtful words, although all the learned of all ages may have been blind, so as to understand and interpret them otherwise. Prevaricate as much as you may, your own conscience, and that of all men, is compelled to acknowledge, if God be not mistaken in that which he foreknows, the *very* thing foreknown must necessarily take place. Else who could trust his promises, who would fear his threatenings, if what he promises or threatens do not necessarily follow? or, how can he promise or threaten, if his foreknowledge deceives him, or can be thwarted by our mutability? This excessive light of undoubted truth manifestly stops every mouth, puts an end to all questions, and decrees a victory in spite of all evasive subtilties. We know very well that the foreknowledge of man is beguiled. We know that an eclipse does not happen because it is foreknown, but is foreknown because it is going to happen. But what have we to do with this sort of foreknowledge? we are arguing about the foreknowledge of God. Deny to this the necessity of the thing foreknown being effected, and you take away the faith and fear of God; you throw down all God's promises and threatenings; nay, you deny the very being of God.— But even Diatribe herself, after a long struggle, in which she has tried all her arts, is at length compelled by the force of truth to make confession of our sentiment, and says;

'The question about the will and purpose of God is a more difficult one. For God wills the same things which he foreknows. And this is what Paul subjoins; "Who resisteth his will, if he pitieth whom he will, and hardeneth whom he will?" For if he were a king, he would do what he liked, so that no one should be able to resist him; he would be said to do what he would. Thus the will of God, as being the principal cause of all events, seems to impose a necessity upon our will.' This is what she says.

And I thank God that Diatribe has at last recovered her senses. What is become of Freewill now? But this eel slips again out of our hands, by saying in a moment;

'But Paul does not resolve this question; on the contrary, he chides the inquirer; nay, but O man, who art thou that repliest against God?'

O exquisite evasion! Is this what you call handling the word of God? to deliver a mere *ipse dixit* in this manner, by your own sole authority, of your own head, without producing testimonies of Scripture, without working miracles? let me rather say, thus to corrupt some of the clearest words that God ever spake? Paul does not resolve this question: what is he doing then? 'He chides the inquirer,' says she. Is not this chiding the most complete resolution of the question? What was in fact asked in this question concerning the will of God? Was it not asked whether he puts a necessity upon our will? Paul answers, that "Thus (that is, because he does so) he hath mercy (He says) on whom he will have mercy, and whom he will he hardeneth. It is not of him that willeth, nor of him that runneth, but of God that sheweth mercy."[y] Not content with having resolved the question, he moreover introduces those who, in opposition to this answer, murmur for Freewill—prating, that neither is there any such thing as merit, neither are we condemned by any fault of our own; and the like—for the very purpose of putting a stop to their indignation and murmurs; saying, "Thou sayest then unto me, why doth he yet find fault? For who shall resist his will?" Do you notice the personification?[z] They, upon hearing that the will of God imposes a necessity upon us, blasphemously murmur and say, "Why doth he yet find fault?" that is, why doth God so press, so drive, so demand, so complain? why doth he accuse? why doth he condemn? as if we men could do what he demands, if we pleased. He has no just cause for this complaint—let him rather accuse his own will—there let him prefer his complaint—there let him press and drive. For who shall resist his will? who can obtain mercy, when he does not choose they should? who can melt himself, if it be his will to harden? It does not lie with us to change His will, much less to resist it: that will chooses that we should be hardened; by that will we are compelled to be hardened—whether we will or no.

If Paul had not resolved this question, or had

[y] Luther makes some confusion in the order of the verses, putting the 18th in the place of the 15th. But his argument is not dependent upon the transposition. The more explicit testimony of verse 18 is implied in verse 15; but verse 18 precedes both the cavil and the reproof.

[z] *Prosopopœia*.] 'The introducing of imaginary persons:' literally, ' the making of persons ;—a well-known figure of rhetoric. Paul had before been simply stating truth in plain language. Now he brings in a supposed objection. Luther asks Erasmus whether he notices this ? It was essential to his correct understanding of the passage, that he should have remarked this change in the Apostle's mode of address: that he *does* personify, and *what sort* of persons he fabricates.

TEXTS AGAINST FREEWILL MAINTAINED. 287

ot unequivocally determined that a necessity is SEC.XIX.
nposed upon us by the divine prescience, what
eed was there to introduce persons as murmur-
ig and alleging that it is impossible to resist
is will? For who would murmur or be indig-
ant, if he did not think that this necessity
ad been determined? The words in which he
peaks of resisting the will of God are not ob-
;ure. Is it doubtful what he means by 'resisting,'
r by 'will;' or 'of whom' he speaks, when he
peaks of the will of God? Let unnumbered
lousands of the most approved doctors be blind
ere, and let them feign that Scripture is not
lear, and let them be afraid of a difficult ques-
on. We have got some most clear words, of this
uport;[1] "He pitieth whom he will; whom he will,
e hardeneth." Also, "Thou sayest to me there-
ire, why doth he find fault? who shall resist his
ill?"

Nor is it a difficult question; nay, nothing can
e plainer to common sense than that this conse-
uence is certain, solid and true: 'If God fore-
nows an event, it necessarily comes to pass;'
hen it has been presupposed, upon the testi-
iony of Scripture, that God neither errs nor is
eceived.[a] I confess that the question is a diffi-
ult one—nay, one which it is impossible to re-
olve—if you should in the same instant determine
) maintain both God's foreknowledge and man's
berty. For what is more difficult, or rather more
npossible, than to contend that contradictions
nd contraries are not at variance with each other;
r that a number is at the same time ten and
ine? There is no difficulty in the question we
re handling, but the difficulty is gone after and

---

[a] *Errat. fallitur*] *Err.* a mistake in his own apprehensions.
all. appearances beguile him. It is not disappointment as to
ie event, which is the subject of remark here, but an ob-
:ct seen afar off made to appear different from what it really
;.

PART IV. brought in, just as ambiguity and obscurity are gone after and introduced by violence into the Scriptures.—So then, he stops the mouths of those wicked ones who have been offended by those most plain words (and why offended, but because they perceive that the divine will is fulfilled by means of our necessity, and because they perceive it to have been unequivocally determined that there is nothing of liberty or of Freewill left to them, but that all things are dependent upon the will of God only); he stops their mouths I say, but it is by bidding them be still, and reverence the Majesty of the divine power and will,[b] over which we have no right of control, whilst it has full power over us, to do what seemeth it good: not that there is any injury done to us by its operations, since it owes us nothing; having received nothing from us, and having promised nothing to us but just so much as it chose and was pleased to do.

SEC XX.

Where true reverence for the Scriptures lies.

Here then is the place, here is the time, for adoring, not the fictitious inhabitants of those Corycian caves, but the real Majesty of God in his fearful wonders, and in his incomprehensible judgments; and for saying "Thy will be done, as in heaven, so in earth." On the other hand, we are never more irreverent and rash, than when we attempt and accuse these very mysteries and judgments, which are unsearchable. Meanwhile, we imagine that we are exercising an incredible degree of reverence in searching the holy Scriptures. Those Scriptures, which God has commanded us to search, we do not search in one direction; but in another, in which he has forbidden us to search them, we do nothing but

---

[b] *Majestatem.*] A form of expression common amongst men, with application to earthly potentates. 'His Majesty' does so and so. It is a sort of personification of the sovereign's state, power, and excellency. So here, of God's power and will.

search them with a perpetual temerity, not to say blasphemy. Is it not such a search, when we rashly endeavour to make that most free foreknowledge of God accord with our liberty; and are ready to detract from the prescience of God if it do not leave us in possession of liberty; or, if it induce necessity, to say with the murmurers and blasphemers, 'Why doth he yet find fault? who shall resist his will? what is become of the most merciful God? what is become of Him who willeth not the death of a sinner? Has he made us that he might delight himself with man's torments?' and the like; which shall be howled out for ever amongst the devils and the damned?

But even natural reason is obliged to confess, that the living and true God must be such an one as to impose necessity upon us, seeing he himself is free: as for instance, that he would be a ridiculous God, or more properly an idol, if he should either foresee future things doubtfully, or be disappointed by events; when even the Gentiles have assigned irresistible fate to their gods.[a] He would be equally ridiculous, if he had not power to do all things, and did not effect all things; or if any thing be really brought to pass without him. Now if the foreknowledge and omnipotency of God be conceded, it follows naturally, by an undeniable consequence, that we were not made by ourselves, neither do we live by ourselves, neither do we perform any thing by ourselves, but all through His omnipotency. And now, since he both knew beforehand that we should be such a sort of people, and goes on to make us such, and to move and govern us as such; what can be imagined in us, pray, that is

[c] *Fatum in-eluctabile*] Even those, who made the fatal sisters superior to Jupiter himself, still had an uncontrolled ordainer of events; inexorable, infallible, invincible fate.

PART IV. free to have a different issue given to it from that which he foreknew, or is now effecting?

So that God's foreknowledge and omnipotency are diametrically opposite to man's Freewill. For either God will be mistaken in his foreknowledge, and disappointed in his actings (which is impossible), or we shall act, and act according to his foreknowledge and agency. By the omnipotency of God, I mean not a power by which he might do many things which he does not; but that acting omnipotency, by which he doeth all things, with power, in all things: it is after this manner, that the Scripture calls him omnipotent. This omnipotency and prescience of God, I say, absolutely abolishes the dogma of Freewill. Nor can the obscurity of Scripture, or the difficulty of the subject, be made a pretext[d] here. The words are most clear, even children know them: the subject matter is plain and easy; one which approves itself even to the natural judgment of common sense: so that, let your series of ages, times and persons, who write and teach otherwise, be never so great, it profiteth you nothing.

SEC. XXI.

What carnal reason hates.

This common sense, or natural reason, is most highly offended forsooth, that God should leave men, should harden them, should damn them, of his own sheer will; as if he were delighted with the sins and torments of the wretched, which are so great and eternal: whereas he is declared to be a God of so great mercy and goodness. It has been deemed unjust, cruel and insufferable to entertain such a sentiment concerning God; with which so many, and those such great men, during so many ages, have also been offended.—And who would not be offended? I myself have been

[d] *Prætext*] Properly, 'a fine web of art spread before a substance to cover, or disguise it.'—*Judicium naturale*, like *ratio naturalis* above, opposes 'natural' to 'spiritual.' The conclusions are so obvious, that we need not the Spirit to draw them.

offended at it, more than once, to the very depth, and lowest depth^e of despair, so as to wish that I had never been created a man: until I learned how salutary that despair was, and how near of kin to grace. Hence all this toil and sweat in putting forward^f the goodness of God, and accusing the will of man: here lay the discovery of those distinctions between God's regulated and absolute will, between the necessity of a consequence and of a consequent, and much of like kind; which have produced no result however, save that the ignorant have been imposed upon by "vain babblings, and by oppositions of science falsely so called."^g Still there has always remained this sting infixed in the deep of their hearts, both to the learned and to the unlearned, if ever they have come to be serious; that they could not believe the prescience and omnipotency of God without perceiving *our* necessity.

Even natural reason, though offended by this necessity, and making such vast efforts to remove it, is compelled to admit its existence, through the conviction of her own private judgment; which would be the same, even if there were no Scrip-

[e] *Abyssum.*] ' *Abyssus* est *profunditas* aquarum *impenetrabilis*, sive speluncæ aquarum latentium, de quibus fontes et flumina procedunt, vel quæ occulte subtereant. Hence applied to ' *the* abyss.' " They besought him that he would not command them to go out into *the abyss* ' (Gr) " Art thou come hither to torment us *before the time* ?"—Luther had felt the very hell of despair.

' And in the lowest deep,
A lower deep still threatening to devour me
Opens wide '

[f] *Pro excusandâ bonitate Dei.*] *Excus.* ' Item, in excusationem affero.'—For regulated and absolute will see above, Sect xix. where he distinguishes these as *volunt. ordin seu signi*, and *volunt. placiti*—For consequence and consequent, see Part i. Sect xi.

[g] 1 Tim. vi. 20 ἀντιθέσεις. ' Doctrina opposita,' ' quæstio quæ ad disceptandum proponitur '—Not what is commonly understood by opposition ; but men setting out to canvass doctrines with a great display of school-learning, and maintaining theses which were opposite to the truth.

ture. For all find this sentiment written in their hearts, so as to recognise and approve it, even against their will, when they hear it discussed: first, that God is omnipotent, not only in what he is able to do, but also in what he actually does, as I have said;[h] else he would be a ridiculous God: secondly, that he knows and foreknows all things, and can neither mistake, nor be misled. These two things being conceded through the testimony of their heart and senses, by and by they are compelled to admit by an inevitable consequence, that we were not made by our own will, but by necessity; and hence, that we do not any thing in right of Freewill, but just as God hath foreknown and doth direct us, by a counsel and an energy which is at once infallible and immutable. So then, we find it written at once in all hearts that there is no such thing as Freewill: although this writing be obscured, through the circumstance of so many contrary disputations, and so many persons of such vast authority having, for so many ages, taught differently. Just as every other law, which (according to Paul's testimony) has been written in our hearts, is recognised when rightly handled, but obscured, when distorted by ungodly teachers and laid hold of by other opinions.[i]

I return to Paul. Now, if he be not solving this question, and concluding human necessity from the prescience and will of God, what need

---

[h] See above, Sect. xx.

[i] Paul's testimony can only respect the fact that a law may be written in our hearts, which is not outwardly taught and professed: for it is neither the same law, of which Paul speaks; neither does he testify any thing about the handling, or about the recognition of that law. (Rom. ii. 13—16.)— Luther supposes this law of necessity to lie at the bottom of our hearts, so that, when we hear it duly and truly set out, we by the exercise of our natural powers accord with it, whilst it may be made illegible, and effaced, by false teaching and prejudice.

has he to introduce the simile of the potter making, out of one and the same lump, one vessel to honour and another to dishonour? Yet the thing made doth not say to its maker 'why hast thou made me thus?' It is men that he is speaking of: whom he compares to clay, and God to the potter. There is no meaning in the comparison; nay, it is absurd and adduced to no purpose, if he do not mean that our liberty is nothing. Nay, Paul's whole argument in support of grace is abortive. The very scope of his whole Epistle is to shew that we can do nothing, yea even then, when we seem to be doing good; as he saith in the same place, ' how that Israel, by following after righteousness, hath not however attained to righteousness; but the Gentiles, which followed not, have attained to it:'[k] of which I shall speak more at large when I produce my own forces.

SC. XXII.
——
resumed. Diatribe dishonest and cowardly— would escape, but cannot

But Diatribe, disguising the whole body of Paul's argument, together with its scope, consoles herself meanwhile with garbled and corrupted words.[l] It is nothing to Diatribe, that Paul afterwards, in Rom. xi. exhorts them, on the other hand; saying, " Thou standest by faith; see that thou art not lifted up." And again: " They also, if they believe, shall be graffed in," &c. He says nothing there about the powers of man; but uses imperative and conjunctive verbs, the effect of which has been sufficiently declared already.[m]

[k] Rom. ix. 30.—I have not marked the words as a *Scripture* quotation, because they are not exact. He says *in the same place:* the intervening verses are all dependent upon verse 24, being so many quotations to shew, that it was God's avowed purpose to call a body of Gentiles into his church, and to save only a remnant of Israel.

[l] *Excisis et depravatis*] *Exc.* words ' cut out' from the text, in which they stand connected with others. *Depr.* ' turned awry,' ' made crooked,' their meaning, through this violent separation, distorted and polluted.

[m] See above, Part iii. Sect. xxxiv.

PART IV. Nay, Paul himself, in the very same place, as if to prevent the vaunters of Freewill, does not say that *they can believe;* but, " God is able to graff them in," says he.—To be short, Diatribe proceeds with so trembling and hesitating a step in handling these texts from Paul's writings, that she seems, in conscience, to dissent from even her own words. For, in those places where she ought most of all to have gone on and proved her doctrine, she almost always breaks off the discourse with a— ' But enough of this;' or, ' I will not investigate this point now;' or, ' It is no part of this subject;' or, ' They would say so and so;' and many like expressions.ⁿ Thus she leaves the matter in the midst, making it doubtful whether she would rather seem to be standing up as a champion for Freewill, or only to be shewing her skill in parrying off Paul with vain words.º 'All this she does after a law and manner of her own; as one who is not in earnest whilst pleading this cause. But we ought not to be thus indifferent; thus to skim the ears of corn; thus to be shaken like a reed with the winds : but, first to assert confidently, steadfastly, fervently; and then to demonstrate by solid, apposite, and abundant proof the doctrine we maintain.ᵖ

Then again, how exquisitely does she contrive to preserve liberty in union with necessity, when she says, Nor does every sort of necessity exclude freedom of will. As for instance, God the Father necessarily begets the Son; but he begets him willingly and freely, inasmuch as he is not compelled to beget him. Are we disputing now,

ⁿ *Excutiam. instituti*] *Excut.* ' concutere, scrutandi et explorandi causâ.' *Inst.* ' scopus, propositum, inceptum.' προαίρεσις·
º *Pro libero arbitrio dicere. Eludere Paulum.*
ᵖ *Super aristas incedere.*] See above, Part iii. Sect. vi. note ᵇ.
' *Certo*' opposed to ' hesitatingly;' *constanter*, to ' variableness of statement;' *ardenter*, to ' indifference;' *solidè*, to ' insubstantial;' *dextrè*, to a ' clumsiness, and want of address;' *copiosè*, to ' scantiness of materials.'

pray, about compulsion and force? Have I not in all my writings testified, that I speak of a necessity of immutability?[q] I know that the Father willingly begets; I know that Judas betrayed Christ through an act of his will. But I affirm that this will was about to be in this very Judas, certainly and infallibly, if God foreknew it. If what I affirm be not yet sufficiently understood, 'let us refer one sort of necessity—that of violence—to the work; another sort of necessity—that of infallibility—to the time.' Let him who hears me understand me to speak of the latter of these two necessities, not of the former; that is, I am not discussing whether Judas became a traitor willingly or unwillingly, but, whether at the time fore-appointed of God it must not infallibly come to pass, that Judas, by an act of his own will, betrays Christ.

But see what Diatribe says here: 'If you look at the infallible foreknowledge of God, Judas was necessarily to become a traitor; but Judas might have changed his will.' Do you even know what you are saying, my Diatribe? To omit, what has been already proved, that the will can but choose evil; how could Judas change his will in consistency with the infallible foreknowledge of God? could he change the foreknowledge of God, and make it fallible? Here Diatribe gives in, deserts her standard, throws away her arms, and flies; referring the discussion, as none of hers, to those scholastic subtilties which distinguish between the necessity of a consequence and the necessity of a consequent:[r] a sort of quibble

---

[q] See above, Part iii Sect. xxxvii. note [h].

[r] In consistency with what has been said before (Part i. Sect. xi.), but with a minute variety in the application, Judas's *treachery*, they would say, was necessary, but he was not a *necessary* traitor: he must betray, but not *therefore* necessarily; that is, according to their account of the matter, *compulsorily*.

PART IV. which she has no mind to pursue. It is very prudent in you doubtless, after having conducted your cause all the way into the midst of a crowded court'—when now a pleader is most of all necessary—to turn your back, and leave the business of replying and defining[t] to others. You should have acted this counsel from the first, and abstained from writing altogether; according to that saying, 'The man who knows not how to contend abstains from the weapons of the field.'[u] It was not expected of Erasmus, that he should remove[v] that difficulty, ' how God with certainty foreknows, yet our actions are contingent.' This difficulty was in the world long before Diatribe's time. But it was expected that he should reply and define. However, being himself a rhetorician, whilst we know nothing about it, he calls in a rhetorical transition to his aid, and—carrying us ignoramuses along with him, as if the matter in debate were one of no moment, and the whole discussion were mere quirk and quibble,—dashes violently out of the midst of the crowd, wearing his crown of ivy and laurel.[x]

[s] The 'mediæ turbæ' are the multitudes surrounding the judicial tribunal ' non usitatâ frequentiâ stipati sumus.'—Cic. ' Perduxeris' expresses the pomp and the labour with which he had dragged on the cause to issue.

[t] *Respondendi et definiendi.*] *Resp* has respect to the adversary's argument, which should be invalidated or *taken off: defin.* is the explanatory statement of the advocate's own case. See above, Part i. Sect. ix.

[u] Hor. Art. Poet. v. 379.

[v] *Moveret.*] There is a peculiar force, if I mistake not, in ' moveret :' he does not say ' remove,' though I have ventured, with good authority, to give it that force ; rather, it is a heavy body which he cannot ' wag.'

[x] Luther thus ridicules his claim to skill and victory. In many sorts of competition, and for many sorts of merit, it was customary to crown the conquerors with various materials— sometimes precious, sometimes of no value—as the highest tribute of honour which could be received. Here therefore he represents Erasmus as *crowning himself;* by a feint of rhetoric abandoning his cause, and assuming to be a conquering

But you have not gained your end by this stratagem, brother! There is no skill in rhetoric so great as to be able to deceive a sincere conscience: the sting of conscience is mightier than eloquence with all her powers and figures. We shall not suffer the rhetorician to pass on here to another topic, that he may hide himself: it is not the place for this exhibition. The hinge of the several matters in dispute, and the head of the cause is attacked here: it is here that Freewill is either extinguished, or shall gain a complete triumph. But instead of meeting this crisis, no sooner do you perceive your danger, or rather perceive that the victory over Freewill is sure; than you pretend to see nothing but metaphysical subtilties in the question. Is this acting the part of a trusty theologian? Are you serious in the cause? How comes it then, that you both leave your hearers in suspense, and the discussion in a state of confusion and exasperation.[y] Still however, you would be thought to have done your work very honourably, and would seem to have carried off the palm. Such cunning and wiliness[z] may be endurable in profane causes; but in theology, where simple and undisguised truth is the object of pursuit—that souls may be saved— it is most hateful and intolerable.

The Sophists also have felt the invincible and insupportable force of this argument; and have therefore feigned this distinction between the

Sect. XXIII.

Much joy to the Sophists and Diatribe in

Bacchus, and an unrivalled Apollo, by wearing the emblems of those divinities.

[y] *Perturbatum et exasperatum.*] *Perturb.* implies want of order and distinctness, no first, second, and third, either in reply or advancement · *exasp.* the heat and ruffle with which it is maintained, we speak of ' angry' debate.

[z] *Vafritia et versutia*] *Vaf.* expresses the subtile invention which devises ; *versut.* the versatility and adroitness with which the crafty counsel is executed : opposed afterwards by *simplex,* ' what is inartificial,' and *aperta,* ' what is manifest to the view.'

PART IV.

their necessity of a consequent.

necessity of a conse*quence* and of a conse*quent*: but how fruitless this distinction is, has been shewn already.[a] They also, like yourself, are not aware what they say, and how much they admit against themselves. For, if you allow the necessity of a consequence, Freewill is vanquished and laid prostrate, and is nothing aided by the consequent's being either necessary or contingent. What is it to me, that Freewill does what she does willingly and not by compulsion? it is enough for me that you concede, ' it must necessarily be that Judas do willingly what he does; and that the event cannot be otherwise, if God hath so foreknown it.' If God foreknows that Judas will betray the Lord, or that he will change his will to betray him; whether of the twain he shall have foreknown, will necessarily come to pass: else God will be mistaken in his foreknowings and foretellings; which is impossible. The necessity of the consequence effects this; if God foreknows an event, that very event necessarily happens. In other words, Freewill is a nothing. This necessity of the consequence is neither obscure, nor ambiguous: if the great doctors in all ages have even been blind, they must still be obliged to admit its existence, since it is so manifest and so certain as to be palpable.[b]

But the necessity of the consequent, with which they comfort themselves, is a mere phantom, and fights, as the saying is, diametrically with the necessity of the consequence. For example; it is the necessity of a consequence, if I say 'God foreknows that Judas will be a traitor; therefore it will certainly and infallibly come to pass, that Judas is a traitor.' In opposition to this neces-

---

[a] See above, note 1.
[b] *Palpari.*] ' What you may stroke with the hand.' The gentlemen which have no eyes may still receive sense-testimony to it.

sity of the consequence, you console yourself in this way; But since Judas may change his will to betray; therefore there is no necessity in the consequent. I demand of you, how these two assertions agree with each other: 'Judas may not be willing to betray;' and 'it is necessary, that Judas be willing to betray.' Do they not directly contradict and fight against each other? 'He shall not be compelled (say you) to betray, against his will.'—What is this to the purpose? You have been affirming something about the *necessity* of a consequent; that *it* is not rendered necessary, forsooth, by the necessity of the consequence; but you have affirmed nothing about the *compulsion* of the consequent. Your answer ought to have been touching the *necessity* of the consequent; and you produce an example which shews *compulsion* in the consequence. I ask one question and you reply to another. All this is the produce of that half asleep half awake state of mind, in which you do not perceive how perfectly inefficient that device is, the necessity of a consequent.

So much for the first of the two passages;[d] which respects the induration of Pharaoh, and

SECT. XXIV.

The other admitted text defended.

[c] *Commentum*] The subtilty means 'Judas has still a will, which is not forced; therefore there is Freewill still '—Who says 'forced?' But can it choose otherwise? A will, that can only make one choice, is in bondage.—The example of Judas is introduced by Erasmus, not Luther.

[d] See Part iv. Sect 1—The course of this long, elaborate, and invincible argument may be traced by the side notes attached to each section; but the reader will forgive me if I endeavour to assist him by the following short summary. Erasmus endeavours to evade this plain text by a trope. 1. Tropical interpretations are *generally* inadmissible. 2. Absurdity of the proposed one. 3. It does not remove the difficulty. 4. Certain illustrations objected to. 5 The causes assigned for introducing it examined. 6 How God hardens explained. 7. Diatribe exposed, and Luther's view maintained by an appeal to the context. Also, by an appeal to Paul's comment; which introduces Erasmus's evasion and that of the Sophists.— In the course of these considerations several topics are ad-

PART IV.

[Margin: Nothing to do with salvation. So Jerome had said.]

involves all the texts of like kind, amounting to a phalanx—and that an invincible one. Let us now examine the second, about Jacob and Esau; of whom, when not yet born, it was said " The elder shall serve the younger." Diatribe evades this passage by saying, ' It has nothing properly to do with the subject of man's salvation. God may will that a man be a servant or a poor man; whether the man will or no, without his being rejected from eternal salvation.'

See how many side-paths and holes of escape a slippery mind seeks after, which is intent upon flying away from truth; but still she does not quite accomplish her flight. Let us suppose, if you will, that this text does not appertain to man's salvation (of which I shall speak hereafter), is it to no purpose then, that Paul adduces it? Shall we make Paul ridiculous, or absurd, in the midst of so serious a discussion? Howbeit, this is a fancy of Jerome's; who, with abundant arrogance on his brow, whilst he is committing sacrilege with his mouth, has the audacity in more places than one to affirm, that those Scriptures which oppose in Paul, do not oppose in their proper places,[e] from which he quotes them.' What is this but to say, that, in laying the foundations of christian doctrine, Paul does but corrupt the divine Scriptures, and beguile the souls of the faithful, by a sentiment which is the coinage of his own brain, and which is intruded upon the Scriptures by violence? Such is the honour, which the Spirit ought to receive, in the person of that holy and choice instrument of God, Paul! Now, whereas Jerome ought to be read with judgment, and this saying of his to be classed

mitted by the way such as the state of man, limits of inquiry, carnal reason's objections, &c ...

[e] *Pugnant.*] Said with reference to some particular doctrine not named—the doctrine of Freewill doubtless, as maintained by Jerome and those who teach like him.

amongst the many which that gentleman (through his listlessness in studying, and his dulness in understanding Scripture) has written impiously; Diatribe snaps up this very saying without any judgment, and does not deign to mitigate it, as she might at least do, with a gloss of some sort, but both judges and qualifies the Scriptures by this saying, as an oracle which precludes all doubt. Thus it is, that we take the ungodly sayings of men as so many rules and measures for interpreting the divine word: and can we any longer wonder that it has become ambiguous and obscure, and that so many of the Fathers are blind to its real meaning, when it is thus made impious and profane?

Let him be anathema therefore who shall say, 'those words do not oppose the doctrine in their original places, which do oppose as quoted by Paul.' This is said, but not proved; and is said by those, who neither understand Paul nor the passages cited by him, but deceive themselves by taking the words in their *own* sense; that is, an impious one. For although this text in particular (Gen. xxv. 21—23.) were meant of temporal servitude[f] only (which is not true); still it is rightly and efficaciously quoted by Paul to prove, that, not for the merits of Jacob or of Esau, but through him that calleth, it was said to Sarah[g] "The

Paul defended in his use of Gen. xxv. 21—23. Nothing gained by supposing the service temporal

---

[f] What is, in fact, gained by this distinction? The principle is the same, ' God of his sovereign will putting a difference.'—Just so it is, with respect to national and personal election. Yet some seem to think that they have hooked a great fish, in discovering, that Great Britain may have been elected to hear the Gospel without any of her children having been elected to receive it!

[g] *Sarah*] Clearly, it should be Rebekah. Sarah was dead when this prophecy was delivered, which is expressly said to have been delivered to Rebekah "And she (Rebekah) said, If it be so, &c. And the Lord said unto her." Gen xxv. 22, 23. The preceding mention of Sarah in Rom. ix. accounts for the mistake.

elder shall serve the younger."—Paul's question is, whether they attained to what is said of them by the virtue or merits of Freewill; and he proves that, not by the virtue or merits of Freewill, but only by the grace of him that called him, Jacob attained to what Esau did not. This he proves by invincible words of Scripture: such as, that they were not yet born; and again, that they had done neither good nor evil. The weight of the matter lies in this proof; this is the point under debate. But Diatribe, through her exquisite skill in rhetoric, passing over and disguising all these things, does not at all debate the question of merits (although she had undertaken to do so, and although Paul's handling of the subject requires it), but quibbles about temporal servitude (as if this were any thing to the purpose); only that she may appear not to be conquered by those most mighty words of Paul. For what could she have to yelp out against Paul, in support of Freewill? what profit was there of Freewill to Jacob? what hurt of the same to Esau? when it had been settled by the foreknowledge and ordination of God what sort of a lot each of them should receive: namely, that the one should serve, and the other should rule; when as yet neither of them was born, or had done any thing. The rewards, which each shall receive, are decreed before the workmen are born, and have begun to work. It is to this point, that Diatribe ought to have directed her reply. This is what Paul insists upon, that they had done nothing good or evil as yet; but still the one is ordained to be the master and the other the servant, by a divine judgment. The question is not, whether this servitude have respect to eternal salvation, but by what merit this servitude is imposed upon a man who has not merited any thing. But it is most

TEXTS AGAINST FREEWILL MAINTAINED. 303

irksome to maintain a conflict with these depraved[h] endeavours to torture and elude Scripture.

SECT. XXVI.

Howbeit, that Moses is not treating of their temporal servitude and dominion only, and that Paul is right in this also, that he understands him to speak with reference to their eternal salvation (although this be not so important to the point in hand, I will not however suffer Paul to be defiled with the calumnies of sacrilegious men[i]), is proved from the text itself. The divine answer[k] given to Rebekah in the book of Moses is, "Two manner of people shall be separated from thy womb; and the one people shall overcome the other people, and the elder shall serve the younger." Here two sorts of people are manifestly distinguished from each other. The one is received into the free favour of God, although the younger, so as to overcome the elder; not by strength, it is true, but through God's befriending him. How else should the younger conquer the elder, except God were with him? Now, since the younger is about to become the people of

The service is not *really* temporal but spiritual.

---

[h] *Pravis.*] Nearly allied in meaning to the *torquendæ Scripturæ* which follows; ' what is crooked and awry.'—No objection, it is obvious, can be drawn from the statement in this paragraph, and from St. Paul's argument, to what has been advanced in a former note (see above, Sect. x. note [z]) on the subject of original sin. The question is about the difference between Jacob and Esau. Both alike fallen and self-destroyed in Adam, the question is how either of these receives distinguishing benefits, whether of a temporal or eternal nature. With respect to manifest existence and distinct personal agency, neither of them, it is plain, had done good or evil, when the words were spoken to Rebekah. That which alone could constitute any difference on a ground of Freewill or merit, there had as yet been no opportunity of displaying.

[i] See last section. The question of Freewill is not affected. Erasmus follows Jerome, whom Luther has pronounced sacrilegious.

[k] *Oraculum.*] It is said of Rebekah, that " she went to inquire of the Lord." *Oraculum* therefore, ' an answer, counsel, or sentence from the Gods,' is the fit term by which to characterise what was said to her.

PART IV. God,[1] it is not only external dominion or servitude, that is treated of here, but every thing which appertaineth to the people of God; that is, the blessing of God, the word, the Spirit, the promise of Christ, and the eternal kingdom: which is even yet more largely confirmed by the Scripture afterwards, where it describes Jacob as being blessed, and as receiving the promises and the kingdom. Paul intimates these several things briefly, when he says, " the elder shall serve the younger:" sending us back to Moses, as one who treats them more at large. So that, in opposition to the sacrilegious [m] comment of Jerome and Diatribe, you may say, that all the passages which Paul adduces fight yet more stoutly against Freewill in their original places, than in his writings. A remark which holds good, not only with respect to Paul, but with respect to all the Apostles; who quote the Scriptures as witnesses to, and assertors of their doctrine. Would not it be ridiculous to quote as a testimony, that which testifies nothing, and does not bear upon the question? If those be accounted ridiculous amongst philosophers, who prove an unknown thing by one yet more unknown, or by an argument which is foreign to the subject; with what face shall we ascribe this absurdity to the chief leaders and authors of the doctrine of Christ; on which the salvation of souls depends? especially in those parts of their writings in which they treat of the main articles of the

---

[1] Isaac's descendants in the line of Jacob were not only to be the typical family—the community which shadowed out the Lord's elect church—but also to be the visible church for a season, and to contain within them the true seed: so that all the spiritual blessings of God were comprehended in this superiority which is announced as the portion of Jacob.

[m] *Sacrilegam.*] ' Qui sacra *legit*,' i. e. *furatur.* Thus, sacrilege is beautifully defined by Johnson to be ' the crime of robbing heaven.' Jerome and those who followed him were guilty of this.

faith. But such insinuations become those, who have no real reverence for the divine Scriptures?" ^{SECT. XXVII.}

That saying of Malachi's which Paul annexes, "Jacob have I loved, but Esau have I hated," she tortures by three distinct productions of her industry.° The first is, 'If you insist upon the letter,ᴾ God does not love as we love; nor does he hate any man: since God is not subject to affections of this kind.'

Diatribe's evasions of Malac 1. 2, 3 Love is by a trope put for effect of love.

What is it I hear? Is it not made the question, how God loves and hates; instead of why he loves and hates? By what merit of ours he loves or hates, is the question. We know very well, that God does not hate or love, as we do; since we both love and hate mutably; but he loves and hates according to his eternal and immutable nature: so far is he from being the subject of accident and affection. And it is this very thing which compels Freewill to be a mere nothing; namely, that the love of God towards men is eternal and immutable, and his hatred towards them eternal; not only prior to the merit and operation of Freewill, but even to the very making of the world; and that every thing is wrought in us necessarily, according to his having either loved us or not loved us, from eternity: insomuch that not only the love of God, but even his manner of loving, brings necessity upon us.—See here

---

ⁿ *Qui sacris scripturis serio non afficiuntur.*] Luther has a peculiar use of the word *afficio*, or rather *afficior*, which I recognise here—'affected to'—denoting a mind interested in, having its affections excited towards an object

° *Triplici industriâ torquet*] A peculiar use of the word *industriâ*—which commonly denotes 'a state, or act, of mind'—to express 'the result of that act;' and this in an unfavourable sense. 'a laboured excogitation, in which there is neither genius, nor the Spirit' (See above, Sect. v. note ᶻ)

ᴾ *Si literam urgeas*] By way of forcing a tropical interpretation of the text, she intimates that the literal cannot possibly stand 'If you *drive* the letter;' that is, force us to take it whether we will or no.

x

PART IV. what Diatribe's attempts at escape have profited her; every where she but runs aground the more, the more she strives to slip away: so unsuccessful a thing is it to struggle against truth. But let your trope be allowed: let the love of God be the effect of love, and the hatred of God the effect of hatred; are these effects wrought without, or beside,[q] the will of God? Will you also say here, God doth not will as we do; neither is he subject to the affection of willing? If these effects take place then, they take place only when he wills: and what he wills, that he either loves or hates. Tell me then, by what merit on their part severally, Jacob is loved and Esau is hated before they are born and perform any act? It appears therefore, that Paul doth most excellently introduce Malachi to support the sentiment of Moses (namely, that God called Jacob before he was born, because he loved him, and not because he was loved before by Jacob, or because he was moved by any merit of his to do so); that it might be shewn in the case of Jacob and Esau, what our Freewill can do.[r]

SECT. XXVIII.

Malachi speaks of temporal affliction.

The second of these laboured excogitations is, 'that Malachi seems not to be speaking of the hatred by which we are eternally damned, but of a temporary affliction. It is a reprehension of those who would build up Edom.'

Here is a second word of reproach for Paul, as doing violence to Scripture: so entirely do we cast off our reverence for the majesty of the Holy Spirit, if we may but establish our own conclu-

---

[q] *Citra et præter.*] More literally, 'on this side and beyond :' implying therefore that they are altogether *of* him and *through* him and *to* him

[r] Erasmus says it is not love and hate, but the effect of these. Luther replies, if effect, it is God's will that effects, and the effect is what he approves : he approves one sort of event to Jacob therefore, and another to Esau.—How much forwarder are you?

TEXTS AGAINST FREEWILL MAINTAINED. 307

sions. But we will bear this insult for a while, and see what good it does. Malachi speaks of temporal affliction. What comes of this? or what is this to the point in hand? Paul is proving from Malachi that this affliction was brought upon Esau without any merit of his, by the mere hatred of God; that he may conclude Freewill to be nothing. Here it is you are pressed: to this point you ought to direct your answer. We are disputing about merit, you speak of reward; and in such a way as not however to elude what you was meaning to elude: nay, in even speaking of reward you acknowledge merit.[s] But you pretend that you do not see this. Tell me then, what was the cause in the divine mind for loving Jacob and hating Esau, when they were not yet in being.—Again; it is false, that Malachi speaks only of temporary affliction; nor is his business with the destruction of Edom: you pervert the whole meaning of the Prophet by this laboured subtilty. The Prophet makes it quite plain what he means, by using the clearest terms: his meaning is to upbraid the Israelites with their ingratitude, because, whilst he has been loving them, they in return are neither loving him as a father, nor fearing him as a master. The fact of his having loved them he proves both by Scripture and by actual performance. For instance, although Jacob and Esau were brothers, as Moses writes in Gen. xxv. he had however loved and chosen Jacob before he was born (as we have just shewn),

SECT XXVIII.

[s] To make this text consist with Freewill, there must be ground of love and of hate in the personal mind and conduct of the two persons —What follows is a master's view of Malachi's prophecy, and decisive as to the question Judah's reproach is that he has been freely, distinguishingly loved, and has been so treacherous The essence of the reproach is the freeness of the love: and what is this *temporality*, which extends from generation to generation, and which comprehends as its central portion 'the eternal God had,' in opposition to 'not had, but had for an enemy?'

x 2

but had so-hated Esau, as to have reduced his country to a wilderness. Moreover he hates, and persists in hating, with such pertinacity, that, after having brought Jacob back from captivity, and restored him, still he suffered not the Edomites to be restored; but, even if they should say, they would build, himself threatens them with destruction. If the Prophet's own plain text[t] does not contain these things, let the whole world charge me with telling a lie. It is not the temerity of the Edomites then, which is reprehended here, but the ingratitude (as I have said) of the sons of Jacob; who do not see what he is conferring upon them, and what he is taking away, from their brothers the Edomites, for no reason but because he hates the one, and loves the other.[u]

How will it now stand good, that the Prophet is speaking of temporary affliction? when he declares in plain terms, that he is speaking about two distinct nations of people, who had descended from the two Patriarchs: that the one of these had been taken up to be his people, and had been preserved; the other had been abandoned, and at length destroyed. Now the act of taking up a people as a people, and not taking them up, as such, has not respect to temporal good or evil only, but to every thing. For our God is not the God of our temporal possessions only, but of every thing we have and look for: nor will he choose to be your God, or to be worshipped by you, with half a shoulder, or a limping foot, but with all your strength and with all your heart; so as to be your God both here and hereafter, in all circumstances, cases, times, and works.

[t] *Textus ipse apertus Prophetæ.*] *Ipse*, without any additions of mine; *apertus*, what requires no opening to make its meaning clear.

[u] *Hic odit, illic amat*] More literally, 'hates in the one quarter, and loves in the other.

·The third of these elaborate excogitations is, 'By a tropological form of expression, he declares that he neither loves all the Gentiles nor hates all the Jews; but some out of each. By this tropical interpretation it is made out, says she, that this testimony has no voice for proving necessity, but for repelling the arrogance of the Jews. Having made this way of escape for herself, she next goes out by it to the length of maintaining, that God is said to hate those who are not yet born, inasmuch as he knows beforehand that they will do things worthy of hatred. Thus the hatred and love of God are no obstacle to Freewill. She comes at last to the conclusion, that the Jews have been cut off from the olive tree by the *merit* of unbelief; that the Gentiles have been graffed into it by the *merit* of faith—making Paul the author of this sentiment—and gives hope to them that have been cut off, that they shall again be graffed in; and fear to them that have been graffed in, lest they should be cut off.'

SC XXIX.
———
Jacob and Esau are a trope for Jews and Gentiles.

'. Let me die, if Diatribe knows herself what she is saying. But perhaps there is here also some rhetorical figure, which teaches scholars to obscure the sense, wherever there is any danger of being entrapped by the word. I see none of those tropical forms of speech here, which Diatribe imagines to herself in her dreams, but does not prove: no wonder then, that the testimony of Malachi does not oppose her, if taken in a tropological sense; when it has no such sense at all. Again; our subject of disputation is not that cutting off and graffing in of which Paul speaks afterwards,ᵛ when he exhorts. We know

ᵛ I insert the word 'afterwards' to give clearness. It is evidently the eleventh chapter to which he refers.—There cannot be a more pernicious practice in the interpretation of Scripture (whilst there is scarcely any more common), than that of dragging in words which are *somewhere thereabouts,* but do really stand in quite a different connection, and have a perfectly dif-

PART IV. that men are graffed in by faith, and are cut off by unbelief, and that they are to be exhorted to believe, that they may not be cut off. But it does not follow from hence, neither is it proved, that they can believe or disbelieve through the power of the free will: which free will is the subject of our debate. We are not discussing who are believers and who not; who are Jews and who are heathens; what follows to believers and to unbelievers; all this belongs to the exhorter. Our question is, by what merit, by what work, men attain to that faith by which they are graffed in; or to that unbelief by which they are cut off. This is what belongs to the teacher. Describe this merit to us. Paul teaches that this befals, not by any work of ours, but only by the love and hatred of God: and, when it has befallen men to believe, exhorts them to perseverance, that they may not be cut off. Still, exhortation proves not what we can do, but what we ought to do. I am forced to use almost more words in withholding my adversary from wandering else whither and leaving his cause, than in pleading the cause itself: howbeit, to have kept him to the point is to have conquered him; so clear and invincible are the words which we have under consideration. Hence it is, that he does almost nothing else but turn aside from it, hurry away in an instant out of sight, and plead another cause than that which he had taken in hand.

SC. XXX.

The simile of clay in

She takes her third passage from Isaiah xlv. "Doth the clay say to its potter, what makest ferent scope; to ascertain the meaning of a proposed text. An argument, or rather an illustrative exhortation of the eleventh chapter, separated from the preceding by many intervening subjects of discussion, is adduced by Erasmus to determine the meaning of an express affirmation in the early part of the ninth.

ˣ According to Paul's distinction of offices in Rom. xii. 6—8. " Having then gifts, &c.; or he that teacheth, on teaching; or he that exhorteth on exhortation."

thou?" And from Jeremiah xviii. "As the clay is in the hand of the potter, so are ye in my hand." 'These words, again, are much stronger combatants in Paul, she says, than in the Prophets from whence they are taken; in the Prophets they are spoken of temporal affliction, but Paul applies them to eternal election and reprobation'—giving Paul a black-eye for his temerity, or for his ignorance.

sc. xxx.
the hand of the potter, Paul does not quote— Temporal afflictions do not evade its force.

But, before we see how she proves that neither of these passages exclude Freewill, let me first observe, that Paul does not appear to have taken this passage from the Prophets, nor does Diatribe prove that he has. Paul is wont to bring in the name of the writer, or to protest that he takes his sentiment from the Scriptures: neither of which he does here. It is therefore more probable that Paul uses this general simile (which different writers adopt for the illustration of different causes), in a sense of his own, for the illustration of the cause which he has in hand. Just as he does with that simile, "A little leaven corrupteth the whole lump;" which, in 1 Cor. v., he adapts to corruptive manners, and elsewhere casts in the teeth of those who were corrupting the word of God: just as Christ also makes mention of the leaven of Herod and of the Pharisees So then, although the Prophets may speak especially of temporal affliction (a point which I decline speaking to now, that I may not be so often occupied and put off with questions foreign to the subject); still Paul uses it in a sense of his own, against Freewill. But, how far it is shewn that Freewill is not taken away, if we be clay to the afflicting hand of God; or why Diatribe insists upon this distinction; I know not: since it is unquestionable, that afflictions come upon us from God against our own will, and put us under the necessity of bearing them, whether we will or no, nor have we it in our own power to avert them; although

PART IV.

SC.XXXI.

The cavil from 2 Tim ii. repelled.

we are exhorted, it is true, to bear them with a willing mind.[y] But it is worth while to hear Diatribe prosecute her cavil, that Paul does not exclude Free-will in his argumentation, by introducing this simile. She objects two absurdities; one of which she gathers from Scripture, the other from reason. The Scriptural one runs thus.

When Paul had said in 2 Tim. ii. that in a great house there are vessels of gold and of silver and of wood and of earth; some for honour, and some for dishonour; he presently adds, "if a man shall have cleansed himself from these he shall be a vessel unto honour, &c." Upon this, Diatribe reasons thus: 'What could be more foolish than if a man should say to an earthen urinal, if thou shalt have purged thyself, thou shalt be a vessel of honour? which however would be rightly enough said to a cask possessed of reason, which has the faculty of accommodating itself to the will of its master, when admonished what that will is.' From these hints she would collect that the simile does not square in all respects, and is so far parried, as to prove nothing. I answer, first, to the exclusion of this cavil, that Paul does not say, if a man shall have cleansed himself from his own filth, but from these; that is, from the vessels of reproach: so that the sense is, if a man shall abide in a state of separation from these ungodly teachers, and shall not have mixed himself with them, he shall be a vessel of honour, &c. But, what if I should also grant that this text of Paul's has no more

[y] Erasmus says the Prophets speak only of temporal afflictions. What of this? You do not disprove bond-will by this distinction, if it be just; rather, you adduce an instance of bond-will. These afflictions come, lie, remain against our will. How much does this shew of freedom?—*Voluntarie*. We are taught indeed to make God's pleasure ours; but, whether we be enabled to do so, or not, his pleasure only is done.

efficacy than Diatribe wishes to give to it; that SC.XXXI.
is, that the simile proves nothing? how will she
prove that Paul means just the same thing in that
passage from Rom. ix. which we are discussing?
Is it enough, to quote another passage, and to
have no care at all whether it have the same
scope or a different one? There is not any easier
or commoner failure in the interpretation of Scripture, as I have often shewn, than that of paral-
lelizing different passages of Scripture, as being
alike;[z] so that similitude of texts (on the ground
of which Diatribe here vaunts herself) is even
more inefficacious than this simile of ours which
she is confuting. But, not to be contentious, let
me grant that each of these passages in Paul's
writings means the same thing: and that a simile
(which without controversy is true) does not
always, and in all particulars, square with the
thing illustrated. Indeed, if it did, it would be
neither simile nor metaphor, but the very thing
itself; according to the proverb, 'Simile halts,
and does not always run upon all fours.'

But here is Diatribe's error and offence; she
overlooks the cause of the comparison which
ought to be looked at more than all the rest, and is
captious and contentious about words: whereas
the meaning is to be sought, as Hilary says, not
only from the words used, but also from the causes
which give occasion to them. Thus the force of a
simile depends upon the cause of the simile. Why
then does Diatribe leave out the matter for the sake
of which Paul uses the simile, and catch at what he
says over and above the cause of the simile.
What he says, 'If a man shall have cleansed
himself,' belongs to exhortation; what he says, 'In
a great house are vessels, &c.' belongs to teaching: so that, from all the circumstances of Paul's

[z] *Velut similes coaptare.*] I have given the idea rather than
the exact word. it is 'pairing, like horses joined together in
a chariot.'.

words and sentiment, you would understand him to be making a declaration about the diversity and use of vessels. The meaning therefore is, 'Since so many are now departing from the faith, we have no consolation but in that we are sure, the foundation of God standeth firm, having this seal to it; the Lord knoweth them that are his, and every one who calleth upon the name of the Lord departeth from iniquity.' Thus far we have the cause and the force of the simile; namely, 'that the Lord knoweth them that are his.' Then follows the simile; namely, 'that there are different vessels, some to honour, and some to disgrace.' Here ends the doctrine; namely, 'that vessels do not prepare themselves, but their master prepares them.' Rom. ix. means also the same thing; 'that the potter hath power, &c.' Thus doth Paul's simile remain unshaken, as most efficacious to prove that Freewill is nothing before God.[a]

After these follows the exhortation, "If any man shall have purged himself from these;" the force of which expressions is well known from what has been said above. It does not follow from

[a] *Coram Deo.*] Referring to a distinction which I have already objected to (See Part i. Sect. xxv. note [i]); as though there were some objects and considerations, with regard to which it is not a nothing.—Erasmus argues against the conclusion drawn from the simile of the potter, chiefly by appealing to 2 Tim. ii. 20, 21. Luther says, 1. You mistake the words "from these." 2. If the simile be inefficacious here, this does not prove it so in Rom. ix. You must prove the similitude which you assume. 3. This passage, rightly interpreted, does mean the same, and does prove the very thing in dispute.—The account which Luther gives of this text, in its connection and construction, is perfectly correct. Ruin aboundeth; "the nevertheless solid foundation of God standeth;" evil does not contradict his will and plan, but fulfils it. In a great house there are vessels of two sorts. God's *eternal* separation of his people is manifested, realized, and consummated by their own God-enabled voluntary separation *in time*—through his Spirit working in due season. Θεμέλιος expresses the whole elect church of God laid by him as a sort of huge foundation-stone with inscriptions. See Zechar. iii. 9.

hence, that he can therefore cleanse himself: nay, if any thing be proved by these words, it is that Freewill can cleanse itself without grace; since he does not say, 'if grace shall have cleansed any one,' but 'if he shall have cleansed himself.' Abundance however has been said about imperative and conjunctive verbs: and the simile, let it be observed, is not expressed in conjunctive verbs, but indicative; 'as there are elect and reprobate, so there are vessels of honour and of ignominy.' In a word, if this evasion be admitted, Paul's whole argument falls to the ground. To what purpose would he introduce persons murmuring against God as the potter, if the fault were seen to be in the vessel and not in the potter? Who would murmur at hearing that one worthy of damnation is damned?[b]

SECT. XXXII.

Diatribe culls a second absurdity from Madam Reason, commonly called Human Reason; namely, 'that the fault is not to be imputed to the vessel but to the potter: especially since he is such a potter as creates the very clay itself and moulds it. Here is a vessel cast into eternal fire, says Diatribe, which has committed no fault but that of not being its own master.'

Reason's cavil from this simile.

Nowhere does Diatribe more openly betray herself than in this place. For here is heard, in other words it is true, but with the same meaning, what Paul represents profane men as saying: "Why doth he find fault? who shall resist his will?" This is that verity which reason can neither apprehend, nor endure. This is what offends so many persons of excellent talents, received for so many ages! Here forsooth they demand of God that he should act according to human law, and do what seemeth right to them; or

Set forth in its audacity.

[b] On the contrary supposition to that assumed and reasoned upon by Paul, the vessel is not the potter's workmanship, as having been made by him just such as he is; but his own. Why defend the potter then?

cease to be God. The secrets of his Majesty shall profit him nothing. Let him give a reason why he is God, or why he wills or does what hath no appearance of justice; as you would call a cobbler or a tailor to come and stand at your judgment-seat. The flesh does not think fit to put such an honour upon God as to believe him just and good, when he speaks and acts above and beyond the rules prescribed in Justinian's Codex, or the fifth book of Aristotle's Ethics. Let the creative majesty give place to one single dreg of his creation, and let the famed Corycian cave change places with its spectators, and stand in awe of *them*, not they of *it!* So then, it is absurd that he damns a person who cannot avoid deserving damnation: and because this is such an absurdity, therefore it must be false that "he hath mercy on whom he will have mercy, and whom he will he hardeneth." But he must be brought to order, and laws must be prescribed to him, that he may not condemn any one who has not first deserved it according to our judgment. Thus only can they be satisfied with Paul and his simile; namely, by his recalling it, and allowing it to have no meaning, but so moderating it, that according to Diatribe's explanation, the potter here makes a vessel to dishonour, on the ground of previous deservings: just as he rejects some Jews for unbelief; and takes up the Gentiles for their faith. But if God's work be such that he have respect to merits, why do they murmur and expostulate? How come they to say, 'Why doth he find fault? who resisteth his will?' What need is there for Paul to stop their mouths? For who wonders, I will not say who is indignant or expostulates, if he be condemned of his own desert? Again; what becomes of the power of the potter to make what he pleases, if he be subjected to merits and laws? He is not suffered to do what he will, but is required to do what he ought.

Respect to merits is quite at variance with the power and liberty of doing what he pleases: as the householder in the parable proves, when he opposes liberty of will in the disposal of his good things to the murmurs of his labourers who demanded a distribution according to right. These are amongst the considerations which invalidate Diatribe's gloss.

SECT. XXXIII.

But let us suppose pray, that God ought to be such an one as hath regard to merits in the damned. Shall we not equally maintain and allow, that he looks at merits also in the saved. If we have a mind to follow Reason, it is equally unjust that the unworthy be crowned, as that the unworthy be punished. Let us conclude then, that God must justify on the ground of previous deservings; or we shall declare him unjust, as being delighted with evil and wicked men, and inviting them to impiety by crowning them with rewards. But woe unto us—who would then be indeed wretched beings—if this were our God. For who then should be saved?—See how good for nothing is the human heart! When God saves the unworthy without merit; nay, when he justifies the ungodly with much demerit; this heart does not accuse him of unfairness: this heart does not then imperiously demand of him why he wills thus—though it be most unfair, according to her own[c] judgment—but, forasmuch as it is advantageous and acceptable to herself, she counts this fair and good. But, when he condemns the undeserving—seeing it is disadvantageous to herself—this is unfair, this is intolerable: here comes in expostulation, murmuring, blasphemy.

Exposed further by asking, why not cavil against the salvation of the saved?

You see then that Diatribe and her friends do not judge according to equity in this cause, but according as their interest is affected. If she had regard to equity, she would expostulate with God for

[c] Luther personifies 'the heart,' or rather 'the wickedness of the heart:' which I have therefore ventured to make feminine.

crowning the unworthy, just as much as she does for condemning the undeserving: she would also commend and extol God for condemning the undeserving, just as much as she does for saving the unworthy. In each case there is equal unfairness, if you refer the matter to our own judgment; unless it be not equally unrighteous to commend Cain for his murder, and make him a king; as it would be to cast innocent Abel into prison, or put him to death. When it is found then, that reason commends God for saving the unworthy, but finds fault with him for condemning the undeserving, she stands convicted of not commending God as God, but as one who promotes her own personal interest; in other words, she looks at self and her own things in God, and commends them; not at God and the things of God. The truth however is, that if you are pleased with God for crowning the unworthy, you ought not to be displeased with him for condemning the undeserving. If he be just in the one case, why not in the other? In the former case, he scatters favour and pity upon the unworthy; in the latter, he scatters wrath and severity upon the undeserving: in both cases excessive and unrighteous according to man's judgment, but just and true according to his own. For, how it be just that he crowns the unworthy, is incomprehensible at present; but we shall see how, when we come to that place, where he will no longer be believed, but with open face beheld. So again, how it be just that he condemns the undeserving, is incomprehensible at present; but we receive it as matter of faith, until the Son of man be revealed.[d]

---

[d] Luther blunders a good deal here, whilst he says many excellent things.—In dealing with this cavil, ' the fault then is in the potter,' he first sets forth its audacity, next repels Erasmus's gloss by it, then maintains that it is an interested judgment, not a judgment of equity, by which God is condemned.—Much of the difficulty is, no doubt, resolvable into

TEXTS AGAINST FREEWILL MAINTAINED. 319

Diatribe however, being sorely displeased with this simile of the potter and the clay, and not a little the sovereignty of God; that sovereignty which is so bitterly offensive to the carnal mind, whilst without the light of it we cannot stir a step in God. Whence came creation in all and every part of its wide range; whence come blessing and cursing, either as foreordained or as fulfilled, whence come heaven and hell, and inhabitants for each, whence comes the devil, whence comes the fall of man; whence comes sealed ruin on the one hand, and whence comes free restoration and glorification on the other, but from him who makes no appeal to the creature for his vindication, but says 'I have lifted up my hand that it shall be so?'—But there is a *worthy* end for all this, which Luther saw not, and therefore did not assign: the sight of which, however, makes the difference of a cruel God and a wise one. (See Part iii. Sect. xxviii. notes $^{t\ v\ x}$.)—It is not true that God condemns the undeserving, or that he crowns the unworthy. Luther did not discern the mystery of the creation and fall of every individual man in Adam (see Part iii Sect xxxviii. note ^{i}, Part iv. Sect. x. note ^{z}), neither did he understand the mystery of the predestinative counsel. Every individual of the human race became a hell-deserving sinner in Adam; every individual of the saved is saved by virtue of new relations assumed by God, and given to him in Christ—as one previously self-ruined, whom Christ has rendered worthy to be taken up from his ruin, by having shared it with him. Predestination is fulfilment forearranged, as is the execution, such was the covenanted design. It is self-destroyed ones therefore that are predestinated to hell; even as it is Christ-made worthy ones that are predestinated to life.—Luther knew nothing about God's assuming relations, much less about his assuming distinct relations; and shews once more how impossible it is to give any consistent account of the salvation of the righteous, on the basis of universal redemption: such a redemption must leave either partiality in God, or merit in man Luther will have it *indignos* to avoid merit, and therefore leaves God 'a respecter of persons'—He does not say a word too much about sovereignty, but he puts it in its wrong place, and omits what ought to be added to it— the end for which it is exercised. The place is, ' God determining to make creatures with opposite destinies—some to everlasting life, and some to shame and everlasting contempt— vessels of wrath and vessels of mercy.' And that we may not even in heart murmur here, we must have an adequate end shewn to us. It *is* shewn to as many as have an eye to see it, ' he determines to make, and he does make them, to his own glory—the manifesting of himself, according to what he really is' " What if God, willing, &c." (Rom. ix 22—24)—In the fulfilment of this design sovereignty is not the hinge; there is nothing from first to last, in the varieties of the way or of the

SECT. XXXIV.

Scripture must be understood with qualifications.

indignant to be so hunted by it, is reduced at length to the extremity of producing different passages from Scripture, of which some seem to ascribe all to man and some all to grace, and then contending in her passion, that both these ought to be understood with a sober explanation,^e and not to be taken strictly. Else, if we urge this simile, she in her turn is prepared to urge us with those imperative and conjunctive texts; especially with that of Paul's, "If a man shall have purged himself from these." Here she represents Paul to contradict himself, and to attribute all to man, except a sober explanation come to his aid. 'If then an explanation of the text be admitted here, so as to leave room for grace, why may not the simile of the potter also admit of qualification, so as to leave room for Freewill?'

'I answer, it is no matter to me whether you take the words in a simple sense, or in a double sense, or in a hundred senses.^f What I say is, you gain nothing, you prove nothing (of what you seek to gain and prove), by this sober explanation. It ought to be proved, that Freewill can will nothing

end, but what approves itself to right reason.—Luther seems to think that the salvation of the righteous escapes animadversion : the fact that there is such a state may ; but if the true nature of that state, and the true way, to it, be faithfully opened, they are scarcely less offensive to the carnal mind, than the damnation of the lost.

^e *Interpretatione sanâ.*] I do not venture to render by 'qualified interpretation,' though this appears to be nearly the meaning : 'a sound,' as opposed to extravagant, sense is to be assigned to the words, in contradistinction to their simple, literal meaning; which, it is implied, would be extravagant and contradictory. A peculiar use of 'interpretatio,' which both Cicero and Quintilian recognise ; from whom Erasmus no doubt borrowed it : 'a giving of the sense, instead of rendering the words ;' much as the Levites did when they read the law to the people after the captivity. Nehem. viii. 7, 8. See Part iii. Sect. xxx. note ^f.

^f *Simpliciter, dupliciter, centuplic.*] Luther puns upon the word *simpliciter* : which is properly opposed to figurative, or tropical.

good. But in this place, "If a man shall have purged himself from these," the form of expression being conjunctive, neither is any thing, neither is nothing proved; Paul is only exhorting. Or if you add Diatribe's consequence and say, 'he exhorts in vain, if man cannot cleanse himself;' then it is proved that Freewill can do every thing without grace. And so, Diatribe disproves *herself*.

I still wait for some passage of Scripture therefore, which teaches this explanation; I do not give credit to those who make it out of their own heads. I deny that any passage is found which ascribes all to man. I deny also that Paul is at variance with himself, when he says "If a man shall have cleansed himself from these." I affirm that the variance in Paul is not less a fiction, than the explanation which she extorts from it is a laboured invention; and that neither of them is demonstrated. This indeed I confess, that, if it be lawful to increase the Scriptures with these consequences and appendages of Diatribe's—as when she says, injunctions are vain if we have not power to fulfil them—then Paul is really at variance with himself, and all Scripture with him, because then the Scripture is made different from what it was before. Then also she proves, that Freewill can do every thing. But what wonder if, in that case, what she says elsewhere be also at variance with her; 'that God is the alone doer of every thing?' But this Scripture, so added to, is not only at war with us, but with Diatribe herself also, who has laid it down that Freewill can will nothing good. Let her therefore deliver herself first of all, and say how these two things agree with Paul, 'Freewill can will nothing good;' and, 'if a man shall have cleansed himself; therefore he can cleanse himself, or else it is said in vain.' You see therefore that Diatribe is plagued to death, and overcome, by this simile of the potter, and that all her effort is to elude the

PART IV.

SECT. XXXV.

Luther has always maintained the perfect consistency of Scripture —illustrates it in affirmed opposites.

force of it; not heeding, in the mean while, how much her interpretation injures the cause which she has undertaken to defend, and how she is confuting and making a jest of herself.[g]

I, on the contrary, as I said before, have never been ambitious of interpretations, nor have I ever spoken after this manner, " extend the hand;" that is, ' grace shall extend it.'[h] ' These are Diatribe's fictions about me, to benefit her own cause. My affirmation has always been, that there is no variance in the words of Scripture, and no need of ' explanation' for the purpose of untying a knot. It is the assertors of Freewill who make knots where there are none,[i] and dream out discrepancies for themselves. For example; those two sayings, " If a man shall have cleansed himself," and " God worketh all in all," are in no wise opposite: nor is it necessary, by way of untying a knot, to say, God does something and man does something. The former of these texts is a conjunctive sentence; which neither affirms nor denies any work or power in man, but prescribes what work or power there ought to be in a man. There is nothing figurative here, nothing which needs explanation; the words are simple, the sense is simple, if you do not add consequences and corruptives after the manner of Diatribe. Then indeed the sense would become unsound: but whose fault would it be? not the text's, but its corrupter's.

The latter text, " God worketh all in all," is an indicative sentence, affirming that all work, all power is God's. In what respect then do two places disagree, of which one has nothing to do

---

[g] All this alleged inconsistency in Scripture is the fruit of your additions; by the aid of which you create inconsistencies, but you also contradict your own positions.

[h] *Affectavimus, extende.*] See above, Sect. iv. text and notes; particularly note [u].

[i] *Nodos in scirpo quærunt.*] See above, Part i. Sect. xxvi. note [l].

with the power of man, and the other ascribes all to God? Rather, do they not most perfectly agree with each other? But Diatribe is so plunged over head and ears, choked and sobbed,[k] by entertaining that carnal thought, 'it is vain to command impossibilities,' as not to be able to restrain herself, whenever she hears an imperative or conjunctive verb, from at once appending her own indicative consequences to it, and saying—'There is something commanded, therefore we can do it, else it would have been folly to command it.' Upon this, she sallies forth and makes boast of her victories every where, as though she had demonstrated that those consequences, together with her own imagination, were as much a settled thing, as the divine authority. Upon this, she does not hesitate to pronounce that in some passages of Scripture every thing is ascribed to man; that there is a discrepancy therefore, a repugnacy in those places, which must be obviated by an explanation: not seeing, that all this is the figment of her own brain, without a single letter of Scripture to confirm it; that it is, besides, a figment of such kind, as, if admitted, would confute no one more stoutly than herself. For, would she not prove by it, if she prove any thing, that Freewill can do every thing?—the express contrary to that which she has undertaken to prove.

Upon the same principle it is, that she so often repeats the words, 'If man does nothing there is no room for merit; where there is no place for merit, there is no place for punishment or for reward.'

Again she does not see how much more stoutly she confutes herself by these carnal arguments,

^k *Corrupta.*] The figure is that of a man drowned; and the last term expresses the state of his substance, when now it has been long under water. It is like Virgil's 'cererem *corruptam undis.*'

than she does me. For what do these consequences prove, save that all attainable merit is by Freewill? What room will there then be for grace? Besides, if you shall say Freewill earns a very little, and grace the rest, why does Freewill receive the whole reward? Shall we also invent a very small degree of reward for her? If there must be place for merit, that there may be place for reward; the merit should be as big as the reward.—But why do I lose my words and my time about a thing of nought? Though even all which Diatribe is contriving should be built up and stand; and though it should be partly man's work, and partly God's work, that we have merit; still they cannot define this very work in which our merit consists, of what sort, and how big it is—so that we are disputing about goats' hair.[1] Well then, since she proves none of those things which she asserts—neither discrepancy, nor qualified interpretation—nor can exhibit a text of Scripture which ascribes all to man; but all these things are phantasms of her own imagination; Paul's simile of the potter and his clay maintains its ground, unhurt and irresistible, as proof that it is not of our own will, what sort of vessels we are formed; and that those exhortations of Paul's, "If a man shall have purged himself" and the like, are models to which we ought to be conformed, but are no proofs of either our performance or our endeavour. Let this suffice with respect to those passages about Pharaoh's hardening, about Esau, and about the potter.

SECT. XXXVII.

Diatribe comes at length to those passages which are cited by Luther in opposition to Freewill, intending to confute *them* also; of which the first is that from Gen. vi. "My Spirit shall not always abide in man, because he is flesh." She confutes this passage in various ways. First, she

---

[1] *Lana caprina.*] See above, Part ii. Sect. iii. note q.

urges that "flesh" does not signify 'sinful affection' here, but 'infirmity.' Secondly, she increases Moses's text: because his saying pertains to the men of that age, not to the whole human race, therefore she would say, 'in those men;' yet again, not applying it to even all the men of that age, since Noah is excepted. Lastly, she urges that this saying imports something else in the Hebrew language; that is to say, the clemency and not the severity of God, according to Jerome: meaning possibly to persuade us, that, as this saying appertaineth not to Noah but to the wicked; so the severity and not the clemency of God appertaineth to Noah, the clemency and not the severity of God appertaineth to the wicked!—But we will pass over these fooleries of Diatribe's, who is every where telling us that she counts the Scriptures a fable. I care not what Jerome says in his trifling way here: it is certain he proves nothing; and we are not inquiring what Jerome thinks, but what the Scripture means. Let the perverters of Scripture pretend, that the Spirit of God means his indignation. I affirm that she fails in her proof two ways: first, in that she cannot produce a single text of Scripture in which the Spirit of God is taken for God's indignation; whilst kindness and sweetness on the contrary are every where ascribed to him: secondly, in that if she could by any means prove, that it is some where or other taken for indignation, still she cannot forthwith prove, that it necessarily follows it must also be taken so here. So again, let her pretend that the flesh is taken for infirmity, still she just in the same degree proves nothing. For, whereas Paul calls the Corinthians carnal, he certainly does not mean to impute infirmity, but fault to them—complaining as he does, that they were oppressed with sects and parties; which is not infirmity, or incapacity to receive more solid doctrine, but the old leaven of

PART IV. malice; which he commands them to purge out.
Let us examine the Hebrew.
"My Spirit shall not always be judging man, because he is flesh." This is word for word what Moses says;[m] and, if we would give up our own

[m] I am disposed to give rather a different turn to the declaration, though in no wise affecting Luther's argument. All he wants to shew is, that they are words of anger, not of pity and palliation. But since the word which we render "strive" and which Luther renders "judge" properly signifies 'debate' or 'judgment given after discussion ;' why might not the sentiment be "My Spirit shall not be always proving that man is flesh ;" or " shall not always be reproving him for *being* flesh ?" The great reason for continuing man in existence after the original and damning transgression was, that he might shew himself what he is, as he has made himself; so different from what God made him. The Lord here says, he will carry on this work of manifestation—this controversy, as it may be called—no longer than for one hundred and twenty years. There seems to be no great importance in the annunciation that he would not strive *because* he is flesh. He was so from the first moment of transgression; and not more so now, than from that moment. But the manifestation having been carried far enough, there was now a reason why it should cease. This trial, or controversy, or judgment, or proof, or reproof, was effected by the divine Spirit both mediately and immediately acting upon their spirit. Luther confines it to the effect of their intercourse with others ; such as Noah, and those of the Lord's people who had lived and were living with those generations of men : in whom the Spirit of God was. But did not that Spirit also act upon these disobedient ones, without their intervention ? that Spirit, which, according to Luther, 'moves and drives' all God's creatures.—'ידן appendere—litem vel causam agere—quomodo ' disceptare ' signift.' et ' judicare.' fut ידון disceptabit. Gen. vi. 3.' (Sim. Lex. Hebr. in loc.)—' ידון Contendit. prop. appendit. 2. Judicavit, i. e. appendit bilance judicii. 3. In judicio contendit. To judge, to strive, to litigate.' (Robertson's Clavis Pentateuch in loco.)
בשגם ' Inasmuch as,' ' for that.' Robertson: Simon derives it rather differently, and explains by ' ἐν τῷ ' seducere eos ; i. e. dum seducit eos ipsa caro.
Luther seems to lose the particular point of the preceding verses, when he speaks of the ' sons of *men* ' marrying wives ; it is the *sons of God* seeing the *daughters of men*, &c. meaning surely those who practised and made profession of his worship.

dreams; the words are sufficiently clear and manifest, I think, as they stand there. But the words which go before and which follow after, connected as they are with the bringing on of the flood, sufficiently shew that they are the expressions of an angry God. They were occasioned by the fact of the sons of men marrying wives through the mere lust of the flesh, and then oppressing the earth with tyranny, so as to compel God to hasten the flood, through his anger; scarcely allowing him to defer for an hundred years what he would otherwise never have brought upon the earth. Read Moses carefully, and you will see that he clearly means this. But what wonder that the Scriptures are obscure, or that you set up not only Freewill, but even Divine will through their means, if you be at liberty to sport with them as if you were looking for scraps and shreds of Virgil in them.[n] This forsooth is untying knots and putting an end to questions by a qualified interpretation! But Jerome and his friend Origen have filled the world with these trifling conceits, and have been the originators of this pestilent precedent for not consulting the simplicity of Scripture.[o]

It was enough for me, that it be proved from this text, that divine authority calls men flesh; and in such manner flesh, that the Spirit of God could not continue amongst them, but at a fixed period must be withdrawn from them. He explains presently what he means by declaring that his Spirit shall not always judge amongst men; by prescribing the space of an hundred and twenty years, as that in which he should still judge. He

SECT. XXXVII.

in opposition to those who had thrown it off. The great offence and provocation seems to have been given by that hypocritical remnant, to and concerning which Enoch, as appears from Jude, verse 15, had previously prophesied.

[n] *Virgilicentonas.*] More literally, '*Virgilian centos.*'
[o] *Simplicitati scripturarum studeretur.*] i. e. taking care to maintain a *plain sense* where it is practicable, in opposition to a figurative one.

opposes the Spirit to the flesh, because men, being flesh, do not receive the Spirit; and he, being Spirit, cannot approve the flesh: whence it would arise, that he must be withdrawn after an hundred and twenty years. So that we may understand the passage in Moses thus : 'My Spirit, which is in Noah and my other saints, reproves. those wicked men by the word they preach, and by the holy life they lead (for to judge amongst men is to exercise the ministry of the word amongst them ᵖ—to reprove, rebuke, and entreat, in season and out of season); but in vain. For they, being blinded and hardened by the flesh, become worse the more they are judged: just as it is, whensoever the word of God comes into the world; men are made worse, the more they are instructed. And this is the cause why the wrath of God is now hastened, just as the flood also was hastened in that day; not only do men sin now-a-days, but even grace is despised, and as Christ says, 'Light is come but men hate light.'

Since men are flesh therefore, as God himself testifieth, they can mind nothing but the flesh; so that Freewill can have no power but to commit sin : and since, with even the Spirit of God calling amongst them and teaching them, they grow worse; what would they do when left to themselves, without the Spirit of God?—Nor is it any thing to the purpose here, that Moses speaks of the men of that age. The same is true of all men, since all are flesh, as Christ says in John iii. 6. " That which is born of the flesh is flesh." How great a malady this is, he teaches us himself on the same occasion, when he says, " No one can enter into the kingdom of God, except he have been born again." Let the Christian know therefore, that Origen and Jerome, and

ᵖ *Officio verbi ;inter eos agere*] Implying, more than mere preaching, he has before said ' per verbum prædicationis et vitam piorum :' it is word administered by mouth and life.

all their tribe, are guilty of a pernicious error in denying that the flesh is to be taken for ungodly affection in these places. For that expression in 1 Cor. iii. "Ye are yet carnal" bespeaks ungodliness. Paul means that they had ungodly persons still amongst them; and further, that the godly, so far as they mind carnal things, are carnal; although they have been justified by the Spirit.

In short, you will observe in Scripture that wheresoever the flesh is treated of in opposition to the Spirit, you may almost always understand by the flesh every thing that is contrary to the Spirit. For instance; "The flesh profiteth nothing." But where it is treated of absolutely, you may know that it denotes the bodily nature and condition: as "They two shall be one flesh." "My flesh is meat indeed." "The word was made flesh." In these places you may change the Hebrew idiom and say 'body,' instead of flesh: the Hebrew language expressing by one word 'flesh,' what we do by the words 'flesh' and 'body.' I wish indeed that it had been so translated, by distinct terms, throughout the whole canon of Scripture, without exception.—So that my text from Gen. vi. will still maintain its place boldly, I think, as the opponent of Freewill: since it is proved, that the flesh, as here spoken of, is that same substance of which Paul says in Romans viii. that "neither can it be subjected to the will of God" (as we shall see when we come to that place); and of which Diatribe says herself, that it can will nothing good.^q

^q It is impossible to understand this text so as that it shall not be a decisive testimony against Freewill. Whether it be that 'God would cease to prove man, what he is,' or 'cease to judge him, because he is such an one;' what he is remains the same; and that is something so vile that God cannot any longer tolerate it.—I confess that I greatly prefer understanding the flesh in Rom. vii. viii. as the bodily part of the saint; which, whilst he remains in this world, is unrenewed. But

PART IV.
SECT. XXXVIII.
Gen. viii. 21. and vi. 5. maintained.

The second passage is from Gen. viii. "The imagination and thought of man's heart are prone to evil from his youth." And in chap. vi. "Every thought of man's heart is intent upon evil continually." She puts off this by saying, "The proneness to evil, which is in most men, does not altogether take away the freedom of the will."

But does God, pray, speak of most men, and not rather of all men, when, as if repenting himself what difference does this make as to the question of Freewill? Every individual man is by natural constitution "enmity against God;" so far as that natural constitution remains in the saint, he also is enmity. The passage under consideration either says, or implies, being he is flesh, he is contrary to the Spirit, and offensive to God. What is the state of his will then?—I would rather understand the word 'flesh' here, of his whole substance or constitution than, as Luther and most other divines do, of 'an affection' of it. Indeed, I consider that much jargon has been introduced into theology by this distinction. It has led to what is called the doctrine of two principles (the term "principle" being a very indefinite one, and a shelter for almost every thing that is unknown or wishes to be obscure); whereas I believe there are few if any places in Scripture, in which it may not be understood of 'the human substance,' either in its complexity as soul and body, or in its dividuality, as body only.—I by no means subscribe to the interpretation which Luther assigns to some of the texts he adduces. "The *flesh* profiteth nothing," is not 'evil affection' but 'the natural substance of man' as contrasted with 'the Spirit.' "The word was made *flesh*," does not declare body in opposition to soul, but that whole human person which the second Person of the ever-blessed Trinity did verily and actually assume into union with himself, when the fulness of the time was come. So "my *flesh* is meat indeed" does not exclude his soul as made an offering for sin: neither does the "*one flesh*" which the church is made to be with Christ exclude him that is joined to the Lord from being one Spirit.— As a hint to shew that, if Luther's interpretation and distinction, with respect to the term 'flesh' be admitted, a third must at least be added (viz. this sense which comprehends the whole human substance, and so constitutes a title which distinguishes man from all other creatures); I would mention Psalm cxlv. 21, Luke iii. 6. Isaiah xl. 5, 6. John xvii. 2. 1 Cor. i. 29. to which others without number might be added.—Luther speaks with sufficient exactness of the presence and withdrawal of the Spirit to make it clear that he did not understand Him to have *dwelt in* the ungodly; whilst he omits a very important part of His agency. (See above, note m.)

after the flood, he promises to those which remained of men, and to those which should come after, that he would not any more bring a flood because of man; subjoining as the reason, that man is prone to evil? As if he should say, 'Were man's wickedness to be regarded, there must never be any cessation from a flood: but I do not mean hereafter to look at man's deservings &c.' So you see God affirms that men were evil both before the flood and after it; making it to be nothing, what Diatribe says about *most men.* Then again, this proneness or propensity to evil seems a matter of small moment to Diatribe; as though it were within the limits of our own power to raise it up[r] or restrain it: whereas the Scripture means to express by this proneness that constant seizure and impulse of the will towards evil. Why has not Diatribe consulted the Hebrew text even here also? in which Moses says nothing about proneness; that you may have no ground for cavilling. For thus it is written in chap. vi. "Every imagination of the thoughts of his heart is only evil all his days." He does not say intent upon, or prone to evil, but absolutely evil; and that nothing but evil is imagined and thought of by man all his life. The nature of its wickedness is described; that it neither does, nor can do otherwise, seeing it is evil: for an evil tree cannot bear any other than evil fruit, according to Christ's testimony. As to Diatribe's cavil, 'Why is space given for repentance, if repentance be in nowise dependent upon the will, but every thing is wrought by necessity?' my reply is, you may say the same of all the precepts of God: why does he enjoin, if all things happen by necessity? He commands, that he may instruct and admonish men what they *ought* to do, that having been humbled by the recognition of their own wickedness they

[r] *Erigere.*] See Part iii. Sect. xxxviii. note n.

PART IV.

SECT. XXXIX.

Isaiah xl.2. maintained.

may attain to grace; as hath been abundantly declared.[s] So that this text, also, still stands its ground invincibly, as the antagonist of Freewill.

The third passage is that of Isai. xl.: "She hath received of the Lord's hand double for all her sins." Jerome, says she, interprets it of divine vengeance, not of grace given in return for evil deeds. This means, 'Jerome says so, therefore it is true.' I affirm that Isaiah asserts a certain proposition in most express words, and Jerome is cast in my teeth; a man, to speak in the gentlest terms, of no judgment or diligence. What is become of that promise, on the faith of which we made a compact that we would plead the Scriptures themselves, not human commentaries?[t]

This whole chapter of Isaiah, according to the Evangelists, speaks of remission of sins as announced by the Gospel; in which they affirm that "the voice of him that crieth," pertaineth to John the Baptist. Now is it to be endured, that Jerome should, after his manner, obtrude Jewish blindnesses upon us as the historical sense of the passage, and then his own silly conceits by way of allegory to it; that, through a perversion of grammar, we may understand a passage, which speaks of remission, to speak of vengeance? What sort of vengeance is it, pray, which has been fulfilled by preaching Christ?[u]—But let us

[s] See above Part iii. Sect. xxii. &c.
[t] See Part ii. Sect. i.
[u] There is a vengeance connected with the preaching of Christ; yea, and a necessary part of that preaching. "To preach the acceptable year of the Lord, and the day of vengeance of our God." The kingdom of God has enemies that would not be reigned over by the King, to be trodden under foot, as well as princes to be seated on thrones. There are souls to be cut off amongst the people by not hearing that Prophet, as well as souls to be gathered by hearing him. "We are unto God a sweet savour of Christ in them that are saved and in them that perish. To the one we are a savour of life unto life; and to the other a savour of death unto death." The Lord Jesus said of his Jewish opposers, "If I had not

look at the words themselves in the Hebrew. Be comforted (says he), be comforted, O my people; or, comfort ye, comfort ye my people, saith your God. I imagine *he* does not inflict vengeance who commands consolation. It follows; "speak to the heart of Jerusalem and proclaim unto her." To speak to the heart is an Hebraism; meaning, to speak good, sweet and soothing things: as, in Genesis xxxiv. Sichem speaks to the heart of Dinah, whom he had defiled; that is, he soothed her in her sadness with soft words—as our translation has it. What those good and sweet things are, which God hath commanded to be spoken for their consolation, he explains by saying, "For her warfare is finished, insomuch that her iniquity is pardoned; seeing, she hath received of the Lord's hand double for all her sins."—' Warfare,' which our manuscript copies exhibit faultily by the word ' malice,' appears to the audacious Jewish grammatists,ᵛ to denote a stated time: for thus they understand that saying in Job vii. The life of man upon the earth is a ' warfare;' that is, there is an appointed time to him. I prefer considering the term ' warfare' to be used literally, according to its grammatical sense; understanding Isaiah to speak of the course and labour of the people under the law, which was like that of combatants in the

---

come and spoken unto them, they had not had sin." The manifestation of what is in man—of the Satanic enmity of the human heart—is peculiarly effected by the preaching of Christ. But it is not the *form* of that dispensation to condemn ("God sent not his Son into the world to condemn the world"), though aggravated guilt and increased condemnation be the *actual result* of his coming. Nor is Luther's argument invalidated by this result the people to be comforted are not objects of vengeance, but of favour.

ᵛ *Grammatistis*] Not gramma*ticus*, but gramma*tista*: a name of reproach, which he applies here to the Jewish Rabbins; who were sciolists in literature, though vast pretenders, and took great liberties with the sacred text. See above, Sect. iv. note ᵗ.

stadium. For thus Paul by choice compares both the preachers and hearers of the word to soldiers; as, when he commands Timothy to fight as a good soldier, and to war a good warfare: and represents the Corinthians to be running in a racecourse. So again, "No man is crowned except he strive lawfully." He clothes both the Ephesians and the Thessalonians with armour, and boasts that he has himself fought the good fight: and the like in other places.[x] So in 1 Kings (1 Samuel), it is written in the Hebrew text, that the sons of Eli slept with the women who were performing service (literally, 'warring') at the door of the tabernacle of the covenant: of whose warfare Moses also maketh mention in Exodus.[y] Hence too, the God of that people is called the Lord of Sabaoth; that is, the Lord of warfare or of armies.

Isaiah therefore declares, that the warfare of a legal people with which they were harassed under the law, as with an insupportable burden (according to the testimony of Peter in Acts xv.), should be finished; and that they, being delivered from the law, should be translated into the new service of the Spirit. Moreover, this end of their most hard service, and this succession of a new and most free one shall not be given them through their merit (since they could not even bear that service), but rather through their demerit; because their warfare is finished in this manner, through their iniquity being freely forgiven them. Here are no obscure or ambiguous words. He says that their warfare shall be finished, because their iniquity is forgiven them; plainly intimating, that they, as soldiers under the law, had not fulfilled the law— neither could have fulfilled it—but had been warring in the service of sin, and had been sinner

[x] 2 Tim. ii. 3. 1 Tim. vi 12. 1 Cor. ix. 24—27. 2 Tim. ii. 5. Ephes. vi. 1 Thess. v. 2 Tim. iv. 7.
[y] Exod. xxxviii. 8. Compare 1 Sam. ii. 22.

soldiers: as if God should say, I am compelled to forgive them their sins, if I would have the law fulfilled by them; nay, I am compelled at the same time to take away the law, because I see that they cannot but sin—and that most of all, when they are militating; that is, labouring to shew the model of the law[z] through their own strength. The Hebrew phrase " her iniquity hath been forgiven," denotes ' gratuitous good pleasure:' by which iniquity ' is made a present of' (forgiven) without any merit, nay with absolute demerit. This is what he subjoins.

"For she hath received of the Lord's hand double for all her sins." This, as I have said, means not only remission of sins, but even a finished warfare; which is nothing else but—the law, which was the strength of sin, being taken away; and sin, which was the sting of death, being forgiven—to reign in twofold liberty, through the victory of Jesus Christ: this is what Esaias means by his " Of the hand of the Lord." They have not obtained these things by their own strength or merits, but have received them through the conquests and free gift of Christ. " In all their sins," is an Hebraism; agreeing to what is expressed in Latin by *for* or *on account* of their sins: just as in Hosea xii. it is said, Jacob served *in* his wife; that is, *for* his wife. And in the 17th Psalm, they have compassed me round *in* my soul; that is, *for* my soul. Isaiah therefore represents our merits, in a figure, to be the procuring cause of this twofold liberty; namely, the finished warfare of the law, and forgiveness of sin; because these (our merits) have been only sins, and all of them sins.

Shall we then suffer this most beautiful and

---

[z] *Legem exprimere.*] Properly, ' to press, wring, strain, or squeeze out;' hence applied figuratively to models in wax, marble, or canvass.

invincible text against Freewill to be polluted with Jewish filth, such as Jerome and Diatribe have daubed upon it? God forbid! On the contrary, my friend Esaias keeps his ground as the conqueror of Freewill, and makes it clear that grace is given, not to the merits or endeavours of Freewill, but to its sins and demerits; and that Freewill can, by its own powers, do nothing but maintain the warfare of sin—insomuch that even the very law, which is supposed to have been given as a help to her, was an intolerable burden, and made her yet more a sinner whilst militating under it.[a]

[a] *Militantem*.] The word 'milito,' which occurs in divers forms throughout this passage, expresses 'the whole state of a soldier' as to doing and suffering, in preparation, conflict, and endurance.—Luther goes far afield for his solution and defence of this text, 1. Warfare is her legal service. 2. She only sinned in that service. 3. She was rewarded for sin, not merit —The truth, if I mistake not, lies nearer home. Why not understand " double for all her sins" as a 'phrase to denote, that ' great and manifold as her sins had been, she was receiving *the double* of them in divine favour.' Double is a finite put for an infinite. (So Isa. lxi. 7. Jerem. xvi. 18. xvii. 18. Zech. ix. 12. Rev. xviii 6) Her *warfare* is the whole interval of her toil and labour —I cannot but think that the prophecy in its *consummation* is still future, though it has already received a *partial* fulfilment. Jerusalem's warfare is not yet accomplished · but the whole space from the Lord's first coming in the flesh to his hereafter coming in glory is comprehended in this prophecy; in which it will at length be seen that the Jerusalem ' which then was' had an interest. The *visible* church received this ' double' at the coming, or rather at the ascension, of the Lord Jesus, when her covenant of condemnation was exchanged for a covenant of righteousness. But the prophecy looks farther, even to the end of that new dispensation which John Baptist began, when the true church—" the church of the first-born, which are written in heaven"—shall receive its consummation and bliss; and the national Israel, which has been running a parallel with it throughout the whole of its history, shall receive and enjoy what it has never yet truly possessed—its Canaan and its Temple Thus, I neither understand the ' warfare,' nor the ' double,' with Luther's strictness; I might rather say, *farfetched-ness:* nor do I place this text where he would place it, as a testimony against Freewill. It is only by implication

TEXTS AGAINST FREEWILL MAINTAINED.

As to what Diatribe argues, that 'although sin abounds through the law, and where sin hath abounded, grace also abounds; but it does not follow hence, that man, assisted by the help of God, cannot, even before grace makes him acceptable, prepare himself, by means of works morally good, for the divine favour:'

SECT. XL.
———
Episode upon God's help — Cornelius rescued.

I shall wonder, if Diatribe be speaking here of her own head, and have not culled this flower from some document sent or obtained from some other quarter; which she has entwined into her own nosegay.[b] She neither sees, nor hears, what her own words mean. If sin aboundeth by the law, how is it possible that a man can prepare himself by moral works for the divine favour? How can works profit, when the law does not profit? or what else is it for sin to abound by the law, but that works done according to the law are sins? But of this in another place.—Then what is it she says, that 'man assisted by the help of God can prepare himself by good works?' Are we arguing about God's help, or about Freewill? What is not possible to the divine help? But this is just what I said, Diatribe despises the cause she is pleading, and therefore snores and gapes so in the midst of her talk.

But she adduces Cornelius the centurion, as an example of a man whose prayers and alms have pleased God, before he was yet baptized, and inspired with the Holy Spirit.

[a] testimony against Freewill; it is a broad, palpable testimony to "reigning grace" sin is requited with *superabounding*, free favour; and it is implied that there has been, and could be, nothing but sin going before —The hypothetical, and therefore questionable, nature of Luther's interpretation is manifested by his own testimonies. all rest upon ' militia,' which he makes *law-service*. But does not he cite the Gospel also called a warfare? To whom are these sayings in Timothy, the Corinthians, Ephesians, &c. addressed?

[b] *Libro suo inseruerit.*] I have ventured to maintain Luther's figure of ' decerpserit.'

PART IV.
I also have read Luke's account in the Acts; but I have never found a single syllable which indicates that the works of Cornelius were morally good without the Holy Spirit, as Diatribe dreams. On the contrary, I find that he was a just man, and one that feared God: for so Luke calls him. But for a man to be called a just man and one that fears God, without the Holy Spirit, is to call Belial Christ.—Then again, the whole argument in that passage goes to prove that Cornelius was one clean in the sight of God: even the vision, which was sent down from heaven to Peter, and which also rebuked him, testifies this; nay, the righteousness and faith of Cornelius are celebrated by Luke in such great words, and by such great deeds, that it is impossible to doubt them. Diatribe however, with her friends the Sophists, contrives to be blind, and to see the contrary, with her eyes open, amidst the clearest light of words and evidence of facts. Such is her want of diligence in reading and observing the Scriptures; which in that case may well be defamed as obscure and ambiguous. What though he had not yet been baptized, and had not yet heard the testimony to Christ's resurrection! Does it follow from thence that he had not the Holy Spirit? On the same principle, you will say that John the Baptist also, with his father and mother—next, Christ's mother and Simeon—had not the Spirit! But away with such thick darkness!^c

SEC. XLI.
My fourth text, taken from the same chapter of Esaias, "All flesh is grass, and all the glory

^c Cornelius, if I distinguish rightly, was a quickened man, but not a converted man. one begotten again from death by the Holy Ghost, but not yet turned to the Lord—for how could he be turned to him whom he knew not? and how could he know him of whom he had not heard? But he had already been brought by the Spirit of Christ into a state to receive Him when he should be manifested by preaching; and the Lord had reserved, and still doth reserve, this honour for his outward word, and for his accredited ambassadors.

thereof as the flower of grass; the grass withereth, and the flower thereof falleth, because the Spirit of the Lord bloweth upon it;" &c. seems to my Diatribe to suffer very great violence when drawn to the subject of grace and Freewill. Why so, pray! Because Jerome, says she, takes the Spirit for indignation, and the flesh for the infirm state of man; which cannot stand against God. Again are the trifling conceits of Jerome produced to me instead of Esaias. I have a harder fight to maintain against the weariness with which Diatribe's carelessness consumes me, than against Diatribe herself. But I have said very lately what I think of Jerome's sentiment.—Let us compare Diatribe's self with herself. Flesh, says she, is the infirm state of man. Spirit is the divine indignation. Has the divine indignation nothing else then to dry up, but only this wretched and infirm condition of man; which it ought rather to raise up than to destroy?

But this is a finer touch still.—' The flower of grass is the glory which arises from prosperity with respect to bodily things. The Jews gloried in their temple, in circumcision, and in their sacrifices: the Greeks in their wisdom.' So then, the flower of grass and the glory of the flesh is the righteousness of works and the wisdom of the world. How is it then, that righteousness and wisdom are called bodily things by Diatribe? What must then be said to Esaias himself, who explains himself in words without figure, where he says, " Truly the people is grass." He does not say, ' Truly the infirm condition of man is grass,' but " the people is grass;" and he asserts it with an oath. What is the people then? Is it only the infirm condition of man? I do not know indeed whether Jerome means ' the creature itself,' or ' the wretched lot and state of man,' by ' the infirm condition of man.'—But, whichsoever of the two it be, the divine indignation ' carries off

SEC. XLI.

Isaiah xl. 6, 7. maintained.

PART IV.

SC. XLII.

The true interpretation.

wonderful praise and ample spoils assuredly,'[d] in drying up a wretched creature, or men that are in a state of unhappiness, instead of scattering the proud and putting down the mighty from their seat, and sending the rich empty away; as Mary sings.[e]

But let us bid adieu to our spectres, and follow Esaias. The people, says he, is grass. Now the people is not merely flesh, or the infirm state of human nature, but comprehends whatsoever is contained in the people; namely, rich men, wise men, just men, holy men: unless the Pharisees, the elders, the princes, the chiefs, the rich, &c. were not of the people of the Jews. Its glory is rightly called the flower of grass; forasmuch as they boasted of their dominion, their government, and especially of their law, of God, of righteousness and wisdom; as Paul argues in Rom. ii. iii. ix. When Esaias therefore says, " all flesh;" what is this else but *all* the grass, or *all* the people? For he does not simply say, " flesh," but " all flesh." Now there pertaineth to the people soul, body, mind, reason, judgment and whatsoever can be mentioned or discovered that is most excellent in man. For he who says " all flesh is grass" excepts no one, but the Spirit which dries it up. So neither does he omit any thing who says, " the people are grass." Let there be Freewill then, let there be whatsoever is accounted highest and lowest in the people, Esaias calls all this flesh and grass: seeing that these three nouns; flesh, grass, people, according to the interpretation of the very author of the book, mean the same thing in this place.

Then again, you affirm your own self, that the wisdom of the Greeks, and the righteousness of the Jews, which were dried up by the Gospel, are grass, or the flower of grass. Do you think

[d] Virg. Æn. iv. 93. [e] Luke i. 51, 52.

that wisdom was not the most excellent thing SC. XLII.
which the Greeks possessed? Do you think that
righteousness was not the most excellent thing
which the Jews could work? Shew me any thing
that was more excellent than these. What becomes of your confidence then, by which you
gave even Philip a black-eye,[f] as I suppose; saying, 'If any man should contend that what is best
in man is nothing else but flesh—that is to say,
wickedness—I will be ready to agree with him,
provided he but shew by Scripture testimonies
that what he asserts is true?'

You have here Esaias proclaiming with a loud
voice that the people which hath not the Spirit of
the Lord is flesh; although even this loud voice
does not make you hear. You have your own
self's confession (made perhaps without knowing
what you was saying), that the wisdom of the
Greeks is grass, or the glory of grass; which is
just the same thing as calling it flesh. Unless
you should choose to contend that the wisdom of
the Greeks does not appertain to reason, or 'the
leading thing,'[g] as you call it by a Greek term;
that is, to the principal part of man. Hear yourself, at least, pray—if you despise me—when as
you have been taken captive by the force of truth,
affirming what is right. You have John declaring,
"That which is born of the flesh is flesh; and
that which is born of the Spirit is Spirit." This
passage, which evidently proves that what is not
born of the Spirit is flesh (else that division of
Christ would not stand, by which he divides all
men into two parties, the flesh and the Spirit)—
this passage, I say, you have the courage to pass
over—as if it did not teach you what you were

---

[f] *Etiam Philippum sugillabas*] Philip Melancthon—who maintained a good deal of friendly intercourse with Erasmus, and was much more to his mind than Luther and the rest of the reformers: this explains *etiam*.

[g] Τὸ ἡγεμονικὸν.

PART IV. demanding[h]—and scurry away, as your manner is, to another subject; holding forth to us in the mean while, how that John says, 'Believers are born of God and made sons of God; yea Gods and new creatures.' You give no heed to the conclusion which the division leads to, but teach us in superfluous words who those are whom the other part of the division comprehends: trusting in your rhetoric, as if there was nobody to observe this most crafty transition and dissimulation of yours.[i]

It is hard to give you credit for not being artful and chameleon-like here. The man, who labours in the Scriptures with the wiliness and hypocrisy which you employ over them, may safely enough

[h] Referring to his challenge above; 'provided he but shew,' &c.

[i] Luther's argument is, Freewill is called 'flesh' here; for it is part of 'the people'—which, with all that is in it, gets the name of 'flesh' here · for 'people,' 'flesh,' 'grass,' are declared by Isaiah himself to be the same thing.—You ought according to your own previous confession therefore to submit, and, with respect to the real nature of flesh, we have it from our Lord's own mouth in John iii.—I do not fall in with his reasoning · if flesh mean what he says it does in John, must it also mean the same here? But why must it mean what he says, in John? why not there as well as here mean 'the whole substance and constitution of man,' not 'body only,' nor 'ungodly affection.' (See above, Sect xxxvii note q) 'All flesh,' is 'all human beings.' 'the people' generally distinguishes the Jews from the rest of the world, and *so* gives emphasis here It is man's mortality, moreover, rather than his sin, which is brought into view here, as set in contrast with the immutability of God (See the whole context from ver. 3 to ver. 8, and compare with 1 Pet. i. 24, 25) The great subject of the prophecy is, THE GLORY Jehovah shall be revealed . God—who is not, like man, grass and a liar—hath spoken it.—In the word 'grass,' I follow our English version, which has the authority of the original text—חָצִיר herba virens a צָצָה viruit. But Luther has *fœnum*; grass in the state of 'cut and withered.' Thus, again we have a testimony against Freewill by implication only · and, though we need not wonder, as Erasmus does, how this should be dragged into the dispute (for if man be grass, what is his will?), I cannot help remarking, what I shall have occasion to do hereafter more freely, that Luther would have done wisely in keeping back some of his witnesses.

profess that he is not yet taught by the Scriptures; but that he wishes to be taught; whereas he wishes nothing less, and only chatters thus, that he may disparage that most clear light which is in the Scriptures, and may give a grace to his own obstinacy. Thus the Jews maintain unto this day, that what Christ and the Apostles and the Church have taught is not proved by the Scriptures. Heretics cannot be taught any thing by the Scriptures. The Papists have not yet been taught by the Scriptures, although even the stones cry out the truth. Perhaps you are waiting for a passage to be produced from the Scriptures, which shall consist of these letters and syllables, ʽ The principal part in man is flesh ;' or ʽ that which is most excellent in man is flesh ;' and till then, mean to march off as an invincible conqueror. Just as though the Jews should demand that a sentence be produced from the Prophets consisting of these letters; ʽ Jesus, the son of a carpenter, born of the Virgin Mary at Bethlehem, is the Messiah, and the Son of God.'

Here, where you are compelled to admit our conclusion, by the manifest sentiment, you prescribe the letters and the syllables which we are to produce to you: elsewhere, when conquered both by the letters and the sentiment, you have your tropes; your knots to untie, and your sober explanation. Every where you find something to oppose to the divine Scriptures: and no wonder, when you do nothing else but seek for something to oppose to them. One while you run to the interpretations of the ancients; another while to the absurdities of reason: when neither of these serve your purpose, you talk about things that are afar off, and things that are nigh, just that you may avoid being confined to the text immediately before you. What shall I say? Proteus is no Proteus, as compared with you. But you cannot slip out of our hands even by these artifices. What victories did the Arians boast, because those letters and syllables ὁμοέσιος were not contained in the Scriptures: not accounting it any thing, that the reality affirmed by that word is most decisively proved by other words. But let even impiety and iniquity herself judge, whether this be the acting of a good mind—I will not say of a pious one—which desires to be instructed.

Take your victory then—I confess myself conquered—these letters and syllables, 'the most excellent thing in man is but flesh,' are not found in the Scriptures. But see thou, what sort of a victory thine is, when I prove that there are found testimonies in the greatest abundance to the fact, that not one portion—or the most excellent thing in man—or the principal part of man—is flesh; but that the whole man is flesh: and not only so, but that the whole people is flesh; and, as though this were not enough, that the whole human race is flesh. For Christ says, "That which is born of the flesh is flesh." Untie thy knots, imagine thy tropes, follow the interpretation of the ancients, or turn else whither, and discourse about the Trojan war, that you may not see or hear the text which is before you. It is not matter of faith with us, but we both see and feel, that the whole human race *is born of the flesh*: we are therefore compelled to believe what we do not see; namely, that the whole human race *is flesh*, upon the authority of Christ's teaching. Now therefore, we leave it to the Sophists to doubt and dispute whether the ἡγεμονικὰ, or leading part in man, be comprehended in the whole man, the whole people, the whole race of man: knowing as we do, that in the subject, 'whole human race,' is comprehended the body and the soul, with all their powers and operations, with all their vices and virtues, with all their folly and wisdom, with all their justice and injustice. All things are flesh; because all things mind the flesh (that is, the things which are their own), and are destitute of the glory of God and of the Spirit of God: as Paul says in Rom. iii.[k]

[k] Luther speaks as the oracles of God, when he says, ' all *things*'—meaning ' all *persons*'—all human beings—are flesh. —I have hinted already (see the last note) that I do not agree with Luther in his interpretation of this most authoritative text (John iii. 6) on which he bottoms his whole argument here, as he did before. He says " That which is born of the flesh is flesh" means ' that which is born of the flesh is sinful, or ungodly, affection ,' in short, is ' wicked,' or ' wickedness' *I* say ' flesh' means the same in the subject and in the predicate , ' that which is born of man is man.' What this is, as to its nature, properties and qualities, must be sought elsewhere : but the next clause gives us a pretty good hint at these, by implying that it is of a nature directly contrary to that of the Holy Ghost; " That which is born of the flesh is flesh , and that which is born of the Spirit is Spirit." The Scripture is, moreover, abundantly explicit in its testimony to what this nature is, by giving us a full and complete history of its creation and depravation, and by asserting in the clearest and strongest terms its total, universal, complicated, and pervasive villainy. Take but these four passages, to which scores might be added, and let them teach us ' what that flesh is which flesh begets, and brings forth.' " What is man, that he should be clean ? and he which is born of a woman, that he should be righteous ? Behold, he putteth no trust in his saints, and the heavens are not clean in his sight : how much more abominable and filthy is man, which drinketh iniquity like water ?" (Job xv 14—16) " Behold I was shapen in iniquity, and in sin did my mother conceive me." (Psalm li 5) " The heart is deceitful above all things, and desperately wicked , who can know it ?" (Jerem xvii. 9) " For from within, out of the heart of man, proceed evil thoughts, adulteries, fornications, murders, thefts, covetousness, wickedness, deceit, lasciviousness, an evil eye, blasphemy, pride, foolishness : all these evil things come from within, and defile the man." (Mark vii. 21—23.)—It is not therefore, that I draw a different testimony from John iii 6. but I make it a *step* to explicit proof, rather than explicit proof itself , and by so doing cut the sinews of objection here, whilst I also preserve simplicity and uniformity in the interpretation of Scripture terms.*

* For a more full consideration of the terms flesh and spirit, I venture to refer the reader to ' Vaughan's Clergyman's Appeal,' chap. iii sect. iii. and chap. v. sect. ii. iv. where some account is given of the nature state of man, and of the sanctification of the Lord's people, which I deem satisfactory.

PART IV.
────
SC.XLIII.

Heathen
virtue is
God's ab-
horrence.

As to what you say therefore, that 'every affec-tion¹ of man is not flesh, but there is which is called soul, there is which is called spirit; by the latter of which we strive after whatsoever things are honourable ᵐ—just as the philosophers strove, who taught that death should be encountered a thousand times sooner than allow ourselves in any base act, even though we knew that men would be ignorant of it, and God forgive it'—.

I reply; it is easy for a man who believes nothing assuredly to believe any thing, and say any thing. Let your friend Lucian,ⁿ not I, ask you, whether you can shew us a single individual out of the whole human race (you shall be twice or seven times over a Socrates yourself, if you please) who hath exhibited what you here mention, and say that they taught. Why do you tell stories then, in vain words? Could those strive after honourable things who did not even know what honourable is? You call it honourable perhaps (to hunt out the most eminent example) that they died for their country, for their wives and children, and for their parents; or that, to avoid belying themselves or betraying these relations, they endured exquisite torments. Such were Q. Scævola, M. Regulus, and others.ᵒ But what can you display in all these, save an outside shew of good works? Have you looked into their

---

¹ *Omnis affectus.*] Not merely what we commonly denote 'affection,' meaning 'appetite and passion;' but all that is liable to be moved and affected in man : 'his whole constitution as a moral being.'

ᵐ *Quo nitimur ad honesta.*] *Honestum* is properly opposed to *turpe* : 'placui tibi, qui turpi secernis honestum'.—Hor. It is the 'honore et laude dignum,' opposed to what is dishonourable : the καλὸν of the Greeks; something more exalted than the πρέπον, even as that was also more exalted than the δίκαιον.

ⁿ See above, Part ii. Sect. xx. note ˣ.

ᵒ It should rather be C. Scævola; that Scævola who hazarded his life to rid his country of Porsenna; that Regulus who dissuaded from peace with Carthage though he went back to die for it.

hearts? Nay, it appeared at the same time on the very outside of their performance that they were doing all these things for their own glory; insomuch that they were not ashamed to confess and to make it their boast, that they were seeking their own glory. For it was glory burning them through and through, which led even these Romans, according to their own testimony, to do whatsoever they did that was virtuous; which same thing is true both of the Greeks also, and of the Jews also, and of the whole human race.

Now, although this be honourable amongst men, still nothing can be more dishonourable in the sight of God; nay, in his sight, it was the most impious and consummate sacrilege, that they did not act for the glory of God, neither did they glorify him as God, but, by the most impious sort of robbery, stole the glory from God and ascribed it to themselves: so that they were never less honourable and more vile, than whilst shining forth in their most exalted virtues. But now, how could they act for the glory of God, when they knew nothing of God and of his glory: not for that these did not appear, but because the flesh did not suffer them to see the glory of God, through the rage and madness with which they were raving after their own glory. Here then, you have the chieftain spirit ($\dot{\eta}\gamma\epsilon\mu o\nu\iota\kappa o\nu$), that principal part of man, striving after things honourable—in other words, exhibiting itself as the robber of God's glory, and the affectant of his Majesty—in the case of those men most of all, who are the most honourable and the most illustrious for their consummate virtues. Deny now, if you can, that these men are flesh, and in a lost state through ungodly affection.

Indeed I imagine that Diatribe was not so much offended with its being said that man is flesh or spirit, when she read it according to the Latin translation, ' man is carnal or spiritual.'

PART IV. For we must grant this peculiarity amongst many others to the Hebrew tongue, that when it says, 'Man is flesh or spirit,' it means the same that we do, when we say, 'Man is carnal or spiritual:' just as the Latins say, 'The wolf is a sad thing for the folds.' 'Moisture is a sweet thing to the sown corn;' or when they say, 'That man is wickedness and malice itself.' Thus, holy Scripture also, by an expression of intensity, calls man flesh as though he were carnality itself; because he has an excessive relish for the things of the flesh, and none for any thing else: just as it also calls him spirit, because he relishes, seeks, does and endures only the things of the Spirit.

She may put this question indeed, which still remains, 'Although the whole man, and that which is most excellent in man, be called flesh; does it follow that whatsoever is flesh must straightway be called ungodly?' Whosoever hath not the Spirit of God, him I call ungodly: for the Scripture declares, that the Spirit is given for this very purpose, that he may justify the ungodly.[p] Again,[q] when Christ distinguishes the Spirit from the flesh, by saying "That which is born of the flesh is flesh;" and adds, that one who is born of the flesh cannot see the kingdom of God; it evidently follows, that whatsoever is flesh, the same is ungodly, is under the wrath of

---

[p] *Ut impium justificet.*] Luther evidently means by 'justify' here, 'making righteous,' and that, as to personal character. I do not know whence he gets his quotation, "believeth on him that justifieth the ungodly." (Rom. iv. 5), is said with quite another meaning: the nearest I can find is 1 Cor. vi. 11. "And such were some of you; but ye are ...justified in the name of the Lord Jesus, and by the Spirit of our God."

[q] *Cùm verò.*] I venture to give it this turn, because it is clearly a new and distinct argument which he here introduces: to call 'flesh' is to call 'wicked;' for it is to say, 1. that he hath not the Spirit (which alone maketh godly); 2. that he is a member of the devil's kingdom.

God, and is far from the kingdom of God. Now, SC.XLIV. if it be far from the kingdom and Spirit of God, it must necessarily follow that it is under the kingdom and spirit of Satan—there being no middle kingdom between the kingdom of God and the kingdom of Satan; which are perpetually fighting against each other. These considerations prove that the most consummate virtues amongst the heathens—the best sayings of their philosophers, and the most eminent actions of their citizens—however they may be spoken well, and may appear honourable in the sight of the world —are truly but flesh in the sight of God, and services rendered to Satan's kingdom; that is, impious and sacrilegious, and in all respects evil.

But pray let us for a moment suppose Diatribe's assertion to stand good, that the whole constitution of man is not flesh; that is, wicked: but that part of it, which we call spirit, is honest and sound. See what absurdity follows hence, not in the sight of human reason it is true; but with reference to the whole religion of Christ, and to the principal articles of the faith. For if the most excellent part in man be not ungodly, lost and damned, but only the flesh; that is, the grosser and inferior affections; what sort of a Redeemer shall we make out Christ to be? Shall we represent the worth of his most precious blood-shedding to be so small that it only redeemed the vilest part in man; whilst the most excellent part in man is strong of itself, and hath no need of Christ? Henceforth then, we must preach Christ, not as the Redeemer of the whole man, but of his most worthless part—that is, the flesh; whilst man is himself his own redeemer in his better part.

Consequences of this assumption respecting a part in man which is not 'flesh.'

Choose which of the two you please. If the better part of man is sound, it does not stand in need of Christ as a Redeemer. If it does not stand in need of Christ, it triumphs over Christ with a glory superior to his—as curing itself, which is the better part, whereas Christ cures only the more worthless. Then again, the kingdom of Satan also will be nothing; as reigning over the viler part of man, whilst it is itself rather ruled by man, as to his better part. Thus it will be brought to pass by this dogma concerning the principal part of man, that man is exalted above both Christ and the devil; that is, he will be made God of Gods, and Lord of Lords.—What becomes then of that approvable opinion, which affirmed that Freewill can will nothing good? Here, on the contrary, she contends that this same Freewill is the principal part, and the sound part, and the honest part; that which hath no need even of Christ, but can do more than God himself and the devil can. I mention this, as in former instances,[r] my Erasmus, that you may see again, how dangerous a thing it is to attempt sacred and divine things without the Spirit of God, under the rash guidance of human reason.— If then Christ be the Lamb of God, who taketh away the sin of the world; it follows that the whole world is under sin, damnation and the devil; and the distinction between principal parts, and not principal parts, avails nothing. For the world signifies men who relish worldly things in all parts of their frame.[s]

'If the whole man, says she, when even regenerated by faith,[t] is nothing else but flesh, what

---

[r] See Part i. Sect xxii. Part iii. Sect. xxxii. Part. iv. Sect. xx. xxxii.

[s] Luther's order in the last two sections is, 1. Your praise of the heathens is false. 2 Man is 'flesh' 'is man is wickedness.' 3. What would follow if your cavil 'not all' were true—There is a good deal of subtilty in this part of his argument, and we are ready to say 'not content with knocking down his adversary, he kicks him when he is down:' but his objections are solid and unanswerable.

[t] There is an ambiguity in the expression 'renatus per

becomes of the spirit which is born of the Spirit? what becomes of the son of God? what fidem.' Faith is the fruit and effect of regeneration strictly and properly so called, that is, ' of that act of God by his Spirit, whereby he begets the soul anew, and so makes it capable of spiritual perceptions, actings and sufferings' But in the more enlarged sense of regeneration, which includes *state* as well as *character* (what is more properly called new *birth, born* again) regeneration may be said to be the *fruit* of faith: " Ye are all the children of God in Christ Jesus by faith;" that is, manifested to be such—visibly and acknowledgedly adopted into his family.—The child as begotten differs from the child as born into the world Regeneration, strictly speaking, is the begetting of the child; speaking more widely, is the birth of it; and Baptism is the sign and seal of this regenerate state—the sign *of*, and the seal that we are *in* it. In its most correct view, it is the sacrament of the Resurrection; of our having died and risen again with Christ—into whom we have been baptized—in a figure, of which, our being in the number of those, for whom and with whom he has died, in order that they might be raised up again from the dead with him and for his sake—at an appointed time—is the reality. By baptism therefore, the Lord's people are sealed to be in the state of those who have risen from the dead; who *already have* that which is to be had in this life of the resurrection from the dead, in possessing, acting and enjoying a risen Spirit—and who have the pledge of God, which cannot lie, that they *shall have* the superabundant residue both in their person (a raised body) and in their state (partakers of the glory which shall be revealed) In whatever form the ordinance be administered, whether by immersion, affusion, or aspersion, it is in effect the same teaching sign; the laver of regeneration being the Lord's blood, and its application to our person denoting our union with him in his death and resurrection. It is this signing, sealing ordinance, I say, to God's elect, and to none else. who, when they have been called by the Spirit (which may be before or after—if one part of the sign must be future, why may not both ?), are led and enabled either to wait upon the Lord in the receiving of it, or to look back to it as a benefit already received.—Hosts of objections will rise up, no doubt, against this testimony. Why then are infants baptized ? Why is baptism administered to the non-elect ?—I am not careful to answer these questions of the natural man. Infant baptism however, I remark, must stand upon its own grounds of vindication; and, for my own part, I am content with God's having commanded every male Israelite to be circumcised on the eighth day.—Administered to non-elect! Why it has been the mystery of God from the beginning to bring out and draw to himself his elect, amidst

SC. XLV.

charged. Authority of the ancients abused, but good for nothing— if good, contradicts Erasmus.

becomes of the new creature? I should like to be informed about these things.' So much for Diatribe.—Whither, whither so fast, my dearest Diatribe? What are you dreaming about? You desire to learn how it is that the spirit in man, which is born of the Spirit of God, can be flesh? O how happy and secure is this victory, under the flush of which you insult over your vanquished one, as though it were impossible that I could stand my ground here! Meanwhile, you would gladly make an ill use of the authority of the ancients, who talk about certain seeds of honesty being sown by nature in the minds of men. First of all, you may, for what I care, *use* or *abuse* the authority of the ancients, if

a multitude of professing hypocrites. Enoch lived amongst such: Judas was one of the twelve. The meaning of the ordinance is not impaired by these mysterious arrangements; and it is just so much of shame, grief and weakness to the spiritual man, if he do not use and enjoy the pregnant sign.—I have mixed this reference to baptism with the subject of regeneration, not only because so mixed by the Fathers and by the Apostles, but because I cannot doubt that the Lord had a reference to it in John iii 5. (Except a man be begotten by the Spirit out of water; *i e.* begotten by the Spirit in and through that water which is the sacramental emblem of my blood; he can have no part or lot in the kingdom of God); and because I consider it as so illustrative of the real nature of regeneration which I cannot allow to be either character or state only, but must regard as, in its more enlarged sense, comprehending both. How simple and how sweet the view thus opened to us of the Lord's sacraments! Baptism, the sacramental introduction of the Lord's people into the resurrection state; and the communion of the body and blood, the sacrament of their continual life therein.—The phrase ' renatus per fidem" then, which both Erasmus and Luther adopt, is allowable as expressive of that state into which the eternally foreknown of God are brought, when, having already been regenerated in Spirit, they, by faith and calling upon God, are regenerated in state. In this state, they live and walk *by* and *in* the Spirit.—Then what has this state of theirs to do with the question of Freewill; or rather, with all that has just been argued about man's being flesh—whatever be meant by that word? He that hath been begotten, or born, of the Spirit is Spirit, and has the Spirit dwelling and walking in him, and serveth God therein.

TEXTS AGAINST FREEWILL MAINTAINED.

you please; it is your look out what you believe, when you believe men who dictate their own opinions without any authority from the word of God: and perhaps it is not a matter of religious anxiety which torments you much, what any man believes; since you so easily give credit to men, without heeding whether what they say be certain or uncertain in the sight of God.—*I* also have my question to propose for information: when did I ever teach what you so freely and so publicly impute to me? Could any one be so mad as to say, that the man who hath been born of the Spirit is nothing but flesh? I decidedly separate flesh and Spirit as substances at variance with each other; and affirm, in unison with the sacred oracle, that the man who hath not been born again by faith is flesh: I affirm further, that the regenerate man is flesh, only so far as pertaineth to that remainder[u] of the flesh in him, which fighteth against the first-fruits of the received Spirit.—I cannot think you so base as wilfully to have feigned this, by way of exciting ill-will against me: else, what could you have imputed to me of a more atrocious nature? But either you know nothing of my matters, or you seem unequal to the weight of the subject; by which you are so pressed and confounded, that you do not sufficiently remember what you say either *against* me, or *for* yourself

---

[u] *Secundùm reliquias*] Luther speaks of this remainder, as many other divines do, in a manner which implies that the work of the Spirit upon the substance of the soul in regeneration is incomplete: whereas it shall receive no increase or alteration for ever. The body only is unrenewed, and shall remain so till the resurrection. The variety is in the energizings of the within-dwelling Spirit which, unto God's glory in our real good, are neither uniform nor perpetual; and give occasion to the unrenewed part of our frame, and to our enemies without, to gain many a transient victory over us.—What I have already said and referred to, about 'flesh' and 'spirit,' will serve to shew that my account of this remainder would differ some little from Luther's.—See above; Sect. xlii. notes [i] and [k]. See also Part ii. Sect i. note [f].

PART IV. self. For in believing, upon the authority of the ancients, that *some* seeds of honesty are implanted in the minds of men by nature, you again speak with a degree of forgetfulness, having asserted before, that Freewill can will nothing good. I do not know how this inability to will any thing good, is compatible with some seeds of honesty. Thus am I perpetually compelled to remind you of the point which is at issue in the cause you have undertaken to plead; from which you are perpetually departing through forgetfulness, and maintaining a proposition different from the one you set out with.[v]

SC. XLVI.
Jeremiah x. 23, 24. defended.

Another passage is in Jeremiah x. "I know, O Lord, that the way of man is not his; nor is it in the power of any man to walk and direct his steps." This text, she says, appertains to prosperity of event, rather than to the power of Freewill.

Here again Diatribe confidently introduces her gloss at pleasure, as if she had a sort of plenipotentiary authority over Scripture. But what need was there of such authoritativeness in the man, to enable him to consider the sense and scope of the Prophet? 'It is enough, says Mr. Erasmus; therefore it is so.' Allow the adversaries of the truth this lust for glossing, and what will they not gain? Let him teach us this gloss then from the context, and we will believe him. On the contrary, I shew from that very context, that whilst the Prophet sees himself engaged in teaching the ungodly with so much importunity to no purpose, he at the same time perceives that his word avails nothing, unless God teach it within; and that it is not at the disposal of man there-

---

[v] Luther defends his interpretation of Isaiah xl. 6, 7. by 1. Making Jerome and Erasmus ridiculous. 2. Maintaining Isaiah. 3. Appealing to Erasmus's vain shew of candour and exposing it. 4. Entertaining the cavil ' not all.' 5. Repelling false charges, and charging inconsistencies.

fore, to hear and to will good. Perceiving this, and alarmed at the thought of God's judgment, he begs of him to correct him with judgment, if he must absolutely be corrected; and that he may not be delivered over to the wrath of God, together with the ungodly, whom God suffers to be hardened and to continue in unbelief.

But let us suppose however, that this passage is to be understood as speaking of prosperous and adverse events: what if this very gloss should most effectually subvert Freewill? This new evasion is invented, it is true, in order that persons unpractised and unskilled in falsehood may fancy they have received a satisfactory explanation of the text—the same sort of trick which is practised in the attempt to evade the necessity of a consequence. They do not see that they are so much the more ensnared and entrapped by these evasions, than by the plain meaning of the words; so misled are they by these new terms! Why, if the event of temporal concerns and transactions, over which man is constituted lord and master (Genesis i.), be not under our own control; how shall that celestial substance, the grace of God, which is dependent upon the will of God alone, be under our control? Can the effort of Freewill obtain eternal salvation, when it cannot keep the printer's dagger, or even a hair of one's head in its place? Have we no power to get possession of the creature, and shall we have[x] power to get possession of the Creator? Why are we so mad? For a man to strive after good or evil, implies by far the greatest degree of mastery over events;[y] because, whichsoever of the two he be striving after, he is much more liable to be deceived, and has less

---

[x] For objections to this distinction, see above, Part i. Sect. xxv. note [1].

[y] *Pertinet igitur*] More literally, ' It most of all pertains to events, that a man strive,' &c.

liberty, than whilst he is striving after money, or glory, or pleasure. What an exquisite escape, then, hath thy gloss effected? which, whilst it denies man's freedom in paltry creature events, proclaims it in the high events of God.* As if you shall say, Codrus cannot pay half a crown, but he can pay millions of guineas. I am surprised too, that Diatribe, who has so persecuted that saying of Wickliff's hitherto, 'all things happen by *necessity*,' should now of her own accord concede, that events are necessary to us.*

'Besides, if you force it never so much, says she, that it may bear upon the subject of Freewill, does not every body confess that no one can maintain an upright course of life without the grace of God? Still however, we strive in the mean while ourselves also, according to our ability; inasmuch as we pray daily, "O Lord my God, direct my way in thy sight." He who sues for help does not lay aside endeavour.'

Diatribe thinks it does not signify a straw what she answers; provided she be not silent, but say something. Having done so, she would be thought to have satisfied every body; so confident is she in her own authority.—The thing to be

---

^z *Creatis eventibus. divinis eventibus.*] Luther has said (see, as at note ˣ), that a dominion has been given to man over the inferior creatures, in the exercise of which he would not object to its being said that he has Freewill. There are creature-events therefore, and God-events; that is, events which are conversant with creatures only, and events which are conversant with God also: these, in which he has to deal with creatures, are of small moment with respect to those in which he has to deal with the Creator. Temporal prosperity is of the former; salvation is of the latter.—I deny the justness of the distinction; and must allow, that we have rather too much of the gladiator in this paragraph. Luther's defence of his text is correct; but to give his adversary another thrust when he is fallen, he goes into refinements which will not stand. Doubtless, spiritual things are higher than temporal things, but each is under the sole dominion of God.

^a See Part iii. Sect. xliv. note ^m.

TEXTS AGAINST FREEWILL MAINTAINED. 357

proved was, whether we strive by means of our own strength; the thing she proves is, that she endeavours something by praying. Is she mocking us, pray? Is she making fun of the Papists? He who prays, prays by means of the Spirit; nay, the Spirit himself prays in us. (Rom. viii. 26.) How is the power of Freewill proved by the endeavour of the Holy Spirit? Is Freewill the same thing as the Holy Spirit in Diatribe's account? Are we at present discussing what the power of the Spirit is? Diatribe leaves me this passage of Jeremiah, therefore, untouched and unconquerable; and only produces this gloss of her own brain, ' We also strive with our own strength;' and Luther is obliged to believe her— if he pleases.[b]

So again, she maintains that the saying in Proverbs xvi. " The preparation of the heart is man's, the government of the tongue is the Lord's;" belongs also to events.

As if we should be satisfied with this *ipse dixit* of hers, and require no other authority! And it is answer more than enough surely, that, if we even grant this to be its meaning, which applies it to events, clearly the victory is mine; according to what I said last: since Freewill is nothing in our own works and events, much more is it nothing in the works and events of God.'[c]

But observe how sharp she is: ' How can it be man's work to prepare the heart, when Luther affirms that every thing is done by necessity?'

I reply; ' Since events are not in our own power, as you acknowledge; how can it be man's work to bring matters to their issue? Take for

SECT. XLVII.

Prov.xvi.1. defended.

---

[b] Luther's order is, 1. To repel Diatribe's gloss. 2. To shew the folly and inconsistency of it, if admitted. 3. To confound Diatribes's confusion. The proof which the text yields is broad and palpable, and only loses force by allowing that it may allow a cavil.
[c] See last section.

PART IV. my answer the answer which you have given me.
Nay verily, we must work especially on this account, because all future things are to us uncertain: as the Preacher says, "In the morning sow thy seed, and in the evening withhold not thine hand, because thou knowest not whether this or that shall spring up." To us, I say, they are uncertain as to knowledge, but necessary as to event. Their necessity inspires us with that fear of God, which is our antidote against presumption and security; whilst their uncertainty begets a confidence, which fortifies our minds against despair.

SECT. XLVIII.

Much in Proverbs for Freewill.

But she returns to her old song, 'that in the book of Proverbs many things are said in favour of Freewill;' such as this, 'Confess thy works unto the Lord.' Dost thou hear, says she? *thy* works.—That is, there are many imperative and conjunctive verbs in that book and many pronouns in the second person: for by such supporters Freewill is proved. As for instance, '"confess;" therefore thou canst confess: "thy works;" therefore thou doest them.' So that saying, '"I am thy God," you will understand to mean, "thou makest me thy God." "Thy faith hath made thee whole;" dost thou hear? "*thy* faith." Expound thus, "thou makest thyself to have faith." And now you have proved Freewill.—I am not mocking here, but shewing that Diatribe is not in earnest, when pleading this cause.

Prov. xvi. 4.

"That saying in the same chapter, "The Lord hath made all things for himself; even the wicked for the day of evil," she absolutely moulds into a new shape by words of her own; urging in excuse for God, that he hath not *made* any creature evil.[d]

As if I spoke of creation, and not rather of that constant operation of God upon things created, by

---

[d] See Part iv. Sect. x. note z.

which God actuates even the wicked; as I have already said about Pharaoh. God makes the wicked man, not by creating evil, or an evil creature, which is impossible; but the seed being corrupted upon which God operates, an evil man is made or created, not by the fault of the Maker, but through the corruptness of the material.

Nor has that saying from the twentieth chapter any efficacy in her view, "The heart of the king is in the hand of the Lord; he inclineth it whithersoever he will." It is not necessary, says she, that he who inclines compel.

As if we were speaking about compulsion, and not rather about a necessity of immutability. By God's inclining of the heart is meant, not that sleepy lazy thing which Diatribe pretends, but that most efficacious operation of God, which the man cannot avoid or change; and by which he necessarily has such a will as God hath given to him, and such a will as God hurries along with his own motion. I have spoken to this point already.[e]

Besides, since Solomon speaks of the *king's* heart, Diatribe thinks that this text is improperly drawn to express a general sentiment; but that it means what Job says in another place, "He maketh a hypocrite to reign for the sins of the people." Job xxxiii. 30. At length she concedes that the king is moved by God to evil, but in some such way as this; 'God suffering the king to be driven by his passions, in order that he may chastise his people.'

I reply; whether God permit or incline, the very act of permitting or inclining arises from the will and operation of God: because the king's will cannot escape the actuation of the omnipotent God; forasmuch as[f] every man's will is

SECT. XLVIII.

Prov. xxi. 1.

---

[e] See above, Sect. xi. note [h].
[f] *Quia.*] I should have liked *quâ* instead of *quia*, if there had been any authority for it.—For the principle maintained, see above, Sect. xi. and note [h].

PART IV. hurried on by him to will and to do, whether it be good or evil. As to my having made a general proposition out of the particular one about the *king's* will; I have done so, as I imagine, neither unseasonably, nor unwisely. For if the king's heart, which seems to be especially free and to have lordship over others, cannot however will otherwise than God shall have inclined it; how much less can any of the rest of men do so? And this same consequence would stand good, not only with respect to the king's will, but also with respect to any man's will. For if one man, however private, cannot will before God^g except as God inclines him, the same must be said of all men. So the fact that Balaam could not speak what he pleased, is an evident proof, contained in the Scriptures, that man is not the free chooser, or doer, of his own law,^h or work: else there would be no such thing as examples in the Scriptures.ⁱ

SECT. XLIX.

John xv. 5. maintained.

After this, having affirmed that many testimonies, such as Luther collects from this book of Proverbs, might indeed be brought together, but they would be such as by a commodious interpretation might be made to stand up *for* Freewill, as well as *against* it; she at length adduces that Achillean and inevitable lance of Luther's from

^g *Coram Deo.*] Referring, I suppose, to the former distinction about divine and created events; as if there were some acts in which God left us at liberty. See above, Sect. xxxi. note ^a.
^h *Sui juris.*] '*Jus* (a jubeo, ut quidam volunt) est universim id quod legibus constitutum est, sive naturalibus, sive divinis, vel gentium, vel civilibus.' 'The law or rule, which he prescribes to himself for the regulation of his conduct.' Hence the expression ' sui juris esse,' i. e. ' liberum esse, suique arbitrii.' ' Ut esset sui juris ac mancipii respublica.'—Cic.
ⁱ Luther defends his quotations from Proverbs, and withdraws the chorus from Erasmus's old song, by 1. Necessity does not preclude human agency, but quickens it. 2. They are imperative and conjunctive verbs. 3. Nature of God's making and operating, in the wicked. 4. The king's heart furnishes an 'à fortiori,' but any man's heart will do.

TEXTS AGAINST FREEWILL MAINTAINED.

John xv. "Without me ye can do nothing." &c. &c. &c.

SECT. XLIX.

I too commend the skill of this exquisite orator of Freewill, in teaching us, first of all, to shape the testimonies of Scripture by convenient interpretations, as seemeth good to our own minds, so that they may in reality stand up for Freewill; that is, may make out, not what they ought to do, but what we please; and then pretending to have such a great dread of one in particular which she calls Achillean, that the stupid reader may hold the rest in exquisite contempt when this has been vanquished. But I shall look sharp after this magniloquous and heroic Diatribe, to see what force it is of hers, by which she gets the better of my Achilles; when she has not yet hit a single common soldier—no not even a Thersites—but has destroyed herself most miserably by her own weapons.

So then, she lays hold of this little word 'nothing,' and slays it by the aid of many words and many examples; dragging it to this result by a commodious interpretation, that 'nothing' may be the same as small and imperfect: that is, she holds forth in other words what the Sophists have heretofore taught thus on this passage—"without me ye can do nothing;" that is, nothing perfectly. Such is the power of her rhetoric, that she contrives to make this gloss, which has now for a long time been stale and mouse-eaten, appear like something new; and insists upon it in such a way, that you might think she has been the first to bring it forwards, that it never was heard of before, and that it is little less than a miracle which she is exhibiting in the production of it. Meanwhile, she is quite careless and thoughtless about the text itself, and its fore and after context; from which the knowledge of it is to be sought: not to mention that her aim is to

What 'nothing' means.

PART IV. hurried on by him to will and to do, whether it be good or evil. As to my having made a general proposition out of the particular one about the *king's* will; I have done so, as I imagine, neither unseasonably, nor unwisely. For if the king's heart, which seems to be especially free and to have lordship over others, cannot however will otherwise than God shall have inclined it; how much less can any of the rest of men do so? And this same consequence would stand good, not only with respect to the king's will, but also with respect to any man's will. For if one man, however private, cannot will before God[g] except as God inclines him, the same must be said of all men. So the fact that Balaam could not speak what he pleased, is an evident proof, contained in the Scriptures, that man is not the free chooser, or doer, of his own law,[h] or work: else there would be no such thing as examples in the Scriptures.[i]

SECT. XLIX.

John xv. 5. maintained.

After this, having affirmed that many testimonies, such as Luther collects from this book, of Proverbs, might indeed be brought together, but they would be such as by a commodious interpretation might be made to stand up *for* Freewill, as well as *against* it; she at length adduces that Achillean and inevitable lance of Luther's from

[g] *Coram Deo.*] Referring, I suppose, to the former distinction about divine and created events; as if there were some acts in which God left us at liberty. See above, Sect. xxxi. note [a].

[h] *Sui juris.*] '*Jus* (a jubeo, ut quidam volunt) est universim id quod legibus constitutum est, sive naturalibus, sive divinis, vel gentium, vel civilibus.' 'The law or rule, which he prescribes to himself for the regulation of his conduct.' Hence the expression 'sui juris esse,' i. e. 'liberum esse, suique arbitrii.' 'Ut esset sui juris ac mancipii respublicæ.'—Cic.

[i] Luther defends his quotations from Proverbs, and withdraws the chorus from Erasmus's old song, by 1. Necessity does not preclude human agency, but quickens it. 2. They are imperative and conjunctive verbs. 3. Nature of God's making and operating, in the wicked. 4. The king's heart furnishes an 'à fortiori,' but any man's heart will do.

John xv. "Without me ye can do nothing." &c. &c. &c.

I too commend the skill of this exquisite orator of Freewill, in teaching us, first of all, to shape the testimonies of Scripture by convenient interpretations, as seemeth good to our own minds, so that they may in reality stand up for Freewill; that is, may make out, not what they ought to do, but what we please; and then pretending to have such a great dread of one in particular which she calls Achillean, that the stupid reader may hold the rest in exquisite contempt when this has been vanquished. But I shall look sharp after this magniloquous and heroic Diatribe, to see what force it is of hers, by which she gets the better of my Achilles; when she has not yet hit a single common soldier—no not even a Thersites—but has destroyed herself most miserably by her own weapons.

So then, she lays hold of this little word 'nothing,' and slays it by the aid of many words and many examples; dragging it to this result by a commodious interpretation, that 'nothing' may be the same as small and imperfect: that is, she holds forth in other words what the Sophists have heretofore taught thus on this passage—"without me ye can do nothing;" that is, nothing perfectly. Such is the power of her rhetoric; that she contrives to make this gloss, which has now for a long time been stale and mouse-eaten, appear like something new; and insists upon it in such a way, that you might think she has been the first to bring it forwards, that it never was heard of before, and that it is little less than a miracle which she is exhibiting in the production of it. Meanwhile, she is quite careless and thoughtless about the text itself, and its fore and after context; from which the knowledge of it is to be sought: not to mention that her aim is to

SECT. XLIX.

What 'nothing' means.

PART IV. shew; by so many words and examples, how 'this word 'nothing' *may* be taken here for 'something small and imperfect;' as 'if,' forsooth, we were disputing about what might be—when the thing to be proved is, whether it ought to be taken, so. The whole of her magnificent interpretation therefore amounts but to this, if to any thing, that this passage of John's is made uncertain and ambiguous: and what wonder, when it is Diatribe's one and alone object, to make out that the Scriptures are every where ambiguous, lest she should be compelled to use them;[k] that the testimonies of the Fathers are decisive, that she may have liberty to abuse them! Strange reverence for God this, which makes His words useless, and man's words profitable!

SECT. L. But the finest thing of all is to see how consistent she is with herself. "Nothing" may be taken for "a little." And in this sense, says she, it is most true that we can do nothing without Christ: for he speaks of Gospel fruit, which befals none but those who are abiding in the Vine; that is, Christ.

Inconsistency charged.

Here, she confesses herself that fruit befals none but those who abide in the Vine; and this she does, in that self-same commodious interpretation by which she proves that 'nothing' means the same with 'small and imperfect.' Perhaps we ought also to interpret the adverb 'not' commodiously, so as to signify that gospel fruit befals men out of Christ in some measure, or in a small and imperfect degree; hereby announcing that ungodly men, without Christ, with the devil reigning in them and fighting against Christ, may yield

[k] *Uti. abuti.*] *Ut.* 'To use according to its real nature.' *Abut.* 'To use contrary to the nature, or first intention of a thing, whether for the better or worse.' The Scripture is authority; she will not use it. The Fathers *are not* authority; she will use them as though they were.

TEXTS AGAINST FREEWILL MAINTAINED.

some portion of the fruits of life; in other words, the enemies of Christ may act for Christ. But no more of this.

I should like to be informed here, how heretics are to be resisted, who shall avail themselves of this law every where in their interpretations of the Scriptures, and insist upon understanding 'nothing' and 'not' to denote an imperfect substance. As 'without him was nothing made;' that is, 'very little.' 'The fool hath said in his heart there is no God;' that is, 'God is imperfect.' 'He hath made us and not we ourselves;' that is, we made 'a very little' of ourselves. And who can number the passages of Scripture in which the words 'nothing' and 'not' occur? Shall we say here, the suitableness of the interpretation is to be looked at. What heretic does not account his own interpretation suitable? What this, I suppose, is an untying of knots, to open such a window of licence to corrupted minds and deceiving spirits![1] To you who make havoc of the certainty of sacred Scripture, I can readily believe that such a licence of interpretation would be commodious: but to us who are labouring to settle the consciences of men, nothing can arise of a more inconvenient, a more hurtful, a more pestilent nature than this commodiousness which you recommend. Hear thou therefore, mighty conqueress of Luther's Achilles; except thou shalt have proved that 'nothing' in this place, not only *may* but *must* be taken for 'a little;' thou shalt get nothing by all this multitude of words and of examples, but that thou hast been fighting fire with dry stubble. What have I to do with thy 'may be;' when thou art required to prove that it 'must be?' Until thou shalt have done this, I stand fast in the natural and grammatical

Advantage given to heretics.

[1] *Corruptis. fallacibus.*] *Cor.* expresses the state of the receiver; *fal.* the wilfulness of the false prophets: we have the tinder ready, and they strike the spark.

PART IV.

More inconsistencies &c.

signification of the word, laughing at thy armies, no less than at thy triumphs!

What is now become of that approvable opinion, which declares that Freewill can will nothing good? But perhaps the principle of commodious interpretation hath arrived here at last, making out that 'nothing good,' means ' something good,' by an altogether unheard of art both of grammar and of logic which explains ' nothing' to mean the same with ' something;' what logicians would account an impossibility, since they are contradictory? What becomes of the assertion, that we believe Satan to be the prince of this world, reigning according to Christ and Paul, in the wills and minds of men, which are his captives and serve him? Will that roaring lion forsooth, the implacable and restless enemy of the grace of God and of man's salvation, suffer it to come to pass, that man, who is his slave and a part of his kingdom, should endeavour after good, by any motion towards it, at any moment, that he may escape his tyranny? Would he not rather incite and urge him, both to will and to do what is contrary to grace, with all his might? The righteous, who act under the influence of the divine Spirit, hardly resist him, so as to will and to do what is good; such is his rage against them.

You who feign that the human will is a thing placed in a free medium, and left to itself, have no difficulty in feigning at the same time, that the effort of the will is towards either side; because you imagine both God and the devil to be afar off as mere spectators of this mutable and free will, and do not believe that they are impellers and agitators of this bond will of ours; each of them most determined warriors on the side on which he acts. Believe this fact only, and our sentiment stands in full strength, with Freewill laid prostrate at its feet: as I have already shewn.

TEXTS AGAINST FREEWILL MAINTAINED.

For, either the kingdom of Satan is a mere nothing in men, and so Christ is a liar: or, if his kingdom be such as Christ describes it to be, Freewill is nothing but Satan's captive packhorse, which cannot have freedom, unless the devil be first of all cast out by the finger of God.

'Thou perceivest from hence, my Diatribe, what it is, and of what power, which thy author in detestation of Luther's positiveness of assertion is wont to say, ' Luther drives on his cause with a mighty force of Scripture, but all his Scripture is pulled to pieces by one little word?'[m] Who does not know that the whole body of Scripture might be pulled to pieces by one little word? We knew this well enough, even before we had ever heard the name of Erasmus. But the question is, whether it be satisfactory that the Scripture should be pulled to pieces by a little word? The matter in dispute is, whether it be rightly pulled to pieces thus, and whether it *must* be pulled to pieces thus. Let a man direct his view to this point, and he will see how easy it is to pull the Scriptures to pieces, and how detestable is Luther's positiveness. But the truth is, he will see that it is not a parcel of little words, nor yet all the gates of hell that can do any thing towards accomplishing this object.

Let us then do what Diatribe cannot for her affirmative, and, though we have no business to do so, let us prove our negative; extorting by force of argument the concession, that the word 'nothing' here not only *may*, but *must* be taken to signify not 'a little,' but what it naturally expresses. This I will do by arguments additional to that invincible one which has already given me victory; namely, that words ought to be kept to

SECT. LI.

Luther proves the negative.

---

[m] *Uno verbulo*] Alluding to this little word 'nothing,' I suppose. All Luther's force, he would say, is in this Achillean lance; which we break by our interpretation of the word 'nothing.'

PART IV.
―――
1. From the nature of the case.

their natural meaning, unless the contrary shall have been demonstrated:[n] which Diatribe neither has done, nor can do here.—First then, I extort this concession from the very nature of the case. It has been proved by testimonies of Scripture, which are neither ambiguous nor obscure, that Satan is by far the most powerful and most crafty prince of the princes of this world;[o] as I have said: under whose reign the human will, which is now no longer free, and its own master, but the slave of sin and Satan, cannot will any thing but what this prince of hers shall be pleased to let her will. Nor will he suffer her to will any thing good: albeit, if Satan did not rule her, sin itself, whose servant man is, would be a sufficient clog upon her to prevent her willing good.[p]

2 From the sequel of the parable.

Secondly, the very sequel of the discourse—which Diatribe in her valour despises,[q] although I had commented upon it very copiously in my assertions—extorts the same concession. For Christ goes on thus in John xv. "If a man abide not in me; he is cast out as a branch, and he withereth, and they gather him up, and cast him into the fire, and he burneth." These words, I say, Diatribe acting the part of a most profound rhetorician has passed over; in hopes that this transition would be incomprehensible to such unlettered readers as the Lutherans. But you

[n] See above, Sect. iii.
[o] *Longè potentiss. et callidiss. mundi*] There is a little ambiguity in the expression; but he clearly means to compare the devil with other earthly Princes.
[p] Luther speaks as others speak; leaving it to be imagined, that sin is a substance, and has a real and positive existence. (See above, Sect. xi. note [b].) The more correct statement is, 'the human soul is itself a substance sinful and devilish; and would remain so—*willing* according to its nature—if Satan and his agency were withdrawn from it.
[q] *Fortiter contemnit.*] The taunt is obscure; but I understand it to insinuate, that Diatribe has a good deal of that 'better part of valour, which is discretion.'

perceive that Christ, becoming himself the interpreter of his own simile of the branch and the vine here, most expressly declares what he would have to be understood by the word 'Nothing;' namely, that a man out of Christ is cast forth and withereth. And what else can this being cast forth and withering mean, but that he is delivered over to the dominion of the devil, and is continually made worse? But to grow worse and worse is not to have power, or to endeavour. The withering branch is made more and more ready for the burning, the more it withereth. If Christ had not thus opened and applied this simile, nobody would have dared to open and apply it so. It is established therefore, that the word 'Nothing' *must* be taken literally here, according to its natural import.'

Let us now look also into the examples by which she proves that 'nothing' is in some places taken for 'a little;' in order to shew, that in this part of her argumentation also Diatribe *is* nothing, and *effects* nothing. Yet, if she had even proved

SECT. LI.

3. By refuting Diatribe's examples.

r I should rather rest the conclusion upon the scope and train of the parable, than upon the interpretation of the figures in any one verse: a good general rule for the interpretation of parables. We may overstrain parts; but we cannot be wrong in seizing the general outline, and maintaining the broad principle which is illustrated; where that can be distinctly ascertained.—Perhaps I should not interpret this parable just as Luther does. I consider it as a representation of the *visible* church; exhibiting two sorts of members, fruitful and unfruitful. The fruitful only are Christ's true ones; and their fruitfulness is dependent altogether upon a real, continued and unobstructed union with himself. It is with reference to their continuance in him, that this *nothingness* is spoken of. Should they be cut off from him—suppose them to have been never so fruitful—(thus the parable speaks) their fruitfulness would cease—entirely cease. Both the end and the way require that the *nothing* be an *absolute nothing*.—Luther cannot state the result of nonunion, or dis-union, more awfully than I would do; but I should question the parable's setting this out with the minuteness which he assigns to it, and do not see it necessary to the conclusion he is sustaining. It is quite enough that the disunited branch is a cast-away waiting for the burning.

PART IV. something here, she would have effected nothing; such a perfect nothing is she, in all her parts and in all her means.[s] 'It is a common saying (she avers) that a man does nothing, if he does not obtain what he seeks after; but still, the man who endeavours frequently makes some way towards his object.'

I reply, I never heard that this is a common saying; you take the liberty of imagining so. Words (so far as they give names to things[t]) must be considered according to the subject matter, and with relation to the intention of the speaker. Now a man never calls that 'nothing,' which he *endeavours* when in action; nor does he speak of his endeavour when he talks about 'nothing,' but of the effect: this is what a man is looking at, when he says '*that* man does nothing, or effects nothing;' that is, 'he has not reached his point, he has not obtained.'—Besides, if your instance proves any thing (which however is not the case), it makes more for me than for you. For this is the very point I am maintaining, and wishing to get proved; that Freewill does many things, which are but nothing in the sight of God.[u] What is the use of her endeavouring, if she does not gain what she seeks?—So that, let Diatribe turn which way she will, she founders and confutes herself, as is usually the case with advocates pleading a bad cause.

Thus again, she is unhappy in her instance

[s] *Per omnia et omnibus modis.*] *Per omn.* the several parts of her argument. *Omn. mod.* the materials of each. Her arguments would not prove her point, if they were sound; but they are not so.

[t] *Verba, ut vocant.*] *Ut voc.* i. e. ' quatenus vocabula sunt, sive dictiones quibus res singulæ vocantur, aut voce efferuntur.'

[u] *Coram Deo.*] Erasmus says, nothing means a little; and so men speak of their performances. Luther replies, this is said of the effect, not of the act: but if it be said of the act, this proves for me: doing, he does not; for in the sight of God his work is nothing. *Coram Deo,* in a former instance (see above, Sect. xxxi. note [a]), referred to God's presence as an agent; here refers to it as a spectator.

which she adduces from Paul, "Neither is he that planteth any thing, nor he that watereth, but God that giveth the increase." What is of very little moment, and useless of itself, he calls 'nothing;' says she.

"Who is this? What you, Diatribe, call the ministry of the word useless of itself, and of small moment; that ministry which Paul extols with such great praises both every where else, and especially in 2 Cor. iii. where he calls it the ministration of life and the ministration of glory?—Again you are guilty of neither considering the subject matter, nor the intention of the speaker. With respect to giving the increase, the planter and the waterer are nothing; but with respect to planting and watering they are not 'nothing:' it being the chief work of the Spirit in the church of God to teach and to exhort. Paul means this, and his words very clearly express this. But granting that this inapplicable example also applies, it again, like the other, will stand on my side. For I am maintaining, that Freewill is nothing—that is, useless—of itself, as you explain this text, before God: for it is of this kind of existence that we speak, well knowing that the ungodly will is 'a something,' and not 'a mere nothing.'ᵛ

So again, with regard to that saying in 1 Cor. xiii. "If I have not charity, I am nothing." I do not see why she adduces this example, except it be that she is in quest of number and multitude, or thinks that we are in want of arms with which to dispatch her. For the man who has not charity is truly and strictly 'nothing' before God. I

ᵛ *Merum nihil*] Erasmus applies this text to the acts of ministering the word, whereas it belongs to the effect of that ministry. But be it, that it illustrates the agency of the free will under the ministry, without grace, this agency is nothing in the sight of God, though not an absolute nothing in itself—This conclusion however is drawn from a double misapplication of the text: it is act, instead of effect; and it is act of the hearer, not of the speaker.

2 B

PART IV. maintain the same thing with respect to Freewill. So that this example also stands up for me against Diatribe herself, unless it be that Diatribe is even yet ignorant what our ground of battle is.[x] We are not speaking of an existence of nature; but of an existence of grace, as they call it. We know that Freewill performs certain natural acts; that she eats, and drinks, and begets children, and rules the house. So that Diatribe might have forborne to mock us with that nonsensical saying, which is like the ramble of a delirium, 'that a man cannot even sin, without Christ,' if we insist upon this word 'nothing;' whereas even Luther admits that Freewill has a power of committing sin, though it hath no other!—The wise Diatribe, you see, must have her joke even upon a serious subject.—What we affirm is, that man without the grace of God still remains under the control of the general omnipotency of God, who performs, who moves, who carries away all things by a necessary and infallible course; but what the man so carried away does, is "nothing"—that is, availeth nothing before God, and is accounted nothing but sin. Thus—with regard to a being of grace—he is nothing who hath not charity.— Why then does Diatribe, after confessing of her own accord that we are in this place treating of evangelical fruit, which is not produced without Christ, here in an instant turn aside from the question at issue, begin a strange song, and cavil about natural operations and human fruits? Why—but that a man destitute of the truth, is never any where consistent with himself?[y]

John iii. 27.

So again, that saying in John iii. " A man can

---

[x] *Quo loco pugnemus.*] The same with 'status causæ;' the question at issue.

[y] We are reasoning about 'existence of grace,' or 'existence before God,' and her argument is about mere natural existence; which is absolute; when she has even avowed the distinction which makes the difference.

receive nothing, except it be given him from heaven."

John speaks of a man, who was something assuredly already, and denies that this man receives any thing; that is to say, the Spirit with his gifts: for it is of this, and not of nature, that he speaks.[z] He had no need of Diatribe's instructions, surely, to teach him that the man already had eyes, nose, ears, mouth, mind, will, reason, and all the other properties of a man. Perhaps Diatribe thinks that when the Baptist spoke of a man, he was so mad as to be thinking of Plato's chaos, or Leucippus's vacuum, or Aristotle's infinite, or some other 'nothing,' which was at last to be made 'something' by a gift from heaven! What, it is bringing examples from Scripture, purposely to make sport in this way upon so weighty a subject!—To what purpose is it then, that she brings forwards such a redundancy of material, by way of teaching us that fire, escape from evil, effort towards good, and the rest, proceed from heaven; as if any man knew

---

[z] *De hoc enim*] We shall see hereafter, that Luther is mistaken in his view of this text, but the conclusion remains: the 'nothing' is distinct from natural endowments.—Plato's chaos is that ' rudis indigestaque moles,' out of which, ' being itself eternal,' he taught that the eternal God, according to an eternal draught or model in his own mind, had, in his own appointed time, created the world—Leucippus of Abdera, A. c 428. was the first who invented the famous system of atoms and a void, which was afterwards more fully explained by Democritus and Epicurus. The void was nothing, till the infinity of eternal atoms rushed into it by a blind and rapid movement, and thus settled into a world.—Aristotle's 'infinite' is his 'first moveable' eternally put into motion by his 'first Mover,' and made to be what it is, at its one first projection, by Him. There is not much of essential difference therefore between Plato's chaos, Leucippus's vacuum, and Aristotle's infinite. they are each a name for some supposed state in which the world that now is subsisted antecedently to its present one.—For some account of Plato, see Preface; see also Part ii Sect. v note [u], where I have followed Seneca's account of his term 'idea.'—For some account of Aristotle, see Part iv. Sect. viii. note [r].

PART IV.

SECT. LIII.

Diatribe's troop of

not, or denied this? I am speaking of grace; or, as she has herself expressed it, of Christ and gospel fruit: but she meanwhile chatters away about nature, that she may get time, protract the cause, and throw dust in the eyes of the unlearned reader. With all this however, she not only fails in adducing a single example of 'nothing' taken for 'a little,' which is what she undertook to do; but even manifestly betrays herself to be one who neither knows, nor cares, what Christ is, or what grace is, or how grace differs from nature: a distinction which the very rudest of the Sophists knew, and beat out in their schools by commonest use.[a] Nor is she in the least aware, at the same time, that 'all her examples make *for* me and *against* herself. Even this saying of the Baptist—" A man can receive nothing except it be given him from heaven "—proves that Freewill is nothing. This is the way to conquer my Achilles—Diatribe puts arms into his hands with which to destroy her in her nakedness and defencelessness. Thus it is, that those Scriptures, by which the inflexible dogmatist Luther drives all before him, are scattered by a single wordling.[b]

After this she details[c] a great many similes; by which all she does is to carry off the foolish

[a] *Detriverunt.*] A figure taken from threshing, or more properly from treading out the pure grain with the feet· " Thou shalt not muzzle the mouth of the ox that treadeth out the corn." Possibly he may have a squift at the name of Diatribe, in his use of this term, ' even the Sophists have trodden the floor· of their schools' to better purpose than she. See Introduction, p. 3, note [a].

[b] Luther maintains his Achillean lance, by 1. Exposing the staleness, unaptness, and unauthorizedness of the evasion which Diatribe proposes. 2. The dangerous conclusions which may be extorted from her concessions. 3 Impossibility of realizing what is thus ascribed to Freewill. 4. 'Nothing' cannot mean 'a little' in this text. 5. Does not in any of the texts which she adduces.

[c] *Enumerat* implies ' the number in full tale '—an ostentatious display of numbers.

reader, as her manner is, into foreign matters, herself meanwhile quite forgetting her cause. As for instance; God preserves the ship it is true, but still the mariner conducts it into port; so that the mariner does something. It is a *distinct* work forsooth, which this simile ascribes to God on the one hand—that of preserving—and to the mariner on the other, that of guiding into port. Besides, if it proves any thing, it proves that the whole work of preserving is God's; the whole work of guiding, the seaman's. But still, it is an exquisite and apt simile!^d

Marginal note: SECT. LIII. similes naught, and against her.— What she ought to have spoken to.

So the husbandman carries the productions of the earth into his barns, but God has given them. Here again, distinct works are ascribed to God and to man; unless she chooses to make the husbandman creator at the same time, and so even joint-giver of the fruits. But let the same works moreover be assigned to God and to man by these similes, what is the amount of them, but that the creature cooperates with the operating God? Are we now disputing about cooperation then? Are we not disputing, rather, about the several force and operation of Freewill? What a flight is this! The orator was to have spoken about a palm tree, but he has talked only of a gourd. A cask was to be turned, why comes there out a pitcher?^e

I also know, that Paul works together with God in teaching the Corinthians; himself preaching without, whilst God teaches within: where the work of the two operators is a different one. In like manner, he also works together with God, when he speaks in the Spirit of God.: and the work is the same. For this is what I assert and maintain, that God, when he works without the

^d There is a double failure in the comparion. the works are two; and the agent in each, one.

^e Hor. Art Poet. v. 22.—I do not find any *classical* allusion for the gourd.

confines of the grace of his Spirit, worketh all in all, even in the wicked; seeing that he, the alone maker of all things, doth also alone move, drive and carry away all things, by the motion of his omnipotency: which they cannot escape or change, but do necessarily follow and obey; each according to the measure of its own power, which God hath given to it. So true is it, that even all wickednesses[f] do work together with him. Again; when he acts by the Spirit of grace in those whom he hath made righteous—that is, in his own kingdom—he in like manner drives and moves them; and they—seeing that they are new creatures—do follow and work together with him; or rather, as Paul says, they are *led* by him.—But this was not the place for these things. Our question is not, what we can do when God worketh, but what we can do, of ourselves; that is, whether, when now created out of nothing, we can do or endeavour any thing, through that general motion of omnipotency, towards preparing ourselves for the new creation of his Spirit? This question should have been answered, instead of turning us aside towards another. For we answer this question, and our answer is this: like as man, before he is created to be a man, does nothing and endeavours nothing towards making himself a creature; and afterwards, when he has been made and created, does nothing and endeavours nothing towards continuing himself in being as a creature; but each of these events takes place by the alone will of the omnipotent might and goodness of God, who creates and preserves us without ourselves, but does not work in us without ourselves— seeing we are those whom he hath created and preserved for this very end, that he may work in us, and we may work together with him; whether this be without the confines of his kingdom

---

[f] *Omnia etiam impia.*] 'All wicked substances.' men and devils.

by the acting of his general omnipotency, or within the confines of that kingdom by the special power of his Spirit—so (we go on to say) man, before he is renewed to become a new creature of the kingdom of the Spirit, does nothing, endeavours nothing, towards preparing himself for that renewal and kingdom; and afterwards, when he has been created anew, does nothing, endeavours nothing, towards continuing himself in that kingdom; but the Spirit alone doeth each of these things in us, both creating us anew without ourselves and preserving us when so created—as James also says, "Of his own will begat he us by the word of his power, that we might be the beginning of his creation;" speaking of the renewed creation.[g] Still he does not work in us without ourselves; seeing we are those whom he hath created anew and doth preserve, to this very end, that he might work in us, and that we might work together with him.[h] Thus, he preaches by us, has pity on the poor by us, comforts the afflicted by us. But what is hereby ascribed to Freewill? rather, what is left to it, but 'nothing;' absolute nothing?

"Read the Diatribe in this part for five or six leaves together, and you will find that all she does is, first by lugging in similes of this sort, and afterwards by citing some of the most beautiful passages and parables from Paul's writings and from the Gospels, to teach us that *innumerable* texts (as she expresses it) are to be found in the Scriptures, which declare the cooperation and helping gifts of God. Now, if I collect from these testimonies,

SECT. LIV.

Inconsistency and audacity of Diatribe— takes up one subject and pursues another— argues by inversion.

[g] *Renovata creatura.*] Sometimes called 'the new creation;' but with less propriety: this new is all made out of the old; which 'new' does not imply, but 'renewed' does.

[h] *Cooperaremur.*] The cooperation in both cases consists in our acting concurrently with God, according to our nature: God, by his own agency, calls out our faculties such as they are, whether natural or renewed, into act and exercise. it is *by*, and not *without*, our faculties that he 'moves, drives and hurries us along.'

PART IV. that man can do nothing without the helping grace of God, therefore no works of man are good; she, on the contrary, using a rhetorical inversion, concludes 'Nay rather, there is nothing which man cannot do with the assistance of God's grace, therefore all man's works *may* be good. Well then, as many passages as there are in the word of God, which make mention of divine assistance; so many are there which maintain Freewill. Now there are such without number. I have conquered therefore, if the question be decided by the number of testimonies.' Thus she.—But do you think Diatribe was quite sober, or of sound mind, when she wrote these words?, For I will not impute it to malice and wickedness in her (except so far as she might have a mind perhaps to destroy me by a perpetual tiresomeness), that she preserves such a perfect consistency throughout her whole performance, always handling other topics than those which she proposed to treat. However, if she has delighted herself with talking nonsense on so grave a subject, it shall be my pleasure, in return, to expose to public scorn the absurdities which she has so wantonly promulgated.[1]

First then, I neither make it a question, nor am ignorant, that all the works of man may be good, if they be done with the help of God's grace. Secondly, I neither make it a question, nor am ignorant, that there is nothing which man cannot do, with the help of God's grace. But I cannot sufficiently admire your negligence, that having commenced to write upon the power of Freewill, you should proceed to write on the power of divine grace: having done which, as if all were stocks and stones, you are audacious enough to

---

[1] *Publicè traducere.*] A peculiar use of *traduc.* 'to expose to ridicule or dishonour, to disgrace.' So 'traducit avos.'—Juv. viii. 17. 'Rideris, multòque magis traduceris,'—Martial. 'Miseram traducere calvam.'—Id.

say publicly, that Freewill is established by those passages of Scripture which extol God's helping grace. Not only have you the audacity to do this, but even to sing your own pæan,[k] as a most glorious, triumphing conqueror! I now know experimentally, through this word and deed of yours, what Freewill is, and what her power. 'She is mad.' What can it be in you, pray, which speaks thus; save this very Freewill?

But, mad as you are, hear your own conclusions. Scripture extols the grace of God; therefore Scripture proves Freewill. Scripture extols the help which is derived from God's grace; therefore Scripture establishes Freewill. What art of logic is it pray, from which you have learned these conclusions? Why might it not be just the reverse? Grace is preached, therefore Freewill is exploded. The help which is afforded by grace is extolled, therefore Freewill is destroyed. For to what end is grace conferred? Is it, that the pride of Freewill, who is sufficiently strong of herself, may frolic and sport at a Bacchanalia,[l] tricked out with grace, as a sort of superfluous ornament?—Well then, *I* also will draw an inference by inversion; and, though confessedly no rhetorician, yet with a more solid rhetoric than yours. As many passages as there are in the divine Scriptures which make mention of divine help; so many there are which exclude Freewill. Now there are such without number. If the question is to be decided by numbers then, I have conquered. For wherefore have we need of grace;

[k] *Encomion.*] A Greek derivative; whence our English word 'encomium'. also: applied peculiarly to the laudatory songs which were sung to the praise of the conqueror amidst the tumultuous revels of his Triumph.—See Introd. p. 4.

[l] Feasts in honour of Bacchus; which were not only drunken bouts, but scenes of proud display, to the praise of the glory of man. They imitated the poetical fictions concerning Bacchus; putting on fawn skins, crowning themselves with garlands and personating men distracted.

PART IV. and wherefore is the help of grace conferred; but because Freewill can do nothing, and, as this very Diatribe has affirmed, in that approvable opinion of hers, cannot will good? When grace therefore is extolled, and the help of grace is proclaimed, the impotency of Freewill is in the same instant proclaimed. This is that sound conclusion, and that legitimate consequence, which not even the gates of hell shall overthrow.

SECT. LV.
Here I make an end of maintaining my own texts against Diatribe's confutation of them, that my book may not grow to an immoderate size: the rest (if there be any worth noticing) shall be considered in the assertion of my own sentiment. As to what Erasmus repeats in his Epilogue, that, if our sentiment stand, there are never so many precepts, never so many threatenings, never so many promises all made vain; there is no place left either for merit, or demerit, for reward, or for punishment—then again, that it is difficult to defend the mercy, or even the justice of God, if God condemns those who sin necessarily—and other disagreeable consequences, which have so moved the greatest men as to overthrow them—

I have given an answer to all these considerations already. Nor do I either tolerate, or receive, that golden mean which advises, with good intention, as I am willing to suppose, that we should concede a very small degree of power to Freewill, in order that the inconsistency of Scripture, and the forementioned inconveniences, may the more easily be removed. The truth is, this golden mean neither assists the cause which it is meant to serve, nor gets us any forwarder in the solution of difficulties. Unless you yield the whole and every thing to Freewill, as the Pelagians do, there still remains inconsistency in the Scriptures, merit and reward are excluded, the mercy and justice of God are abrogated, and all those inconveniences which we aim to avoid by allowing a very small and inefficacious power to Freewill remain in force; as I have already shewn. We must therefore come to the extremity of denying Freewill altogether, and referring every thing to God; and then we shall find that the Scriptures are not inconsistent with themselves, and that our inconveniences are either removed or rendered tolerable.

There is one thing, however, which I deprecate, my Erasmus, and that is, your persuading yourself that I plead this cause with more of zeal than of judgment. I cannot endure that I should be charged with such hypocrisy as to think one thing and write another: nor is it true what you write of me, that I have been carried forwards by the heat of self-defence to the point of now for the first time denying Freewill wholly, whereas I had hitherto ascribed something to it. You will not shew this something, I well know, in any of my publications. There are theses and questions of mine extant, in which I have been perpetually asserting, up to this very hour, that Freewill is a nothing, and a matter of mere name; such was the term which I then used about it. Overcome by truth; provoked and compelled by disputation; thus I have been brought to think, and thus I have been brought to write. That I have discussed the matter with a considerable degree of vehemence, if it be a crime, is a crime to which I plead guilty: nay, it is my marvellous joy, that this testimony should be borne to me by the world, in the cause of God. May God himself confirm this testimony in the last day! So shall none be then more blessed than Luther; who is so greatly extolled by the testimony of his own age as one that hath not pleaded the cause of truth sluggishly or deceitfully, but with a high degree, it may be with an excess of vehemence. Then shall I happily escape that judgment spoken of by Jeremiah: Cursed is the man, who doeth the work of the Lord negligently.^m

Now if I shall also seem a little severe upon your Diatribe, you must pardon me. It is not from ill-will to you that I am so: but I have been stirred up to it, by the conviction that you were mightily depressing this cause, which is the cause of Christ, by your authority; whilst your knowledge and the matter you put forthⁿ are not such as to entitle you to any superior consideration.— And then, who has such a command of temper every where, as not in some places to grow warm? Your desire of moderation has made you almost cold as ice in this treatise; but you not unfrequently contrive to hurl fiery and exceeding bitter darts, so as to seem absolutely virulent to your reader, except he regard you with peculiar favour and indulgence. But all this has nothing to do with the cause: we ought to forgive these asperities mutually, seeing we are but men, and nothing different from humanity is found in us.^o

^m *Negligenter.*] Our version says deceitfully, but has negligently in the margin.
ⁿ *Re ipsâ.*] 'The material which he worked up:' as distinguished not only from his name, but from the dress of language which he put upon it.
^o *Nihil humani alienum.*] ' Homo sum, nihil a me humani alienum puto,' has furnished Luther with a sentiment which requires a little correction. As a called child of God he had surely something *in him* more than human.—He only means to make full confession of his humanity—and that another name for sin of all kinds.

PART V.

FREEWILL PROVED TO BE A LIE.

SECTION I.

How Luther proposes to conduct the fight.

We are now arrived at the last part of this treatise, in which, according to promise, I ought to lead out my own forces against Freewill. But I shall not produce them all; for who could do this in a small work, when the whole Scripture is on my side, every point and letter of it. Nor is there any need to do so, since Freewill has already been vanquished and laid prostrate by a twofold victory; vanquished, by my having proved that all is against her, which she thought was for her; vanquished again, by my having shewn that all those proofs which she had a mind to confute remain still invincible. Besides, even if she were not already vanquished, it were enough that she should be prostrated by one or two lances. For what need is there, when an enemy has been slain by some single weapon, to pierce him through and through as he lies dead, with many more. I shall therefore be short now, if the subject will allow me; and out of the vast variety of armies, which I might lead forth into the field, I shall summon two general officers only, with a select portion of their legions: these are Paul and John the Evangelist.

Paul, writing to the Romans, thus enters upon his argument in behalf of the grace of God against Freewill. "The wrath of God, says he,

SECT II.

Rom. i. 18. pro-

PART V.

nounces sentence upon Freewill.

is revealed from heaven upon all ungodliness and unrighteousness of men, who hold the truth in unrighteousness." In these words you hear a general sentence pronounced upon all men, that they are under the wrath of God. What is this else, but that they are worthy of wrath and punishment? He assigns as the cause of this anger, that they do nothing but what is worthy of wrath and punishment; that all, forsooth, are ungodly and unjust, and hold the truth in unrighteousness. Where now is that power of Freewill which endeavours after something good? Paul represents it to be deserving of the wrath of God, and passes sentence upon it as ungodly and unjust. Now that which is ungodly, and deserves wrath, endeavours and hath power, not *for* grace, but *against* it.[a]

Luther will be laughed at here for his carelessness, as not having examined Paul's text sufficiently; and some will say, that Paul does not speak of all men, nor of all their endeavours, in this passage, but only of those who are ungodly and unjust: of those, as his words express it, who detain the truth in unrighteousness; and so it does not follow that all are of this character. Upon which I remark, that, with Paul it is the same thing to say, 'upon all ungodliness of men,' as to say, 'upon the ungodliness of all men;' for Paul *hebraizes* almost every where:[b] so that his meaning is, 'all men are ungodly and unjust, and detain the truth in unrighteousness; therefore all men are worthy of wrath.' Besides, it is not the relative that is used in the Greek text—

---

[a] Luther's argument is, 'Paul declares that wrath is revealed upon "all men." If so, it is revealed upon Freewill.—His labour therefore is to shew that this text means so much.—That it does mean so much is shewn, 1. From the very words. 2. From the preceding context.

[b] *Ebraicatur.*] I should not say 'hebraizes' here; for it is Greek as well as Hebrew—perhaps nearly all languages—thus to speak: grammarians call it Hyperbaton.

FREEWILL PROVED TO BE A LIE. 383

of those who—but the article; as thus, 'The SECT II. wrath of God is revealed upon the ungodliness and injustice of men, detaining *as they do* the truth in unrighteousness.'—So that this is a sort of epithet applied to all men, 'That they detain the truth in unrighteousness:' just as it is an epithet when it is said, 'Our Father which art in heaven;' which might otherwise be expressed thus, 'Our heavenly Father,' or 'Our Father in the heavens.'[c] For the expression is used to distinguish them from those who believe and are godly.

But let these suggestions be frivolous and vain, if the very thread of Paul's argument do not constrain and prove them. He had said just before, "The Gospel is the power of God, unto salvation, to every one that believeth; to the Jew first and also to the Greek." The words here used are not obscure or ambiguous: 'To the Jews and to the

[c] An epithet which implies the reason of the Lord's conduct; and which I should venture to render by '*for that* they detain, &c.' in Latin 'utpote qui;' 'seeing that they are those who, &c.'—I do not agree with Luther in the distinction which he here understands the Apostle to make: I consider him to be speaking strictly of all men, even as he is proceeding to shew that all men without exception are *in their nature state* chargeable with holding the truth in unrighteousness. It is the nature state of man, the state of man without the Gospel, of which the Apostle treats, till he comes to the twenty-first verse of the third chapter. The true connection is, I shall be glad to come to Rome, for I am not ashamed of the Gospel, for that Gospel is the power of God unto salvation; that salvation which all men want; which all men want because the wrath of God is revealed upon all men for their ungodliness; for their ungodliness and unrighteousness, because they hold 'the truth' in unrighteousness, they hold the truth in unrighteousness because God has made himself manifest to them, but they have not dealt with him according to that manifestation. His great charge therefore, which he goes on to maintain against man universally—both Jew and Gentile—considered as yet without the preached Gospel—is, that they hold the truth in unrighteousness— This account of the context does not at all invalidate Luther's application of the text. All he wants is "all men:" and this he clearly has.

Greeks—that is, to all men—the Gospel of the power of God is necessary, in order that believers may be saved from the wrath which is revealed.' When he declares the Jews—who excelled other nations in righteousness, in the law of God, and in the power of Freewill—to be, without any difference, both destitute' of the power of God and in need of it, that they may be saved from the revealed wrath—making that power necessary to them—does he not reckon them to be under wrath; pray? What men will you assume to be unobnoxious to the wrath of God, when you are compelled to believe that the greatest men in the world—the Jews and the Greeks for instance—are not so? Again; whom will you except amidst those Jews and Greeks, when Paul embraces them all without any distinction under one name, and subjects them all to the same sentence? Is it to be supposed, that there were no individuals in these two most eminent nations,[d] who strove after honesty?[e] Were there none that endeavoured, to the uttermost of Freewill? Yet Paul does not heed this at all; he sends all under wrath; he pronounces all ungodly and unjust. Must we not suppose, that the rest of the Apostles also did, by a like sentence, cast all the other nations also, and each individual of them in his lot, as one mass of

[d] *Istis duabus*] I should rather understand the Greeks in this connection to be the representatives of the Gentile world, selected as the most favourable or enlightened specimen of it; Jew and Greek, like Jew and Gentile, comprehending the whole human race. Luther understands Paul to express that nation in its individuality, and argues by induction thence to the rest of the nations.—The frequent use of this antithesis—Jew and Greek—favours my view. but Luther's argument is not affected by the distinction. *His* refined Greek is included amongst *my* promiscuous Gentiles

[e] *Qui ad honesta niterentur*] Referring to Erasmus's noble defence of the heathens and their philosophers, as such great sticklers and strivers for the 'honestum.' See Part iv. Sect. xliii. note [m]. See also Part ii. Sect. viii.

condemnation under the curse and dominion of this wrath?

A published Gospel proves want of knowledge in the natural man, as well as want of power.

This passage of Paul's therefore stands boldly, and insists that Freewill, or the most excellent thing in men, even in those who are most eminent, even in those who are endowed with the law, justice, wisdom and all virtues, is ungodly and unjust, and deserves the wrath of God: else Paul's argument falls to the ground; whereas if it stand, his division, by which he distributes salvation to those who believe the Gospel and wrath to all the rest, leaves no man in the midway between them. He represents believers as righteous, unbelievers as ungodly, unrighteous, and subject to wrath. For all he means to say is, 'the righteousness of God is revealed in the Gospel, that it is of faith:' therefore all men are ungodly and unrighteous; seeing it would be foolish in God to reveal righteousness to men, which they either knew, or possessed the seeds of already. But seeing that God is no fool, and yet he reveals a righteousness of salvation; it is manifest that Freewill, even in the chiefest of men, not only has nothing and can do nothing, but does not even know what is just in the sight of God. Unless you shall choose to say, that the righteousness of God is not revealed to those chiefest of men, but only to the baser sort; in opposition to Paul's boast, that he is a debtor to the Jew and to the Greek, to the wise and to the unwise, to the barbarian and to the Greek.ᶠ So then Paul, comprehending all men without exception in one mass here, concludes that all of them are ungodly, unjust, and ignorant of righteousness and faith; so far are they from being

---

ᶠ The allusion is to Romans 1. 14.—I do not find any text in which he speaks of himself as *debtor to Jews and Greeks.* Luther seems to have confounded the fourteenth verse with the sixteenth, and with some expressions in Rom. ii. 1 Cor. 1. Galat. iii. Coloss. iii.

PART V. able to will or to do any good thing: a firm conclusion from the premise, that God reveals a righteousness of salvation to them, as being ignorant and sitting in darkness—why then of themselves they are ignorant. Now those that know not a righteousness of salvation are assuredly under wrath and damnation; and cannot extricate themselves therefrom through their ignorance, or even endeavour to be extricated. For what endeavour can you make, if you know not what, where, whither, or how far you are to endeavour.

SECT IV. Fact and experience agree with this conclusion.

Experience confirms Paul's argument. Freewill neither conceives the truth, nor can endure it.

Shew me a single individual out of the whole race of mortals, though he be the most holy and righteous of all men, who ever conceived that this is the way to righteousness and salvation—forsooth to believe in Him, who is at the same time God and man; who has died for the sins of men, and who has risen again, and is seated at the right hand of the Father—or who ever dreamed of this wrath of God, which Paul here declares to be revealed from heaven? Look at the Jews, continually taught as they have been by so many miracles, by so many Prophets; what do they think of this way? Not only have they declined accepting it, but they even hate it, to such a degree that there is not a nation under heaven which has persecuted Christ more atrociously unto this very day. And yet who would dare to say that there hath not been a single individual in such a multitude of people, who hath cultivated his free will, and endeavoured to effect something by its power? How comes it then, that all men try after something different from this, and that the most excellent of the most excellent of men have not only neglected to cultivate this method of righteousness, yea, and been ignorant of it; but, when now it has been published and revealed, have repelled it with the most consummate hatred, and have been eager to destroy it? So that Paul, in 1 Cor. i. declares this way to be to the Jews a stumbling-block, and to the Gentiles foolishness.

Now, since he makes mention of Gentiles and Jews indiscriminately, and since it is certain that the Jews and the Gentiles are the chief people under heaven; it is at the same time certain, that Freewill is nothing but the chiefest enemy of righteousness and of man's salvation; because it cannot be, but that some amongst these Jews and Gentiles have acted and endeavoured with the uttermost power of Freewill; and yet with this very Freewill have done nothing but wage war against grace. Go now, and say that Freewill endeavours after good, when goodness and righteousness itself is a stumbling-block and foolishness to her! Nor can you say that this saying pertains to some, but not to all. Paul speaks indiscriminately of all, when he says, " to the Gentiles foolishness, and to the Jews a stumbling-block;" excepting none but those that believe. " To us, says he; that is, to the called and sanctified; he is the power and wisdom of God." He does not say, ' to some Gentiles, to some Jews;' but simply, ' to the Gentiles and to the Jews who are not of us'—making a division, which is very plain, between the believing and the unbelieving, and leaving not a single individual in the midway between the two. Now we are talking about Gentiles who have not the grace of God: Paul says that the righteousness of God is foolishness to them, and they abhor it! So much for this laudable endeavour of Freewill after good.[g]

[g] Luther's account of this text is, 1. The words are a testimony. 2 This testimony is confirmed by (1.) the preceding context (2) fact and experience.—I deem him mistaken in his view, both of the text and context. (See above, note [c].) The text does not refer to ' the truth' as preached by the Gospel, neither does it make any division or exception. It is the

388

BONDAGE OF THE WILL.

PART V.
SECT. V.

Paul expressly

Again; see whether he does not himself adduce the very chiefest of the Greeks as examples' nature state of 'all men' that is here described, and described as a reason for Paul's willingness to preach the Gospel at Rome, or any where Luther was misled, possibly, by the word ' truth ;' " who hold *the truth* in unrighteousness ;" as if it must necessarily mean the Gospel. What, is there no teacher of truth but the Gospel ? and is ' the truth' identical with the Gospel ? " The truth" is either ' the substance of God,'* or ' the doctrine of that substance'—what states it out; and consequently, what states out or displays any part of this—so far as it *does* state this out—may in this inferior sense (I call doctrine *of* or *about* THE REALITY inferior to THE REALITY itself) be called ' the truth.' Now some of the invisible things of God were thus shewn, or stated out, in creation; and are shewn by what we call the works of nature (that is, works of God in creation as distinguished from those of super-creation or redemption.) So that those who had not the Gospel might still be charged with holding the truth in unrighteousness: they had it, and did not act it.—That this is Paul's reference and meaning here, appears from what follows. He goes on to say, " Because that which may be known of God is manifest in them, for God hath shewed it unto them. For the invisible things of him from the creation of the world are clearly seen, being understood by the things that are made, even his eternal power and Godhead so that they are without excuse ' He then sets out the conduct of the Gentiles under this knowledge, having thus previously shewn, that if they sinned, it was without excuse —Luther is guilty here of the very error which he charges upon Erasmus in Part. iv. Sect. xxx , that of assuming parallelisms without proof: because Jew and Greek are opposed in 1 Cor i, and also here, he assumes that it must be with just the same reference and scope in each; whereas it is there the rejecting infidel, here the un-evangelized neglecter and contemner of God, that is the subject of remark —Still the testimony against Freewill is entire. Even the conclusion from the sixteenth verse, and from the seventeenth verse, is not abated : " The Gospel is the power of God unto salvation to every one that believeth ; to the Jew first, and also to the Greek;" therefore both Jew and Greek needeth salvation—therefore they neither have, nor know it by Freewill. " Therein is the righteousness of God revealed from faith to faith ;" therefore righteousness is not known without it—is not known by Freewill; it is by faith—and

---

* I do not forget that the Lord Jesus Christ is both personally and mystically called THE TRUTH; but if this title be examined, it will be found that He has it, in both these regards, *subordinately*, as the grand Displayer, Declarer, Word, and Glory of God the Father—the created image of the Uncreated Reality.

FREEWILL PROVED TO BE A LIE.

of his assertion, when he says that the more wise of them were made foolish, and their heart was darkened: also that that they were made vain by their reasonings; that is, by their wily disputations.[h] *(SECT. V. — names the chiefest of the Greeks, and afterwards condemns the Jews indiscriminately.)*

What, does he not here lay his hands upon what is highest and most excellent amongst the Greeks, when he lays hold of their reasonings? These are their highest and best thoughts and opinions, which they accounted solid wisdom. But this wisdom, which he elsewhere calls foolish in them,[i] he here calls vain; and says, that with much endeavouring it got from bad to worse: so that at length their heart was darkened,

that faith is not of Freewill, but opposed to it —But what says the text itself in its grammatical sense as led to and supported by a just view of the context? 'The wrath of God is revealed against all men in their nature state, for that they hold the truth in unrighteousness they manifest themselves to be what they are—children of wrath and curse, through original sin and guilt—by blinding themselves to that display of God which is made by the visible, and otherwise sensible, things of his hand.'

[h] Luther does not quote the words in the order in which we have them in our version, and in which they stand in the original text. "Because that, when they knew God, they glorified him not as God, neither were thankful but became vain in their imaginations, and their foolish heart was darkened. Professing themselves to be wise, they became fools, and changed the glory of the uncorruptible God, &c."—I doubt the propriety of Luther's distinction here between the wiser of them, and the rest of the nation He appears to have understood the words ' φάσκοντες εἶναι σοφοί,' as expressing those who said they were wise amongst them. But there is nothing *partitive* in the form here. It is a description applied to the persons of whom he had spoken in the preceding verse, and of whom he continues to speak in the following verses The whole nation, which was a refined and philosophical nation, boasted itself of its wisdom. The philosophers led the way in much of the idolatry and sin, but the people followed them; and it is of the whole, *inclusively* but not *exclusively* of the philosophers, that the Apostle delivers his testimony. Luther's argument, however, is not affected by this distinction, he only wants to have it secured that the greatest and best of their community are comprehended in the censure.

[i] 1 Cor. iii. 18—20.

and they worshipped idols, and performed the monstrous acts which he records in the following verses.[k] If the best endeavours and performance, then, in the best of the Gentiles be evil and wicked; what do you think of the remaining multitude? being, as they were, even a worse sort of heathens. For neither here again does he make any difference between the better sort; whilst without any respect of persons he condemns their search after wisdom. Now, when the very act or endeavour is condemned, the endeavourers, whosoever they be, are condemned also, although they may have done what they did with the uttermost might of Freewill. Their very best effort, I say, is declared to be faulty; how much more the persons employed in it!

Presently he in like manner rejects the Jews also without any distinction, as being Jews in the letter and not in the spirit. " Thou, by the letter and circumcision, dishonourest God," says he. And again; " For he is not a Jew who is a Jew openly, but who is a Jew secretly."— What can be plainer than this division? The outside Jew is a transgressor of the law. But how many Jews were there, think you, who had no faith, men of the greatest wisdom, devotion and honesty, who strove after justice and truth with the greatest earnestness of endeavour? Just as he often bears them record, that they have a zeal for God, that they follow after the righteousness of the law, that they are labouring day and night to obtain salvation, that they live blameless![l] And yet they are transgressors of the

[k] *Sequentia monstra, quæ.*] The form is ambiguous; it *might* express that their horrific abominations were the natural consequence of their idolatries: which is true, though I do not consider him as affirming it. The form as I have rendered it, though not grammatical, is common.

[l] *Quod sine quereld vivant.*] Ambiguous—might mean without a murmur—but seems clearly to refer to such passages as Philipp. iii. 6. Luke i. 6.—Luther's representation of these

law, because not in spirit Jews, but even obstinate in their resistance to the righteousness of faith. What remains then, but that Freewill is the worst when it is best, and the more it endeavours the worse it is made. The words are clear, the division is one which admits of no doubt, there is not any thing which can be controverted.

But let us hear Paul himself in the character of his own interpreter. Making a sort of epilogue[m] to his argument, in chap. iii. he says, "What then? do we excel them? By no means. For we have charged[n] both Jews and Greeks with being all under sin."

Paul's epilogue establishes his meaning.

Jews requires chastening · they yielded but an outward observance to the law, either in its ceremonial, or in its moral requirements. They did not really fulfil the commandment any more than they entered into the spirit of the ritual. The real Jew, the spiritual Israelite, was enlightened by the Holy Ghost to see, understand, receive, use and enjoy Christ in both, by faith; having faith bestowed upon him, by an exercise of grace which was distinct from and beyond his covenant. (See above, Part iii. Sect. xxviii. note [v].) But the others were *transgressors of the law*, not because they had not faith: "For the law is not of faith; but the man that doeth them shall live in them." (Galat iii. 12) One of the objects proposed by the law was to make them superabounding transgressors (Rom. v. 20.), and they were constituted such, not by lack of faith in Christ, but by lack of spiritual obedience to its spiritual requirements Luther confounds Law and Gospel here . the *spirit*-faith of Abraham with the *letter*-morality of Moses ! It suits his view of the Apostle's argument, but that view is incorrect. (See above, Sect ii. note [c]) The Apostle is shewing that the law-having Jew is no better than the uncovenanted Gentile · " but if thou be a breaker of the law, thy circumcision is made uncircumcision " (Rom ii. 25.)

[m] *Velut epilogum faciens*] *Epil.* ' Postrema pars orationis quâ congregantur et repetuntur ea, quæ dicta sunt; Latinè peroratio, cumulus, conclusio ab ἐπιλέγω, insuper dico, dictis addo, repeto.'

[n] *Causati sumus.*] προητιασάμεθα —*We* say, proved; but Luther is more correct, as appears both from the etymology of the word and from the discourse which follows . προαιτ *ante causam affero; ante arguo.* Most commentators however, and Sleusner amongst the rest, assign a sense to it like ours, although this be the only place in the New Testament where the

PART V. What is become of Freewill now? All Jews and Greeks, says he, are under sin. Are there any tropes, or knots here? What can a qualified interpretation, in which the whole world should join, avail against this sentence which is so plain? He who says '*all*' excepts none. He who lays it down that they are under sin; that is, servants of sin, leaves nothing good in them. But where has he preferred this charge that all the Jews and the Gentiles are under sin? Nowhere else, save where I have shewn that he does so; that is, when he says, "The wrath of God is revealed from heaven upon all ungodliness and unrighteousness of men." In the words which follow he proves this by experience; for that they, being displeasing to God, were subjected to so many vices, being convicted as it were by the fruits of their ungodliness, that they will and do nothing but evil.º He then enters into judgment with the Jews separately, charging the Jew with being a transgressor of the letter; and this he in like manner proves by their fruits, and by experience: "Thou preachest that man should not steal, and stealest. Thou abhorrest idols, and committest sacrilege;" excepting none, unless they be in spirit Jews. Nor have you any outlet of escape here, by saying, 'Although they be under sin, still what is best in them, as reason and will, has endeavour towards good:' for, if good endeavour be remaining in them, his assertion that they are under sin is false. For when he specifies Jews and Gentiles, he by that mention comprehends whatsoever is in Jews and Gentiles: unless you would invert his words, and suppose him to have

word occurs. Paul enters forthwith into proof, which looks as if he considered what had preceded as little more than laying a charge.—Some MSS. read the simple verb ητιασ. which Luther seems to have followed.

º *Velut fructibus impietatis convicti*] Their abandonment of God, under which they did such vile things, proved what they were, with respect to God, who had been provoked to give them up.

written, 'The flesh of all Jews and Greeks'—that is, their grosser affections—'are under sin.' But the wrath of God, which is revealed from heaven upon them, will condemn their whole substance; except they be justified by the Spirit: and this would not be so unless their whole substance were under sin.

SEC. VII.

But let us see how Paul proves his sentiment from the Scriptures; whether the words are more to the point as we read them in Paul, than as we read them in their own places. "As it is written, says he; for there is none righteous, no not one; there is none that understandeth: there is none that seeketh after God. They are all gone out of the way; they are together become abominable; there is none that doeth good; no, not one." And the rest.

Paul justified in his quotations.

Let who can give me a commodious interpretation here; let who dares invent his tropes; complain that the words are ambiguous and obscure, and defend Freewill against these severe condemnations. Then will I also willingly yield and recant, and myself become a confessor and assertor of Freewill. It is clear these things are said of all men; for the Prophet introduces God looking forth upon all men, and pronouncing this sentence upon them. Thus he speaks in Psalm xiv. "The Lord looked forth from heaven upon the sons of men, to see if there were any that understandeth or seeketh after God. But they are all gone out of the way, &c." And Paul prevents the Jews from thinking that these things do not belong to them, by asserting that they do especially belong to them. "We know, says he, that whatsoever the law saith, it saith unto them that are under the law." He meant the same, where he said; "To the Jew first, and also to the Greek."[p]

[p] That I deny: here he speaks of Jews only; there, by the combination of the two names he comprehended all men.

You hear therefore, that all the sons of men, all who are under the law—that is, Gentiles as well as Jews—are in the judgment of God such as be unjust, do not understand, do not seek after God—no, not even one of them—but all go out of the way, and are unprofitable. I suppose now, that amongst the sons of men, and those who be under the law, are numbered those also who are the best and most honourable; those who by the power of Freewill endeavour after what is honourable and good, and those whom Diatribe makes her boast of, as having the sense and the seeds of honesty implanted in them: unless, peradventure, she maintain that those are sons of angels![q]

The very force of the argument consists in its exclusiveness. The Jews would say, those Scriptures do not belong to us, but to the heathens. Nay, says he, they are addressed to you: "Whatsoever the law saith, it saith to them that are under the law, that every mouth may be stopped, and all the world may become guilty before God." Do not excuse *yourselves;* it is meant for *you* chiefly. Why should that be spoken to you, which belongs to *others*, but not to *you?* Your excuse therefore cannot be admitted.—It is a common and current mistake that the law was given to every body: given to Adam in creation, and through him to the whole race. But this is apocryphal, and not canonical Scripture. It was never given but to the Jews, that is, to the church; the elect and covenanted nation of Israel which was for its hour (a space of fifteen hundred years) the visible church (even as the whole community of professed Christians is that church now); which was the type of the church of the first-born—the true church—and in which the several and individual members of that same church—the people of God during that period existent in the flesh—were *chiefly*, if not *exclusively*, gathered into realized union with Christ.—Here at least, it is plain that the Apostle distinguishes between the two parts of mankind—Jews and heathens—by means of this badge. If the rest of mankind be supposed to be dealt with according to this law, and as though they were under it, this must be by a tacit reference to it in the divine mind, not on the ground of any positive and express enactment which had given it to them : in which they are plainly differenced from the Jews, who are here the subjects of remark.

[q] My objection with respect to the law does not affect the universality of the charge. Paul is dealing with a Jewish objector: with respect to the guilt of the heathens no question

How can those endeavour after good then, who are all universally ignorant of God, and neither care for, nor seek after him? How can those possess a power which is profitable for good, who all turn away from good, and are altogether unprofitable? Do we not know what this meaneth—to be ignorant of God, not to understand, not to seek after God, not to fear God, to turn aside out of the way, and to be unprofitable? Are not the words most plain, and do they not teach that all men are both ignorant of God and despise God; and then, as the next step, turn aside towards evil, and are unprofitable for good? We are not talking now about ignorance in seeking food, or about contempt of money; but about ignorance and contempt of religion and piety: an ignorance and contempt which, beyond all question, are not seated in the flesh, and in the inferior and grosser affections, but in those highest and most excellent powers of man in which justice, piety, the knowledge and the reverence of God ought to reign; that is, in the rational faculty and in the will—and so, in the very power of Freewill itself; in the very seed of honesty, or in the very heart of that which is most excellent in man.

Where art thou now, my Diatribe, who before promisedst, that thou wouldest willingly agree, as concerning the most excellent thing in man, that it is flesh—that is, ungodly—if it should be proved by Scripture. Agree to this now therefore, hearing as you do, that the most excellent thing in all men is not only impious, but ignorant of God, a contemner of God, turned towards evil, and unprofitable as to good. For what is it to be unjust, but that the will, which is one of the most excellent things in man, is unjust? What is it to have no understanding of God and of

is entertained the Scriptures which he quotes have established the guilt of the Jews also. He has therefore made good his charge, that ' all men' hold the truth in unrighteousness.

PART V. good, but that the understanding, which is another of the most excellent things in man, is ignorant of God and of good; that is, blind to the knowledge of godliness? What is it to be gone out of the way, and to be unprofitable, but for men not to have any power in any part of them—and least of all in those parts of them which are most excellent—to do good, but only to do evil? What is it not to fear God, but for men in all parts of them—and especially in those better parts of yours—to be despisers of God? Now to be despisers of God is to be at the same time despisers of all the things of God; for instance, of the words, works, laws, precepts, and will of God. Now what can the understanding dictate that is right, when she is herself blind and ignorant? What can the will choose that is good, when she is herself evil and unprofitable? Nay, what can the will follow after, when the understanding dictates nothing to her, save the darkness of her own blindness and ignorance? If the understanding then be in a state of error, and the will in a state of averseness, what good can the man either do or attempt?

SEC. VIII.

The Prophet's condemnation includes power as well as act.

But some one may perhaps venture upon a sophistical distinction, and say, that, although the will turn aside and the understanding be ignorant in action, the will notwithstanding is able to endeavour, and the understanding to get knowledge, by their own powers respectively: seeing we have power to do many things which we do not however actually perform, whilst our question forsooth is about power, not performance.

I reply; the words of the Prophet include both act and power; and it is the same thing to say 'Man does not seek after God,' as it would be to say 'Man cannot seek after God:' an assertion which may be collected hence; 'If there were a power or force in man to will good—seeing he is not suffered to rest, or take his pastime, through the impulse of the divine omnipotency, as I have shewn above[r]—it could not be, but that this power were moved *towards* something, or at least *in* some one thing, and were displayed by some sort of use. This however is not the case; because God looketh down from heaven, and seeth not even one who seeks after him, or endeavours. It follows therefore, that this power which endeavours, or is willing to seek after God, is nowhere to be found; but rather all men go out of the way. Again; if Paul be not understood to speak of want of power as well as want of act, his argument would avail nothing. His whole bent is to prove grace necessary to all men. Now if men could begin any thing of themselves, grace would not be necessary. But as it is—since they cannot—grace is necessary to them. So then Freewill, you perceive, is quite eradicated by this passage, and nothing of goodness or honesty is left in man; he being declared to be unrighteous, ignorant of God, a despiser of God, averse from him, and unprofitable in his sight. The Prophet is a pretty strong antagonist, therefore, in his own text as well as under Paul's allegation of him.—Nor is it a small matter, when man is said to be ignorant of God, and to despise Him: these are the fountains of all wickednesses, the sink of sin, yea, the very hell of evil. What evil will be left undone, where there is ignorance and contempt of God? In a word, the empire which Satan has in men could not have been described in fewer or fuller words, than by his calling them ignorant and despisers of God. In this is included unbelief; in this, disobedience; in this, sacrilege; in this, blasphemy towards God; in this, cruelty and want of compassion towards our neighbour; in this, the love of self pervading all things both divine and human.

[r] See above, Part iv. Sect. xi.

PART V.
SECT IX

Paul's big words in Rom. iii. 19, 20 insisted upon.

But Paul goes on to testify that he is speaking of all men, and especially of the best and most excellent of men;[s] saying, "That every mouth may be stopped, and all the world may become guilty before God. Because by the deeds of the law is no flesh justified before him."

How is every mouth stopped, pray, if there still remains a power in us, by which we can do something? For a person may say to God, 'It is not an absolute nothing which is here: here is something which you cannot condemn; seeing it is what you have your own self given me, that it might be able to do something. This at least shall not be silent, nor shall it be guilty before thee. If this power of Freewill be whole, and can do something, it is false that the whole world is guilty, or under charge of guilt before God;[t] since this power is no small thing, nor is it in a small part of the world, but is in all the world, a most excellent possession held by all in common, whose mouth ought not to be stopped. On the other hand, if its mouth ought to be stopped, then must it, together with the whole world, be criminal and guilty before God. But with what right shall it be called guilty, except it be unrighteous and ungodly; that is, worthy of punishment and vengeance? Let her look to it, pray, by what explanation this power of man's is absolved from the guilt with which the whole word is charged at the suit

[s] I object, as before, to Luther's interpretation of this text: it is the Jews of whom he is speaking, not of the best and most excellent of men generally. These testimonies are borne to, and concerning Jews, that they also may have their mouths stopped. Of the Gentile mouths being stopped there could be no question, and was none with the Jews; though they shifted off their own charges from themselves to others. But the argument, again, is not affected by this distinction: the whole world is declared guilty, which is all he wants.

[t] *Deo obnoxius seu reus*] ὑπόδικος τῷ Θεῷ. *Obnox.* in this distinction expresses 'liable to charge.' *Reus,* 'one actually arraigned' Υπόδ. τ. Θ. comprehends the two, 'one charged with crime at the suit of God.'

of God,ᵘ or by what art it is excepted from being enclosed within the circle of the whole world. These words of Paul's are mighty thunders and penetrating lightnings, and are truly that "hammer which breaketh the rock in pieces," as Jeremiah says: "They are all gone out of the way," "The whole world is guilty," "There is none righteous." By these words all that is, not only in any one man, or in some men, or in some part of them, but all that is in the whole world, in all men, without the exception of a single individual absolutely, is broken in pieces; so that the whole world ought to tremble, to fear, and to flee at them. What bigger words, what mightier words, could be uttered than these; the whole world is guilty, all the sons of men are turned aside and unprofitable, none feareth God, none is righteous, none understandeth, none seeketh after God? Yet such hath been, and still is, the hardness and insensible obstinacy of the human heart, that we neither hear nor perceive these thunders and lightnings, but join in extolling and asserting Freewill and its powers against all these, so as truly to fulfil that saying of Malachi i. "They build, I will throw down?"ᵛ

ᵘ *Quâ interp. reata obstrictus*] *Interp.* See above, Part iv. Sect xxxiv. note ᵉ. *Re* 'the state of the 'reus' or accused : *obst.* one tied and bound with the chain of crime solemnly charged, or imputed '

ᵛ Luther should not say 'fulfil,' it is a mere accommodation of Malachi's words, which have no reference to this subject.—Luther refines here too much, and is again guilty of arguing *per sequelam.* 'The whole world is guilty. Why then, if there be any good thing in them, any good part in their substance, or any good affection of their substance, it ought to be excepted. else this part, &c. has an answer for God.'—But why may they not have abused this good part ? the testimony is against their spirit and conduct By inference, their whole substance and all its affections must be bad, but this is not asserted. Just so, in the last section ; 'Man seeketh not after God' is the same as saying 'Man cannot seek after God;' which he proves by argument and inference.

There is the same bigness of speech in that saying also; "By the deeds of the law no flesh is justified before him." It is a big saying, "By the deeds of the law;" just as is that also, 'The whole world;' or that 'All the sons of men.'—It is observable, that Paul abstains from speaking of persons, and mentions the things they are seeking after; meaning, forsooth, to involve all persons, and whatsoever is most excellent in them. For had he said, 'the common people amongst the Jews,' or 'the Pharisees,' or 'some of the wicked,' are not justified; he might seem to have left some out, as not altogether unprofitable, through the power of Freewill and the propping-up of the law. But when he condemns the very deeds of the law, and makes them wicked before God, it becomes manifest that he condemns all who excelled in zeal for the law and its deeds: and yet those only who were the best and most excellent had a zeal for the law and its deeds; and that only in the best and most excellent parts of their frames, even their understanding and their will.

If then, those who exercised themselves in the law and its deeds with the greatest zeal and endeavour of the understanding and of the will—that is, with the whole power of Freewill—and were even assisted by the law itself, as a sort of divine helper, which instructed and encouraged them; if these persons, I say, be charged with ungodliness, in that they are said not to be justified, but are declared to be flesh in the sight of God—what remains, pray, in the whole human race, which is not flesh and ungodliness? We see all alike condemned, who are of the deeds of the law. Whether they exercise themselves with the greatest zeal, or with moderate zeal, or with no zeal at all, it matters not: all could yield but a performance of the deeds of the law; and the deeds of the law do not justify. If they do not justify, they prove their fulfillers to be ungodly, and leave them so. But the ungodly are guilty persons, and deserving of God's wrath.—These things are so plain, that no one can even mutter ought against them.[x]

But it is common to elude Paul here, and to get out by saying, that by the deeds of the law he means the ceremonial ordinances, which have become deadly since the death of Christ.

I reply; this is that ignorant mistake of Jerome's, which, in spite of Augustine's bold resistance, hath, through God's departure and Satan's ascendency, flowed abroad into the world, and continued to this day: by which it hath also been brought to pass, that Paul could not possibly be understood, and that the knowledge of Christ has necessarily been obscured. Nay, had there been no error besides in the church, this one was sufficiently pestilent and powerful to make havoc of the Gospel; by which, except a special grace hath interposed, Jerome has earned hell rather than heaven—so far am I from venturing to canonize him, or to call him a saint. It is not true then, that Paul speaks only of ceremonial works; else how will his argument stand, by which he comes to the conclusion, that all are unrighteous,

Evasion, that it is ceremonial law of which Paul speaks.

---

[x] Luther misapprehends the condemnation here pronounced by the Apostle. It is not that the works of the law are evil; or that the works of men, so far as they be a fulfilment of it, are evil; but that they do not really perform these works. If they really performed these works, such testimonies as those above would not have been borne against them. The fact that such testimonies have been borne (which he has shewn to be designed especially for them) proves that they are not keepers of the law but breakers of it, and as breakers, not as keepers, are condemned by it—Luther is again in error about the word 'flesh;' it is not sinful affection here, any more than in the former instances it is a name for the human species, "no flesh" is 'no human being.' The argument however is not shaken. If the deeds of the law be never so good, but man and Freewill instead of attaining to them are condemned by them, what is man, and what is Freewill?

and have need of grace? A man might say, I grant we are not justified by ceremonial deeds; still a man might be justified by the moral deeds of the decalogue. So that you have not proved grace necessary to us by your reasoning. Besides, what would be the use of that grace, which has only freed us from the ceremonial ordinances? Those are the easiest of all, and may at least be extorted from us by fear or self-love.

Again, it is a mistake to say that the ceremonial ordinances have become deadly and unlawful since the death of Christ. Paul has never said this. He says, that they do not justify; and that they do not profit a man before God, so as to free him from the charge of ungodliness. It is perfectly consistent with this, that a man may do them, and do nothing unlawful in doing so: Just as eating and drinking are works which do not justify, and do not commend us to God; but a man does not therefore commit an unlawful act in eating and drinking.

They err also, inasmuch as the ceremonial works were enjoined and exacted by the old law equally with the decalogue; so that the latter had neither less nor more authority than the former: and Paul speaks *first* to the Jews; as he says in Romans i.[y]—Let no one doubt therefore, that " by the deeds of the law" is meant ' all the works of the whole law:' for they must not be even called works of the law, if the law hath been abolished, and is deadly: an abrogated law is now no longer a law, as Paul knew very well; and therefore he does not speak of an abrogated

---

[y] *I* say, ' to the Jews *only*;' (see above, Sect. ii. note [c], and Sect. vii. note [p]), though Luther will have it, to both: clearly, however, both had it not *in the same form*; and the Jew had the ceremonial, which the Gentile confessedly had not. It was necessary to Luther's argument therefore, that he should mark the distinction.—He goes on, ' Nor had this been abrogated.'

law, when he makes mention of the deeds of the law, but of a law which is still in force, and regnant. Else, how easy would it have been for him to say, ' The law itself is now abrogated!' which would have been plain and clear.—But let us adduce Paul himself, his own best interpreter, who says in Galatians iii. " As many as are of the works of the law are under the curse: for it is written, Cursed is every one who shall not have continued in all things which are written in the book of the law, to do them." You observe that Paul here, where he is pleading just the same cause as to the Romans, and in the same words, speaks of all the laws which are written in the book of the law, as often as he mentions the works of the law.

What is still more wonderful, he absolutely cites Moses when pronouncing a curse upon those who *continue not* in the law, whereas he himself pronounces those cursed who *are of* the deeds of the law, adducing an opposite passage to confirm his opposing sentiment; inasmuch as the former (Moses) is negative, the latter (Paul) is affirmative.—But he does so, because the matter stands thus before God: those who are most zealous of the deeds of the law do least of all fulfil the law; for that they lack the Spirit, who is the fulfiller of the law: which they may attempt, it is true, to fulfil through their own powers, but can effect nothing. Thus each saying is true: according to Moses they be accursed who do not continue; according to Paul they be accursed who are of the deeds of the law: for each of these writers requires the Spirit in his performer. Without this Spirit, the deeds of the law, how much soever be done, do not justify, as Paul says: and for the same reason, they do not continue in all the things which are written, as Moses says.[z]

[z] The cavil is, Paul speaks of ceremonial works exclusively; Luther's answer is, 1. Paul's argument would be defective

PART V.
SECT. XI.
———
Paul's meaning is, 'works of the law, done in the flesh, condemn.'

In fine, Paul abundantly confirms what I am here advancing, by his own division of persons.

2. Grace would be a mere trifle. 3. These works have not become deathly. 4. They were a part of the law requirements as much as the decalogue, and have never been abrogated. 5. When treating the same subject in Galatians iii. he expressly says, ' All things which are written in the book of the law.' The true and short answer to this cavil is, the whole law ceremonial and moral is one institution, and Paul makes no exceptions or distinctions. Luther goes wide, and says many exceptionable things. What he says about ' not abrogated,' is ambiguous, inconclusive, and unnecessary. Does he mean that the law in both its parts is still standing, just as it was ? Was it the Apostle's place here to say, ' not abrogated,' if he, considered it so? as he does explicitly in Romans vi. vii. 2 Cor. iii. Ephes. ii. Colos ii Galat. iv. 1 Tim. i. Is it true, that what has been the law shall not be spoken of under the name of the law, except it be still in force and reigning? Did the Jews, to whom *I* say *only*, he says *firstly* (see last note), this argument is addressed, require any assertion of its authority ?—What he says to reconcile the apparent discrepancy between Paul and Moses, which forms the basis of his interpretation and position here, he says under a misapprehension of both Paul's and Moses's meaning, and says unwisely and untruly. (Compare Deut xxvii. 1—26, with Galat. iii. 10.) Paul has it not for his object to condemn as many as are *doers* of the law, but " as many as are *of the works* of the law ;" that is, 'all those who are looking for justification, in whole or in part, from their obedience to the law.' What inconsistency is there between this interdict of Paul's, and Moses's curse, denounced upon every one that continueth not in all things, &c.'—Paul neither takes away this curse, nor condemns the fulfiller: he condemns the attempt to fulfil, not because it succeeds, but because it fails, and must ever fail.—' They both require the Spirit in their performer: Moses's cursed continues not, because he has not the Spirit; Paul's cursed is not justified, because he does the works without the Spirit.' Now there is no consideration about either *power* or *motive*, in either. Moses in effect says, ' fulfil,' without inquiring or teaching *how:* and Paul says, ' aiming to be justified by the law curses, because man cannot fulfil it, and there is a curse upon him who doth not.' But so far is the Spirit from being the law fulfiller (*legis consummator*), as Luther entitles him; that he who hath the Spirit, *after justification*, does not "continue in all things," and would be condemned still, if that were required of him ; nor is it in any wise his aim to do so. His aim is to do the whole will of God, in that relation into which he has now manifestly and consciously been brought by Him in Christ, as God shall be pleased

He divides men who are the doers of the law into two parties: the one he makes spiritual doers, the other carnal doers; leaving none between the two. For thus he speaks, " By the deeds of the law shall no flesh be justified." What does this mean, but that they work at the law without the Spirit, seeing they are *flesh;* that is, ungodly and ignorant of God: whom those works profit nothing? Thus, in Gal. iii. using the same division, he says, " Received ye the Spirit from the deeds of the law, or from the hearing of faith?" And again, Rom. iii. " Now the righteousness of God without the law is manifested." And again, " We judge that a man is justified by faith without the deeds of the law." From all which, as put together, it becomes plain and clear, that the Spirit is opposed by Paul to the works of the law—just as it is to all other things which are not spiritual, and to all the powers and pretences of the flesh—so as to make it certain, that this is the sentiment of Paul, agreeing with Christ in John iii. that all which is not of the Spirit (be it never so specious, so holy and so excellent) is flesh; and therefore, that even the most beautiful

to make known that will to him, and to enable him, by his Spirit which dwelleth and walketh in him: a rule, if rule it can be called, far more extensive and copious than the law, and of a totally different character, the law of an eternally saved and glorified sinner, walking in Christ with God—his Father, his Friend, his Portion, his exceeding Joy.—What he says here, and in other places, about the justification of the Spirit, is fallacious. His language implies that, if the obedience of those who are " of the works of the law " were yielded in the Spirit, it would justify, and that it was for lack of this gift, that Moses's worshippers did not escape their curse, by " continuing in all things." Now, though it be true that the Spirit justifies the Lord's called people (1 Cor. vi. 11), as it did " God manifest in the flesh" (1 Tim. iii. 16.), by proving whose, and who, and what they are, this is perfectly distinct from any act of obedience which removes curse, or earns acceptance.—All he wants from Galatians, however, he has: ' Paul, treating the same subject there, expressly comprehends the whole law.'

PART V. works of the divine law are of this character, by whatsoever powers they may happen to have been wrung out. For the Spirit of Christ is necessary; without which they are all deserving only of damnation. Let it be a settled point then, that Paul means by the deeds of the law not those which are ceremonial only, but all the works of the whole law. It will at the same time be settled, that whatsoever be done without the Spirit, in doing the deeds of the law, is condemned. But this power of Freewill—the most excellent thing forsooth in man—seeing it is of Freewill properly so called that we are now treating, is without the Spirit. Whereas, to be of the works of the law is such a thing, that nothing better can be said of a man. He does not say, you observe, 'as many as are of sins and of transgression against the law;' but "as many as are of the deeds of the law;" that is, the best of men—men zealous for the law— who, besides the power of Freewill, have even been assisted by the law; that is, instructed and exercised therein.[a]

[a] I object to Luther's interpretations and conclusions in this section. He infers a division of law workers from the words *no flesh;* by which Paul expresses not division, but universality. *No flesh* (see above, Part iv. Sect. xxxvii. note [k]) is no human being. The argument drawn from this supposed division therefore— that it is the deeds of the law done without the Spirit, which fail to justify, and do absolutely condemn—falls to the ground. In the several passages which he quotes, the opposition is not between the Spirit and the deeds of the law, but between the Law and the Gospel. (Gal. iii. Rom. iii.) Nor do I allow the parallel between this text and John iii. 6. any further than that the word 'flesh' is used in the same sense in both; but that, not Luther's sense. I must object to the assertion, that it is the absence of the Spirit which makes the deeds of the law damnable; which would not be damnable, if He were present in them : as if any works of man in the flesh, performed with or without the Spirit, ' could endure the severity of God's judgment!'—All I can allow to Luther, therefore, in this section is, 'By the deeds of the law shall no flesh be justified in his sight;' therefore Freewill, even with the help of the law, is still condemned; for with that help she cannot justify. Then what is she without it?—*And is not this enough?*

FREEWILL PROVED TO BE A LIE.

If then Freewill assisted by the law, and occupied in the law with all its might, profits nothing, and does not justify, but is left in ungodliness and flesh; what are we to think that it can do alone, and without the law?

SECT. XII.

All the law does is to shew sin.

"By the law, says he, is the knowledge of sin." He shews here, how much, and how far, the law profits a man: in other words, that Freewill is so blind, when left to herself, as not even to know sin, but to stand in need of the law for a teacher. Now what can he endeavour towards the taking away of sin, who does not know what sin is? This is what he can do; he can take sin for no sin, and what is not sin for sin; as experience abundantly shews. How does the world persecute the righteousness of God which is preached in the Gospel, vilifying it as heresy, error, and all other the worst possible names, by the instrumentality of those very persons, whom she accounts the best of men, and the most zealous for righteousness and godliness. Meanwhile, she makes a boast and brag of her own works and actions, which are in reality sin and error, as though they were righteousness and wisdom. Paul doth therefore stop the mouth of Freewill with this word of his, by teaching that sin is shewn her by the law; she being herself one who does not know what is sin: so far is he from

Luther misapprehends the scope of the Apostle's argument. He is not reasoning and declaring about man as with, and as without, the Spirit but having shewn what man is, both Jew and Gentile, from Scripture; he is arguing, how impossible it is that he should be justified by the law. The argument is against justification by the law, as preparatory to his opening of justification by the Gospel; not against man's natural impotency and imbecility, whilst without the Spirit.—Luther makes 'not justified' to mean the same as 'damned.' It implies damnation, certainly, but Luther's expressions and argument intimate, that damnation is brought and incurred by doing these deeds without the Spirit; whereas, in fact, that damnation had already been incurred, before the law came; and was only *continued* and *manifested* thereby, instead of being removed.

PART V. granting to her any power of striving after good.

And here that question of Diatribe's; so often repeated throughout her whole treatise, 'If we can do nothing, what is the use of so many laws, so many precepts, so many threatenings, so many promises,' is answered. Paul here replies, "By the law is the knowledge of sin." He gives a far different answer to this question, from what man, or Freewill, thinks for. Freewill is not proved, says he, by the law; she does not work together with it unto righteousness: for righteousness is not by the law, but the knowlege of sin. This is the benefit, this the effect, this the office of the law, to be a light to the ignorant and blind: and such a light, as shews disease, sin, wickedness, death, hell, the wrath of God, to be ours; but does not help, or release us from them. She is contented with having shewn us what our state is. Upon this, the man knowing his disease of sin, is sad, is afflicted, yea despairs. The law does not help him; much less can he help himself. Another light is necessary to shew him his remedy. This is the word of the Gospel, displaying Christ as the deliverer from all these. It is not Reason or Freewill which makes Him known: nay, how should she make him known, when she herself is very darkness, needing the light of the law to shew her that self-disease, which she sees not by her own light, but imagines to be soundness.[b]

[b] How clearly do these latter words of Paul confirm the view given in the former note as to his meaning and design! 'The law cannot justify, for it exposes this state of man which I have been charging upon him, it just manifests what he is.' He does not say makes sin, or makes him a sinner; but *is*, or *leads to*, knowledge and acknowledgment of sin. What connection would this clause have with the preceding sentence, if the object were to shew, that man's law deeds done *without* the Spirit do not justify, implying that *with* the Spirit they do?— But how strong is the argument, when correctly opened, against Freewill! She does not even know, what is sinful and what is not; nor how vile she is, through her propensity to it.—

In Galatians too, he treats the same question in just the same way, when he says, what then is the law? and answers this question, not as Diatribe would, by saying that it proves there is such a thing as Freewill, but by saying, "It was ordained for the sake of transgressions, until the seed should come, to which he had made the promise." For the sake of transgressions, he says: not to restrain them, as Jerome dreams (since Paul maintains, that it was promised to the Seed which should come, that He should take away and should restrain sin, by the free gift of righteousness); but to increase transgressions, as he writes in Rom. v. "The law stole in, that sin might abound."[c] Not that there were no sins, or that

SECT. XIII.

Confirmed by Gal. iii. 19. and Rom. v. 20.

Luther reads the word "justified" in the present tense, for which I do not find any authority: the future defines the sense both of διότι and of ἐπίγνωσις; that it is *therefore*, not *because*, and '.increased or perfected knowledge,' not ' acknowledgment.' The law not only shews what *is* sin to a greater extent, but also its power over us, and its malignity, or " exceeding sinfulness:" it exacerbates and excites by forbidding and requiring (see Rom. vii. 7—12.) ; and what must that soul, or Freewill be, which is provoked to evil by such a cause ?

[c] Luther does not see quite the whole of this great text, though he sees much of it. To understand it, we must connect what has gone before with it; beginning with verse 12. "Wherefore, as by one man sin entered into the world, and death by sin : even so death passed upon all men through him in whom all sinned. For until the law sin was in the world ; but sin is not imputed when there is no law."—Man—the whole race—sinned *in* and *with* the first man ; each individual, distinctly and personally, having been created with, and being inseparable from him, when he personally committed the one transgression.—Though sins were committed afterwards by the several individuals of the race, as brought out, one after another, into manifest existence; these were not imputed, but they were dealt with on the ground of the first transgression, in which they were distinctly, individually and personally, parties; by means of their union and unity with Adam.—The law afterwards " stole in," that *the offence might be multiplied;* or, as in Galatians, *because of offences ;*[*] that

[*] With whatever little variety this text may be read and understood—whether *added because of*, or *put into the hand of a Mediator* because of—it must imply, if it do not express, the same broad truth, that the law had no other effect and design than to multiply transgressions.—Again, the application of

PART V. sins did not abound, without the law, but inasmuch as transgressions were not known to be transgressions, or such great offences, but the greater part, and the greatest of them, were accounted righteousnesses. Now if sin be not known, there is no room for remedy, and no hope, because they would not bear the hand of the physician; as being whole in their own eyes, and having no need of a physician. The law, therefore is necessary in order to make sin known; that, by knowing the baseness and vastness of his sin, the proud man, who seemeth whole in his own eyes, may be humbled, and may sigh and pant after the grace which is set before him in Christ.

See what a simple sentence is here! "By the law is the knowledge of sin." Yet this sentence of itself is quite powerful enough to confound and overturn Freewill. For if it be true, that she knows not of herself what sin and wickedness is, as Paul says both here, and in Rom. vii. ("I had not known lust to be sin, except the law had said, Thou shalt not covet") how shall she ever know

is, that there might be more than one offence; that many offences might be added to the first. It is not, therefore, merely the communication of the knowledge of sin, that was sought and conveyed by that institution, but multiplication of transgression, that, with regard to the Lord's people, who are the displayers of God, specially as that God which is love—love to the uttermost—love in the way of grace and mercy—the God of all grace might be shewn as what He is, in the much more abounding of grace, where sin hath abounded —Sin has never been imputed by God to man, any more than by man to himself, without express and absolute enactment. The command, or prohibition, in the garden was of this sort; and there hath been none given since, save the law—which was confined to one family, the seed of Abraham, for a while the visible church— and a second, declaredly an universal one, "Repent ye and believe the Gospel." On the former of these universal commands' death was suspended, on the latter, life. He that believeth—which implies repentance—shall be saved; he that believeth not—which implies impenitence—shall perish.

Rom vii 7. is equally just when that text is understood in its fulness—the provocation which the law gives to sin—as in its inferior and more common interpretation, of mere teaching.

FREEWILL PROVED TO BE A LIE.

what is righteousness and goodness? If she does not know what righteouness is, how shall she ever strive after it? We know not sin—in which we have been born, in which we live and move and have our being; say rather, which lives and moves and reigns in us—how then should we know righteousness which reigns without us, in the heavens! What a mere nothing, and less than nothing, do these words make of that wretched thing called Freewill!^d [d]

SECT. XIV.

These things being so, Paul makes proclamation with full confidence and authority, saying, " But now the righteousness of God without the law is manifested, being witnessed by the law and the Prophets; the righteousness of God, I say, by faith in Jesus Christ, unto all and upon all them that believe in him. For there is no distinction: for all have sinned and come short of the glory of God; being justified freely by his grace, through the redemption which is in Christ Jesus; whom God hath set forth as a propitiation by faith in his blood, &c."

Rom. iii. 21—25. contains many thunderbolts against Freewill.

Here Paul utters nothing but thunderbolts against Freewill. First, the righteousness of God without the law, says he, is manifested: he separates the righteousness of God from the righteousness of the law; because the righteousness of faith comes by grace, without the law. What he says, "without the law," can mean nothing else, than that Christian righteousness is perfectly independent of the works of the law; so as that the

First thunderbolt.

---

[d] The whole force of the argument from this clause, "By the law, &c." is, ' if the law, which does so little, be necessary, what is Freewill by itself?' Luther, however, did not thoroughly apprehend the nature and design of that interposed covenant and dispensation; its twofold relation to Israel, as the elect nation, and as the visible church—its universal typicality—its strict temporariness—and its precise adaptedness to teach sin ;- that is, to teach those who have made themselves sinners before they are born into the world, and as such are under the wrath of God, how just that wrath is.

works of the law are of no worth or power for the obtaining of it. As he says soon after, "We determine that a man is justified by faith without the works of the law:" and as he has said already, "By the deeds of the law no flesh is justified before him." From all which it is most plain, that the endeavour or desire of Freewill is absolutely nothing: for, if the righteousness of God consists without the law and without the works of the law, how shall it not much more consist without Freewill? Since it is the highest endeavour of Freewill to be exercised about a moral righteousness, or the works of the law; by which its blindness and impotency is aided. This word 'without' clears away works morally good, clears away moral righteousness, clears away preparations for grace: in short, invent what you may as a performance which Freewill is equal to, Paul will persist in saying, 'the righteousness of God has nothing to do with this.'

Now, although I should grant that Freewill might by its own endeavour make advances some whither; that is, to good works, or the righteousness of the civil law or the moral law; still it advances no way at all towards the righteousness of God, nor does God account its endeavours worthy of any regard towards obtaining his righteousness, when he says that his righteousness availeth without the law. If then Freewill maketh no advances towards the righteousness of God, what would it be profited by advancing through its own performances and endeavours (were this possible) even to the holiness of angels?—These surely are no obscure or ambiguous words; here is no place left for any tropes. Paul manifestly distinguishes two sorts of righteousness; ascribing the one to the law, the other to grace: affirming, that the latter is freely given without the former and its works; but that the former does not justify or avail any thing, without the latter:—

Let me be made to see then, how Freewill can subsist and be defended amidst these objections.

The second thunderbolt is, that he says the righteousness of God is manifested, and is in force, unto all and upon all who believe in Christ; and that there is no difference.

Again he in the clearest terms divides the whole human race into two parts, and gives the righteousness of God to believers, whilst he takes it away from unbelievers. Is any one so mad then, as to doubt that the power or endeavour of Freewill is something different from faith in Christ? Now Paul denies that any thing, which subsists without the limits of this faith, is righteous before God; and, if not righteous before God, it must be sin. For with God there is nothing left in the midway between righteousness and sin, as a sort of neutral substance, which is neither righteousness, nor sin. Else, Paul's whole argument would fail, which proceeds upon this division of things; namely, that whatsoever is done and carried on amongst men, is either righteousness or sin: righteousness, if it be done in faith; sin, if done without it. With men indeed there are actions, it is true, of a middle and neutral character, in which they neither owe nor yield any thing to each other mutually; but the ungodly man sins against God, whether he eat or drink, or whatsoever he do, because he is perpetually using God's creatures wickedly and ungratefully, without giving glory to God from his heart at any moment.[e]

SECT. XV.

Second thunderbolt.

---

[e] The believer alone is righteous before God. It is not pretended by those, with whom Luther reasons, that Freewill makes any man a believer: it is a power and exercise distinct from, and prior to faith. If the faithful man, then, alone is just, what is the Freewill man—and of what character is his act?—It is scarcely necessary to notice here, that Luther speaks of God's *manifested* righteous ones Those who have been justified from everlasting, in the covenant transactions between the divine persons, referred to the Father and to the Lord Jesus Christ

414 BONDAGE OF THE WILL.

PART V.
SECT. XVI.

Third thunderbolt.

This also is no light thunderbolt, that he says, "All have sinned and are come short of the glory of God: neither is there any difference." What could be said more clearly, pray?—I will suppose a man to act by his Freewill; tell me, whether this man sins in that self-endeavour of his. If he does not sin, why does Paul not except, but involve him amongst the rest, without any distinction? Assuredly, he who says all have sinned excepts none in any place, at any time, for any performance, for any endeavour. If you except a man for any endeavour or work, you make Paul a liar; because this Freewill worker, or endeavourer, is also numbered amongst the all, and in the all, and Paul ought to have given him reverence, and not to have numbered him so freely, and so generally, amongst the sinners.

Fourth bolt.

So again, it is no light thunderbolt, his saying that they are devoid of the glory of God.—The glory of God may be understood with a difference here, actively and passively. Paul contrives this by his use of the Hebrew idioms, in which he is frequent. Actively, the glory of God is that with which God glories in us; passively, that with which we glory in him. I think it should be understood passively here: just as the faith of Christ, in Latin, expresses the faith which Christ has; but by the Hebrews the faith of Christ is understood to mean the faith which we have towards Christ. So the righteousness of God, in

(the Father's will appointing to receive them as just, through the merits of the most precious death and passion of his dear Son) are manifested to be such, by the blessed Spirit's acting *upon* and *within* them in due season, and thereby enabling, yea constraining them to believe. Now therefore they have conformed with that edict of God, described above (Sect xiii. note ᶜ), which says, " Repent ye and believe the Gospel ." nor is it until this manifestation has thus been made, that any of their personal actings become the acts of the righteous, or can in in any sort, consequently, be accounted as righteous acts. The acts of Freewill therefore, being performed before the man has entered into this state, are acts of sin.

Latin, means the righteousness which God possesses: but by the Hebrews is understood to mean the righteousness which we have from God, and before God. Thus I understand the glory of God, not Latin-wise but Hebrew-wise, as denoting the glory which we have in God, and before God, and which may be called glory in God. He, then, glories in God, who knows of a surety, that God has a favour towards him, and counts him worthy of a kind regard, so that what he does is pleasing in his sight, or what displeases is freely forgiven and borne with.

If then the endeavours of Freewill be not sin, but goodness, in the sight of God, assuredly she may boast, and with confidence in that glory may say, 'this pleases God,' 'God looks with an eye of favour upon this,' 'God ascribes a worthiness to this and accepts it, or at least bears with and forgives it.' For this is the sort of glory which the faithful have in God; which they who have not, are rather confounded before him. But Paul denies this to all men here, affirming that they are absolutely devoid of this glory: which experience also proves. Ask all the party of Freewill endeavourers without exception, and, if you can shew me one, who seriously from his heart can say of any one desire and endeavour of his, 'I know this is well pleasing to God;' I will acknowledge myself conquered, and will yield the palm to you. But I know that no such man will be found. Now, if this glory be wanting, so that conscience dares not certainly to know or to be confident, that this particular act is pleasing to God, we may be sure that it does not please God. Because, as the man believes, so it is with him: for he does not believe that he certainly pleases God—which, however, is necessary; since this is the very crime of unbelief, to doubt of the favour of God: who would have us believe with the most assured faith, that he favoureth us. Thus we prove by the very testimony of their own conscience, that, since Freewill is desti-

PART V.
———
Fifth bolt.

tute of the glory of God, she is perpetually subjecting herself to the charge of unbelief, together with all her powers, desires and endeavours.' But what will the defenders of Freewill say at last to that which follows; " being justified freely by his grace?" What is this " freely?" What is this " by his grace?" How do endeavour and merit square with a gratuitous and freely given righteousness? Perhaps they will say here, that they ascribe the least thing possible to Freewill; by no means a merit of condignity. But these are empty words; for the very aim of Freewill is to make room for merit. This has been Diatribe's perpetual complaint and expostulation,— ' If there be not freedom in the will, what place is there for merit? If there be not place for merit, what place for reward? To what shall it be imputed, if a man is justified without merit?'

Paul replies here, that there is absolutely no such thing as merit, but that all men are justified freely, as many as are justified; and that this is not imputed to any thing but the grace of God: but with the gift of righteousness is bestowed at the same time the kingdom, and eternal life. Where is now the endeavour, the desire, the pains, and the merit of Freewill? What is the use of these things? You cannot complain of obscurity and ambiguity; the matter and the words are most clear and most simple. For what if they do attribute the least thing possible to Freewill; still they teach us that we can obtain righteousness and

f It will be seen presently, that I consider Luther wrong in the account which he here gives of " the glory of God '," but he is excessive and erroneous, even upon his own representation of his thunderbolt. Freewill, he says, is evil because destitute of ' the glory of God,' by which he understands ' assurance that we please God.' She is in fact guilty of unbelief, in not having it. This is outrageous: because faith is not ' I believe God has a favour to me ,' but ' I believe in God .'' neither is it true that God has a favour to every body. What are Luther's reprobates? Then, if every body is to believe this, many are to believe a lie.

grace by this very little thing. For they do not resolve that question 'Why does God justify this man and leave the other in his sins,' otherwise than by setting up Freewill; that is to say, that the one man has endeavoured, and the other has not: and that God respects the one of these characters for his endeavour, and despises the other, that he may not be unjust, as he would be if he acted otherwise. Yea although they pretend both in their writings and in their speakings, that they do not obtain grace by merit of condignity, and do not call it merit of condignity, still they mock us with a word, and do not less hold fast the thing. For what excuse is it, that they do not call it merit of condignity, when they still ascribe to it every thing which belongs to merit of condignity? for instance, that he who endeavours finds favour with God; he who does not endeavour finds none. Is not this plainly merit of worth? Do they not make God a respecter of works, of merits, and of persons? For instance; that the one has himself to blame for lacking grace, because he hath not endeavoured; the other, because he hath endeavoured, gets grace; who would not have had it, if he had not endeavoured. If this be not merit of worth, I should be glad to know what can be called merit of worth. You might trifle in this manner with all sorts of words, and say, it is not indeed really merit of condignity, but it does what merit of condignity usually does. The thorn is not a bad tree, it only does what a bad tree does. The fig-tree is not a sound tree, but it does what a good tree usually does. Diatribe forsooth is not an abandoned woman, but only says and does what abandoned women are wont to do.[g]

[g] Luther's bolts are five; 1. The righteousness of God is here declared to be perfectly distinct from the righteousness of the law. 2 Whatsoever is not of faith is sin 3. All have sinned. 4. All have come short of the glory of God. 5. The

PART V.

SC. XVII.

Sophists worse than the Pelagians.

These defenders of Freewill have met with the misfortune described in that old saying, 'He justified are all justified freely.—I should rather consider this magnificent and comprehensive passage as one vast bolt, the very emission of which lays Freewill prostrate, because it declares what her state was, to give occasion to such emission. This vast bolt, however, may be considered as expanding itself into several smaller bolts, each of which contuses Freewill— Luther breaks the shock of this bolt, in some measure, by not exactly discerning the order of the Apostle's argument. He considers Paul as speaking of the preached Gospel, in its reception and effects, from chap. i. 16; whereas from i. 18. to iii. 20. he is setting out the condemnation of all men, first of the Greek, and secondly of the Jew, as without the Gospel. and then, having previously shewn that there is nothing but condemnation without it, both without and with the law, he proceeds to open the Gospel as the revelation of the counsel and performances of God's free favour, with which Freewill neither has, nor can have, any thing to do, and which her necessities have rendered necessary, if every individual of mankind—already shewn to be in a damned state—were not to be continued in that damned state for ever and ever.—Some of his bolts also I consider Luther as interpreting erroneously; whilst each, truly interpreted, is a bolt indeed!

"But now the righteousness of God without the law is manifested, being witnessed by the law and the Prophets" The righteousness of God is that righteousness which God freely bestows, which, on many accounts, might specially be called HIS; but which is specially so called, in opposition to man's own righteousness—a law righteousness—the result of a man's own personal obedience. "Not having mine own righteousness which is of the law, but that which is through the faith of Christ, the righteousness which is of God by faith." (Phil. iii. 9)—Luther speaks much of distinctness and opposition, but he did not discern the extent of this; and was for bringing the law in again, after having cast it out. But the words χωρὶς νόμȣ banish all connection with the law for ever, just as χωρὶς χριϛȣ̃ (Ephes ii. 12) and χωρὶς ἐμȣ̃ (John xv. 5.) declare entire severance from Christ· indeed what is severance, except it be perfect?—" Even the righteousness of God, which is by faith of Jesus Christ, unto all and upon all them that believe."—*I* say, by *the* faith of Jesus Christ, meaning the Gospel, as strictly opposed to the Law, and so preserving a distinctness from that which follows, " them that believe"—the distinguishing character of those to whom the Gospel is made the power of God unto salvation   it is *unto* these—preached especially for their benefit—they are as it were its point of rest, and *upon* these—they are efficaciously, consciously, and manifestatively invested with it, even as they

falls into Scylla by wishing to avoid Charybdis.' Through a desire of dissenting from the Pela-

SC. XVII.

have covenantly, secretly, and to the eye of God and his Christ, possessed it from all eternity. "Inherit the kingdom prepared for you from the foundation of the world;" "According to his own purpose and grace which was given us in Christ Jesus before the world began."—(Matt xxv. 34 2 Tim. i 9)—"For there is no difference . for all have sinned, and come short of the glory of God." The Jew and the Greek are invested with this righteousness alike, through the instrumentality of this preached Gospel He is hereby shewn and declared to be the God of the Gentile as well as of the Jew, and to be no respecter of persons ; even as all—that is, both Jew and Gentile alike—have manifested themselves to be sinners, and nothing but sinners (for those who had the law transgressed it, as well as those who had it not), so proving that there was no possibility of acceptance with God—that is, of being made righteous—in any other way. I consider the sin here spoken of to be the sin committed by every individual man whilst living and acting in this world, which rendered it impossible that he should obtain the glory of God on a law ground, even if his original sin and guilt were remitted which it was the special design of the law covenant and dispensation to make manifest The word ἥμαρτον denotes a time prior to this manifestation of God's righteousness it is not *are sinning*, or *have sinned*, but *have in time past been sinning*—as the Apostle has shewn distinctly of both these parties, which together constitute the whole human race—and are now therefore "left behind in the race" by the glory of God This is the proper import of the word ὑστεροῦνται which applies specially to the Jews who had the covenant of eternal life—that is, " of the glory of God"—proposed to them, on the ground of their own personal obedience; which could not be so properly said of the Gentiles, whilst their conduct had been such as to make it manifest that they could have no claim under such a covenant if they had been allowed to be candidates and competitors for its prize.— I do not accord with Luther in his idea of this glory : it is the same thing which is spoken of, Rom v. 2. ("rejoice in hope of the glory of God"), and in 1 Peter v 1 (" a partaker of the glory which shall be revealed.") It is that manifested excellency which God has provided for his people ; and which is with the greatest fitness called His glory—the glory of God—because the state into which He will in due time introduce his human people will be one of His most glorious manifesters : they will in their measure, both individually and collectively, when thus brought into, and displayed in, the completeness of their union with the Image of the Invisible One, shew Him forth as He is By this glory—which, if it be to be received upon a law ground, requires spotless perfection

2 E 2

gians, they began with denying merit of condignity, and, by the very ground on which they deny,

in him who wins it—they had all been outstripped and overcome, so as to have no part in it —" Being justified freely by his grace through the redemption which is in Christ Jesus" These words open the nature of God's righteousness, as well as the origin and ground of its bestowal. *Justified* is from the same root with *righteousness*, and expresses properly ' making the unjust just .' it is God's method of absolving a sinner from his offences by taking them clean away ; the origin of this removal is free favour, and the way of it is Christ's blood-shedding. It is a cleansing which we receive without money and without price, from, and unto the display of, that portion of God which we distinguish by the name of grace , but it is a cleansing which he has rendered himself just in freely bestowing— that is, which he freely bestows in perfect consistency with his justice—through the price which Christ paid, by joining himself to them in their damned state, living with them as The Righteous One *in* and *under* their curse, and at length dying *with* them, and *for* them, a death of shame, agony, and complicated torments. The expression is peculiar, " The redemption which is in Christ Jesus ;" marking the peculiar and elect objects of this redemption : it is a deliverance, through payment of a valuable consideration, had and received by means of union with Christ Jesus—sought and obtained, therefore, for those only, to whom the Father (as both Covenant and Scripture speak) hath vouchsafed this most precious of all gifts, which implies and conveys all the rest—union *with*, being *in*, Christ. " According as he hath chosen us *in Him*"—that is, to be in Him , that we should be in Him—" before the foundation of the world "—Hereby, as it is afterwards declared, God is shewn to be righteous, though the justifier of sinners; who are manifested to have had this covenant union, of His free gift, from everlasting, and therefore to have been of the number of those, for the sake of whom He did so come, live, and die—by having faith given to them in due season, through the regeneration and within agency of the Holy Ghost, and so differencing themselves from others, to whom, according to the will of God, the free grace proclamation is made, and the second *universal* commandment (which the more private and peculiar one of the law had established to be the only practicable method of salvation and glory)—Repent ye and believe the Gospel—hath been in common with them delivered, whilst it is by them exclusively obeyed.

Thus doth this ordinance text of Luther's fire a sort of volley against Freewill, of which every shot is death. ' Righteousness of God'—' without the law '—' the faith of Jesus Christ'— all them that believe'—' no difference'—' all have sinned '—' all come short of glory '—' justified freely'—' by His grace '—

do more strongly affirm it; denying with word
and pen what in reality and in heart they affirm,
and making themselves twofold worse than the
Pelagians. First, inasmuch as the Pelagians simply, candidly, and ingenuously confess and assert
merit of condignity, calling a boat a boat, a fig-tree a fig-tree; and teaching what they think. But
our friends,[h] though they think and teach the same
thing as these, beguile us meanwhile with lying
words, and with a false shew of dissenting from the
Pelagians, when in reality they do nothing less than
this; so that, if you look at the character we personate, you see in us the most determined enemies of the Pelagians; if you look at our real
mind, we are double Pelagians. Secondly, inasmuch as, by this assumption, we estimate and
purchase the grace of God at a far lower rate
than the Pelagians. They assert, that it is not
some small thing which is in us, whereby we obtain grace, but many great, whole, full, and perfect endeavours and performances. Our friends,
on the contrary, account it to be a very small
thing, and next to nothing, by which we earn
grace.

If we must be in error therefore, those persons
err more honestly and with less pride, who affirm
that the grace of God is purchased at a great
price, reckoning it to be dear and precious; than
those who teach that it is bought for a little, and
for a very little, accounting it mean and contemptible. But Paul beats them both together

' through the redemption'—' a propitiation by blood'—' that
he might be just'—' the justifier of him that believeth·' here
are no less than thirteen bolts, thirteen death-blows for Free-will, whilst the very existence of the Gospel declares the Free-will state of those to whom it is sent.

[h] *Nostri verò*] *Friends,* inasmuch as they profess to be antagonists of the Pelagians *together with us*—What follows—' si
hypocrisin spectes'—' hâc hypocrisi'—is by a figure taken
from the histrionic art, that peculiar species of simulation, of
which the stage-player is guilty, when he puts on his mask,
and personates a character in the drama.

PART V. into one mass by a single word, when he says that " all are justified freely ;" and again, " that they are justified without the law ;" " without the deeds of the law." In asserting a free justification as the justifier of all men, he leaves none to work, or merit, or prepare themselves, and leaves no work that can be called congruous or deserving, but breaks in pieces, by one stroke of this thunderbolt, both the Pelagians with their entire merit, and the Sophists with their little modicum of merit. Free justification does not allow you to set up workers of any sort; inasmuch as ' free gift,' and ' prepare yourself by some work,' are manifest opposites. Again; justification by grace allows not of any personal worthiness: as he says afterwards also, in chap. xi. " If by grace, then is it no more of works; otherwise grace is no more grace:" just as also in chap. iv. he says, " Now to him that worketh is the reward reckoned, not of grace, but of debt." So that my friend Paul stands up as the invincible destroyer of Freewill, laying two whole armies flat on their faces, with a single word. For if we be justified without works, all works are condemned; both small and great; he excepts none, but fulminates equally against all.

SC.XVIII. See here, also, how drowsy all our friends have been ; and of what profit it is to a man, if he have
Fathers overlooked Paul. leaned upon the authority of the old Fathers, approved as those have been, through ' such a series of ages.' Have not they also been all equally blind; rather, have not they also overlooked Paul's most clear and most express words? Is it possible, that any thing could be said clearly and expressly for grace, in opposition to Freewill, pray, if Paul's discourse be not clear and express? He pursues his argument in a way of comparison,' making his boast of grace in

---

i *Per contentionem.*] Referring to Paul's continual and repeated opposition of grace to works, in this and the following

opposition to works; and then, in the clearest and plainest terms, declares, 'that we are justified freely; and that grace is not grace, if it be procured by our works—most explicitly excluding all works in the matter of justification, that he may establish only grace, and gratuitous justification:[k] and do we still look for darkness in the midst of this light; and, when we cannot ascribe great things and every thing to ourselves, do we endeavour to ascribe very small and inconsiderable things to ourselves, just to carry the point that justification is not free, and without works, by the grace of God? As if, forsooth, the man who denies that we are supplied with the greater things, and the all things which are necessary to justification, doth not much more deny, that we are supplied with the little things and the few—when he is maintaining all the while, that we are justified only by his grace, without works of any kind, and even without the law itself; in which all works, both great and small, both works of congruity, and works of condignity, are comprehended?—Go now and boast of the authority of the ancients, and trust to their sayings; all of whom to a man, as you perceive, have overlooked Paul, that most clear and explicit doctor! Nay, they have, as it were, designedly got out of the way of this day-star, or rather of this sun; being engrossed, forsooth, with the carnal imagination, that it seemed absurd there should be no place left for merits.

Let me adduce the example of Abraham, which Paul subsequently adduces. "If Abraham, says

Paul's citation of the example of

chapter, as also in chapters x. xi Contention, or comparison, is a figure which Paul abounds in, letter and spirit, law and faith, God's righteousness and their own righteousness; life and death, flesh and Spirit, &c &c. are set out by him in the most forcible manner, through this sort of competition.

[k] *Solam gratiam gratuitam justificationem*] *Sol. gr.* as opposed to grace mixed with works. *gr. just.* justification without any personal worth.

PART V.

Abraham searched and applied.

he, was justified by works, he hath glory; but not before God. For what saith the Scripture? Abraham believed God, and it was counted to him for righteousness."

Here again, observe Paul's division; he distinctly mentions two righteousnesses of Abraham: one of works, which is moral and civil, but by which he denies that he was justified before God, though just before men by it. Moreover, he has glory with men, although even this man also comes short of the glory of God, by this righteousness. Nor can any one say, that the works[1] of the ceremonial law are here condemned; since Abraham lived so many years before the law. Paul speaks simply of the works of Abraham; and those, none other than his best. It would be ridiculous to reason whether a man be justified by bad works. If then Abraham be not just by any works of his, but, except he be clothed with another righteousness, that of pure faith, be left, both as to his person and as to all his works, under the charge of ungodliness; it is plain, that no man makes any advances towards righteousness, by his own works: and further, that no works, no desires, no endeavours of Freewill are of any avail before God; but are all accounted ungodly, unjust and wicked. If the man be not just, his works and desires are not just; if not just, they are damnable, and worthy of wrath. The other righteousness is that of faith, which doth not stand in any works, but in God's favour and manner of accounting of us, through grace. And see how Paul dwells upon that word 'accounting

---

[1] *Gloriam apud homines Vacat gloriâ Dei.*] Here again, Luther has the mistake already noticed (see notes g h), respecting the glory of God. It is quite in another sense that all are said to come short, and Abraham not to boast. He had no cause of boasting before God, because he was not justified to God by his works, else he would have had: as he might boast himself before men, because he was shewing himself to be one justified to God, by his works done after justification.

FREEWILL PROVED TO BE A LIE.

of us;' how he urges, repeats, and beats it into us.

"To him who worketh, says he, is the reward reckoned not of grace but of debt. But to him that worketh not, but believeth on him who justifieth the ungodly, his faith is counted for righteousness; according to the purpose of the grace of God." Then he adduces David speaking in like manner of the reckoning of grace;[m] and saying, "Blessed is the man to whom the Lord hath not imputed sin, &c."

Nearly ten times in that same chapter he repeats the word 'imputation.' To be short; Paul compares the worker and the non-worker: leaving none between these two. He denies that righteousness is imputed to the worker: to the non-worker he asserts that righteousness is imputed, if he but believe. It is not possible for Freewill to escape or slip away here with her endeavour, or pains: for she must be numbered either with the worker, or the non-worker. If with the worker, you hear in this place that no righteousness is imputed to her; if with the non-worker, who however believes in God, righteousness is imputed to her. But then she will not be Freewill; she will be the new creature—the soul renewed by faith.[n] Now, if righteousness be not imputed to him that worketh, it is plain that his works are nothing but sins, wicked and ungodly acts in the sight of God.

Nor is it possible for any Sophist to turn saucy, and say, 'though the man be wicked, yet his

---

[m] *Reputatione gratiæ*] 'The account which grace takes of character '—*rep* is most correctly englished by 'reckon;' but Luther uses it throughout the whole of this passage interchangeably with 'imputo'

[n] *Renovata creatura per fidem*] As if the Lord's people were *renewed* by faith! whence comes their faith then? So he had said above, acquiescing in Erasmus's term, 'renatus per fidem;' which I there called ambiguous, but we now see to have been meant wrongly.—See above, Part iv. Sect. xlv. note t.

PART V. work may not be wicked.' For Paul lays hold, not on the person of the man simply, but on the man at work, for this very purpose, that he may declare in the most explicit terms, how that the very works and endeavours of the man are condemned, whatsoever those may be, and under whatsoever name or species they may be classed. Moreover, it is of good works that he treats, because it is of justification and merit that he is discoursing—and when he speaks of a man that worketh, he speaks universally of all working men, and of all their works; but especially of good and honest works: else his division into worker and non-worker would not stand.

SEC. XX.

Luther omits much which he might insist upon.

I here omit those most powerful arguments which are drawn from the purpose of grace, from promise, from the power of the law, from original sin, and from the election of God; of which there is not one, but what alone, and by itself, utterly takes away Freewill. For if grace comes from the purpose or predestination of God, it comes by necessity, not by our pains or endeavour; as I have already shewn. So, if God promised grace before the law, as Paul argues both here and in Galatians; then it does not come from our works, or from the law; else the promise will be nothing. So, faith also will be nothing (yet it is said that Abraham was justified by it before the law), if works have any efficacy. So, whereas the law is the strength of sin, only manifesting, and not taking away, sin; it makes the conscience guilty before God, and threatens wrath: this is what is meant by that saying, " The law worketh wrath." How then could it be, that righteousness is obtained by the law? And, if we are not profited by the law, how can we be profited by Freewill when acting without it.º

º ' No Freewill' follows from God's " purpose and grace:" " Whom he did foreknow, them he did predestinate; whom he did predestinate, them he also called." The calling is of

Again; seeing, we are all under sin and damnation through the one offence of the one man Adam, how can we attempt any thing which is not sin, and which is not damnable? For when he says all, he excepts no one; neither the power of Freewill, nor any workman; whether he work or work not, endeavour or endeavour not, he will necessarily be comprehended amongst the all, with the others. Nor could we have sinned, and been condemned, by that single sin of Adam's, unless it were our sin. For who could be condemned for another man's sin, especially in the sight of God? But that sin is not made ours by imitation, or by some subsequent act of ours; since this could not be that one sin of Adam, as being that which we, and not he, hath done: it becomes ours, by birth. But this is not the place for discussing that question. However, original sin suffers not that Freewill do any thing else, save sin and be damned.ᵖ

predestination therefore, not of Freewill; " according to the eternal purpose which he purposed in Christ Jesus our Lord." —' No Freewill' follows from God's promise, which was antecedent to the law, and therefore cannot be dependent upon our works, which are *by* the law · indeed, in its very nature, as Paul argues, *promise* is opposed to *work*.—' No Freewill' follows from faith (" the just shall live by faith ," " they which be of faith are blessed with faithful Abraham") , of which the law—that is, works—is not. (Galat. iii. 11, 12.)—' No Freewill' follows from the law . for even the law worketh wrath—and yet she is a help, Freewill does not even know what sin is, without her.

ᵖ Luther has his eye, all the way, upon Romans v. 12—19. His account is, Adam's sin is ours ' *nascendo*'—by our being born of him, as we are; *born of him who did it*. making *us* voluntary agents in being born, and *God* the propagator of sin, in causing that we should be born from him—or, as he has described it, making us out of him (See above, Part iv. Sect. x., and, for objections to his statement, note ᶻ thereupon.) However, Luther's conclusion is right, though he arrives less correctly at it . the truth is, we are born having previously sinned, guilty, " children of wrath;" how then can we do any thing good ? Luther—how near is he to the truth, yet does not reach it ! Observe, he will not have it ' sin after birth,' and he will have it ' our own and not Adam's only .' but

PART V. These arguments, then, I omit, because they are most manifest, and most powerful: besides, I have said something about them already. Now, if I had a mind to recite all that Paul only has said to the subversion of Freewill, I could not do this better, than by discussing the whole of Paul's writings in the form of a perpetual commentary, and shewing that this so vaunted power of Freewill is confuted in almost every single word of his: just as I have done in these third and fourth chapters. My special object in thus exhibiting these chapters has been; first, to shew the stupid drowsiness with which we have all nodded over his writings—reading them, clear as they are, in such a way as not to have the least idea that they contain the strongest possible arguments against Freewill—secondly, to shew the folly of that confidence which leans on the authority and writings of the old doctors—and thirdly, that I might leave it as matter of thought, what these most manifest arguments are capable of effecting, if handled with diligence and judgment.

SEC XXI.

Luther's own view of Paul.

For my own part I am greatly astonished, that, whereas Paul so often uses those universal terms ' All,' ' None,' ' Not,' ' Nowhere,' ' Without;' as for instance, "They are all gone out of the way," "There is none righteous," "There is none that doeth good, no not one," "All have been made sinners, and damned, by the offence of one." "We are justified by faith without the law, without works;" (so that, if a man had a mind to speak otherwise, he could not however speak more clearly, or more explicitly); it is a matter of surprise to me, I say, how it hath come to pass, that,

he has not 'that distinct individuality of subsistence given to us in the creation of the *Man*, which makes us truly one with him in his deed,' neither has he 'the power and order before given;' neither has he ' God's veracity to be shewn in inflicting the curse' (See as above.) He is somewhat clearer, however, than our ninth Article; which wants distinctness, as well as fulness.

in opposition to these universal words and sentiments, contrary, nay contradictory, ones have prevailed. As for instance; 'There are some who do not go out of the way, who are not unjust, not wicked, not sinners, not damned. There is something in man which is good, and leans towards good:' as if the man, whosoever he be, that inclines to good, were not comprehended in that saying 'All,' 'None,' 'Not.' *I*, for my part, should not have any thing to oppose or reply to Paul, if I wished it; but should be compelled to comprehend the power of my Freewill, together with its endeavour, amongst those 'alls' and 'nones,' of which Paul speaks; unless some new art of grammar, or some new use of speech, be introduced.

One might perhaps be allowed to suspect a trope, and to torture the words, which I have selected, into some other meaning, if he used such an expression but once, or only in one place. But, in fact, he uses such expressions perpetually—and not only so, but uses both affirmatives and negatives together; so handling his sentiment in a way of contrast and distribution—by which he arrays the several parts against each other, on both sides—that not only the nature of the words, and the sentence itself, but the subsequent, preceding, and immediate context also, together with the scope and very body of the whole discussion, unite in establishing one common conclusion, that Paul means, 'without faith in Christ there is nothing but sin and damnation.[q] It was in this

[q] The words above cited are a sufficient illustration of Luther's meaning in the several terms—'words,' 'sentence,' 'contrast,' 'division,' 'context,' 'scope,' 'discussion at large,' 'mind of the writer'—*Extra fidem Christi*, I translate according to Luther's meaning, not according to my own view of the Apostle's argument Both here and in Galatians, it is common to represent Paul as speaking of 'faith in Christ' as opposed to 'works.' But in both places it is 'the Law' as opposed to 'the Gospel,' of which he is speaking: in both places he is shewing, in opposition to Judaizers, 'that the Law cannot

BONDAGE OF THE WILL.

PART V.

SC. XXII.

Paul's
crown.

way, that I promised to confute Freewill, so that all my adversaries should not be able to resist me. I think I have done so: even though they should not yield to my sentiment, as vanquished; or hold their peace. It is not within the compass of my power to bring them to this: this is the gift of God's Spirit.

But, before we hear the Evangelist John, let us add Paul's finish to his argument on this subject, as contained in that Epistle; prepared, where this shall not satisfy, to set the whole of Paul's writings in array against Freewill, by a perpetual commentary. In Romans viii. after[r] dividing the whole human race into two parts, flesh and Spirit, as Christ also does in John iii. he speaks thus: 'They that are after the flesh do mind the things of the flesh; but they that are after the Spirit do mind the things of the Spirit.'

save, the Gospel only can.'—But then, that this Gospel may save, ' it must be believed with the heart;' ' Christ must be believed *in* and *into*.' Under the right interpretation of these passages then, two steps are wanting to Luther's conclusion, ' Paul condemns Freewill ' Paul *says* only, ' Without the faith of Christ there is nothing but sin and damnation.' But that faith must be received, or obeyed, before it can save; and that reception or obedience is ' not of the nature power of Freewill, but of the supernature power of God's Spirit.'—There are texts, more than enough, to prove both these points , I would rather say, Scripture is explicit enough in her witness to both these points—("Taking vengeance on those that know not God, and those that obey not the Gospel of our Lord Jesus Christ"— " No man *can* come unto me, except the Father, which hath sent me, draw him ") so that there can be no question what is truth in this matter , though Luther does not come at˜his conclusion legitimately, through misuse of his premises.

[r] *Ubi genus*] Referring to the preceding verses, " Them which are in Christ Jesus, who walk not after the flesh, but after the Spirit."—As to what follows, it has been seen already (Part iv Sect xlii notes [i] [k]) that I do not admit the parallel. Paul clearly divides men into two classes, but the Lord, in John iii is shewing the necessity of a new and spiritual birth. The opposition is not between those who have, and those who have not, this birth, but between nature power of procreation, and Spirit power of procreation, Adam produces his like, and the Holy Ghost produces *His* like.

That Paul, here, calls all carnal who are not spiritual, is plain both from the division and opposition between flesh and Spirit, and also from Paul's own words which follow. " Ye are not in the flesh, but in the Spirit, if but the Spirit of Christ dwell in you. Now if any man have not the Spirit of Christ, he is none of his." For what else does he mean here, by the words ' Ye are not in the flesh, but in the Spirit,' than that those who have not the Spirit are necessarily in the flesh? But he who is not Christ's—whose is he else, than the devil's? It stands good therefore, that those who have not the Spirit are in the flesh, and under Satan.

Let us now see, what he thinks of the endeavour and power of Freewill in the carnal. " They that are in the flesh cannot please God." And again; " The mind of the flesh is death:" and again, " The mind of the flesh is enmity against God." Again, " It is not subject to the law of God, neither indeed can be."ˢ Let the advocate for Freewill answer me here, how that which is death, which is displeasing to God, which is enmity against God, which is disobedient to God, and which cannot obey him; can endeavour after good! For he has not been pleased to say, ' the mind of the flesh is dead, or hostile to God;' but " is death itself, is enmity itself:" to which it is impossible, that it be subjected to the law of God, or please God; as he had also said just before, " For what the law could not do, in that it was

---

ˢ *Sensus carnis. non est subjectus*] Sensus, ' the mind in action;' or rather the result of that action; ' what it thinks or desires.' It is not so properly the mind, or desire, that is not and cannot be subject (as is commonly understood), but the flesh, that is, the unrenewed body itself. φρόνημα, according to the analogy of language, should be ' the desire formed,' not ' the faculty forming it,' and therefore, it is not this φρόνημα but the substance that forms it (the flesh—σάρξ), which ought to be subject, but is not.

PART V. made weak by the flesh, God hath done,ᵗ &c. I know, as well you do, Origen's tale about three

> ᵗ *Legi impossibile.*] Luther does not explain, as we might have wished him to do, this most difficult text: but the considerations which we have already entertained respecting the flesh and the Spirit will assist us to unravel it.—In the preceding chapter, Paul had been describing a very remarkable temptation, with which, for his own good and that of the church, he had been visited since his conversion. He had been tempted to think that he must still obey the law; and, having been put upon trying to do this, had acquired a deep knowledge of his own state: which is also that of every called child of God. He discovered, that he had a law in his members (his body) which warred against the law of his mind, and brought him into captivity to the law of sin which was in his members. He sighed for deliverance from that body—fitly called a *dead* body—whose law made him so wretched. He was assured that he should one day possess it, through the gift of God in Christ Jesus. At present, however, his state was that of a person serving two laws, in the two distinct parts of his frame. But still, even now, he was not condemned. Why? because he was a man in Christ * Why, as a man in Christ, had he no condemnation? Because the Holy Ghost, as *had* by him in Christ, had delivered him from the thraldom and bondage of that law which still reigned in his members. Why had he the Holy Ghost in Christ Jesus? Because God, by sending his own Son in flesh of sin, had condemned sin in the flesh, that is, had executed sentence of death upon this sinful flesh, and could now, in consideration of that sentence so borne, raise up both Him and that people for whom and with whom he had borne that sentence, into a new state of being, in which they should be the subjects of spiritual influences in both parts of their frame: in whom even here, whilst tabernacling in their flesh of sin, the foretaste and firstfruits of this grace is shewn in their being renewed, and dwelt in, by the Holy Ghost.† Thus, they have that done for them which the law could not do, because it was weak through our flesh's being what it is, they are enabled to fulfil the righteousness of the law—or rather to yield to God a service

---

* I perfectly approve Griesbach's improved reading, which casts " Who walk not after the flesh, but after the Spirit," as read in chap. viii. 1. into the interior margin. It breaks the connection of the argument; and may very naturally be supposed to have been interpolated from verse 4

† I have here stated the reality, which is more commonly set forth by the Holy Ghost in figure; the dying, quickening, rising, and now sitting of the Lord's elect *in* and *with* Him. (See Rom vi. Ephes i. ii. Coloss ii iii) God's eternal, covenanted design of raising them up, *in Christ*, from that death into which they were contemplated as having brought themselves by their fall *in* and *with* Adam, is the basis and element of this reality.

sorts of affection, one of which is called the flesh by him; another, the soul; another, the spirit; and of which is far more righteous, because more adapted to that full manifestation which He has now made of himself, than a law obedience would, or could be—Hereafter, as he proceeds to shew most triumphantly, in the progress of this chapter, the other part of their frame will also have its triumph : the body which has death in it, and has yet assuredly to die, shall be quickened by the same Spirit which hath already quickened and dwelt in their souls, and shall live. This, which had been glanced at in chap. vii. 25. and is so distinctly affirmed in vv. 11. 21. 23 of this chapter, receives its seal and crown in 1 Cor. xv. where the pæan is sung, and the victory ascribed to its giver and communicator. " But thanks be to God which giveth us the victory, through our Lord Jesus Christ."—I have found it impossible to render a consistent account of these two chapters (to which the precedent sixth may be added), verse by verse, and clause by clause, on any other principle than this; which makes ' flesh' the substance of the body, and 'spirit' the renewed mind. (See Part iv. Sect. xxxvii xli. xlii and much that has elsewhere gone before) There is much emphasis in verse 1. *Howbeit* * (that is, although with the flesh they serve the law of sin) *there is now* (opposed to I thank God, chap. vii. 25. for what shall be) *no condemnation* (all these out-breakings and manifestations of evil are forgiven, and not allowed abidingly to mar the peace of their souls—for " Who shall lay any thing, &c. &c." viii. 33—39) *to them which are in Christ Jesus*.† (It is of the Lord's called that he here bears this testimony, as appears from the context · a testimony, which is in the Lord's time realized to all his elect, and for the same reason—God *has* condemned their sin which is in their flesh—" Who is he that condemneth' It is Christ that died.") *Hath made me free*: an

---

* The argument is closely connected and compacted from verse 24 of the preceding chapter He pants He thanks God. He sums up his state. ἄρα οὖν οὐδὲν ἄρα νῦν.

† The people of God are said to be in Christ Jesus, with reference to two distinct states *in Him*, by covenant and predestinative union from before the worlds (" According as he hath chosen us in Him, &c " " Grace which was given us in Him, &c "); *in Him* by realized, conscious and efficacious union, through the calling of the Holy Ghost (" Andronicus and Junia... who also were in Christ before me " " I knew a man in Christ, &c.") A third state may be distinguished as that of sacramental union (see Part iv Sect xlv note †), which is distinct and separable from the other two : bearing analogy to that entrance which the Lord had into his kingdom, by his baptism.—The blessedness here described belongs to his called, but it is he ordained, earned and waiting portion of all his elect ; who, as they are one by one brought by the Holy Ghost into the knowledge of this grace, regard themselves as those who have virtually died *in* and *with* Christ, and who therefore are dead, and have their life hid with Christ in God Hence they live and walk after that part of their frame which lives—into which He has already been introduced, not according to that which is virtually dead.

which the soul is the middle one—what may be turned towards either side, the flesh or the spirit. But these are his own dreams; he only tells, he does not prove them. Paul here calls whatsoever has not the Spirit flesh, as I have already shewn." So

habitual deliverance is not incompatible with an occasional *ravished* subjection—such as he has described in chap. vii. *The law of sin and death* is clearly the law of evil which is in the members, or flesh, or body. *The impossibility of the law*—the law gave no power, and therefore could not possibly get itself to be obeyed by a creature whose substance is such as fallen man's. *Likeness of flesh of sin* does not deny *reality* any more than in Philip. ii. 7. *Condemned* etc. not only passed the sentence but inflicted the judgment.* *Righteousness of the law* is not what is commonly meant by it, 'the act, or ground, of justification;' but 'the enactment'—'the matter of the statute'—δικαίωμα, not δικαιοσύνη. *Who walk*—denoting habitual conduct, aim and principle.—Their conformity with the law is circuitous, not direct; incidental, not deliberate and designed. They "walk in the Spirit" (Gal. v, 16.); that is, 'in or *after* their renewed mind:' just as it is said here, *Who walk not after the flesh, but after the Spirit.*—I cannot forbear remarking what a close parallel that whole chapter (Gal, v,) is to this seventh and eighth of Romans, and how truly the whole rule or law of the Lord's called ones ("Ye have been called unto liberty") is set out in the four words which I have recited above. For what is, not only the whole law, but even the whole volume of Scripture to us, save so far as it is apprehended and received by our renewed mind, through the inspiration of the Holy Ghost?

^u I cannot agree with Luther here. Origen is more nearly right than he, if by soul may be understood 'the will with its affections;' and the distinction is surely recognised in Scripture, when Paul prays for the Thessalonians "that their whole spirit and soul and body may be preserved blameless unto the coming of our Lord Jesus Christ." (1 Thess. v. 23.) According to Luther, 'those that are after the flesh,' and 'the flesh,' are the same substance; whereas, in truth, the distinction of character is made by these constituent parts of their frame, according to which they walk (that is, habitually act) severally. The natural man (ψυχικὸς) lives after his flesh, and is carnal:

* Compare 1 Peter iv. 1—6. also iii. 18—22. 'Christ's *flesh* condemned, and made to suffer or die,' is not only the burden of Scripture, but *the essence of the reality of the foundation of God's new creation transactions in Him:* even as the knowledge of this body of ours, what it was in its formation, what it was *in* and became *by* the Fall, what it is to the unregenerate, and specially what it is to the regenerated sons and daughters of Adam, is one of the great keys to the mystery of man, and to christian experience.

that those highest virtues of the best of men are 'in the flesh;' that is, are dead, enemies to God, not subject to the law of God, nor capable of being subjected to it, and displeasing to God. For Paul does not only say that they are not subjected, but that neither can they be subjected. So Christ also in Matthew vii. "A corrupt tree cannot bring forth good fruit." And in Matthew xii. "How can ye, being evil, speak good things?" You see here, that we not only speak evil, but even cannot speak good. And he who in another place says, that we, being evil, know how to give good gifts to our children, still denies that we do good even in the very act of giving good things; inasmuch as the creature of God (which we give) is good; but neither are we ourselves good, nor do we give our good things well: and when so saying, he speaks to all; yea, even to his disciples. So that these twin sentiments of Paul stand good: "The just lives by faith;" and "Whatsoever is not of faith is sin:" of which the latter flows from the former. For if there is nothing but faith by which we can be justified; it is evident, that those who have not

the spiritual man ($\pi\nu\epsilon\nu\mu\alpha\tau\iota\kappa\grave{o}s$)—he who has a $\pi\nu\epsilon\hat{\nu}\mu\alpha$—that is, 'an Holy-Ghost-renewed spirit'—lives after his renewed spirit, and is spiritual. Thus the spirit and the man, and the flesh and the man, are distinct substances severally; though the one includes the other.—Still, Luther's conclusion is not affected. He who does not live after the spirit, but after the flesh, does only evil, because that flesh, after which he lives is only evil; 'defecated' evil and, *except* and *until* a man be renewed in the spirit of his mind, and thus be made spiritual, he neither does, nor can do any thing good. Nay further, if he be thus renewed, and when he hath been thus renewed, it is only so far as his renewed spirit be impelled and sustained by the Holy Ghost, that he either resisteth evil, or worketh good. There are seasons, when, for the fuller manifestation of God unto his *real* good, the Holy Ghost, who never *leaves* his temple, is but as the friend who sitteth by, neither speaking, nor putting out a finger to help. So far as he is left to the endeavour and power of Freewill, therefore, all that is here said by Paul about not pleasing God, &c. belongs to him.

PART V.

SC.XXIII.

Grace exemplified in Jews

faith are not yet justified. Now those who are not justified are still sinners; and sinners are corrupt trees, which can do nothing but sin, and bear corrupt fruit. So then, Freewill is nothing but the servant of sin, death and Satan: which neither doeth, nor is able to do or to attempt, any thing but evil.*

Add that example in chapter x. taken from Esaias, " I have been found of them that sought me not; I have been made manifest to those

* Luther adduces these expressions in Romans viii. as the crown of Paul's testimony against Freewill. The flesh—meaning, as I maintain, the natural, unrenewed substance of man, with all that is in it (and the unrenewed man has nothing else)—is enmity against God.—He confirms this saying by two of Christ's, which say we can do nothing else; not merely that we do evil, but that we *can do* nothing else, from our very composition; being like 'corrupt trees,' "being evil." And in another place: 'Ye "being evil," do evil, even whilst ye are giving good gifts.'—Then, by insinuation and implication, he proves the same from Paul's twin sayings. If the just man lives by faith, he that hath not faith is not just; and, if not just, he is a sinner.—If whatsoever be not of faith is sin, whatever is done by mere Freewill is sin; because Freewill has nothing to do with faith, but is by the supposition perfectly distinct from it · neither has faith any thing to do with Freewill, but has another origin Whatsoever it doth therefore, not being of faith, is sin. So that Freewill is only sin.— I object to the application of these two texts in this connection. It is the eternal state of the already justified person, which is proclaimed by " shall live " (See Habak ii. 4. Galat. iii. 11. Heb. x. 38) Faith then is the acceptable principle, without which (it is implied) there shall be no acceptance to any man. Freewill has no faith; therefore does nothing acceptable —But still the fair application is, *shall not live;* not *does only sin.*— "Whatsoever is not of faith, &c" *if Luther interprets rightly,* proves his point; because Freewill, not acting *in* and *by* faith, can do nothing, therefore, but what is sin —But that text means, 'if a man is not satisfied as to the rectitude of his own act, but doubts about it,' it is sin —This text therefore does not fairly apply; because Freewill may have no doubts—yet still is damned, whether she doubt or not. On the other hand, a person may sin in some particular act, by acting without faith, yet not be a condemned person : it is of such that Paul speaks.—Thus, although the principles which Luther would establish from these two texts be true ; these texts, rightly understood, do not prove them.

who inquired not after me." He says these things about the Gentiles; because it hath been given to them to know and hear of Christ, when they could not even think of him before, much less seek after him, or prepare themselves for him, by the power of Freewill. It is abundantly plain from this example, that grace comes so truly gratuitously, that not even a thought about it, much less any thing of endeavour or pains precedes its approach. Thus Paul also, when he was Saul, what did he by that most exalted degree of Freewill which he possessed? Assuredly, he was revolving the best and most honest things in his mind, if mere reason be inquired of. But see what endeavour it is of his, by which he finds grace: he is not seeking it; nay, it is even by raving like a madman against it, that he receives his portion. On the other hand, speaking of the Jews in the ninth chapter, he says that the Gentiles which did not follow after righteousness have attained to righteousness, even the righteousness which is of faith; but that Israel which followed after the law of righteousness hath not attained to the law of righteousness. What can any advocate for Freewill mutter against these sayings? The Gentiles, when filled to the full with impiety and all sorts of vices, receive righteousness freely from a pitying God. The Jews, seeking after righteousness with the greatest pains and endeavours, are disappointed. Is not this just to say, that the endeavour of Freewill is vain, whilst endeavouring after the best things; and that she herself rather makes bad worse, stumbles and runs backward.[x] No one can say that they have not tried hard, with the utmost power of Freewill. Paul himself bears them this testimony in his tenth chapter, "That they have a zeal for God, but not

SC XXIII.
rejected—
Gentiles
called.

[x] *Sublapsum referri.*] 'Omnia rursus
    In pejus ruere, ac retro sublapsa referri.'
                        Virg. G. I. v. 200, 201.

438 BONDAGE OF THE WILL.

PART V.
according to knowledge." In the Jews therefore, none of those excellencies are wanting which we ascribe to Freewill, and yet nothing follows; nay, the contrary result follows. In the Gentiles none of those excellencies which we ascribe to Freewill are present, but still the righteousness of God follows. What is this, but to have it confirmed, as well by the most manifest example of both nations, as by the clearest testimony of Paul at the same time, that 'grace is bestowed freely upon the undeserving, nay upon the unworthiest of human beings; whilst it is not obtained by any pains, endeavours, or performances, great or small, even of the best and most respectable of men, though seeking and following after righteousness with a burning zeal.'[y]

SC XXIV.

John a devourer.

Let us also come to John, who is of himself an abundant and able devastator of Freewill. In the very beginning of his Gospel, he ascribes such a blindness to Freewill, as that she is not able to see the light of truth—so far is she from having power to endeavour after it. For thus speaks he, " The light shineth in darkness, but the darkness comprehendeth it not." And presently: " He was in the world, and the world knew him not. He came unto his own, and his own received him not."

What does he mean, think you, by the world? Will you except any man from the number included under this name, except he be created anew by the Holy Ghost? Indeed, it is a peculiar use[z] which this Apostle makes of the word

[y] For some considerations which seem desirable, to mitigate the harshness of this statement, see above, Part iv. Sect. xxxiv. note [d], also Part iv. Sect. x. Part iii. Sect. xxxviii. note [1].

[z] *Peculiaris*] Luther means *peculiar* to this Apostle, as contrasted with the other sacred writers: but it is not confined to John. Paul has it also, Ephes ii. 12. Coloss. i. 6. It may be doubted too, whether he ever speaks of the world *universally*, that is, of a strict ' all men,' ' all mankind ;' though his contrast is varied. Sometimes it is the world at

'world,' expressing the whole race of man, without exception, by it. Whatever he says about the world, therefore, is meant concerning Freewill, as that which is the most excellent thing in man. Now it is said by this Apostle, 'that the world knew not the true light. The world hateth Christ and his people. The world knoweth not, neither seeth the Holy Ghost. The whole world lieth in wickedness; or in the wicked one. All that is in the world is the lust of the flesh, the lust of the eyes, and the pride of life.—Love not the world.' Again; " Ye are of the world, saith he. The world cannot hate you; but me it hateth, because I testify of it that its deeds are evil." All these and many like sayings, then, are so many proclamations about Freewill; that is, about the principal constituent part, which reigneth in the world, under the empire of Satan. For even this John speaks of the world in a way of opposition; meaning by it, whatsoever of the world is not translated into the Spirit;[a] as Christ says to his

large, opposed to the Jews; sometimes the multitude of the unregenerate, opposed to the called people of God, as Luther afterwards distinguishes ("*Nam et ipse Johannes, &c.*") which is a more correct distinction than Christ's people, and the seed of the wicked one. For, until called by the effectual working of the Holy Ghost, the children of the kingdom are often found to be as fierce opponents of the truth, and of its children, as the devil's seed. What was Paul?—Luther does not notice the former of these oppositions, but it is a necessary one to mark. Clearly, it obtains in the words under consideration. " He was in the world (that is, in the material world—on the earth) and *the world* knew him not he came unto his own, &c." The contrast here is between the world at large, and his peculiarly connected ones, the Jews And so, in John iii " God so loved the world, &c " It is all kindreds and tongues, and languages, &c contrasted with the natural seed of Abraham. The clear sense here assists in establishing this use of the term, and serves to confirm the ascription of it to John iii 16, &c.

[a] *Translatum in spiritum.*] We might render 'made spiritual,' but this would efface the distinction which he means to mark. He opposes Christ to the world; making Christ the Spirit, in contrast with Adam, the flesh. So, by realized union with Christ, we are transferred from the *world* into the *Spirit.*

Apostles, " I have taken you out of the world, and have constituted you, &c." . If now there were any in the world, who strove for good by the power of Freewill—as must be the case if Freewill could really do any thing—John ought properly to have moderated his expression out of respect to these, that he might not involve them by a general expression in the multitude of crimes, of which he accuses the world. From his not doing so, it is evident that he charges Free- will with all the crimes with which he charges the world; since whatever the world does, it does by the power of Freewill; that is, by the under- standing and the will, the most excellent of its constituent parts. It follows:

" But as many as received him, to them gave he power to become the sons of God; even to them which believe in his name: which were born not of bloods, nor of the will of the flesh, nor of the will of man, but of God."

Having made this division, he rejects from the kingdom of Christ ' bloods,' ' the will of the flesh,' and ' the will of man.' By ' bloods' I suppose him to mean the Jews; that is, those who had a mind to be sons of the kingdom, be- cause they were sons of Abraham and of the Fathers; boasting forsooth of their descent.— By ' the will of the flesh' I understand the pains with which that people exercised themselves in law works. For the flesh, here, signifies carnal persons which have not the Spirit; as being those who have will and endeavour, but, since there is no Holy Ghost in this will and endeavour, have them carnally. By ' the will of man,' I under- stand the pains which mankind in general, all men take—whether under the law, or without the law—the Gentiles, say, or whom you will—to find favour with God. The meaning therefore is, neither by a birth of the flesh, nor by a zeal for the law, nor by any other human means, are they made sons of God, but only by a divine birth. If then

FREEWILL PROVED TO BE A LIE.

they are not born of the flesh, nor trained by the law, nor obtained by any human discipline, but are born again of God; it is plain that Freewill is of no avail here. For I think the word 'man,' here, is taken, in the Hebrew acceptation, for any one whatsoever; just as 'flesh' is taken, by contrast, for the people of Israel not having the Spirit: and 'will,' again, for the highest power in man; that is, the principal ingredient in Freewill.

But grant that we may not understand each word correctly, still the sum and substance of the assertion is most plain; namely, that John, by this division, rejects whatsoever is not of divine begetting, in saying that men are not made the sons of God but by being born of God; which is effected, according to his own interpretation, by believing in his name. Now in this rejection, the will of man, or Freewill, not being a thing born of God, nor yet faith, is necessarily included. If Freewill availed any thing, the will of man ought not to be rejected by John; neither ought men to be withdrawn from it, and sent to faith and new birth only: else that might be said to him, which was said in Isaiah v. "Woe unto you who call good evil." But now, since he equally rejects 'bloods,' 'the will of the flesh,' and 'the will of man;' it is certain, that the will of man has no more power towards making sons of God, than bloods or fleshly nativity. Now, no one counts it doubtful whether fleshly birth makes, or doth not make, sons of God; as Paul also tells us in Romans ix. "They which are the children of the flesh, these are not the children of God:" which he proves by the examples of Ishmael and Esau.[b]

---

[b] 'The will of the flesh' and 'the will of man' separated and distinguished, and both named, must, upon every conceivable interpretation of those terms, exclude every thing belonging to the human will from this generative power, and therefore decide the question as to the power of Freewill, in bringing us

BONDAGE OF THE WILL.

PART V.
SC. XXV.

John Baptist's testimony.

The same John introduces the Baptist speaking thus ; " Of whose fulness have all we received, grace for grace."

He speaks of grace received by us out of the fulness of Christ; but for the sake of what merit, or endeavour? For the grace, says he, forsooth of Christ :[c] just as Paul also speaks in Romans v. " The grace of God, and the gift by grace of one man Jesus Christ, hath abounded unto many." Where now is the endeavour of Freewill, by

to the inheritance of God's children. But I should rather understand ' bloods' to express natural birth generally (we have not it by descent from our parents) ; ' will of the flesh' for our own personal and individual will, which we have by nature ; and ' will of man' for the ordinance and appointment of man generally. it is not a human device ; what men have chosen and procured for themselves, or what can, in any individual instance, be conferred by man, one or many, willing it to another. A man may leave his estate at death, or confer a liberal gift in his lifetime, but he cannot *will* or *bestow* new birth — Luther speaks as if we were ' begotten' by believing (' nascendo ex Deo, quod fit credendo in nomine ejus') ; like Erasmus's ' renatus per fidem,' which, as we saw, he does not object to : but the truth is, we must be begotten again before we can believe; and then, believing, we take our place amongst God's adopted children. So that there is a sense in which we are regenerated by faith, inasmuch as it is by faith we are *manifested* to be of the Lord's children · but the birth, or *generation* more properly, spoken of in verse 13. is prior to faith ; so that it cannot in this view be said, ' nascor ex Deo, credendo in nomine Jesu Christi ' (See above, Part iv. Sect. xlv. note [t]; also Part v. Sect. xix. note [n].)

[c] *Pro gratiâ scilicet Christi.*] Luther seems to understand him as saying 'grace in return for, or on account of, his grace ;' that is, the grace which Christ has himself shewn. So he clearly explains himself afterwards, when he says ' gratiam eis impetrat per suum sanguinem.' In this view, it is parallel with the passage which he cites from Romans v —It is more commonly interpreted ' grace for grace ,' that is, one degree or measure of grace for another. But Luther is the more correct : although the grace which we have from Christ is in reality grace given to us by the Father in the same instant in which the grace is given to Christ, by means of which he has done and endured every thing personally; still it comes to us, and is actually conferred upon us, in the way of fruit and consequence of his actings—grace bestowed on us, for the sake of grace acted previously by himself.

which grace is procured? Here John says, not only that grace is received without any endeavour of ours, but even by another's grace, or another's merit; namely, that of one man, Jesus Christ. Either therefore it is false, that we receive our grace for the sake of another's grace; or it is evident that Freewill is nothing; for the two cannot stand together—that the grace of God is on the one hand so cheap, as to be obtained commonly, and every where, by the paltry endeavour of any man you please; and on the other so dear, as to be freely bestowed upon us *for* and *by* the grace of one so great a man only.

I would at the same time admonish the advocates of Freewill in this place, that in asserting Freewill they are deniers of Christ. For, if I obtain the grace of God through my own endeavour, what need is there of the grace of Christ for my receiving of grace? or, what is wanting to me, when I have obtained the grace of God? But Diatribe has said, all the Sophists also say, that we obtain the grace of God by our own endeavour, and are prepared for the reception of it, not of condignity indeed, but of congruity: which is absolutely denying Christ, for whose grace's sake the Baptist here testifies that we receive grace. For, as to that figment about condignity and congruity, I have already confuted it; shewing that these are empty words which in reality mean merit of condignity,[d] and have more impiety in them than the Pelagian assertions; as I have declared. So that the impious Sophists, with Diatribe at their head, deny the Lord Christ who bought us, more than the Pelagians, or any heretics have done: so utterly incompatible is grace with any particle or power of Freewill.—Howbeit, that the advocates for Freewill

---

[d] *Meritum condignum*] 'Worthy merit,' i. e. 'merit worthy of the reward which is proposed to be given to it;' 'merit of worth to the uttermost.'—See above, Sect. xvi.

deny Christ, is proved not only by this Scripture but by their own life. Hence it is, that they make Christ to be no longer a sweet Mediator, but a tremendous Judge; whom they are endeavouring to appease by the intercessions of his Virgin Mother, and of the Saints; moreover by many works, rites, superstitions, vows of their own invention: the object of all which is to make Christ favourable to them, that he may give them his grace. On the other hand, they do not believe that he intercedes with God, and obtains grace for them through his blood; and grace, as it is here said, for grace. And as they believe, so it is done unto them. They have Christ truly and deservedly for their inexorable Judge; whilst they forsake him in his office of most powerful Mediator and Saviour, and account his blood and grace a more worthless thing than the pains and endeavours of Freewill.

SC. XXVI.
Nicodemus's case.

Let us also hear an example of Freewill. Nicodemus, I warrant you, is a man in whom nothing was wanting which Freewill can effect: what is it of pains or endeavour, which this man omits? He confesses Christ to be a true witness, and to have come from God; he makes mention of his miracles, he comes by night to hear and to compare the rest. Does not this man seem to have sought the things which belong to piety and salvation, by the power of Freewill? But see how he founders! When he hears the true way of salvation by new birth pointed out to him by Christ, does he recognise that way, or confess that he has ever sought it? Nay, he so revolts from it, and is confounded, that he not only says he does not understand it, but even turns away from it, as impossible.—How can these things be, says he? And no wonder indeed: for who ever heard that a man must be born again of water and of the Spirit, if he would be saved? Who ever thought that the Son of God must be lifted up, to the end that all that believe in him might not perish, but have eternal life. Have the acutest and best of philosophers ever made mention of this? Have the princes of this world ever learned this science? Has any man's Freewill ever made an attempt at it? Does not Paul confess it to be wisdom hidden in a mystery? foretold, it is true, by the Prophets, but revealed by the Gospel; so as to have been from eternity kept secret and unknown to the world.^e

What shall I say? Shall we consult experience? Even the whole world, even human reason, even Freewill herself is compelled to acknowledge, that she neither knew nor heard of Christ, before the Gospel came into the world. Now, if she did not know, much less hath she sought, or been able to seek, or to endeavour after him. But Christ is the way, the truth, the life and the salvation. She confesses therefore, whether she would or no, that by her own powers she has neither known, nor been able to seek those things, which are belonging to the way, the truth and the salvation. Still however, in opposition to this very confession and our own experience, we play the madman; and maintain, by a mere war of words, that we have a certain power remaining in us, which both knows and can apply itself to the things that appertain to salvation: which is as good as saying, knows and can apply itself to Christ the Son of God,

^e It is most true, that the Gospel mystery is strictly matter of revelation, and not within the discovery of natural reason. But it is also true, that it has been the will of God there should be intimations, of this mystery, hereafter to be revealed, and traces of such intimations amidst all nations, from the beginning. The kingdom of God was announced immediately after the fall, in the denunciation upon the serpent, and it has been part of the counsel and work of God, that it should be spoken of, and looked for, and that the eternal separation between the two parts of the human race into hell and into heaven, should be made on the ground of it.—Still, it is not that Freewill has found this out—but God has shewn it.

PART V. who was lifted up for us;[f] whereas no one has ever known, or could have thought of such a person. Still, this ignorance is not ignorance, but knowledge of Christ; that is, of the things which appertain to salvation! Do you not even yet see, and almost feel with your hands, that the assertors of Freewill are downright mad; when they call that knowledge, which they confess themselves to be ignorance. Is not this to call darkness light? (Isaiah v.) So mightily doth God shut the mouth of Freewill, according to her own confession and experience; but, with all this, she will not hold her tongue, and give glory to God.[g]

SECT. XXVII.

John xiv. forestalled. Way, truth, &c are exclusive.

Again, when Christ is called the way, the truth, and the life; and that, by way of comparison—so that whatever is not Christ, is neither way, but out of the way; nor truth, but a lie; nor life, but death—Freewill, being neither Christ, nor in Christ, must have its dwelling place in error, falsehood and death. Where then is to be found, and whence is to be proved, that middle and neutral substance—this substance of Freewill forsooth—which not being Christ (that is, the way, the truth and the life), still does not necessarily become error, falsehood and death? For, if what is said about Christ and his grace were not all said by way of comparison, in opposition to their contraries; as for example, that out of Christ there is none but the devil; out of grace, there is nothing but wrath; out of light, there is nothing but darkness; out of the way, there is nothing but error; out of the truth, there is nothing but

[f] *Pro nobis exaltatum.*] *Exalt.* is a word of doubtful meaning, which might refer to his seat at the Father's right hand; but I understand it with allusion to the Lord's words, "And I if I be lifted up" (ὑψωθῶ, John xii. 32.), as explained by the comment, "this he said, signifying what death he should die."

[g] *Nec sic tamen tacere*] A sort of ὀξύμωρον, like 'stremna inertia,' 'concordia discors,' but there is no real inconsistency: Freewill should be silent for herself, and give glory to God.

falsehood; out of life, there is nothing but death:[h] what would all the discourses of the Apostles, and all Scripture amount to? all surely would be said in vain, since it would not force the conclusion that Christ is necessary to us (which however is their great object); inasmuch as some middle substance might be discovered, which of itself is neither evil nor good, belongs neither to Christ nor to Satan, is neither true nor false, neither alive nor dead—yea, perhaps, is neither any thing nor nothing—yet shall be called the noblest and most excellent endowment of all that is found in the whole human race.

Choose which you will, therefore: if you grant that the Scriptures speak by way of comparison, you can ascribe nothing to Freewill which is not contrary to what is in Christ; you must say of it, that error, death, Satan, and all evil reigns in it. If you do not grant that they speak by way of comparison, you in that case enervate the Scriptures to such a degree, that they effect nothing, and do not prove Christ to be necessary. And thus, in establishing Freewill, you make Christ void, and tread all Scripture under foot. Again; whilst you pretend in words to be confessing Christ, you *really* and *with your heart* deny him: for, if Freewill is not all error and damnation, but sees and wills things honest and good, and things which pertain to salvation, she is whole, and has no need of Christ for her doctor; nor hath Christ redeemed that part of our nature: for what *need* is there of light and life, where there *is* light and life?

Now, if this be not redeemed by Christ, the best ingredient in the composition of man is not redeemed; but is of itself good and sound. In this case, God, also, is unjust in condemning any man, because he condemns that which is best in

---

[h] The word *extra* is used throughout the whole of this passage, to denote distinctness: there are but two sorts of substances; to be *without* the one, is to be *within* the other.

man, and which is sound; in other words, he condemns the innocent. For there is no man who has not Freewill: and, though a bad man abuses his Freewill, still we are taught that the power itself is not extinguished in him, so as neither to strive, nor be able to strive, for good. Now if it be such, without doubt it is holy, just and good; and therefore ought not to be condemned; but to be separated from the man that is to be condemned. But this cannot be; and if it could be, in that case the man, no longer having Freewill, would no longer be a man, and would neither merit evil nor good; neither be damned nor saved, but must be an absolute brute, and no longer an immortal being. It remains therefore, that God is unjust who condemns that holy, just and good power, which has no need of Christ, *in* and *with* a bad man.[i]

SECT. XXVIII.

John iii. 18. 36.

But let us go on with John. "He who believeth on him, says he, is not judged. He who believeth not, hath been judged already,[k] because he believeth not in the name of the only begotten Son of God."

[i] Luther's argument is, Scripture speaks by way of comparison (See above, Sect. xviii. note [i]); therefore Freewill, which confessedly is *out of* Christ, must be sin, death, Satan, error, &c. &c. If you deny that Scripture speaks by comparison, 1. You make Scripture void. 2. You deny Christ. 3. You make God unjust.—His reasoning is subtile, but conclusive.—See the same sort of argument pursued, and remarked upon, Part iv. Sect. xliv. note *.

[k] *Jam judicatus est.*] *Already* as opposed to the *judgment day:* he need not wait for that; the preaching of Christ tries him, of what sort he is, whether he be a doer of evil, or a doer of the truth—as appears from vv. 20, 21. The secret is, a regenerated soul, when Christ is preached, knows, owns and receives him : he who rejects Christ, thereby proves that he is not regenerated, but is in his nature state ; devilish, and possessed by the devil.—It is supposed, that the state here described is the abiding, unchanged, yea dying state of the man. Every deliberate rejection of Christ, when preached, gives ground of awful apprehension ; but it is final rejection, which stamps this judgment. Such being his mind towards Christ, he needs not the process of the last judgment to declare whether he be "in God," or not.

FREEWILL PROVED TO BE A LIE.

SECT. XXVIII.

Tell me, whether Freewill is in the number of the believers, or no? If she be, again she has no need of grace, seeing she believes in Christ of herself, which Christ, however, she of herself neither knows, nor has any conception of. If she be not, she has been judged already: and what is this, but that she hath been condemned before God? Now God condemns nothing but what is wicked. She is wicked therefore: and what pious act can an impious thing attempt? Nor can Freewill, I suppose, be excepted here; since he speaks of the whole man, which he says is condemned. Besides, unbelief is not a gross affection, but that highest sort of affection which sitteth and reigneth in the citadel of the will and understanding; just as its contrary, faith, does. Now to be unbelieving, is to deny God and make him a liar. (1 John i. 10.) If we believe not, we make God a liar.[1] Now, how can that power which is contrary to God, and which makes him a liar, strive after good? If this power were not unbelieving and ungodly, he ought not to have said of the whole man, " he hath been judged already," but to have spoken thus: 'the man hath been judged already with respect to his gross affections; but with respect to his best and most excellent one, he is not judged, because it strives after faith, or rather is even now believing.'

Thus, as often as the Scripture says, " Every man is a liar," we shall say upon the authority of Freewill, 'On the contrary, the Scripture rather lies, because man is not a liar in his best part, that is, in his understanding and will, but only in his flesh, blood and marrow; so that all from whence man has his name—that is, understanding and will—is sound and holy.' So, in that saying

[1] Luther refers only to 1 John i. But the testimony is equally strong 1 John v. 10. "He that believeth not God hath made him a liar, because he believeth not the record that God gave of his Son."

of the Baptist's, "He that believeth on the Son, hath everlasting life: but he that believeth not the Son, shall not see life, but the wrath of God abideth on him;" by 'upon him' we must understand, 'upon his gross affections the wrath of God remaineth;' but upon that eminent power of Freewill—upon his understanding and will forsooth—grace and eternal life abideth. It appears from this example, that, in order to maintain Freewill, you, by a synecdoche,[m] turn and twist what is said in the Scriptures against ungodly men so as to confine it to the brutish part of man; hereby keeping the rational and truly human part of him safe and sound. In this case, I will render my thanks to the assertors of Freewill; since I shall not feel the least concern for my sin, being confident that my understanding and will, that is, my Freewill, cannot be condemned, inasmuch as it is never extinguished, but always remains sound, just and holy. But if my understanding and will are to be happy, I shall rejoice that my filthy and brutish flesh is separated and condemned; so far am I from wishing that Christ should be its redeemer. You see whither the dogma of Freewill carries us, even to the denying of all divine and human, temporal and eternal realities, and to the deluding of itself with so many monstrous fictions!

So again, the Baptist says, "a man cannot receive any thing except it shall have been given him from heaven."

Cease, Diatribe, to display your great fluency here, by enumerating all the things which we receive from heaven! We are not arguing about nature, but about grace; we are not inquiring what sort of persons we are upon earth, but what in heaven and before God. We know that man is constituted lord of the things beneath him;

---

[m] *Per synecdochen.*] *Syn.* 'A figure by which part is taken for the whole, or the whole for part:' here, Diatribe makes it the whole of man put for his grosser part.

over which he has power and Freewill, that they may obey him, and may do what he wills and thinks. But this is our question, whether he has Freewill towards God, so that God obeys and does what man wills; or, whether God, rather, has Freewill over man, so that he wills and does what God wills, and can do nothing but what God shall have willed and done. Here the Baptist says, that he can receive nothing, except it be given him from heaven: so that Freewill is nothing.[n]

So again, " He that is of the earth is earthly, and speaketh of the earth; he that cometh from heaven is above all." John iii. 31.

Here again he makes all earthly (and says that they mind and speak earthly things) who are not of Christ, and leaves none between the two. But Freewill, surely, is not he that cometh from heaven. So that it must be of the earth, and must mind and speak the things of the earth. Now, if there

[n] *Hic dicit*] That is, according to Luther (who assumes that the things here spoken of are things of God, not of the creature), determines this question; it is God's will, not man's, that is done.—I have already objected many times to the distinction which Luther here again resorts to (see above, Part iv. Sect xlvi. note [x]), nor can I allow this text to be a direct testimony against Freewill —John is accounting for the superior honour paid to Jesus above himself. he had just been informed concerning Jesus, " All men come to Him." The principle of the remark therefore is, I can have no more of honour than it is the will of God to bestow upon me. And he goes on to say, that he never claimed to be Christ, and consequently never claimed to receive the honour which it had been the Father's good pleasure to appropriate to Him. It is honour and distinction therefore, not spiritual power and capacity, of which John here speaks.—But it is honour *in* and *of* the kingdom of God; which is preceded by a gift of super-creation power exciting and leading to it. As the honour, so the precedent power is of God, and according to the measure in which he has ordained to bestow, and does produce it.—However, *non tali auxilio* If Luther understands it, ' we must have power given to enable us to receive power,' it is a testimony: but its meaning is far simpler than this. What we have, we have received: if another has more, it is because God has given it.

PART V. were any power in any man, which at any time, in any place, in any work, did not mind earthly things, the Baptist ought to have excepted this man, and not to have said generally concerning all out of Christ, that they are earthly, and speak of the earth.°

John viii. 23.

So, afterwards in chap. viii. Christ also says, " Ye are of the world; I am not of the world: ye are from beneath, I am from above."

The persons to whom he spake had Freewill, to wit, understanding and will; and yet he says " they were of the world." Now what news would it be, if he should say they were of the world, with respect to their flesh and gross affections? Did not the whole world know this before? Besides, what need is there to say, that men are of the world in that part in which they are

---

° This is a testimony borne to Jesus by John, in contrast with himself: though filled with the Holy Ghost even from his mother's womb, and having the hand of the Lord with him (Luke i. 15. 66), he had not been born 'by the Holy Ghost's coming upon a virgin mother, and the power of the Highest's overshadowing her;' ' he had not come down from heaven,' he had not ' come from above,' ' come from heaven,' (and, as compared with Him, was earthly in his words (see Luke i 35. John iii. 13 31. vi 38 41, 42 *), as well as in his frame and formation.) Luther misunderstands the text—does not see its glory, and does not elicit its testimony against Freewill correctly. It *is* however a testimony: if John only so far as he had a gift from heaven was other than earthly, and had comparatively so little of this gift as fitly to call himself earthly— what is 'Freewill,' 'nature man,' ' that which is nothing but earth,' instead of being such an one as John by the grace of God had been made. It is not ' Christ's people,' and ' the world,' which are opposed to each other here by the names ' earthly' and ' heavenly,' but Christ and John singly: John was a man in nowise different from other men as to his natural frame, he was truly and solely a son of Adam: but Christ's human person, as to its spiritual part, was from heaven.

* I do not refer to 1 Cor. xv. 47. because I consider it as belonging to another subject—Christ the *risen* head of his *risen* people, come down the second time from heaven to raise his dead ones —it is of Christ as walking upon this earth that the Baptist here testifies, he *cometh* or (what is the same in import *here*) *hath come* from heaven; and so in the other passages to which I have referred.

brutish; when, at this rate, the beasts also are of the world?ᵖ

Again, what does that saying of Christ's in John vi. " No one cometh unto me, except my Father shall have drawn him," leave to Freewill?ᑫ He says, it is necessary that a man hear and learn from the Father himself; and afterwards, that all must be taught of God. (vv. 44, 45.) Here forsooth he teaches that not only the works and pains of Freewill are vain, but that even the word of the Gospel (of which he is here treating) is heard in vain, except the Father himself speak, teach, and draw within. No man *can* come, says he: that power forsooth, by which a man is enabled to make any endeavour after Christ; that is, after those things which are appertinent to salvation; is asserted to be nothing. Nor is that saying of Augustine's which Diatribe adduces for the purpose of blurring this most clear and most mighty passage—that God draweth just as we draw a sheep by shewing it a bough—of any service to Freewill. She will have it, that this simile proves there is a power in us to follow the drawing of God. But this simile is of no avail here: forasmuch as God shews us not one good thing only, but all his good things, and even Christ himself—

ᵖ Surely the Lord means more by 'from beneath' here, than the Baptist did; who spake of himself—or, according to Luther, 'of himself and all that are Christ's.' The Lord speaks of these Jews as the devil's seed, whose throne and habitation are beneath the earth whilst his own origin, as well as throne, was and is heaven (See that whole discourse John viii. especially from v. 21 to the end of the chapter)—Luther's conclusion however is correct. He bore this testimony to their best and finer part, not to the grosser An objection may indeed be taken 'These were expressly and emphatically children of the wicked one, and therefore their case is somewhat different from that of the children of the kingdom The answer is, not as it respects nature—Freewill and all nature powers.

ᑫ *Venit ad me*] The original text is stronger; "*is able to* come unto me."

PART V. his Son; but still no man follows him, unless the Father shew him something else within, and in other ways draw him: nay, the whole world persecutes that Son, whom he shews. This comparison of Augustine's squares perfectly enough with the case of the godly; who are now sheep, and know their shepherd God. These, who live by the Spirit and are moved by the Spirit, follow whithersoever God willeth, and whatsoever he shall have shewn them. But the ungodly cometh not, even when he hath heard the word, except the Father draw and teach within; which he does by bestowing the Spirit. In them is another drawing, distinct from that which is without; in them Christ is shewn by the illumination of the Spirit, through which the man is married off to Christ by a most delightful ravishment, and rather *endures* the act of a speaking teacher and a drawing God, than performs one himself by seeking and running.[r]

[r] *Illuminationem Spiritûs.*] Not 'the enlightening of the man's own soul,' but 'the throwing of light upon Christ:' the blessed Spirit casts his bright beams upon the face, or person, of the Lord Jesus Christ; and so wins to him.—A most beautiful and accurate description this, of that Holy Ghost violence, with which the soul is converted. One can hardly help saying to Luther, *O si sic omnia!* A single testimony, like this broad and irresistible one, opened as he opens it, is worth a hundred abstruse and obscure ones, of which it is a question in the first place, whether they bear *at all* upon the subject—secondly, *how* they exactly bear upon it—and thirdly, with what degree of *effect*.—I am not meaning to disparage Luther's testimonies—which, with a few exceptions, are clear, and strong to the point; but I think the question might be safely rested upon this single text—*considered in its connection*—and that, on such a subject, to bring those which will admit of a doubt, or of a possible misconstruction—in short to use any other implement than a sledge-hammer—is unwise. Even Luther might have made his proofs clearer and stronger; and they would have lost nothing by being fewer. The impression is weakened by being extended; and many small blows, of which one or two beat the air, render the victory doubtful, in the sight of the by-standers. (See above, Part iv. Sect. xlii. note [1])—But what have we here? It is not only that the words are so express it is impossible to evade them, and that to cite them

FREEWILL PROVED TO BE A LIE.

SECT. XXX.

I will bring yet one more text from this same John, who in his sixteenth chapter says, "The spirit shall reprove the world of sin, because they have not believed in me." (John xvi. 9.) Here you see it is sin not to believe in Christ. But this sin, surely, is not fixed in the skin or in the hair, but in the very understanding and will. Now, when he charges the whole world with this sin, and it is ascertained by experience that this sin of theirs is as unknown to the world as Christ himself—seeing it is that which is revealed by the reproving of the Spirit—it is plain that Freewill, together with its will and understanding, is considered as captured, and condemned for this sin, before God. So then, whilst Freewill is ignorant of Christ and does not believe in him, she cannot will or endeavour after any good thing, but is necessarily the slave of this unknown sin. In short, since the Scriptures preach Christ in a way of comparison and opposition every where, as I have said; representing every thing which hath not the Spirit of Christ as the subject of Satan, ungodliness, error, darkness, sin and the wrath of God; how many soever testimonies there be which speak of Christ, these will, all and every of them, fight against Freewill. Now such testimonies are innumerable; nay, they make up the whole of

John xvi.9.

is even more impressive than to enlarge upon them, but they *must* mean what they say—'There is no power whatsoever in the natural man to come to Christ'—because otherwise they have no meaning at all, in this context.—The Lord is accounting for their murmurs, in which they muttered out a rejection of him. 'You reject me! What wonder? It cannot be otherwise, seeing ye are not drawn to me of God.'—And when he repeats the same sentiment at the 65th verse, it is to account for the same fact, and is followed by a consequence which would naturally result from such a declaration, but which no other sentiment would account for. "From that time many of his disciples went back and walked no more with him. Then said Jesus unto the twelve, "Will ye also go away?" The testimony therefore is so unequivocal, as well as so decisive, that Freewill has not even a heel to lift up against it.

Scripture. So that if we try this cause at the judgment seat of Scripture, I shall conquer every way;[s] there not being a single jot or tittle remaining, but what condemns the dogma of Freewill.

Now although our great theologians and maintainers of Freewill either know not, or pretend not to know, that the Scripture thus preaches Christ in the way of comparison and opposition, still all Christians know this, and publicly confess it. They know I say, that there are two kingdoms in the world, which are most adversative to each other; that Satan reigns in the one, and is on this account called by Christ the Prince of this world, and by Paul the God of this age; holding all men captive at his will, who have not been torn from him by the Spirit of Christ, as the same Paul witnesseth; and not suffering them to be torn from him by any force, save by the Spirit of God; as Christ testifies in his parable of the strong man keeping his palace in peace. In the other reigneth Christ: whose kingdom is continually resisting and fighting with that of Satan. Into this kingdom we are translated, not by our own power, but by the grace of God; by which we are delivered from this present wicked age, and snatched out of the hands of the power of darkness. The knowledge and confession of these kingdoms, as fighting perpetually against each other with such might and resolution, would be of itself sufficient to confute the dogma of Freewill: seeing that we are compelled to serve in the kingdom of Satan, unless we be rescued from it by a divine power. These

---

[s] *Omnibus modis vicero*] *Omn mod.* like παντὶ τρόπῳ, or κατὰ παντα τρόπον, of the Greeks, expresses the manner in which any act is done, or event accomplished : 'By what arts and means soever, or with what spirit and turn of mind soever, the contest be carried on, I shall have conquered so as not to leave a single jot or tittle for Freewill'—The argument is, Scripture preaches Christ by antithesis; therefore, whatsoever preaches Christ excludes Freewill. But Christ is preached every where : therefore Freewill is opposed every where.

things, I say, the vulgar know, and by their proverbs, prayers, efforts and whole life, abundantly confess.ᵗ

I omit that truly Achillean argument of mine, which Diatribe in her noble courage has left untouched; namely, that in Romans vii. and Galatians v. Paul teaches us that the conflict between flesh and spirit is so mighty in the sanctified and godly, that they cannot do the things which they would. I argue thus from it: if the nature of man is so wicked, that in those who have been born again of the Spirit, not only it does not endeavour after good, but even fights against and opposes good; how should it endeavour after good in those who, being not yet regenerated, are serving under Satan, in the old man? For Paul does not speak of the gross affections only in that place, through which as a sort of common outlet Diatribe is wont to slip like an eel out of the hands of every Scripture; but reckons heresy, idolatry, dissensions, contentions, mischiefs, which reign in those highest powers of the soul—the understanding and the will, say— amongst the works of the flesh. If then the flesh maintains a conflict against the spirit, by means of

Side note: Omits to argue from the conflict between flesh and spirit, because no attempt has yet been made to repel what he has said about it.

ᵗ How strange that this enlightened and enlightening view of the two kingdoms should be so little realized, substantiated and applied! this, which needs only to be carried back to the period of the fall, and thence continued downwards to the end of the world, with an understanding, that this is not the creation state of man, and the things of man, but the counsel and scheme of God as made way for by the creation and the fall—to render all Scripture, history, observation and experience, simple and intelligible !—Luther evidently did not comprehend them in the fulness of their origination, design, operations and results, but the substance is here—and we can scarcely help breathing out the vain wish that he had, for his own comfort, and that of others whom the Lord hath not disdained to edify by his writings, been enabled to put the elements, with which he here furnishes us, together, in their beginning and endings, and in the connection of the intermediate parts, in a workmanlike manner. He has the materials ; but he neither models, nor lays the foundation, nor buildeth thereon. Still, what grace in *his* day to have seen so much!

these affections, in the saints; much more will it fight against God in the ungodly, and their Freewill. On this account Rom. viii. calls it enmity against God.[u]

I should be glad, I say, if any body would take off this argument for me, and defend Freewill from it.

For my own part, I confess that, if it could any how be, I should be unwilling to have Freewill given to me, or any thing left in my own hand, which might enable me to endeavour after salvation: not only because in the midst of so many dangers and adversities on the one hand, and of so many assaulting devils on the other, I should not be strong enough to maintain my standing and keep my hold of it (for one devil is mightier than all men put together, and not a single individual of mankind would be saved); but because, if there were even no dangers, and no adversities, and no devils, still I should be compelled to toil for ever as uncertainly, and to fight as one that beateth the air.[v] For, though I should live and work to eternity, my own conscience would never be sure and secure how much she ought to do, that God might be satisfied with her. Do what she might, there would still be left an anxious doubt, whether it pleased God, or whether he required any thing more; as the experience of all self-righteous persons[x] proves, and as I, to my

---

[u] I have already shewn that I do not coincide with Luther in his representation of the flesh and the spirit: that I consider the flesh and the spirit to be the unrenewed body and the renewed mind, severally, of the Lord's called people. But this difference does not affect the argument here. If the renewed man, who has the Spirit, have this conflict to maintain; what is the wholly unrenewed man before God, and what his endeavour after good?

[v] *Laborare.*] The allusion is evidently to 1 Cor. ix. 26.—but he does not use the word *currere.* Paul says τρέχω.

[x] *Justitiariorum.*] I do not find the word, except as bad Latin for 'a justice!' but the connection determines it to mean

own great misery, have learned abundantly by so many years of conflict.

But now, since God has taken my salvation out of the hands of my own will, and has received it into those of his own; and has promised to save me, not by my own work or running, but by his own grace and mercy; I am at ease and certain, because he is faithful and will not lie to me, and because he is moreover great and powerful, so that no number of devils, no number of adversities, can either wear *Him* out, or pluck *me* out of his hand. No one,[y] says he, shall pluck them out of my hand; for my Father who gave them me, is greater than all. Thus it comes to pass, that, if all are not saved, some, however, nay, many are; whereas by the power of Freewill none absolutely would be, but we should all to a man be lost? Moreover, we are fearlessly sure that we please God, not by the merit of our own work, but by the favour of his mercy, which he hath promised us; and that, if we do less than we ought, or ought amiss, he does not impute it to us, but with a fatherly mind forgives and amends it. Such is the boast of every saint in his God.[z]

here, 'persons who are going about to establish their own righteousness,' in opposition to 'those who have learned that there is a God-righteousness and have been led to submit to it.'—'Justicers,' or 'righteousness-mongers.'

[y] Οὐδεὶς· implies more than no *man;* no *person*, man or devil.

[z] The defects of Luther's theology are apparent in this paragraph. He gives quietness, but not triumph; quietness too, we know not why—when a reason might be assigned. We *are to live*, assuredly to live, we do not yet live · we are to work too, that we *may* live; and our workings must be forgiven and amended —He did not see Christ's peculiar and peculiarizing headship he did not see that the efficacy of Christ is his enabling God, *by His dying*, to raise up the cursed from their curse after suffering a part of it; that they live, even now, in a risen Christ as though they had risen with him; and that it is eternal life already received and acted—just in such measure as He is pleased to bestow of it—which constitutes the acceptable service they are now rendering: which service He, as he hath appointed, and just in such measure and manner

PART V.
SECT. XXXII.

Difficulty stated.

Exposed.

But if this disturb us, that, it is difficult to maintain the mercy and equity of God, in that he damns the undeserving—namely, ungodly men who are even of such a sort, that, being born in ungodliness, they cannot by any means help being ungodly, remaining so, and being damned; yea, being compelled by the necessity of their nature to sin and perish (as Paul speaks, "We were all the sons of wrath even as others"), being created such as they are, by God himself, out of a seed which became corrupted through that sin which was Adam's only—

In this state of things, we must honour and reverence the exceeding great mercy of God in his dealings with those whom he justifies and saves although most unworthy of such benefits, and must at least make some small concession to his divine wisdom, believing him to be just, when to us he seems unjust. For, if his justice were indeed such as might by human apprehension be pronounced just when it is judged, it would clearly not be divine justice, but would differ nothing from that of man. Now, seeing that God is the one true God, and is moreover totally incomprehensible, and inaccessible to human reason; it is natural, nay it is necessary, that his justice also be incomprehensible: just as Paul also cries out, saying, "O the depth of the riches both of the wisdom and knowledge of God, how incomprehensible are his judgments and his ways unsearchable." (Rom. xi. 33.)

Now they would not be incomprehensible, if we could, throughout the whole of them, conceive why

---

as he hath appointed, will reward.—But all this upon the basis of Christ's super-creation headship, and their relations to God, in Him the merit of their acceptance having been wrought already, to the uttermost, by Him only; and they having only to enter into and enjoy their portion—a mixed one here, an unmixed one hereafter. See Part iii. Sect. xxxviii. note [1]. John iii. 36. v. 24. x. 28. xvii. 3. 1 John v. 10.

they are just. What is man compared with God? What is our power capable of, as compared with his? What is our strength compared with his might? What is our knowledge compared with his wisdom? What is our substance compared with his substance? In short, what is every thing of ours, as compared with every thing of his?[a]

SECT. XXXIII.

Now if, with no other preceptress than nature, we confess that man's power, strength, wisdom, knowledge, substance and every thing of ours is absolutely nothing, when compared with God's power, God's strength, God's wisdom, knowledge, and substance; what is this perverseness of ours, that we pull and hale God's justice and judgment only,[b] arrogating so much to our own judgment as to try whether we cannot comprehend, judge and estimate the judgment of God? Why do we not in like manner say here also; our judgment is nothing, if it be compared with the divine judgment? Ask reason herself, whether she be not compelled by conviction to acknowledge, that she is foolish and rash in not allowing the judgment of God to be incomprehensible, when she confesses all the other properties of God to be incomprehensible? What! in all other things we concede a divine majesty to God; it is in his judgment only, that we are prepared to deny it to him, and cannot, even for this little while, give him credit for being just, when he has promised us, that, after he shall have revealed his glory, it shall come to pass, that we all of us do then both see and feel, that he has been, and is just.

Reproved.

I will give an example to confirm this belief, and to console that evil eye,[c] which suspects God

And palliated by example.

---

[a] *Ad illius omnia.*] I do not venture to render, 'as compared with its like of His,' but Luther means so, presuming that our image-ship extends to every divine property.

[b] *Justitiam et judicium.*] *Just.* The principle of justice; *jud.* the faculty of judgment.

[c] *Ad consolandum.*] An odd expression in this connection; but he means, to console the spirit which is tempted to see with

PART V. of injustice. Behold, God so governs this material world in outward things, that, if you observe and follow the judgment of human reason, you are compelled to say, either there is no God, or there is an unjust God; as that poet says, "I am often solicited to think that there are no Gods." For, see how true it is, that the wicked are most prosperous, and the good, on the other hand, most unfortunate; even proverbs, and experience, who is the mother of proverbs, testifying, that 'the wickeder men are, the more fortunate.' "The tabernacles of the wicked abound," says Job; and the 73d Psalm complains that sinners abound with riches, in this world.[d] Is it not most unjust in the judgment of all men, pray, that the wicked should be prospered and the good afflicted?[e] Yet

evil eye: 'an evil eye is one which is either unsound *generally*, or is infected with the particular disease of envy, malice and blasphemy.' See Matt. vi. 23. xx. 15. Mark vii. 22.

[d] Job xii. 6. Psalm lxxiii. 12. Our version says, "The tabernacles of robbers prosper." "Behold, these are the ungodly who prosper in the world; they increase in riches."

[e] Luther feels a difficulty in reconciling the condemnation of the reprobate with God's justice. In fact he acknowledges that he cannot; begs off, and makes unwarrantable concessions. This difficulty arises from his imperfect conception of the creation and fall of man. If every individual of the human race had a distinct personal subsistence given to him, in the creation of Adam; and, consequently, had a distinct personal subsistence in him, when he brake his commandment; and, as this distinct substance, was one with him who by his alone personal agency did break that commandment (the union of these many distinct substances *in* and *with* his one substance nowise contradicting the alone and distinct agency of the one first man, Adam); where is the injustice of God's bringing out each of these distinct individuals, one after another, into manifest existence and distinct personal agency, and—having given to them individually, for the most part, the opportunity of shewing what they are according to their own making of themselves, not according to his making of them—inflicting upon them the judgment which he had distinctly fore-announced, which by their disobedience as one with Adam they had wilfully incurred, and which for the most part they have by their own subsequent actings in this world proved to be their due, suitable, and self-made portion? If

such is the course of the world. It is here, that even the greatest wits have fallen to the depth of

God has been pleased to make provision for the mitigation, removal and reversal of this sentence in some of those who have justly incurred it, clearly they who suffer have justly incurred it; and therefore God is only just in inflicting it.—Through not discerning the mystery of the creation, Luther accounted God the creator of these wicked ones, as we have several times seen; and, through not, in consequence, discerning their participation in the fall, he accounted God their debtor to give them an equivalent for that Freewill, or rather that knowledge of only good, which Adam had possessed, and which he did not see how they had forfeited. I say knowledge of only good, because Adam had no more of Freewill properly so called, than we have, as hath been shewn. With respect to the justice of God in this transaction then, there can be no question, though Luther makes one Justice is the fulfilment of relations; God had fulfilled all His, when man incurred his fore-announced curse—then what does justice require, but that it be exacted? Again; with respect to God's right of instituting such relations as He did between himself and the human race in Adam, there can be no question. God has a *right* to form any creature that he is pleased and has power to form. To be consistent with himself, he will give them due relations, and will fulfil his own part in those relations. Now, what was wanting in the relations he gave to Adam? Did He not give him reason and knowledge, by which he ought to have resisted the temptation? And if Adam had enough, what could the distinct substances which were in him complain, if God put their safety upon the issue of his obedience? What difference would there have been, or could they pretend that there would have been, in the result, if each of them distinctly and personally had undergone the same trial?—But I do not deem this consideration at all necessary; it is the union and unity of each individual of the human race, still retaining his individuality, with Adam, which constitutes his original sin and his original guilt; and from which the loss of his creation state and of his creation character was derived —The only question that can be asked in all this mystery respects the goodness, that is, the loving-kindness of God. It is here that Paul puts the difficulty, here that he calls for submission; and here that he assigns the principle of the procedure. "Is there not unrighteousness?" For it will come to this, no man hath done otherwise than God designed. The answer is, God has exercised his right of the potter, and has exercised it for a great and wise reason — " What if etc. ?"—The man whose eyes the Lord hath opened will see, and will search into, these things, and will justify God at his heart. Nor will Paul, with his Isaiah, condemn him. He is using what God hath done and hath revealed unto the very

PART V. denying that there is a God, and of feigning that Fortune turns and twists every thing, as the whim takes her: such were the Epicureans and Pliny. Following close upon these, Aristotle,' to deliver that first Being of his from misery, is of opinion, that he does not see any of the things that exist, but himself; because he considers that it would be most painful to him to see so much of evil, so much of injustice.[f]

The Prophets, on the other hand, who believed that there is a God, are more tempted with the suggestion of God's injustice: as Jeremiah, Job, David, Asaph and others. What do you imagine Demosthenes and Cicero to have thought, when, after having done all they could, they received such wages as they did, in a wretched death?[g] Yet this injustice of God, which is exceedingly probable, and inferred by such arguments as no power of reason or light of nature can resist, is most easily removed by the light of the Gospel and the knowledge of grace; which teaches us, that the wicked flourish, it is true, in their body,

end for which He hath done and hath revealed it. See Part iii. Sect. xxxviii. note [l]. Part iv. Sect. x. note [z], Sect. xi. note [h], and Sect. xxxiv. note [d].

[f] Luther's mention makes it doubtful to which of the two Plinies he refers; whether to the great naturalist or his nephew neither of them, however, saw in the works of nature any thing more than matter both were amiable, as natural men, and the former was a monument of philosophy and industry, called by some the martyr of nature, but more fitly called the martyr of curiosity and self-will. The latter, was a wellbred, lettered persecutor of Christians; but too proud to inquire into their doctrines, and not afraid, though reluctant, to shed their blood. For some excellent remarks upon his character, see Miln. Eccl. Hist. vol. 1. pp. 166—172.—For a hint at the Epicureans, who were like their master—' Epicuri de grege porcus '—See above, Part i. Sect. v. note [q].—For a confirmation of what is here said about Aristotle, see above, Part iv. Sect. viii. note [r].

[g] Demosthenes, abandoned in fact by his countrymen, after having fled to the temple of Neptune in Calauria, sucked his poisoned quill: Cicero was delivered up to his philippicized Antony.

but they perish in their souls: so that we have the brief solution of all this insolvable question in a single short sentence, 'There is a life after this life, in which whatsoever hath not been punished and rewarded here shall hereafter be punished and rewarded; seeing that this life is nothing but the precurse, or rather beginning, of the life to come.' If the light of the Gospel then, which owes all its power to the word and faith, be so efficacious, that this question, handled as it had been in all ages but never answered, is so thoroughly made an end of and laid to sleep; what will happen, think you, when the light of the word and of faith shall have ceased, and when the reality, even the divine Majesty itself, shall be revealed as it is? Do you not think, that the light of glory will then be able to solve, with the greatest ease, that question which in the light of the word, or of grace, is insolvable; seeing that the light of grace hath so readily solved a question, which could not be solved by the light of nature? Let it be conceded, that there are three great lights—the light of nature, the light of grace, and the light of glory—according to the common distinction, which is a good one. In the light of nature, it is a fact not to be explained, that it is just the good man be afflicted, and the bad man prosper. But the light of grace resolves this question. In the light of grace it is inexplicable, how God condemns the man, who cannot, by any power of his own, do otherwise than sin, and be guilty. In this case, the light of nature, as well as the light of grace, declares that the fault is not in wretched man but in unjust God. For how can they judge otherwise of God? seeing he crowns a wicked man gratuitously without any merits, and does not crown another but condemns him—who perhaps is less, or at the worst not more wicked.—But the light of glory proclaims something else, and, when it arrives, will shew God, whose judgment is for the present that of incomprehensible justice, to be only that of most just and most manifest justice; teaching us, in the mean time, to believe, the certainty of this event, admonished and confirmed, as we are, in and unto the expectation of it, by the example of the light of grace, which accomplishes a like prodigy with respect to the light of nature.[h]

SECT. XXXIV

Sum of the argument.

Here I shall put an end to this treatise; prepared, if need be, to plead the cause yet further; although I consider, that I have in this said abundantly enough to satisfy the pious mind, which is willing to yield to the force of truth without pertinacity. For, if we believe it to be true, that God foreknows and predestinates every thing; moreover, that he can neither be mistaken, nor hindered, in his foreknowledge and predestination; and, once more, that nothing is done without his will (a truth which reason herself is compelled to yield); it follows, from the testimony of the selfsame reason, that there can be no such thing as Freewill in man or angel, or any creature. So again; if we believe Satan to be the

---

[h] If the observations of the preceding note be correct, we do not want Luther's illustration, with its distinctions. We need not wait for the decision and discoveries of the great day, to see God just. Nor are his assumptions admissible. God has never left the eternity of man and the future judgment without witness. If these things have been obscured, it is not by God's having put them into the dark, but because men have wilfully shut their eyes to them. The new creation kingdom was announced at the fall—and has been variously preached ever since, to the whole earth. The kingdom of grace does not leave God under the suspicion of injustice; man has made himself that damned thing which he is. The elect are not crowned sinners. The union of the elect with Christ, and the lack of this union, with its consequent self-left state, in the reprobate, explains both dooms, in perfect consistency with divine equity. The illustration, therefore, is both unneeded and untrue: unneeded, inasmuch as the spiritual man even now sees the inflexible justice of God to be without spot—what it assuredly is; and untrue, inasmuch as Luther's insolvable questions are resolved under those lights which he declares to be severally inadequate.

Prince of this world, who is perpetually plotting and fighting against the kingdom of Christ, with all his might, so that he doth not let his captives of human kind go, unless he be driven out by a divine power; again it is manifest, that there can be no such thing as Freewill.

So again, if we believe original sin[i] to have so ruined us, as to make most troublesome work even for those who are led by the Spirit, through striving, as it does, against good in them; it is clear, that nothing is left in man as devoid of the Spirit, which can turn itself to good, but only what turns itself to evil. Again; if the Jews, who followed after righteousness with all their might, have fallen headlong the rather into unrighteousnes; and the Gentiles, who were following after unrighteousness, have freely and unhopedly attained to righteousness; it is manifest, as in the former instances, by very deed and experience, that man without grace can will nothing but evil. In fine; if we believe Christ to have redeemed man by his blood, we are obliged to confess that the whole man was undone; else we shall make Christ either superfluous, or the redeemer of the vilest part in man: which is blasphemous and sacrilegious.[k]

[i] A still inferior view to what he has given us before of original sin, but a very common one : he here takes it for that vitiation of nature, which is the consequence of it—instead of that *first* sin, which gave origin to the vitiation.—But the argument against Freewill is not affected; the consequent vitiation is in nowise less than he represents it to be.

[k] He briefly recites certain additional considerations, which must, each of them, be conclusive upon this subject. 1. God's foreknowledge and predestination. 2. Satan's lordship over the world. 3. Original sin. 4. The case of the apostate and rejected Jews, as contrasted with the conversion of the Gentiles. 5. Christ the Redeemer unnecessary, or his benefit vilified.

CONCLUSION.

Luther admonishes, thanks, counsels, prays.

Now therefore I beseech thee in the name of Christ, my Erasmus, that thou wouldest at length perform what thou hast promised: thou promisedest that thou wouldest be willing to submit thyself to the man who should teach thee better things. Have done with respect of persons. I confess, thou art a great man, adorned with many of the noblest gifts by God; not to mention others, with genius, and learning, and eloquence, even to a miracle. On the other hand, *I* have nothing, and *am* nothing; save that I could almost glory in being a Christian. Again; I greatly commend and extol you for this thing also, that you are the only man of all my antagonists that hath attacked the heart of the subject, the head of the cause; instead of wearing me out with those extraneous points, the Papacy, Purgatory, Indulgences, and a number of like topics, which may more fitly be called trifles, than matters of debate: a sort of chase, in which nearly all my opponents have been hunting me hitherto in vain. You are that single and solitary individual, who hath seen the hinge of the matters in dispute, and hath aimed at the neck: I thank you for this from my heart—it is far more to my taste to be occupied in debating this question, so far as time and leisure are accorded me. If those who have heretofore attacked me had done the same; if those who are just at this time making their boast of new spirits, and new revelations, would do so; we should have less of sedition and divisions, as well as more of peace and concord. But God thus stirs up Satan to punish our ingratitude.[a]

Howbeit, unless you can plead this cause in a style somewhat different from your Diatribe, I could earnestly wish that you would be content with your own proper good, and would cultivate, adorn and advance the cause of literature and the languages, as you have heretofore done, with great profit and praise. By this pursuit of yours you have even served *me* not a little; insomuch that I confess myself greatly your debtor, even as I most assuredly venerate you, and sincerely look up to you as my superior, in that particular. God hath not yet willed, nor given to you, that you should be equal to this cause! Pray do not think that I say this with any arrogancy.

And yet I do implore the Lord to make you as much my superior in this particular speedily, as you already are in all others. Nor is it any thing new, that God should instruct a Moses by Jethro, or a Paul by Ananias. As to what you say, that you have failed, miserably indeed, of your aim, if you do not know Christ; I think, you must be

---

[a] *Ita per Satanam*] Very true as to instrumentality But whence then comes this ingratitude? Could not God cure it? Could not he drive out the Canaanite altogether from the land? Regenerate man, and a revived church, is still Adam; and it is the glory of God to save and glorify an Adam. He must be shewn therefore, or rather must shew himself what he is. 'His Canaan is not yet the Lord's world—neither is he yet the risen God-man. The time of ingratitude is yet, and is yet, because the Lord's real and designed glory requires that it should be so.—There is something satisfying, and cheering, and enlightening, in this view of the Lord's present dealings with his church and people, which reconciles us to what must otherwise be a constant burden and distress—and which leaves no more questions to be asked. Luther had not distinct perceptions of the origin, and nature, and design of evil, and whilst he talked much of Satan, did not understand him well enough to put him in his place.

aware yourself what sort of a saying this is. All will not *therefore* be in the wrong, because you or I, if it be so, are in the wrong. God is declared to be a God that is wonderful in his saints; so that we *may* count those for saints, who are the farthest off from saintship. Nor is it hard to suppose, that you, being a man, may neither rightly understand, nor with sufficient diligence observe, either the Scriptures or the sayings of the Fathers, by whose guidance you imagine that you have obtained your aim. We have a pretty good hint to this effect, when you write that you do not assert at all, but confer. The man who sees clearly through the whole of his subject, and understands it correctly, does not write thus. I, for my part, have not conferred, but asserted, in this book; yea, and I do assert. Neither is it my desire to appoint any man judge in this cause: I persuade all to receive my decree. The Lord, whose cause this is, shine upon you—and make you a vessel unto honour and glory! Amen.

London: Printed by A Applegath, Stamford-street.

CPSIA information can be obtained
at www.ICGtesting.com
Printed in the USA
LVHW082215160322
713672LV00021B/215